JERUSALEM THRONE GAMES

The Battle of Bible Stories after the Death of David

Peter Feinman

OXBOW | books
Oxford & Philadelphia

To my father who didn't live to see this,

To my mother who did.

Published in the United Kingdom in 2017 by
OXBOW BOOKS
The Old Music Hall, 106–108 Cowley Road, Oxford, OX4 1JE

and in the United States by
OXBOW BOOKS
1950 Lawrence Road, Havertown, PA 19083

© Oxbow Books and Peter Feinman 2017

Paperback Edition: ISBN 978-1-785706-16-5
Digital Edition: ISBN 978-1-78570-617-2 (epub)

A CIP record for this book is available from the British Library

Printed in the United Kingdom by TJ International

For a complete list of Oxbow books, please contact:

United Kingdom
OXBOW BOOKS
Telephone (01865) 241249
Fax (01865) 794449
Email: oxbow@oxbowbooks.com
www.oxbowbooks.com

United States of America
OXBOW BOOKS
Telephone (800) 791-9354
Fax (610) 853-9146
Email: queries@casemateacademic.com
www.casemateacademic.com/oxbow

Oxbow Books is part of the Casemate group

CONTENTS

CONTENTS

PREFACE

'When I was at Teheran, I realized for the first time what a very small country this is. On one hand the big Russian bear with its paws outstretched – on the other the great American Elephant – & between them the poor little English donkey – who is the only one that knows the right way home.'

Winston Churchill to Violet Bonham-Carter several months after the Conference, in her diary entry for 1 August 1944.[1]

Jerusalem Throne Games: The Battle of Bible Stories after the Death of David is about exactly what the title states. David was one of the most extraordinary human beings who ever lived. He changed the course of human history although he did not know it at the time. Then he died. Now what?

Queen Bathsheba was an intensely ambitious person. She could not become king but she could marry one and become mother of one. In modern parlance the manner in which she installed her son on the throne following the death of her husband is called a *coup*. Her actions generated a vigorous response that failed politically. However, stories were written in the aftermath of her success. Six of them are the basis of this study.

The stories were written in the language and conventions of their time. It was a time before abstract language where a picture is worth a thousand words and a story a thousand footnotes. If you saw an image of an elephant stomping a donkey, what would come to mind? Would you consider such action an unusual occurrence within the animal kingdom? Would you alert the appropriate animal authorities? Would you record the event and upload it to the web? Suppose the animals were red and blue?

Most likely, if you are an American, you would recognize that the elephant and the donkey symbolize the two leading national political parties as of the time of this writing. Most likely you would understand that the image is a comment on the recent presidential election, as of this writing. Most likely you would know that literal animal concerns were not pertinent to the message being delivered. But suppose you are not an American, then would you understand its message? Suppose it is the year 3016, 4016, or 5016? Will people 3000 years from now be better equipped to understand our time than we are to understand David's?

As it turns out there is a biblical donkey story in the Book of Numbers, Chapter 22. In that story the prophet Balaam is riding his donkey when they come upon a messenger of the Lord. At least the donkey sees the armed messenger of the Lord, the prophet does not. The donkey then stops in the presence of the divine messenger and is berated by the

---

1. Violet Bonham Carter, *Champion Redoubtable: The Diaries and Letters of Violet Bonham-Carter, 1914–45*, edited by Mark Pottle. (London: Weidenfeld & Nicolson, 1998), 313.

prophet who does not see him. Amazingly, the donkey then speaks. Like the serpent in the garden, the donkey possesses the power of speech. After a dialog ensues, the prophet's eyes are opened and he sees the light, he sees the messenger of the Lord and responds accordingly.

Typically, this incident is viewed as a folktale because of the talking animal. This makes about as much as sense as deciding the elephant and donkey are just two animals in the wild. Ancient Israel had political parties, too. Here they are symbolized by a donkey and a wilderness (Transjordanian) prophet in the area where writing in the name of Balaam has been found at Deir Alla. In this instance, the donkey prevails. He is beaten by the prophet but he sees the truth and convinces the prophet of the error of his ways. Contrary to traditional exegesis, the story is a political one and not a folktale.

Sometimes the stakes were higher. A short time later in the narrative sequence (Num. 25), still in the wilderness, Phinehas, the priest and grandson of Aaron, spears a man and a woman at the tent of meeting. One presumes that the man and woman who were killed with a single spear were engaged in activities deemed inappropriate in that setting. Phinehas is rewarded with the covenant of eternal priesthood. The woman was a Midianite, the same as the wife of the prophet Moses, the giver of the covenant. The brutal death of Cozbi, a daughter of Midian, has become a *cause celebre* for feminists. However, contrary to feminist exegesis, the story is a political one and not a folktale. Here the priest and prophet parties are represented by Phinehas, grandson of Aaron, and a Midian from the family of Moses.

The wisdom of judgement story of Solomon similarly is political. Visually one sees a graphically striking image of an infant perhaps on the verge of being rendered asunder, chopped in half. Once again, the literal reading conveys a story that is abhorrent to modern sensibilities. Once again, the story is about a political situation. What story would you tell if part of your country sought to separate or secede? What story would you tell if you wanted to separate from a larger Union? Given that emotions involved are likely to have been intense, it is equally likely that the story of a division is likely to have been intense as well. When the kingdom separated after the death of Solomon, the emotions involved were just as raw and intense as they are today when similar actions occur. The writers of the biblical stories in this book expressed strong feelings and they did so through the story, not the tweet, the blog, the op-ed piece, or the essay.

Politics makes for strange bedfellows as the pairings in biblical stories often reveal. Unfortunately, the political basis for the stories is often overlooked in the emphasis on folk, myth and sin. In politics, there are winners and losers and then they may switch sides. The storytelling in the battle for power after the death of David has no counterpart in the ancient world. The stories enable us to enter a 3000-year-old world by reading the words of specific human beings battling for power in the royal arena in Jerusalem. This book is dedicated to the journey to see the truth of those stories as they originally were created.

Jin Canrong, a professor of international relations at Renmin University in Beijing, told Global Times: 'China is a dragon. America is an eagle. Britain is a lion. When the dragon wakes up, the others are all snacks.' (Chris Buckley, 'Trump's and Xi's differences magnify uncertainties between US and China,' *NYT* 12/20/16)

Peter Feinman
January 2017

ABBREVIATIONS

AASOR	Annual of the American Schools of Oriental Research
AB	Anchor Bible
ABD	David Noel Freedman, ed., *Anchor Bible Dictionary* (New York: Doubleday, 1992, 6 volumes)
AfO	Archiv für Orientforschung
AIL	Ancient Israel and its Literature
AJSL	American Journal of Semitic Languages
ALH	American Literary History
AnBib	Analecta Biblica
ANEM	Ancient Near East Monographs
AOAT	Alter Orient und Altes Testament
AOS	American Oriental Series
AOTC	Apollos Old Testament Commentary
ASOR	American Schools of Oriental Research
BA	Biblical Archaeologist
BAR	Biblical Archaeology Review
BASOR	Bulletin of the American Schools of Oriental Research
BBR	Bulletin for Biblical Research
BES	Bulletin of the Egyptological Seminar of New York
Bib	Biblica
BibInt	Biblical Interpretation
BiIntS	Biblical Interpretation Series
BJS	Brown Judaic Studies
BN	Biblische Notizen
BO	Bibliotheca Orientalis
BSac	Bibliotheca Sacra
BTB	Biblical Theology Bulletin
BZ	Biblische Zeitschrift
BZAW	Beihefte zur Zeitschrift für die alttestamentliche Wissenschaft
CA	Current Anthropology
CANE	Jack Sasson, ed., *Civilizations of the Ancient Near East* (Peabody, MA: Hendrickson Publishers, 1995, 4 volumes)
CBQ	Catholic Biblical Quarterly
CHANE	Culture and History of the Ancient Near East
ConBot	Coniectanea biblica: Old Testament Series
CSSH	Comparative Studies in Society and History
CTQ	Concordia Theological Quarterly
DDD	Karel van der Toorn, Bob Becking, Pieter W. Van der Horst, eds, *Dictionary of Deities and Demons in the Bible*, (Leiden: Brill, 1999, 2nd edn)
EA	El Amarna
ErIsr	Eretz-Israel
ET	Expository Times

FAT	Forschungen zum Alten Testament
FZPhTh	Freiburgere Zeitschrift für Philosophie und Theologie
HBM	Hebrew Bible Monographs
HeBAI	Hebrew Bible and Ancient Israel
HS	Hebrew Studies
HSCP	Harvard Studies in Classical Philology
HSM	Harvard Semitic Monographs
HSS	Harvard Semitic Studies
HTR	Harvard Theological Review
HUCA	Hebrew Union College Annual
IEJ	Israel Exploration Journal
Int	Interpretation
JA	Journal asiatique
JAAR	Journal of the American Academy of Religion
JAEI	Journal of Ancient Egyptian Interconnections
JANER	Journal of Ancient Near East Religions
JANES	Journal of the Ancient Near East Society
JAOS	Journal of the American Oriental Society
JARCE	Journal of the American Research Center in Egypt
JBL	Journal of Biblical Literature
JBQ	Jewish Bible Quarterly
JCS	Journal of Cuneiform Studies
JEA	Journal of Egyptian Archaeology
JEGH	Journal of Egyptian History
JESHO	Journal of Economic and Social History of the Orient
JETS	Journal of the Evangelical Theological Society
JHS	Journal of Hebrew Scriptures
JIAS	Journal of the Institute of Asian Studies
JJS	Journal of Jewish Studies
JNES	Journal of Near Eastern Studies
JPOS	Journal of the Palestine Oriental Society
JRT	Journal of Religious Thought
JQR	Jewish Quarterly Review
JRAS	Journal of the Royal Asiatic Society of Great Britain and Ireland
JSOT	Journal for the Study of the Old Testament
JSS	Journal of Semitic Studies
JSSEA	Journal of the Society for the Study of Egyptian Antiquities
JTS	Journal of Theological Studies
JTVI	Journal of the Transactions of the Victoria Institute
KDB	King David Bible
KJV	King James Version
LHBOTS	Library of Hebrew Bible/Old Testament Studies
LXX	Septuagint
MT	Masoretic Text
MVHR	Mississippi Valley Historical Review
NEA	Near Eastern Archaeology

NRSV	New Revised Standard Version
NYT	New York Times
OEANE	Eric M. Meyers, ed., *The Oxford Encyclopedia of Archaeology in the Near East* (New York: Oxford University Press, 1997, 5 volumes)
OIS	Oriental Institute Seminars
OJA	Oxford Journal of Archaeology
OLA	Orientalia Lovaniensia Analecta
Or	Orientalia
OTS	Old Testament Studies
OtSt	Oudtestamentische Studiën
PEGLMBS	Proceedings Eastern Great Lakes Bible (and Midwest Bible) Societies
PEQ	Palestine Exploration Quarterly
PRSt	Perspectives in Religious Studies
PSBA	Proceedings of the Society of Biblical Archaeology
PSCF	Perspectives on Science and Christian Faith
RB	Revue biblique
Rev Assyriol Archeol Orient	Revue D'Assyriologie et D'Archeologie Orientale
RSV	Revised Standard Version
SAAS	State Archives of Assyria Studies
SAOC	Studies in Ancient Oriental Civilization
SBLABS	Society of Biblical Literature Archaeology and Biblical Studies
SBLDS	Society of Biblical Literature Dissertation Series
SBLRBS	Society of Biblical Literature Resources for Biblical Studies
SBLSymS	Society of Biblical Literature Symposium Series
SBTS	Sources for Biblical and Theological Study
Sem	Semitica
SJOT	Scandinavian Journal of the Old Testament
SP	Samaritan Pentateuch
SPCK	Society for Promoting Christian Knowledge
ST	Studia Theologica
SVT	Vetus Testamentum Supplements
SWBA	Social World of Biblical Antiquity
TA	Tel Aviv
TBN	Themes in Biblical Narrative
TS	Theological Studies
TSBA	Transactions of the Society of Biblical Archaeology
TynBul	Tyndale Bulletin
UF	Ugarit-Forschungen
VT	Vetus Testamentum
WMQ	William and Mary Quarterly
WTJ	Westminster Theological Journal
YES	Yale Egyptological Studies
ZA	Zeitschrift für Assyriologie
ZAW	Zeitschrift für die alttestamentliche Wissenschaft
ZDPV	Zeitschrift des Deutschen Palästina-Vereins

Books of the Bible

Gen.	Genesis
Chr.	Chronicles
Deut.	Deuteronomy
Ex.	Exodus
Ezek.	Ezekiel
Jer.	Jeremiah
Judg.	Judges
Kgs	Kings
Num.	Numbers
Phil.	Philippians
Sam.	Samuel

Other

Ant	Jewish Antiquities, Josephus
Bab. Bat.	Babylonian Talmud Tractate Baba Batra
Dtr	Deuteronomist
Gen Rab	Genesis Rabbah
Midr Agadah	Midrash Aggadah
Pes	Babylonian Talmud Tractate Pesachim
San	Babylonian Talmud Tractate Sanhedrin

All boldface in biblical passages quoted in the book has been added.

THE DOCUMENTARY HYPOTHESIS

'When a book is studied in a high school or university class, one usually learns something of the author's life, and generally this contributes to the understanding of the book... [M]ost readers seem to find it significant to be able to see connections between the author's life and the world that the author depicts in his or her work... The more obvious this seems, the more striking is the fact that this information has been largely lacking in the case of the Bible... [H]ow did the author come to have an idea of what happened? ...How much did the events of the author's own day affect the way in which the author told the story?'

Richard Elliott Friedman, *Who Wrote the Bible?*, 16, 17

Who Wrote the Bible? is the title of a book written by Richard Elliott Friedman. Its purpose was to bring to the attention of the general public the research by biblical scholars directed to answering this question.[1] Through this book, readers would have the opportunity (i) to retrace the path taken by these scholars in the attempt to answer the question, (ii) to learn the answers which had been developed, and (iii) to be exposed to an original idea by the author himself. The book helped bridge the gap between what was occurring in the ivory tower and what was known in the general educated public.

The study undertaken here seeks to build on that foundation and to continue the journey in solving the question of 'who wrote the Bible?' through the analysis of six specific stories (see Chapter 1). To begin with, it is necessary to clarify the meaning of some terms and to become familiar with the behind-the-scenes decisions and conclusions which have been reached along the way. Based on these clarifications, it will then be possible to achieve the intended goals of the study.

Background information

In the beginning was the word 'the'. It seems like such a simple word, this frequently used common article preceding a common or proper noun. There is no mystery to the word but its presence in the title may provide a misleading impression. To speak or write of '*the* Bible' suggests that there is only one. That is not exactly true. For example, for a given faith community there may indeed be one and only one Bible. However there are

---

1. Richard Elliott Friedman, *Who Wrote the Bible?* (New York: Summit Books, 1987), 13. These exact words begin a similar investigation by Karel van der Toorn a generation later. He cites Friedman's book in his first footnote. As it turns out the two studies unintentionally complement each other particularly through the focus on the Levites (see Chapter 9) (Karel van der Toorn, *Scribal Culture and the Making of the Hebrew Bible* [Cambridge, MA: Harvard University Press, 2007], 1 and 267).

multiple faith communities that share the use of the term 'Bible' without their agreeing on precisely what the Bible is.

The starting point for defining the different Bibles is the Jewish Bible, the oldest one. Jews do not always use this term to designate the writings they deem holy or sacred. Judaism often uses the term 'tanakh'. The word is an acronym constructed from the first letter in Hebrew of the three components of the Jewish Bible: the Torah, the Prophets (*Nevi'im*), and the Writings (*Ketuvim*). Bible is a term recognized and understood within the Jewish community as well. All Jews share the same Bible or set of sacred writings regardless of their denomination within Judaism.

With Christianity, the story is different. All Christian denominations share the Jewish Bible in common. They also share many additional books in common such as the Gospels. But the Christian faiths, primarily Catholic, Eastern Orthodox, Protestant, and possibly Mormon, do not share a completely identical set of writings. These differences are not germane to the study undertaken here except to point out one important fact: people who refer to *the* Bible are not necessarily referring to the same writings. It is important for the reader or listener to know what the speaker or author means when employing that term.

Given this clarification of 'the', there is a second issue of what 'Bible' itself means. 'Bible' is an English version of the Greek term τὰ βιβλία or tà biblía. In Greek, the word is a plural noun meaning 'books' while the common English usage is in the singular 'book'. Apparently the Greeks chose the term 'byblos', their word for papyrus, as the basis for *biblia*. They selected it because the Egyptian shipments of papyrus used for writing passed through the city of that name on the coast of modern Lebanon. They named the product from the last known city associated with it before it reached Greece. One notes the common consonantal root BBL between the two words **Bible** and **Byblos**. The residents of the city did not refer to themselves as living in Byblos but Gubla, as best can be determined from the Egyptian records referring to the city. Byblos like Egypt, Phoenicia, and Mesopotamia is a Greek name which has been applied to non-Greek areas and peoples and which has become the name by which the city is known.

In ancient times when people used the term *biblia* it referred to a collection of books. This sense of the Bible being a collection of books is maintained today as one might refer to 'the Book of Genesis' or 'the Book of Ruth'. When biblical scholars raise the question of 'who wrote the Bible?', generally they are not referring to all the individual books of the Bible, not even of the shortest or Jewish Bible. The focus of the investigation has been on the Torah, also called the Pentateuch meaning Five Books or the Five Books of Moses: Genesis, Exodus, Leviticus, Numbers, and Deuteronomy. All the biblical religions share these books in common as the first books of the Bible. This study will focus on the early portions of the Book of Genesis and also draw on material outside the Pentateuch such as in the Books of Samuel and Kings.

None of these books was written originally in English. This seemingly obvious statement may be overlooked in the attempt to ascertain the meaning of biblical texts. There is a long history of how the texts one reads as the Bible in English came to be written in English. In 2011, biblical scholars and others celebrated the quadricentennial of the King James Version

(KJV), the best-known English version. One should recognize that the English language is older than 400 years, meaning there were English translations prior to it. The Geneva Bible (1560), for example, was a translation produced by Protestants in exile from Queen Mary. It became the Bible of Shakespeare and the Puritans who came to America. One may glimpse in this accounting a subtext of political and religious considerations in the process of the creation of a Protestant English translation in exile and a Catholic English translation commissioned by the king. These two manuscript versions remained separate and never have been combined into one. The political aspect to the translation of the Bible into English is somewhat reminiscent of the political process by which the original stories were created as will be explained in this study.

Since the Geneva and KJV translations centuries ago, there have been numerous developments and changes impacting translations. Some are due to a change in style. 'Thou' and 'ye' are dead giveaways that the speaker is affecting ancient airs or at least pretending to be part of a hallowed tradition. Sometimes the translations have changed because of better information. Since the discovery of the Rosetta Stone in 1799 and the translation of hieroglyphics in 1824, the world of ancient Egypt was revealed. With the archaeological discoveries in the 1840s and the translation of cuneiform in the 1850s, the world of the ancient Near East was resurrected. There have been less-known but still important texts from the past discovered in other locations in modern Syria. Collectively they reveal a world with stories similar to the biblical stories, words similar to biblical words, and names both human and divine also found in the biblical passages. One major difference, especially with the stories of Baal, is these stories from other cultures are from their point of view instead of Israel's. These discoveries have helped elucidate the perplexing meanings of biblical texts. Translations also have changed because of change in values. One problematic result may be to force the ancient text conform to values in the present. The goal here is to understand the stories for what they meant at the time of their writing and not how they have been interpreted, retold, or retranslated over the centuries and millennia.

Translated from what? Regardless of what modern language is used in a biblical translation, it expresses a translation from something. The primary source documents for the translation of the Five Books of Moses into English (or any other language) are in Hebrew, Greek, and Latin. While Hebrew was the original language of the Jewish Bible, the Hebrew manuscript that provides the starting point is fairly recent. The text used is called the Masoretic text (MT) after the Masoretes who wrote in Tiberias. The specific text used has been the Leningrad Codex (1008/9), which is located in the National Library of Russia in St Petersburg, Russia. It is still called that even though Leningrad no longer is the name of the city. Cities do change names, like New Amsterdam to New York, and name changes occurred in biblical times as well:

> *And they named the city Dan, after the name of Dan their ancestor, who was born to Israel; but the name of the city was Laish at the first* (Judges 18: 29)

The most famous example of a city name change is Jebus/Salem/Jerusalem becoming the City of David. This city is the stage on which the battle for power will be played (see Chapter 8).

The MT has gained increasing prominence as the definitive but not sole source text for biblical scholarship. The Hebrew text is used as the basis for translations into English by Jews as one might expect. Protestants also use it. The Protestant usage expressed the liberation from the Latin Catholic texts by going back to the presumed original Hebrew. However, beginning in the 20th century, Catholics began to use the MT as well as the authoritative text. So do scholars. The Aleppo Codex, another Hebrew-language manuscript, is slightly older version of the MT but is no longer complete.

Two additional Hebrew language texts bear notice. One is the famous Dead Sea Scrolls discovered at Qumran beginning in 1946. These numerous scrolls are dated generally to Hasmonean (140–37 BCE) and Herodian times (37 BCE–100 CE), concurrent with the settlement of Qumran in the last centuries BCE ending with Jewish War against Rome around 70 CE. The Dead Sea Scrolls therefore pushed back the date for the oldest existing Hebrew texts by over a millennium. They do not always agree with the MT. The second is the Samaritan Pentateuch (SP), 'discovered' in 1616. The SP is the Bible of the Samaritans and includes only the Five Books of Moses. Scholars debate its date of origin and the related issue of the post-Assyrian destruction of Samaria, capital of Israel in 722 BCE. It too differs from the MT and demonstrates that extremely similar narratives with different perspectives are possible.

In addition to the Hebrew manuscripts, there is a Greek version of the Bible known as the Septuagint or LXX. This designation derives from the legendary story of how the translation came to be. It involves 70 or LXX, sometimes 72, translators working independently in the time of Pharaoh Ptolemy II Philadelphus (283–246 BCE). The 70 simultaneously produced identical translations. It is a miracle. The Greek version, too, differs from the MT and SP. While many of the variants are minor, some differences are more extensive. Fortunately, the differences in the stories under analysis in this study tend to be minor. They will be addressed as appropriate in Part II as part of the exegesis of each biblical writer.

Finally, in western Christianity, there is the Latin version famously produced by Jerome in the 4th century CE. Pope Damasus I commissioned him in 382 CE to produce a standard version that the Church could use. Jerome lived in a time of multiple Old Latin versions that lacked consistency. By studying Hebrew, he sought to produce a definitive Latin version for the Church. He succeeded in creating the Vulgate. It did not become the official or canonized Catholic version of the Bible until the Council of Trent (1545–1563). The Church's decision happened after Luther had created a Protestant German-language Bible. The Vulgate canonization provides another example of a biblical text being produced as a result of political conflicts between priesthoods and religions just as occurred in ancient times.

These varying and differing versions plus additional ones in the eastern and Aramaic traditions reveal the existence of numerous 'Bibles'. The existence of multiple biblical texts may seem overwhelming to someone steeped in the tradition of one and only one Bible with one and only one ancient language version and one and only one authorized version in English or whatever language one happens to use. As a rule, in the beginning of any book with a biblical translation, there will be a preface or introduction that readers tend to ignore. The editorial committee or author who produced the translation writes it to explain the decisions made about ancient language manuscripts used and the decisions made when differences occurred. As might be expected, not all the ancient manuscripts are complete. In addition there are even multiple copies of some manuscripts in the same language that are generally in good agreement with each other but are not identical. There is a sub-division within biblical scholarship for people who focus on these different manuscripts. In short, producing a modern language version of the Bible requires a great many human decisions that usually are forgotten or ignored by those who read the finished product.

With this brief background in mind, it is now possible to turn to the book that Friedman wrote about 'Who Wrote the Bible', where he focused on the Five Books of Moses.

Who wrote the Bible?

The traditional answer to the question 'who wrote the Five Books of Moses?' is that Moses was the author. This conclusion indeed was the common tradition in both Jewish and Christian religions. One should note that the attribution to Moses is a non-pentateuchal tradition of unknown origin which biblical scholars seek to reconstruct. For example, after the wilderness battle against the Amalekites, the biblical account states:

> *And Yahweh said to Moses: 'Write this as a memorial in a book and recite it in the ears of Joshua, that I will utterly blot out the remembrance of Amalek from under heaven'.* (Ex. 17: 14)

One might easily conclude from this verse that Moses did write but not in other passages lacking the divine instruction. There is a story to be told about how Moses came to be considered the author of the entire Pentateuch but it remains conjectural at present.[2]

Long before modern biblical scholarship, questions arose about the validity of the tradition of Mosaic authorship. The presence of certain verses just did not seem quite kosher with the view that he was the author. Prominent among them is:

> *So Moses the servant of Yahweh died there in the land of Moab … and he buried him in the valley in the land of Moab opposite Bethpeor* (Deut. 34: 5–6)

Why 'there' and not 'here in the land of Moab' since the people had not yet crossed the Jordan? Where was the author located when he wrote this? Jerusalem or Moab? How did Moses know who buried him? The suggestion that Moses wrote his own obituary in advance and communicated it to the people he led is more morbid than prophetic.

> *but no man knows the place of his burial to this day.* (Deut. 34: 6)

What day is that? In any book other than the Hebrew Bible one would automatically recognize the perspective of a writer looking back on the death of Moses from the vantage point of the writer's present west of the Jordan River. The intent is not hidden or obscure. The verse is not prophecy by Moses, it is a claim made by an author long after the death of Moses.

---

2   For a recent attempt at recreating this process see, Joel S. Baden, *The Composition of the Pentateuch: Renewing the Documentary Hypothesis* (Anchor Bible Reference Library; New Haven: Yale University Press, 2012), 14–16.

And the people of Israel wept for Moses in the plains of Moab thirty days; then the days of weeping and mourning for Moses were ended. (Deut. 34: 8)

Now, not only did he write his death notice, he described his funeral service as well!

Understanding the Hebrew Bible should not require the suspension of common sense or the insulting of one's intelligence. The rabbis were cognizant of the problems in attributing these verses to Moses. They responded in the Talmud by crediting the final eight verses of the Pentateuch (Deut. 34: 5–12) to Joshua (*b. Bab. Bat. 14b*). Of course, once they adopted such a solution, they inevitably had taken a first step on a slippery slope leading to additional suspect verses.

Now the man Moses was very meek, more than all men that were on the face of the earth. (Num. 12: 3)

Is that something a meek or humble person would write about himself?

Now consider the human dynamics of the story. Let us suppose, for example, that Moses wrote the Five Books of Moses at Sinai as part of the covenant and not at Nebo just before he died. Suppose Moses wrote '*all the words of Yahweh*' (Ex. 24: 4) and that '*the tablets were the work of God, and the writing was the writing of God, graven upon the tables*' (Ex. 32: 16) simultaneously. Combined, these two verses indicate that both he and Yahweh or God wrote something perhaps on two occasions at the mount of Yahweh or God. People have the opportunity to interpret the meaning of these words in different ways, and those interpretations are exactly that: interpretations.

For the moment, let us chose to interpret those words and tablets as not just meaning a covenant, but as what is now the entire Five Books of Moses. Let us assume that the entire history of the people up to that point was meant, including the events just lived through by the people.

Further, let us ignore the technological challenge of the effort required to write all verses on stone. Let us ignore the time required to write on papyrus with an endlessly replenished supply of ink. Let us ignore how any human being could read it all. Instead let us focus instead simply on the human dynamic. Certainly Moses would have known the words written for there is absolutely no indication in the stories that such knowledge was denied him. No one knew the words better than he did. But look at what he had read. Moses had seen the future. He had read tomorrow's newspaper today!

When Moses wrote the words the first time, he learned that he was going to destroy the tablets when he returned from the mount to face the golden calves! Imagine all that effort to write Genesis and Exodus 1–32 only to then discover in Exodus 33 that your handiwork would be destroyed when you climbed down the mount. What incentive would you have to continue writing Exodus 34–40, Leviticus, and Deuteronomy? Why bother? Would you consider such a god merciful? Who was being punished here?

Moses knew who was going to lead the rebellion in the wilderness against him! He had read it in advance. He knew their names, he knew when, he knew where, and he knew how. Of course, he also knew that he would prevail. For that matter, he knew that by striking the rock he would be condemned to die in the wilderness and that he would never enter the promised land. He even knew what the spies would find and how the people would react … he had seen the future … including the funeral at his death. However, there is no sense in any of these stories that Moses was experiencing *déjà vu*.

Issues like the ones just presented here led rabbis and others to ponder alternative explanations for the writing of the Pentateuch. Friedman titles one section of his opening chapter 'Six Hundred Years of Investigation.'[3] He reports various religious people did struggle to make sense of various anomalies. These disturbances included references to Moses in the third person, mentioning of places he did not visit, and his death. Friedman notes that the old tradition that Joshua composed the death scene was itself rejected since it was not so easy to excise those verses from the text since they were written in the same style as the remaining verses. For Baruch Spinoza, 'And there has not arisen a prophet since in Israel like Moses' (Deut. 34: 10) seemed to have been written long after the death of Moses. Also it was hardly worthy of the humblest man on earth.

In response to the efforts by rabbis and church fathers to ameliorate the issues raised by a close reading of the text, Richard Simon, a French priest in the 17th century, wrote:

> 'I don't believe that it would be necessary, or even wise, to resort to these kinds of ways around the problem, since the most knowledgeable Fathers have freely admitted that the Pentateuch, at least in the form it is now, cannot be attributed to Moses.
>
> The challenge confronting the people who took the Bible seriously was to develop a coherent theory that could rationally explain what they could clearly see if not openly admit.'[4]

The closer one scrutinized the text, the more questions were asked undermining the validity of Mosaic authorship. Friedman refers to these developments in a section entitled 'Sources', the next section in his book. Here Friedman observes that exegetes detected doublets, two versions of the same story. Examples include the creation (Gen. 1–2: 4a and 2: 4b–3), Sarah as Abraham's sister (claim to Pharaoh in Gen. 12: 10–20 and to Abimelech of Gerar in Gen. 20), two revelations to Jacob involving Bethel (the famous dream story in Gen. 28: 11–20 and in Gen. 35: 1–8). The list could be extended. Upon further observation, people like Jean Astruc noticed that different names were used for the deity in the doublets, Yaheweh and Elohim. Each usage became the definer of a source document which perhaps Moses had used. 'Documents' meant the writing was fragmentary but coherent and continuous in some way. He published his conjecture anonymously in 1753. Then in a doctoral dissertation published in 1805, Wilhelm de Wette proposed that the Book of Deuteronomy, which included the death of Moses, represented a third source written in distinctly different language (more like a sermon than a story). Finally, in 1853, Hermann Hupfeld suggested that the proposed Elohim source really consisted to two distinct components (contrast the creation story in the beginning, the genealogies, and laws with actual stories). The stage was being set for someone to put the pieces together and devise a comprehensive documentary source hypothesis.[5]

---

3 Friedman, *Who Wrote the Bible?*, 18–21.

4 Richard Simon, *Histoire Critique du Vieux Testament* (Rotterdam: n.p., 1685; reprint Frankfurt: Minerva, 1967), 32, quoted in Baden, *The Composition of the Pentateuch*, 14.

5 Friedman, *Who Wrote the Bible?*, 22–24. For a review of additional suspect texts see Baden, *The Composition*

During the time of this investigation there arose within early 19th-century Germany, the idea that German texts in the present might not have been originally written in their final form. Instead there may have been a process whereby different texts or sources over time became part of longer texts. The challenge for the scholar of German history and culture was to identify these sources now contained within the extant text. This process accelerated with the simultaneous invention of the graduate school as the place where such research would occur. This development did not happen in a vacuum either. The time from Napoleon's defeat of Prussia at Jena in 1806 to German unification in 1871 following the Franco-Prussian War coincided with this quest into Germany's past through the identification of sources. The investigation to determine what actually happened in German history was applied to the biblical text as well.

The result was the Documentary Hypothesis, most prominently associated with Julius Wellhausen (1844–1918).[6] Wellhausen was not the first to identify the sources but he was the one who put the pieces together to create a coherent whole of sequentially dated sources or originally-independent documents. The hypothesis also is called JEDP after the first letter of the four sources postulated by Wellhausen. In the remainder of his book, Friedman seeks to explain the context in which these four different authors wrote, the message(s) they delivered, and the verses that are to be assigned to each of the sources. In so doing he drew on a century-old tradition of biblical scholarship that had reached a consensus on which author had written what. A similar approach will be followed in this book for the six J-stories under consideration. Although this study is on texts assigned to the J author who was the first or oldest author in this hypothesis, it is worth providing a brief overview on each of the writers anyway. Some of the patterns and priesthoods with the Documentary Hypothesis apply to the J Documentary Hypothesis proposed in this study (see Chapter 9).

The progression will be examined in reverse chronological order. It begins with the person believed to have combined the different individual narratives into one. Portions of the stories presented in this study derive not from the original authors but from the redaction process when they were combined.

R

In biblical scholarship the redactor is designed as 'R.' Friedman defines the redactor as follows:

> 'The person who assembled the four sources into the Five Books of Moses is known as the redactor. The redactor is harder to trace than any of the authors of the sources. For the most part, the redactor was arranging texts that already existed, not writing very much of his or her own, and so there is little evidence to shed light on who he [or she] was… To start with, the redactor came from the circle of Aaronid priests.'[7]

---

of the Pentateuch, chapter I: the Documentary Hypothesis (13–33) which provides numerous examples of the verses that tried the rabbis' souls.

6   This section is called 'The hypothesis,' in Friedman, *Who Wrote the Bible?*, 24–27.

7   Friedman, *Who Wrote the Bible?*, 218.

Typically, scholars imagine a lone individual surrounded by papyrus (not paper) documents wrestling them into a coherent whole. After all, scholars today perform the same tasks when they bring together different source documents, books, articles, and ancient texts, all carefully footnoted to create a unified finished product, the scholar's own book or article. The familiar model of academic research and composition, then, has been retrojected to ancient times whereby an individual redactor is presumed to have done something similar but without the footnotes identifying the sources used by scholars today.[8]

The political approach taken here yields a different understanding of the redactor from the ivory-tower one. In a political redaction process, there is no such thing as 'the individual'. Everything is by committee. Suppose one sought to combine multiple sources such as the American view of the American Revolution and the British view or the Northern view of the American Civil War and the Confederate view of the War of Northern Aggression, into a single text, how many people would be involved? One can be sure that advocates for each side would demand a seat at the table in the room where it happened. So it was in ancient times as well.

The biblical sources identified in the Documentary Hypothesis were combined by a committee, probably more than once at different time periods. One member of final committee was likely to have been an Aaronid priest of the temple in Jerusalem as Friedman suggests. As will be seen, the temple priests also were known as Zadokites, a separate but related group. The investigation into the writings of the six stories analyzed in the book addresses the contentious issue of the relationship between the Aaronids and the Zadokites. Regardless of that relationship, the political faction of temple priests was centuries old at the time of the final redaction. The temple priest redaction committee member was a later representative of the political party that existed at the time that the stories to be investigated in this analysis originated. He would not have been the only member of the committee. People who disagreed with the temple-based approach would have participated also. The operation of this committee for the six son stories in this study will be presented in the final chapter of the book when the pieces are put together.

P

Friedman identified the P or Priest writer as being from the same circle of Aaronid priests as R. P is not known as a great storyteller. The verses most frequently associated with the author are genealogies or temple rituals such as those in the Book of Leviticus. The most famous passage attributed to P is the story of creation that begins the Bible in the Book of Genesis, Chapter 1.[9]

Scholars subsequently have suggested the existence or more than one P author. The designation H is used for the Holiness Code in the Book of Leviticus, chapters 17–26. They consider these chapters to have been an independent text now incorporated into

---

8 Sometimes scholars edit a book where each chapter clearly was written by a different person and there often is barely any connection between the chapters except that they are published in a single book. Readers often read, photocopy, scan, or download specific individual chapters as needed.

9 Friedman, *Who Wrote the Bible?*, 50–60, 188.

the P document. They ascertained the distinction through the analysis of the vocabulary and specifications of the laws in the chapters compared to those elsewhere in Leviticus. The details of the analysis are not germane here. What is of significance is the scholarly recognition that within a given source document, in this instance, P, there may be multiple voices.[10]

From the political perspective, P and Friedman's R have clear focuses and concerns. The Davidic dynasty, the Solomonic temple, and the legitimacy and rituals of the temple priesthood all loom large. By no coincidence whatsoever, these are the exact same issues which were addressed centuries earlier when the Davidic dynasty was first established, when his son Solomon succeeded him, when the temple was first built by Solomon, and when Zadok became the chief priest of the temple in Jerusalem. All of these concerns originated when the very institutions they deal with first occurred in history, in the time of Solomon. P is a descendant of those who fought the good fight on behalf of the Davidic dynasty, the Solomonic temple, and the Zadokite priesthood when they were first established.

D

Like P, D or the Deuteronomist (Dtr) is not known for being a good storyteller. The name is derived from the Book of Deuteronomy. The book is mainly a sermon or series of sermons by Moses proclaiming the law to the people before he dies after having seen the land he will never enter. D frequently is presumed to have been involved with the formation of books beyond the Five Books of Moses including Joshua, Judges, Samuel, and Kings. The exact nature of that involvement is part of the current scholarly discourse. Sometimes Dtr is considered a compiler as well for consolidating the already-existing stories that comprised the history of Israel and Judah from the conquest by Joshua to the exile after the temple in Jerusalem was destroyed. Sometimes Dtr is considered to be different peoples in different times belonging to a school of scribes who wrote before and after Nebuchadnezzar II destroyed the Solomonic temple in 587 BCE.

The Book of Deuteronomy appears to champion the Levites and that is where Friedman assigns authorship. But which Levites or priests? Friedman observes that the laws in the book do not mention Aaron, the high priest at the temple or the objects that would be in the temple. Instead Friedman writes: 'the High Priest of Jerusalem had been Aaronid ever since the day when King Solomon expelled the priest Abiathar and made the Aaronid priest Zadok the sole High Priest'.[11] One critical insight applied in the analysis of the stories selected for study here is based precisely on this observation. There was a political conflict expressed through stories by the Abiathar, Zadok, and Aaronid factions or priesthoods after the death of David.

Friedman connects the author of D with the priests of Shiloh, a national religious center in the time of Samuel prior to the monarchies of first Saul and then David. These priests were not wedded to the monarchy. After all, Israel had existed for centuries without having

---

10 The Holiness Code is not a factor in Friedman's analysis. For the Holiness Code see Israel Knohl, *The Sanctuary of Silence: The Priestly Torah and the Holiness School* (Minneapolis: Fortress Press, 1995).

11 Friedman, *Who Wrote the Bible?*, 121.

a king and the odds of there being no priests during that time are zero. Friedman expresses the view that the Shiloh priesthood could have survived even after Abiathar's exile and that the source of legitimacy was from Moses and not Aaron.[12]

The issue raised by Friedman's observation is exactly how could that priesthood have survived in exile from the capital. The American political system provides a partial answer. In American terms the ancestral claim for legitimacy would be a little like two political parties tracing their heritage back to different Founding Fathers from the American Revolution, Thomas Jefferson or Alexander Hamilton. 'Priests' and politicians today comment directly about ancestral American figures or claim to speak 'in the spirit of' them. Ancient Israelite writers engaged in the same practice of delivering their message in the name of revered ancestral figures but in the story format. Their stories could be set in the past, including the Exodus or those selected for study here, or be set in the present. Friedman's Abiathar in exile could not have survived by remaining silent and the presumption here is that he did not.

Friedman also envisions the author of D continuing in the tradition of E, the next author to be described.[13] So whereas one writer might emphasize the temple and the king, another might prefer the covenant and Moses. This disagreement between priest and prophet goes back to the time when Israel first had a king. The proponents of the temple and the covenant both would have had a seat at the redaction table.

E

The E or Elohist is known as a story-teller, at least more so than D or P and less so than J. He is called the Elohist because in the verses assigned to him, the deity is designated as *elohim*. To refer to God as *elohim* was a little strange to biblical scholars because the word is in the plural form: *el* would be the more familiar singular form as in Beth-el or Isra-el. However, despite *elohim* being in the plural, it is used in Hebrew in the singular because the verb is singular not plural: 'they writes' third person plural subject and first person singular verb is an odd combination. In the English translations the plural noun is translated in the singular form 'God' and not 'Gods' and the singular verb form is used. What is less clear is why this author used the plural form to represent a singular being.

To understand the significance of E's actions, it is beneficial to examine a more recent and recognizable parallel. The comparable American example is 'the United States'. Once that was a plural name and now it is a singular. Once one said 'The United States are a country'. Now one says 'The United States *is* a country'. Europeans still refer to America as 'the States' in the plural. This transformation of the United States of America in the plural to in the singular is attributed to one person at one place at one moment in time: President Abraham Lincoln at Gettysburg. His emphasis on the Union of the people irrevocably changed the country.[14] The change had political implications. Whether E was Israel's Lincoln as the originator of the biblical transformation of *elohim* from plural to

---

12 Friedman, *Who Wrote the Bible?*, 122–124, 129.
13 Friedman, *Who Wrote the Bible?*, 122.
14 Garry Wills, *Lincoln at Gettysburg: The Words that Remade America* (New York: Simon & Schuster, 1992), 145.

singular cannot be determined from the stories analyzed in this study. Nonetheless, it is important to recognize that there would be political ramifications for a change in the name of something as crucial as the deity of a people. The name of a deity in a story can be critical to understanding the message of the story even within one of the individual sources.

Friedman assigns E to the priests of Shiloh. He suggests these priests thought of Moses as their own ancestor.[15] Even if Moses had not existed, these people may have considered themselves sons of Moses the same way in other cultures an Alexander or Aeneas might be perceived a descendant of Zeus or Venus. Moses, of course, was renowned for challenging truth to power, the power being that of Pharaoh. So if any individual was to challenge or confront the power of the king, be it the prophets Ahijah (I Kgs 11: 28–30 and 14: 1–16), Elijah (I Kgs 17–19, 21), or Jeremiah (Jer. 21–22 and 26) over the centuries, it is likely that they would have done so in the name or the tradition of Moses.

One diagnostic in identifying the authors of the biblical stories is the attitude toward Moses conveyed in a story. Regardless of the historicity of Moses, his name carried meaning with the biblical tradition beyond 'lawgiver'. In effect, his name may be considered a metaphor for 'one who challenges kings'. It also could mean, 'one who defends the weak from the strong' similar to Robin Hood meaning 'to rob from the rich and give to the poor' regardless of the historical validity. As Friedman points out, Ahijah of Shiloh in the biblical tradition confronted two sitting kings: first Rehoboam, son of Solomon, by supporting Jeroboam in creating a new kingdom (I Kgs 11: 28–30) and then Jeroboam himself (I Kgs 14: 1–16) when he wanted his own people in the priesthood and not the Shiloh priests.[16] Prophets could claim to speak in the name of Moses when challenging a contemporary 'Pharaoh' for an abuse of power. They could be a formidable foe if the Israelite people believed the prophet really spoke in the name of Moses. Some scholars have suggested that E should be associated with the time of Jeroboam.[17]

The Israelite attitude towards kingship directly contributed to the son stories in this study. Regardless of the merits of the E–Jeroboam link or if E even existed, the salient point is the significant distinction between biblical writings and the texts of the other cultures from the ancient Near East. In no other culture is there such a persistent castigation of kings as in the biblical tradition. That action could only occur once Israel actually had a king. Between Pharaoh and Saul there was no opportunity or need to challenge an Israelite king. Just as Americans may have favorite founding fathers or other hallowed figures from the past, so competing political factions in Israel may have justified themselves through different figures in the past. One group may have done so through Aaron, another through Moses. Their stories would be different.

As Friedman observes, Moses is at the center of the tradition when the name Yahweh became known. In the E narrative, the deity is *elohim* until the burning bush, when the name Yahweh is revealed to Moses.[18] This datum is significant. As will be seen, the name

15 Friedman, *Who Wrote the Bible?*, 79.
16 Friedman, *Who Wrote the Bible?*, 47–48.
17 Robert Coote, *In Defense of Revolution: The Elohist History* (Minneapolis: Fortress Press, 1991); Alan W. Jenks, 'Elohist,' in *ABD* II: 478–482.
18 Friedman, *Who Wrote the Bible?*, 81.

Yahweh appears several times in the dialogue in stories from the beginning of the Book of Genesis analyzed in this study. That analysis therefore must ascertain who are the individuals who used the name Yahweh prior to the story of the burning bush and what was the purpose in doing so.

Friedman, along with many biblical scholars, presumes that E did not contribute any stories to the early part of Genesis.[19] The political approach yields a different interpretation. As indicated above, R was not an individual but a committee. That committee would have consisted of representatives from the main political parties, in this case D and P. Friedman specifically mentions the creation and flood stories as not having an E component. Nonetheless, one should keep in mind the possibility that the E and J stories of the garden and the deluge were similar except for the name of the deity. As will be seen in the analysis of the son stories in this study, there is a prophetic layer in them. As soon as there was a king to abuse power, there was a prophet to call him to task.

J

By all accounts J or the Yahwist is the greatest storyteller in the Bible and one of the great human storytellers. Generally the best-known stories are from him, such as the Garden of Eden, Cain and Abel, and the Flood. The designation 'J' instead of 'Y' is due to the German origin of the Documentary Hypothesis where the letter 'J' is used instead of 'Y'. English-language biblical writers call the author 'J' and the deity 'Yahweh'.

In a second book (yes, a person can write on more than one occasion including in ancient times as well), entitled *The Hidden Book in the Bible: The Discovery of the First Prose Masterpiece*, Friedman reassess the writings to be assigned to J. His analysis extends J's narrative far beyond the life of Moses into the time of Solomon. Friedman calls this masterpiece 'the first work of prose' which is far from being 'a rudimentary piece of writing'.[20] He refers to this once unified narrative as the 'first known attempt at history writing'.[21] Scholars previously have posited the existence of a Hexateuch (Six Books) and not a Pentateuch, meaning the Book of Joshua should be considered a continuation of the previous books with the same writers and the true ending of the narrative sequence. Now Friedman sought to push the envelope even further into the Books of Samuel and Kings. Scholars refer to the entirety of Genesis through Kings as the Primary History or Enneateuch (Nine Books).

Friedman's moment of epiphany transpired when a student suggested to him that the language of the story of David's rise to power and challenges in maintaining his royal position (conventionally I Sam. 16: 14–II Sam. 5, II Sam. 10–20, and I Kgs 1–2) was similar to J. When Friedman commenced his own investigation of this possibility he realized that the idea had been suggested before. He cited most prominently the German scholar Karl

---

19 Friedman, *Who Wrote the Bible?*, 83.
20 Richard Elliott Friedman, *The Hidden Book in the Bible: The Discovery of the First Prose Masterpiece* (New York: HarperCollins, 1998), 3.
21 Friedman, *The Hidden Book*, 4.

Budde (1850–1935).[22] The implication of his observations is that Budde's interpretation never attained mainstream status as part of scholarly biblical paradigm like JEDP. Friedman discovered that the language was similar, the styles were similar, and the plots were similar. As he researched the scholarship on the Books of Joshua, Judges, Samuel, and Kings, he discerned the hand of a single author until he concluded:

> '…the text that is known as J is just the beginning of a story that starts with the creation of the world in Genesis and continues all the way to the establishment of David's kingdom on earth.'[23]

This masterpiece begins with the garden in Gen. 2: 4b and ends with the kingdom secure in the hand of Solomon in I Kings 2: 46. When attempting to understand the message of a writer, it is useful to know the beginning and the ending of the text. It makes a difference whether a narrative begins in garden, with Abraham, or the Exodus. Similarly a narrative delivers a different message if it ends with David with the ark at Zion, Solomon in the temple, or the people in exile after the temple is destroyed.

Friedman rejects the idea that multiple people might have contributed to the writing of this extended J:

> '…there is a limit as to just how many literary geniuses we can ascribe to ancient Israel. In biblical scholarship we have been asserting a scenario in which a very small country produced an unparalleled number of exceptional authors and each one of them composed only one short surviving work.'[24]

Friedman is headed in the right direction but he is still bound by his one-author belief. As Friedman notes, biblical scholars have often debated the existence of multiple Js as if J had been produced by a school. He rejects this possibility, asserting that the J narrative is unified and complete in itself. He discerns no convincing analysis that demonstrates smaller units or multiple hands within J.[25]

Jerusalem Throne Games

By contrast, this study offers a different interpretation. There was an exceptional genius who produced a literary masterpiece that began in the garden but it ended with David installing the ark at Zion and not Solomon and the temple, the latter was an extension of the former. The narrative will be designated as the King David Bible (KDB) (see Chapter 9). It extends beyond the confines of the Pentateuch and includes material not assigned to J but included in Friedman's more extensive narrative. The KDB does not include all texts included by Friedman. The difference in approaches is in the number of authors.

---

22 Friedman, *The Hidden Book*, 13.
23 Friedman, *The Hidden Book*, 11.
24 Friedman, *The Hidden Book*, 28–29.
25 Friedman, *Who Wrote the Bible?*, 85. Over the years there have been variations proposed on the JEDP hypothesis. These include the existence of multiple Js, the non-existence of E, and a variety of other letter sources, L (lay source), K (Kenite source), S (Seir source), and N (nomadic source) that are not directly germane to this study.

Friedman proposes one person at one time. By contrast, one genius created the KDB. Politics did not cease when that author died. After his death other people added to the narrative including the six son stories of this study. Literature was politics, politics was literature.[26] The additions included new stories, such as the ones to be analyzed here, and revisions to existing stories. To determine the precise verses to be assigned to the KDB is massive endeavor. The focus here will be narrower.

Friedman's proposed narrative ends with Solomon secure in the throne. That ending sufficed only for the political faction that supported him, his temple, his priesthood, his marriage to Pharaoh's daughter, and his manner of ruling as recounted in I Kings: 3–10. The opposition to all of that also continued as recounted in I Kings: 11–12 with the division of the kingdom. These competing factions jockeying for power in Jerusalem supplemented the KDB. In Part I, the six stories selected for the study will be identified along with the scholarship about those stories. In Part II, the four writers responsible for those six stories will be identified. These people will be placed in historical context to provide the background that caused these stories to be written by them. Finally the writings of each of these four people will be analyzed to determine what they meant at the time these people wrote them. The focus will be the battle of bible stories after the death of David as part of Jerusalem throne games.

> 'I like Wellhausen's version of the Documentary Hypothesis, or a refinement such as Friedman's, because it can be easily explained and grasped… But we must disabuse ourselves of the conceit that we will ever know exactly how the Torah came to be'.
>
> William H. C. Propp, *Exodus 19–40* (New York: Doubleday, 2006), 2A: 734

---

26 The sentence comes from the title of a book, see David S. Vanderhooft and Abraham Winitzer, eds, *Literature as Politics, Politics as Literature: Essays on the Ancient Near East in Honor of Peter Machinist* (Winona Lake: Eisenbrauns, 2013). The biblical stories in this study are analyzed in accordance with that title phrase.

PART I

INTERPRETING THE STORIES

Chapter 1

BATTLEFIELD STORIES OF THE BIBLE

Sons of J Stories

The subject of this study is six 'son' stories from the first cycle of J in the Book of Genesis commonly referred to as Primeval History.[1] Primeval history is a non-biblical designation used by scholars. It derives from the standard perceptions that the stories are about the dawn of the human existence and may even have survived in oral form from hoary antiquity before being written down. The approach here, to be detailed in Part II, is that (i) all these stories supplemented the original KDB narrative cycle which consisted of the garden, Cain and Abel, and the flood, and (ii) all of them are political in purpose written as acts of conscious will. These stories are grouped together and called 'son' stories for convenience sake. They involve descendants of the three primary male characters in the original KDB narrative. They are sons of Adam, Cain, or Noah.

These stories are:

Gen. 4: 17–24	the sons of Cain
Gen. 4: 25–26	the sons of Seth
Gen. 6: 1–4	the sons of God
Gen. 9: 20–27	the sons of Noah
Gen. 10: 8–10	the sons of Cush (Nimrod)
Gen. 11: 1–9	the sons of men (Tower of Babel).[2]

The 'son' stories continue beyond the first cycle. They appear in the second or Abram cycle with the sons of Terah (Gen. 11: 27–32) and the sons of Abram (Gen. 16, 21, 24). They exist in the third or Jacob cycle with the sons of Jacob (various, interspersed). These 'son' stories can be compared and contrasted for the messages they delivered about the critical issues of importance to the Israelite community such as kingship, covenant, temple, and ethnic constituency. The reasons for these supplemental stories to the core stories of the garden, the murder, and the Flood need to be determined if one is to understood Israelite history and the writing of the Hebrew Bible.

---

1 Ron Hendel uses the term 'Primeval Cycle' rather than 'Primeval History' since the stories are myths and not history and since they form a coherent cycle (Ronald S. Hendel, 'Of demigods and the deluge: toward an interpretation of Genesis 6: 1–4', *JBL* 106, 1987, 13–26, here 14). The term 'first cycle' is used in this study because the stories are not about primeval times and are the first in a series of cycles that comprise the KDB.
2 A reviewer of the manuscript asked 'And what about "daughters" Without them the "sons" can't have descendants'. In the Cain story there are three wives, two of whom are named, and no parents are identified for them to be the daughters of. There also is one sister in the Cain line. In the Seth story there is one unnamed wife presumed to be Eve and she is not a daughter. In the sons of God story there are anonymous daughters of men. In the remaining stories no female figures, wives, daughters, sisters, or otherwise, are identified. All these figures are included in the analyses in Part II.

Each of the six stories chosen for this study will be analyzed following the same template. First a writing from antiquity will be presented with its version of the biblical account. For this study, the author chosen is Josephus, the 1st century CE Jewish writer perhaps best known for his story of Masada. In addition to writing about the Jewish War against Rome in which he was a participant, he also wrote a history of the Jews in antiquity. Josephus is one of the non-Greco-Roman 'historians' who sought to write a history of their own peoples to validate their identity and importance (Manetho of Egypt, Berossus of Babylon, and Philo of Byblos are others). He also was part of group within the Jewish community who rewrote all or part of the biblical narrative (other examples are Jubilees, Genesis Apocryphon, and the Samaritan Pentateuch). Finally he responded to the trauma of the destruction of the Temple and the search for explanations and answers as other writers from that time period did. Because he was remembered by the Jewish community as a traitor who defected to the Roman side and because he mentioned various Christian figures like John the Baptist, James the brother of Jesus, and Jesus, Christians, not Jews, were responsible for the preservation of his writings.

Second, the rabbinic versions of the stories will be presented. This midrash arose as rabbis who scrutinized the stories asked many of the same questions later secular scholars would. However, the rabbis operated within a specific religious parameter distinct from the modern scholarly one. In some cases, the rabbis delved into the mysteries of the stories at a time when information from the ancient world had been lost. Ironically, since the advent of archaeology, people today may know more about the ancient Near East than the people of the early 1st millennium CE knew. Sometimes the stories the rabbis told have become as well known as the biblical story and have been completely integrated into the biblical account in the popular understanding.

The rabbinic Midrash has been collected by others so it is not necessary to scour the Talmud in search of their comments about these biblical stories. The two leading collections that serve as reference guides for this study are Louis Ginzberg, *The Legends of the Jews: I Bible Times and Characters from the Creation to Jacob* and Hyman E. Goldin, *The Book of Legends: Tales from the Talmud and Midrash Part I: The Biblical Period.*

Ginzberg declares that he has made an attempt to gather from the original sources all Jewish legends about biblical persons and events. This gathering includes first and foremost from Talmudic-Midrashic literature covering the second to 14th centuries and includes apocryphal and pseudepigraphic sources as well. Goldin expresses similar thoughts on the Haggadah or legend/stories of the Talmud.[3]

Third, a series of modern commentaries will be presented. This series includes individual commentaries from the dawn of modern biblical scholarship over a century ago. As these commentaries were being written, five new developments occurred during the 19th century which altered the manner in which biblical exegesis happened:

---

3 Louis Ginzberg, *The Legends of the Jews: I Bible Times and Characters from the Creation to Jacob* (Philadelphia: Jewish Publication Society of America, 1954, first published 1909), xi–xiii; Hyman E. Goldin, *The Book of Legends: Tales from the Talmud and Midrash Part I: The Biblical Period* (New York: Hebrew Publishing Company, 1929), iii.

1. The development of German nationalism culminating in the creation of the German nation at the same time German biblical scholars studied the tribes of Israel becoming a kingdom. The development of the German state has contributed to the perception of the state as the standard by which ancient Israel should be evaluated.

2. The development of a new methodology for analysis and re-creation of the past through the investigation of written sources to determine what really happened. This German-dominated effort occurred parallel to the development of German nationalism and found a home in the creation of the German graduate school. An unexpected development within biblical scholarship has been the tendency to perceive the biblical writers as ancient versions of the scholars who, instead of writing in the ivory tower as professors, wrote in the temple as scribes.

3. The formalization of the science of geology and the discovery of the Ice Age in the 1830s and 1840s changed the secular understanding of the past. These new scientific understandings affected biblical commentaries, especially of the Book of Genesis. The 19th century commentaries often began with lengthy introductions in which the author sought to incorporate the new geological information. The most impacted areas were the chronologies, the creation, and the flood stories.

4. The uncovering of the ancient past through archaeology changed the secular understanding of it. Archaeological excavations led to the discovery of previously unknown ancient peoples like the Sumerians and the Akkadians, previously unknown ancient stories like *Gilgamesh* and *Enuma Elish*, and previously unknown political configurations from the time before Israel existed. These discoveries continued into the 20th century with the discovery of the Ebla and Mari archives, the Ugaritic texts, and Dead Sea Scrolls. Biblical scholars have been constantly trying to understand the relationship between the biblical texts and non-biblical inscriptions and writings. The material culture exposed in the physicality of the archaeological excavations has provided a more concrete context to the biblical world.

5. The widespread acceptance of the Documentary Hypothesis culminated a centuries-old effort to unravel the sources behind the composition of the Hebrew Bible, especially the Five Books of Moses. Wellhausen's JEDP theory did not spring forth fully-formed from scratch but was part of a long process of suggestions, proposals, and theories before he created his biblical theory of compositional unity. It then became routine for biblical scholars to refer to these designations in their analysis of a Pentateuchal text.

Beginning in the second half of the 19th century, each author of a Genesis commentary grappled with this fluid environment. Any day could result in a new discovery, such as the Code of Hammurabi, a shift in the accepted chronologies of human civilizations by centuries, or the appearance of a non-biblical flood story that matched portions of the biblical one. To digest all the information from a moving database was a Herculean challenge indeed. Scholars also were products of their time influenced by their own immediate situation in life as well as the world around them. The three exegetes chosen in this study from this time period are some of the critical Genesis commentators who helped set the stage for future commentaries.

Franz Delitzsch (1813–1890)

Franz Delitzsch was born Jewish and converted to Lutheranism. His biblical studies focused on the Old Testament and the celebration of the 300th anniversary of the Reformation in 1839. He authored *Genesis* in 1852 with the fifth and final edition being published in German in 1887 and in English the following year. In his Preface to the last edition, Delitzsch singles out August Dillmann (see below) for praise perhaps having been influenced by Dillmann's commentary just published in 1882. Despite the changes as a result of Wellhausen and archaeology, Delitzsch declared in his opening paragraph that 'the spirit of this Commentary remains unaltered'. The paragraph concludes with the affirmation:

> 'I am a believer in two orders of things ... I believe in the Easter announcement, and I accept its deductions.'[4]

One may conclude that Delitzsch's analysis supported his convictions. Not all biblical scholars are as forthright in stating their convictions so clearly and openly.

Delitzsch began as a believer in the unity of the book but by the end of his career had come to accept a version of the Documentary Hypothesis. For him the Hypothesis meant a foundation document with its origin in the time of Moses and a Yahwistic source in the time of Joshua. Delitzsch changed his mind over time especially with the publication of Wellhausen's hypothesis. As a result, various views are expressed in various editions of his Genesis commentaries.

In this final edition, the 59-page Introduction to his Genesis commentary is dominated by Moses, the writings of Moses, and the writings in the name of Moses by those who followed in his ways. Genesis belatedly first appears on page 57. Delitzsch calls Genesis the incomparable historical work of any people in antiquity; it also expresses an essential truth of Christianity. Here he takes issue with both Charles Lyell, the founder of the science of geology, and Charles Darwin. To abandon the child-like innocence of the first-created pair in the garden for the cannibalism of the half-brutal manhood of the stone period and the struggling for existence over millions of years condemns the Christian view of the world as untenable. That Christian view is based on the redemption of Adamic mankind. Delitzsch approvingly quotes Menken (no first name or bibliographical information provided) on the importance of Gen. 1–3:

> 'If the first three chapters of Genesis are taken out of the Bible, it is deprived of the *terminus a quo*; if the last three chapters of the Apocalypse are taken away, it is deprived of the *terminus ad quem*.'

Through this quotation, Delitzsch reveals the enormity of the stakes in Genesis exegesis. Without a beginning or an ending, what is left? While the specific exegesis may address a word, a phrase, or a verse, the entirety of Christianity may be at risk from the consequences.[5]

---

4 Franz Delitzsch, *New Commentary on Genesis* (New York: Schribner & Welford, 1889), v; Raymond F. Sturmburg, 'The influence of the two Delitzsches on Biblical and Near Eastern studies', *CTQ* 47 1983: 225–240, here 225–230.
5 Delitzsch, *New Commentary on Genesis*, 1–59, quotation from 58; Sturmburg, 'The influence of the two Delitzsches', 225–230.

August Dillmann (1823–1894)

Based on Dillmann's career, one would not immediately have thought of his becoming the author of a Genesis commentary.[6] He was a student of Georg Heinrich August Ewald (1803–1875), a leading German orientalist and biblical exegete. After his graduation he became a minister before returning to school for advanced study. His focus was Ethiopic and he devoted considerable time to studying the related manuscripts in England and France. Dillmann sought to discover the Book of Enoch. He succeeded and then published it 1851. In so doing he became a proficient Semitic philologist, a skill he brought to biblical studies. He published *Die Genesis* in 1875 revising a previously published commentary by August Knobel. Eventually, he produced commentaries covering each of the six books of the Hexateuch. He authored three more Genesis editions including the 1882 publication, which probably influenced Delitzsch. His final version in 1892 was translated into English in 1897. Dillmann's learning, lucidity, conciseness, and thoroughness made him a highly respected and regarded figure in biblical exegesis.[7]

Dillmann thought the Book of Genesis was the first of six books concluding with Joshua in the Hexateuch. Narrowing the focus, Dillmann claimed Gen. 1–11 prefaced Hebrew history with a universal primitive history. Multiple authors contributed to the text whom he labeled A, B, C comparable to P, E, and J in the Documentary Hypothesis. He maintained his designations which he had used prior to Wellhausen's JEDP sigla, to provide uniformity with his other commentaries which already had been published. Dillmann claimed that C or J, the Yahwist, borrowed from B or E, the Elohist. If so, then J was the younger than E contrary to Wellhausen. Dillmann located the author in Judah in approximately 750 BCE. Nonetheless, some of the stories in the primeval history of J were heterogeneous sections or older, specifically the sons of Cain, the sons of God and sons of men/Tower of Babel. According to Dillmann, the theme of sin and grace for the saving purpose of God ran through the narrative.[8]

Hermann Gunkel (1862–1932)

Gunkel became a seminal figure in biblical exegesis in the 20th century particularly for his work on the Book of Genesis. Early in his career, he belonged to a religio-historical circle of scholars who opposed the dry-as-dust historical criticism approach which ignored the spiritual. His resistance to the Wellhauseun dogma led to the educational authorities encouraging him to pursue his academic career in a different direction. Gunkel forged a new path by immersing himself in the fields of ancient Near Eastern studies, the classics, and Germanics. As a result, he learned from people outside his area of specialization.

Gunkel's major contribution was to reconstruct the oral background to the Genesis text.

6   This information comes from his obituary: George L. Robinson, 'August Dillmann (Obituary)', *The Biblical World* 4 1894: 244–258.

7   This information and these observations come from Robinson, 'August Dillmann', 244–258 and William B. Stevenson, 'Preface', in Friedrich August Dillmann, *Genesis: Critically and Exegetically Expounded* (Edinburgh: T&T Clark, 1897), v–vii.

8   These comments come from the 'Preface' and 'Preliminary remarks' at the beginning of the commentary, see Dillmann, *Genesis*, 1–26; Stevenson, 'Preface', v–vii.

In part he was reacting to the textual hypothesis of Wellhausen, the dominant method of biblical exegesis for Genesis. By contrast, Gunkel champions the oral prehistory of the sources designated by Wellhausen especially behind the J source. A people's culture did not just begin with written records. He supports the great antiquity of these stories by attempting to determine the life setting or *Sitz im Leben* in which they originated. Historical considerations or the personalities of the individual authors were secondary to the earlier setting in which these myths, sagas, and legends were first told in frequently short and self-contained stories or cycles. Gunkel accepts the existence of multiple sources behind individual writers such as J who then collected these independent units while adding his own viewpoint to the mix.

Gunkel recognizes that his reconstructions of his pre-J sources were speculative. He proposed different reconstructions in the each of the first three editions of his Genesis commentary beginning in 1901. The third edition was translated into English in 1997, nearly one century later. Gunkel's foreword to that edition begins with 'I have carefully and thoroughly revised the whole work over the course of several years'. Furthermore, if he had been able to produce a fourth version, it would have differed even more. One area of change occurred with etiologies. Gunkel starts by attributing many stories to having originated as explanations for the way things were. He later diminished that emphasis in favor of folktales.[9]

The opening section of his introduction to the Genesis commentary is entitled 'Genesis is a Collection of Legends'. Gunkel starkly declares that 'Israelite historical traditions concerning the primordial times cannot be seriously discussed.' His introduction continually stresses oral, primal, and collecting for the early chapters. For Gunkel, 'Israel surely did not produce a very large segment of these legends, but received them from abroad'. The name 'Yahweh' was secondarily imprinted on primal legends influenced by Babylonia. As for J, it is neither a unified work nor does it trace back to an older self-contained unified work. It is a combination of multiple hands consisting of three sources in the primal history. Starting with the garden story, J^e is the primary source, coherent and well-rounded. By contrast, a second source, J^j, is fragmentary and mythical. The final narrator, the third writer, who combined them is the gifted master who expelled the foreign and the barbarian. But Gunkel thought even J^e itself is woven from two traditions.[10] He was firmly convinced that multiple people contributed to the J source.

Gunkel concludes his introduction to his Genesis commentary with a lament:

> 'One may regret that the last great poetic genius who could have formed a true "Israelite national epic" from the individual stories did not appear. Israel produced great religious reformers who created a comprehensive unity in religious spirit from the dispersed traditions of their people. But it did not produce a Homer.'[11]

---

9 Quotation from Hermann Gunkel, *Genesis* (Macon, GA: Mercer University Press, 1997; originally published in 1901), v. Background information from M. J. Buss, 'Gunkel, Herman (1862–1932)', in Donald K. McKim, ed., *Historical Handbook of Major Biblical Interpreters* (Leicester, England: InterVarsity Press, 1998), 487–491; Ernest W. Nicholson, 'Foreword to the English translation', in Gunkel, *Genesis*, 3–9.

10 Gunkel, *Genesis*, ix, xlviii–l, lxxii–lxxiii, 25–28, quotations from ix and xlviii.

11 Gunkel, *Genesis*, lxxxvi.

Gunkel considers this a blessing:

> 'This is fortunate for our scholarship at any rate. Precisely because there was no poetic whole and the passages were left in an essentially unfused stated [*sic*], we are able to discern the history of the whole process.'[12]

In the approach taken in this study there was a 'poetic whole' of multiple original stories. To retrieve the original KDB whole requires peeling back the additions, an enormous task in which this study is but one small step.

Gunkel joins with Delitzsch in stressing the importance of the beginning of the faith story with its conclusion. In biblical terms that means the connection between the Books of Genesis and Revelation. Gunkel's publication of *Schöpfung und Chaos in Urzeit und Endzeit/ Creation and Chaos in the Primeval Era and the Eschaton: A Religio-historical Study of Genesis 1 and Revelation 12* attests this link. The Christian focus on Gen. 1–3 as a fundamental truth that undergirds the belief in the Apocalypse de-emphasizes the other stories in the primeval history as Claus Westermann points out (see below). One would be remiss in an analysis of these Genesis exegetes if one ignores the literal end game in Revelation. These Genesis commentaries did not simply happen by chance. The stakes were high for Christians.

A second group of modern commentaries represents the 'canonical' works mainly from the second half of the 20th century which became the standards in the academic world. They tend to be based on or presume the previous works of Wellhausen (literary criticism) and Gunkel (form criticism).

John Skinner (1851–1925)

Skinner began his commentary in 1904 and completed it six years later as part of the International Critical Commentary series. He notes that during that interim there were no important new commentaries either in German or English. Skinner acknowledges his debt to the existing commentaries of Driver and Gunkel and claims his commentary will not supersede those books. Gunkel's

> 'aesthetic appreciation of the genius of the narratives, [his] wider historical horizons, and [his] illuminating use of mythological and folklore parallels, has breathed a new spirit into the investigation of Genesis, whose influence no writer on the subject can hope or wish to escape.'

Skinner also cites Dillmann and Delitzsch. One may observe from these references, an intention to stand on the work of his predecessors and to bring it to the attention of the English-speaking audiences.[13]

One significant change had occurred. During the 19th century, it was not uncommon for Genesis commentaries to have extensive geology sections. In the beginning of the commentary, the exegete wrestled with the issue of the reconcilement of the first chapters of Genesis with developments in modern science. Skinner elected to forgo addressing the controversies involving the compatibility of the two disciplines. Interested readers were

---

12 Gunkel, *Genesis*, lxxxvi.

13 John Skinner, *A Critical and Exegetical Commentary on Genesis* (New York: Charles Scribner's Sons, 1910), vii.

referred to the writings of Driver who had included them. Instead, Skinner's focus was to be 'the recent reaction against the critical analysis of the Pentateuch'.[14] By this comment, Skinner means the negative response to the Documentary Hypothesis which he considers to be an essentially sound hypothesis.

Despite such protestations, Skinner's commentary is that of a believer. He advises the reader to retain one's

> 'faith in this inspiration of this part of Scripture, to recognize that the Divine Spirit has enshrined a part of His Revelation to men in such forms as these. It is only by a frank acceptance of this truth that the Book of Genesis can be made a means of religious edification to the educated mind of our age.'[15]

Before delving into the texts themselves, Skinner provides some background on his approach. He contrasts the story of David in Samuel and the beginning of Kings with the Genesis material. For Skinner, the former resembles history by contemporary authorities who write in a convincingly realistic style that conveys first-hand information from the evidence of eyewitnesses.[16] He ascribes no such verisimilitude to the Genesis writings. These writings reflect the mass of popular narrative talk about the past in which all the races of the world engage. Those traditions, stories, legends persist in the cultural memory of the people into historic times as a remnant of the pre-literary and uncritical stage of society. Skinner avers that this literature which is frequently mistaken for history has in some respects a greater value than history for it reveals the soul of a people.[17]

Skinner supports the standard view on foreign mythology in the Bible, especially Gen. 1–11. Archaeological discoveries clearly reveal the borrowing by bible writers of the stories of others. He postulates that the Canaanites were the medium through which Israel acquired its knowledge of the Babylonian stories. Yet he is reluctant to designate the biblical versions as myths 'because the spirit of Hebrew monotheism has exorcised the polytheistic notions of the deity, apart from which true mythology cannot survive.'[18] Only scattered fragments of the old heathen concepts remain. Skinner is pleased to announce that these remnants 'only serve to show how completely the religious beliefs of Israel have transformed and purified the crude speculations of pagan theology, and adapted them to the ideas of an ethical and monotheistic faith.'[19]

---

14 Skinner, *A Critical and Exegetical Commentary*, viii.
15 Skinner, *A Critical and Exegetical Commentary*, ix.
16 Skinner, *A Critical and Exegetical Commentary*, iii–iv.
17 Skinner, *A Critical and Exegetical Commentary*, viii. A few years after Skinner wrote these words, John Ronald Reuel Tolkien participated in the Battle of Somme in the 'war to end all wars'. After he returned home in a weakened state he began to write his first mythology. It would be decades later and another world war before he wrote *The Lord of the Rings*, books from the 1950s that became movie blockbusters in the 21st century. If Skinner had lived to witness the books and the movie, one wonders if he would have realized that Tolkien was writing about his present through the past and not about England's past. By contrast, Winston Churchill, officer, politician, writer, of the same era, wrote directly about contemporary events and a history of the English people. Sometimes animal farms and Lilliputians are not figures from hoary antiquity but originate in the present of the writer as a comment on the present.
18 Skinner, *A Critical and Exegetical Commentary*, ix.
19 Skinner, *A Critical and Exegetical Commentary*, ix.

One of the critical issues in this study is the existence of multiple writers within the J narrative. Skinner, as with many other exegetes from that time period, acknowledges that J itself is a composite work based on older collections of Hebrew traditions. He specifically sites some of the very considerations to be addressed in subsequent chapters:

1. The parallel Cainite and Sethite genealogies
2. The incompatibility of the Cainite genealogy and the Deluge tradition
3. The mutually exclusive explanations in the Table of Nations and Tower of Babel for the diversity of languages
4. Enosh's introduction of the worship of Yahweh.

Skinner recounts the various efforts by previous luminaries to develop a theory of multiple authorship or origin which would account for these inconsistencies. He sees, following Gunkel, links connecting the Sethite genealogy (Gen. 4: 25–26) and the naming of Noah (Gen. 5: 29), then back to the cursing of the first man (Gen. 3: 17) and forward to Noah the vintner (Gen. 9: 20). In effect, he has identified one core document within the J narrative (or supplement to the KDB). In the end, Skinner proposes a four level scheme which he admits is 'in the highest degree precarious and uncertain; and can only be regarded as tentative explanations of problems for which it is probable that no final solution will be found.' This study continues that subsequently abandoned quest to bring order to the chaos of discrepancies and discontinuities which Skinner and others identified by shifting the starting point from myths from hoary antiquity to politics as literature, literature as politics.[20]

Gerhard von Rad (1901–1971)

Von Rad entered the pastorate in 1925 and his religious values infused his scholarship. He exalted Israel's confessions of saving acts in history by its God. He was active in the underground opposition to the Nazis. Despite his actions, he ended up serving his country and became a prisoner of war. Following the war, he resumed his scholarship. Von Rad opposed the atomization of analysis which he saw in the work of Gunkel. The search for minute oral snippets behind the written text undermined his theological approach based on the final text shedding light on God's actions in history. The memory of the Nazis also was one which remained with him. He professed an era of humanism and enlightenment in the court of Solomon in the 10th century BCE when J was written as a narrative about Yahweh, a God in history. Sinai, the covenant, David, and ark at Zion were highlights and the Canaanite fertility religion was a constant threat to Israel to be overcome. Von Rad's J was a true author and theologian whose writing spanned Genesis to Joshua in the Hexateuch, His J was the Homer whom Gunkel never saw. This Old Testament writing became the foundation for the New Testament.[21]

The opening section of the Introduction to his commentary is entitled 'Genesis as

---

20 Skinner, *A Critical and Exegetical Commentary*, 2–4, quotation from 4.

21 J. L. Crenshaw, 'Von Rad, Gerhard (1901–1971)', in Donald K. McKim, ed., *Historical Handbook of Major Biblical Interpreters* (Leicester, England: InterVarsity Press, 1998), 526–531.

Part of the Hexateuch'. On the first page he criticizes the atomistic approach which has been taken in the exposition of Genesis. In the next three pages, he identifies the three confessions in history (professions of faith) which dominate his analysis: Deut. 6: 20–24 and 26: 5–9 and Josh. 24: 2–13. These credos recounting Israel's history are crucial to von Rad's thinking about the formation of the narrative portion of the Hebrew Bible. None of them appears in Genesis.

As far as J is concerned, von Rad focuses on the critical formation of the Israelite state as a time of great crisis. It led to the Solomonic era enlightenment when J was produced. By including the primeval history in his narrative, von Rad claims that J shows the greatest independence of the sacred traditions of Israel that began with the patriarchs. He fashioned multiple elements into a sequence of stories delivering a message on sin and salvation. As a result of the genius of J, the (universal) primeval history he has created dovetails with the sacred history (of Israel) that begins with Abraham. Von Rad concludes his Introduction asserting these patriarchal narratives in Genesis lead to 'God's revelation of himself in Jesus Christ.'[22]

Ephraim A. Speiser (1902–1965)

Ephraim Avigdor Speiser was born in Galicia. It was part of Austrian Poland when he was born and part of the Ukrainian Soviet Socialist Republic when he died.[23] He arrived in the United States in 1920. In his academic career, he taught at the University of Pennsylvania and belonged to the American Schools of Oriental Research (ASOR). His excavations focused on ancient Mesopotamia in the newly formed country of Iraq and he served as president of the American Oriental Society. As one might expect, Speiser brought a Mesopotamian perspective to his biblical exegesis. For the early stories in J, that orientation was expressed in his writings on the garden, Nimrod, and the movement of peoples, perhaps an interest due to his own life's experiences as a wandering Jew from the east who emigrated to God's New Israel, a city on a hill.

Speiser did not initiate the idea for a Genesis commentary. The book was part of a larger effort. The still-ongoing Anchor Bible series of biblical commentaries originated as an American effort to make the Bible 'accessible to the modern reader'. Its target audience was the 'general reader' who had no specialized training in biblical studies. Yet the production of each volume was to be held to 'the most exacting standards of scholarship, reflecting the highest technical accomplishment'. The series was intended to be 'international and interfaith in scope'.[24] While many of these objectives have been met, the volumes are scarcely for the general reader and have become ever longer, more exhaustive, and more exhausting.[25]

22 Gerhard von Rad, *Genesis: A Commentary* (Philadelphia: Westminster Press, 1972, first published 1961), 13–43.

23 See Moshe Greenberg, 'In memory of E. A. Speiser', *JAOS* 88 1968: 1–2.

24 William Foxwell Albright and David Noel Friedman, in E. A. Speiser, *Genesis: Introduction, Translation, and Notes* (AB I; Garden City: Doubleday & Co., 1964) (William Foxwell Albright and David Noel Freedman, General Editors), II.

25 An updated and vastly revised Genesis commentary is being prepared by Ron Hendel but it has not been published at the time of this writing. Hendel was a student of Frank Moore Cross who along with David Noel

In his preface to the Genesis commentary, Speiser wrote, 'The study follows in the main the moderate school of documentary criticism.'[26] Each author in the series provides his/her own translation of the biblical text. In this instance the translation closely resembled the Jewish Publication Society of America version published in 1962 where Speiser served on the small committee which produced it. In the Introduction to the volume, Speiser recounts the history of biblical criticism especially the Documentary Hypothesis which provides the basis for his analysis. He strongly stresses both the Mesopotamian world and the historicity of the patriarchs. His expertise in that region is part of the reason why the general editors, William F. Foxwell and David Noel Freedman, selected him for this volume. Spesier lists some of the distinguished Genesis commentaries which he has frequently consulted including those by Dillmann, Gunkel, Skinner and von Rad, and by S. R. Driver who appears frequently in the analysis in Part II.[27]

Claus Westermann (1909–2000)

Claus Westermann was the son of a missionary, became a pastor, and is one of the most influential biblical interpreters in the 20th century. His theological writings developed in the context of Nazi Germany which he opposed. His interest in the Old Testament was disparaged as devotion to a Jewish book. He served in the military and was a Russian POW. During these times his focus was on the Psalms and prophets. Later his three-volume commentary on Genesis became a standard not only for his own interpretations but for the exhaustive background material of previous scholarship included in his own exegesis. His commentary on Gen. 1–11 was published in 1974. The second edition from 1976 was then published in English in 1984.[28]

In his Genesis commentary, Westermann calls for a revision of the Documentary Hypothesis criteria for the separation of sources. He surveys the previous failed attempts to revise it and also calls for recognizing that simply to assert an oral stage of tradition preceding the written one is not enough. He frequently references Gunkel. Westermann gently mocks classical literary criticism for its obsession on the name of God for source classification and its ceaseless discovery of new sources. This relentless postulation of sources generated a false trail which Pentateuchal criticism has followed based on literary criticism. He affirms that 'arguments that aim at confirming such a division of sources within J are likewise untenable'. J is both a collector and writer and cannot be divided. Westermann prefers to focus on the unity of the texts which J produced from the stories that had previously circulated independently. In some cases these stories developed in primitive cultures prior to the existence of Israel. He expresses his awe at the Yahwist for being 'the

Freedman were students of William Foxwell Albright. Hendel's forthcoming commentary will be the first fully American one to join the pantheon of Genesis commentaries that have dominated modern scholarship.

26 Speiser, *Genesis*, V.

27 Speiser, *Genesis*, xvii–lxxvi.

28 J. Limburg, 'Westermann, Claus (b. 1909)', in Donald K. McKim, ed., *Historical Handbook of Major Biblical Interpreters* (Leicester, England: InterVarsity Press, 1998), 535–540; Claus Westermann, *Genesis 1–11: A Commentary* (Minneapolis: Augsburg Publishing House, 1984, first published 1974).

first, as far as we know, in the history of the world to bring together a historical whole that compasses several quite different epochs'. This broad sweeping view was only possible from the era of David and Solomon.[29]

In the opening paragraph of his 'Introduction to the Story of the Primeval Events', Westermann dates the Yahwist (J) to the 10th–9th century BCE. He does so in the context of asserting the unbroken continuity of the biblical primeval story from antiquity to modern times. The paragraph ends with the ringing declaration:

> 'The Christian Churches throughout the world continue in their formal worship to acknowledge their belief in God, the creator of heaven and earth, and every attempt to detach faith in the creator from faith in Christ has miscarried.
>
> To understand how Jesus Christ came as the savior of all humanity, one must understand the beginning of the story in the Book of Genesis, in the primeval stories.'[30]

Westermann considers the primeval stories to be 'a separate element of the Pentateuch' that form 'a relatively self-contained unity'. He recognizes that the Christian emphasis on the creation and fall contributed to the diminution of the intrinsic value of Gen. 4–11 (the section containing the stories under study here). As for the texts, there are two main types: the numerative ones (genealogies) and the narratives with J tending towards the narrative.[31]

What strikes Westermann above all else in these stories are the parallels between the biblical stories of universal origin and those of all religions. His concern is the history of religions and therefore of the human need to understand how the world came to be what it is in the present. It is not only that these stories are about primeval times but that they originated nearer to these primitive times than did other portions of the Bible. Undoubtedly the ancient Israelite awareness of the antiquity of the stories contributed to their separateness from the Israelite story commencing with Abraham.[32]

Westermann states the Genesis genealogies of J have not been preserved in their entirety. He lists the verses as (in the terminology used here):

4: 1–2	Adam and Eve, Cain and Abel
4: 17–24	sons of Cain
4: 25–26	sons of Seth (with 4: 26 probably the remnant of a narrative)
5: 29; 9 :18–19	sons of Noah
10: 8–30	table of nations including the sons of Cush (Nimrod)
11: 28–30	sons of Terah (beyond the scope of this study and Westermann does not even include these verses in volume 1 of his commentary on Gen. 1–11).

The sons of God (6: 1–4) and the sons of men/Tower of Babel (11: 1–9) form the narrative portions of J's primeval stories included in this study. In Westermann's opinion, '(a)ll the narrative stories in Gen. 1–11 are concerned in some way with crime and punishment.' They also all are etiological. This portion of his introduction is dominated by the theme

---

29 Westermann, *Genesis 1–11*, 570–592, quotations from 581 and 589.
30 Westermann, *Genesis 1–11*, 1.
31 Westermann, *Genesis 1–11*, 2–3, quotation from 2.
32 Westermann, *Genesis 1–11*, 4–6.

of crime and punishment as reflected in the earliest myths of humanity from Africa and not those of Egypt and Mesopotamia.[33]

Westermann links the Tower of Babel and the Cainite genealogy as myths of human achievement. Nimrod is not included here. His focus is the contrast between these biblical stories and those of other cultures such as the Sumerians. The sons of Cain and the sons of men build cities and a tower and originate crafts and professions on their own initiative and not by divine command. The biblical stories simultaneously tell the tale of human revolt and human progress. His bold pronouncement clearly differentiates the biblical text from its neighbors: 'Faced with the mythology of the Ancient Near East, the Bible takes the same stand as does the modern secular scholar: all progress in civilization is a human achievement.'[34]

These developments do not occur in isolation from what is to follow. The primeval story is linked to history with the call to Abram in Gen. 12. God's saving action begins 'in the beginning' and much of Westermann's introduction delves into the creation stories of humanity. He ends his introduction by returning to his opening paragraph: 'One can understand then how this history leads ultimately to God becoming human.' By prefixing the non-Israelite primeval history to Israel's history, J has universalized Israel's history. This universalism anticipates the Apocalypse which also is universal (as mentioned in the second to last paragraph of his introduction). Only in this context can God's universal action from the beginning to the end and the work of Jesus Christ be understood (the final paragraph of his introduction).[35]

The final commentaries in this study are the briefer study guides. Two of them are from biblical faith communities and one from a secular organization devoted to the study of the Bible. These guides cover all the books of the Bible as defined by the editors of these communities with Genesis being one in each of them. Individual commentators analyze each biblical book but with the Book of Genesis, there are two writers in one study guide.

The Jewish Publication Society

Editors Adele Berlin and Marc Zvi Brettler inform the reader in the 'Introduction', that there 'is no official Jewish interpretation of the Bible' and 'no authorized Jewish translation of the Bible into English.'[36] This study guide published in 2004 is a revision of the 1917 publication. According to the JPS website:

> 'Since 1888 the mission of JPS has been to enhance Jewish literacy and self-understanding with the JPS TANAKH, the most widely read English translation of the Hebrew Bible, Bible commentaries, and hundreds of classic books about Jewish history and thought.'[37]

---

33 Westermann, *Genesis 1–11*, 9, 12, 18, 47, 53, quotation from 47.
34 Westermann, *Genesis 1–11*, 56–61, quotation from 61.
35 Westermann, *Genesis 1–11*, 65, 68, 606, quotation from 68.
36 Adele Berlin and Marc Zvi Brettler, eds, *The Jewish Study Bible* (Oxford: Oxford University Press, 2004), ix–x.
37 https://jps.org/about/mission-and-vision/

The volume provides information about the history of scholarship, translations, and multiple essays on different topics. The exegete selected for the Book of Genesis is Jon D. Levenson. No information is provided about him. He was a student of Frank Moore Cross.[38]

The New Jerome Biblical Commentary

The New Jerome Biblical Commentary is dedicated to Popes Pius XII and Paul VI. It draws its inspiration from the Second Vatican Council and the admonition to avoid arid literalism that kills.[39] It is a revision of the 1968 version. Although not an officially-designated commentary, it serves as an authoritative one within the English-speaking Catholic religion. The volume provides information about the history of scholarship, translations, and multiple essays on different topics. Two writers were selected for the Book of Genesis, Richard J. Clifford and Roland E. Murphy. Clifford is responsible for the commentary on the son of J stories included in this study. He is identified as a Professor of Old Testament, Weston School of Theology, Cambridge, MA. He also was a student of Frank Moore Cross.[40]

Society of Biblical Literature

The Society of Biblical Literature was founded in 1880. It appears that Frederic Gardiner of Berkeley Divinity School in Middletown, Connecticut, initiated conversations with Philip Schaff and Charles Augustus Briggs of Union Theological Seminary in New York about the need for such a group. The outcome was a preliminary meeting held in Schaff's study in New York City on the second of January, 1880, 'to take into consideration the formation of a Society for the promotion of study in Biblical Literature and Exegesis.'[41]

From that humble beginning it has become an organization of thousands from many countries with a comparably-sized annual conference, American regional and international conferences, an academic journal and book publications.

One such publication is *The HarperCollins Study Bible: New Revised Standard Version.*[42] The introductory sections explain the decisions made by the editorial committee in selecting the NRSV as the English-language textual basis for the study guide. That committee included multiple confessional traditions with all members dedicated to pursuing open scholarship. No specific information is provided about Joel W. Rosenberg, the individual selected to comment on Genesis beyond his being an associate professor of Hebrew Literature and Judaic Studies at Tufts University.[43]

---

38 Jon D. Levenson, 'Genesis', in Berlin and Brettler, eds, *The Jewish Study Bible*, 8–101.

39 Carlo Maria Cardinal Martini, 'Foreword to *The New Jerome Biblical Commentary*', in Raymond E. Brown, Joseph A. Fitzmyer, and Roland E. Murphy, eds, *The New Jerome Biblical Commentary* (Englewood Cliffs, NJ: Prentice Hall, 1990), xv–xvi, here xv.

40 Richard J. Clifford and Roland E. Murphy, 'Genesis', in Brown, Fitzmyer and Murphy, eds, *The New Jerome Biblical Commentary*, 8–43.

41 Ernest W. Saunders, *Searching the Scriptures: A History of the Society of Biblical Literature* (Chico, CA: Scholars Press, 1982), 3.

42 Wayne A. Meeks, ed., *The HarperCollins Study Bible: New Revised Standard Version* (New York: Harper Collins, 1993).

43 Joel W. Rosenberg, 'Genesis', in Meeks, ed., *The HarperCollins Study Bible: New Revised Standard Version*, 3–76.

The citations in this study to these study guides will be to the individual writer personally and not to the institutional publishing organization.

Together, these commentaries provide the basis for attempting a reconstruction of the six individual son stories selected for this study. There are, of course, additional commentaries which could be included both from earlier times and from more recently. These selections exclude defining and older voices from some biblical faith communities (Augustine, Luther, Calvin, and Adam Clarke). They exclude the multiplicity of often niche commentaries which have arisen more recently that have not attained the prominence of the ones selected here. Naturally, these choices are subject to legitimate debate.

Before the exegesis of the six son stories in Part I, it is beneficial to draw some summary conclusions from the individuals who have been so pivotal.

1. The 'public-audience' selections in this study (Josephus and the rabbis) were written by storytellers. Their versions of the biblical account routinely are embellished and result in stories intended to hold the attention of a public audience.
2. The scholarly selections for this study are from members of the academic guild. These commentaries are difficult to read straight through and often serve as reference books when one is interested in a particular passage or even a word. As a result, their Introductions and Prefaces often are not read.
3. Scholars frequently seek to understand the stories as deriving in some way from the dawn of human existence. The present location of the stories under study here following the P creation story 'In the beginning' in Gen. 1 strongly encourages that perception. The J stories have been subsumed within a P framework in scholarship just as in the biblical text itself. The issue arises most frequently concerning the existence of other human beings in the time of Cain and his immediate descendants.
4. Scholars, especially from a Christian background, tend to see sin and salvation everywhere. The human characters constantly are rebelling against God, demonstrating their hubris, and otherwise being uppity. Time and time again they need to be put in their place.
5. Scholars are receptive to the idea of multiple peoples participating in the writing of J but with no agreement on who these individuals were and what exactly they wrote.
6. Scholars are receptive to the idea of the pentateuchal narrative originally extending beyond the Five Books of Moses into the Book of Joshua.
7. Scholars wonder whether or not Israel had a 'Homer' rather than a collector/editor of existing stories.

The political approach taken in this study yields a vastly different understanding of the origin of these stories than the ones expressed by these people. Israel did indeed have a 'Homer' and before Greece had one. The original narrative did extend beyond the Five Books of Moses. The authors were not collectors but writers. The main topic was not sin but politics. The analysis to substantiate these claims begins by applying the template presented in this chapter to each of the six stories (Part I) and then by examining the political context of the four people who wrote them and what these people meant by these stories (Part II).

Chapter 2

WHO ARE THE SONS OF CAIN?

Genesis 4: *[17] Cain knew his wife, and she conceived and bore Enoch; and he built a city, and called the name of the city after the name of his son, Enoch. [18] To Enoch was born Irad; and Irad was the father of Mehujael, and Mehujael the father of Methushael, and Methushael the father of Lamech. [19] And Lamech took two wives; the name of the one was Adah, and the name of the other Zillah. [20] Adah bore Jabal; he was the father of those who dwell in tents and have cattle. [21] His brother's name was Jubal; he was the father of all those who play the lyre and pipe. [22] Zillah bore Tubalcain; he was the forger of all instruments of bronze and iron. The sister of Tubalcain was Naamah. [23] Lamech said to his wives: 'Adah and Zillah, hear my voice; you wives of Lamech, hearken to what I say: I have slain a man for wounding me, a young man for striking me. [24] If Cain is avenged sevenfold, truly Lamech seventy-sevenfold.'*

The story of the sons of Cain combines diverse genres. At first it appears to be a routine genealogy involving obscure names and the building of a city, perhaps the first city ever. Then it branches out to encompass not a location but various types of activities or professions most closely associated in ancient times with non-city dwellers. Finally it ends with a defiant song of warning to anyone who would violate Lamech. The passage begins and ends with Cain and follows immediately on the story of Cain and Abel.

Understanding the diverse elements within this pericope or extracted passage from the Bible has proved a challenge. Standard questions raised by commentators throughout the ages have honed in on the apparent tensions within the verses. The detected issues include:

1. Where did all these other people come from? – the people from whom Cain needed protection, the people from whom Cain got his wife (she did have human parents didn't she?), the people needed to build a city?
2. Why would people do Cain's bidding to build a city and why would Cain even approach them if he feared for his life?
3. Why all this fuss about people and their inventions if it all was going to be washed away in the Flood?
4. What was the purpose of the violent Song of Lamech?

In addition to these traditional questions regarding the text, one may add:

What political message was being delivered through the communication of this story? Or how did it help one political faction, the Cainites, in the time of Solomon against the other ones? Besides the cut-and-dry claims from the genealogy, there does seem to be some strong emotion involved. The longstanding effort to contrast the sons of Cain to the sons of Seth complicates the attempt to discern the original meaning of the text (see Chapter 3).

The tracking of the attempts by exegetes to understand this passage will begin in ancient times with Josephus, proceed to the rabbis, and continue with modern scholarship from the end of the 19th century to the canonical commentaries of the 20th.

Josephus

Ant 1: 60 *And when Cain had travelled over many countries, he, with his wife, built a city, named Nod, which is a place so called, and there he settled his abode; where also he had children. However, he did not accept his punishment in order to amend his behaviour, but to increase his wickedness; for he only aimed to procure everything that was for his own bodily pleasure, though it obliged him to be injurious to his neighbours.* [61] *He augmented his household substance with much wealth, by rapine and violence; he excited his acquaintance to procure pleasures and spoils by robbery, and became a great leader of men into wicked actions.*

Josephus portrays a thoroughly unrepentant Cain who wreaks havoc on the world he is condemned to wander. The description of his life is shocking and worthy of reprobation in its own right separate from the murder of his brother. There is really nothing positive to say about the life of Cain in this non-biblical portrait. The Josephus depiction establishes a precedent which will continue across generations.

Ant 1: 61 *He also introduced a change in that way of simplicity wherein men lived before; and was the author of measures and weights. And whereas they lived innocently and generously while they knew nothing of such arts, he changed the world into cunning craftiness.*[62] *He first of all set boundaries about lands; he built a city, and fortified it with walls, and he compelled his family to come together to it; and called that city Enoch, after the name of his oldest son Enoch.*

According to Josephus, Cain truly left his mark on the world. While Cain evidenced some wisdom in devising a system of weights and measure, for Josephus the establishment of the commercial world was a great negative. Actually, the world Cain creates would be right at home with the Roman world in which Josephus lived, so one wonders what his message really was in this negative portrayal of Cain.

Ant 1: 63 *Now Jared was the son of Enoch; whose son was Mahalaleel, whose son was Methuselah; whose son was Lamech; who had seventy-seven children by two wives, Silla and Ada.* [64] *Of those children by Ada, one was Jabal; he erected tents, and loved the life of a shepherd. But Jubal, who was born of the same mother with him, exercised himself in music; {b} and invented the psaltery and the harp. But Tubal, one of his children by the other wife, exceeded all men in strength, and was very expert and famous in martial performances. He procured what tended to the pleasures of the body by that method; and first of all invented the art of making brass.* [65] *Lamech was also the father of a daughter, whose name was Naamah.*

This description of the further descendants of Cain including the family of Lamech is almost idyllic. They loved the simple life of the shepherd, the playing of music. They were inventive and strong. One wonders how such a reprobate as Cain produced exemplary descendants. Be that as it may, the world so depicted would not long endure.

Ant 1: 65 *and because he was so skilful in matters of divine revelation, that he knew he was to be punished for Cain's murder of his brother, he made that known to his wives.* [66] *Nay, even while Adam was alive, it came to pass that the posterity of Cain became exceedingly wicked, everyone successively dying, one after another, more wicked than the former. They were intolerable in war, and vehement in robberies; and if anyone was slow to murder people, yet was he bold in his profligate behaviour, in acting unjustly, and doing injuries for gain.*

All-in-all and with his additions to the biblical text, Josephus casts Cain and his descendants in a wicked life neither deserving nor seeking redemption. Based on Josephus's description the world clearly would be a better place with the destruction of that genealogical line in the Flood.

Rabbis

The rabbinic tradition focuses on two descendants of Cain: Enoch and Lamech. The Enoch traditions will not be addressed in this study because they derive primarily from references to him in a P genealogy (see Gen. 5: 21–24) and not a J story.

The sons of Cain reference by the rabbis that is relevant here refers to Enoch as a city-builder. According to the rabbinic account, he constructed seven cities surrounded by a wall. People (from where?) considered Enoch's construction to be a godless deed. Indeed, all Enoch's acts were deemed 'impious' as he led a life of sin, wickedness, and violence. What is most interesting in the rabbinic portrayal of Enoch as a thoroughly reprehensible person is his stature as a 'great leader of men'. Implicit in these rabbinic comments is a larger world teeming with people including his mother, the wife of Cain who appears out of nowhere in the story. The existence of all these other people of unknown origins suggests that is was not an issue of importance to the rabbis. The real concern in the narrative was the people who mattered to the audience of the midrash and not the need to provide detailed explanations for the origins of everything.[1]

The rabbis fill the gap in the story of Lamech by explaining the circumstances in which the killing mentioned in the song occurred. It seems that one day the blind Lamech was hunting aided by his son. The son who could see clearly would identify targets for his father who would then shoot with his bow and arrow according to the instructions he received. On one such occasion, the son successfully directed his father to shoot a distant target he could not see clearly. When Lamech and his son approached the slain figure, the son exclaimed that the killed beast was a human with a horn on its forehead. The distraught father quickly realized that he had killed his own ancestor Cain who had been marked by God with a horn. In his despair as he clasped his hands together, Lamech inadvertently then killed his own son too.

The story gets worse. The calamity intensifies. The earth then opens to swallow up the three generations of Cain identified in this genealogy: Enoch, Irad, Mehujael, and Methushael, Lamech's own father. The blind Lamech is forced to remain by the corpses of Cain and his son until his wives find him. Once they realize what had transpired, they

---

1 Ginzberg, *The Legends of the Jews*, I, 115–116.

immediately seek to put as much distance between them and Lamech as they can since any child of Lamech is a descendant of Cain and doomed to destruction. Lamech pleads with them to remain in the song that is part of the biblical text. In response they all adjourn to Adam for him to render judgment on the situation, He decides the case in favor of Lamech.

The story then continues as life goes on.

The two wives, Adah and Zillah, then bore Lamech four children (which wife bore the son who Lamech killed is not stated).

Jabal, son of Adah, became the first to erect temples to idols (not mentioned in the biblical account).

Jubal, son of Adah, invented and played music (agrees with the biblical account).

Tubal-cain, son of Zillah, carried on in the tradition of his ancestor Cain, the murderer, by fashioning iron and copper instruments of war (the editorial comment is not in the biblical account).

Naamah, daughter of Zillah, meaning 'lovely' created sweet sounds from her cymbals which she used to call people to the worship of idols (not in the biblical account).

All in all, the rabbis like Josephus paint a horrendous picture of a family gone degenerate and worthy of being destroyed in the coming deluge. They are irredeemable, beyond saving or salvation. Whereas the Josephus revisions are set in a Roman milieu, the rabbinic enhancements appear outside of time and space beyond the ceaseless need to cope with the unexpected vagaries of life.[2]

Modern scholarship has tended to focus on the literary and textual issues since there does not seem to be much archaeology with which to work. Exegetes may discuss general considerations on the origins of cities, musical instruments, and metallurgy. However the details of the story itself do not provide the specificity that lends them to archaeological investigation. These items are more anthropological in nature and engender discussion on the origin of human civilization. Of all the stories in the study, it is Gen. 4: 17–24 that appears to reflect events which transpired at the dawn of human civilization.

Delitzsch

Delitzsch asks some of the same questions the rabbis were forced to deal with but his solutions were not necessarily kosher. For example, he does wonder from whence came Cain's wife. Delitzsch plaintively asks if Cain found her in the land of Nod. He chooses not to speculate on such questions declaring that the essence of the biblical account is the descent of the entire human race from Adam. Simply put, the wife of Cain must be a daughter of Adam and Cain's sister since there is no other option. Given a single-pair origin of the species, incest was inevitable if the species were to continue.[3]

One significant change since rabbinic times had occurred. The recent discovery through archaeological excavations of multiple formerly-dead languages provides Delitzsch with the opportunity to observe what the rabbis could not have known. He is struck by the fact that

---

2   Ginzberg, *The Legends of the Jews*, I, 116–118.
3   Delitzsch, *New Commentary on Genesis*, 189–190.

the names of the progenitors of the human race were not Hebrew or that of any Semitic language. Delitzsch concludes that the names derived from a now-vanished prediluvian language.[4]

Citing German biblical scholar Karl Budde, Delitzsch ponders if Cain was the original ancestor of humanity before the generic האדם, 'the adam' or 'man' became the proper name 'Adam'.' He rejects the idea as an arbitrary expedient.[5]

He comments that Lamech's bigamy (Gen, 4: 19) represents a violation of the monogamy expressed in Gen. 2: 24 and the first step in the perversion of this fundamental law.[6]

Delitzsch's ruminations on the meaning of the names of the descendants displays the fascination in attempting to make sense of them by drawing on the philological database as it then existed. Of more import is his observation that the 'progress of civilisation has never kept equal pace with that of religion'. Humanity's first song is 'Lemech [as he spells the name]'s boastful defiance by reason of the newly-invented weapon of vengeance'. After all, the safety of the wives to whom the song is sung depends on Lamech's use of the metal arms that his son had invented. Delitzsch mocks the rabbinic interpretation that Lamech killed both his son and Cain. Instead he avers Lamech's declaration means that he will pay back every attack on him by slaying the one who makes it. These deaths will derive by his own power. As a result Lamech has made himself more inviolable than even Cain was with the mark of God.[7]

Delitzsch appreciates that the origin of music was followed by that of metallurgy. Amazingly, even though Lamech did not speak Hebrew, the lyric poetry of the language of the song remains although the form may have changed when converted to Hebrew.[8]

To those who claim that the story of Cain and Abel and the following genealogy are not in harmony, Delitzsch counters that the reference to Cain at the conclusion of the song 'binds the two supposed discrepant pieces of history in close connection'. He is fairly brutal in his condemnation of the Cainite line:

> 'The Cainite development starts from murder and culminates in that murderous lust of war, in which the ascendancy of the animal instinct in human nature manifests itself.'

No subtlety here. Delitzsch posits that whereas the unity of the Cainite and Sethite genealogies are invented by the biblical author, the Cainite unity itself is original, real and deplorable.[9]

Dillmann

As might be expected, Dillmann expresses concern over the same questions that challenged previous exegetes. He expresses some of the same conclusions as Delitzsch but without the

---

4   Delitzsch, *New Commentary on Genesis*, 193.
5   Delitzsch, *New Commentary on Genesis*, 192.
6   Delitzsch, *New Commentary on Genesis*, 194.
7   Delitzsch, *New Commentary on Genesis*, 197–198, quotations from 197.
8   Deliztsch, *New Commentary on Genesis*, 199–200.
9   Delitzsch, *New Commentary on Genesis*, 200.

same negative casting of judgment. For example, as previously noted, the biblical text does not state where Cain obtained a wife. The logical solution in this context is that she was a daughter of Adam and sister of Cain. But contrary to Delitzsch, Dillmann suggests such a marriage would not have been considered offensive at the time.[10]

Cain as the builder of the city deservedly draws attention by Dillmann as well. Two challenges for the exegete are the implications 'that there were already with Cain such a number of people as made it worthwhile to build a city, and further, that Cain does exactly the opposite of that to which, in ver. 12, he was sentenced'.[11] Dillmann resolves the situation by positing traces of second source in the narrative. He recognizes that the city name may be based on obscure information about a city with a similar name. His comment suggests he was not yet aware of the existence of the now archaeologically-identified Sumerian city of Eridu equated with Irad, son of Enoch (in the time before vowels were written).[12]

The names in the genealogy challenge Dillmann. For the names of the descendants in Gen. 4: 18, Dillmann really has nothing to contribute. They were a mystery in ancient times as they continue to be today. By contrast, Dillmann suggests the names of the wives in Gen. 4: 19 are indispensable for the understanding the Song of Lamech. Dillmann is puzzled that a son of Lamech and Adeh could be a nomad given the rise of human culture and civilization (Gen. 4: 20).[13]

For Dillmann, this development of culture and civilization is key to the story. It is not about individuals in history or even peoples, but instead the story traces the beginning of culture and the important discoveries in art and occupations at the dawn of time. The human origin of civilization in the biblical account contrasts with other ancient peoples who trace such events to the time when gods ruled the earth. Dillmann differentiates between the invention of tools/weapons and their use in Gen. 4: 22. He postulates that what is objectionable develops out of the usage and not the invention, a still common argument.[14]

Dillmann raises the issue of multiple authorship in this pericope. First, he cannot imagine one writer creating both the Cainite and Sethite genealogies. Second, he cannot reconcile Cain the unsettled fugitive in the Cain and Abel story with Cain the builder here. Third, 'this is the only place where the continuity of human history is unbroken by the Flood'. What difference would these pre-Flood demonstrations of human cultural progress make if they all were washed away in an universal Flood? Based on these observations, he cites the frequent proposal positing two authors called J[1] and J[2]. J[1], the sons of Cain author, also is responsible for the Tower of Babel story involving building another city. While this division does render the J primitive history comprehensible, Dillmann has no explanation for the substantial similarity in style by these authors.[15]

The breakdown of the verses becomes even more complicated. Dillmann avers that the Song of Lamech (Gen. 4: 23–24) was not created by the biblical writer but was transmitted

---

10　Dillmann, *Genesis*, 196–197.
11　Dillmann, *Genesis*, 197.
12　Dillmann, *Genesis*, 197–198.
13　Dillmann, *Genesis*, 199–200, 202.
14　Dillmann, *Genesis*, 204.
15　Dillmann, *Genesis*, 179–180.

to him. According to the song, Lamech considers himself superior to his ancestor Cain and capable of providing his own protection without a divine mark. The song expresses the savage custom of blood revenge against which a barrier was to be reared.[16] The author is invoking a distant past that is relevant to his audience by drawing on sources and traditions which he has fashioned into a new story.

Many of these observations by Dillmann may be viewed as preliminary or foundational to the proposed breakdown of the four authors of the six stories in Part II. He is aware of the tensions within the text and struggling to bring order to it. He does not consider the possibility that the author of the text might be a Cainite who asserted a proud claim that his people were responsible for great developments at the dawn of human civilization ... meaning that Mesopotamians and Egyptians were not.

Gunkel

Gunkel continues the idea that the passage originally was an independent narrative. He posits that once there had to have been many legends connected with the individuals named in these verses. The biblical story drew on ancient traditions and was not a recent invention. Based on the presence of related names elsewhere, he deduces that these tribal names are connected to the south and east of Palestine, the name for the area used by the Ottoman Empire at the time Gunkel was writing. Such tribal names derive from the earliest period of Israel's history.[17]

Despite the local geographical setting of the passage, Gunkel perceives that ancient Israel as with many other civilizations, pondered the question of the origin of human culture. Naturally the commencement of this quest occurred a long long time ago before the formation of Israel, a very young country. The focus of these verses is on nomads, smiths, and musicians, three classes of people of the desert. The passage then reflects a Bedouin perspective.[18]

Gunkel regards the Song of Lamech as separate from these considerations. It is not a song of inventions but of fierce vengeance. Lamech is the proud powerful warrior who will not be intimidated, an attitude that expresses the beliefs of Israel at its beginning. Similar values are expressed in other biblical stories. Gunkel first cites the Midianites in their confrontation with Gideon as they 'proudly await death and Gideon's son is to learn blood vengeance' (see Additional Readings: Midian):

> **Judges 8: 18** *Then he [Gideon] said to Zebah and Zalmunna [kings of Midian], 'Where are the men whom you slew at Tabor?' They answered, 'As you are, so were they, every one of them; they resembled the sons of a king.' *[19]* And he said, 'They were my brothers, the sons of my mother; as Yahweh lives, if you had saved them alive, I would not slay you.' *[20]* And he [Gideon] said to Jether his first-born, 'Rise, and slay them.' But the youth (naar) did not draw his sword; for he was afraid, because he was still a youth (naar).*

Gunkel's second example is Samson's humorous-violent victory song:

---

16 Dillmann, *Genesis*, 205–207.
17 Gunkel, *Genesis*, 50–51.
18 Gunkel, *Genesis*, 51–52.

Judges 15: 16 *And Samson said, 'With the jawbone of an ass, heaps upon heaps, with the jawbone of an ass have I slain a thousand men.'*

Unlike Gideon's son, Samson has no problem singing about men he has slain.

Gunkel avers that the Song of Lamech shows that Cain was not considered to have been the ancestor of Lamech. The song is not expressing inappropriate boasting over one's ancestor. Instead the reference to Cain in the song is to a contemporary foreigner, perhaps a rival who also was a fierce warrior with his own incident of celebrated blood vengeance. Gunkel imagines the song was sung on the return to camp by the blood-spattered warrior who announces his proud victory to his adoring family. By contrast, Gunkel's 'collector' of the song for the biblical narrative lived in a softer more civilized time. He used the song in its new narrative sequence to portray the frightful decay of the human race leading to the punishment of the Flood.[19]

Yet, Gunkel is puzzled by the presence of the city-builder amidst all these desert reminiscences collected by one hand. He speculates the existence of an old city 'Enoch' whose location was not only unknown in Gunkel's time but probably to the collector of the traditions as well. Enoch may then have been the patron deity of the city. His musing raises the question of why Cain and not Enoch was designated as the builder in the biblical account. Regardless of the reason, the implication is that this note was added to the text.[20]

As to the inevitable question, if the narrator had been asked about where Cain got his wife, the answer would have been she was his sister.[21]

Gunkel sums up the history of the passages as follows:

1. Cain originally was the progenitor of the Kenites [a people who appear in subsequent biblical texts regarding the wife of Moses, the Song of Deborah, and the time of Saul and David].
2. In the legend, Cain is cursed for fratricide and famed for being a fierce warrior, a legacy that was carried on in the Song of Lamech.
3. Cain means 'smith' thereby explaining his later connection with metalworking figures in the story.
4. Kenan, a variant of Cain, changes Cain into a city-builder through this new linkage to Enoch who gave his name to the city.
5. Later the Cain and Seth genealogies were interwoven with Cain becoming the godless one [whose line is destroyed in the Flood] and Seth the pious one [whose lineage survives].[22]

This breakdown of the Cain verses is in accord with Gunkel's perception of J as a collector of traditions who creates a new tradition based on what stories he chooses to combine, in what sequence, and with what additions of his own. Now suppose that the author of the song was a Kenite and he was delivering a message in his present through the Song of Lamech about the action he was willing to take against his foes or those who would seek to kill him. Gunkel is so focused on the past, he cannot see the fierce declaration being made in the present.

---

19 Gunkel, *Genesis*, 52–53.
20 Gunkel, *Genesis*, 53.
21 Gunkel, *Genesis*, 53.
22 Gunkel, *Genesis*, 54.

Skinner

Skinner divides Gen. 4 into three sections which have been woven together: Cain and Abel, the Cainite genealogy, and the Sethite genealogy fragment. The Cainite genealogy has no explicit sequel. As a seven-generation sequence it is complete in and of itself. It functions to record the introduction of the various arts and industries which comprise the civilized life. Skinner rejects the notion that it consists of generations of sinners in contrast to the Sethite genealogy as has been proposed. Both genealogies derive from a common original. Skinner also rejects the notion that two separate genealogies in J were amalgamated by a redactor. He questions whether the genealogy originally was a continuation of the garden story and declares that an essential connection cannot be affirmed.[23]

Skinner raises the intriguing possibility of one writer imitating another whether consciously or unconsciously. He accepts that the story of Cain and Abel originally existed independent of the garden story. Someone incorporated it into the narrative and linked the name to the genealogy. Whether that incorporation included the entire genealogy or not is impossible to say. One may observe in these ruminations, the exegete wrestling to bring order to diverse threads and disparate traditions but within the confines of the mythical rubric which dominated scholarship.[24]

Skinner seeks to understand the place of Cain within the Bedouin world. Seemingly modern counterparts in the Arab world can be found in low-caste tribes called 'Sleyb' who are part hunters, part smiths, part gypsy-laborers who have no property save some assess and no cattle. They wander the entire Arabian Peninsula but are not 'Cains' because they do not and lack the means to engage in the blood-feud with the stronger tribes.[25] Furthermore, those Bedouins who do engage in such actions are not 'Cains' either. They are not fugitives and vagabonds as prescribed by the biblical injunction: they raise sheep, the profession of Abel, and they possesses a proud spirit as surely the Hebrews knew. For Skinner, 'Cain is the impersonation of an inferior race of nomads, maintaining a miserable existence by the chase, and practising a peculiarly ferocious form of blood-feud.'[26] Given the friendly relationship between the Kenites and the Israelites in biblical texts and that 'they seemed to have cherished the most ardent attachment to Yahwism, it becomes incredible that they should have been conceived as resting under a special curse.'[27]

Skinner sees an obvious incongruity between the banished Cain of the Cain and Abel story and the city-builder Cain of the Cainite genealogy. However he avers that undue emphasis has been placed on the proposed identity of Cain with the Kenites. Cain does represent the nomadic life but it is a doomed life of wandering the uncultivated regions beyond the pale of civilization.[28]

Lamech brings a new dimension to the story. No judgment is passed on Lamech's bigamy, and probably none was intended in the text. He wonders if the two female names are a relic

---

23 Skinner, *A Critical and Exegetical Commentary*, 98–99.
24 Skinner, *A Critical and Exegetical Commentary*, 101.
25 Skinner, *A Critical and Exegetical Commentary*, 113.
26 Skinner, *A Critical and Exegetical Commentary*, 112.
27 Skinner, *A Critical and Exegetical Commentary*, 114.
28 Skinner, *A Critical and Exegetical Commentary*, 100, 111–112.

of a nature myth. He sees in Jabal the origin of the Bedouin way of life. Skinner rejects the presumption that Tubal-cain's metallurgical prowess automatically equates to the invention of weapons. He concludes that Lamech's three sons do not represent the highest stage of social evolution but rather express three picturesque modes of life.[29]

With the Song of Lamech, Skinner's passions are more aroused. It is an 'appalling development of the spirit of blood-revenge, which could hardly be considered an advance in culture' and may more rightfully be considered 'an exhibition of human depravity'.[30] The Song has a doubtful connection with the genealogy previously delineated. It simply enunciates 'the fierce implacable spirit of revenge that forms the chief part of the Bedouin's code of honour'.[31] By attributing the Song to the Bedouin, Skinner negates the proposition that it is a remnant exulting in the revelation of the primitive ferocity of a stone-age savage triumphantly dancing over the corpse of his victim.[32]

Von Rad

For von Rad this genealogy enables the narrator to present his view of the development of man, his culture, and his mental attitude. Today, the reader may observe the 'the distinctive features and subtleties of the Yahwistic narrative' and in so doing recognize that 'it arose by a combination of several different traditions'. For example the story of Cain's crime and the genealogy must have different origins given their different forms. In this melding effort, 'the Yahwist saw nothing strange in the fact that the genealogy speaks of Cain's wife, as though the reader had already heard of her'. The narrator's voice is best heard through the composition as a whole than in the individual parts.[33]

The purpose of the Kenite genealogy in 4: 17–22 is to answer fundamental questions of human history: the origin of the city and division of the population into professions. Von Rad asks the reader to experience the cultural progress of man. The city arises and the smith is alongside the shepherd. Art appears. This genealogy therefore is an important one for understanding the development of human civilization.[34]

Beyond the name 'Cain' at the forefront of this list, nothing else links it to the preceding story. One may debate whether the establishment of a city contradicts the curse of Cain to be a wanderer and von Rad cites I Sam. 30: 29 as an example of Kenite cities:

> *in Racal, in the cities of the Jerahmeelites, in the cities of the Kenites.*

He equates the list with the skills practiced by the Kenites in the area between wilderness and the cultivated land. The absence of a connection with the preceding story also raises questions about the link to the subsequent stories. The introduction of these professions and the connections to the Kenites in the time of David 'does not reckon with the Flood and

---

29 Skinner, *A Critical and Exegetical Commentary*, 118, 120–121, 123.
30 Skinner, *A Critical and Exegetical Commentary*, 115.
31 Skinner, *A Critical and Exegetical Commentary*, 120.
32 Skinner, *A Critical and Exegetical Commentary*, 122.
33 Von Rad, *Genesis*, 110.
34 Von Rad, *Genesis*, 110–111.

the annihilation of all living beings'. Von Rad does not expect there to be a link between people who must have been destroyed by the Flood with a people living well after it. He does not consider the possibility that in the narrative of this author there is no universal Flood and that one purpose of the genealogy was precisely to extol the Kenites as the founders of civilization.[35]

Von Rad suggests the 'Song of the Sword' at the end of the genealogy (4: 23–24) had to have been a very ancient song of revenge which became known to the narrator. It serves to present the opposite side of the coin of human development. Lamech operates independently of the Lord and ignores the divine promise of protection which had been extended to Cain. Technically, the divine promise of protection was only for Cain with no provision for any descendants. This may be of one of the occasions where the details in the melding process need to be ignored for the sake of the compositional whole. Von Rad makes a point that Lamech executed vengeance on his own and did so recklessly. He praises the Yahwist who incorporated the song into his narrative for allowing the song to speak for itself.[36]

Naturally for von Rad, this song is another in the sequence of increased sin and disturbance of the natural order beginning with the Fall. He suggests Jesus alludes to the Song of Lamech in Matthew 18: 22 with the reference to forgiving seventy times seven:

Jesus said to him, 'I do not say to you seven times, but seventy times seven.[37]

Speiser

Speiser is quite blunt and to the point in his assessment of this passage: 'This short section poses many problems'. He sees multiple sources, long periods of oral transmission, and telescoping of traditions involving the Cainite and Sethite lines. What is clear is its dependence on Mesopotamian traditions about the kings who ruled before the Flood. The transmission process from Mesopotamia to biblical author included a change in names but not core features. For example, in 4: 20, 'It is worth noting that Mesopotamian king lists sometimes interrupt their statistics with similar incidental comment about a given entity'.[38]

A common purpose was to trace the line between pre- and post-flood people. This continuity took priority over the validity of cultural details that were appended to the genealogy.

> 'While the Cainite line is singled out here as the vehicle for mankind's technological progress, it is evident that the account was not conceived as a summary of cultural achievements. It is derivative in every respect, repeating what tradition managed to hand down. And since some of the sources go back to the 3rd millennium BCE, the scientific perspective is often archaic. At other times the results are anachronistic…'[39]

---

35 Von Rad, *Genesis*, 110–111.
36 Von Rad, *Genesis*, 111.
37 Von Rad, *Genesis*, 111–112.
38 Speiser. *Genesis*, 35–36, quotations from 35.
39 Speiser. *Genesis*, 36.

Speiser's distinctive view anchors the passage in both Mesopotamian culture and with the development of human civilization.

By contrast, Speiser declares the Song of Lamech to be an anomaly, separate from the genealogical verses. The 'Song of the Sword' lacks the Mesopotamian basis. It sings to the vengeance by a triumphant tribesman over his enemy. Its origins may even be to the south of Palestine where the Kenites were known to live. Exactly why or how it became linked to the preceding verses is unknown beyond the specific reference to Cain in the song.[40]

Westermann

Westermann includes the Cainite genealogy in 4: 17–24 and the Seth genealogy in 4: 25–26 together in his commentary. He recognizes that they 'each have an independent origin and are to be understood independently of each other'. He understands the material to focus on primeval times. He concludes that the perspective is of the sedentary farmer and the city taking precedence over the nomad, while simultaneously esteem is shown for the nomad way of life. Even within 4: 17–24, Westermann discerns two traditions – one of genealogy and one of the origin of civilization, each of which had its own rich history before only a few excerpts were retained by the biblical writer.[41]

Westermann draws several insights from the genealogy. He acknowledges the theory postulated by Gunkel that the Cain family tree rose from defunct stories. He posits the author was aware of the Sumerian traditions with its seven *apkallu*, the sages or demigods created to bring civilization to humans. The Cain genealogy functions as a seminal notion of the history of human civilization. The verses exhibit an awareness of the great age of the inventions and discoveries that serve as the basis of that civilization. Strikingly, the author makes no attempt to designate Israel itself or the ancestors of Israel as being responsible for this great leap forward. Quite the contrary, Israel is heir to the same common founding of the civilization as non-Israelites.[42]

The perennial question of the Flood rendering meaningless this effort to describe the pre-Flood origin of civilization obligates Westermann to respond to the previous exegetes. He references the Babylonian traditions which describe the world before the flood as well as after it. If the Babylonians traced culture and civilization to the primeval period, then evidently the Flood was not the disruptive force in the continuity of the human history that it was thought to be by some exegetes. In a further observation, he postulates the independent existence of these narrative traditions. As a result the relevance of myths of the primeval times could be raised as an issue only if they were brought together in a chronological sequence prior to the Flood. The net result of this compilation is a history of cultural achievements. For Westermann, the author has demonstrated a recognition of the advance of human civilization that exceeds any individual accomplishment subsumed within it.[43]

40　Speiser. *Genesis*, 37.
41　Westermann, *Genesis 1–11*, 323, 324, 330, quotation from 323.
42　Westermann, *Genesis 1–11*, 324–325.
43　Westermann, *Genesis 1–11*, 325.

These observations still leave the place of the independent Song of Lamech undefined. That song was placed as the end of the genealogy for a purpose. Indeed, it was meant to conclude the entire chapter of Cain and Abel (meaning it was separate from Gen. 4: 25–26 about Seth). Westermann endeavors to understand the passage through the historical reality of increased killing deriving from the growing complexity of human civilization. His approach extends the meaning of the story beyond the context of the development of metallurgy by Tubal-cain. Through J's insertion of the braggart song, it became a comment on the violent dangers facing humanity even as it progresses.[44] One detects here an appreciation by the 20th-century German biblical scholar for the ancient biblical writer who addressed fundamental questions on the nature of human civilization and history.

The Jewish Study Bible

Levenson entitles the section encompassing 4: 17–26 'The growth of culture'. The concept is proffered that the biblical text is a highly compressed passage that may be the epitome of well-known legends which have not survived. There is a Mesopotamian flavor to the pre-flood sages who founded the basic institutions of civilization in the emergence of the occupations and technologies. The Song of Lamech attests the ongoing violence from Cain and the increasing evil of the human race.[45]

The New Jerome Biblical Commentary

The potential Mesopotamian influences are striking in this brief passage.

1. Irad corresponds to Eridu, the first antediluvian city according to the Sumerian King List.
2. The seven sages or *apkallu*, who are believed to have founded the elements of culture in antediluvian times, resemble the seven generations of Cain.

The genealogy is used not to convey biological information as one might seek to document one's own family, but to determine domestic, politico-jural, and religious matters.[46]

Clifford notes the question regarding who built the first city. 'He built a city' seems to refer to Enoch and not Cain. He named the city after his son Irad comparable to Sumerian-city Eridu. The naming of the city after Enoch appears to be a gloss.[47] Such a change would make Enoch the founder of civilization. If so, then this combination raises the possibility that a biblical writer linked the Enoch tradition to the Cain story.

Finally, Lamech's celebration of his own violence suggests the effects of the curse of Cain lived on through his descendants thereby anticipating the Flood.[48]

---

44 Westermann, *Genesis 1–11*, 335–337.
45 Levenson, 'Genesis', 19–20.
46 Clifford and Murphy, 'Genesis', 13.
47 Clifford and Murphy, 'Genesis', 13.
48 Clifford and Murphy, 'Genesis', 13.

The Harper Collins Study Bible

Rosenberg makes two observations:

1. The specific professions mentioned of stock-breeding and artisan trades were vital to the rise of cities.
2. The Song of Lamech was a boastful one which 'typifies the world's multiplication of violence, despite God's effort in 4.15 to restrain blood vengeance.'[49]

The significance of these observations is left to the reader.

Conclusion

This review of the sons of Cain exegesis over the millennia reveals significant commonalities, some differences in interpretations, and open questions. These observations may be summarized as follows.

1. The earlier commentators such as Josephus and the rabbis were storytellers in their own right. They sought to smooth the way by filling in gaps through expository creations. They anticipated the questions an audience might ask reading or hearing the story as part of the existing canonized narrative.
2. Modern scholars recognize the presence of multiple voices within J's account. The Song of Lamech and the genealogies seemed to have been independent originally. The nomadic and the city verses reflected separate perspectives. The text is a passage of multiple origins that a collector brought together.
3. Everyone tends to agree that the story is about the dawn of human civilization whether the story is a mythical folktale or the word of God.
4. Modern scholars who perceive the story to be mythical tend to assume that it derives from older traditions which have been truncated.
5. Modern scholars tend to discern Mesopotamian and Kenite elements within the story.

Beyond the concern for sin and fall that is inevitable in biblical exegesis there still are several presuppositions, considerations, and revisions which should be taken into account.

1. There is a presupposition that the story of the sons of Cain follows one generation after the story of Cain and Abel which follows one generation after the story of Adam and Eve. That may not have been true in the KDB where the sons of Cain story did not yet exist and the garden story and Cain and Abel may have been temporally separate.
2. There is a presupposition that the story of the sons of Cain is about primeval times and the origin of civilization. This presupposition seems perfectly valid with the references to city-building and metallurgy in particular. There is a possibility that within Israel there may have been different peoples, priesthoods and political factions who looked to the wilderness or to Mesopotamia for the origin of civilization and the story of the sons of Cain was part of that discussion.
3. The story may not have been about the first biological human beings so there would have been no problem with the presence of other people outside the Cain line.

---

49 Rosenberg, 'Genesis, 11'.

4. There is a possibility that for the author of the sons of Cain, the Flood may not have been global.

Perhaps the most significant presupposition regarding the story is the attitude of the exegetes towards nomads. After Wellhausen proposed the Documentary Hypothesis, he became an 'Arabist'. The late 19th to early 20th century was a time of European imperialism in the Middle East with consequences which resonate to this very day. Thanks to the steamship, tourists also began to travel to the Holy Land. As Europeans and Americans traveled these now readily-accessible lands, they brought with them deeply-seated ideas about who and what they were encountering in the Holy Land. One persistent conception was the journey was one not only in space but in time where they were able to see the past come to life and witness a presumed unchanging world in the millennia since biblical times. It was as if the people of the past were alive today. They were traveling not only to the Holy Land in their present but to as it was in biblical times. At any given moment, one might observe a modern Abraham emerging from a tent or a Rachel drawing water from a well. The Middle East was not a Disney theme park or a Colonial Williamsburg yet alone a Jurassic Park or Westworld, but a living world frozen in time for all these millennia that scholars could now observe in the present to understand the past. This mindset became a recurring framework through which stories from primitive times should be understood (see Additional Readings: Holy Land).

Such attitudes also communicated a relationship that was not one of equals. In this scenario, the visitors from the west were at the forefront of modern civilization while the local inhabitants were the relic of a primitive past. As one reads the scholarly commentaries on the story of the sons of Cain, one cannot help but notice the secondary position of the nomads vis-à-vis the scholars. The west has left their world behind. Their story belongs to the primeval stage at the dawn of human civilization, but since Abraham, mankind has progressed (these scholars were male), his journey has removed him from this primitive way of life. The very separation of the story of the sons of Cain and the other stories of this study into the routinely-designated 'Primeval' section of the Bible automatically encourages interpretations in a certain derogatory direction. The oral and folk traditions championed by Gunkel only exaggerated this sense of superiority to the world of the stories and their original audiences.

Another problem is to treat a story individually. The tendency to analyze the Cainite passage in isolation from other passages may contribute to a skewed understanding of it. To some extent, such analysis in unavoidable as reflected in the separate chapters for each of the six son stories in this study. One observes glimpses of scholars addressing this challenge in references to the stories of Seth, the Flood, and the Tower of Babel. Precisely as Friedman stated, in each instance it is important to learn something of the author's life to understand the writing, to see connections between the author's life and the world that the author depicts in his or her work. How did the author come to have an idea of what happened? How much did the events of the author's own day affect the way in which the author told the story? Part II directly addresses these issues raised here.

One goal in this study is to understand the stories in their own terms. The effort includes the recognition that the stories are political in nature. Lamech is not a generic figure from hoary antiquity, he represents the voice of the author who is issuing a rather vigorous warning in the present of what is to happen. He is drawing a line in the sand. Another approach is to see him as a person of Kenite heritage who defines himself as not-Sethite. He is proud of his Kenite legacy and is responding to those who champion a Mesopotamian legacy. In elephant/donkey terms, this author is from the prophet or pro-Moses political party. Based on the Song of Lamech, it is reasonable to conclude that he was engaged in a battle for power with another political party which looked elsewhere for its legitimation. He expressed that battle in fighting terms that left no room for doubt. With these thoughts in mind, one can now turn to Cain's sister story, the sons of his brother Seth.

Chapter 3

WHO ARE THE SONS OF SETH?

Genesis 4: *[25] And Adam knew his wife again, and she bore a son and called his name Seth, for she said, 'God has appointed for me another child instead of Abel, for Cain slew him.' [26] To Seth also a son was born, and he called his name Enosh. At that time men began to call upon the name of Yahweh.*

The figure of Seth from these verses does not loom large in the analysis in ancient or modern times. His diminished presence is reflective of the lack of stories attributed to him in the biblical account. The verses are more of an announcement of a three-generation genealogy with one action than an actual story: there is the founder, a new son to replace his dead and murdered predecessor, and a third-generation son. During the time of Seth and his son, people begin the worship of Yahweh by name. End of pericope.

Seth lives in the shadow of his older brothers. Cain and Abel have generated enormous attention over the centuries and millennia. Together their names have crossed over into popular culture along with the mark of Cain and the penultimate question 'Am I my brother's keeper?' By contrast, there is little to say about Seth. What little prominence he is accorded derives from discussions about his lineage versus that of Cain's family in the preceding passage. That comparison is made because of its ramifications for the story of the sons of God (see Chapter 4). Nonetheless, despite his dullness, someone made the effort to create the Seth line, someone who knew the stories of the garden, Cain and Abel, and the Flood. That makes Seth a figure of importance.

Despite the brevity of the verses, commentators have raised questions about the significance of the story. The detected issues include:

1. What is the relationship between Seth and his surviving older brother Cain?
2. What action does calling on the name of Yahweh mean before the name was revealed to Moses at the burning bush?
3. Who were these men who did the calling? What is their relationship to the men who presumably aided in the building of a city or to one of whom was a victim to Lamech?
4. What was the purpose of the calling on the name of Yahweh?

In addition to these traditional questions regarding the text, one may add:

What political message was being delivered through the communication of this story? Or how did it help one political faction, the Sethites, in the time of Solomon against the other ones? Above all other considerations, the longstanding effort to contrast the sons of Seth to the sons of Cain complicates the attempt to discern the original meaning of the text.

The tracking of the attempts by exegetes to understand this passage will begin in ancient times with Josephus, proceed to the rabbis, and continue with modern scholarship from the end of the 19th century to the canonical commentaries of the 20th.

Josephus

Despite the scant information contained within the biblical text, Josephus wrote extensively about Seth.

> **Ant 1: 68** *He [Adam following the murder of Abel and Cain's departure] had indeed many other children, but Seth in particular. As for the rest, it would be tedious to name them; I will therefore only endeavour to give an account of those who proceeded from Seth. Now this Seth, when he was brought up, and came to those years in which he could discern what was good, became a virtuous man; and as he was himself of an excellent character, so did he leave children behind him who imitated his virtues.[69] All these proved to be of good dispositions. They also inhabited the same country without dissensions, and in a happy condition, without any misfortunes falling upon them till they died. They also were the inventors of that peculiar sort of wisdom which is concerned with the heavenly bodies, and their order.[70] And that their inventions might not be lost before they were sufficiently known, upon Adam's prediction that the world was to be destroyed at one time by the force of fire, and at another time by the violence and quantity of water, they made two pillars, the one of brick, the other of stone: they inscribed their discoveries on them both,[71] that in case the pillar of brick should be destroyed by the flood, the pillar of stone might remain, and exhibit those discoveries to mankind; and also inform them that there was another pillar of brick erected by them. Now this remains in the land of Siriad to this day.*

One observes here Josephus's efforts to place Seth in a social context of multiple people at the dawn of civilization. He needed to mention that there were more people around than identified in the biblical narrative. If he had not, the story would not make sense to an audience that thought the story was about the first human beings.

Josephus sought to make sense of the story by filling in the gaps. The numerous other children too tedious to name also may be a way of coping with the fact that the adult Cain and Abel were a generation older than Seth. The youngest son was not born until after adult Cain murdered adult Abel. One presumes that the significance of the generation age difference was not lost on the original audience. That difference also implies that Eve gave birth over an extended period of time which was a common practice in human history.

The biblical verses attribute nothing to Seth about the origin of civilization that Josephus mentions. It is far easier to discuss the origin of the civilized world through the verses from the sons of Cain story (see Chapter 2). In contrast to his treatment of the Kenites, Josephus emphasizes Seth's wisdom, his ability to discern good from evil. He comments favorably on the wisdom Seth and his generation have accumulated and of their precautions to ensure that such knowledge would survive any calamity which befell them. Since Josephus was writing following the destruction of the Jerusalem temple by Rome, one wonders how audiences in his present were to understand his elaborations on the biblical passages about Cain and Seth.

Josephus also skips over Enosh, the son of Seth mentioned in the biblical verses. He concludes by making some general comments about Seth's extended lineage.

> **Ant 1: 72** *Now this posterity of Seth continued to esteem God as the Lord of the universe, and to have an entire regard to virtue, for seven generations; but in process of time they were perverted, and forsook the practices of their forefathers, and did neither pay those honours to God which were appointed them, nor had they any concern to do justice toward men. But for what degree of zeal they had formerly shown for virtue, they now showed by their actions a double degree of wickedness; whereby they made God to be their enemy.*

So despite the virtuous start, in the end, the sons of Seth are no better than anyone else. Josephus quickly then moves to the Flood story. Now the catastrophic destruction of humanity has a justifiable basis given this description of the behavior of the Seth line. Perhaps those who survived the destruction will discover those pillars of brick and stone and share the inscribed wisdom with the world.

Rabbis

The rabbinic tales integrate the biblical chronologies into the stories thereby including information not identified as part of the Seth story. Seth becomes important within Jewish tradition since he, and not Cain or Abel, would become the ancestor of the messiah. According to the rabbis, his birth was unusual in human history in that there was no need for circumcision. Seth was different from Cain:

> *Thus Seth became, in a genuine sense, the father of the human race, especially the father of the pious, while the depraved and godless are descended from Cain.*[1]

This dichotomy within the human race therefore is traced back to in the beginning. Both the first pair of children, Cain and Abel, and the second pair, Cain and Seth, exhibit distinctive and distinguishing characteristics. It remains interesting to note this distinction given the presumed global flood to follow. In that event the Cain line is eliminated so its character would seem to be irrelevant beyond demonstrating that it deserved to be destroyed. However, in a local flood tradition, the descendants of both Cain and Seth would be important. The possibility of separate authors for the two genealogies correlates with the possibility of local and global flood traditions.

As for the life of Seth, the rabbinic versions essentially match the description of that provided by Josephus. The difference occurs with Enosh, the son of Seth. As the rabbis tell it, there came a time when people inquired of him how it came to be that his grandparents (and one would think their grandparents as well!) came to be. In his responses, Enosh sought physically to replicate the creation story in the presence of the questioners. His method was to breathe into clumps of earth which he had fashioned into images. He was unsuccessful in his efforts. Satan, however, seized the initiative and entered one of these images which became alive. The people then worshiped this walking image and the rabbis deemed them the first idol worshipers. The results were calamitous. The cosmic order had been ripped

---

1   Ginzberg, *The Legends of the Jews*, I: 121.

asunder and the age of depravity commenced. Devolution resulted. The people started to resemble apes since they were no longer in the image of God.[2]

Both Josephus and the rabbis started with the same lone biblical verse describing an action which occurred during Enosh's life. From that brief notice, they spun elaborate tales of Satan, angels, and mastery over the sun, the moons, and stars. Their skill as storytellers has become part of the challenge in reversing the process to arrive at the plain truth.

Modern scholarship has tended to focus on the literary and textual issues since there does not seem to be much archaeology with which to work. Exegetes did address the calling of the name of Yahweh. This action frequently was religious in nature engendering discussion on the origin of religion in human civilization.

Unexpectedly, archaeology did contribute to the discussion. Its impact was greater in the 20th century than the 19th. Its impact occurred because of the discovery of the name 'Yahweh' in the Egyptian inscriptions, something that would not have been known to Josephus or the rabbis. Archaeologically one can make the case that the name Yahweh dates back at least to the time of Pharaoh Amenhotep III in the 14th century BCE and that he was the deity of the Shasu people, a wilderness people associated in the Egyptian record with Seir and Edom (see Additional Readings: Shasu). That connection parallels multiple biblical references which also locate Yahweh in the wilderness of Seir and Edom, the area where Israel wandered:

> He [Moses] said, 'Yahweh came from Sinai, and dawned from Seir upon us' (Deut. 33: 2)
>
> Yahweh, when thou didst go forth from Seir, when thou didst march from the region of Edom (Judges 5: 4)

and the area where Esau was at home:

> And Jacob sent messengers before him to Esau his brother in the land of Seir, the country of Edom (Gen. 32:3)
>
> Let my lord pass on before his servant, and I will lead on slowly, according to the pace of the cattle which are before me and according to the pace of the children, until I come to my lord in Seir… So Esau returned that day on his way to Seir. (Gen. 33: 14, 16)
>
> So Esau dwelt in the hill country of Seir; Esau is Edom (Gen. 36: 8)
>
> Then we turned, and journeyed into the wilderness in the direction of the Red Sea, as Yahweh told me; and for many days we went about Mount Seir. [2] Then Yahweh said to me, [3] 'You have been going about this mountain country long enough; turn northward. [4] And command the people, You are about to pass through the territory of your brethren the sons of Esau, who live in Seir; and they will be afraid of you. So take good heed; [5] do not contend with them; for I will not give you any of their land, no, not so much as for the sole of the foot to tread on, because I have given Mount Seir to Esau as a possession'. (Deut. 2: 1–5)

The archaeological discoveries of Yah(weh), Seir, and Edom in the Egyptian record provided new information to modern exegetes. The debate on the meaning of calling the name of

---

2   Ginzberg, *The Legends of the Jews*, 123–124. See also Goldin, *The Book of Legends*, 37–38.

Yahweh prior to Moses expanded to include the significance of the name outside the biblical narrative. Now one needs to keep in mind two distinctive but related issues:

1. The historical question of the connection of Israel to Yahweh of Seir and Edom in the archaeological record;
2. The knowledge of the authors of this verse in the story of Seth and elsewhere in the six son stories about the Yahweh.

The topic will be revisited with the story of Nimrod as well as with the relationship of the Kenites and Israel (see Additional Readings: Yahweh).

Delitzsch

For Delitzsch, Seth 'was indeed a gift of the God of promise'. He takes the position that the expression of the proclaiming of the name of the Lord represents 'the first link in a chain' of such pronouncements. Such declarations are not simply the exposition of his name but a beginning of 'the formal and solemn common worship of God'. Left unaddressed in his analysis is exactly who are the people doing this worship. Identifying the unsung masses praising the name of the Lord in the time of the second generation and after the birth of third generation is part of the key to determining the meaning of the verse.[3]

Dillmann

Dillmann titles his section on Gen. 4 in his Genesis commentary 'The Growth of Sin among Men and the History of the Wicked Patriarchs...'. He contrasts the evil Cainite line with the moral and righteous Sethite line. The dichotomy exemplifies the perennial opposition between the paths of good and of evil that exists through human history.[4] For Dillmann, Israel at the time of the writing of the story was a young people in the ancient Near East. Under the influence of Mosaism, Israel successfully curtailed the use of primitive myths that had been standard for the civilizations of the time. Dillmann concludes that the old stories on which Gen. 4 was based were not told for their own sake which explains why they were difficult and incomplete.[5]

As previously stated (see Chapter 2), Dillmann questions whether one writer could have written both the Sethite and Cainite genealogies (Gen. 4: 17–24). He attributes the sons of Seth to J[2] and the sons of Cain to J[1]. Even beyond that differentiation, he still has no explanation for Gen. 4: 26b (*At that time men began to call upon the name of Yahweh*), a text that clearly states that the worship of Yahweh had commenced without the presence of Moses. For Dillmann, it is entirely consistent that the Yahwist should write of the public worship of Yahweh beginning in the third generation of humanity. He recognizes that observation still leaves unanswered the question of authorship of the verse. He wonders if

3 Delitzsch, *New Commentary on Genesis*, 202, 204.
4 Cited in Westermann, *Genesis 1–11*, 338. Westermann does not provide the bibliographical data for this citation. Dillmann does draw a distinction between the Sethite line of the patriarchs and its 'antithesis of the Canaanites' (*Genesis*, 175).
5 Dillmann, *Genesis*, 172–174.

perhaps it was an addition to the text. Dillmann has raised the precise issue to be resolved in this study (Part II) since he is absolutely right about multiple authors being responsible for the writing of Gen. 4: 17–24 (the Kenites), 25–26a (the Sethites), and 26b (the worship of Yahweh).[6]

Gunkel

Gunkel's commentary on these verses is brief. He does not address the quality of the character of Seth or Enosh the way Josephus and the rabbis did. He considers the Seth genealogy to be a variant of the Cain genealogy. Gunkel wonders why the proper name 'Adam' is used instead of the common הֵָאדָם, the adam or man, which J normally used. His bigger concern is the beginning of the worship of Yahweh in contrast to the view that Moses at the burning bush was the first to know that name.

> 'This note is extremely interesting from a religiohistorical standpoint. It contradicts, at least in wording, the usual assertion (Exod 3: 4; 6: 12) that Moses was the first to employ the name Yahweh. We cannot state the reason for associating the name Yahweh with Enosh. We have here the oldest deliberation about the age of Yahweh worship, and the impression reflected in this note that the same Yahweh traces back to the primeval period and is older than Moses and the people Israel is assuredly correct.'[7]

Gunkel confesses no knowledge about why such Yahweh worship was attributed to Enosh in the primeval period. As it turns out, he has precisely identified one of the critical issues in the battle for power among the competing priesthoods: the battle over the name of the deity to be worshiped.

Finally, Gunkel includes the naming of Noah as part of this Seth genealogy by Jᵉ, the primary source for J:

> **Genesis 5: 29** *and called his name Noah, saying, 'Out of the ground which Yahweh has cursed this one shall bring us relief from our work and from the toil of our hands'.*

Gunkel's inclusion of this verse demonstrates one of the enduring challenges in biblical exegesis: the difficulty in limiting one's focus. Try as one might to confine oneself to a particular verse, text, passage, story, or genre, the lure of the abundant biblical material is hard to resist. According to the parameters of this study, the calling of Noah lies outside the purview of the son stories. Yet it has been attributed to J and must belong somewhere. The verse cannot stand on its own unattached to any story or isolated in the P genealogy in Gen. 5. To assign the verse its proper place in an extended J narrative is part of the requirement to effectively discern the intent of the biblical author of this verse. Gunkel is correct that the naming of Noah follows upon men calling on the name of Yahweh in the time of Enosh but without recognizing the political significance of such an assertion.

---

6   Dillmann, *Genesis*, 179, 182, 209.
7   Gunkel, *Genesis*, 54.

Skinner

For Skinner the very verses that have proved troubling to earlier exegetes contain the reason for their preservation. First, the verses provide an important notification of the origin of the worship of Yahweh. Without the redactor placing the Sethite verses here in the narrative, the existence of the Sethite genealogy would not have been known and the course of J-analysis in its component strata might have followed a different course. Still Skinner is left to wonder 'What historic reminiscence (if any) lies behind this remarkable statement' and he is forced to admit 'we can not conjecture' although he does. Should it be attributed to events at Sinai? Kadesh?[8]

It is even conceivable that Seth was the first born 'once suspicious elements are eliminated. His birth verse corresponds with Gen. 4: 1 on the birth of Cain'. Skinner links the name to Num. 24: 17 as a synonym for Moab:

> *I see him, but not now; I behold him, but not nigh: a star shall come forth out of Jacob, and a scepter shall rise out of Israel; it shall crush the forehead of Moab, and break down all the sons of Sheth.*

He wonders if the mother naming the child is a relic of the matriarchate. He debates whether קנה should be understood as 'to create/produce' or 'to acquire'. Skinner identifies a strikingly similar phrase in a Babylonian creation story suggesting a more mythically-tinged language in the text than generally accepted.[9]

He notes without comment that the Sethite fragment extends to Gen. 5: 29 and the use of the term 'elohim' in dialog (Gen. 4: 25) as in garden story. Skinner accepts the possibility that the garden recension including Gen. 3: 20:

> *The man called his wife's name Eve, because she was the mother of all living*

continued in Gen. 4:1 with Eve becoming a mother giving birth to Cain with Yahweh's assistance. With these observations about all these verses, Skinner has glimpsed the multitude of writers who composed what he calls J but without any way to identify them. They will be untangled in Part II but for now identifying the authors and determining the meaning must be held in abeyance.[10]

Von Rad

Von Rad takes a different tact in his analysis. He also refers to the 'Yahwistic Sethite list' as a fragment. Only a shell of the original genealogical list remains here following the redaction process. The incorporation of Seth into the Priestly Sethite genealogy in Gen. 5 stripped the genealogy of extraneous material not relevant to P's purpose.

A second focus and significant difference by von Rad in his exegesis is the effort to locate the people of Seth within the ancient Near East context. He attempts to situate the Sethites through a possible connection with the same-name people in the prophecy of Balaam in Num. 24: 17 just quoted in the Skinner section. Based on that potential link, von Rad

---

8 Skinner, *A Critical and Exegetical Commentary*, 125–127, quotations from 126.
9 Skinner, *A Critical and Exegetical Commentary*, 102, 126, quotations from 126.
10 Skinner, *A Critical and Exegetical Commentary*, 98, 124–125.

surmises a reasonable candidate for the Sethites is the Guti. Von Rad identifies the Guti as a disruptive Aramaean nomadic people in the 2nd millennium BCE who wreaked havoc in the civilized world west and north of the Arabian Desert. The location of the people there makes Seth an Aramaean tribal leader in contrast to Cain of the Kenites a people with a northern Arabian background. These two peoples would have been rivals, a geopolitical relationship obscured in the present text. Exegetical efforts suffer from the difficulty in determining the associations the original audience would have made to the story. If characters are named after the Hatfields and the McCoys without the knowledge that those name mean 'feuding families' in American English, one will miss the point of the selection the names.[11]

Von Rad recognizes that the existence of the two ancestral genealogies of the Sethites and the Kenites has been an issue for the Church. He notes the parallelism of the two genealogies but is significantly more concerned with theological considerations of sin, salvation, and prefiguration. Putting aside his Christian emphasis, one is struck with his references to 'the narrator' and 'our narrator' thereby rejecting the previous scholars who had discerned multiple writers in the text. He despairs of ascertaining the correct meaning of this individual's composition.

Here is where von Rad had the opportunity to take the next step. Given that he assigned J to Solomonic times, what did these two genealogies mean then? Apparently it did not occur to him that even though he identified Sutu/Seth and Kenite backgrounds to the genealogies that there might be two authors involved. The two authors might reflect two peoples of different heritages battling for power within a single political entity in part through stories of the great founding ancestors somewhat like the Sons of Hamilton and the Sons of Jefferson in the American tradition.

Von Rad's focus on a single narrator leads to another 'strange' situation which 'can scarcely be rightly explained'. He is referring to the 'notice about the beginning of the Yahweh cult'. He presumes as with Gunkel that the Yahwist inherited this tradition of a Yahweh cult existing prior to Moses, prior to the patriarchs, all the way back in primeval times. Von Rad adds a parenthetical note referencing the Kenites with a question mark about whether the religion has its roots with them, the people into whom Moses married. Strangely he does not comment on the Yahweh attribution belonging to the Seth line and not the Cain or Kenite line where it more typically is located given Zipporah was a Kenite. Apparently it did not occur to him that this attestation of Yahweh worship also might be connected to the battle for power at the time of the writing of the story which he puts in Solomonic times. Here one may observe the restrictive impact of the mythical/folk approach where biblical writers are said to inherit material rather than the political one where biblical writers were creators in their own right.[12]

---

11 One wrinkle with sequence is that von Rad actually referred to the Suti rather than the Guti. A misreading of the German script led to a misprinting in the English translation. The Suti, more commonly written as Shutu, were a Transjordanian people living in close proximity to the rival Kenites. This realization renders the juxtaposition of the two names not a chance occurrence. See John Day, *From Creation to Babel: Studies in Genesis 1–11* (London: Bloomsbury T&T Clark, 2013), 56 n.10. This train of thought will be elaborated on in Part II.

12 Von Rad, *Genesis*, 112.

Speiser

In his commentary on the Book of Genesis, Speiser has nothing really to say. He never even mentions Seth or Enosh. The worship of Yahweh draws his attention. Speiser posits an original worship of Yahweh confined to 'a small body of searchers under the aegis of the patriarchs' which was recorded by J. When Moses fashioned Israel 'out of an amorphous conglomerate of sundry ethnic and tribal elements', he connected the religion of the forefathers already tied to Promised Land with Yahweh. As a result, Speiser differentiates the personal revelation to Moses as part of the Exodus nation-building with the older religion of the 'patriarchal pioneers'. This rubric enables Speiser to render the text coherent within the larger biblical narrative.[13]

Westermann

Westermann deems the Sethite genealogy an independent, self-contained, and altered fragment which may include the naming of Noah in Gen. 5: 29 as Gunkel claimed. He rejects the proposals that the Sethite genealogy demonstrated the moral development of humanity in opposition to the Cainite line as biological expressions of good and evil. Westermann asserts that the text itself does not support that interpretation. Westermann further rejects the proposition that the Sethites are to be connected with the Aramaean nomads as suggested by von Rad. The story is about primeval events and not relations among peoples in the historical times of the author.[14]

Westermann's perception that the story is about primeval times enables him to wrestle into reconcilement the dual traditions of Moses at the burning bush and the time of Enosh. The former is a comment about the origin in history of the people Israel who worship Yahweh; the latter is a primeval statement. It is not meant to be about the beginning of the worship of Yahweh but of a cult or religion, a heritage which belongs to all peoples in every time as the normal part of the human experience. Westermann's J is stating that even though many peoples have many gods with many names there can be only one creator god and that deity's name is Yahweh.[15]

There should be no underestimating how important it is to Westermann to resolve satisfactorily the tension between the Enosh and Moses traditions on Yahweh. He first enlists two of the commentators included here to buttress his claim:

> 'As F. Delitzsch and A. Dillmann had already seen, 4: 26 is not referring to the worship of Yahweh, properly so called but to the worship or cult in the most general sense.'

Westermann then notes Gunkel's disagreement quoting him with the same quotation on 'a religiohistorical standpoint' by him cited above.[16] Westermann pursues this topic in several pages of detailed small-print analysis. Obviously it is of great importance to him. He remains firmly convinced that these texts reveal the history of religion (and civilization)

---

13 Speiser, *Genesis*, 37–38, quotations from 37 and 38 respectively.
14 Westermann, *Genesis 1–11*, 338.
15 Westermann, *Genesis 1–11*, 339–340.
16 Westermann, *Genesis 1–11*, 340.

from primeval times. He is wedded to Gunkel's J as a collector of myths from hoary antiquity. The possibility of two competing priesthoods battling for power expressing alternate views on when the worship of Yahweh began, with Moses in the wilderness or at a cultic place in the time of the birth of the third-generation of the Adam-Seth-Enosh line, is not part of his analysis. In modern parlance, Westermann is not thinking outside the box, he is confined to it.

The Jewish Study Bible

Levenson offers only a brief note and only on verse 4: 26. The culmination 'of what is, in the Jewish view, the most important of these: the proper worship of the true God' follows the growth of culture delineated in the Cain genealogy.[17] No comment is made regarding the early appearance of the proper worship of the true God long before Abraham or Moses. No comment is made about who these people are who worship the true God.

The New Jerome Biblical Commentary

Clifford entitles this section 'Seth and the Introduction of Worship'. Once again the focus is on the 'most important cultural institution of civilization, authentic worship'. The appearance of this authentic worship before Moses is dutifully noted.[18]

The HarperCollins Study Bible

Rosenberg observes that this worship of YHWH 'long anticipates the Israelite religion' without specifically mentioning Moses.[19]

Conclusion

This review of the sons of Seth exegesis over the millennia reveals significant commonalities, some differences in interpretations, and open questions. These observations may be summarized as follows.

1. The earlier commentators such as Josephus and the rabbis were storytellers in their own right. They sought to smooth the way by filling in gaps through expository creations. They anticipated the questions an audience might ask reading or hearing the story as part of the existing canonized narrative.
2. Modern scholars are divided on the presence of multiple writers within J's account. The idea that the stories of the sons of Seth and the sons of Cain were written by different people perhaps of different backgrounds seems reasonable but unprovable or difficult to flesh out.

---

17 Levenson, 'Genesis', 19.
18 Clifford and Murphy, 'Genesis', 13.
19 Rosenberg, 'Genesis', 11.

3.   Everyone tends to agree that the story is about the dawn of human civilization whether the story is a mythical folktale or the word of God with the exception of von Rad who sought to determine a specific historical setting.

4.   Modern scholars who perceive the story to be mythical tend to assume that it derives from an older tradition part of which may be missing.

5.   Modern scholars are divided on the significance of the calling on the name of Yahweh pre-Moses. This act may be considered of great importance for its apparent contradiction of subsequent biblical text or treated in a 'ho hum' fashion as something to note but not to get worked up over for its theological implications.

There are major implications generated from this seemingly insignificant short text:

1.   There is a Seth line different from the Cain line.

2.   There are two traditions of the origin of the worship of Yahweh – one based on the man Moses in the wilderness and one based on men acting in an organized or cultic manner.

3.   There is a three generation genealogy of Adam-Seth-Enosh that is important. In it the second generation male directs men to construct a cultic place where Yahweh can be worshiped and does so after the third generation male is born.

4.   The position of Gen. 5: 29, the naming of Noah, before it was incorporated into the P genealogy needs to be determined.

Analyzing a story in isolation from what else an author may have written and the sequence in writing in response to others or before others responded to him, may skew the understanding of the story. Precisely as Friedman stated, in each instance it is important to learn something of the author's life to understand the writing, to see connections between the author's life and the world that the author depicts in his or her work. How did the author come to have an idea of what happened? How much did the events of the author's own day affect the way in which the author told the story?

Perhaps the key to understanding the story of the sons of Seth is the author's selection of Seth for the name of the younger brother of Cain. Von Rad attempts to identify the Seth people among the peoples of the ancient Near East. Regardless of the accuracy of his endeavor, his effort is correct. Again there is an elephant/donkey scenario where the author presumed his audience would understand his choice of the Seth people while thousands of years later we have to struggle to make sense of the name. Clearly this author rejects the pro-Moses viewpoint of the Kenite author. Instead of a covenant-based people, he proposes an origin of Yahweh worship not with Moses in a wilderness but when people build something in the time of the second generation male (king?) and after the birth of the third generation son. In the battle for power, these two parties were in opposition to each other. With these thoughts in mind, one can now turn to the brief and even more complex story of the sons of God.

Chapter 4

WHO ARE THE SONS OF GOD?

> **Genesis 6:** *¹ When men began to multiply on the face of the ground, and daughters were born to them,² the sons of God saw that the daughters of men were fair; and they took to wife such of them as they chose. ³ Then Yahweh said, 'My spirit shall not abide in man for ever, for he is flesh, but his days shall be a hundred and twenty years.'⁴ The Nephilim were on the earth in those days, and also afterward, when the sons of God came in to the daughters of men, and they bore children to them. These were the mighty men [gibborim] that were of old, the men of renown.*

This short and seemingly abbreviated story has been a troubling one for both scholars and ministers. The behavior exhibited in the story is difficult to teach in Sunday School, to reconcile with the values expressed elsewhere in the biblical narrative. Even for people who take the Bible literally, the story has proved a challenge in determining exactly what is meant (in English) by the phrase 'sons of God'. Similarly, the academic debate has ranged over multiple possibilities in the quest to discern its meaning in what has been deemed 'one of the obscurest sections of the Torah'.[1]

The legacy of the sons of God has been a poor one. One observes a consistency of ill-will and negative thoughts directed against beings who routinely are considered to be divine in some manner. Scholars have searched throughout the ancient Near East and the Aegean to find parallels that might elucidate the 'true' meaning of this disturbing story.[2] Are they gods of some kind? What is their relationship to Yahweh? Are they human beings? If so, what kind of human beings? The apparent ambiguity of the phrase has fostered a plethora of interpretations even in ancient times before there were Jewish rabbis, Catholic priests, Protestant ministers, and university scholars to ponder the dilemma in religious and academic terms (see Additional Readings: Sons of God and also Nephilim).

In addition to the traditional questions regarding the text, one may add:

What political message was being delivered through the communication of this story? Or what political factions in the time of Solomon did it help? The longstanding effort to determine what exactly terms like sons of God, Nephilim, and *gibborim* mean complicates the attempt to discern the original meaning of the text.

---

1   Umberto Cassuto, 'The episode of the sons of God and the daughters of Man', in *Biblical and Oriental Studies* (Jerusalem: Magnes, 1973), I: 17–28, here 17.

2   For a history of the interpretation of the pericope see Jaap Doedens, *The Sons of God in Genesis 6: 1–4* (Dissertation Theologische Universiteit van de Gereformeerde Kerken, 2013), 89–178; Westermann, *Genesis 1–11*, 371–373; L. R. Wickham, 'The sons of God and the daughters of Men: Genesis VI 2 in early Christian exegesis', *OtSt* 19 1974: 135–147.

The tracking of the attempts by exegetes to understand this passage will begin in ancient times with Josephus, proceed to the rabbis, and continue with modern scholarship from the end of the 19th century to the canonical commentaries of the 20th.

Josephus

Josephus expresses the condemnation that is the legacy of the story.

> **Ant 1: 73** *for many angels {a} of God accompanied with women, and begat sons that proved unjust, and despisers of all that was good, on account of the confidence they had in their own strength; for the tradition is, that these men did what resembled the acts of those whom the Greeks call giants.* [74] *But Noah was very uneasy at what they did; and, being displeased at their conduct, persuaded them to change their dispositions and their acts for the better; but seeing they did not yield to him, but were slaves to their wicked pleasures, he was afraid they would kill him, together with his wife and children, and those they had married; so he departed out of that land.*

There are four key points to observe in this rendition of the biblical account.

1. Josephus refers to these sons of gods as angels. This identification apparently is the definitive one in ancient times for as far back as it can be traced in the exegetical record.[3] This definition reflects an ongoing debate about the nature of these beings from ancient times through the religious writings of Jews and Christians to the academic scholars.
2. Josephus equates these biblical beings with those the Greeks call 'giants'. This equation did not originate with Josephus but apparently comes from the Septuagint, a Greek version of the Hebrew Bible, in which the relevant biblical verse reads:

> *The giants were on the earth in those days, and after that, when the sons of God went into the daughters of men.*[4]

The Greek-based identification of these beings as giants enabled the biblical narrative to be integrated into the Greek cultural traditions. An extensive Greek mythological corpus existed involving giants and Titans who ruled before the Olympians rebelled and took power. Now the biblical account had similar beings who also would meet their fate: none of them was on Noah's ark so presumably none of them could have survived the Flood. Umberto Cassuto concluded that the pericope was a polemic against pagan giant legends.

The appeal of the Greek mythical tradition may also be due to a story in Hesiod's *Catalogue of Women* where gods do take the daughters of men to produce a new race of semi-divine beings. Zeus then devises the Trojan War to destroy the demigods and to prevent a repeat occurrence. Interestingly, the Trojan War also has been likened to a type of Deluge which is the next story in the biblical sequence.[5]

---

3 Philip S. Alexander, 'The targumim and early exegesis of "sons of God" in Genesis 6', *JJS* 23, 1972: 60–71, here 61.

4 The term appears about 40 times in the Septuagint but not always to translate the same word. It may have been used in reference to the Nephilim, Rephaim, Anaqim, and *gibborim* (Gerard Mussies, 'Giants', *DDD*, 343–345; Archie T. Wright, *The Origin of Evil Spirits: The Reception of Genesis 6.1–4 in Early Jewish Literature* (Tübingen, Mohr Siebeck, 2005), 83–86; Brian Doak, 'The embarrassing and alluring biblical giant', http://www.bibleinterp.com/articles/2015/12/doa398002.shtml. Of course, if the Nephilim were not giants then any interpretation based on their having been giants is rendered moot.

5 Cassuto, 'The episode of the sons of God and the daughters of Man', 28; Hendel, 'Of demigods and the deluge', 18–20; Ronald Hendel, 'The Nephilim were on the Earth: Genesis 6: 1–4 and its Near Eastern context',

3. Josephus quite dramatically joins the story of the sons of God with Noah. He has the latter alive in the time of the former. The connection between these two stories would be a much debated one over the alleged sins of the sons of Gods supposedly leading to the punishment of humanity in the Flood. Josephus clearly links the disdainful behavior of the sons of the Gods with the punishment of the Flood to follow.[6]

4. Josephus's Noah is aghast at the behavior of these beings just as non-biblical Abraham would be at the behavior of Nimrod (see Chapter 6). Both non-biblical Noah and Abraham flee for fear for their lives. The biblical commentators have now provided both of the heroes with the rationality for their otherwise inexplicable decisions to leave home.

In summary, the sons of gods are angels or giants and defiant of God. Their impact beyond the story contributes to the justification for the Flood and creates a sons-of-god/Noah and Nimrod/Abraham parallel.

Rabbis

The rabbis vividly detailed the degeneracy of the sons of God. They wove stories together to highlight the shortcomings of these beings. The storytelling ability is really quite remarkable and evidences the ability of the human mind to grow the barest of facts into the most elaborate of tales. Consider below the compendium of legends of the Jews accumulated from the Midrash, Talmud, and other Jewish writings.[7]

As previously seen (Chapter 3), Enosh begins the time of idol-worshiping. The deterioration accelerates afterwards. The depravity of humanity increases monstrously in the time of his grandson Jared, by reason of the fallen angels. The rabbinic traditions continue the story with 200 angels descending to the summit of Mount Hermon.

> *Under the leadership of twenty captains they defile themselves with the daughters of men, unto whom they taught charms, conjuring formulas, how to cut roots, and the efficacy of plants. The issue from these mixed marriages is a race of giants, three thousand ells tall, who consume the possessions of men.*[8]

These Prometheus-like beings are impious evil-doers who corrupt humanity. Their story then becomes intertwined with Enoch of whom the Hebrew Bible says in a non-J account:

> **Genesis 5:18** *When Jared had lived a hundred and sixty-two years he became the father of Enoch.*

in Christoph Auffarth and Loren T. Stuckenbruck, eds, *The Fall of Angels* (Leiden: Brill, 2004), 11–34, here 30–32; David Melvin, 'The Gilgamesh traditions and the pre-history of Genesis 6: 1–4', *PRSt* 38/1, 2011: 23–32, here 23; R. Scodel, 'The Achaean Wall and the myth of destruction', *HSCP* 86, 1982: 33–50.

6   Hendel supports this linkage claiming the passage originally introduced the Flood story until a more suitable cause for the Deluge was inserted in Gen. 6: 16–17 ('The Nephilim were on the Earth…', 12–13; Hendel, 'Of demigods and the deluge', 23). Yet as Melvin notes, the known flood stories from the ancient Near East do not involve mating of gods and humans so it could not have been part of a single narrative adapted to Israelite purposes (Melvin, 'The Gilgamesh traditions', 23 n.4).

7   For examples of the treatment of the sons of God in ancient times see, James L. Kugel, *The Bible as It Was* (Cambridge MA: Harvard University Press, 1997), 110–114; for the rabbinic and early Christian debate on angelology see Alexander, 'The targumim and early exegesis of "sons of God"', 61–71.

8   Ginzberg, *The Legends of the Jews*, I: 124–125.

[19] *Jared lived after the birth of Enoch eight hundred years, and had other sons and daughters.* [20] *Thus all the days of Jared were nine hundred and sixty-two years; and he died.* [21] *When Enoch had lived sixty-five years, he became the father of Methuselah.* [22] *Enoch walked with God after the birth of Methuselah three hundred years, and had other sons and daughters.* [23] *Thus all the days of Enoch were three hundred and sixty-five years.* [24] *Enoch walked with God; and he was not, for God took him.*

Extraordinary tales sprung forth from this description of the 365-year-old man who walked with God. In particular, non-biblical *I Enoch* 6–11 may be regarded as an elaborate midrash on Gen. 6: 1–4 in which the sons of Gods also are angels as part of an apocalyptic eschatology of evil and cosmic restoration.[9] With these developments in Hellenistic times and afterwards, the story of the sons of Gods becomes even more fanciful and fantastic and even less relevant to determining who they were in their original supplement to the first cycle of the KDB narrative. The goal here is to determine that meaning.

Modern scholarship has tended to focus on the literary and textual issues since there does not seem to be much archaeology with which to work. Exegetes may address general considerations on the nature of the beings included in the story. These beings are more mythical in nature and engender discussion on the early human religions. Indeed, it is this story, more so than others in this study, where the boundaries between the human and the divine are most vividly crossed.

Because of the seminal nature of Wellhausen's contribution to the study of the sons of God, the recap of the modern exegesis begins with him.

Wellhausen

The untangling of the verses in this short pericope Gen. 6: 1-4 has proved a challenge for biblical scholars. For Wellhausen, the story was '(a)nother strange erratic boulder'. He thought the story had only the 'loosest' connection to the 'Jehovist' narrative. Furthermore, 'it is in entire disagreement with the preceding part' since its story of 'a second fall of man' expresses 'a point of view morally and mentally so different from that of the first, that this story can in no wise be regarded as supplementing or continuing that one'. These views, more-or-less, have become staples within biblical scholarship and have complicated the challenge to realize how integral the sons of God story is to understanding Israelite history and the writing of the Hebrew Bible.[10]

---

9   Alexander, 'The targumim and early exegesis…', 60; John J. Collins, 'The sons of God and the daughters of Men', in Marti Nissinen, ed., *Sacred Marriages: The Divine: Human Sexual Metaphor from Sumer to Early Christianity* (Winona Lake: Eisenbrauns, 2008), 259–274, here 263–274; Paul D. Hanson, 'Rebellion in Heaven, Azazel, and euhemeristic heroes in I Enoch 6–11', *JBL* 96, 1977: 185–233, here 197 and 232–233. Melvin contends that similarities of I Enoch 6–11 and Gen. 6: 1–4 are due to both deriving from Gilgamesh ('The Gilgamesh traditions', 25–32).

10 Julius Wellhausen, *Prolegomena to the History of Israel* (Atlanta: Scholars Press, 1994; reprint of 1885 edition), 317.

Delitzsch

In his Genesis commentary, Delitzsch includes these verses with the following verses in Gen. 6: 5–8 leading up to the Flood:

> *Yahweh saw that the wickedness of man was great in the earth, and that every imagination of the thoughts of his heart was only evil continually.* [6] *And Yahweh was sorry that he had made man on the earth, and it grieved him to his heart.* [7] *So Yahweh said, 'I will blot out man whom I have created from the face of the ground, man and beast and creeping things and birds of the air, for I am sorry that I have made them.'* [8] *But Noah found favor in the eyes of Yahweh.*

He entitles the section 'Judgment called Forth, The Long-Suffering of God, and the Decree of Judgment, VI. 1–8'. He rejects the idea that the original narrator lacked knowledge of the Flood. This division of verses combining 6: 1–4 and 5–8 instantly raises the question of whether the story of the sons of God should be understood as an independent pericope or as part of the larger story. Furthermore, as a larger story, does it end the story of the generations of Adam or does it begin the story of the generations of Noah and the Deluge? The divisions of the texts into units is a construct imposed upon the text and in so doing may influence how the narratives are interpreted.[11]

For Delitzsch, the story continues the story of sin. Could angels have carnal intercourse with human women? Perhaps the sons of God should be understood in a spiritual sense. He agrees with the interpretation that 'to take women' refers to real marriages and not random or isolated sexual acts. That physical interaction leads to the assumption of angelic incarnation for repeated and sustained acts of unnatural relations over extended time. For Delitzsch the assertion in 6:3 that Yahweh will take his spirit from man is the equivalent of inflicting extermination upon the human race.[12]

Delitzsch concludes his analysis with the pending destruction of humanity. He paints a dark picture because he says the biblical text does so in 6: 5–7 before Noah is introduced in 6: 8. The second section of Genesis draws to a close and a new section beginning with Noah commences. But Delitzsch never really demonstrates the connection of the sons of God to 6: 5–8 and the Flood. The relationship remains an open question. The issue of where the Flood story actually begins is part of the challenge of determining who wrote some of the verses in the sons of J stories.[13]

Dillmann

In his Genesis commentary, Dillmann labels the section 'The Corruption of Men Before the Flood, VI. 1–8'. He avers that the intention was to provide a foundation for the judgement to be rendered in the next episode, the Flood. Nonetheless, Dillmann remains unsure of the story's origins. In the present position, the story is 'obscure, disconnected, and contains gaps ... hav[ing] the appearance of being hardly more than an extract from a fuller account'. These observations lead him to conclude it is part of a separate parallel

---

11 Delitzsch, *New Commentary on Genesis*, 226, 230.
12 Delitzsch, *New Commentary on Genesis*, 222–223, 225, 229.
13 Delitzsch, *New Commentary on Genesis*, 233–234.

account to the garden story and part of the same tradition as the sons of Cain (Gen. 4: 17–24). Apparently Dillmann's author C (J) chose only to extract the portion of the story which suited his needs.[14]

Dillmann further observes that many ancient peoples told stories of giant races that had preceded them. The farther back in time one goes, the more monstrous characteristics they possess. As a result, Dillmann postulates that the story did not originate with Mosaism but from the old legends such as the Greeks had. Once one recognizes this relationship, one should equally recognize that by 'his acceptance of this history, the author has certainly shown his belief in the possibility of such a horrible perversion of all order'.[15]

Following these preliminary comments, Dillmann proceeds to analyze the story verse by verse, word by word. He acknowledges the traditional view that the sons of God were angels as well as the disgust to Christian consciousness of carnal intercourse between such beings and human women. Hence the compelling need to obviate this discordant situation with a suitable explanation. Despite that need, he declares that there is no basis to interpreting the story as portraying a contrast between the virtuous sons of Seth and worldly women of Cain who then corrupted the entire human race.

Then he seeks to situate the Nephilim in Gen. 6: 4 within this universe. They could not have been produced by the union of Sethite men and Cainite women. These beings are part of a verse that was an external addition to the story and their very name derives from an early period or Canaanite dialect. Instead these Nephilim are the fruits of the marriages between the sons of God and the daughters of men. Dillmann thinks the audience already possessed this information from a non-biblical Nephilim legend. Since it already was known, the narrator simply decided to omit an express reference to it as part of his intention to treat the distasteful event with brevity.[16]

One may observe here Dillmann struggling to make sense of these divergent threads in this brief story. He is on the right track in discerning anomalies in the text as he was in the sons of Seth story, anomalies which can be cleared once the actual authors and their political contexts are identified (see Part II).

Gunkel

Gunkel labels his section on the story 'The Angel Marriages 6: 1–6 J'.[17] In its present location, the story introduces the Flood story which begins in 6: 5. It functions as an illustration of the corruption of the human race which thereby warrants the Flood.[18]

For Gunkel, 'The piece is a torso. It can hardly be called a story'.[19] The extant shrunken

---

14 Dillmann, *Genesis*, 230–231, quotation from 231–232.
15 Dillmann, *Genesis*, 231–232, quotation from 232.
16 Dillmann, *Genesis*, 233–234, 240–241.
17 This heading appears to contain a typographical error in the English version as his analysis concludes with 6: 4 and the next section begins with 6: 5. The German version has 6: 1–4 (*Genesis* [Göttingen: Vandenhoeck & Ruprecht, 1901], 50).
18 Gunkel, Genesis, 59.
19 Gunkel, *Genesis*, 59.

version leads him to conclude that the 'original narrative must have been much richer'.[20] From this conclusion, Gunkel opines that the 'further development of religion in Israel suppressed mythology and left standing only a very minimal remnant like milestones of the way traveled' before reaching a more elevated level.[21] This mythical origin of the story means the ancient and original narrative had become 'half-forgotten in the narrator's time'.[22] The simple explanation for the mutilation of the myth of angels and humans producing Nephilim is its offensiveness. Since Israel felt 'disgust for the interbreeding of divine and human', the narrator judiciously incorporated just enough to suggest the whole legend without having to wallow in its demeaning storyline.[23] Gunkel ponders which of the two collections within the J narrative, J^j or J^e to assign 'this fragment … of very inferior value' and decides on J^j although he acknowledges it could have been inserted later.[24]

Skinner

Skinner copes with the story by stating:

> 'The disconnectedness of the narrative is probably due to the drastic abridgement either by the original writer or the later editors to whom its crudely mythological character was objectionable, and who were interested in retaining no more than was needful to account for the origin of the giants'.

It contains an aetiological explanation of the Nephilim who perhaps originally were called 'elohim' or 'gods'. But this pagan coloring is too pronounced for him. It leads Skinner to seek solace in the Greek and Latin myths with their stories of giants and intermarriage in the heroic age.[25]

He clearly states that the story imputes no sin to mankind or their daughters in the depicted relationships. The humans committed no sin. Repeat: *the humans committed no sin.* There is no doubt that the divine element is masculine. There is no doubt that the mingling of divine and human beings occurred. It is illicit, leads to disorder, and requires divine resolution. It also appears to have continued to occur beyond the confines of this story as evident by the existence of Nephilim in Num. 13: 33 during the wandering in the wilderness:

> *And there [in the land of Canaan] we [the spies] saw the Nephilim (the sons of Anak, who come from the Nephilim); and we seemed to ourselves like grasshoppers, and so we seemed to them.*

Skinner presumes that the Nephilim in the story of the sons of God are the offspring of the mating of the sons of Gods and the daughters of man but that the sentence specifying that development has been dropped from the story.[26]

---

20 Gunkel, *Genesis*, 59.
21 Gunkel, *Genesis*, 56.
22 Gunkel, *Genesis*, 59.
23 Gunkel, *Genesis*, 59.
24 Gunkel, *Genesis*, 59–60.
25 Skinner, *A Critical and Exegetical Commentary*, 140–141, quotation from 141.
26 Skinner, *A Critical and Exegetical Commentary*, 142–143, 145–147.

Skinner makes two observations which are exactly right without having a conceptual framework to understand their significance. His impression is that the introductory clause to the story of the sons of God in Gen. 6: 1 is closely preceded by the J creation story of man in the garden (Gen. 2–3). Without the Kenite material in Gen. 4: 17–24, the proximity of the garden and sons of God stories would be even clearer. Furthermore, he finds nothing in the passage to indicate that the Flood story is its sequel. Skinner goes so far as to state the story 'belongs to a stratum of J which knows nothing of a flood…' With these observations, Skinner has glimpsed the multitude of writers who composed what he calls J but without any way to identify them.[27]

Von Rad

Von Rad's analysis reveals the difficulty in separating the values of the observer from the text observed. He titles the section 'The Angel Marriages'. He sees in these verses 'wild licentiousness' whereas the text is much more neutral in its depiction. After all, they do marry! Despite the absence of debauchery or orgy in the text, this 'wild licentiousness' among beings who marry produces 'bastards born to those marriages'. Perhaps he might have explored how marriage worked in primeval times and when marriages do and do not produce bastards. Adam knew his wife (Gen. 4: 1, 25), Cain knew his wife (Gen. 4: 16), and while it is not specified, one presumes Seth did, too (Gen. 4: 26 before the birth of Enosh. All that 'knowing' occurred without any bastards being produced in these 'undocumented marriages' involving neither priesthood nor government.[28]

Clearly, von Rad has sin on his mind and it colors his view. These sons of God belong to the world of the Elohim or gods. They have been enticed by women into a new Fall requiring a new punishment. This 'disturbance caused by sin' evidences the general corruption of man which was the message the Yahwist sought to deliver. Von Rad's sympathies are with the judgement decree in Gen. 6: 3 as he understands it and the Flood to follow.[29]

Speiser

The title of his section on the story is 'Prelude to Disaster'. By this designation, Speiser indicates that this story must be understood in connection with the pending Deluge. The story is a moral indictment that provides 'a compelling motive for the forthcoming disaster'. Speiser's understanding is a logical outcome of the location of the story combined with the identity of the Nephilim.[30]

For Speiser, the 'undisguised mythology of this isolated fragment makes it not only atypical

---

27 Skinner, *A Critical and Exegetical Commentary*, 141.
28 Von Rad, *Genesis*, 114–115.
29 Von Rad, *Genesis*, 114–115. The objection to the punishment of humanity for the actions of the sons of God goes to the heart of the issue of who these beings are; see Clines, 'The significance of the "sons of God episode"', 34. Hendel states, 'the sexual mingling with mortal women is not explicitly condemned' ('Of demigods and the deluge', 16); Kraeling considers the punishment 'rather harsh' (Emil G. Kraeling, 'The significance and origins of Gen. 6: 1–4', *JNES* 6 1947, 197). Petersen notes that the perpetrators are not punished and no human agents are culpable ('Genesis 6: 1–4, Yahweh and the organization of the cosmos', 49).
30 Speiser, *Genesis,* 46.

of the Bible as a whole but also puzzling and controversial in the extreme. Its problems are legion!' He wonders if it was the full account or merely an excerpt. He wonders why 'such a stark piece' even had been included in the narrative. Speiser sees the answers emerging in the LXX translation of the Nephilim as 'giants'. For him this opens up the Greek traditions of giants or Titans from primordial times. Hittite texts with Hurrian myths contain a mid-2nd millennium BCE account of a 'bloodthirsty' conflict for heavenly rule that provide the basis for Phoenician and Greek myths. Furthermore such traditions 'could hardly have been a stranger to J or his own immediate sources'. Its popularity forced J to respond to the 'depravity that it reflected'. He was so filled with horror that the world 'could entertain such notions [that] it deserved to be wiped out'. As a result, J incorporated this 'fragment' immediately prior to the Flood as a story of moral indictment that justified the pending disaster. Speiser takes solace in the recognition that unlike the Mesopotamian parallels, the biblical flood account has a moral basis. He never does explain what the human males did in this scenario or why the human females who were taken deserved to be punished.[31]

Westermann

Westermann's section title is 'The Sons of the Gods and the Giants' so he too follows the Greek tradition. For Westermann, the purpose of the pericope is to describe the origin of the *gibborim*, the mighty men. He regards the note about them in Gen. 6: 4a as out of context in the final version hence rendering the connection between the Nephilim and *gibborim* unexplained. Verse 3 has no relationship to the narrative leaving vv. 1–2, and 4a as the core story without a connection to the mighty men but connected to the offspring of the sons of God and the daughters of man. Westermann considers the debate over the nature of these 'sons of God' as angels or Sethites to be over: despite all the machinations to absolve divine beings of such heinous behavior, the determination to make them humans can no longer be sustained, the sons of God indeed are angels.[32]

The focus of his analysis is the actions of the sons of God: they saw and they took. Westermann compares this sequence with the meeting of Jacob and Rachel at the well (Gen. 29) whereupon Jacob agrees to serve Laban, her father. He compares this interaction with the meeting of Pharaoh and the wife of Abram where the former did take the woman of the latter (Gen. 12). He compares this situation with the meeting of David and Bathsheba where once again the beautiful woman ended up with the more powerful male (II Sam. 11). Apparently only Jacob, who was a physically mighty man at the well (Gen. 29: 10), played by the rules. Westermann contrasts the male behavior exhibited in this story with garden story of a man and a woman becoming one (Gen. 2: 18–24), a passage which remains to

---

31 Speiser, *Genesis*, 45–46. The modern literary pursuit of giants in mythology involved such luminaries as Emil Kraeling who related the Nephilim to 'primeval figures of huge size (best known to us from Greek mythology) who were cast down into Hades by a deity they dared to oppose' ('The significance and origins of Gen. 6: 1–4', 208). For a response, see David L. Petersen, 'Genesis 6: 1–4, Yahweh and the organization of the cosmos', *JSOT* 13 1979: 47–64, here 50–52. Kraeling concurs with Speiser stating that Gen. 6: 1–4 had been 'chosen' by J[1], not 'written', to prepare the way for the Flood story ('The significance and origins of Gen. 6: 1–4', 195).

32 Westermann, *Genesis 1–11*, 365–366, 371–373.

this very day an idealized and positive way of expressing a male–female relationship. The Gen. 6: 1–4 pericope showcases 'the other pole: the potentate can choose among the many beauties who take his fancy; he can do this even where there are barriers, simply because he is powerful'. Sometimes men can grab and seize women because the ordinary rules do not apply to them.[33]

Based on these examples, Westermann concludes that the already short story consists of two narrative threads addressing two concerns that have been interwoven. First is the etiological explanation of the giants; second is the mythical story where a dangerous transgression of boundaries results in the intervention of God. The mythical story likely was Canaanite in origin to which the etiological element was added. In the present form, Westermann states that 'the narrator and listeners in the period of the monarchy' would have recognized that the:

> 'only really divine thing about them is their superior power that enables them to take whichever woman they like, just as in the parallel stories of the Pharaoh and David. What is decisive for the older form of the story is the infringement that superior power makes possible.'[34]

Westermann, more so than the other exegetes has raised the possibility of understanding the story within a political context. Despite any supposed mythical or etiological considerations, the true meaning for an audience in the time of the monarchy has to do with power. Does a man in power have the right to covet? Does the man in power have the right to take what he covets? If he does not, then can he be held accountable? If he does, then what kind of society is it? Whether the story of the sons of God truly raises these questions or not, Westermann's reference to the audience of the story in the time of the monarchy suggests an alternate way of understanding the story than traditionally has been done.

The Jewish Study Bible

Levenson agrees with those who regard the story as a condensation of a longer and well-known myth. A breach of the boundaries between the divine and the human has occurred. The story explains the origin of a preternatural giants in the land of Canaan along with the shorter lifespan of humans. He links 6: 1–4 and 5–8 together in a section entitled 'The Prelude to the Flood'.[35]

The New Jerome Biblical Commentary

Clifford unequivocally equates the sons of God with divine beings in the Canaanite tradition. He interprets the divine judgment in 6: 3 to indicate the presumption of sin having occurred. He then links the lifespan limitation in 6: 3 with the divine judgment in 3: 22:

> *Then Yahweh Elohim said, 'Behold, the man has become like one of us, knowing good and evil; and now, lest he put forth his hand and take also of the tree of life, and eat, and live for ever.'*

---

33 Westermann, *Genesis 1–11*, 366–368, 370–371.
34 Westermann, *Genesis 1–11*, 368–369, 372–373.
35 Levenson, 'Genesis', 21.

Once again a breach of the boundary between the human and divine has occurred with a resulting punishment.[36]

Clifford also opens the door to an archaeological component in the quest to decipher the meaning of the story. In the story of the sons of Seth there was no archaeological consideration unless one sought to locate the temple or place from which men called the name of God. In this case, the search is for giants. Clifford observes that pre-conquest Canaanites are biblically referred to as giants (Deut. 2: 10–11, 20–21; 3: 11; and Josh. 12: 4 and 17: 15). He may also have recalled the earlier archaeological work of George Ernst Wright, a fellow Harvard student from the 1930s who became a teacher there, who 'discovered' such giants in the land. Clifford added that recognition should also be given to the legitimate efforts of people struggling to understand a long-vanished past.[37]

The HarperCollins Study Bible

Rosenberg attributes the 'retrograde' angel interpretation to later times and by implication was not intended as part of the original meaning. Instead, he sees the connection with the ironically now nearly-forgotten legacy of the ancient heroes of renown.[38]

Conclusion

This review of the sons of God exegesis over the millennia reveals significant commonalities, some differences in interpretations, and open questions. These observations may be summarized as follows.

1. The earlier commentators such as Josephus and the rabbis were storytellers in their own right. They sought to smooth the way by filling in gaps through expository creations. They anticipated the questions an audience might raise reading or hearing the story within the context of the existing canonized narrative. They were very concerned about the violation of angel–human relations which the story suggests happened.
2. Modern scholars are divided on the presence of multiple writers within the sons of God story. Gen. 6: 3 in particular seems out of place to many exegetes while the awkwardness of the construction of 6: 4 raises eyebrows.
3. Everyone tends to agree that the story is about the dawn of human civilization whether the story is a mythical folktale or the word of God. Westermann raises the issue of the meaning to the audience in monarchic times regardless of the date of origin of the story.

---

36 Clifford and Murphy, 'Genesis', 14.
37 Clifford and Murphy, 'Genesis', 14. For the possibility of actual giants inhabiting the land of Canaan in ancient times, see G. E. Wright, 'The troglodytes of Gezer', *PEQ* 69 1937: 67–78 and G. E. Wright, 'Troglodytes and giants in Palestine', *JBL* 57 1938: 305–309. For an updated version involving the memory of *Homo sapiens/* Neanderthal interbreeding, see Shubert Spero, 'Sons of God, daughters of Men?', *JBQ* 40 2012: 15–18, here 17–18. As genetic testing increasingly is applied to Neanderthals and humans the reality of such interbreeding has become scientifically established. For the effort to understand the past see Matthew J. Goff, 'Ben Sira and the giants of the land: a note on Ben Sira 16: 7', *JBL* 129 2010: 645–655.
38 Rosenberg, 'Genesis', 12.

4. Everyone tends to agree that the story is in some way connected to the story of the Flood.
5. Modern scholars also are divided about the fairness of the divine pronouncement in 6: 3. They have trouble identifying exactly what either the human males or females did to warrant being punished. This puzzlement is based on the virtually unanimous opinion that 6: 3 is a punishment and not simply a statement of fact or description of the human condition as Yahweh created it.
6. Modern scholars who perceive the story to be mythical tend to assume that it derives from an older tradition part of which may be missing. The canonical version is a (very) shortened version of a longer non-biblical story that J incorporated into his narrative while cleansing it of its mythology and folktale attributes as much as a possible. One gets the impression that the exegetes would prefer that the story was not in the narrative at all rather than have to deal with it in some way.

Even putting aside the sin and fall perspective that is inevitable in biblical exegesis there still are several presuppositions, considerations, and revisions which should be taken into account. The tendency to attribute the story to an independent origin obscures links to other biblical stories.

1. There are biblical stories involving individual named men taking women as some exegetes noted:

    Pharaoh and Sarah (Gen. 12)
    Abimelech and Sarah (Gen. 20)
    Abimelech and Rebekah (Gen. 26)
    Shechem and Dinah (Gen. 34)
    Jacob and Tamar (Gen. 38)
    David and Bathsheba (II Sam. 11)
    Amnon and Tamar (II Sam. 13).

    These texts all are part of the ongoing political debate for power of which the sons of God story is merely one example. To isolate the story from its context undermines its meaning and degrades its significance.
2. The story is not about one son of God taking one woman, it is a collective act. There are biblical stories of unnamed groups of men taking or threatening to take women.

    The anonymous men of Sodom threaten the anonymous daughters of Lot. They are prevented from raping the women because of the intervention of two messengers of Yahweh (Gen. 19).

    The anonymous men of Gibeah 'which belongs to Benjamin' (and was Saul's capital) ravage the anonymous concubine of Bethlehem (home of David) leading to the Levite (priest of Shiloh) to call for avenging this monstrosity (presumably with the assistance of a man of Bethlehem) (Judges 19–20).

    The anonymous men of Benjamin took the daughters of Shiloh who were dancing the dances at the yearly feast of Yahweh as their wives and thereby rebuilt their tribe (Judges 21).

    These stories may be deemed 'texts of terror'. Part of the challenge in understanding the story of the sons of God is to determine if it is like the personal stories of named individual males and women or the group encounters of unnamed male and female beings.[39]

---

39 See Phyllis Trible, *Texts of Terror: Literary-Feminist Readings of Biblical Narratives* (Philadelphia: Fortress Press, 1984). One may add to this list the slavegirl of Kirk Douglas's Spartacus and Roman imperialism and

3. The continued existence of the Nephilim after the Flood (Num. 13: 33) as with the emphasis of the Kenite genealogy Gen. 4: 17–24) prior to the Flood raises the possibility of a local flood story before it became a universal one.

4. The odd presence of Gen. 6: 3 raises the question, as it did for Gen. 5: 29, of where that verse might have been before it was placed in this story. Originally there were no isolated verses. A verse was always part of a larger prose narrative even if of only two verses. Whenever one encounters what appears to be a stand-alone prose verse, the challenge is to determine where it belongs before being placed in its present position. These two examples are verses which go beyond mere redaction for editorial smoothing. They were integral to their original respective stories.

5. The paradigmatic application of some mythical or folk tradition to the presence of Nephilim as giants from days of yore in the land of Canaan may be misguided. Maybe they were heroes to the author.

Analyzing a story in isolation from what else the author may have written and the sequence in writing in response to others or before others responded to him may skew the understanding of the story. Precisely as Friedman stated, in each instance it is important to learn something of the author's life to understand the writing, to see connections between the author's life and the world that the author depicts in his or her work. How did the author come to have an idea of what happened? How much did the events of the author's own day affect the way in which the author told the story? What if it is not a fragmented folktale from hoary antiquity?

With three stories reviewed so far, now it is time to take stock of what has been revealed and to glimpse what is to come. The story of the sons of Cain consists of three components: the city builders, the descendants, and the Song of Warning. Each is told in its own turn. The mentioning of Cain at the conclusion refers to the sequence beginning with Cain's killing of Abel. The Kenite presence suggests a connection to Moses who first experienced Yahweh in the wilderness. Based on the presumption of the story as a supplement to the KDB in the time of Solomon, the working hypothesis is that this story originated with a political faction or priesthood loyal to Moses and his prominence in the religion and history of Israel.

In the second story, we are introduced to an alternative view. Based on the selection of the name Seth, the author defines himself in opposition to the Kenites. During the life of Seth, the name of Yahweh is called upon. Based on the presumption of the story as a supplement to the KDB in the time of Solomon, the working hypothesis is that this story originated with a political faction or priesthood loyal to Solomon, supportive of the temple, and anti-Israel or at least to Israel based on Moses.

In the third story, the lines are less clear. The story is awkward and does not flow easily. It leaves much unanswered. The fixation on sin and separation probably were irrelevant to the audience in Solomonic times unless it has something to do with his mother. Unlike with the first two stories, this one seems more like noise rather than music where one has to struggle to make sense of the discordant sounds emanating from it. Deciding exactly who wrote what and why in the battle for power after the death of David is more of a challenge. With these thoughts in mind, one can now turn to the also troublesome story of the sons of Noah.

---

the wife of Mel Gibson's William Wallace and English imperialism. Some storylines have not changed.

Chapter 5

WHO ARE THE SONS OF NOAH?

Genesis 9: *[18] The sons of Noah who went forth from the ark were Shem, Ham, and Japheth. Ham was the father of Canaan. [19] These three were the sons of Noah; and from these the whole earth was peopled. [20] Noah was the first tiller of the soil. He planted a vineyard; [21] and he drank of the wine, and became drunk, and lay uncovered in his tent. [22] And Ham, the father of Canaan, saw the nakedness of his father, and told his two brothers outside. [23] Then Shem and Japheth took a garment, laid it upon both their shoulders, and walked backward and covered the nakedness of their father; their faces were turned away, and they did not see their father's nakedness. [24] When Noah awoke from his wine and knew what his youngest son had done to him, [25] he said, 'Cursed be Canaan; a slave of slaves shall he be to his brothers.' [26] He also said, 'Blessed by Yahweh God be Shem; and let Canaan be his slave. [27] God enlarge Japheth, and let him dwell in the tents of Shem; and let Canaan be his slave.'*

The story of the sons of Noah is another one of the biblical stories best omitted from Sunday School. The story seems to cross the line on acceptable behavior and it is important to maintain a safe zone to protect young people from exposure to such activities. Perhaps biblical stories should come with warning labels or trigger alerts so the unsuspecting will not be subject to the more unpleasant and unsavory aspects of the biblical narrative. Better to eliminate the abhorrent than to understand it.

The downside of such treatment is although the story is in the Bible and it was created by adults for adults, its importance is minimized. Unfortunately the mythic, folk, sex-sin-fall-punishment syndrome that defines so many biblical commentators has distorted the meaning of the story until it bears little resemblance to its original intent. Like the story of the sons of God, the story of the sons of Noah is extraordinarily revealing of the Israelite history and the writing of the Hebrew Bible. To see these lessons, one must cast aside mistaken interpretations which have obscured, hidden, and undermined the original intent. Standard questions raised by commentators throughout the ages have honed in on the apparent tensions within the verses. Issue arise such as:

1. What exactly did Ham do?
2. How did Noah know what had been done and who did it?
3. Why is Canaan cursed for something Ham did?
4. Why is Canaan denounced twice?
5. How could the hero of the Flood story sink so low so quickly?
6. Where are the wives of Noah during all this?

In addition to these traditional questions regarding the text, one may add:

What political message was being delivered through the communication of this story? Or what political factions in the time of Solomon did it help and what political faction did it attack? There does seem to be some strong emotion involved here as in the Song of Lamech. It is precisely through these passages that one gains access into the intensity of the battle for power after the death of David. Unfortunately, the longstanding effort to understand exactly who these sons are in a mythical-sin format complicates the attempt to discern the original meaning of the text to the audience hearing the story in the time of Solomon.

The tracking of the attempts by exegetes to understand this passage will begin in ancient times with Josephus, proceed to the rabbis, and continue with modern scholarship from the end of the 19th century to the canonical commentaries of the 20th.

Josephus

For Josephus, the story sets the stage for events to come, a typical approach for commentators.

> **Ant 1: 140** *Noah, when, after the Deluge, the earth was resettled in its former condition, set about its cultivation; and when he had planted it with vines, and when the fruit was ripe, and he had gathered the grapes in their season, and the wine was ready for use, he offered sacrifice, and feasted,* [141] *and being drunk, he fell asleep, and lay naked in an unseemly manner. When his youngest son saw this, he came laughing, and showed him to his brethren; but they covered their father's nakedness.* [142] *And when Noah was made sensible of what had been done, he prayed for prosperity to his other sons; but for Ham, he did not curse him by reason of his nearness in blood, but cursed his prosperity. And when the rest of them escaped that curse, God inflicted it on the children of Canaan. But as to these matters, we shall speak more hereafter.*

The laughing son who shows of the comically abysmal state of the father to his two brothers fleshes out the Josephus-figure from the biblical one. Critical to note is that even though the cursing of Canaan is absent, Canaan, not Ham, bears the brunt of the curse because of the reason Josephus provides. Tellingly, Josephus concludes that this infliction is a harbinger of things to come.

Rabbis

For the rabbis, the story of the sons of Noah was an unpleasant one to consider.[1] The pious Noah who heroically had preserved humanity quickly had degenerated into a drunken stupor who upon reviving introduced slavery into humanity's second chance at life.[2] The link between the new world and old world before the flood was strong here. Noah was said to have planted a vine from Eden which Adam had taken when he left the garden (Pirqe Rabbi Eliezer 23). In fact, God admonishes Noah for following in the footsteps of Adam:

> God said to Noah: 'You should have been warned by the example of Adam whose perdition came about through eating the fruit of the vine'. It is taught that the tree from which the original Adam ate was the vine, for there is nothing which brings man as much misery as wine (San. 70a).

1   David H. Aaron, 'Early Rabbinic exegesis on Noah's son Ham and the so-called "Hamitic Myth"', *JAAR* 63 1995: 721–759.
2   Ginzberg, *The Legends of the Jews*, I: 167.

Exactly how Noah would have been aware of Adam's action is part of the fascinating backdrop to the transmission of traditions which is presumed to have occurred.

To keep the story moving, only a single day was required for the planted vine to bear fruit! Noah immediately then employed his wine-press (Were there two in the ark? When did he build it?) with the assistance of Satan.[3] Clearly this is no minor incident. Then Ham who had observed his father enter the tent of his mother with the goal of producing son number 4, 'added to this sin of irreverence the still greater outrage of attempting to perform an operation upon his father designed to prevent procreation'.[4] The post-diluvial tabula rasa had not remained a clean slate for long. What had man learned since Gen. 6:5:

> *Yahweh saw that the wickedness of man was great in the earth, and that every imagination of the thoughts of his heart was only evil continually,*

assuming it already had been written?

Would another fresh start be required? Noah could not harm Ham: '…for God had conferred a blessing upon Noah and his three sons as they departed from the ark' (Note: this claim derives from Gen. 9: 1 normally attributed to P, a different biblical writer, but JEDP was not part of the rabbinic lexicon). Therefore he put the curse upon the last-born son of the son that had prevented him from begetting a younger son than the three he had.[5]

On a certain level there is a moral balance to such reasoning but only based on the need to make sense of a canonical text in a strained way. Here is a situation where common sense is secondary to the obligation to understand not only why Noah and Ham did what they did, but why Canaan was the one who was punished.

In the rabbinic tradition, the punishment incurred by Canaan therefore was a balanced one in accord with an eye for eye, a tooth for tooth, measure for measure that makes sense on paper but not in the real world:

Canaan's red eyes were because Ham had looked upon his father's nakedness;
Canaan's misshapen lips were because Ham had spoken of what he had seen;
Canaan's twisted curly hair was because Ham had twisted his head to see his father's nakedness;
Canaan's nakedness was because Ham had not covered his naked father.

Later, the naked descendants of Ham, the Egyptians and Ethiopians, are led away captive and into exile by the king of Assyria. But before Canaan dies he addresses his children reading his last will and testament which includes:

'Speak not the truth; hold not yourselves aloof from theft; lead a dissolute life; hate your master with an exceeding great hate; and love one another.'[6]

By contrast, Shem was praised as was his descendant Solomon who would build the temple and Cyrus, a descendant of Japheth, who would be critical for the building of the second temple.[7]

---

3   Ginzberg, *The Legends of the Jews*, I: 167–168.
4   Ginzberg, *The Legends of the Jews*, I: 168. See Gen. Rab. 36.7.
5   Ginzberg, *The Legends of the Jews*, I: 169.
6   Ginzberg, *The Legends of the Jews*, I: 169.
7   Ginzberg, *The Legends of the Jews*, I: 170.

Modern scholarship has tended to focus on the literary and textual issues since there does not seem to be much archaeology with which to work. There are general considerations on the identity of the figures named in the story. These figures are more representational in nature (like Uncle Sam) and engender discussion about who are what peoples they represent. Indeed, it is with this story, more so than the others in this study, where the identities of the peoples in the time of the audience and the characters in the story are most frequently linked.

Delitzsch

Delitzsch characterizes this story as representing a transfer from stories about humanity before the Flood to stories about the fate of nations after the Flood. In the original version he suggests that Canaan not Ham transgressed against Noah. Biblical scholars commonly subscribe to the interpretation of Canaan's guilt. Delitzsch notes that to refer to Noah as a husbandman or cultivator of the field as a farmer is incorrect since he cultivated the vine which apparently originated in Armenia. The issue of 'national sin' is of some significance to him. Here Delitzsch refers to the 'pro-slavery advocates' of his own time. He observes that the national misfortune of vassalage can become the means to a blessing. A positive ending occurs only if one does not participate in the national sin as Rahab did not and was saved. He is referring to her assistance to the spies Joshua had dispatched before the fall of Jericho. In Delitzsch's commentary, one may recognize how stories about nations or peoples in the past may become part of the discussion about nations or peoples in the present. The 'curse of Ham' played a significant role in American history and in the debate over slavery.[8]

Dillmann

Dillmann sees two hands at work in the pericope. He is struck by the fact that Canaan is the only actual name of an historically real people in the story whereas Shem and Japheth are not. One is therefore forced to conjecture who the brothers represent until the information is detailed later in the Table of Nations (Gen. 10). Presumably when the story was first told, the audience required no such elaborations. They did not need to wait. They knew instantaneously upon hearing the names exactly what person or peoples were meant.

According to Dillmann, in the original story, Canaan is more likely to have been the primary actor. Such behavior is to be expected given 'the miserable condition into which the peoples of the Canaanitish race had already sunk by the time of our author...' Dillmann castigates the Canaanites for their 'moral perversity', 'licentiousness', and 'shameful customs' which are not new developments in the time of the audience 'but which can be traced back to their very beginnings'. These beginnings did not extend back to pre-Deluge times

---

8 Delitzsch, *New Commentary*, 290–292, 295. On slavery, see Aaron, 'Early Rabbinic exegesis on Noah's son Ham', 721–759; Benjamin Braude, 'The sons of Noah and the construction of ethnic and geographical identities in the medieval and early modern periods', *WMQ* 54 1997: 103–142; Gene Rice, 'The curse that never was (Genesis 9: 18–27)', *JRT* 29 1972: 5–27.

but commenced with the first ancestor after the Flood. The result is an author telling the story about the dismal Canaanites in the present of the author being heirs to their dismal origin as documented in the story of the sons of Noah.[9] Dillmann does not address the possibility that the story of the reprobate Canaan originated in the time when Israel and Canaan were in conflict. Nor does he seek to identify more narrowly the specific Canaanites who might have been the target of original author's ire.

Gunkel

Gunkel considers Gen. 9: 18–19 to be the conclusion to the J Flood narrative. The peopling of the whole earth catches his attention given a similar dissemination to occur in the story of the Tower of Babel (see Chapter 7). Gunkel approvingly cites Dillmann on recognizing the transformation of moral Noah of the Flood to the drunk one here. He notes the change in marital status of the sons from married in the ark to single afterwards and the shift from Canaan to Ham as one of the original three sons. The alteration in marital status is frequently observed by biblical scholars. For Gunkel, the combination of themes and these changes are indicators of independent traditions and multiple authors.[10]

Besides his analysis of the story verse by verse, Gunkel extensively engages in the debate to determine the current situation presupposed by the blessings and curses involving Shem Japheth, Ham, and Canaan. He states that the narrator considered himself a Shemite, the first-born of Noah. Now Japheth, the second son has subjugated Canaan, the third and youngest son, and has driven out Shem from his land. The standard view in Gunkel's time was that Shem was Israel and Japheth was either the Phoenicians or the Philistines. Gunkel acknowledges that:

> 'Certainly, the ancient Israelite who heard this legend would have understood the son whose god is Yahweh and who rules Canaan to be the progenitor of his people [why not to be his people Israel?] just as he interpreted the legend of Esau and Jacob in relation to Edom and Israel.'[11]

However, Gunkel raises the issue of even if that is how the audience interpreted the story, is that what it originally meant? He rejects the common view asserting that neither Shem nor Japheth was a transmitted name for either Israel or the Philistines. He rejects that they are 'secret names' as suggested by Budde. He rejects the Phoenician interpretation because such a territorial configuration among these peoples never occurred. Gunkel presumes Israel knew the Canaanites and the Phoenicians were the same people. He is open to exploring the hypothesis that Japheth relates to the nations of north (apparently meaning the Sea Peoples who included the Philistines), but he advises caution. All the various geopolitical machinations are fraught with danger. He concludes that 'the effort to relate these sayings to Israel's historical situation may be considered a failure'.[12]

---

9   Dillmann, *Genesis*, 301–303, quotations from 303.
10 Gunkel, *Genesis*, 79.
11 Gunkel, *Genesis*, 82.
12 Gunkel, *Genesis*, 83.

Gunkel prefers to examine the prehistorical situation. The Flood hero Noah is the first farmer and wine grower. The sons are part of Noah's story from primeval times when they become the progenitors of all peoples of the world as outlined in the Table of Nations (Gen. 10). For Gunkel, the three original sons, Shem, Japheth, and Canaan were primitive peoples from days of yore. Yet Gunkel must address one incongruity: while the names of Shem and Japheth did not persist into the historical record, the name Canaan certainly did continue from primitive to historical times.[13]

This realization forces Gunkel, the great proponent of myth and folktales, into the world of archaeology. The archaeological world he describes is in a state of flux. Gunkel deals with the Egyptian, Mesopotamian, and biblical geographical information available to him and arrives at two conclusions:

1.   Canaan has a dual sense as the name of a people and of a region.
2.   The 2nd millennium BCE is the best chronological fit for Canaan.

These two observations have stood the test of time as the 1st millennium BCE references to Canaan by name generally are from the Bible and not archaeology. This change thereby raises the issue of what the word meant in the biblical context when no political entity Canaan existed and the kingdoms of Israel and/or Judah did. Gunkel concludes that the story contains the oldest biblical report of the relationships among nations and was probably preserved because of the poetry of the curses and blessings.[14]

After all this investigation and ruminations, Gunkel at last ends his section on the story of the sons of Noah with his view of Noah:

> 'He was originally a Syro-Canaanite figure, the first farmer and wine grower, progenitor of Syro-Canaanite humanity, then of all humanity, for this reason he then made his way into the Babylonian Flood legend, which originally did not contain his name.'[15]

Gunkel never really addresses the issue: if the audience knew who Canaan was, did not they also know who Noah, Shem, Japheth, and Ham were in their own time?

Skinner

Skinner addresses many of the questions which continue to be discussed on the centennial of his commentary. For Skinner, the story of Noah's sons 'almost certainly comes from a different cycle of tradition from the righteous and blameless patriarch who is the hero of the Flood'.[16] The now unmarried sons living in the tent of the father makes this a story of juvenile depravity.

Ham is the gloss in the text with the cursing of Canaan, the youngest son being the dominant feature of the original story. For Skinner, Gen. 9: 18 closes the J flood story with either the Table of Nations or Tower of Babel in Gen. 10 and 11 respectively as

---

13   Gunkel, *Genesis*, 83.
14   Gunkel, *Genesis*, 83–84.
15   Gunkel, *Genesis*, 84–85.
16   Skinner, *A Critical and Exegetical Commentary*, 181.

the next stories. The story of Noah's sons expresses no knowledge of the Flood. It is an 'independent legend, originating amidst Palestinian surroundings'. Presumably the redactor who combined the two J documents also inserted the gloss of Ham as the father of Canaan.[17]

Skinner approaches the story from a theological and anthropological basis. This Noah is an entirely new character who originates the wine culture. His action demarcates a fresh advance in human civilization. The story expresses the transition from nomadic to agricultural life whereby the simpler forms of agriculture are supplemented by the grape. Skinner uses this advance to contrast the Israelites with the Canaanites and the 'orgiastic character' of their agriculturally-based religion. 'It exhibits the repugnance of a healthy-minded race towards the excesses of a debased civilisation'. Given the authorial representation of these divergent lifestyles, Skinner seizes the opportunity to explain how it came to be that one culture succumbed to such depravity while the other rose above it:

> 'The sons of the desert who then served themselves heirs by conquest to the Canaanitish civilisation escaped the protracted evolution of vine-growing from primitive tillage, and stepped into the possession of the farm and vineyard at once. From this point of view the story of Noah's drunkenness expresses the healthy recoil of primitive Semitic morality from the licentious habit engendered by a civilisation of which a salient feature was the enjoyment and abuse of wine. Canaan is the prototype of the population which had succumbed to these enervating influences, and is doomed by its vices to enslavement at the hands of the hardier and more virtuous races.'

The moral implications from this recognition of cultural evolution are not to be ignored; nor are the moral judgments being rendered by the scholars who are dismissive of the repugnant and inferior peoples.[18]

What Noah accomplished as evidenced by the definition of his name in Gen. 5: 29 ('Out of the ground which Yahweh has cursed this one shall bring us relief from our work and from the toil of our hands') should be understood 'as an advance or refinement on the tillage of the ground to which man was sentenced in consequence of his first transgression'. The transition is not merely reported but is accompanied with a serious message to 'convey an emphatic warning against the moral dangers attending this new step in human development'. Canaan and the people he represents thereby serve as a retardant on the progress of human civilization. One wonders how this message resonated in a time of imperialism in the late 19th and early 20th centuries in the very same part of the world where these stories were presumed to have occurred (see Additional Readings: Holy Land).[19]

Biblical scholars wrestled with the archaeological data to determine when this transition occurred. Skinner posits the ethnographic subjugation of the Canaanites by Israel in the early days of the monarchy meaning the time of David and Solomon. To integrate the dominion by Japheth whom he equates with the Philistines over Canaan dwelling in Shem whom he equates with the Hebrews proves problematical in history. When could

---

17 Skinner, *A Critical and Exegetical Commentary*, 182–184, quotation from 183.

18 Skinner, *A Critical and Exegetical Commentary*, 181–185, quotations from 183 and 185.

19 Quotations from Skinner, *A Critical and Exegetical Commentary*, 185, 186.

such dominion have occurred? What geopolitical context was in accord with this proposed configuration of Philistines, Israel, and Canaan?

Skinner recognizes the problem. He avers 'that the Hebrews should have wished for an enlargement of the Philistines at their own expense is incredible' and he rejects the Phoenicians linkage for Japheth. A better alternative explanation existed. 'A better defined background would be the struggle for the mastery of Syria in the 14th cent. BC' as revealed in the diplomatic texts discovered from the Amarna Age (see Chapter 8). The equation of the *habiri* from those texts with the Hebrews may be a factor in determining the historical setting (see Additional Readings: Habiru). Regardless of the merits of Skinner's chronological setting, the critical observation is his determination to situate the story in an historically-defined context that would have been known to the original audience.[20]

Von Rad

Von Rad absolves Noah from moral condemnation on the grounds that ignorance is an excuse. How could Noah know the effect of wine? He considers the story somewhat more 'loosely inserted in the large teleological, Yahwistic narrative context of the primeval traditions than the other traditions … It is filled with difficulties and obscurities for which the final explanatory word has not yet been spoken'. One such problem is the tension between the ecumenical scheme versus the local one revolving around the character of Canaan. A second is the sons of Noah changing from being married in the flood story to being single in this story.[21]

As for the tensions generated by the story, von Rad offers an explanation that 'The traditions that the Yahwist united to form a great composition were complex, and he had much less need to reconcile them absolutely with one another from within'.[22] Then 'because of a subsequent revision the notion of the three families of nations has become disunified'.[23] Somehow an 'older ethnological narrative [wa]s stripped of its specific ethnological character and expanded into something primevally historical and human'. Von Rad's own interpretation then leaves him befuddled. He has no idea where the name Noah, which is not the name of the Babylonian flood hero, originated or how he became part of the Israelite tradition.[24] This story is a classic illustration of the difference between the perception of a single writer collecting stories versus the conscious will in the political arena approach proposed here. Von Rad is so deeply trapped within his paradigm that when stumped he sees no way out.

Speiser

Speiser envisions this story as constituting a link between the Flood and the Table of Nations (see Chapter 6). But there are problems: the story does not agree with the Flood story since

---

20 Skinner, *A Critical and Exegetical Commentary on Genesis*, 186–187.
21 Von Rad, *Genesis*, 135–136, quotation from 136.
22 Von Rad, *Genesis*, 136.
23 Von Rad, *Genesis*, 135.
24 Von Rad, *Genesis*, 139.

the married sons are now single. He laments that '(c)onnecting passages can be puzzling precisely because they are meant to bridge gaps, and they usually are laconic'. He compares the story to Gen. 4: 17–24 in this regard (see Chapter 2). Once again he imagines there once was a more substantial narrative of which this is merely a splinter. Speiser notes the problem of Noah identifying the youngest son as the violator and Canaan being the one whom Noah curses in 9: 25. Therefore he asks, 'Have two divergent traditions been fused, or was the Canaan the original offender? At all events, the moral of the story is actually aimed at Canaan and, by extension, at the Canaanites.'[25]

Given this conclusion, Speiser hones in on the date of the story. He asserts that 'the burden of it is not so much to justify an accomplished political fact, as it is to stigmatize distasteful practices on the part of the older inhabitants of the land'. Speiser then seeks to identify the historical setting when Shem and Japheth cooperated at the expense of Canaan. His answer is the 12th century BCE when the Philistines arrived and Israel was struggling against Canaan. A century later was too late: Canaan had ceased to be a major political factor and Israel and the Philistines were arrivals. The verses now can be dated 'with reasonable accuracy'. He does not consider the possibility that the author is delivering a message about the political facts in his present by stigmatizing the Canaanite faction in Israel. Similarly Speiser is prone as are other exegetes to identify Shem, Japheth, and Canaan with historical peoples while ignoring the figure of Noah, the figure of authority.[26]

Speiser cannot explain what this local story is doing here 'in marked contrast with the bulk of Primeval History, for which the ultimate inspiration came from Mesopotamia'. Perhaps the singular achievement of the story which 'is abundantly clear' is its local background.[27]

Westermann

In general terms and consistent with others, Westermann sees the story as the setting for the post-diluvial stage of humanity. The story addresses an event of some import and its significance should not be limited to a genealogical occurrence. The story is one of the history and progress of human civilization. So for a short story, it possesses critical information for tracing human progress.[28]Westermann also wrestles with the apparent tensions of the story. He envisions a coalescence of three components within the story: the three sons, the history of civilization, and the theme of crime and punishment, curse and blessings. Unfortunately, he has no generally accepted solution how these pieces fit together into a coherent whole. As a result Westermann is forced to a significant conclusion: 'This solution seems so convincing that it cannot be countered by tradition criticism. One must conclude that there are two different traditions about the order of Noah's sons in 9: 20–27'. In the combining of these two different traditions, the author or redactor was obligated

25 Quotations from Speiser, *Genesis*, 61 and 62.
26 Quotations from Speiser, *Genesis*, 62 and 63.
27 Speiser, *Genesis*, 62.
28 Westermann, *Genesis 1–11*, 482, 483, 485.

to retain the contradiction involving Ham and Canaan.[29] It is interesting to observe how frequently scholars detect two hands but remain committed to the mythical or folk genesis of what turns out to be a political story with more than one writer.

The Jewish Study Bible

Levenson builds on rabbinic tradition. Noah serves as an object lesson for the dangers of intoxication. But is it fair to hold accountable the first person to grow grapes for becoming drunk? Presumably he was justifiably ignorant of the degrading consequences of excessive alcohol consumption. Following along the lines of Josephus, the main story 'serves as an explanation of the sexual perverseness that the Israelite culture sometimes thought to be typical of Canaanites'. Such presumed wanton sexuality of the Canaanite religion and people has been used to understand the stories of the sons of God and Noah as well as the Canaanites dwelling in the land of Canaan prior to the arrival of the Israelites.[30]

Plaut in *The Torah: A Modern Commentary* concurs. While Ham's punishment 'seems harsh in the extreme … this harshness suggests that the Bible was referring to a transgression far more serious than seeing one's father naked and in a drunken stupor'. This commentary appears to being following in the tradition of Speiser as seen in his analysis of the story of the sons of God. Plaut notes that 'an old Canaanite myth [what would be a 'new Canaanite myth'?] … told how the god El-Kronos had emasculated his father' and 'the Hurrian legend that told how Kumarbis severed the genitals of his father, the god Anu'. He postulates a direct connection between pagan myths and biblical text: 'Evidently these old mythic traditions were current millennia after they were first told, and we may assume that they were familiar to the biblical author'. A more detailed version of the tale may have been expurgated given the brevity of the canonical version but the message of the story was still delivered. It is a story of sexual perversion which subtly asserted that the Hamites, meaning Egyptians, and the Canaanites were the descendants of sexual deviates in this polemic 'against Israel's nearest neighbors and dearest enemies'. The commentary concludes with a reference to the story of Lot's daughters, another story of sex following a drunken stupor where the eastern neighbors Moabites and Ammonites similarly are castigated as peoples 'of indecent sexual background' (Gen. 19: 32–38).[31]

The New Jerome Biblical Commentary

Clifford joins with others in absolving Noah of wrong doing. According to Clifford, the first cultivator of the grape could not be expected to know of the intoxicating impact of the grape whereas Ham knew exactly what he was doing. Despite the nakedness and incest prohibitions in Lev. 20: 17–21, Ham's actions should not be construed as meaning sexual

---

29 Westermann, *Genesis 1–11*, 483–484, quotation from 483.

30 Levenson, 'Genesis', 25–26, quotation from 26.

31 W. Gunther Plaut, ed., *The Torah: A Modern Commentary* (New York: Union of American Hebrew Congregations, 1981), 70. *The Schocken Bible* takes a similarly dismal view of this 'bizarre' event and notes the connection to Gen. 19 (Everett Fox, *The Five Books of Moses* [New York: Schocken Books, 1995], 44).

intercourse occurred between the son and his drunken father. The affront Ham committed was twofold: first in what he saw and second in what he spoke, serious offenses which implied contempt for the father. Despite Ham being at fault, the exegesis of these verses in this commentary concludes: 'Canaan's offense prefigures the sexual license of the latter Canaanites, against which Israel is repeatedly warned'. Once again wanton sexuality raises its ugly head as an underlying theme of the story and it is projected onto the Canaanites. One wonders what the people experiencing the story for the first time were expected to think particularly if there were Canaanites present at the time of the telling.[32]

The HarperCollins Study Bible

Rosenberg takes a less judgmental approach. He states that the story of Noah's sons was 'an originally independent legend'. He contrasts the blameless Noah of the Flood story with the post-Flood Noah shown 'quickly succumbing to the bad habits of settled society'. This depiction suggests the commentator sees the vineyard as a synecdoche for the very civilization which Noah had left. The possibility of a sexual act by Ham with his father is noted but the author focuses more on the vocabulary of two key words: saw and knew:

> the woman *saw* the tree was good for food and a delight to the eye (Gen. 3: 6)
> the sons of God *saw* the daughters of man were fair (Gen. 6: 2)
> Yahweh *saw* the wickedness of man was great in the earth (Gen. 6: 5)
> Ham *saw* the nakedness of his father (Gen. 9: 22)
> and the word *knew* from the garden (3: 5, 7, 22), Cain (4: 1, 17), and Noah (8: 1).

No comment is made about these occurrences but the implication is there is a connection. Any connection calls into question the claim previously made about the story originally having been an independent legend. Did this story just happen by chance to share a common vocabulary with the other stories? Was that shared vocabulary imposed by the redactor writing in a single style? Was the shared vocabulary an expression of multiple authors commenting on a single theme of contention? Regardless of the answer(s), Rosenberg suggests the story of the sons of Noah should not be understood in isolation from other stories of the first cycle of J.[33]

Gunkel refers to the 'narrator repeatedly employ[ing] a whole chain of words'. Such usage provides the 'impression of the account's unity'. He attributes this practice to 'the poverty of the language' available to the writer. By contrast, Hendel argues that the presence of this distinctive literary technique called *leitwort* was deliberately intended to create precisely such a unifying literary structure by guiding the reader. This technique is critical to identifying the authors of the stories and their relations to each other but with a twist. One writer in a political context might deliberately draw from the language of a foe to undermine the other's position. In this technique, one uses the very words of one's opponent to make them eat their words.[34]

---

32 Clifford and Murphy, 'Genesis', 17.
33 Rosenberg, 'Genesis', 16.
34 Gunkel, *Genesis*, xl; Ronald Hendel, 'The *Leitwort* style and literary structure in the J Primeval Narrative',

Rosenberg suggests a further area of study as well. He notes that the 'Canaanites, viewed by the biblical tradition as later Israel's immediate predecessors in the land are the chief preoccupation here' and '[t]he hostility toward Canaan is rooted in Israel's memory of Canaan's onetime hegemony in the land under the protection of Egyptian might'. The reader is advised to follow this insight to his note on Gen. 10: 6, which states that 'Egypt's close relationship with Canaan before the Amarna period and exodus era (14th–13th centuries BCE) accounts for their kinship here [in the Table of Nations]'. Rosenberg's comments imply the so-called primeval story has an historical context specific to the land of Canaan and those who controlled it, more specifically Egypt versus Israel. One consequence is that in the effort to understand the story of the sons of Noah it is essential to understand the meaning of 'Canaan' just as Gunkel wrestled with a century earlier.[35]

Conclusion

This review of the sons of Noah exegesis over the millennia reveals significant commonalities, some differences in interpretations, and open questions. These observations may be summarized as follows.

1. The earlier commentators such as Josephus and the rabbis were storytellers in their own right. They sought to smooth the way by filling in gaps through expository creations. They anticipated the questions an audience might raise reading or hearing the story within the existing canonized narrative. They were very concerned about Noah's change in behavior and seemed almost eager to castigate the Canaanites.
2. Modern scholars are divided on the presence of multiple writers within the sons of Noah story. The introduction in 9: 18–19 and the series of curses in 9: 25–27 raise eyebrows to many exegetes and the presence of Ham as the father of Canaan in 9: 18 and 22 seems awkward.
3. Modern scholars tend to be united that Canaan was the original source of ire for the narrator.
4. Modern scholars tend to be divided as to whether the story is about the dawn of human civilization, whether the story is a mythical folktale or the word of God, or whether it can be situated in some specific historical context.
5. While modern scholars frequently accept that the sons of Noah represent peoples, there is little or no effort to identify who Noah, the figure of authority, represents.
6. Given the drunkenness, the story of the sons of Noah needs to be understood within the context of other stories of drunkenness such as the story of Lot's daughters in Gen.19: 30–38 mentioned in some of the commentaries and Gaal at Shechem (Judges 9: 26–41).
7. Given the significance of Canaan to the story the meaning of Canaan needs to be determined particularly as specified in multiple expressions in Gen. 10. Based on the definition of Canaan, the story of the sons of Noah then can be understood within the Canaanite geopolitical context.

---

in Shawna Dolansky, ed., *Sacred History, Sacred Literature: Essays on Ancient Israel, the Bible and Religion in Honor of Richard E. Friedman* (Winona Lake: Eisenbrauns, 2008), 95–109, here 95–96; see also Ronald Hendel, 'Is the "J" Primeval Narrative an independent composition? A critique of Crüsemann's "Die Eigenständigkeit der Urgeschichte"', in Thomas B. Dozeman, Konrad Schmid with Baruch J. Schwartz, eds, *The Pentateuch: International Perspectives on Current Research* (FAT 78; Tübingen: Mohr Siebeck, 2011), 181–205.

35 Quotations from Rosenberg, 'Genesis', 16 and 17.

Given these concerns and considerations specified above, the idea of a sons of Noah story as an independent folk tale that a skilled writer/collector incorporated into the narrative seems less and less likely. The allusions to the garden with its pronouncement on work, the meaning of the name of Noah (Gen. 5: 29), the various biblical alcohol and sex stories are more suggestive of writers commenting on common themes and issues rather than plucking ancient folk tales out of a hat. In a world where the abstractions of academic discourse had yet to be invented, the language of discourse was storytelling. Ideas were expressed in human stories involving families, biology, and sex. What today might seem like a frivolous folk tale might in ancient times have been just as serious as the writings of Plato or Machiavelli seeking to explain human conduct. Regarding any potential sexual allusions in biblical stories, one should be guided here by the ancient words of wisdom that politics makes strange bedfellows and that sometimes a banana isn't a banana.[36]

Exegetes demonstrate some unusual tap dancing in their maneuvering to make sense of the story. Noah's not knowing the effect of alcohol can be rationalized since no one ever drank before. However, Ham and Canaan can be judged by a law code which does not yet exist and which would not have applied to them anyhow since they were not Israelite and had not entered into the covenant community. Given these machinations, one wonders although the story nominally is set in primeval times, it really is not about them all. To uncover the truth of the story of Noah's sons, one must uncover the setting in which the story was written and recognize its political origin. The animosity towards the Canaanites in the story matched the animosity towards the Canaanites in the time of the writers. Friedman cautions exegetes of the need to learn about the world of the writers to successfully connect that world and the written word. One reasonable supposition that whatever is meant by Canaan in the political arena at that time was something these Israelite writers truly despised. These same considerations apply as the focus shifts to stories with a more pronounced historical setting, the stories of Nimrod and the Tower of Babel.

---

36 A modern America example is the political bear. Everyone knows a political commercial with a bear is about Russia. It is not a folk image from hoary antiquity but is about a current political issue. In ancient times, the story of the bear would have expanded into a more elaborate and extensive story including a hunter. Or one could simply have a picture of a hunter looking like Uncle Sam holding a bear rug thus proving the adage that a picture is worth a thousand words.

Chapter 6

NIMROD: WHO IS THE SON OF CUSH?

> **Genesis 10**: *⁸ Cush became the father of Nimrod; he was the first on earth to be a mighty man. ⁹ He was a mighty hunter before Yahweh; therefore it is said, 'Like Nimrod a mighty hunter before Yahweh'. ¹⁰ The beginning of his kingdom was Babel, Erech, and Accad and Calneh, all of them in the land of Shinar.*

Nimrod has been a source of fascination for centuries. Who is this person who appears out of nowhere and disappears so quickly leaving behind a slew of important names and extraordinary attributes? Few individuals outside the direct line from first man to Abram appear in J's first cycle beyond simply being part of a list of some kind. Even fewer have some story to tell, who have an identity, who have a 'name'. Therefore, it is reasonable to focus on those who stand above the crowd and outside the routine. The isolating of such figures renders it possible to determine their function in the narrative given that their absence would not be noticed (see Additional Readings: Nimrod).

Standard questions raised by commentators throughout the ages have included such issues as:

1. Why was this non-Israelite and non-ancestor of an Israelite included in the biblical narrative?
2. Is there any connection between Nimrod and the building of the Tower of Babel?
   Is there any evidence for Nimrod in the archaeological record?

Although Nimrod might seem to be a minor figure quickly passed over, he turns out to be an integral part of the debate about the origins of civilization, its meaning for Israel, the writing of the Bible and Israelite history.

In addition to the traditional questions regarding the text, one may add:

1. Was Nimrod's legacy meant to be an example to Israelite kings of what to emulate or of what to disavow?
2. Was the story of Nimrod an insert into the narrative or part of a longer supplement?
3. Were the stories of Nimrod and the Tower of Babel written by the same person or enemies?
4. What did Nimrod actually do that was so bad?

What political message was being delivered through the communication of this story? Or how did it help one political faction in the time of Solomon? Complicating the attempt to discern the original meaning of the text is the longstanding efforts to isolate it from the surrounding narrative or to combine it with the Tower of Babel story.

The tracking of the attempts by exegetes to understand this passage will begin in ancient times with Josephus, proceed to the rabbis, and continue with modern scholarship from the end of the 19th century to the canonical commentaries of the 20th.

6. Nimrod. Who Is the Son of Cush?

87

The legacy of Nimrod has been a poor one. When one turns to non-biblical sources from ancient times, one observes a consistency of ill-will and negative thoughts directed against this person who is remembered as having done something wrong although there is no specific mention of any infraction in the text.

Josephus

The quest to understand him and his significance is an ancient one. As it turns out, far more has been written about Nimrod outside the Bible than in the Bible itself. For example, according to Josephus:

> **Ant. 1: 113** *Now it was Nimrod who excited them to such an affront and contempt of God. He was the grandson of Ham, the son of Noah – a bold man, and of great strength of hand. He persuaded them not to ascribe to God, as if it was through his means they were happy, but to believe that it was their own courage which procured that happiness.[114] He also gradually changed the government into tyranny, seeing no other way of turning men from the fear of God, but to bring them into a constant dependence on his power. He also said he would be revenged on God, if he should have a mind to drown the world again; for that he would build a tower too high for the waters to be able to reach! and that he would avenge himself on God for killing their forefathers! [115] Now the multitude were very ready to follow the determination of Nimrod, and to esteem it a piece of cowardice to submit to God; and they built a tower, neither sparing any pains, nor being in any degree negligent about the work; and by reason of the multitude of hands employed in it, it grew very high, sooner than anyone could expect.*

This Nimrod led people astray, established tyrannical rule, pledged revenge against God for the Flood, and initiated the building of a tower to accomplish that goal. This harsh portrayal became the standard view of Nimrod. He was an evil person and responsible for the building of the Tower of Babel in Gen. 11 (see Chapter 7). Various other ancient luminaries such as Philo, Pseudo-Philo, Jerome, and Augustine expressed similar views.[1] This Nimrod is depicted as an arrogant person against, not before, the Lord.

Rabbis

Rabbinic traditions partook of the same understanding. Nimrod consistently was portrayed in the negative. He is the prototype of a rebellious people, his name being interpreted as 'he who made all the people rebellious against God' (Pes. 94b). His vaunted deeds as a hunter before Yahweh are interpreted to mean he was the one who introduced the eating of meat by man ... when he was not busy being the first to make war on other people (Midr. Agadah to Gen. x. 9).

The rabbis even went so far as to create a youth for Nimrod. He was not born to the dark side, far from it. During his innocent years, he freely sacrificed to Yahweh the animals he had hunted. Whereas blind Lamech required the assistance of a sighted-son to successfully hunt, Nimrod's own prowess was sufficient. But he did have an edge. Back in the garden,

---

1   The negative portrayals and comments on Nimrod have been collected in Kugel, *The Bible as It Was*, 126–127.

Yahweh had fashioned garments of skins for the man and woman to wear (Gen. 3: 21). These garments became a legacy item somewhat like the vine Adam had taken from the garden. He bequeathed the garments to Enoch who passed them to Methusaleh. Eventually both vine and garments came into the possession of Noah, who took them with him into the ark. In both cases the vile Ham upset the applecart. He saw his father drunk and he stole the garments. Ham then gave the garments to his son Cush who gave them to his son Nimrod. Now when the animals saw Nimrod clothed in the skins of animals, they crouched before the invincible and irresistible figure and he had no difficulty in catching them. Jacob would use similar garments resembling those of his hunter-brother Esau to deceive the blind Isaac. In fact, according to one rabbinic tradition, Nimrod was slain by the jealous Esau as is the wont of alpha-males with related physical skills. As with Isaac, the people in the time of Nimrod also were deceived. They perceived Nimrod's hunting prowess to be due to his extraordinary strength. In recognition of his demonstrated superiority, the people made him their king.

As king, Nimrod did not fare well in rabbinic eyes. Rabbi Akiba said: 'They cast off the sovereignty of Heaven and made Nimrod king over themselves' (Pirqe Rabbi Eliezer 24). He became the first mortal to rule world as one day the Messiah would rule it but better! Nimrod sought to convert the world to his brand of iniquity where men no longer trusted God but had faith in their own ability. In fact there was no need to worship God since he himself should be worshiped as a god. The height of his hubris was his command to build a tower to reach the heavens.

The rabbinic tales sought to bring order to the chronology of the Bible, substance to the ellipse between Gen. 10: 8–12 and Abram in Gen. 12, and an explanation for what would transpire. They designated Nimrod as the builder of the Tower of Babel in the time of Abraham. According to the rabbis, Terah was a high official in the court of King Nimrod. Then his son Abraham broke all Terah's idols forcing the father to plea for his son before Nimrod. After a direct face-to-face encounter between Abraham and Nimrod, Abraham survived the fiery furnace punishment and hid when Nimrod had a fearful dream about him. Given all these experiences, Abraham's decision to leave and never see the face of Nimrod again seems quite reasonable.[2]

The Nimrod stories became fairly fanciful, elaboration upon elaboration until one shakes one's head in wonder at the tales the rabbis have spun. Altogether, Nimrod ends up being linked to the garden, Noah, the Tower of Babel, Abraham, Chedorlaomer, the king from the east in Gen. 14, and Esau. They all become part of a single continuous narrative. Abraham's actions in leaving Ur now could be explained in the context of one who rebelled against the harsh rule of the tower-builder based on the Hebrew meaning of Nimrod's name, *mrd*, 'to rebel'. He had the vision and courage to leave the land of oppression for a better way of life, a theme that resonated well with the people of the Exodus. So the rabbinic midrash anticipates the rebellion against Pharaoh, too. This understanding became an accepted part

2　For the supplemental stories to the biblical accounts see, Goldin, *The Book of Legends*, I: 61–79; Ginzberg, *The Legends of the Jews*, I: 177–181, 193–203; Emil G. Hirsch, M. Seligsohn and Wilhelm Bacher, 'Nimrod', in Joseph Jacobs, ed., *The Jewish Encyclopedia* (New York: Funk & Wagnalls, 1906), 309–311.

of rabbinic lore and provided a rational explanation for the otherwise unexpected and inexplicable journey that launched the new religion.

Regardless of the specific details, the rabbis have provided an immeasurably valuable contribution towards understanding the writing of the Hebrew Bible in general, the KDB, and the supplements to it. They envisioned the narrative as a whole. As they filled in the blanks in the story of Nimrod, they connected him to a wide range of other stories. Gunkel's atomistic approach with the collection of small stories molded into a incoherent whole. One visionary can create a single story that transcends time. More than Gilgamesh, more the Iliad, more than the Odyssey, more than the plays about the House of Atreus or the kings of England, one story line in a single work can encompass multiple generations, locations, and events. The rabbinic effort to connect the dots across a vast array of stories continues the work of the original authors. The linkages that the rabbis forged among various stories updated the linkages which existed when they originally were written. Nimrod is a pivotal figure because the author who told that story also wrote other stories including ones beyond the scope of this study. So did those who opposed the very way of life exemplified by Nimrod. From a literary and story-telling perspective, the reign of Solomon was an extraordinary time to be alive; from a political perspective it was a dangerous one as the factions battled for power when the price for losing was death itself.

The archaeological search for Nimrod

The Nimrod exegesis encompasses an extensive archaeological component that differentiates it from other stories. With the sons of Cain, Seth, God, and Noah stories, there was little in the way of direct archaeology to elucidate the meaning on the stories. Philology was crucial in understanding the meaning of various words and terms; anthropology was critical in understanding the development of human civilization as reflected in stories presumed to be from hoary antiquity; and theology was important in understanding the messages of separation, sin and salvation being delivered. Archaeology, however, did not loom large in these considerations. All that changed with Nimrod: here was a biblical figure who potentially could be discovered archaeologically.

Nimrod is the only leader of renown mentioned in the first cycle of stories. No Pharaoh is named and no other Mesopotamian leader is named either. No Sumerian. No Akkadian. No Amorite. No Kassite. No Babylonian. No Assyrian. No Chaldean. No one. Therefore to link the biblical name to some archaeological artifact was an irresistible lure to biblical scholars just as the search for the four kings of Gen. 14 mentioned by name and location was in the late 19th and early 20th centuries.[3] Perhaps nowhere else could archaeology

---

3   As an example of the quest to unravel the mystery of Gen. 14 to link it to the secular, i.e., archaeological, record thereby providing an anchor for the patriarchal saga, consider a 61-page chapter of a dissertation devoted solely to the efforts of William Foxwell Albright. Even this chapter is incomplete because it was submitted in 1965 before Albright died and had stopped searching and only covered the period until 1958 (Stanley E. Hardwick, *Change and Constancy in William Foxwell Albright's Treatment of Early Old Testament History and Religion, 1918–1958* [Ph.D. dissertation, New York University, 1958], 130–190).

prove as successful in identifying a biblical figure in the secular record. Here was a chance to connect the Bible to history in a scientific manner. The search was underway.

The commencement of modern archaeology and the search for Nimrod were practically simultaneous. At times, reputable people thought that they had discovered him. No sooner did archaeologists begin excavating the Mesopotamian past when they seemingly struck paydirt. In the 1840s Austen Henry Layard started his excavations at what he thought was Assyrian Nineveh but turned out to be Calah, both cities that were part of the Nimrod legacy.[4] The cry of Layard's worker, 'Hasten, O Bey … hasten to the diggers, for they have found Nimrod himself' remains forever part of archaeological lore.[5] Imagine the excitement when on virtually Day One of the dig, Layard had discovered a physical remnant of this mysterious biblical figure from the earliest chapters of the Book of Genesis!

Divine providence seemingly provided such a link when George Smith, of the British Museum, addressed the Society of Biblical Archaeology in London on December 3, 1872. In an august setting with the Prime Minister of England in attendance following press releases announcing the discovery of something big, this British Museum Assistant revealed the existence of a Mesopotamian flood story with parallels to Noah. Those parallels raised a number of questions regarding the historicity of the Flood and the relationship between Mesopotamia and the Bible. Smith himself raised a relevant issue to this study:

> 'From the heading of the tablets giving his history, I suppose that Izdubar [now spelled Gilgamesh] lived in the epoch immediately following the Flood, and I think, likewise, that he may have been the founder of the Babylonian monarchy, perhaps the Nimrod of Scripture. This, however, is pure conjecture.'[6]

Amidst the swirl of this extraordinary revelation about the Mesopotamian flood story, a more obscure question also was asked. Surely the hero king of the ancient Mesopotamian epic had to be Nimrod. Who else could he be? No other name was known from the Bible. Scholars were quick to link the epic hero to the biblical account. Initially, archaeologists/Assyriologists took for granted that there was an historical Nimrod. Therefore the challenge was simply to find him in the vast cuneiform record which was being discovered. Certainly the most prominent person at the dawn of Mesopotamian civilization who also appeared at the dawn of archaeology was Gilgamesh. The identification of this great king made him the prime candidate to be Nimrod. Prolific author and Assyriologist A. H. Sayce authored a paper entitled 'Nimrod and the Assyrian Inscriptions'. He presented it a few months later on April 1, 1873 with the assertion:

> 'The identification of the Biblical Nimrod is one of the problems connected with Assyrian research which still await their solution.'[7]

---

4   Austen Henry Layard, *Nineveh and Its Remains: with an Account of a Visit to the Chaldean Christians of Kurdistan, and the Yezidis, or Devil-worshipers; and an Inquiry Into the Manners and Arts of the Ancient Assyrians* (London: J. Murray, 1849), I: 24.

5   Layard, *Nineveh and Its Remains*, I: 65. See also 'Chapter 2: They have found Nimrod himself', in Gordon Waterfield, *Layard of Nineveh* (New York: Frederick A. Praeger, 1963), 128–140.

6   George Smith, 'The Chaldean account of the Deluge', *TSBA* 2 1873: 213–234, here 215; reprinted in Alan Dundes, ed., *The Flood Myth* (Berkeley: University of California, 1988), 29–48, here 32.

7   A. H. Sayce, 'Nimrod and the Assyrian inscriptions', *TSBA* 2 1873: 243–249, here 243.

His conclusion, stated at the end of the first paragraph, was that Nimrod was to be identified with Merodach (Marduk), a divine not historical being. In another article a few months later this time focusing on the relation of the two flood stories, Sayce tentatively acknowledged a non-flood biblical link to the document revealed by Smith:

> 'The document appears to have been the special property of Erech, and it is curious that a tetrapolis similar to that of these old Babylonian tablets is mentioned by the inserter of the notice about Nimrod in Gen. X.'[8]

His concern here seems to have less about identifying an historical Nimrod than specifying the time an author inserted the Nimrod passage into the 'Jehovist' [J] narrative.

By contrast, Smith focused on the potential Izdubar-Nimrod equation in an historical context. The year following Sayce's publications, Smith published some notes on the paper he had presented in 1872 first revealing the Babylonian flood story. He attempted to show some similarity between the sound of the second element of Izdubar and the final two consonants of Nimrod, but otherwise he did not stress any historical identity for Nimrod.[9] The extended title of his publication in 1875, *The Chaldean Account of Genesis: Containing the Description of the Creation, the Fall of Man, the Deluge, the Tower of Babel, the Times of the Patriarchs, and Nimrod: Babylonian Fables, and Legends of the Gods, from the Cuneiform Inscriptions*, expresses the effort to intertwine the biblical and Mesopotamian stories on a more comprehensive scale. In his chapter on the Izdubar legends, after an opening paragraph about his discovery, he stated at the beginning of the second paragraph:

> 'The Izdubar legends give, I believe, the history of the Biblical hero Nimrod.'[10]

His concluding comment in the paragraph is more revealing of the author than the archaeology.

> 'He appears to me to be the monarch who bears the closest resemblance in his fame and actions to the Nimrod of the Bible.'[11]

One may observe here the predisposition to find the biblical Nimrod in the historical record. Smith accepted the historical validity of the biblical account. For him the challenge was simply to find in the archaeological record the figure who came closest to matching the biblical account, a quite different approach than Sayce had exhibited so far. After all, according to Smith, 'as Nimrod was always known as a famous sovereign it was necessary to find a definite place for him in any chronological scheme'.[12] Smith meant that people

---

8   A. H. Sayce, 'The Chaldean account of the Deluge, and its relation to the Old Testament, *Theological Review* 42 1873: 364–377, here 375. See also Josef Grivel, 'Nemrod et les écritures cunéiformes', *TSBA* 3 1874: 136–144. Smith cited both of them (*The Chaldean Account of Genesis: Containing the Description of the Creation, the Fall of Man, the Deluge, the Tower of Babel, the Times of the Patriarchs, and Nimrod: Babylonian Fables, and Legends of the Gods, from the Cuneiform Inscriptions* [New York: Scribner, Armstrong & Co., 1876], 180).

9   George Smith, 'The eleventh tablet of the Izdubar legends: the Chaldean account of the Deluge – text and notes to accompany paper read 3rd December, 1872', *TSBA* 3 1874: 530–596, here 588.

10 Smith, *The Chaldean account of Genesis*, 167.

11 Smith, *The Chaldean account of Genesis*, 168.

12 Smith, *The Chaldean account of Genesis*, 177.

from Josephus to early Christian writers such as Africanus (*c*. CE 160–240) to Eusebius (*c*. CE 263–339) among others who relied on the biblical narrative always had integrated Nimrod into their narratives. So should Assyriologists today. 'Considering that Nimrod was the most famous of the Babylonian kings in tradition, it is evident that no history of the country can be complete without some notice of him'.[13] Smith rejected the Mesopotamian deity Marduk option proposed by Sayce and Joseph Grivel preferring to focus on the similar geography, character, and traits of Gilgamesh and Nimrod.[14]

Smith's investigations enabled him to propose the following historical chronology:

> 2450 BCE – Elamites overrun Babylonia
> 2280 BCE – Kudur-nanhundi, king of Elam ravages Erech
> 2250 BCE – Izdubar/Nimrod slays Humba-ba, the final Elamite king, and restores Chaldean power with the story of this most famous of Babylonian kings composed in *c*. 2000 BCE.[15]

Smith concluded that Izdubar/Nimrod 'owed a great portion of his fame … to his slaying Humbaba' and his heroic action provided the impetus to unify the country 'as the people saw the evils of disunion, which weakened them and laid them open to foreign invasion'.[16] The king of the land then was able to extend his authority from the Persian Gulf to the Armenian mountains with Erech as his capital.[17] Smith acknowledged that this conjecture was '(t)he most hazardous of these theories [referring to his other theories in the book]'[18] and he took comfort from the fact that his conjecture 'has since been adopted by several other scholars'.[19] The discoverer of the Mesopotamian flood story had found the link between Bible and history in primeval times even before Abram fought the kings of the east. Quite an achievement for one individual!

Even one-time skeptic Sayce had come around to locating Nimrod in an historical setting. He opined, 'There are grounds for thinking that Mr. George Smith was right in seeing in him the prototype of the Biblical Nimrod'.[20] His thinking on the subject continued

---

13 Smith, *The Chaldean account of Genesis*, 180.
14 Grivel proposed Nimrod was Marduk in 1871 even prior to Smith's flood announcement in 1872. The suggestion appeared in the appendix of his article entitled 'Le plus ancien dictionnaire' that he wrote for the *Revue de la Suisse catholique* (August 1871); see Grivel, 'Nemrod et les ecritures cuneiformes', 136.
15 Smith, *The Chaldean Account of Genesis*, 189 and 302.
16 Smith, *The Chaldean Account of Genesis*, 302; see also the posthumously published, *The History of Babylonia* (London: Society for Promoting Christian Knowledge, no date), 55, 61.
17 Smith, *The Chaldean Account of Genesis*, 309.
18 Smith, *The Chaldean Account of Genesis*, 301.
19 George Smith, *The Chaldean Account of Genesis: Containing the Description of the Creation, the Fall of Man, the Deluge, the Tower of Babel, the Times of the Patriarchs, and Nimrod: Babylonian Fables, and Legends of the Gods, from the Cuneiform Inscriptions* (London: Sampson Low, Marston, Searle, and Rivington, 1880), 190. This claim does not appear in the 1876 edition.
20 A. H. Sayce, *Lectures on the Origin and Growth of Religion as Illustrated by the Religion of the Ancient Babylonians* (London: Williams & Norgate, 1887), 8. Knohl also uses the term 'prototype' for the Mesopotamian king who builds cities and hunts (Israel Knohl, 'Nimrod, son of Cush, King of Mesopotamia, and the dates of P and J', in Chaim Cohen, ed., *Birkat Shalom: Studies in the Bible, Ancient Near Eastern Literature, and Post-Biblical Judaism, Presented to Shalom M. Paul on the Occasion of His Seventieth Birthday* (Winona Lake: Eisenbrauns, 2008), 45–52, here 46.

to evolve as the issue was more than one of academic curiosity to him. Sayce's goals were clearly stated as evidenced by the very extended title of his 1883 publication *Fresh Light from Ancient Monuments: A Sketch of the Most Striking Confirmations of the Bible, from Recent Discoveries in Egypt, Palestine, Assyria, Babylonia, Asia Minor.* For his opening lines, Sayce wrote:

> 'The object of this little book is explained by its title. Discovery after discovery has been pouring in upon us from Oriental lands, and the accounts given only ten years ago of the results of Oriental research are already beginning to be antiquated... The same spirit of scepticism which had rejected the early legends of Greece and Rome had laid its hands also on the Old Testament, and had determined that the sacred histories themselves were but a collection of myths and fables. But suddenly, as with the wand of a magician, the ancient eastern world has been reawakened to life by the spade of the explorer and patient skill of the decipherer, and we now find ourselves in the presence of monuments which bear the names or recount the deeds of the heroes of Scripture.'[21]

Both the title of the book and the opening lines of the author signify that more was at stake than simply an ivory-tower exercise in finding a figure in the archaeological record.

Nonetheless, Sayce could not deny that 'His name has not yet been discovered in the cuneiform records'.[22] He did not state the name 'has not been' discovered, but 'has not *yet* been discovered'. He had genuine reason to believe that based on the flood of discoveries so far, it was possible that on any given day one might witness the emergence of Nimrod's name in the cuneiform record.[23] His next sentence further illuminates the context: 'Some Assyrian scholars have wished to identify him with Gisdhubar ...' but such an equation was not valid.[24] The expression of the 'wish' goes to the heart of the scholarship of the time. Sayce's consolation was that 'If, however, little light has been thrown by modern research on the person of Nimrod, this is by no means the case as regards Abraham'.[25] Sayce meant archaeology had demonstrated the link between the biblical patriarch and secular history through the story of Genesis 14.

The work of Theophilus G. Pinches had been particularly instrumental in demonstrating the putative archaeological confirmation of the kings of the east in Gen. 14. Sayce's interest in the battle between Abraham and the four kings in Gen. 14 may even have exceeded his interest in Nimrod. Even ignoring his articles on the figure of Jerusalem priest-king Melchizedek in that chapter, Sayce wrote about Chedorlaomer on numerous occasions (see Additional Readings: Gen. 14).

---

21 A. H. Sayce, *Fresh Light from Ancient Monuments: A Sketch of the Most Striking Confirmations of the Bible, from Recent Discoveries in Egypt, Palestine, Assyria, Babylonia, Asia Minor* (London: Religious Tract Society, 1883), 3.

22 A. H. Sayce, *Fresh Light from Ancient Monuments*, 51. See also, A. H. Sayce, *The First Book of Moses Called Genesis* (London: J. M. Dent, 1901), 150.

23 William Rainey Harper also uses the word 'yet' and suggests that Nimrod had two names, a biblical one and a Babylonian one (William Rainey Harper, 'Notices of Babylon in Genesis X, 8–10', *The Old Testament Student* 5 1885: 35–36, here 36.

24 Sayce, *Fresh Light from Ancient Monuments*, 51.

25 Sayce, *Fresh Light from Ancient Monuments*, 52–53.

Sayce continued to seek Nimrod in the archaeological record and sought to resolve his identity on scientific grounds. First he declared the attempt to equate the pronunciation of the hero's name in the great Chaldean epic with Nimrod had to be abandoned as unworkable. The geographical details rather than history or ethnology were the key to Nimrod's introduction into the narrative.[26] Sayce seemed fascinated by the manner in which the Nimrod interpolation disrupted the three-part geographical schema created via the sons of Noah.[27] He stated that the 'continuity of the [geographic] chart is broken by the episode of Nimrod' and that the 'episode clearly is an insertion'.[28]

Given the insertion and Nimrod not being Gilgamesh, certain specific questions then were raised about Nimrod.

1. What was his background? – For Sayce, Nimrod was an ethnic Kassite and not a Cushite, a Mesopotamian and not an Ethiopian.[29]

2. When did the Hebrews learn of Nimrod, the Kassite? – Sayce favored the Amarna period in the 14th century BCE when people in the land of Canaan knew cuneiform script and Mesopotamian stories. At one point, Sayce dated the composition of the Gilgamesh Epic to the time of Hammurabi (now dated to the 18th century BCE but then dated to the 3rd millennium BCE) whom he identified as a contemporary of Chedorlaomer from Genesis 14.[30] But Sayce attributed the mention of the Philistines in The Table of Nations (Gen. 10: 14) to the time of Ramses III (12th century BCE) prior to the Hebrew conquest of Canaan. Therefore the Late Bronze Age (today 1550–1200 BCE) should be considered the time of Nimrod as well, long after the Gilgamesh Epic had been written.[31] During the Late Bronze period, Shalmaneser I built Calah and restored Nineveh. His father was a contemporary of the Kassite king of Babylonia, Nazi-Maruddas. Since names were 'greatly abbreviated and transformed in the pronunciation of their Semitic subjects… It does not therefore, seem improbable that in Canaanite Nazi-Maruddas may have become Na-Maruda or Nimrod' in the time of Ramses II (1353–1327 BCE as he was dated then), the Pharaoh of the Oppression.[32]

3. When was this 2nd-millennium figure inserted into the biblical narrative? – Sayce placed the insertion of the Kassite Nimrod into Gen. 10 when Nineveh thrived in Neo-Assyrian times during the 1st millennium BCE, probably by the same author in Jerusalem in Hezekiah's reign after the Assyrian destruction of Israel. The inserter was the same person who was re-editing the old texts from the royal library.[33] Sayce's position here is at variance with his own previously-expressed idea that the material might have been inserted by the original author of the biblical text himself and not inserted by the final editor.[34]

---

26 A. H. Sayce, *The Races of the Old Testament* (London: Religious Tract Society, 1891), 66–67.

27 A. H. Sayce, *The 'Higher Criticism'*, 148–149.

28 A. H. Sayce, 'Archaeological commentary on Genesis', *ET* 8 1896: 83. Sayce did not refer to the Merneptah Stele discovered in 1896 prior to the publication of this article but not necessarily before its writing and submission.

29 Sayce, *The 'Higher Criticism'*, 149, 171; Sayce, 'The tenth chapter of Genesis', *JBL* 44 1925: 193–202, here 202.

30 A. H. Sayce, 'Archaeological commentary on Genesis', *ET* 7 1896: 264–267, 366–268, and 461–465, here 264, 366, and 462. These same-named articles were part of a series of articles on the first chapters of Genesis.

31 Sayce, 'Archaeological commentary on Genesis', *ET* 8, 82.

32 Sayce, 'Archaeological commentary on Genesis', *ET* 8, 180–182, here 180.

33 Sayce, 'The tenth chapter of Genesis', 202.

34 Sayce, *The 'Higher Criticism'*, 172.

4.   Who is responsible for the presence of Babylonian elements in Genesis? – Sayce characterized Nimrod as one of the Babylonian elements in the Book of Genesis.[35] Eden, the Flood, and Chedorlaomer's campaign also formed part of the Babylonian stratum 'directly dependent on the cuneiform records of the Chaldaean scribes'.[36] He also might have added from the Eden story the insertions of the rivers with the Tigris and Euphrates in Gen. 2: 10–14.[37]

As a result from these observations, Sayce concluded that archaeology had disproved 'higher criticism': 'Nimrod is no myth, but a historical personage, and the historical character of Chedorlaomer's campaign has been amply vindicated',[38] a reminder that Nimrod should not be analyzed in isolation from other Mesopotamian elements in the Bible, especially the story of Gen. 14.

As for the writing of the texts, Sayce suggested a modification of the Wellhausen documentary hypothesis (JEDP) to include 'Babylonian, Canaanite, and other similar elements. The author of the fourteenth chapter must be the same author of the history of the Fall or of the rise of the power of Nimrod'.[39] This insight proves critical in resolving the question of 'Who is Nimrod?' just as it does for other biblical questions like 'Where is Eden?' and 'Who are the sons of God?' Sayce's observations raise the intriguing possibility of a dialogue within the Israelite community among people of different cultural backgrounds. Just as the American Founding Fathers drew on the legacy, examples, and history of differing nations and cultures (England, France, and biblical Israel), so individual writers in ancient Israel might have drawn on Canaanite, Mesopotamian, and older Israelite traditions.

Sayce like the rabbis recognized a critical component to the writing of the Hebrew Bible. He has identified different voices within the narrative. Sayce views these voices as legacies from the past, perhaps as recent as the 14th century BCE. In accordance with the exegetical paradigm of his time, he was seeking an historical context in the past of the writer. In this study, the question is who are the people in the present who look to Canaan, Babylonia, or elsewhere (Egypt, Israel) for inspiration. The question to be addressed in this study is not the one Sayce and Smith so strenuously pursued. Rather it is what did the character of Nimrod mean in the time of Solomon?

Since Sayce and his contemporaries, the search for historical Nimrod has continued. Scholars have proposed a variety of candidates of different ethnicities and time periods. Fritz Hommel repeatedly asserted that Gilgamesh was to be equated with Nimrod.[40] According to Gunkel, 'He has, not without reason, been identified with the national hero Gilgamesh…'[41] T. G. Pinches writing for a highly-regarded Bible dictionary of the times identified him as

---

35 Sayce, *The 'Higher Criticism'*, 152.

36 Sayce, *The 'Higher Criticism'*, 153.

37 See Peter Feinman, 'Where's Eden?' in JoAnn Scurlock and Richard H. Beal, eds, *Creation and Chaos: A Reconsideration of Hermann Gunkel's Chaos Kampf Hypothesis* (Winona Lake: Eisenbrauns, 2013), 172–189.

38 Sayce, *The 'Higher Criticism'*, 171.

39 Sayce, *The 'Higher Criticism'*, 171–172.

40 Fritz Hommel, 'The Babylonian Gish-du-barra to be identified with biblical Nimrod', *PSBA* 8 1886: 119–120; Fritz Hommel, 'Gish-Dubarra, Gilbil-Gamish, Nimrod', *PSBA* 15 1893: 291–300; Fritz Hommel, 'A supplementary note to Gibil-Gamish', *PSBA* 16 1893: 13–15.

41 Hermann Gunkel, *Creation and Chaos in the Primeval Era and the Eschaton* (Grand Rapids: William B. Eerdmans, 2006), 96; see also Hermann Gunkel, *Genesis* (Macon, GA: Mercer University Press, 1997), 90.

Gilgamesh.[42] Leading German and American Assyriologist Paul Haupt from his inaugural address at Göttingen in 1880 through American Oriental Society conferences in the 20th century referred to *The Gilgamesh Epic* as 'the babylonian Nimrod Epic'.[43] Leading American Assyriologist Morris Jastrow, Jr of the University of Pennsylvania denied Gilgamesh was Nimrod, but instead claimed Gilgamesh 'evidently influenced' the description of Nimrod 'who is viewed as the type of Babylonian power and of the extension of Babylonian culture to the north'.[44] Indeed who else could have been the basis for Nimrod?

As other figures from Mesopotamian history emerged from archaeological excavations, so too the candidates for Nimrod expanded. After Gilgamesh (2600 BCE), the next most prominent person discovered was Sargon the Great (2334–2279 BCE). He was the Akkadian hero who had created an empire encompassing Sumer, Akkad, and other parts of the ancient Near East, a figure who became legendary as had historical Gilgamesh. Yigal Levin suggested that Nimrod combined Sargon the Great and his grandson Naram-Sin (2254–2218 BCE) from the Sargonid Dynasty. C. van Gelderen preferred the descendant and almost equally famous Naram-Sin to the dynastic founder. So perhaps instead of being Sumerian, Nimrod was Akkadian and Semitic.[45]

The names kept coming. A third figure who has received attention is Tukulti-Ninurta (1243–1207 BCE), the great Middle Assyrian leader who captured Babylon. He was the first Assyrian king to invoke the deity in his throne-name.[46] Speiser championed this interpretation in his articles and Genesis commentary.[47] Such an identification also raised the issue of the link between Nimrod and Ninurta, the Mesopotamian war deity, somewhat eclipsed by Marduk when Nebuchadnezzar I (1126–1105 BCE) of Babylon became the dominant figure in Mesopotamia. He was a warrior deity who defeated the monster forces of chaos. His victorious royal human counterpart triumphantly returned to the city and the temple the statue of Marduk that the Elamites previously had captured. In a footnote,

---

42 T. G. Pinches, 'Nimrod', in James Hastings, ed., *A Dictionary of the Bible* (New York: Charles Scribner's Sons, 1903), III: 552–553.

43 Paul Haupt, 'The Cuneiform account of the Deluge', *OTS* 7/3 1883: 77–85; Paul Haupt, 'The beginning of the Babylonian Nimrod Epic', *JAOS* 22 1901: 7–12; Paul Haupt, 'The introductory lines of the Cuneiform account of the Deluge', *JAOS* 25 1904: 68–75. He also reported that The Johns Hopkins Press had plaster casts for sale of 'the eleventh tablet of the Babylonian Nimrod Epic' (Paul Haupt, 'On a modern reproduction of the eleventh tablet of the Babylonian Nimrod Epic and a new fragment of the Chaldean account of the Deluge', *JAOS* 16 1896: ix–xii.

44 Morris Jastrow, Jr, *The Religion of Babylonia and Assyria* (New York: Ginn & Co., 1898), II: 515.

45 C. van Gelderen, 'Who was Nimrod?', *The Expositor* 8 1914: 274–282; Yigal Levin, 'Nimrod the Mighty, King of Kish, King of Sumer and Akkad', *VT* 52 2002: 350–366. For Sargon, Naram-Sin, and the Akkadians see, Benjamin Foster, 'Akkadians', in *OEANE*, 49–54; Sabina Franke, 'Kings of Akkad: Sargon and Naram-Sin', in *CANE*, 831–841.

46 William Hallo, book review of *The Return of Ninurta to Nippur* by Jerrold Cooper, *JAOS* 101 1981: 253–257, here 254. For Tukulti-Ninurta see also Peter Machinist, 'Literature as politics: the Tukulti-Ninurta Epic and the Bible', *CBQ* 38: 455–482; W. G. Lambert, 'The enigma of Tulki-Ninurta I', in Grant Frame, ed., *From the Upper Sea to the Lower Sea: Studies on the History of Assyria and Babylonia in Honour A. K. Grayson* (Leiden: Nederlands Instituut voor het Nabije Oosten, 2004), 197–202.

47 He claimed Tukulti-Ninurta became Ninos in classical sources (Speiser, *Genesis*, 72–73; E. A. Speiser, 'In search of Nimrod', 45–52.

W. G. Lambert stated, 'The present writer prefers the more usual opinion that the Sumero-Babylonian war god Ninurta is meant' than Tukulti-Ninurta.[48] Christoph Uehlinger concurred based on circumstantial evidence with what he thought was the reasonable view of the majority.[49] Aron Pinker raised the intriguing idea that MRDK became NMRD when the ending *kaf* became the first letter and then became a *nun* which it resembled.[50]

In summary, one perceives from these varied attempts to identify Nimrod with an historical figure, no consensus. Over the course of more than a century of scholarship, he has been associated with the Sumerian Gilgamesh, the Akkadians Sargon the Great and Naram-Sin, the Assyrian Tukulti-Ninurta, and the god Ninurta along with Marduk, Nuzi-marutash, Orion, Pharaoh Amenhotep III and Ninos.[51] Interestingly for a ruler of Babel in the chapter before the story of the Tower of Babel, he has not been linked specifically to a Babylonian ruler such as Amorite Hammurabi or to Nebuchadnezzar I of Isin. Perhaps the former was omitted because of the extensive effort in the late 19th century and early 20th century to link Hammurabi to Amraphel as one of the kings of the east in Genesis 14;[52] perhaps the latter was omitted because when this search began, little was known about Nebuchadnezzar I who emerged later on in the process of historical discoveries.

Part of the fascination in observing this effort with a century of hindsight is documenting the heroic efforts of these learned people writing dignified articles laboring to make sense of it all as a stream of new discoveries constantly changed the archaeological cosmos. The presumption of a connection obligated them to create order from chaos involving a moving target, a difficult objective to fulfill in the best of circumstances. The effort was rendered more complicated by the *a priori* conviction that Nimrod was an historical figure who therefore had to exist in the archaeological record. In viewing the wide range of choices covering the major peoples of 3rd and 2nd millennium BCE Mesopotamia, perhaps the answer is in the old saying about not being able to see the forest for the trees. Maybe as with the story of the seven blind people and the elephant, all the guesses touch one part of the truth but to see the overall picture all the pieces need to be assembled (see Part II).

---

48 W. G. Lambert, 'The Babylonian background of Genesis', *JTS* 16 1965: 287–300, here 298–299 n.2.

49 Christoph Uehlinger 'Nimrod', in *DDD*, 627–630, here 627.

50 Aron Pinker, 'Nimrod found?' *JBQ* 26 1998: 237–245. Porter notes 'The importance of the One God: Ninurta' and 'The importance of the One God: Marduk' (Barbara N. Porter, 'The anxiety of multiplicity: concepts of divinity as one and many in Ancient Assyria', in Barbara N. Porter, ed., *One God or Many? Concepts of Divinity in the Ancient World* (Chebeague Island, ME: Transactions of the Casco Bay Archaeological Institute, 2000), 211–271, here 240–254.

51 Westermann, *Genesis 1–11*, 515.

52 George Barton summed up the failed effort to equate Hammurabi and Amraphel: 'Another point in which archaeology confirms [higher] criticism is the instance of the 14th chapter of Genesis. In spite of all that has been written to the contrary, the kings who are said to have fought with Abraham, have not been brought to light by archaeology in a way to confirm that chapter' ('Higher archaeology and the verdict of criticism', *JBL* 32 1913: 244–260, here 254).

The textual search for Nimrod

This archaeological search for Nimrod differentiates this story from some of the other son stories. No such comparable investigation has been undertaken to locate Seth, the sons of God, or the sons of Noah. Certainly extensive efforts have been made to find the ark but such a discovery would not substantiate the story of the sons of Noah. The situation is different here. With Nimrod there appeared to be an opportunity to anchor bible chronology to secular time regardless of one's faith or lack of one. These actions provide a backdrop to the literary commentaries which were being written as these archaeological discoveries were being made and debated.

Delitzsch

Delitzsch claims 'the Hamite of the extract, vv. 8–12, is a person of world-wide importance'. Delitzsch expresses awareness of the effort to identify Nimrod with Izdubar but points out that an inscription with the name Nimrod has not been found. He is, however, curious about the possible connection with the Babylonian Marad (meaning the god Marduk). The characterization of Nimrod as a hunter distinctly contrasts him with the proverbial peaceful shepherd life. That makes Nimrod a prototype for the Babylonian and Assyrian kings. It is this hunter without equal who becomes the founder of the first state. So Nimrod does not represent simply a people (as the sons of Noah are sometimes considered to be) 'but a *great* empire'.[53] He does not mention David as a hunter/shepherd/founding king as Nimrod's counterpart.

Dillmann

Dillmann's first observation is that the subject is a (legendary) personage and not a person. His second observation is that any identification with Izdubar is pure conjecture and with Marduk is far-fetched. Instead he surmises that to the Hebrews, Nimrod personified the king and people of the earliest founded empire, an empire to be associated with the Kassites of Mesopotamia and not the Kushites of Africa. Nonetheless, he is unable to determine if the Israelites first knew Nimrod in his hunter persona or as the founder of a state.[54]

As a ruler, Dillmann states Nimrod 'founded a kingdom by power and violence' and should be considered a 'despot or tyrant'.[55] There is no indication if this description also applied to Otto von Bismarck and the founding of the German Empire in 1871. Dillmann's observation written in a book published in Berlin that the formation of states was a new movement in history beginning with Nimrod correlates with the events in the world around him. Undoubtedly that is not a coincidence.

---

53 Delitzsch, *New Commentary of Genesis*, 321, 323, 327, quotations from 321 and 327, emphasis original.
54 Dillmann, *Genesis*, 349–351, 353.
55 Dillmann, *Genesis*, 351.

Gunkel

Gunkel detects a two-stage process in the creation of the story. First Nimrod was the hunter with a hunter deity probably being named rather than Yahweh in the original version. Second, there was the Babylonian tradition of a primeval king like Gilgamesh as a likely identification for Nimrod. Gunkel remains puzzled as how the two traditions related to each other and the circumstances in which they would be combined. Perhaps the puzzlement is unavoidable since only meager comments survive from an original narrative tradition.[56]

Skinner

Skinner regards the Nimrod interpolation as an historical document 'of the highest importance'. It provides 'the most systematic record of the political geography of the Hebrews at different stages of their history' and reflects the unity of mankind. Nimrod was an individual human being and not a symbol or representative of a people. He became famous for being the originator of the idea of the military state, based on arbitrary force. One should not equate him with the *gibbor* of Gen. 6: 4 who are mighty men like Nimrod. Skinner concentrates on the idea of violent, tyrannical power.[57]

He acknowledges that the search for the historical Nimrod has proved unsuccessful so far. Nimrod probably lived after the Kassite conquest of Babylonia in the 17th century BCE. Although Nimrod ruled over these various cities he should not be considered the founder of any of them. Skinner links the interpolation of hunting verse 9 into the text as an expression of the true prototype of the Assyrian monarch. He has no explanation for the reference to Yahweh. The odds are he anticipates that additional archaeological discoveries would shed light on this crucial but still obscure person in human history who managed to be included in the story of Israel.[58]

Von Rad

Von Rad treats Nimrod as an individual who already was a remote and legendary figure to the Israelites. Only part of his historical achievements were remembered. The key is that he was 'the first wielder of power on earth, the first ruler of historical significance, the first in the series of those great men who will become determinative for the fate of entire nations'. Since he takes the J Table of Nations quite seriously as the work of a single individual, von Rad has great difficulty trying to fit Nimrod into an historic and geographically valid setting.[59]

Speiser

Speiser considers Nimrod as fully human and therefore rejects any effort to link him to Ninurta. Based on that approach and recognizing the 'obviously authentic' appended

---

56 Gunkel, *Genesis*, 90–91.
57 Skinner, *A Critical and Exegetical Commentary*, 194, 207, quotations from 194.
58 Skinner, *A Critical and Exegetical Commentary*, 192, 208–210.
59 Von Rad, *Genesis*, 146–147, quotation from 146.

detail, he declares the presence of various capital cities as 'clear proof of a sound historical background'. That realization enables Speiser to identify Nimrod as Tukulti-Ninurta I in the 13th century, the first Assyrian conqueror of Babylon. He hails Tukulti-Ninurta as a conqueror and builder who became the subject of an epic extolling his exploits. Speiser lived before the time when enough was known to make a similar claim for Nebuchadnezzar I in the 12th century, closer to the time of the Israelite monarchy. His view suggests a positive image of the figure in the story in contrast to the negative expressions elsewhere.[60]

Westermann

According to Westermann, the Nimrod narrative is self-contained episode that reports the origins of oriental empires. The empire is born, the foundation is established, the empire expands. These actions represent something new and progressive in human history that occurred due to the seizure of power by an individual. Yet that individual is not to be pinned down to an historical figure.[61]

The Jewish Study Bible

Levenson identifies Nimrod as one of the inventors of culture. He is linked with both Noah and the sons of Cain in this regard, an important observation. Levenon's insight raises the possibilities worth additional investigation. It permits various options where one person was responsible for all these stories or that different people were in competition with each in their assertions on where human culture originated (see Part II). Levenson acknowledges the midrash based on the derivation of Nimrod from 'to rebel' but sagely counsels the wisdom of Rabbi Abraham Ibn Ezra, 'Don't look for a reason for every name.'[62]

The New Jerome Biblical Commentary

Clifford similarly observes J's characteristic interest in the founders of culture. He compares Nimrod to Gilgamesh as a hunter but for an historical personage cites Speiser's identification of Tukulti-Ninurta.[63]

The HarperCollins Study Bible

Rosenberg reports on the various efforts to identify Nimrod in the historical and mythical record. He does compare the 'power and fearsomeness' of Nimrod's rule to that of Gilgamesh.[64] Part of the fascination with this portrayal is that the text itself simply touts Nimrod prowess as a hunter and warrior but makes no mention of how he rules over the

---

60 Speiser, *Genesis*, 72.
61 Westermann, *Genesis 1–11*, 515.
62 Levenson, 'Genesis', 28.
63 Clifford and Murphy, 'Genesis', 17.
64 Rosenberg, 'Genesis', 17.

people in his kingdom. Despite the consistent negative portrayal, it is just as easy to make the case that the author who created this story from scratch admired the figure.

Conclusion

This review of Nimrod, son of Cush, exegesis over the millennia reveals significant commonalities, some differences in interpretations, and open questions. In addition to the standard literary and textual considerations there are archaeological ones as well. These observations may be summarized as follows.

1. The earlier commentators such as Josephus and the rabbis were storytellers in their own right. They sought to smooth the way by filling in gaps through expository creations. They anticipated the questions an audience might raise reading or hearing the story within the existing canonized narrative. They did not view Nimrod in isolation but connected him to the subsequent stories of the Tower of Babel and Abram. However, they do not necessarily see the invasion by the kings of east in Gen. 14 as related to Abram's departure from the east in Gen. 12.
2. Modern scholars are divided on the presence of verse 9 hunting proverb as an insertion or not.
3. Modern scholars debate whether the founding of the state was a good thing or not. They do not compare it to the debate Israel had over the founding of a monarchy and state.
4. Modern scholars are less likely to attribute the story to the dawn of human civilization or to a mythical folktale. They are quite willing to entertain the notion of a secular origin by a pagan people which possibly can be situated in some specific historical context in the 3rd or 2nd millennium BCE.
5. Modern scholars express some awareness of the possibility that Nimrod may be a symbolic or metaphorical figure for the founding of a state, possibly derived from an historical personage.

Interestingly, we now have a second occasion for the use of the name of Yahweh prior to Moses at the burning bush. In the first instance, people in the time of Seth called his name; in the second instance the king is linked to Yahweh and people call his name as well as that of the Lord. One may glean from these episodes that the worship of Yahweh and the connection between Yahweh and the king were battlegrounds of importance in the time of Solomon. One faction emphasizes the calling or worship such as at a temple built by Solomon; the other plays to the glory of the king himself who is heralded as a mighty man who founds a kingdom suggesting David more than Solomon. Contrary to the depictions by Josephus and the rabbis, this author's Nimrod is a giant in history to be respected for his achievements.

The scholarship about Nimrod did not occur in a vacuum. As with the negative attitude of the scholars towards nomads, they bring their biases to the story of Nimrod. He routinely is referred to negatively. He routinely is regarded as a despot. He routinely is presumed to have oppressed his people. Yet nowhere in the biblical text is there even a hint of any nefarious deed perpetrated by this king. As an eastern or oriental king, it simply is taken for granted that he is despicable. This perception, perhaps originating with the clash between the ancient Greeks and the Persians, has distorted the understanding of biblical Nimrod. After all, it was the Persian Cyrus the Great who permitted the exiled Judeans to return home.

In the story of Esther, Haman is the villain, not the Persian king. Instead of denigrating Nimrod, one should be open to the possibility that an author exalted the Mesopotamian ideal king who ruled like a god on earth knowing good from evil. The 'mighty hunter before Yahweh' who ruled the world could be considered an admirable figure, even a role model.

The geographic scope of the Nimrod story with four cities extends far beyond simply the land of Canaan. This generates the question of who would seek to situate Israel within a larger world context, when, and why. It further raises the question of the possible connection to other such geographically expansive expressions such as the four rivers of the garden (Gen. 2) and four kings of the east against Abram (Gen. 14). Perhaps, Yahweh is not simply a wilderness deity who brought the people Israel out of the land of Egypt or who established at Zion his kingdom in the land Canaan. Perhaps he was a deity of all the world for all time and Israel could learn from the example of Mesopotamia. Or at least so claimed one author of biblical stories. Then again, there was the story of the Tower of Babel which suggested another author who thought otherwise.

Chapter 7

WHO ARE THE SONS OF MEN BUILDING THE TOWER OF BABEL?

Genesis 11: 1: *Now the whole earth had one language and few words.* ² *And as men migrated from the east, they found a plain in the land of Shinar and settled there.* ³ *And they said to one another, 'Come, let us make bricks, and burn them thoroughly'. And they had brick for stone, and bitumen for mortar.* ⁴ *Then they said, 'Come, let us build ourselves a city, and a tower with its top in the heavens, and let us make a name for ourselves, lest we be scattered abroad upon the face of the whole earth'.* ⁵ *And Yahweh came down to see the city and the tower, which the sons of men had built.* ⁶ *And Yahweh said, 'Behold, they are one people, and they have all one language; and this is only the beginning of what they will do; and nothing that they propose to do will now be impossible for them.* ⁷ *Come, let us go down, and there confuse their language, that they may not understand one another's speech'.* ⁸ *So Yahweh scattered them abroad from there over the face of all the earth, and they left off building the city.* ⁹ *Therefore its name was called Babel, because there Yahweh confused the language of all the earth; and from there Yahweh scattered them abroad over the face of all the earth.*

The story of the Tower of Babel is another one of the biblical narratives that has crossed over into popular culture. Even if the details are not clearly remembered the concept of a 'babel', of the noise of people speaking without understanding each other, is one which resonates even in non-religious settings. Indeed, even people who speak the same language are expert at speaking past each other without listening to or understanding the words of the other. The Tower of Babel is a story that could stand on its own independent of the biblical narrative and yet be readily understood by all who heard its words or saw the images depicting its message. One does not need the biblical narrative to grasp its message. With the Tower, a picture truly is worth a thousand words.

Standard questions raised by commentators throughout the ages have included such issues as:

1. Can the Tower of Babel be connected with a tower which can be archaeologically identified?
2. How does the scattering of the people in this story relate to the scattering meticulously detailed in the Table of Nations in the preceding story?
3. What is the relationship between the city building by the sons of Cain and the city building here by the sons of men?
4. Did the author and audience of the story have to have seen a tower to understand the story?
5. Who are the 'us' the author has Yahweh mention?

In addition to these traditional questions regarding the text, one may add:

What political message was being delivered through the communication of this story? Or how did it help one political faction in the time of Solomon? It is difficult to imagine that this author supported the building of the temple. It is fascinating to observe that in a religion where the destruction of the Jerusalem temple first by the Babylonians in 587 BCE and then by the Romans in 70 CE, there also are the stories of Samson (Judg. 16) and the Tower of Babel. Undoubtedly the debate whether or not to build a temple after centuries of not having one must have been as robust as the one whether to have a king or not. The longstanding effort to connect Nimrod and the Tower of Babel further complicates the attempt to discern the original meaning of the text.

The tracking of the attempts by exegetes to understand this passage will begin in ancient times with Josephus, proceed to the rabbis, and continue with modern scholarship from the end of the 19th century to the canonical commentaries of the 20th.

Josephus

Before examining the writings of Josephus, one should keep in mind that he lived in a time that knew the building projects of both Caesars and Herod and of the destruction of the temple built by the latter and then destroyed by a Roman general who became emperor. While this is not a study of the writings of Josephus in his context, it is a reminder that knowing the world of writer is essential for understanding that person's writings. People do not write 'timeless', they write stories that may become timeless and which may be removed from their original context and meaning.

> **Ant 1: 113** *Now it was Nimrod who excited them to such an affront and contempt of God. He was the grandson of Ham, the son of Noah – a bold man, and of great strength of hand. He persuaded them not to ascribe to God, as if it was through his means they were happy, but to believe that it was their own courage which procured that happiness.* [114] *He also gradually changed the government into tyranny, seeing no other way of turning men from the fear of God, but to bring them into a constant dependence on his power. He also said he would be revenged on God, if he should have a mind to drown the world again; for that he would build a tower too high for the waters to be able to reach! and that he would avenge himself on God for killing their forefathers!*

As part of the condemnation of Nimrod, Josephus mentions that he initiated the building of a tower with the specific purpose of negating the power of God to destroy humanity again through a flood. Josephus wrote these words while the scattered Jewish community was debating what to do next following the destruction of their temple. Part of that debate included whether or not the temple should be rebuilt. Or should it be replaced and, if so, by whom or what? What did God want?

Regardless of the actual intentions of Josephus, it is reasonable to conclude that his audience might infer a message in the present. One notes that Josephus proceeded to castigate those who had followed the direction of Nimrod in this evil quest.

> **Ant 1: 115** *Now the multitude were very ready to follow the determination of Nimrod, and to esteem it a piece of cowardice to submit to God; and they built a tower, neither sparing any pains, nor being in any degree negligent about the work; and by reason of the multitude of hands employed in it, it grew very high, sooner than anyone could expect;* [116] *but the thickness of it was so great, and it was so strongly built, that thereby its great height seemed, upon the view, to be less than it really was. It was built of burnt brick, cemented together with mortar, made of bitumen, that it*

might not be liable to admit water. When God saw that they acted so madly, he did not resolve to destroy them utterly, since they were not grown wiser by the destruction of the former sinners; [117] *but he caused a tumult among them, by producing in them various languages, and causing that, through the multitude of those languages, they should not be able to understand one another. The place wherein they built the tower is now called Babylon; because of the confusion of that language which they readily understood before; for the Hebrews mean by the word Babel, Confusion.*

The people who assisted Nimrod in this act of defiance do not fare much better than the ruler himself in this version. They have learned nothing from the experience of the Flood and the destruction of those sinners. They act madly, and follow the dictates of the human ruler and not the Lord. The result of this disobedience was another destruction followed by a dispersal of the sinners, the world's first diaspora. Again, one may reasonably speculate how the telling of this story could be interpreted politically as a message about what has transpired in the present of the audience.

Ant 1:118 *The Sibyl also makes mention of this tower, and of the confusion of the language, when she says thus:– 'When all men were of one language, some of them built a high tower, as if they would thereby ascend up to heaven; but the gods sent storms of wind and overthrew the tower, and gave everyone a peculiar language; and for this reason it was that the city was called Babylon'.* [119] *But as to the plan of Shinar, in the country of Babylonia, Hestiaeus mentions it, when he says thus:– 'Such of the priests as were saved, took the sacred vessels of Jupiter, (Enyalius,) or conqueror and came to Shinar of Babylonia'.* [120] *After this they were dispersed abroad, on account of their languages, and went out by colonies everywhere; and each colony took possession of that land which they came to, and to which God led them; so that the whole continent was filled with them, both the inland and the maritime countries. There were some also who crossed over the sea in ships, and inhabited the islands;*

In these verses Josephus documents his claims by drawing on previous and non-biblical writings on the same topic. Essentially he is substantiating his text through footnotes. Other writers had expressed similar views to his. The common refrain has been that the building of the tower itself was an affront to Yahweh since it was intended to reach the heavens. The implication is that the mere mortals would climb the tower like a ladder and storm the heavens to replace the rule of the divine with the rule of the human.

Other Jewish writings reflect the same attitudes.

They spoke sharp words … against the Lord our God… It does not rest with Him alone to choose the upper for Himself and allot to us the nether spheres. Come, then, let us build a tower, at the top of which we will set an idol with a sword in hand, so appearing to wage war with Him (Genesis Rabbah 38: 6)

For they had emigrated from the land of Ararat [following the flood] toward the east, to Shinar, and … they built the city and tower saying, 'Let us ascend on it into heaven'. (Jubilees 10: 19)

This desire to ascend to the heavens was perceived to be a driving force behind the construction of the tower.

They were all of one language and they wanted to go up to starry heaven (Sibyline Oracles 3: 99–100)

Once these humans had succeed in building this structure and ascended to the heavens, the natural question would be, 'What would they do when they were there?' The proposed answers did not reflect well on the nature of humanity.

> *And they had taken an augur, and sought to pierce the heaven, saying, 'Let us see whether the heaven is made of clay, or of brass, or of iron.'* (3 Baruch 3: 7)

Perhaps through their ignorance these builders of the tower would cause to be a new flood.

> *They said: let us build a tower and climb to the firmament and strike it with hatchets until its waters flow forth.* (b. Sanhedrin 109a)

The last time waters had flowed forth from the firmament had not proved so beneficial for humanity and here they were potentially seeking to replicate that deluge.[1]

War was the common refrain in the attempt to understand the intent of the builders.

> *He who is zealous for earthly and corruptible things always fights against and war on heavenly things and praiseworthy and wonderful natures, and builds walls and towers on earth against heaven.*
>
> Philo, *Questions and Answers in Genesis* 2: 82

> *These are the ones who built the tower of the war against God and the Lord removed them.* (3 Baruch [Greek] 2: 7)

> *And they said: Come, let us build ourselves a city, and a tower whose top will reach the heavens, and let us make for ourselves at its top an idol and we will put a sword in its hand, and make war against Him.* (Targum Neophyti Gen. 11: 4[2])

These citations leave no doubt that the tower was viewed in opposition to God and its builders were considered combatants against the Lord.

A final consideration is that Nimrod the leader of the rebellion against the Lord in the building of the tower also is remembered as a giant. This is due to the references to him as a mighty hunter and man. Just as 'Nephilim' has been translated as 'giants' in the LXX (see Chapter 4), so too Nimrod became a giant in the LXX version:

> **Genesis 10: 8** *And Cush begot Nimrod: he began to be a giant upon the earth.* [9] *He was a giant hunter before the Lord God; therefore they say, As Nimrod the giant hunter before the Lord.*

Thus it became common to perceive a group of giants banding together to erect the tower.

> *The Assyrian city of Babylon was first founded by those who escaped the flood. They were giants, and the built the tower well known in history. When the tower was destroyed by God's power, these giants were scattered over the whole earth.*
>
> Pseudo-Eupolemus cited in Eusebius, *Praeparatio* 9: 17: 2–3[3]

---

1   These fragmentary examples from hoary antiquity were collected by James Kugel; see James L. Kugel, *How to Read the Bible: A Guide to Scripture Then and Now* (New York: Free Press, 2007), 83–84; Kugel, *The Bible as It Was*, 124.

2   These fragmentary examples from hoary antiquity also were collected by Kugel, *The Bible as It Was*, 124.

3   Quoted in Kugel, *The Bible as It Was*, 128.

In Greco-Roman times there was a confusion of Assyria and Babylon. However, there is still the issue of how giants escaped the Flood even with their great height since the Flood story as it exists does not permit any such exemption, On the other hand, this escaping is biblically supported. The word 'Nephilim', the beings in the story of the sons of God who apparently survived the flood and were present in the land of Canaan (Num. 13: 33), also is translated as 'giants' in the LXX version of that verse. The extraction of this pericope from its context proves more complicated than one might expect after reading the story alone.

Rabbis

Rabbinic traditions partook of the same understanding as Josephus. The rabbis sought to bring order to the chronology of the Bible and substance to the ellipse between Gen. 10: 8–12 and Gen. 12 by designating Nimrod as the builder of the Tower of Babel in the time of Abraham (see Chapter 6). Once Nimrod had become and championed the building of the tower, then the work began. Six hundred thousand men (Sefer ha-Yashar 12a) were engaged for 43 years (Book of Jubilees x) in building the Tower. The Tower had reached such a height that it took a whole year to hoist up necessary building material to the top. No one took notice if a man should fall to his death. The true tragedy occurred when something of value fell: a fallen brick meant one year would transpire before its replacement could reach the summit. They behaved heartlessly toward the weak and sick who could not assist in the grand enterprise. Even pregnant women were obligated to power through their travail. She was to tie the new-born round her body with a sheet and continue to mold the bricks needed to complete the Nimrod-appointed task.

Initially, God watched the humans building ever higher and higher, drawing nearer and nearer to the heavenly abode. He hoped the people had learned the lessons of the past and would desist from yet another sinful undertaking. Still they pressed on and his faith was for naught. The punishments the Lord levied against the humans went beyond those recounted in the biblical narrative. Those men who had called for ascending to the heavens to place their idols there turned into apes, evil spirits, demons, and ghosts walking by night. Those men who were to lead the assault to wrest control of the heavens from God were instead forced into combat with each other. Those who were to fight in heaven itself once men had gained access instead were scattered throughout the world. The fate of the tower itself varied. Perhaps it was blown down by the winds. Perhaps one-third of the tower was consumed by fire, one-third sank into the earth, and one-third remained standing. The fact that a remnant was thought to still stand suggests that maybe rabbis in Mesopotamia had glimpsed the once mighty ziggurats which populated the land, a physical witness to the power of the Almighty.[4]

---

4   For the supplemental stories to the biblical accounts see, Goldin, *The Book of Legends*, I: 61–63; Ginzberg, *The Legends of the Jews*, I: 179–181; Morris Jastrow, Jr, Ira Maurice Price, Marcus Jastrow, Louis Ginzberg and Duncan B. McDonald, 'Tower of Babel', in Joseph Jacobs, ed., *The Jewish Encyclopedia* (New York: Funk & Wagnalls, 1906), 395–398.

The archaeological search for the Tower of Babel

As with the Nimrod, the story of the Tower of Babel provided an archaeological opportunity. In this case, the evidence was in abundance and one did not need to look far to find Babel-like structures with Babel-like aims in the land of Mesopotamia.

> *At the time my lord Marduk told me [Nabopolassar] in regard to Etemenanki, the ziggurat of Babylon, which before my day was (already) very weak and badly buckled, to ground its bottom on the breast of the netherworld, to make its top vie with the heavens ... I had them shape mud bricks without number and mould baked bricks like countless raindrops. I had the river Arahtu bear asphalt and bitumen like a mighty flood.*[5]

Ziggurats were standard throughout Mesopotamia. Archaeologists have discovered over 30 of them stretching across the millennia and the land.[6] The function was to provide a connection between heaven and earth. Since no text delineates its exact meaning, John Walton proposes the following:

> 'The ziggurat was a structure that was built to support the stairway (*simmiltu*) which was believed to be used by the gods to travel from one realm to the other. It was solely for the convenience of the gods and was maintained in order to provide the deity with the amenities that would refresh him along the way... The stairway led at the top to the gate of the gods, the entrance to the divine abode.'[7]

Walton's definition and the actual practices of the Mesopotamians suggest the structure was built in support of the deity, that it was something the deity wanted to occur, and that kings and the people were right to take pride in its construction. Such divine revelation and consent was an essential component of the standard Mesopotamian building account.[8] Apparently it was conceptually impossible for them to imagine a world where the gods would not want a ziggurat to be built. One notes that there was no specific mention of a tower in the city of Enoch so perhaps it was possible for a non-Mesopotamian deity, the wilderness god Yahweh, not to need a tower. In any event, in the biblical account the proposed structure is not sanctioned by Yahweh it is not referred to as a temple either.

As in the biblical account of the Tower of Babel, bricks were the essential item in Mesopotamia for the construction of the ziggurats. Brick-making was not something lightly undertaken in the ancient Near East. When it did occur there was sure to be a king or deity around. Egypt was the land of building in stone like the pyramids, Canaan was the

---

5   Quotation from Babylonian king Nabopolassar's inscription from the 8th century BCE in A. R. George, 'The Tower of Babel: archaeology, history and cuneiform texts', *AFO* 51 2005–2006: 75–95, here 83–84.

6   John H. Walton, 'The Mesopotamian background of the Tower of Babel account and its implications', *BBR* 5 1995: 155–175, here 156. For a history of the famous Etememanki ziggurat at Babylon see George, 'The Tower of Babel', 75–95.

7   Walton, 'The Mesopotamian background', 162. 'Gate of Gods' became the name of city Babylon (see I. J. Gelb, 'The name of Babylon', in Richard S. Hess and David Toshio Tsumura, ed., *I Studied Inscriptions from Before the Flood: Ancient Near Eastern, Literary, and Linguistic Approaches to Genesis 1–11* (SBTS 4; Winona Lake: Eisenbrauns, 1994), 266–269, reprinted from *JIAS* 1 1955: 1–4.

8   Andrew Giorgetti, 'The "mock building account" of Genesis 11: 1–9: polemic against Mesopotamian royal ideology', *VT* 64 2014: 1–20, here 10.

land of fieldstones which seemed to mushroom overnight in the fields and made farming a challenge. Mesopotamia was the land of brick-making for ziggurats, the temples that reach the heavens.

Eridu Genesis

> May they come and build cities and cult places,
> that I may cool myself in their shade;
> may they lay the bricks for the cult cities in pure spots ...
> He *the king* [regularly] performed to perfection
> the August divine services and offices,
> laid [the bricks] of those cities ...[9]

Epic of Atra-hasis

In this epic, humans are created for the specific purpose to do the work the lesser gods no longer want to do. These gods complain about their burdens but the humans multiply exceedingly without complaining while performing these tasks ... unless one chooses to define their noise as a sign of rebellion. Bricks are not specifically mentioned in the building efforts but one is mentioned several times in the birthing process of humans by Mami, Mistress-of-all-the Gods. The humans are fashioned from clay and the blood of a slaughtered god and are themselves a form of a brick.[10]

Enuma Elish

The victorious Marduk celebrates his victory by building a house, a temple to signify his sovereignty. The description of the building process by the lesser gods includes:

> Construct Babylon, whose building you have requested,
> let its brick work be fashioned...
> The Annunaki applied the implement;
> for one whole year they molded bricks.
> When the second year arrived,
> they raised high the head of Esagila equaling Apsu

VI 60–62[11]

The *Enuma Elish* composition from the time of Nebuchadnezzar I (12th century BCE) easily could have been known in 10th century Israel.[12] 'Thus even in Palestine there was legendary knowledge of its [Babylon's] gigantic cultural achievements [in the 2nd millennium BCE], especially of the mighty stepped towers in which the united civilized will of this strong

---

9   See the myth of *Eridu Genesis* in Bill T. Arnold and Bryan E. Beyer, eds., *Readings from the Ancient Near East: Primary Sources for Old Testament Study* (Grand Rapids MN; Baker Academic, 2002), 13.

10   See the myth of *Atrahasis* in Arnold and Beyer, *Readings from the Ancient Near East*, 24–25.

11   See the myth of *Enuma Elish* in Arnold and Beyer, *Readings from the Ancient Near East*, 43.

12   Victor Avigdor Hurowitz, 'Babylon in Bethel – new light on Jacob's dream', in Steven W. Holloway, ed., *Orientalism, Assyriology and the Bible* (HBM 10; Sheffield: Sheffield Phoenix Press, 2006), 436–448, here 447.

nation had created an enduring monument.'[13] Awareness is not equivalent to detailed technical knowledge of the construction process.[14]

The first brick used in particular was one of special sacredness. Speiser comments, 'For the ceremonial and year-long preparation of the sacral bricks and the solemn laying of the first brick were standard practices bound up with the religious architecture of Mesopotamia.'[15] The responsibility for the molding of the first brick belonged to the king.

> The sun-god was overjoyed with the brick which he (Gudea) had placed in the mold.
> Out of the mold, he lifted the brick:
> Like a pure crown lifted toward the sky, he lifted the brick.
> He brought it to his people.[16]

Again and again throughout the millennia in Mesopotamia, the king was the one on seals, reliefs, and inscriptions who fulfilled the divine obligation. One of the questions to be asked in the biblical exegesis of the story of the Tower of Babel is how familiar was the author of the story and his audience with these Mesopotamian traditions of ziggurats, bricks, and bitumen. The follow up question is what would a story of ziggurats, bricks, bitumen, and human labor against Yahweh mean in the time when Solomon ruled.[17]

The textual search for the Tower of Babel

Modern scholarship has tended to combine literary and textual issues with the anthropological and archaeological. As a narrative story it stands out compared to the others in this study because of its length and unity. It raises questions about the origin of organized religion and the role of high places in the worship of God. Of all the stories in this study, the story of the Tower of Babel is the only one where some of the action occurs in the heavens. A story with two locations differentiates it from the other stories and begs the questions of the nature of this second realm, who populates it, and how do movements between the two realms occur. Overall, this story generates more thought-provoking questions than some of the other stories and one appreciates the superior skill of the author in raising them.

Delitzsch

Delitzsch takes the perspective that the immediate descendants of Noah still would have been one family with one language. He stresses the role of languages in the development of multiplicity of thoughts and aspirations leading to the creation of nations. Delitzsch deems comparative philology as being incapable of reconstructing that original unified language. He considers it even possible that the Nimrod story originally followed the Tower of Babel

---

13   Von Rad, *Genesis*, 150.

14   Day points out that there is no bitumen in the *Enuma Elish* account unlike the biblical account or other Mesopotamian accounts. He then suggests that more than a literary borrowing was involved, there had to be actual knowledge of how a ziggurat was constructed (Day, *From Creation to Babel*, 176).

15   Speiser, *Genesis*, 76.

16   Quoted in Henri Frankfort, *Kingship and the Gods: A Study of Ancient Near Eastern Religion as the Integration of Society and Nature* (Chicago: University of Chicago Press, 1978), 273.

17   Frankfort, *Kingship and the Gods*, 272–274.

story. This reversal means that Nimrod instead of being the leader in the building of the tower as in many interpretations instead was the first imperial leader after the dispersal because of the failed construction.[18]

According to Delitzsch, the story itself was written from a Palestinian orientation. Special prominence is given to the new manner of building. The tower is conceived not simply for reaching the heavens but as a means of securing the unified people from dissolution. But the result is a shattered humanity into hostile groups. God pronounces judgment on the world-city and the babel ensues. He recognizes that the ruins which archaeologists and travelers recently had discovered including at Babylon may be remnants of this story or at least similar in style to the tower described in the story.[19]

Delitzsch concludes his commentary with an unusual observation. Although comparative philology cannot reconstruct the original human language, there remains the possibility for its 'resurrection' anyway. He is referring to the Pentecostal Church and the speaking in tongues. The unity of the original language is to be found outside the science of language. Delitzsch exults in the prospect of this resurrection.[20]

Dillmann

Dillmann begins his exegesis by asserting the author of this story is different from the author of Gen. 10 with the detailed Table of Nations. He is particularly struck by the absence of any reference to the three sons of Noah who had figured so prominently in the two preceding chapters. Instead humanity is still a unity here. He concludes that the tower legend originally circulated independently of the flood legend and the three sons of Noah. But he rejects the common suggestions that it is a continuation of the sons of Cain in Gen. 4: 17–24 with the city-building in some way. It makes no sense that the unified city builders in one story and who had developed a civilization suddenly became an unbroken unity in a completely different location in another story. His point is well-taken if both cities had been built by the same people. However whereas one was built by the sons of Cain and would have survived a local flood story and the other was built by the sons of men. That difference in location and builders means one person could have written both stories and be separate from the author of the Nimrod story.[21]

As Dillmann understands it, the natural order for men is to spread over the world. He bases his opinion on Gen. 1: 28 and 9: 1 with the divine charge to be fruitful and multiply and have dominion over the earth. These verses normally are attributed to P and not J as he knew. The concept of human dominion over the earth means humanity remaining settled in one city is an act of defiance which warrants punishment. This punishment then generates the exact action God decreed in the first place: dispersal over the earth.[22] Dillmann then takes his analysis to the next level. True the separation into various peoples leads to

---

18 Delitzsch, *New Commentary on Genesis*, 346–347, 355.
19 Delitzsch, *New Commentary on Genesis*, 348–353.
20 Delitzsch, *New Commentary on Genesis*, 355–356.
21 Dillmann, *Genesis*, 384–386.
22 Dillmann, *Genesis*, 386.

international strife, but there is more involved. 'Diversity of language leads to diversity in mental processes and modes of thought.' For Dillmann, this is a blessing. Nonetheless, he recognizes the horror that natives have towards those who speak a foreign language. One cannot help but wonder how the times in which he lived in Europe with new nations being formed often with a linguistic basis factored into his analysis.[23]

Dillmann's musing about the details of the story are based on the archaeological discoveries of his time as would be expected. He imagined there were faint historical reminiscences to the story from the land of Shinar where Semites and Kushites intermixed. Ruins from the northern part of the city of Babîl probably were at the basis of the story but he admits that there could be another unknown ruin which was.[24]

One interesting observation is Dillmann's rejection of various interpreters who claim that Hebrew was the original language spoken by humans before the dispersal and the confusion of languages occurred.[25]

Gunkel

Gunkel approaches the story as a composite of two similar but different stories. One fragment focuses on the city and the confusion of languages, the other on the tower and the dispersion of the humanity over the earth. He further states that neither version is directly related to the Table of Nations in Gen. 10 which also depicts a dispersion of humanity and in quite specific detail.[26]

The discovery of brickmaking is recounted in the city version but in an extremely naive manner. That discovery leads to the idea of building a city and to making a name for themselves or gaining eternal fame. Name has a physical component whether it is here or in the calling the name of Yahweh in the story of the sons of Seth. It is easy today to think of making a name for oneself as acquiring fame or by being a celebrity braggart. To understand the meaning of this verse in ancient times, we need to recognize that the process of making a name for oneself was a physical one and generally reserved to kings who built canals, walls, palaces, temples, and occasionally, new cities.

The results of this human-initiated action are calamitous. For Gunkel, the 'let us come down' signifies the most ancient elements of the story born in a polytheistic world where multiple divine beings descend from the heavens as they would in the Canaanite religion. The result is the name of the city becoming not a designation of fame and honor but of disgrace and shame.[27]

Gunkel regards the tower fragment as older than the city version, but both follow the same sequence. The goal of the construction projection is to keep humanity together. In unity there is strength.[28] Gunkel stresses the amazement by people in the land of Canaan

---

23 Dillmann, *Genesis*, 386–387.
24 Dillmann, *Genesis*, 387, 389–390.
25 Dillmann, *Genesis*, 395.
26 Gunkel, *Genesis*, 95.
27 Gunkel, *Genesis*, 96–97.
28 Gunkel does not mention it but a case can be made that the nation-wide effort to build the pyramids

that the Babylonians could build the most glorious palaces and temples while using such an inferior material as bricks and that they possessed such a strong adhesive as asphalt. Clearly the structure meant by the story was the ziggurat. He suggests the great ziggurat of Babylon was *Esagil*, the temple of Marduk. The disrepair of the ancient and most famous structure in Babylon at the time of the story became part of the message of the story. For the Israelite audience of the story, Babel was an ancient city with a massive structure from time immemorial.[29]

Gunkel has no doubt that the origin of the legend should be attributed to Babylonia. The story pre-supposes the use of Babylonian construction materials. One would expect a native writer who knew the scope and size of Babylon first hand, the city which is named by implication in the story, to be heralding the greatness of the city. Instead the author is a non-Babylonian foreigner for whom the great and powerful city of Babylon signifies wickedness and deserves divine judgment. Gunkel posits that the Aramaeans who wandered from land to land in the ancient Near East during the 2nd millennium BCE brought these images with them to Israel. There the legend was 'intensely Hebraized' by a people amazed by the remarkable Babylonian construction material they had never seen.[30]

The message then was a powerful one. Gunkel avers that 'in the narrator's time, Babylonian despots forced whole nations into servitude to erect structures intended to transmit the fame of the builder to the most distant future'. He adds that these human structures were perceived as works of rebellious wickedness against the deity. The story delivers the message that the fate of the tower and its builders is the fate of any great human plans to have an eternal name and be almighty. He does not appear to consider the possibly of this message being delivered by a prophet at the time when Pharaoh Solomon used forced labor to make his own name great throughout the world.[31]

Skinner

The first consideration for Skinner is the physical reality of the monuments of Mesopotamia. These imposing edifices would have impressed the Semitic nomads gazing upon them from their wilderness wanderings. Quite possibly the ziggurat at Ur was the basis for the story. (However, if biblical Abraham lived in that city he would have grown up with such monuments and they would not have had the same effect on him as Skinner postulates

---

helped unite Egypt although at a tremendous cost. For the despotism of the Pharaohs in the building of the pyramids, see Toby Wilkinson, *The Rise and Fall of Ancient Egypt* (New York: Random House Trade Paperbacks, 2013), 'Chapter 4: Heaven on Earth', 57–76, especially 62–63, 70–71. Less-despotic American examples of nation building through construction include the Transcontinental Railroad, the Interstate Highway, and the Apollo Moon Mission.

29 Gunkel, *Genesis*, 95, 97–98, 100–101.

30 Gunkel, *Genesis*, 101. The story of the Aramaeans is closely intertwined with Israel's as expressed in 'A wandering Aramean was my father; and he went down into Egypt and sojourned there, few in number; and there he became a nation, great, mighty, and populous' (Deut. 26: 5). For the Aramaeans see Wayne T. Pitard, 'Arameans', in *OEANE*, 184–187.

31 Gunkel, *Genesis*, 100.

for the Semitic nomads.) Skinner finds no parallel story in Babylonian tradition rendering the story uniquely Israelite.[32]

Skinner observes the Hebrew reaction to this wondrous construction in the story they told about it. It is an example of the 'unsophisticated reasoning of nomadic Semites who had penetrated into the country and formed their own notions about the wonders they beheld there [in Babylon]'. Gen. 11: 3 expresses with great naïveté, the (city-) legend describing the invention of bricks, and then in the next verse as an afterthought the project of building with them. However it does show that the legend took shape among a people familiar with stone masonry.[33]

The involvement of Yahweh in Gen. 11: 5 marks the turning point in the story. His intervention reveals the true message of the story. To 'the purer faith of the Hebrews', the ziggurat exemplified human pride and presumption. The builders deserve the divine judgment for their 'presumptuous impiety which inspired these early manifestations' of genius and enterprise. Skinner renders his judgement on the Hebrew creation of the story:

> '[A] highly dramatic polytheistic recension has here been toned down by the omission of some of its most characteristic incidents – a document so saturated with pagan theology as the supposed Bab. original must have been. It is more natural to believe that the elimination of polytheistic representations was effected in the course of oral transmission, through the spontaneous action of the Hebrew mind controlled by spiritual faith.'

All this being said, Skinner still is floundered by the fundamental irreconcilability of the Tower of Babel story with the independent of Table of Nations in Gen. 10. He has no explanation for the juxtaposition of these alternate stories. Skinner has glimpsed the multitude of writers who composed what he calls J but without any way to identify them.[34]

Von Rad

Von Rad declares that this tale 'consists of older material which had first to be boldly hewn and recast'. Despite that, when it was incorporated into the Yahwist primeval history it was not done so in detail but rather through its primary ideas. He dismisses the irregularities because of the dispersion of humanity in the Table of Nations preceding this story with the explanation that 'our narrator has freely welded single traditions into a primeval history, and in doing it, he paid much more attention to the inner theological orientation of the whole rather than to precise harmonizing of the details'.[35]

Contrary to Gunkel, von Rad operates from the assumption that the Tower of Babel is a single story. He avers that the use of stone for the construction of larger buildings was standard operating procedure. The violation of prescribed procedures means the use of a perishable material was unsatisfactory. He refers to 'the penetrating judgement of our narrator' in recognizing that the basic forces of what is called culture contain a rebellion

---

32 Skinner, *A Critical and Exegetical Commentary*, 223, 229–230.
33 Skinner, *A Critical and Exegetical Commentary*, 225, 228, quotation from 228.
34 Skinner, *A Critical and Exegetical Commentary*, 223–224, 226–227, quotations from 223 and 227.
35 Quotations from von Rad, *Genesis*, 148.

against God. The punishment for this sinful action is the confusion of languages which adds a new dimension beyond the description in the Table of Nations. The theological message concerning human rebellion against God trumps all other considerations.[36]

As is his custom, von Rad seeks to locate the story in space and time. During the 2nd millennium BCE in particular, Babylon 'was the heart of the ancient world and its center of power'. The legendary knowledge of the gigantic cultural achievements of the Babylonians had spread far and wide. Von Rad described this as 'the rays of its culture went out far into neighbouring lands'. Specifically, these 'mighty stepped towers' such as from Hammurabi (18th century BCE) were the 'united civilized will of this strong nation' which 'created an enduring monument'. He suggests the oldest version of the narrative presents the actions as a danger and threat to the gods (notice the plural). However, in the J revision of the older myth, it is no longer clear exactly what man's sin was. Although Babylon is portrayed as the center of human cultural history, the story no longer concerns Babylon itself as it has assumed universal import.[37]

Speiser

For Speiser, this story 'points more concretely to Babylonia than does any other portion of Primeval History, and the background that is here sketched proves to be authentic beyond all expectations'. This Assyriologist practically rejoices in the Mesopotamian elements contained in the story. He rejects the association with the 1st-millennium BCE ziggurat Entemenanki at Babylon as being too late for the J author. He prefers the earlier versions as described in *Enuma Elish*, the Babylonian creation story, and the construction of Esagila temple, Sumerian for 'the structure with upraised head'. Speiser cites the Akkadian tradition of ceremonial and year-long preparation of the sacral bricks and the first laying of the brick in such constructions. Clearly the story involves sacred actions of the highest order. It is precisely that background which the narrator calls to task for exemplifying man's folly and presumption. So the narrator drew directly from cuneiform sources to deliver a message for an Israelite audience: do not build a temple.[38]

Westermann

Westermann operates on the basis that all these stories are primeval and etiological in nature. They focus on how the present emerged from the distant past. The standard mode is through crime and punishment. These stories are not to be considered historical but explanatory about the nature of human existence. In this instance, the norm is violated as direct contact with human history is rendered through the name Babel in the land of Shinar. Westermann suggests the story of the Tower of Babel still would be complete even if the explanation for word 'babel' had not been included in the story. The presence of this historical element in this etiological tale is indicative of different stages of growth. He

---

36 Von Rad, *Genesis*, 149, 152, quotation from 149.
37 Von Rad, *Genesis*, 150–151, quotations from 150.
38 Speiser, *Genesis*, 75–76.

identifies two themes which have been joined together in a single story: dispersion and multiple languages.[39] The dispersion motif is a carryover from the flood story while the multiple languages only exists here. He sees the dispersion motif being assumed in the tower-building narrative. The dispersion references elsewhere were not depicted negatively:

Genesis 9: 19 *These three were the sons of Noah; and from these the whole earth was peopled.*

Genesis 10: 25 *To Eber were born two sons: the name of the one was Peleg, for in his days the earth was divided, and his brother's name was Joktan.*

Only in this story does it become something to be avoided. In the current version the building of the tower, the dispersion of the people and the multiple languages all have been joined together in a single story.[40]

Westermann then seeks to understand how all these components were fused into that single story. Besides reviewing existing biblical scholarship, he turns to non-biblical stories of the dispersion of humanity over the face of the earth. His global review leads him to observe that the dispersion motif frequently concludes a flood story as in the Old Testament and that dispersion and confusion are closely connected. Of course, one may ask, how much the global dispersion by missionaries and colonists itself of the Old Testament into multiple languages contributed to peoples around the world having stories that followed a similar sequence.[41]

The tower motif provides a third element. Westermann scours the globe searching for other similar stories. The data he collects suggest a differentiation between the tower story and dispersion/confusion stories often associated with the flood. He deems the tower component to be a non-etiological independent element addressing the separation of the human and divine realms. The making of a name for oneself by building a tower to avoid being scattered attempts to bridge the gap between these different concerns and create a single story.[42]

The closest resemblance to the story Westermann finds among Israel's neighbors is a Sumerian one on the confusion of languages, the Epic of Enmerkar. Once upon a time, the people lived without fear and with one language in the land of Martu (the west). In this instance it was a rivalry among the gods Enki of Nippur and Enlil of Eridu that led to the confusion of languages and not the actions of men as in the biblical account. Westermann concludes that this example demonstrates that the confusion element was not only was independent from the tower-building, but once may have part of a narrative tradition about the gods.[43]

After having identified these different components in the one story, Westermann then seeks to understand how J put the pieces together. He rejects the scholarly conclusion that the story originated in Babylon as well as the one that it originated as an anti-Babylonian polemic. He castigates both 'schools of thought' for the same methodological error: making Babylon the theme or center of the narrative, which it is not. He is equally dismissive of

---

39 Westermann, *Genesis 1–11*, 535.
40 Westermann, *Genesis 1–11*, 535–536.
41 Westermann, *Genesis 1–11*, 537–538.
42 Westermann, *Genesis 1–11*, 538–539.
43 Westermann, *Genesis 1–11*, 539.

the attempts to identify a specific ziggurat now in ruins as the basis for the story. The biblical story does not end with the tower in ruins so it cannot be an etiology about a ruined ziggurat in Babylonia.[44]

Westermann ends his general comments on the story by referring to oral tradition in Israel. Although the story did not originate in Babylon and was not about a tower in Babylon, Israel was aware of the existence of huge towers in Mesopotamia especially Babylon. But the subject of the story is 'the sons of man', or humankind, whom he locates in primeval times. He envisions a long process of tradition history before the story was set in stone. Since he attributes the story to the dawn of time about a building project by humanity, he cannot consider the possibility of the story being about the present time and a building project of Israel. For him, the story 'is clearly part of the transition from primeval event to history'.[45]

In this regard he distinguishes between the founding of a city in the Cain tradition (see Chapter 2) with the city here. This city presumes a degree of technical prowess and mathematical skill accompanied by a shared group will to construct such an edifice. As a result, this city differs from the Cain one in that it seeks a summit that will touch the heavens and express the builder's greatness. These values are expressed by the prophet Isaiah:

> **Isaiah 14: 13** *You said in your heart, 'I will ascend to heaven; above the stars of God I will set my throne on high; I will sit on the mount of assembly in the far north;* [14] *I will ascend above the heights of the clouds, I will make myself like the Most High [Elyon].'*

Westermann connects the words of the serpent in Gen. 3: 5 that Yahweh does not want the man and the women to be like God knowing good from evil and the professed desire of humanity in Gen. 11: 4 to make a name for itself with Isaiah's pronouncement. He opines that J delivered the message that on their own, human beings faced great danger. Their aspiration to exceed their designated limits, to be like God and reach the heavens instead of merely standing before God invited repercussions.[46] What Westermann does not do is to compare this ascent via construction of a high place with that of Moses who ascends a mountain of God and encounters the deity who has descended. The temple and the covenant provide contrasting perceptions in Israelite history which Westermann does not see due to his fixation on the transition from the primeval time to history in the setting of a story that really is about the author's present.

Instead Westermann voices a Christian perspective. The dispersion of humanity is a preventive action to minimize the threat that humanity will engage in a rash action with disastrous consequences. By contrast the human race now exists as a plurality of peoples scattered over the face of the earth filled with an abundance of potential. The plurality of languages is by necessity part of the plurality of peoples. Westermann cites Delitzsch quoting the Sybilline Oracles 3.99f:

> *They were all the same in speech and wanted to climb the up to the starry heavens.*

---

44 Westermann, *Genesis 1–11*, 540–541.
45 Westermann, *Genesis 1–11*, 543.
46 Westermann, *Genesis 1–11*, 554–555.

Since that situation was not the case, people developed the concept that the lack of unity must have been a punishment. But perhaps one day in the endtime, the condition created in the primeval time would cease.

> **Zephaniah 3: 8** *'Therefore wait for me', says Yahweh, 'for the day when I arise as a witness. For my decision is to gather nations, to assemble kingdoms, to pour out upon them my indignation, all the heat of my anger; for in the fire of my jealous wrath all the earth shall be consumed'. ⁹ Yea, at that time I will change the speech of the peoples to a pure speech, that all of them may call on the name of Yahweh and serve him with one accord.*[47]

Westermann ends his commentary on The Tower of Babel story with the good news that through Christ the language barriers have been burst.

> **Acts 2: 11** *(W)e hear them telling in our own tongues the mighty works of God.*

On the day of the Pentecost, devout Jews from all the nations of the world gather in one place. There they hear the sound of the multitude but it was not a babel since they hear them each speaking their own language. Thanks to the divine universal translator the multiplicity of languages remains but all can be understood. For Westermann, Acts 2 corresponds with Gen. 11: 1–9 in recognizing the positive benefit to humanity of multiple languages that with the new understanding through Jesus that renounces individual ambition and fame.[48] There are no footnotes documenting how if at all the experience of having been an anti-Nazi Russian POW in World War II affected this German exegete who began his Genesis commentary in the 1950s. One wonders if the author of the story of the Tower of Babel may have had a more immediate purpose in mind when he composed the story.

The Jewish Study Bible

Levenson characterizes the building action as 'an act of Promethean hubris on the part of a humankind still unwilling to accept subordination to their Creator'. He likens the ambition of the builders to the prideful boast of the king of Babylon that Westermann had cited in Isa. 14: 13–14. The advanced technological level of the Babylonians astonishes the author but there also is an awareness of the grave danger it presents when not accompanied by a reverence for the Lord. The author is amused that despite the vaunted erection, the deity still must descend![49]

Levenson sees a series of connections between this story at the end of the first cycle with the Abram stories at the beginning of the second cycle. Both involve the theme making a name great (Gen. 11: 4 and 12: 2). Both involve a departure (from Babel here and from Ur for Abram, Gen. 12: 1). Both involve a world view (dispersion here and blessing of all the nations via Abram, Gen. 12: 2–3). The implication from these observations is that the story of the Tower of Babel should not be analyzed independently of its surroundings.[50]

---

47 Westermann, *Genesis 1–11*, 556.
48 Westermann, *Genesis 1–11*, 557.
49 Levenson, 'Genesis', 29.
50 Levenson, 'Genesis', 29.

The New Jerome Biblical Commentary

Clifford entitles his commentary 'The Prideful City with the Tower'. The people have refused to disperse to their apportioned lands described in Gen. 10, The Table of Nations. Instead they choose to congregate in a single city. This migration and settling in the land of Shinar directly contradicts the divine instruction. Clearly no good can come of this decision. Clifford contrasts two parallel actions by the humans and the Lord:

> **Genesis 11: 4** *Then they said, 'Come, let us build ourselves a city, and a tower with its top in the heavens, and let us make a name for ourselves, lest we be scattered abroad upon the face of the whole earth'.*

> **Genesis 11: 7** *Come, let us go down, and there confuse their language, that they may not understand one another's speech.*

He adds that from a distance, the Mesopotamian temples on the flat Babylonian plains indeed must have looked as if they had reached the heavens.[51]

A second contrast is between Abram and the tower-builders. The latter act in disobedience to God by seeking on their own to make a name for themselves. By contrast, Abram obeys the word of the Lord which includes the promise of the divine action making the human name great (Gen. 12: 2). The human builders are punished for their pride and expelled as were the man and woman from the garden. Just as they cannot return to the garden again to challenge the divine role, so too, the scattered humans will never again be able to launch their physical challenge.[52]

The HarperCollins Study Bible

Rosenberg refers to the story as a 'brief allegorical tale about the separation of languages and people already described in ch. 10'. He compares it to the garden story as a folktale expressing human pride and folly with an antiurban bias. He cites the ziggurat such as Entemenanki and the wordplay on the Akkadian Bab-ilani, 'Gate of the gods' for the Hebrew 'confusion' from Babel.[53]

Conclusion

This review of the Tower of Babel exegesis over the millennia reveals significant commonalities, some differences in interpretations, and open questions. In addition to the standard literary and textual considerations there are archaeological ones as well. These observations may be summarized as follows.

1. The earlier commentators such as Josephus and the rabbis were storytellers in their own right. They sought to smooth the way by filling in gaps through expository creations. They anticipated the questions an audience might raise reading or hearing the story within the context of the existing canonized narrative. They did not view Tower of Babel in isolation but connected it to the previous and subsequent stories of Nimrod and Abram.

---

51 Clifford and Murphy, 'Genesis', 18.
52 Clifford and Murphy, 'Genesis', 18.
53 Rosenberg, 'Genesis', 18.

2. Modern scholars are divided on the unity of the story or if it derives from two independent traditions with the unity side tending to predominate.
3. Modern scholars debate whether the building of a tower and a city was a good thing or not.
4. Modern scholars tend to be divided as to whether the story is about the dawn of human civilization, whether the story is a mythical folktale, whether the story is the word of God or whether it can be situated in some specific historical context.
5. Modern scholars express some awareness of the possibility that Tower may be a symbolic or metaphorical structure possibly derived from an actual structure in Mesopotamia.

Even putting aside the sin and fall perspective that is inevitable in biblical exegesis there still are several presuppositions, considerations, and revisions which should be taken into account. The tendency to attribute the story to an independent origin obscures links to other biblical stories.

1. The story of the Tower of Babel shares common motifs and vocabulary with other biblical stories:

   Movements eastward or from the east: Garden, Cain, Lot and, by implication, Abram from Ur (Gen. 2: 8, 14, 24; 4:16; 13:11)
   Shinar: in Nimrod, the war with the kings from the east and the conquest (Gen. 10: 10, 14: 1, 9; Joshua 7: 21)
   Brick(s): in the Exodus (Ex. 1: 14 and 5 [6 times])
   Bitumen: in the war with kings from the east and in the Exodus (Gen. 14: 10; Ex. 2: 3)
   Towers: Gideon and Shechem in Judges 8–9.

   The presence of these common elements at least presents the possibility that the stories are connected in some manner. One individual may have been responsible for all of them. A second individual may have sought to invalidate the argument of the first author by using that author's own words to undermine his message. Both suggestions may be true as well once all the items can be fully analyzed in conjunction with each other.
2. Following the guidelines just mentioned above, the second story of dispersion in the Tower of Babel may have originated by a second author in reaction to the story of Nimrod and not as a continuation of it. Just as with the sons of Cain and the sons of Seth and with the double cursing of Canaan in the sons of Noah, the stories of Nimrod and Babel may reflect the diversity of views within the Israelite polity.
3. The story of the building project may have resonated with the original audience because of what it had just experienced in their own lives. Simply because the story was set in Mesopotamia does not mean it was about an event in Mesopotamia. Stories tend to be about the present of the audience regardless of the setting in space, time, or iconography.
4. The position of the Tower of Babel as the concluding story in the first cycle of the KDB in the supplement by this author should not be treated as happenstance or coincidence. Someone made a deliberate decision not only to create the story but to situate it here. First the sons of Noah and cursed Canaan had become the new ending for the cycle. Then the story of Nimrod and world geography had. Now the Tower of Babel had with dispersed humanity. All these changes were inserted between the end of KDB's first cycle and the onset of the story of Abram in the second.

The story of the Tower of Babel ends and therefore helps define the first cycle of stories while setting the stage for the second cycle about the warrior-shepherd from Hebron. Another author had sought to accomplish the same with his story of Nimrod. There is no inherent reason to presume that Nimrod and the Tower of Babel originally were part of the same manuscript. American Protestant churches separated in the 1840s, well before the country divided politically into North and South in the 1860s. Nimrod and Babel concluded separate supplements to the KDB by competing factions in the battle for power following the death of David in the time of Solomon just before the kingdom split politically into north and south.

This review of the Tower of Babel is a fitting end to the review of the six son stories in the first cycle of the KDB. The pursuit of sin and salvation or myths from the dawn of human civilization are methodologically suspect. Instead one may approach the stories as political expressions by specific individuals who can be named. The application of a politically-based methodology drawing on the scholarship but not necessarily the interpretations of the primarily Protestant-based exegesis inevitably produces different results. The biblical writers lived in a time before the abstract essay had been invented, before op-ed pieces in newspapers, and before blogs on the internet. Nonetheless, they were quite capable of engaging in battles for power in Jerusalem. These battles were expressed through the information technology available to them, the newly established alphabet prose narrative format. These battles were fought by people who created, amended, and responded to stories by other combatants. In the world from ancient Egypt to Mesopotamia, there was nothing comparable to what occurred in 10th century BCE Israel and the stories they told have become part of the global legacy of humanity. These writers can be identified and their writings can be understood in the political context which led to their creation.

Chapter 8

DAVID'S JERUSALEM:
SETTING THE JERUSALEM STAGE

David is a critical person for this historical reconstruction. After extensive contentious debate and discussion, scholars have reached the following consensus about the controversial figure of David: (i) he was king of Israel but not Judah; (ii) he was king of Judah but not Israel; (iii) he was king of Israel and Judah; (iv) he was a chieftain and never became a king; (v) he never existed. It does seem certain that he was not an alien from another planet. The historical reconstruction presented below is based on the premise that David was king of Judah and Israel and that the KDB was a work of genius which changed the course of human history. That is too big a topic to address in one book so this study is merely an introduction to the larger story (see Additional Readings: David).

The battle for power was fought in the capital city of the kingdom. At some point it became clear that a house divided cannot stand and the kingdom split into two parts. Since the stories were written and played out in the Jerusalem beltway it is necessary to understand the stage on which the battles were fought before turning to the writers themselves in Part II. This chapter provides an overview of the history of the political arena.

Jerusalem before Israel

Typically Jerusalem is translated as 'City of Peace'. Another possibility is 'Founded by the god Salem' which would be a more appropriate designation in ancient times. In the Ugaritic tradition (see below) Šalim is most closely associated with the evening star or Venus in partnership with Šahar, the morning star. Two of David's sons, Absalom, born in Hebron, and Solomon, born in Jerusalem, bear names derived from this deity. The suggestion has been made that the term 'City of David' originally only referred to the fortress or citadel where David had his palace and later was extended to encompass the entire city. That proposal is somewhat comparable to the often interchangeable uses of The White House (a building) and Washington (the city) in the United States, when one really means The President. The context then should indicate when the text refers to a specific building or person versus the entire city (see Additional Readings: Salem).

By the time of David, Jerusalem already had a long history. For the most part, that history is known through archaeology and from texts not found in Jerusalem itself. Some of these texts may have been composed by the ruler of the city, meaning by the scribe working on behalf of the king, and found elsewhere. Certainly there is nothing comparable for pre-Israelite Jerusalem to the biblical writings about the united kingdom and the kings of Judah in the Books of Samuel and Kings and to the references in Psalms and by the prophets to it. John Schmitt claims:

> 'The weight of probability seems to be those who would maintain some kind of cultural and religious continuity between pre-Israelite Jerusalem and Israelite Jerusalem.'

Similar views have been written by numerous biblical scholars. That supposition is a pillar of this study. The present chapter seeks to portray that continuity through the time of David; Part II addresses the conflicts which arose due to that continuity after David's death expressed through the son stories.[1]

Jerusalem was located in the land of Canaan. Defining exactly what 'Canaan' means has been problematic. The issues of the land, people(s), and culture of Canaan have been contentious ones in biblical scholarship. At stake are not simply the standard academic disagreements one might expect to find in any subject nor the routine personality clashes and battles of egos. The subtexts of these discussions always are the Bible and Israel, both ancient and today. Depending on how one defines Canaan, its culture and its people, automatically impacts one's definition of Israel, its culture and its people. For example, in Part I, we saw numerous examples of Genesis commentators describing everything about Canaan in vile, repulsive, and derogatory terms. Given the view of debauched Canaanites and their orgiastic culture one can easily justify Noah's curse of the Canaanites and Israel's possession of the land. As a result, any change in Canaan's status in biblical scholarship automatically generates a change in Israel's status, which may be the very goal of the biblical scholar.

The word Canaan itself is not known in the archaeological record until the 2nd millennium BCE. It appeared first in the 19th/18th century archives at Mari, a city on the Euphrates River in Syria near Iraq based on current borders. The usage connotes people perceived to be traders or merchants who plied their wares outside their homeland. In the archaeological record the name 'Canaan' was used most extensively by Egypt in reference to the land it ruled during the New Kingdom (1550–1139 BCE) when it occupied the land. Egypt ruled it from an administrative center in the city of Gaza, 'the Canaan', still a traditional boundary. After the end of Egyptian imperialism in the Late Bronze Age (1550–1200 BCE) the name 'Canaan' disappeared from the archaeological record.[2]

The biblical record is somewhat comparable to the archaeological one. Canaan, specifically 'the land of Canaan', occurs throughout the stories of the Patriarchs, the Exodus, and the Conquest. It appears a few times in the Book of Judges particularly in the song and narrative of Deborah where is it linked to the word 'king' and not land (Judg. 4: 2, 23–24; 5: 19). It does not appear at all in the Books of Samuel and Kings when Israel and Judah have kings who reign in the former land of Canaan. The biblical usage raises the question of exactly to whom the word 'Canaan' applied when Noah was cursing him and the Table of Nations was defining him (see Part II) (see Additional Readings: Canaan).

At no time during Canaan's 2nd millennium BCE existence was there ever a country

---

1   John Schmitt, 'Pre-Israelite Jerusalem', in Carl Evans, William Hallo, and John White, eds, *Scripture in Context: Essays on the Comparative Method* (Pittsburgh: Pickwick Press, 1980), 101–121, quotation 109.

2   Dating schemes vary from specialty to specialty. Round numbers are convenient but not always meaningful. A comparable example for Americans would be dating the onset of the 21st century to 9/11 in 2001.

or kingdom of Canaan encompassing the entire land of Canaan. The area consisted of numerous cities along the coast, in the Jezreel Valley, the Galilee, and sometimes the highlands. It was a land of city-states where each one was independent, dominant over the surrounding daughter villages, and with vacant lands in-between them. Typically each major city had a king, walls, controlled access to water and a temple. The people in the land of Canaan did not think of themselves as belonging to a single cultural, ethnic, political, or social Canaanite entity but as residents of a given city or village. The configuration of Canaanite city-states prior to Israel also has been a subject of contention among biblical scholars (see Additional Readings: Canaanite City-States).

Jerusalem was one of the cities within this mix of Canaanite cities. It lay off the beaten trail of the main roads of commerce and invasion which ran along the coast and through Megiddo. Its location in the interior along a north–south road and with a perennial source of water did make it a location of some significance. Its closest comparable city in the highlands was Shechem which became the capital city of the northern kingdom of Israel (I Kings 12). It did interact with other Canaanite cities as will be seen below.

The city first appears by name in the literary record in the Execration Texts of Middle Kingdom kings of Egypt (the term 'Pharaoh' had not yet been invented). These texts functioned as a form of magic or voodoo. The king asserted his dominion over his enemies by first inscribing the names of his foes on a bowl or figurine which then would be destroyed and buried as part of an imperial ritual of conquest. The name 'Rušalimum' appears twice on these inscriptions on a 19th-century BCE ceramic bowl and 18th-century BCE terracotta figure. Traditionally the people named on these texts are considered to be ethnic Amorites, part of a migration westward towards the Mediterranean and eastward towards Mesopotamia (Hammurabi was one) in the beginning of the 2nd millennium BCE. Egypt ritually dealt with these newcomers into its sphere of influence because it lacked the military power to confront, subjugate, and dominate them. These texts may have been a continuation of a longstanding Egyptian practice of denouncing various peoples or cities by rote so care must be taken in determining the actual political circumstances at the time of these pronouncements. As a result, the presence of Jerusalem in these Middle Bronze Age (2000–1550 BCE) texts may reflect an even older Early Bronze Age existence in the 3rd millennium BCE (see Additional Readings for the Amorites and for the Execration Texts).

The city was located on a narrow ridge surrounded by deep valleys. The exception was the north where it was more exposed on the plateau.[3] Archaeological excavations in Jerusalem from the Middle Bronze Age have revealed it to be a typical city in the land of Canaan. It had a wall, massive gates, and a massive water system that was protected and partially underground. The protection was necessitated by the potential exposure of the Gihon spring, the perennial source of water, being located outside the city. The spring was not easily accessible from the high point where one normally would expect the people to live and the temple would later be built. Its location further down the slope dictated living in close proximity to it and to building projects there. This configuration would continue

---

3   For a description of the site see Hillel Geva, 'Jerusalem', in Ephraim Stern, ed., *The New Encyclopedia of Archaeological Excavations in the Holy Land* (Jerusalem: Israel Exploration Society and Carta, 1993), 701–716; Kathleen Kenyon, *Royal Cities of the Old Testament* (New York: Schocken Books, 1971), 13–52.

to define the city over the centuries (see Additional Readings: Jerusalem – Middle Bronze Age Archaeology).

According to the biblical text, the city of Jerusalem had acquired another name even before it became the City of David. Its name was Jebus. The only times this name appears in the Bible is as an equivalent to Jerusalem.[4]

1. In the allocation after the conquest: **Joshua 18: 28** *Zela, Haeleph,* **Jebus** *(that is,* **Jerusalem***), Gibeah and Kiriathjearim – fourteen cities with their villages. This is the inheritance of the tribe of Benjamin according to its families.*
2. In the story of the rape of the Bethlemite concubine: **Judges 19: 10** *But the man would not spend the night; he rose up and departed, and arrived opposite* **Jebus** *(that is,* **Jerusalem***). He had with him a couple of saddled asses, and his concubine was with him.* [11] *When they were near* **Jebus***, the day was far spent, and the servant said to his master, 'Come now, let us turn aside to this city of the* **Jebusites***, and spend the night in it'.*
3. In the story of David's conquest: **1 Chronicles 11: 4** *And David and all Israel went to* **Jerusalem***, that is* **Jebus***, where the* **Jebusites** *were, the inhabitants of the land.* [5] *The inhabitants of* **Jebus** *said to David, 'You will not come in here'. Nevertheless David took the stronghold of Zion, that is, the city of David.*[5]

The biblical writers equated Jerusalem, Jebus, and the city of David. An analogous American example would be 'New Amsterdam, that is New York'.

The inhabitants of the city were called Jebusites. There is no archaeological record of the Jebusites by that name. They do not appear in any non-biblical text either. Nadav Na'aman notes that some scholars see a similarity with the clan name Yabisa/Yabasa/Yabusu in the same Mari documents where 'Canaan' first appears. He postulates a possible derivation from the verb *YBŚ*, 'to be dry'. A similar root is found with the Jabeshites or Yabeshites in Gilead. He disavows any connection between these Middle Bronze Age Amorites in Upper Mesopotamia and the people in Iron Age Jerusalem (1000–586 BCE). His observations raise intriguing questions about the relationship among (i) the Benjaminites who also are traced to the Mari archives, (ii) the Jebusites in the city that became the capital city after Saul of Benjamin died, and (iii) the Jabeshites whom Saul had rescued (I Sam. 11) and who retrieved the body of the dead Saul after a battle with the Philistines (I Sam. 31). Avi Offer claims the Jebusites settled in a mass migration from Anatolia or north Syria in the 12th century BCE. That migration places them in Jerusalem after the Amarna Age and Israel's emergence in the land (see below). In the Bible, the Jebusites appear most frequently in conjunction with other peoples as part of a litany of pre-Israelite peoples in the land of Canaan. Some of the other peoples named are the Girgashites, Hivites, Amorites, and Perrizites.[6]

---

4   Nadav Na'aman, 'Jebusites and Jabeshites in the Saul and David story cycles', *Bib* 95 2014: 481–497, here 481.
5   The parentheses in the English translations are a modern convention applied to the biblical text. They are meant to suggest that the enclosed words are a gloss or later addition to the original text. The bold emphasis is added.
6   Na'aman, 'Jebusites and Jabeshites', 484, 493; Avi Offer, '"All the hill country of Judah": from a settlement fringe to a prosperous monarchy', in Israel Finkelstein and Nadav Na'aman, eds, *From Nomadism to Monarchy:*

It is not known when these Jebusites asserted themselves in the city of Jerusalem known from the Execration Texts. One reasonable possibility is presented by another set of Egyptian writings, the Amarna Letters. This diplomatic correspondence originated during the reigns of Amenhotep III and his son Amenhotep IV who became Akhnaton. It consists of cuneiform copies of letters from various other political entities, especially cities in the land of Canaan which Egypt ruled. These Akkadian-script letters demonstrates the capability of writing in these cities in the 1340s–1330s BCE using a Canaanized syntax and vocabulary. Scholars have numbered the letters to facilitate references to them (see Additional Readings: Amarna Letters).

Six of the known letters were from Abdi-Heba, the king of Jerusalem. He was considered a 'mayor' (*hazannu*) in the Egyptian context. His name has been translated as 'Servant of [the Hurrian goddess] Heba' suggesting a possible (dynastic) connection to the biblical Araunah (see below). Two other letters from Gath mentioned Jerusalem. These letters reveal a relationship between the city which became David's capital and Egypt. The actual scribe who wrote these letters may have been a foreigner himself from north Syria. He is said to have shown 'political skill' crafting these 'diplomatic gems' and in 'presenting the interests of Jerusalem in the best possible light. It seems that this writer really had outstanding abilities well above his contemporaries in south and central Canaan'.[7] One notes that this political writing was the work of a single individual and did not require a vast number of scribes. It is possible that the king had been educated in Egypt consistent with the Egyptian policy of taking princes as hostages to be inculcated in Egyptian values (see Additional Readings: Amarna Letters and Jerusalem).

William Moran concludes from his analysis of the letters, that Abdi-Heba had a military background and had been brought to the Jerusalem throne on that basis. He dates the letters to the beginning of the reign of Akhnaton. His dating suggests an installation in the time of Amenhotep III. One notes that Amenhotep III exchanged diplomatic correspondence with the king of Mitanni which led to a marriage to his daughter who was accompanied by 317 ladies-in waiting. Perhaps this relationship contributed to the northern Syria influences demonstrated in the writing by the Jerusalem scribe according to Moran.[8]

In this correspondence, Abdi-Heba acknowledges that his kingship was due to 'the strong arm' of the Egyptian king (EA 286, 288). The metaphor is a traditional one to express the power of Pharaoh. He used his power here to install a ruler in Canaan. Whether Abdi-Heba was referring to himself personally or to his dynasty may be debated. The letters describe an incident with the Nubian/Cushite soldiers garrisoned by Pharaoh in Jerusalem that led to their withdrawal (EA 285). The extent of military assistance requested, 50 archers,

Archaeological and Historical Aspects of Early Israel (Jerusalem: Israel Exploration Society, 1994), 92–121, here 110.

7   Nadav Na'aman, 'Jerusalem in the Amara period', in Caroline Amould-Béhar and André Lemaire, eds, *Jerusalem Antique et Medievale: Mélanges en l'honneur d'Ernest-Marie Laperrousaz* (Paris: Peeters, 2011), 31–48, here 35.

8   See William L. Moran, 'The Syrian scribe of the Jerusalem Amarna Letters', in Hans Goedicke and J. J. M. Roberts, eds, *Unity and Diversity: Essays in the History, Literature, and Religion of the Ancient Near East* (Baltimore: Johns Hopkins University Press, 1975), 146–166.

may be indicative of the real size of armed forces necessary to assert control in that part of the world. Abdi-Heba's problem also reveals that Jerusalem had the resources to house an Egyptian military force and that Egypt controlled some buildings within the city. He also claimed that Egyptian vassal kings who had been deserted and left without protection had been assassinated by the *habiru* (EA 280).[9]

The diplomatic correspondence between Jerusalem and other Canaanite cities with Pharaoh highlights a critical issue in the historical reconstruction of pre-Davidic Jerusalem. Na'aman avers that one 'would never have guessed from the excavations of Jerusalem [and Shechem] that any scribal activity took place there in LBA II [during the Amarna Age]'. He observes the identical discrepancy between archaeology and Amarna texts with Lachish and Gezer as well. These disconnects should serve as cautionary warnings on the limits and challenges in historical reconstructions based solely on archaeological data. To posit an interpretation of the history of Israel and Jerusalem solely based on the material remains generates a skewed picture. Imagine if the Amarna Letters had not been discovered in Egypt how much less would be known about Jerusalem during the Late Bronze Age. Imagine if diplomatic correspondence from more than just these few decades had been discovered how much more would be known about Jerusalem and Israel.[10]

The Amarna Letters provide a window into the relationship of Jerusalem to other Canaanite cities and to how cities responded to threats. Additional Amarna Letters including from other Canaanite cities highlight the tensions between Jerusalem and its neighbors such as Gezer and Gath including the defections with competing alliances. During such encounters, a Canaanite city could beseech Pharaoh for permission to engage the 'rebels' even without direct Egyptian participation (EA 279, 280). Abdi-Heba singled out Gezer, Ashkelon, and Lachish for assisting the rebels and blamed Shechem for instigating the rebellion (EA 287, 289). One result was the creation of a coalition of Canaanite cities acting with Pharaoh's blessing against the rebels. One may anticipate that a Jerusalem-led coalition just as easily could act with Pharaoh's blessing against Israel when it emerged in history. Similarly such conflicts and rivalries between cities within the land of Canaan did not disappear when Jerusalem became the capital city of a kingdom encompassing the land of Canaan.[11]

One also should recognize that there could come a time when Canaanite cities themselves were insufficient to thwart any rebellions or incursions and more direct Egyptian involvement was required. The Late Bronze Age was a period of Egyptian domination of the land of Canaan. It was less a time of destruction than administration. Egypt responded against occasionally recalcitrant cities who disrupted the Egyptian sense of *ma'at*, an

---

9   Daniel Bodi, 'Outraging the resident-alien: King David, Uriah the Hittite, and an El-Amarna parallel', *UF* 35 2003: 29–56, here 34.

10   Nadav Na'aman, 'The contribution of the Amarna Letters to the debate on Jerusalem's political position in the tenth century BCE', *BASOR* 304 1996: 17–27, here 21; Nadav Na'aman, 'The Shephelah according to the Amarna Letters', in Israel Finkelstein and Nadav Na'aman, eds, *The Fire Signals of Lachish: Studies in the Archaeology and History of Israel in the Late Bronze Age, Iron Age, and Persian Period in Honor of David Ussishkin* (Winona Lake: Eisenbrauns, 2011), 281–299, here 287–289.

11   Na'aman, 'The Shephelah', 289–292.

ordered universe of harmony. During the 13th and 12th centuries, Egypt augmented its presence in the land of Canaan. The time from Ramses II to Ramses IV witnessed the strengthening of the Egyptian hold in the lowlands where the bulk of the Canaanite cities were located precisely when Israel was emerging in history in the highlands. Egypt's vigorous exploitation of the land amounted to a defacto annexation that clearly delineated the hill country where the Egyptian presence was less felt and the low country where it was heavier. Cities like Gaza, Megiddo, and Beth-Shean served as direct outposts of Egyptian rule. It is reasonable to conclude that the arrivals of new entities in the land at this time, Israel and the Philistines, contributed to this renewed activity. This time period is one that drew the Genesis commentators trying to make sense of Japheth (the Philistines?), Shem (Israel?), and Canaan in the story of the sons of Noah. Nonetheless, despite all the Egyptian maneuvering, its age of dominance came to an end around 1139 BCE. As a result from that point forward, the one-time vassal cities now were on their own, responsible for their own security (see Additional Readings: Late Bronze Age).[12]

The supposition that 'the Egyptian withdrawal from Canaan was a great relief to all its inhabitants and opened the era for a new era in history' is half true.[13] Egyptian imperialism had taken its toll economically and demographically. Still the withdrawal of the Egyptian garrisons from Canaanite cities posed a danger. At that point, Jerusalem was devoid of imperial forces and protection meaning it was exposed to external threats. One anticipates here the continued need for a skilled writer to entreat Pharaoh to return the city to his good graces. When Abdi-Heba was threatened, he turned to the king of Egypt for help. He specifically sought help against the outsider *habiru* as well as other Canaanite cities such as Shechem. At times cities sought Pharaoh's assistance against Jerusalem. One may expect that the presence of the Philistines and Israel did not eliminate these factors. The challenge for Jerusalem was what would it do when it had nowhere to turn.

The Amarna letters detail that even during the time of Egyptian hegemony, Canaanite cities fought with each other. Once the superior power of Egypt was removed, there was no constraining force to maintain control. There is no validity to the idea that the time between Ramses VI and Israelite monarchy (1139 to *c.* 1000 BCE) was one devoid of internal conflicts. It was a time of every city, tribe, and clan for itself. Any collective alliance would automatically give its members an edge. If an attack on one was perceived as an attack on all, meaning the members of the alliance, that group possessed an advantage over villages, towns, cities, tribes on their own. At least if the confederates heeded their obligations to assemble and fight collectively. The decades between Ramses III's Canaan campaign in 1177 BCE and Egyptian withdrawal from Canaan in 1139 BCE marked a transition to a new Canaanite order. The time created an opportunity for the emerging coastal Philistine and hill-country Israel entities to assert themselves at Gath and Shiloh

12 Gabriel Barkay suggests there may have been an Egyptian temple in Jerusalem at this time as part of the increased Egyptian involvement in the area due to the emergence of Israel in history in the land of Canaan (see Gabriel Barkay, 'A Late Bronze Age Egyptian temple in Jerusalem?', *IEJ* 46 1996: 23–43). His suggestion remains under discussion within the discipline.

13 Nadav Na'aman, 'The Exodus story: between historical memory and historiographical composition', *JANER* 11 2011: 39–69, here 55.

respectively while exposing the now unprotected pro-Egyptian vassal cities. Everyone now needed to determine how to survive in the new circumstances.

The overview of the situation during the Late Bronze Age reveals precedents for the situation when Israel emerged in history and in the time of David during the Ion Age I (1200–1000 BCE).

1.   When Jerusalem was faced with external threats it sought help from Egypt.
2.   Jerusalem held no leadership position over the Canaanite cities.
3.   Hebron, the future capital of David's kingdom of Judah, and Shechem, the future capital of Jeroboam's kingdom of Israel, were outside Jerusalem's sphere of influence.
4.   Differences were expressed in political diplomacy through writing but not storytelling.

The first three conditions continued to be true during the 13th–10th centuries BCE even when Egypt's power declined.

Jerusalem and Israel before David

Historical reconstructions of Israel during this time period are a contentious issue among biblical scholars. In biblical terms, the period encompasses the setting in the Books of Joshua and Judges. In archaeological terms, Israel's appearance in history commenced in the time of Pharaoh Merneptah (1212–1202 BCE) who claimed to have destroyed the seed of Israel. The discovery in 1896 of Merneptah's Stele containing the oldest mention of Israel in the archaeological record has led to continual debate. Where were these people located? Who they were? What was their relationship to the cities in Canaan, those mentioned in the stele and those listed in previous Egyptian conquests? What deity did these people worship? (see Additional Readings: Merneptah Stele).

The discussions about the meaning of the term 'Israel' in the Merneptah Stele at times may be myopic. After all, additional names were mentioned. As Egyptologist Ellen Morris points out, Gezer and Yenoam had appeared before in the Egyptian records as periodic irritants dating back to the 15th century BCE. The newcomer to the Canaanite city-list was Ashkelon, a day's march from the Egyptian stronghold at Gaza, the border between Egypt and Canaan. She suggests that a city in such close proximity to a major Egyptian military base only would have rebelled if 'something had gone fundamentally wrong in Egypt's maintenance of its northern empire… Ashkelon would never have attempted insurrection had Egypt been in full fighting form'. She posits that the joint attack by the (non-Arab) Libyans and the Sea Peoples on Egypt created a window of opportunity for Ashkelon given the magnitude of Egyptian forces committed to resisting those intrusions. Morris wonders if Ashkelon expected aid from Gezer and notes that these two cities warred against Jerusalem in the Amarna Age. One may add that Israel would have been an eyewitness to these machinations among the Canaanite cities, Egypt, and the Sea Peoples and these actions potentially were part of its collective memory. To isolate Israel from the surrounding political developments creates a skewed understanding of Israel's early history. Israel was not alone in its opposition to Egypt and there is no inherent reason that these different entities were not as aware of each other as their counterparts had been during the Amarna Age.[14]

There has been an ongoing 'discussion' about the role of archaeology in deciphering the history of Israel from Merneptah to monarchy (Iron I, 1200–1000 BCE) in particular. The extent of writing and the differences between Israel and its neighbors in material culture, values and lifestyle, all have generated intense differences of opinion expressed vocally and in print. Rather than become even more entangled in the extensive debate on these issues, for purposes of this study there are four working assumptions which will be followed. The working assumptions presented here will be vociferously objected by those with alternate paradigms and agendas.

1. There was a people who identified itself as Israel in the 13th century BCE in the land of Canaan in the hill-country land of the Rachel tribes, Benjamin and Joseph (Ephraim and Manasseh).
2. The Israelite people worshiped Yahweh.
3. Over time, there were additional peoples who identified as or allied with Israel of their own free will during the time of continued Egyptian hegemony in the land ending with Ramses VI in 1139 BCE.
4. After centuries of not having a king, there came a time when Israel did have a king.
5. During the Iron I period from Merneptah to monarchy, there were peoples who did not become Israelite and who remained loyal vassals of Egypt when Israel emerged in history as an enemy of Egypt.

In sum, Israel originated, acted, and remembered within the context of this secular reality. The events in the 13th–12th centuries when Israel did not have a king and when Egypt still ruled Canaan became part of Israel's cultural legacy (see Additional Readings: Israelite History – Iron I).

According to the biblical account there was an altercation between Israel and Jerusalem during this time period:

> **Joshua 10: 1** *When **Adonizedek king of Jerusalem** heard how Joshua had taken Ai, and had utterly destroyed it, doing to Ai and its king as he had done to Jericho and its king, and how the inhabitants of Gibeon had made peace with Israel and were among them,* [2] *he feared greatly, because Gibeon was a great city, like one of the royal cities, and because it was greater than Ai, and all its men were mighty.* [3] *So Adonizedek king of Jerusalem sent to Hoham king of Hebron, to Piram king of Jarmuth, to Japhia king of Lachish, and to Debir king of Eglon, saying,* [4] *'Come up to me, and help me, and let us smite Gibeon; for it has made peace with Joshua and with the people of Israel.'* [5] *Then **the five kings of the Amorites, the king of Jerusalem**, the king of Hebron, the king of Jarmuth, the king of Lachish, and the king of Eglon, gathered their forces, and went up with all their armies and encamped against Gibeon, and made war against it.*

This narrative text does not date to the time of the confrontation. Nonetheless, it is a valuable source of information.

The idea of an alliance among Canaanite cites against a common foe with the blessing of Pharaoh is consistent with the *modus operandi* during the Amarna Age a century earlier.

---

14 Ellen Morris, *The Architecture of Imperialism: Military Bases and the Evolution of Foreign Policy in Egypt's New Kingdom* (Leiden: Brill, 2005), 379–381, quotations from 379.

Whether Merneptah sponsored this coalition as part of his quest to destroy the seed of Israel or another Pharaoh did afterwards given Merneptah's failure, the coalition presented in the narrative served the needs of Egypt. Na'aman notes that 'once Pharaoh decided to operate and start organizing a campaign to Asia, internal conflicts [in Canaan] abruptly ceased'. Merneptah's campaign to destroy Israel certainly signaled his desires. The responsibility of the vassal cities was to assist Pharaoh in his endeavors dated back to Thutmose III in the 15th century BCE, continued through the Amarna Age in the 14th century BCE, and presumably still functioned in the 13th–12th centuries BCE until Egypt withdrew from the land of Canaan. If Merneptah was confronted with threats from Nubia, Libya, the Sea Peoples and Canaan, all the more reason for the beleaguered king to outsource the military response to his vassals whenever possible. The weaker kings who followed him would have been even more willing for the coalition of Canaanite cities to pick up the slack against Israel (see Additional Readings: Merneptah's Canaanite Coalition versus Israel).[15]

Merneptah even has left images of the Canaanite military forces which would have participated in such an encounter. Besides his textual legacy of the campaign against Israel, Merneptah had images of the campaign against the three Canaanite cities and Israel at the Cour de la Cachette, a wall at Karnak, the site where multiple Pharaohs left images of their victories (see Additional Readings: Merneptah: Cour de la Cachette). They bear witness to the military forces which Canaanite cities that resisted him could bring to bear in battle. One may reasonably conclude that Canaanite cities which supported him possessed similar military capabilities. One notes in the biblical passage, the reference to Gibeon as a great city like a royal city filled with mighty men or *gibborim* (see Chapter 4). Gibeon was the site where the mighty men of David and Ishbaal, Saul's son, would battle over succession after Saul died (II Sam. 2). It was the site where Solomon sacrificed at a great altar before his dream when Yahweh granted him wisdom (I Kings 3: 4–5). There were serious geopolitical consequences to a formidable city like Gibeon joining Israel in an anti-Egyptian alliance.

One should be cognizant that the author of this passage was delivering a message in the present of its writing. He was not an eyewitness to the battle. Furthermore it is reasonable to conclude that the author intended the message to be taken seriously and not be rejected as fraudulent, a lie he just made up. Regardless of the date of origin of the text, it describes what became the City of David and capital of the kingdom of Judah initiating a campaign against the Israelite emergence in the land of Canaan by attacking its ally, the great royal city of Gibeon. In American terms, this would be roughly comparable to an historian/ politician during the Civil War accusing Confederates of having been Loyalists to King George III and not Patriots during the American Revolution. The story of an attack by Jerusalem against Israel is a story which attacks Jerusalem at the time of the writing of the story. It draws on the historical reality that Jerusalem did not welcome Israel when it first appeared in the land of Canaan.[16]

---

15 Nadav Na'aman, 'The Egyptian–Canaanite correspondence', in Raymond Cohen and Raymond Westbrook, eds, *Amarna Diplomacy: The Beginnings of International Relations* (Baltimore: Johns Hopkins University Press, 2000), 125–138, here 137.

16 Na'aman claims the story was intended to positively depict Jerusalem as at the center of events in ancient times for the purpose of glorifying the city in the present (Nadav Na'aman, 'Jerusalem in the Amara period',

In the biblical version, the results of the Jerusalem initiative were not favorable for the Canaanite–Amorite coalition arrayed against Israel. In this encounter Yahweh fought for Israel and prevailed. A song commemorated the victory:

Joshua 10: 12–14 *Then spoke Joshua to Yahweh in the day when Yahweh gave the Amorites over to the men of Israel; and he said in the sight of Israel, 'Sun, stand thou still at Gibeon, and thou Moon in the valley of Aijalon'. And the sun stood still, and the moon stayed, until the nation took vengeance on their enemies. Is this not written in the Book of Jashar? The sun stayed in the midst of heaven, and did not hasten to go down for about a whole day. There has been no day like it before or since, when Yahweh hearkened to the voice of a man; for Yawheh fought for Israel.*

As one might expect, the biblical claim of the sun and moon standing still has been the source of much speculation. Some exegetes seek to document a literal event in astronomical terms; others focus on the metaphorical meaning within the context of neighboring cultures as well as the Israelite tradition linking victories on earth with cosmic events. Thomas Römer posits as one possibility that the sun (Shamash) and moon (Yarah) were the deities of Jerusalem. Therefore the song sings to the triumph of Yahweh over the gods of Jerusalem. Michael Astour wonders if the sun and the moon had been the deities of Benjamin before Benjamin became part of Israel. When victory was achieved on its land, Benjamin then sang to its old deities along with its new one. Benjamin's song of victory may be understood as a counterpart to Miriam's song of victory in the Exodus (Ex. 15: 20–21). These songs become part of the story of the writing of the Hebrew Bible in narrative prose format including the six son stories in this study (see Chapter 9) (see Additional Readings: Valley of Aijalon).[17]

The Book of Jashar containing this song of victory deserves a second look. The site of the confrontation was Gibeon, a city assigned to the tribe of Benjamin (Josh. 18: 25). The only other reference to the Book of Jashar is David's lamentation over the deaths of Benjaminites Saul and Jonathan (I Sam. 1: 17–18). A possible third instance reference to the Book of Jashar occurs with Solomon's prayer at the dedication of the temple (I Kings 8: 12–13). The LXX version directs the reader to the Book of Song with Hebrew 'song' containing the same three consonants as 'Jashar' but with the first two transposed.[18] All three examples of this archaic poetry have then have a Benjaminite connection: a battle is fought there at Gibeon in support of its Gibeonite allies when Israel first appears in the land of Canaan, an elegy praises the deceased Benjaminite king and his son, and Solomon has his dream of a temple at Gibeon in the land of Benjamin. One reasonable conclusion is that Benjamin sang a song of victory in the name of Yahweh against a Jerusalem-led coalition which was first written in the (Song) Book of Jashar and later became part of an anti-Jerusalem Benjamin narrative.

---

in Caroline Amould-Béhar and André Lemaire, eds, *Jerusalem Antique et Medievale: Mélanges en l'honneur d'Ernest-Marie Laperrousaz* (Paris: Peeters, 2011), 31–48; here 48). His interpretation fails to recognize the possibility that putting Jerusalem in a leadership position against Israel was intended as an assault on those who praised the Canaanite city at the expense of Israel.

17 Michael Astour, 'Benê-iamina et Jéricho', *Semitica* 9 1959: 5–20; Thomas Römer, *The Invention of God* (Cambridge, MA: Harvard University Press, 2015), 126–127.

18 Duane L. Christensen, 'Jashar', in *ABD* III: 646–647.

Based on the Book of Jashar and other biblical songs, William Schniedewind posits that a national scroll of ancient Israelite songs existed. It comprised an oral repertoire for temple singers who performed Israel's epic myths at festivals and other cultic occasions. It existed already by the 10th century BCE when Israel became a monarchy. Actually, nothing in the songs Schniedewind refers to requires the existence of a temple. It is unlikely that Israel existed for centuries without songs to sing especially after Pharaoh Merneptah claimed to have destroyed them and failed. It is precisely these papyrus scrolls of poetic songs from Israel's beginnings as a people that would have been sources for the prose narrative scrolls when Israel became a monarchy. I suggest Benjamin's anti-Jerusalem proclivities and writing continued into the monarchy when the prose narratives were written.[19]

Regardless of the dates or origins of the presumably older songs and subsequent narrative texts, they bespeak a legacy of animosity between Israel and Jerusalem from the dawn of Israel's appearance in the land. The battles against the Jerusalem-initiated Canaanite coalition at Gibeon in what became the land of Benjamin and the Canaanite kings near Megiddo (Song of Deborah, Judg. 5) undoubtedly were remembered by both sides. Jerusalem may have taken pride in its mighty men resisting Israel but such praise of its heroes of yore was unlikely to have been received favorably by Israelites with different memories. One can appreciate the challenge in getting Merneptah's Israel to later accept a Canaanite city as its capital after at least two centuries of existence in the hill-country without having a capital city. The challenge was magnified if that city had been an opponent of Israel.

Niels Peter Lemche suggests it is possible to trace the anti-Canaanite sentiments in the biblical narrative back to the Late Bronze Age. Canaanites should be defined not as an ethnic group, not as a geographical term, and not as merchants or traders. Instead they are the people whom the Egyptians selected from among the people they encountered in the cities to serve as their agents or representatives in the administration of their empire. 'The local inhabitants may therefore have used the term "Canaanites" to denote their foreign oppressors and especially their local lackeys'. These Canaanites were always understood to be the enemies of Israel. Lemche's insight contributes to understanding the cursing of Canaan in the story of the sons of Noah and the antipathy to the pre-Israelite pro-Egypt Jebusite leaders in Jerusalem.[20]

The strong Egyptian presence which had been maintained through the reign of Ramses III in the 12th century BCE abruptly ended during the reign of Ramses VI by 1139 BCE. Morris characterizes the end of Egyptian rule as 'a short and bloody affair'. Her survey of Egyptian military bases in Canaan indicates that virtually every one was torched. Her interpretation of the situation bears witness to how people might react if similar circumstances were to be repeated:

> '[T]he local populations must have seized the opportunity of Egypt's internal weakness to rid themselves of their overlords. Without Egyptian taxation, corvée labor demands, co-option

---

19 William M. Schniedewind, *How the Bible Became a Book* (New York: Cambridge University Press, 2004), 52–56.

20 Niels Peter Lemche, 'City-dwellers or administrators: further light on the Canaanites', in André Lemaire and Benedikt Otzen, eds, *History and Traditions of Early Israel: Studies Presented to Eduard Nielsen, May 8th 1993* (SVT 50; Leiden: E. J. Brill, 1993), 76–89, quotation from 89.

of local industries and resources, and interference in local politics, the inhabitants of Canaan must surely have believed that their lots would improve significantly.'

One may add that it is reasonable to expect that Israelites would react the same way if they ever experienced such rule in the land of Canaan under their own 'Pharaoh'.[21]

The appearance of Jerusalem changed after the withdrawal of Egyptian forces from the land of Canaan. Two monumental structures in the city from this time period have been discovered by archaeologists. The first is the Stone Stepped Structure. This terraced construction on the eastern slope of the city was built possibly as an integral part of the city's fortification system. It is dated to the Iron I period, meaning the 12th or 11th centuries BCE, prior to the creation of the Israelite kingdom. The structure consists of two parts: a stone mantle and rampart built on a terracing system. Theoretically the two components could have been built separately. Such a construction project demonstrates the capabilities of the city government to initiate an organized effort on a massive scale just as it had done centuries earlier when it build the walls and gates which protected the perennial water source at Gihon (see Additional Readings: Stone Stepped Structure).

The second building is the more recently discovered Large Stone Structure. The two structures generally are perceived to be one entity with the more extensively-preserved Stone Stepped Structure serving as a support for the mostly-vanished Large Stone Structure on the summit. This view is consistent with the biblical text referring the fortress of Zion:

> **II Samuel 5: 9** *And David dwelt in the stronghold, and called it the city of David. And David built the city round about from the Millo inward.*

Na'aman suggests that David built the Large Stone Structure as his palace separate from the Jebusite stronghold of Zion and that its importance in the First Temple Period has been ignored. Together the two structures reveal part of the city David would make his capital (see Additional Readings: Large Stone Structure).

A natural question to ask is 'Why did the Jebusites build it?' Amihai Mazar decisively declares its magnitude and uniqueness had no parallel from the 12th to early 9th centuries BCE in the Levant. Its construction was an impressive and monumental achievement. One should keep in mind that the Jerusalem inhabitants during the 12th and 11th centuries were aware of the growing presence of the Israelites (and Philistines) and the withdrawal of the Egyptian forces. One reasonable conclusion is that Jebusites faced with the realization that they were on their own decided to act to protect themselves by constructing the Stone Stepped Structure and the Large Stone Structure.[22]

---

21 Morris, *The Architecture of Imperialism*, 546–586, 709, quotations from 709.

22 Amihai Mazar, 'Archaeology and the Biblical narrative: the case of the united monarchy', in Reinhard G. Kratz and Hermann Spieckermann, eds, *One God – One Cult – One Nation: Archaeological and Biblical Perspectives* (BZAW 405; Berlin: Walter de Gruyter, 2010), 29–58, here 45. Mazar employs identical words in publications in 2006 and 2007: Amihai Mazar, 'Jerusalem in the 10th century BCE: the glass half full', in Yairah Amit and Nadav Na'aman, eds, *Essays on Ancient Israel in its Near Eastern Context: A Tribute to Nadav Na'aman* (Winona Lake: Eisenbrauns, 2006), 255–272, here 264, and 'The spade and the text: the interaction between archaeology and Israelite history relating to the tenth–ninth centuries BCE', in H. G. M. Williamson, ed., *Understanding the History of Ancient Israel* (Oxford: Oxford University Press, 2007), 143–171, here 152–153.

While earthly assistance from Pharaoh may not have been available anymore, there always was divine assistance. Israel invoked it through Yahweh against Jerusalem and the Canaanites in the biblical narrative. It is reasonable to conclude that the residents of Jerusalem worshiped a god prior to the city becoming the capital of the kingdom of David. There are no archaeological records to indicate who that deity might be. The Bible suggests the deity might be Elyon.

> **Genesis 14: 18** *And Melchizedek king of Salem brought out bread and wine; he was priest of God Most High.* [19] *And he blessed him and said, 'Blessed be Abram by God Elyon, maker of heaven and earth;* [20] *and blessed be God Elyon, who has delivered your enemies into your hand!' And Abram gave him a tenth of everything.*

This passage identifies Elyon as the deity of Salem or Jerusalem and who is the creator of the universe and who is served by the king/priest.[23] Such a description is exalted to say the least (see Additional Readings: Elyon).

This Elyon is roughly comparable to El known from the Ugaritic texts who is the chief deity of the pantheon (see Additional Readings: for Ugaritic Texts and for El). That El had a consort, Asherah also known as Athirat, the mother of the gods, probably of Amorite origin (see Additional Readings: Asherah). She was antagonistic towards Baal (see Additional Readings: Baal). There has been extensive discussion among biblical scholars about Asherah also becoming the consort of Yahweh due to the archaeological discoveries of the cultic stands at Pella and Tanaach and the inscriptions at Khirbet el-Qom and Kuntillet Ajrud. The process commenced in the 10th century BCE, meaning at the time David made Jerusalem the capital of his kingdom of Israel. If Yahweh and El are to be equated, then El's wife needed to be addressed in some way. It is reasonable to conclude that the Canaanite inhabitants of Jerusalem prior to David worshiped an El-based deity with a female consort Asherah. The complexities of these relationships would become part of the contention in the battle for power after David died.

The day of reckoning for the Jebusites was fast approaching. New settlements attributed to Israel had exploded across the landscape in areas allocated to the Rachel tribes, the lands of Benjamin and Joseph (Ephraim and Manasseh). During this time Jerusalem was not part of Israel. As previously mentioned, Jebus and Jerusalem are equated in the story of the rape of the Bethlemite woman (Judg. 19: 10–11). In the next verse, the author makes clear that Jebus is not an Israelite city either:

> **Judges 19: 12** *And his master said to him, 'We will not turn aside into the city of foreigners, who do not belong to the people of Israel; but we will pass on to Gibeah.'*

If written prior to Jerusalem becoming the capital of Israel, this verse would simply be a statement of fact providing geographical information. If written while Jerusalem was the capital of Israel, this verse mocks the city that led a coalition of Canaanite cities against

---

23 Kirkland contests the equation of Salem and Jerusalem and advances the claim that Shechem is meant. As for the double meetings at Salem (Gen. 14: 18–20) and Sodom (Gen. 14: 17, 21–24) in this story, Kirkland proposes variant endings to the same story which is the exact methodological approach followed in this study – writers in dialog with each other (J. R. Kirkland, 'The incident at Salem: a re-examination of Genesis 14: 18–20', *Studia Biblica et Theologica* 7 1977: 3–23.

Israel as not really Israelite. The verse also implies that the Levite and the woman under his care will be protected in Gibeah, the capital of Saul's kingdom, and not in foreign Jerusalem. That presumption proves false.

According to another biblical text, even though the city of the Jebusites was assigned to the tribe of Benjamin, the tribe had been unsuccessful in its efforts to dislodge them:

> **Joshua 18: 28** *Zela, Haeleph, Jebus (that is, Jerusalem), Gibeah and Kiriathjearim – fourteen cities with their villages. This is the inheritance of the tribe of Benjamin according to its families.*

> **Judges 1: 21** *But the people of Benjamin did not drive out the Jebusites who dwelt in Jerusalem; so the Jebusites have dwelt with the people of Benjamin in Jerusalem to this day.*

One notes the failure of the Benjaminite rebellions against David in Jerusalem (Shimei who rebelled in II Sam. 16, repented in II Sam. 19, supported Solomon in I Kings 1 and was killed on Solomon's orders in I Kings 2). Benjamin's success in establishing its presence in Jerusalem had failed. If these verses were written while Jerusalem was the capital of Israel, then they mocked the military prowess of Benjamin and in effect blame Benjamin for the predicament of the Jebusites with their Canaanite ways still being around in the capital of the kingdom. One presumes Benjamin would wish to remove that stain from its record.[24]

As it turns out, the city also was assigned to the tribe of Judah which experienced similar failure in dislodging the Jebusites:

> **Joshua 15: 8** *then the boundary goes up by the valley of the son of Hinnom at the southern shoulder of the Jebusite (that is, Jerusalem); and the boundary goes up to the top of the mountain that lies over against the valley of Hinnom, on the west, at the northern end of the valley of Rephaim;*

> **Joshua 15: 63** *But the Jebusites, the inhabitants of Jerusalem, the people of Judah could not drive out; so the Jebusites dwell with the people of Judah at Jerusalem to this day.*

Judah fares no better than Benjamin in dislodging the Jebusites. These conflicting passages in the Books of Joshua and Judges reveal tensions concerning the cultural memory of ownership of the city, the failure to conquer it, and who is to blame for the continued presence of the non-Israelite Jebusites. One should keep in mind that the tribe of Judah and the kingdom of Judah based at Hebron under David both excluded Jerusalem. It is incorrect to presume that the mention of Judah in a story automatically refers to the kingdom of Judah including Jerusalem when obviously here it does not.

Strangely there is one tradition of a conquest of Jerusalem:

> **Judges 1: 8** *And the men [sons] of Judah fought against Jerusalem, and took it, and smote it with the **edge of the sword**, and set the city on fire.*

There are a couple of dozen 'edge of the sword' conquests in the biblical narrative. The battle victories often are quite comprehensive in their destructiveness and annihilation. In so far as Jerusalem is concerned, outside of this isolated verse which seems to bear no relation to the verses in Joshua, there is nothing to indicate textually or archaeologically that Jerusalem experienced such a violent defeat. The closest non-David example of a conquest of Jerusalem occurred when his son Absalom was temporarily successful in his Hebron-

---

24 See Marc Brettler, 'The Book of Judges: literature as politics', *JBL* 108 1989: 395–418, here 402.

based rebellion (II Sam. 15: 7–11). All things considered, the overwhelmingly impression of the biblical narrative is that Jerusalem was not part of Israel until David.

David's Canaan, Israel, and Jerusalem

Prior to David no individual had ruled all the land of Canaan save for various Pharaohs. Now that someone within the land of Canaan ruled it, it raised the issue where he would reside. David's selection of Jerusalem as his capital city sometimes is likened to the decision by the Founding Fathers of the United States to make the City of Washington the capital. These decisions to pick neutral turfs that neither side, north nor south, could lay claim to, are considered politically astute resolutions to divisive issues. However, the decisions were starkly different. Washington was founded on empty land. By contrast, the City of David was a renamed city of longstanding in the land of Canaan that is still better known by its non-Israelite name, Jerusalem. While there is no story to the City of Washington before it became the nation's capital, there is a story to the City of David before it became the kingdom's capital.

A second major difference in the selection of Jerusalem and Washington was the domain of the capital city. In the American example, the new city of Washington became the capital of a people who had rebelled against English rule. Indeed, the city was named after the commander of the army of the rebellion. In the biblical example, the old city of Jerusalem became the capital of a people it previously had fought against and had remained separate from for two centuries. A more relevant question to ask is why David would even choose an anti-Israelite Canaanite city to be his capital of his kingdom of Israel? Then given that decision, how did he succeed to make it so?

There is no tradition of Jerusalem welcoming Israel. There is a tradition of Jerusalem being a loyal vassal to Egypt. There is a tradition of Jerusalem turning to Egypt for help when threatened. If there was diplomatic correspondence from the 13th and 12th centuries BCE between the Canaanite cities and the king of Egypt undoubtedly it would have included requests from Jerusalem for help against the Israelites as it did in the 14th century against the unrelated *habiru*. In addition we are missing from both periods the correspondence between the Egyptians stationed in Canaan and the home office about the situation on the ground. Such correspondence would have reiterated the cause for concern about Israel contained in the diplomatic correspondence. What then made Jerusalem an attractive choice to David for his capital?[25]

David's kingdom consisted of four parts (or at least, that is how I choose to divide it).

---

25 Baruch Halpern makes the same point about the Philistines as I do about the Israelites: 'had we an archive comparable to that of Amarna for the twelfth and eleventh centuries, we should likely be hearing a greater deal about competition and conflict even among the Philistines', Baruch Halpern, 'The dawn of an age: Megiddo in the Iron Age I', in J. David Schloen and Lawrence E. Stager (eds), *Exploring the Long Durée: Essays in Honor of Lawrence E. Stager* (Winona Lake: Eisenbrauns, 2009), 151–163, here 157. Morris observes that 'the Egyptian government must have relied heavily on reports from officials based in the area [in the Amarna Period] … [and] there is no reason to suggest that this situation would have been significantly dissimilar in the Nineteenth Dynasty' (*The Architecture of Imperialism*, 462, also 481).

1. Merneptah's Israel

Originally, Israel in the land of Canaan was a hill-country region consisting of the Rachel tribes, Benjamin and Joseph (Ephraim and Manasseh). When Saul became king of Israel he choose his home town of Gibeah in the land of Benjamin for his capital.

A list of tribes identified by name comprising the kingdom of Israel appears in II Sam. 2: 9. One option for David was to choose his home town of Bethlehem for his capital. Bethlehem appears infrequently in the biblical narrative except for David, Ruth, and some stories in Judges 17 and 19 where it is normally identified as 'in Judah'. A Philistine garrison once held the city and three of David's mighty men attacked it without exactly liberating it (II Sam. 24: 14–16). After that it effectively disappears from the narrative.

One Israelite city which David might have considered is Bethel, the second most frequently named city in the biblical narrative (71 times). It is located on the border between Benjamin and Ephraim and jurisdiction over it seems to have shifted over time. Bethel figures prominently in some of the patriarchal stories which had not yet been written when David made his decision about a capital city for his kingdom of Israel.

> Abram built a sanctuary there to Yahweh after he arrived in land of Canaan. He and Lot then allocated the lands for each of them (Gen. 12: 8 and 13).

Jacob had his famous stairway to heaven dream there and actually is credited with naming the site Bethel, house of God (Gen. 28: 11–22). Later. God even identifies himself as the 'God of Bethel' (Gen. 31: 13). In a confusing chapter of multiple important actions (Gen. 35), God instructs Jacob to return to Bethel and build an altar, Deborah, the nurse of Rebecca is buried there, and Jacob's wife Rachel dies on the journey from Bethel to Ephrath that is Bethlehem while giving birth to Benjamin.[26]

Bethel figures in additional stories involving Joshua (7–8) and a showdown between Benjamin and the rest of Israel (Judg. 20–21). Samuel's annual circuit linked Bethel, Gilgal and Mizpah (I Sam. 7: 16). It then becomes a sanctuary city for Jeroboam when the kingdom splits after the death of Solomon (I Kings 12). His placement of golden calves, a derogatory put down of the bulls, probably derives from the sites identification with El who is represented by a bull in Ugaritic tradition and archaeological discoveries. For Jeroboam, then the God El is responsible for the Exodus and his site Bethel is a fitting location for the sanctuary of the kingdom of Israel. All things considered, Bethel seems like an excellent choice for a capital city for the kingdom of Israel. But David did not choose it (see Additional Readings: Bethel).

2. Deborah's Israel

The Song of Deborah (Judg. 5) identifies a number of tribes by name as part of Israel including the Rachel tribes. The names are more extensive than those in the list of tribes in the chronologically-later Saul's kingdom (above). I see the Deborah grouping as comparable to an American-led anti-Soviet Union NATO coalition consisting of Israel and other anti-

---

26 In addition to all the Genesis commentaries which have sections on the Jacob chapters, see Baden, *The Composition of the Pentateuch*, 230–245, for Gen. 35.

Egyptian peoples on both sides of the Jordan River. As with NATO, when the leader calls members to battle, they do not always honor their commitments. Since there was no king or central command structure, the likelihood is that there was no change in the lives of the people in this coalition. It is also quite likely that these non-Rachel tribes did not consider themselves to be Israelite as much as to be allies of Israel which perhaps is why not all of them belonged to Saul's kingdom.

Looking at Deborah's Israel, there are several cities which come to mind as candidates for capital of the kingdom once all the tribes became part of the Israelite political entity. Starting in the north, the first city is Hazor. The prominence of the city dates back to the Middle Bronze Age when it is listed in the Mari Archives. Its orientation may have been to Mesopotamia rather than to Egypt. In fact, during the 13th century BCE when the city was under the sway of Egypt, a massive conflagration of intense heat burnt not just the city in general but the mutilated Egyptian statues in particular. The attack was so fierce and concentrated as to suggest that the Egyptian rulers were the target. So vehement and thorough was the assault on all things Egyptian that the uprising might be considered the first Arab Spring except none of the people involved was an Arab.

The identity of the people who committed the attack is debated. Israel figures in the discussion. I favor an interpretation of the people as being un-Jerusalemites. Just as there were Canaanite cities which supported Pharaoh, so there were those who opposed Egyptian rule. It would be a mistake to presume that Ramses II listed in his monuments all the Canaanite cities which opposed his rule. In Hazor we have an example, possibly inspired by Israel, of local inhabitants who took matters into their own hands to cleanse the city of any and all signs of Egypt. Once they were done and their city had been destroyed in the process, they became refugees, people who voted with their feet and emigrated to join Israel.

According to the biblical narrative, Hazor was 'king of all those kingdoms' (Josh. 11: 10).

Solomon builds a wall at Hazor (I Kings 9: 15) and the six-chambered gates which have been discovered there have become embroiled in a bitter imbroglio among biblical scholars as to the date of the construction. Joshua is remembered for having burned Hazor to the ground in his defeat of Jabin, king of Hazor (Josh. 11). The Kenite woman Jael is remembered for having slain Sisera, the ally of Jabin, king of Hazor, in the prose version of the Song of Deborah (Judg. 4). One gets the impression that Hazor remained a battleground in Israelite politics long after the city actually had been burned to the ground. In any event, David did not chose Hazor to be his capital (see Additional Readings: Hazor).

Shechem, in the hill country, is one other Canaanite city worth mentioning as a possible candidate for capital of David's Kingdom of Israel. As with Jerusalem, the city is mentioned in the Execration Texts and also by an officer of Pharaoh Sesostris III regarding a military campaign there. As with Jerusalem, the city is mentioned in the Amarna Texts. In fact, Shechem's imperial aggrandizement within the land of Canaan made the city and its king Labayu prominent topics of discussion in the correspondence. Canaanite cities joined the pro-Shechem alliance or the anti-Shechem alliance in this dispute. The war of words and on the ground continued until Pharaoh became involved and the anti-Canaanite coalition prevailed apparently with the destruction of the city. Then a few centuries later in the Iron I period, the city itself was temporarily destroyed.

Typically overlooked in the archaeology of the site is the mention of Jacob-el and Joseph-el in the Egyptian records. Thutmose III in the 15th century BCE included them in a list of the cities (or peoples) in the land of Canaan he had conquered.[27] Unfortunately there is no way to know exactly where these people were located not what happened to them (brought as captives to Egypt?). In any event, the names are suggestive of El-worshiping people in the land. Jacob and Joseph are two names closely tied with the biblical traditions of Shechem.

Given its location smack in the middle of the tribe of Joseph and its anti-Egyptian history, the Canaanite city of Shechem was a natural candidate to join forces with Israel. Certainly it became intricately intertwined into Israelite history according to the biblical narrative without actually being part of Israel.

> Abram passes through Shechem on his way to Bethel and southward (Gen. 12: 6).
> Jacob purchases land and builds an altar there after separating from Esau (Gen. 33: 18–20.)
> Jacob's sons pasture his sheep there in the story of Joseph (Gen. 37: 12–13).
> The city is on the boundary of Manasseh (Josh. 17: 7) in the hill country of Ephraim (Josh. 20: 7).
> Joshua gathers the tribes of Israel there and enters into a covenant with them before he dies (Josh. 24).
> Joseph's bones which had been brought from Egypt are buried at Shechem on the land Jacob had purchased and the land became an inheritance for his descendants (Josh. 24: 32).

Rehoboam meets the Israelite people who have gathered at Shechem. Instead of the son of Solomon being recognized as king by them, they withdraw from the kingdom. Jeroboam becomes king of Israel with his capital at Shechem, the city David did not choose (I Kings 12). Ironically, this event marks the first time in the narrative tradition when Shechem really seems to be an Israelite city.

Shechem as an individual is a leading figure in the story typically referred to as 'The Rape of Dinah' (Gen. 34). In this story he is the son of Hamor which means 'donkey'. These names are clues that the story is politically-based and not a biologically- or physically-based one. Shechem seeks Dinah, the daughter of Jacob, to be is wife. Negotiations between the appropriate parties ensue. One may glimpse behind this story the honorable and peaceful settlement of Israel in the vicinity of Shechem followed by the virtually inevitable mingling of the two peoples. This situation is what one would expect when the two anti-Egypt peoples first met. However, the story also presents a dominant claim by Shechem as he is the husband in the story and Israel the female wife. Keeping in mind that political stories are expressed through kin relationships, the Shechem dominance scenario is likely the one the established city pursued when newcomer Israel first appeared proclaiming its anti-Egyptian hegemony message.

---

27 James B. Pritchard, ed., *Near Eastern Texts Relating to the Old Testament* (Princeton: Princeton University Press, 1955), 242.

The story humiliates Shechem for pursuit of dominance over Israel. The two peoples agree to enter into a covenant or alliance. To signify its participation, all the males of the city agree to be circumcised. During their sore time, they are in a vulnerable position, just as the drunk Noah had been. Here, they are exposed to the sons of Jacob. The brothers Simeon and Levi kill them. The story of the rape of Dinah ends badly for the city of Shechem with the males slain and the city plundered. According to Jacob, Simeon and Levi have made Jacob's people odious to the inhabitants of the land and exposed them to attack by the Canaanites and Perizzites. This story of the sons and a daughter of Jacob is comparable to the six supplemental son stories in this study. It attests the war of words after the death of David could become fairly intense in the battle for power and sheds light on Shechem's unsuitability for a capital city. As a supplement ot the KDB it would have written precisely when Shechem became the capital of Israel and Jeroboam did not choose the Levites to be his priests (I Kings 12: 31). Excavating Gen. 34 would require another chapter in Part I and lengthen Part II.

The story does raise the issue of how Shechem became part of Israel. According to Gen. 33: 18–20, the verses immediately prior to the story, Jacob purchased land at Shechem. In Gen. 35: 1, the verse immediately after the story, God instructs Jacob to go to Bethel as noted above. These two verses suggest the story of Shechem was inserted into the narrative as the sudden focus on Jacob's children disrupts the narrative flow. In Gen. 48: 22, when Jacob is nearing the end of his life, he blesses Ephraim and Manasseh (Shechem is on the border between the two tribes):

> Moreover I have given to you rather than to your brothers one mountain slope which I took from the hand of the Amorites with my sword and with my bow.

While Jacob does not name the mountain slope, one possibility to keep in mind is that was referring to Shechem and a violent conquest of it.

Shechem also plays a significant role in another story of violence in Judges 9. Excavating it also would require another chapter in Part I and lengthen Part II considerably. The story has been interpreted as originally a showdown between deities through human agents. In what is believed to be the oldest portion of the story the issue of kingship is raised:

> **Judges 9: 27** And they went out into the field, and gathered the grapes from their vineyards and trod them, and held festival, and went into the house of their god, and ate and drank and reviled Abimelech.[28] And Gaal the son of Ebed said, 'Who is Abimelech, and who are we of Shechem, that we should serve him? Did not the son of Jerubbaal and Zebul his officer serve the men of Hamor the father of Shechem? Why then should we serve him?'

During what may be construed as the Canaanite new year festival at the navel of the land (Judg. 9: 37), the cosmic center, Gaal directly challenges the authority of the ruling king, Abimelech, 'my father is king', in the name of the Shechemites. In divine terms, his action is comparable to Baal challenging El for the kingship. 'Zebul' or 'prince' in the Ugaritic tradition refers to Baal. One should keep in mind the likelihood that with Egypt withdrawn from the land and the Philistines in the land, Canaanite cities may have 'debated' with which side to ally. Canaanite cities were quite capable of conflicts without the direct military presence of Israel.

A similar predicament to Gaal's declaration occurs in the Israelite political world after the death of Solomon. As mentioned, his son Rehoboam journeys to Shechem to meet with 'all Israel'. The negotiations go badly and end with a rejection of royal authority:

> **1 Kings 12: 16** *And when all Israel saw that the king did not hearken to them, the people answered the king, 'What portion have we in David? We have no inheritance in the son of Jesse. To your tents, O Israel! Look now to your own house, David.' So Israel departed to their tents.*

Regardless of the specific dates of the stories, they strongly suggest intense situations about Shechem's place within Israel and royal rule.

Part of the fascination with the Abimelech story is the appearance of a deity Baal-Berith, or a covenant god in the name of Baal. The appellation is especially interesting given the story of a covenant at Shechem between Joshua and Israel (above). The relevant verses are:

> **Judges 8: 33** *As soon as Gideon died, the people of Israel turned again and played the harlot after the Baals, and made **Baalberith** their god.*

> **Judges 9: 4** *And they gave him seventy pieces of silver out of the house of **Baalberith** with which Abimelech hired worthless and reckless fellows, who followed him.*

> **Judges 9: 46** *When all the people of the Tower of Shechem heard of it, they entered the stronghold of the house of **Elberith [not Baal].** [47] Abimelech was told that all the people of the Tower of Shechem were gathered together. [48] And Abimelech went up to Mount Zalmon, he and all the men that were with him; and Abimelech took an axe in his hand, and cut down a bundle of brushwood, and took it up and laid it on his shoulder. And he said to the men that were with him, 'What you have seen me do, make haste to do, as I have done.'*

Also related to this deity at Shechem are the connection between the people in the story and those in the Shechem-based story of the rape of Dinah in Judges 9: 28 (above). Combined, these verses tell the story of a non-Jacob population who served Baal and opposed the father-king in the form of Abimelech. What should one make of this deity and the people who served him?

R. E. Clements, perhaps the first modern scholar to fully address the topic, concludes that 'the covenant of Baal-Berith was a local "ruler" covenant to which much of the Israelite ethos and tradition was opposed'.[28] Theodore Lewis, who pointedly refers to Clements as being the 'notable exception to the dearth of probing work on this deity' echoes his conclusion by affirming 'that the god Baal was present in pre-Israelite Shechem'. In addition to the question of the covenant, Lewis focuses on the people who would have entered into a covenant. The sons of Hamor or sons of the ass/donkey, are part of a donkey-covenant tradition dating back to Mari. He notes the existence of another covenant alliance among humans in the story of Abram:

> **Genesis 14: 13** *Then one who had escaped came, and told Abram the Hebrew, who was living by the oaks of Mamre the Amorite, brother of Eshcol and of Aner; these were allies of Abram.*[29]

---

28 R. E. Clements, 'Baal-Berith of Shechem', *JSS* 13 1968: 21–32, here 32.
29 Theodore J. Lewis, 'The identity and function of El/Baal Berith', *JBL* 115 1996: 401–423, quotations from 401 and 422.

The translation of *berith* into 'allies' in English in this verse obscures the connection to Baal-berith where the word is not translated. So Abram the Hebrew at Mamre which is Hebron enters into a covenant with Amorites in the course of a battle to free his nephew Lot who had been captured by the kings of the east.

A biological literal approach to understanding the political messages being delivered in these stories is of no value. De-ciphering the meaning of these names in the political arena would require an additional chapter or more. Abimelech, 'my father is king', may just as easily have been referring to a deity as to human father especially if the original story was independent of the Gideon narrative. Even if the drunk buffoon Gaal and Abimelech are human counterparts to deities in a cosmic showdown in the original version that does not mean Abimelech who is killed when a woman drops a millstone from the city wall on his head is still a deity and not a human king when he dies. The deeply felt and expressed revulsion and contempt for Abimelech reminds one of the intensity expressed by Lamech in his song and by Noah against Canaan in his curses. The stories of the battle in Jerusalem Throne Games extend beyond the six son stories included in this study.

Shechem presents a different scenario than Jerusalem. Both were Canaanite cities named in Egyptian records and regional powers. Both became part of Israel. But prior to Jerusalem becoming the capital of Israel, the city remained populated with Jebusites and Canaanites and no intermixing with Israelites. The Shechem situation differs. Instead there are a variety of stories of both peaceful and violent interactions between Israelites and Shechemites. Drawing a line separating the populations after a few centuries might have been very difficult given Shechem's location smack in the middle of the Israelite hill-country settlements. Similarly, sorting all the stories to trace the history of the Israel-Shechem relationship from Pharaoh Merneptah to the showdown with King Rehoboam is equally vexing.

One may wonder why in a chapter about Jerusalem I am devoting so much space to the city David did not choose for his capital. Consider again the American example. During the American Revolution, Philadelphia had served as the defacto capital. After the Revolution, New York which had been occupied territory during the war, temporarily became the capital. And, of course, there was Boston, the proverbial city on hill. It had been in the forefront of the confrontation from the Boston Massacre, Boston Tea Party, and Paul Revere. Boston was English Puritan, Philadelphia was English Quaker, New York was Dutch, demographically mixed, and conquered by England from the Dutch before being occupied a century later during the Revolution. These cities had complex relationships with each other and England, different ethnicities, different religions, different material cultures, and different ways of life. Even with voluminous documents in English from the time period, American historians still debate what all this means. It is reasonable to conclude the situation in David's times had similarities to the American one but without the abundance of written records to help us navigate through the morass. The absence of such detailed records from ancient Israel does not mean similar tensions between cities did not apply.

Here, then, is my historical reconstruction of this sequence and its implications for the time of David. During the Amarna Age, Shechem and its allies aggressively sought to expand their domain in the land of Canaan. Jerusalem was part of an anti-Shechem coalition just as it later would be part of one against Israel. When Israel first appeared in history, it expected Shechem to be an ally against Egypt. Israel even entered into a covenant at Mount Ebal (Deut. 27) immediately adjacent to Shechem expecting the center of the opposition to be based there. Scarabs of Ramses II and Ramses III have been discovered at Ebal. However, since only one alpha male can be king of the mountain at a time, I suggest that Shechem and Israel had a falling out where the former chose not to follow the lead of Israel against Egypt. Just because Deborah would call the coalition to arms does not mean Shechem would follow the Israelite woman's lead.

The destruction in the story in Judges 9 has been linked to the archaeologically-discovered destruction of the city from the mid-12th century. This destruction is around the time Egypt withdrew from the land and when Shiloh became the primary cultic site of Israel. One can easily imagine a showdown between Israel and Shechem at that time when the Egyptian withdrawal created a political vacuum. One can easily understand why Israel would relocate its cultic center from Ebal to Shiloh. Given that hostility and competition between Israel and Shechem culminating in a forced confrontation and destroying of a city, one can understand why David would not seek to make Shechem his capital. It also easy to understand why Israel would assemble at Shechem after Solomon died to voice their objections to rule by Jerusalem. Shechem and Jerusalem were longstanding rivals. The political context had changed. Now Shechem was part of Israel in alliance against Jerusalem (see Additional Readings: Ebal, Shechem, Shiloh).

3. David's Judah

David's first kingdom does not garner much attention in biblical studies. In general terms, it is viewed as a short-term way station on the journey from being a fugitive from Saul to becoming king of all Israel in Jerusalem. As a tribe, Judah is not included in the Song of Deborah. Typically it is considered not to have been part of Israel at that time. David receives the credit for the formation of the kingdom making it a comparative newcomer to the story.

The demographics of the population of this kingdom has drawn some attention. It's population has less of a Canaanite background and more of a wilderness origin. The very title of Lars Eric Axelsson's book *The Lord Rose up from Seir: Studies in the History and Traditions of the Negev and Southern Judah* bespeak a different tradition than Joshua crossing the Jordan. His chapter 'The Conquest from the South' emphasizes the non-Joshua 'Calebite' perspective. Simultaneous with Israel establishing its presence in the hill country, different wilderness peoples such as the Kenites, Simeonites, and Kenizzites including the Calebites were establishing themselves in the south at Arad (Judg. 1:16 and Num. 10: 29–32), Hormah (Num. 21: 1–3; Judg. 1: 17; Num. 14: 39–45), and Hebron (Josh. 14: 13–15; Judg. 1: 10, 20). These people may be considered Shasu from Seir home of Yahweh (Song of Deborah, Judg. 5: 4, also Deut. 33: 2). Tryggve N. D. Mettinger concludes that the Yahweh worshipers in Israel and Judah arrived at their worship differently: for Israel, it was connected to the exodus/covenant tradition; for Judah, Yahweh always had been their deity as a wilderness people. In this regard, one may perceive David's Judah to be less of foreign turf than Canaanite–Jebusite Jerusalem.[30]

The capital of David's first kingdom was Hebron. According to the biblical narrative, Abram builds an altar there too (Gen. 13: 8). He ventures forth from there to rescue his nephew Lot in the following chapter (Gen. 14). Abram purchases land there for a family burial site starting with Sarah (Gen. 23). Isaac, Jacob and Joseph are there at various times. The spies fear the Anakites who are located there and so inform Moses when they return to the wilderness. They seem puny compared to the Nephilim who are there, the same Nephilim from the sons of God story before the Flood. The Nephilim did not drown but lived to intimidate Israel (Num. 13: 22–33). Hebron joins the Jerusalem-led Amorite coalition against Israel (Josh. 10). David becomes king of Judah with Hebron as his capital. One notes that David's Calebite wife Abigail follows David in his journeys from Carmel where she had lived to the Philistine city of Gath when David serves Achish there and to Hebron where she bears his son (I Sam. 25; 27: 3; 30: 5; II Sam. 2: 2 and 3: 3). Then she disappears from the narrative. There is no record of her in Jerusalem. It is reasonable to conclude she died in Hebron and was buried in a plot David had purchased there, just as the husband does for his wife in the story of Abraham and Sarah.

David remains in Hebron during his battle against Saul's son Ishbaal and his general Abner until at last he prevails. At that point the people of Israel come to Hebron to have their shepherd, a word for king in the biblical narratives and not nomad, become king over them. David accepts the position and the immediately attacks the Jebusites of Jerusalem (II Sam. 2–5). No explanation is provided for this action. Nothing in the narrative establishes Jerusalem as the next logical step in the process of becoming king. Virtually out of nowhere, David makes his first act as king of all Israel, the attack on the Jebusites of Jerusalem. Not only does he take it, he does so with the intention of making the city his capital. Why?

4. David's Israel

In the biblical account, only one Jebusite individual is identified by name. He has an important role to play in Israelite history and biblical writing.

> **II Samuel 24: 16** *And when the angel [messenger] stretched forth his hand toward Jerusalem to destroy it, Yahweh repented of the evil, and said to the angel [messenger] who was working destruction among the people, 'It is enough; now stay your hand'. And the angel [messenger] of Yahweh was by the threshing floor of **Araunah the Jebusite**.* [17] *Then David spoke to Yahweh when he saw the angel [messenger] who was smiting the people, and said, 'Lo, I have sinned, and I have done wickedly; but these sheep, what have they done? Let thy hand, I pray thee, be against me and*

---

30 Lars Eric Axelsson, *The Lord Rose up from Seir: Studies in the History and Tradition of the Negev and Southern Judah* (ConBOT Series 25; Stockholm: Almquist & Wiksell International, 1987), especially Chapter VI, 'The conquest from the south', 125–142, and Chapter VII 'David and the south', 143–169; Tryggve N. D. Mettinger, 'The elusive essence: YHWH, El and Baal and the distinctiveness of Israelite faith', in Erhard Blum, Christina Macholz and Ekkehard W. Stegeman, eds, *Die Hebräische Bibel und ihre Zweifache Nachgeschichte: Festschrift für Rolf Rendtorff zum 65. Geburstag* (Neukirchen-Vluyn: Neukirchener Verlag, 1990), 393–417, here 405–409.

*against my father's house.'¹⁸ And [the prophet] Gad came that day to David, and said to him, 'Go up, rear an altar to Yahweh on the threshing floor of **Araunah the Jebusite**'.*

The messenger of destruction against Jerusalem calls to mind the destroyer or messenger who passed over the households of the Israelites in the final plague during the Exodus (Ex. 12: 23). André Caquot and Phippe de Robert then suggest the sparing of Jerusalem while the rest of the country was ravaged by the plague was intended to assert divine preference for the city and was a Zadokite redaction of the original text meaning a revision by the priests of Jerusalem. The identity of these Zadokites figures prominently in the proposed historical reconstruction of the writing of the Hebrew Bible (see Chapter 9).³¹

One would think based on this passage that Araunah the Jebusite was a person of some import. A standard explanation is that Araunah was the Jebusite king of Jerusalem, and the transaction was one between kings. P. Kyle McCarter assumes Araunah was a pre-Israelite Jebusite resident of Jerusalem who may have been either of Hurrian or Hittite ancestry. Caquot and de Robert accept the Hittite or Hurrian origin and concur with the understanding of Araunah as a king. The prophet Ezekiel in the 6th century BCE attributes Hittite and Amorite ancestry to Jerusalem (Ezek. 16: 3, 45) so the memory of the city's pre-Israelite existence appears to have lasted for centuries.³²

Another suggestion is that 'Araunah' is not a proper noun or name of an individual but a title based on the Old Hurrian for 'the Lord'. This Jebusite may be considered the last pre-Israelite king of Jerusalem. Yeivin suggests that the untranslated land of 'Moriah' (*hammoriyya*, Gen. 22: 2 where Abraham is to sacrifice his son) draws on the same Hurrian royal title. The Hurrian 'ma' means 'this' so the biblical phrase should read as 'the land of this king' or 'the mountain of this king' in II Chr. 3: 1), the only other verse where 'Moriah' appears. The royal definitions render the exchange a royal one.

An interesting and overlook facet of the negotiations is that the dialog occurs unmediated. There is no sign of a universal translator or even a human one. The Israelite and the Jebusite converse unaided just as David and Philistine Goliath do. Based on the Tower of Babel, one would think such conversations impossible. Biblical writers were aware of the communication problem (Deut. 28: 49; Isa. 33: 19; Jer. 5: 15). In fact, when Assyria besieges Jerusalem in the time of King Hezekiah (701 BCE), the defenders beseech the Assyrian negotiator to speak in a foreign language:

> **II Kings 18: 26** *Then Eliakim the son of Hilkiah, and Shebnah, and Joah, said to the Rabshakeh, 'Pray, speak to your servants in the Aramaic language, for we understand it; do not speak to us in the language of Judah within the hearing of the people who are on the wall'.*

Nothing comparable occurs between David and Araunah. Is it because the Tower of Babel story had not been written? Or was not known to the author of this story? Or was known but rejected? Or it does not mean what we think it means? Or is it like science fiction

---

31 André Caquot and Phippe de Robert, *Les Livres de Samuel* (Geneva: Labor et Fides, 1994), 638–640; see also P. Kyle McCarter, Jr, *II Samuel* (Garden City, NY: Doubleday & Company, 1984, AB9), 511.

32 Caquot and de Robert, *Les Livres de Samuel*, 640–642; McCarter, *II Samuel*, 512. See also Roy Rosenberg, 'The God Ṣedeq', *HUCA* 36 1965: 161–177, here 166; N. Wyatt, '"Araunah the Jebusite," and the Throne of David', *Studia Theologica* 39 1985: 39–53.

stories where if we get hung up on details, the story falls apart? The message of the story takes priority.

The Jebusite not only speaks to David without use of a translator or evidence of bilingual skills, he uses the name of the Israelite deity while clearly referring to Yahweh as god of David.

> **II Samuel 24:23** *And Araunah said to the king, 'Yahweh your God accept you'.* [24] *But the king said to Araunah, 'No, but I will buy it of you for a price; I will not offer burnt offerings to Yahweh my God which cost me nothing.' So David bought the threshing floor and the oxen for fifty shekels of silver.* [25] *And David built there an altar to Yahweh and offered burnt offerings and peace offerings.*

This negotiation between David and Araunah, the possible Hittite-titled king in David's second capital city calls to mind the negotiation between the warrior-shepherd and Ephron the Hittite sitting at the gate, a sign of authority, at Hebron, David's first capital city (above). In the parallel account in the Book of Chronicles, the Jebusite owner of the threshing floor David purchases is named Ornan (I Chr. 21: 15, 18, 28). In this instance, David acts on the express command of the Lord communicated through his messenger/angel. The stakes here are whether or not to destroy the city. Either way, one may interpret the verses as describing the conquering king negotiating an exchange with the conquered (priest-)king over the fate of the city.[33]

Today, it is easy to overlook the importance of threshing floors in ancient times. They were not simply a place where wheat was threshed; they were a place where people gave thanks for life at the conclusion of a harvest. In his analysis of the origin of the Greek theater, B. H. Stricker highlights the essential core of the sacred threshing floor experience.

> 'The oldest theatres are all situated in the vicinity of a sanctuary, and in the temenos of it ... In each theatre an altar was set up in the middle of the orchestra, on which a sacrifice was made before and after the ceremony. The performance took place ... only once a year, on the festival day of the god worshipped in the temple...
>
> The theatre was a sacred place, the actor were sacred persons, their action was sacred action, and it was performed at a sacred time.'[34]

He relates the orchestra to the threshing floor and reviews the ancient literature of Greece, Egypt, and Israel to demonstrate its role in sacred dramatic performances.[35]

According to Stricker, the circular threshing-floor theater matched the people's images of the world with them at the center. On this stage the cosmic story of creation unfolded with the triumph over the forces of chaos and the celebration of the origin and continuation of life.[36] The exact details of the celebration of life varies from culture to culture but in one way or another every culture will celebrate it. Israel was no exception to that human necessity.

---

33 Caquot and de Robert, *Les Livres de Samuel*, 640–641; Cline, *Jerusalem Besieged*, 313 n.9; McCarter, *II Samuel*, 512; Gary Rendsburg, 'The Genesis of the Bible, inaugural lecture of the Blanch and Irving Laurie Chair in Jewish History, October 28, 2004', (Rutgers: The Allen and Joan Bilder Center for the Study of Jewish Life, 2005), 15–16; Sh. Yeivin, 'The threshing floor of Araunah', *Journal of Educational Sociology* 36 1963: 396–400, here 399–400.

34 B. H. Stricker, 'The origin of the Greek theatre', *JEA* 41 1955: 34–47, here 36.

35 Stricker, 'The origin of the Greek theatre', 39–45.

36 Stricker, 'The origin of Greek theatre', 46.

The same considerations apply to the threshing floors in Canaan and Israel in general and to the one in Jerusalem in particular. Once people switched from a primarily hunting society to a primarily agricultural one, the harvest became critical to life. Truly the belief that one would survive to the next harvest due to the bounty of the current one was worth giving thanks for. The threshing floor was the place where a community learned if it would live or die. In a world of 24/7 supermarkets it is difficult to convey the significance of that knowledge to people in ancient times. The promise of certainty by one's deity was not something to take lightly.

Threshing floors mattered in ancient Canaan and Israel. They were the places of assembly, thanksgiving, celebration, storytelling, and finding mates for children in the villages, towns, and cities throughout the land especially at new year. They resemble the post-harvest camp meetings which occurred in the early decades of the 19th century in the Mississippi Valley. They are best appreciated by people who live in isolation from other families in their day-to-day life and welcome the opportunity to socialize (see Additional Readings: Camp Meetings).

Threshing floors were not necessarily small either. Large numbers of people could stand on one as part of a cultic celebration. Consider the number of people involved in Jacob's funeral procession:

> **Genesis 50: 7** *So Joseph went up to bury his father; and with him went up all the servants of Pharaoh, the elders of his household, and all the elders of the land of Egypt,* [8] *as well as all the household of Joseph, his brothers, and his father's household; only their children, their flocks, and their herds were left in the land of Goshen.* [9] *And there went up with him both chariots and horsemen; it was a very great company.* [10] *When they came to the **threshing floor** of Atad, which is beyond the Jordan, they lamented there with a very great and sorrowful lamentation; and he made a mourning for his father seven days.* [11] *When the inhabitants of the land, the Canaanites, saw the mourning on the threshing floor of Atad, they said, 'This is a grievous mourning to the Egyptians'. Therefore the place was named Abelmizraim; it is beyond the Jordan.*

The biblical text even provides a more exact number of the people a threshing floor could hold:

> **I Kings 22: 6** *Then the king of Israel gathered the prophets together, about four hundred men...* [10] *Now the king of Israel and Jehoshaphat the king of Judah were sitting on their thrones, arrayed in their robes, at **the threshing floor** at the entrance of the gate of Samaria; and all the prophets were prophesying before them.*

Here again, a substantial number of people are involved and again the threshing floor is not used for food-producing purposes.

Non-food related examples of threshing floor in the biblical narrative include:

1. The place where the judge Gideon was called to arms (Judg. 6: 36)
2. A stop on the journey of the ark to Zion (II Sam. 6: 6)
3. Where Ruth and Boaz became close (Ruth 3)
4. What the Philistines target at Keilah precisely because they were aware of its essential nature (I Sam. 23: 1).

The previously-mentioned burial procession of Jacob and the royal decision about going to war or not add to the list of activities which could occur at the threshing floor. These examples attest the importance of the threshing floor in ancient times. The threshing floor was a traditional site of theophany where divine messages were received in biblical and Ugaritic tradition.

The use of threshing floors has led to the suggestion that the traditional sacred place of the Jebusites became the sacred place of the Israelites where the temple of Solomon would be built.

> **II Chronicles 3: 1** *Then Solomon began to build the house of Yahweh in Jerusalem on Mount Moriah, where he had appeared to David his father, at the place that David had appointed, on the* **threshing floor of Ornan the Jebusite**.

It is reasonable to conclude that the Israelites, who did not displace the native population, repurposed the existing sacred site in accordance with its traditions and rituals once they took over from the Jebusites.

The Israelite repurposing of the Jerusalem threshing floor raises several important questions. It means the site already was a sacred one even though there was no temple there. It means the people of Jerusalem already worshiped a deity there (Elyon) prior to Israel's establishing the worship of Yahweh there. It means the site was located outside the city walls probably by a city gate. A large infrequently used site simply could not fit within the city-wall complex. Space was too precious. Given the configuration of the city on a ridge, the logical location for the threshing floor was to the north of settled city which is precisely where the temple was built. The transformation of the openly-accessed community-used threshing floor into a permanent restricted-access temple with a priesthood would change the power dynamics of the city. On a practical level, the construction of the temple outside the city walls necessitated the rebuilding of the city walls to contain it. According to the biblical narrative, such an action by Solomon is exactly what happened when he built the temple:

> **I Kings 3: 1** *Solomon made a marriage alliance with Pharaoh king of Egypt; he took Pharaoh's daughter, and brought her into the city of David, until he had finished building his own house and the house of Yahweh and the wall around Jerusalem.*

The threshing floor which been outside the city gate and walls through the time of David now was inside the city walls in the time of Solomon and had become a temple (see Additional Readings: Threshing Floors).[37]

The laconic version of David's conquest of Jerusalem leaves much to the imagination.

> **II Samuel 5:6** *And the king [David] and his men [ish]went to* **Jerusalem against the Jebusites**, *the inhabitants of the land, who said to David, 'You will not come in here, but the blind and the lame will ward you off – thinking, 'David cannot come in here'.* [7] *Nevertheless David took the stronghold of Zion, that is, the city of David.* [8] *And David said on that day, 'Whoever would* **smite**

---

37 Eilat Mazar, 'The Solomonic Wall in Jerusalem', in Aren M. Maeir and Pierre de Miroschedi, eds, *I Will Speak Riddles of Ancient Times: Archaeological and Historical Studies in Honor of Amihai Mazar on the Occasion of his Sixtieth Birthday* (Winona Lake: Eisenbrauns, 2006), 775–786.

the Jebusites, let him get up the water shaft to attack the lame and the blind, who are hated by David's soul'. Therefore it is said, 'The blind and the lame shall not come into the house'. ⁹ *And David dwelt in the stronghold, and called it the city of David. And David built the city round about from the Millo inward.*[38]

How would you stage this event in telling the story?

Exactly how David captured the city remains an archaeological and philological puzzle. These are very difficult verses with obscure references that have challenged the ingenuity of interpreters since ancient times. Bible scholars still debate the meaning of the stronghold, watershaft, the saying about the lame and the blind, and the Millo closely associated with building projects of Solomon (I Kings 9: 15, 24; 11: 27; 12: 20). One notes that Ehud the Benjaminite engineered the capture of a city apparently involving a water passage from the throne room (Judges 3: 12–29). Did the spring-fed pools serve as the defacto infirmary for the city where the ill gathered to immerse themselves in the soothing waters? Prophets are supposed to see the truth but sometimes they cannot (Balaam in Num. 22: 31). Are the Elyon priests who cannot see the truth or dance the religious dances being mocked here or are the warriors of David being mocked for being weak? David does later allow Mephibosheth, the lame son of Jonathan, into his abode (II Sam. 4: 9 and 9: 1–13). Is this text a unity or are multiple hands involved? Daniel Pioske likens David's utterances to a taunting of the Jebusites (like Lamech?). He observes that the scribes responsible for this text 'did not follow the common ideological conventions' by portraying a heroic conquest by the king who then launched a series of impressive building projects.[39]

The missing element in these hypotheses is the political. David was the consummate politician. He was playing four-dimensional chess in the real world while others were playing checkers. If he had been born first, he would have tried to become king of Israel before Saul. He was ambitious. Plus his conception of Israel exceeded that of Saul. The kingdom of Saul included no Canaanite cities Saul had conquered. He defended Israel but he did not reach out beyond it. David was different. It was possible for people before Alexander to have vision and the ability to fulfill one.

David had known success in royal capitals … up to a point. He was successful in the court of Saul at Gibeah but he never could replace Jonathan as Saul's son. He was successful in the court of Achish at Gath, the premier Philistine city then, but he could never become king of the Philistines. He was successful in the court at Hebron in the kingdom of Judah he created, but it was not the same as being king of Israel. If he had just wanted to be king of Merneptah's Israel or Deborah's Israel he could have made Bethel his capital. He wanted to be king of Egypt's Canaan and make it Israel. That made choosing a Canaanite

---

38   In the account in the Book of Chronicles, David's chief warrior, Joab, is the one smites the Jebusites and thereby becomes chief (I Chr. 11: 6). Cahill suggests the stronghold of Zion is the Stepped-Stone Structure (Jane Cahill, 'Jerusalem in David's and Solomon's time', BAR 30/6 2004: 20–31, 62–63, here 25–26.

39   See W. Emery Barnes, 'The Jebusite "citadel" of Zion', *The Expositor* 1914 Ser. 8 7: 29–39; Christian E. Hauer, Jr, 'Jerusalem, the stronghold and Rephaim', *CBQ* 32 1970: 571–578; McCarter, *II Samuel*, 137; Daniel D. Pioske *David's Jerusalem: Between Memory and History* (New York: Routledge, 2015), 94, 111–112, 230; John C. Poirier, 'David's "hatred" for the lame and the blind (2 Sam. 5.8A)', *PEQ* 138 2006: 27–33; Shmuel Vargon, 'The blind and the lame', *VT* 46 1996: 498–514.

city as a capital attractive. Shechem had been anti-Egypt but the competition between Israel and Shechem became violent; Jerusalem had both pro-Egypt and anti-Israel but no confrontation at the city had occurred. After Israel beseeched David to become its king, David agreed to, decided on Jerusalem as his capital, and made the king of the city a deal: give me the city and I will make you the capital of Canaan, of all Israel.

David as the king of Israel inherited the Jerusalem infrastructure. In a rapid survey of Jerusalem from the 4th millennium BCE to Roman times, Lester Grabbe concludes that Jerusalem became part of Israel relatively late under David, continued to include the pre-Israelite Jebusite people within the Israelite polity, that Araunah was the last Jebusite king, and that Jebusite Zadok became a high priest under David. The missing step in Grabbe's analysis is the recognition that everything he proposes directly contributed to writing of the Hebrew Bible when the city became Israelite (see Chapter 9).[40]

David knew he faced challenges. Hebron worshiped Yahweh but not the exodus/covenant one. Canaanite cities worshiped Baal. Israel worshiped Yahweh of the exodus/covenant. Shechem may have worshiped El. The Jebusites worshiped Elyon. Creating one people from many was part of the impetus for creating the KDB (see Chapter 9). Now he needed a capital and he picked Jerusalem.

He knew changes were needed. He needed to transform the city (its threshing floor) into a place where Yahweh was worshiped. Israelites would resist being ruled by a city that had been their enemy; he needed to show that Yahweh was king and his throne was in Jerusalem. Canaanite cities had never accepted the supremacy of one Canaanite city over them; he needed to show that being king over them did not mean taxes, the draft, or forced labor and did mean safety from foreign attack. Once the great warrior king died, why should these cities continue to accept the rule of Jerusalem over them? Was the son a great warrior too? The aftermath of the death of the warrior-king would be a propitious time for the Jebusites to engineer a new diplomatic alliance with Egypt to restore the glory days of the New Kingdom in the land of Canaan. The change would be a hegemony under Canaanite leadership in Jerusalem supported by Egyptian 'muscle'. Not everyone agreed. Stories would be written to address these questions.

Conclusion

This overview of the history of Jerusalem through David reflects competing influences and heritages. There were circumstances of long term duration based on the geographical and geological configuration of the city and its surroundings. There were circumstances of medium term duration due to the end of Egyptian dominance in the land of Canaan after centuries and to the emergence of Israel as a new player in its own right in a way distinctly different from the Canaanite city-state system. Finally, there were circumstances of immediate consideration and individual agency with the death of the charismatic and

---

40 Lester L. Grabbe, 'Ethnic groups in Jerusalem', in Thomas Thompson, ed., *Jerusalem in Ancient History and Tradition* (JSOT Sup. Series 381 and Copenhagen International Seminar13; London: T&T Clarke, 2013), 145–163, here 155, 157, and 162.

innovative genius David and there being no single individual capable of replacing him.

David may be regarded as a watershed figure in both Israelite history and biblical writing. Regardless of his religion, he was the first native-born person to rule in one way or another the land of Canaan. This development triggered various issues that never before had been debated by the people of the land. Most significantly there now was one king in one capital city. In American terms, think of the situation when colonies which had been ruled by the English king now had their own president in a capital city. Why should colonies with independent legislatures now defer to a central legislature and to one located first in New York and then in Washington? Why should Canaanite cities with independent kings now defer to a central king and to one located in Jerusalem? Was this issue resolved in silence or solely in blood?

The focus of the study now shifts to the combatants and their weapon of war in the resolution of these challenges. First we turn to the weapon of war wielded in the battle for power, the alphabet prose narrative. Then we turn to the groups of people who comprised the various political factions engaged in the battle for power who uniquely wielded this weapon. No other civilization in the ancient Near East deployed this weapon in the battle for power at the capital city. Alpha males may have sought the mountaintop of kingship elsewhere but not because they had different visions of what they might see when they stood at the summit but because they wanted to be king of mountain as the goal in its own right. At the birth of the United States, Federalists and Anti-Federalists battled for power through the written word and those writings and differences continue to be part of the American story to this very day. In ancient Israel, the vision of a king and the battle for power after his death gave the world what became the Bible. These are their stories. Who were their authors?

> 'There is still much to be discovered about who wrote (the oldest narratives of the Hebrew Bible). We do not know the precise dates when they lived, and we do not know their names. I think that what we do know is more important. We know something about their world and about how that world produced these stories that still delight and teach us. Still, we may be dissatisfied until we can be more specific about the writers.'[41]

---

41 Friedman, *Who Wrote the Bible?*, 88.

PART II

WRITING THE STORIES

THE J DOCUMENTARY HYPOTHESIS: THE WRITERS AND THE GENESIS OF THE BIBLICAL PROSE NARRATIVE

> 'Each narrative contains a multitude of historical claims that stand in stark contradiction to those of the other sources, but these can be demonstrated only through the detailed study of a given passage'
>
> Baden, *The Composition of the Pentateuch* 25, referring to JEDP but applicable within J as well

The J Documentary Hypothesis is my attempt to understand Israelite history and how the Bible was written. The Documentary Hypothesis is inadequate to explain the composition of the J strand within the four-source JEDP schema and needs to be refined. So far in this quest, I have presented:

1. The Documentary Hypothesis of Wellhausen as explained by Friedman in the Introduction
2. The exegesis by people from ancient times to the 20th century of six stories from the beginning of the Book of Genesis attributed to the J author in Part I
   The history of Jerusalem to David in Setting the Jerusalem Stage.

The current chapter will trace my journey from the Documentary Hypothesis to the J Documentary Hypothesis. The new hypothesis will identify the factions who contributed to the J narrative and the weapon they deployed in the political arena. Pioske, drawing on the work of Jack Sasson, concludes that biblical scholars remain locked into the models created in the 19th century when Germany was becoming a country and the scientific study of history was developing. These ivory tower models fail to recognize that sometimes political players like Theodore Roosevelt and Winston Churchill write histories, too, that sometimes contemporary commentators like Howard Fast and Arthur Miller write about the present through stories in the past, and that sometimes writers create metaphors and symbols like Big Brother, animal farm, and Lilliputians.[1]

The J Documentary Hypothesis relentlessly concentrates on the political arena. It combines one genius, multiple priesthoods, and the alphabet prose narrative at a specific point in time and space. The hypothesis then will be applied in the remaining chapters of Part II to document the creation of the six son stories by four people. Since the application is limited to the six supplemental stories, my study should be considered only as a step towards the full expression of the 'J' narrative in each of its four supplemental strands as has been done by Pentateuch scholars with the J, E, D, and P strands on a larger scale.

---

1   Pioske, *David's Jerusalem*, 15–17; Jack M. Sasson, 'On choosing models for recreating Israelite pre-monarchic history', *JSOT* 21 1981: 3–24.

The Documentary Hypothesis

The Documentary Hypothesis arose from the challenges confronting biblical scholars that Moses was the sole author of the Five Books of Moses. As people scrutinized the texts several anomalies became apparent that suggested perhaps the prevailing view was in error. Some of the more egregious examples were the passages about the death and burial of Moses, his claim of his own meekness, and the lack of any reference in the Pentateuch claiming Mosaic authorship for the entire five books. Duplicate interwoven stories and separate parallel stories with conflicting information proved troublesome, most particularly the Flood story. Different vocabulary and the varied names used to designate the deity of the people contributed mightily to the effort to untangle the various strands which comprised the Pentateuch. The culminating hypothesis was the Documentary Hypothesis which hypothesized (it is not a theorem or scientific/mathematical law) that the Five Books of Moses were composed by four people and at least one redactor who combined the four narratives.

The application: six case studies

The next step in this process was the application of the Documentary Hypothesis to the biblical text. In Part I of this study, I selected six examples from the beginning of the Book of Genesis for review. The selection was not an arbitrary one. I already had thoughts about what would become the J Documentary Hypothesis based on my own readings over the years. The focus on these six stories arose directly from a conference of the Middle West Branch of the American Oriental Society in 2011. The theme of the conference was 'Creation and Cosmos: Reconsideration of Hermann Gunkel's *Chaoskampf* Hypothesis'. For my paper, I chose 'The Torch Has Been Passed to a New Cosmic Center' with the following abstract:

'At the time when Hermann Gunkel was developing his ideas about the significance of creation and chaos in the stories/poetry of the ancient Near East, the dominant interpretation of biblical writing in the academic arena was the still formidable Documentary Hypothesis by Julius Wellhausen. Some of the first stories in Genesis attributed to the P and J writers in this Hypothesis not only addressed the theme of creation but bore resemblance to stories from the Mesopotamian world. This resemblance help generate the Pan-Babylonian school which postulated a direct borrowing by the biblical writers from the Mesopotamian culture. While Pan-Babylonianism has long since bit the dust, the issue of the relationship between the biblical and Mesopotamian traditions remains.

This paper will examine the Mesopotamian motifs in the J writer in Genesis 2–11 and 14. The analysis will seek to determine the historical context in which such motifs were used, meaning that their presence in the biblical narrative is not by chance or coincidence but design. It will attempt to show that one individual in a specific historical context can be held responsible for the introduction of these motifs into an already existing narrative and that he did so with a specific political agenda in mind. This analysis will conclude that while elements within the Israelite/Judahite community were familiar with and responded favorably to such Mesopotamian motifs, other elements had a distinctly different perspective. Thus the inclusion of these Mesopotamian motifs may be seen as part of a war of words related to where the cosmic center in the culture was and the means whereby the people and the deity were linked'.

In the course of attempting to do what I had proposed, I learned that I could not do what I had actually proposed to do. I discovered that my allotted time as well as the page limitations for the conference book did not permit a review of all the motifs. At the time, I assigned these motifs to a writer I designated as Mesopotamia J.[2]

More accurately, I assigned the positive use of Mesopotamian motifs to one writer. By implication, there was a second writer with a diametrically opposed view. Later I would call that writer Prophet J. My investigations more formally documented the reality that contrary points of view could be expressed within the J narrative. On one hand, there could be the global influence of a Mesopotamian-based universe, the four rivers of Eden, the four kingdom cities of Nimrod, the four foes of Abraham, the universal Flood, the awareness of the stories of Gilgamesh and Atrahasis; but on the other hand, there were the cherubs at the garden's border and the Tower of Babel. My awareness of these alternate perceptions led me to the conclusion that there were multiple and opposing authors who composed the J stories in the so-called primeval cycle which were not accounted for in the traditional Documentary Hypothesis.

I pursued my investigation of the topic on two levels. Since my published article was about the Garden of Eden, I researched that story following the same template I use in this study. Simultaneously, I presented papers at different conferences about several of the 'son' stories included here. In one such presentation at ASOR (American Schools of Oriental Research) in 2014, the editor of the publisher of this book was in the audience. Afterwards she approached me and ask if I would be interested in writing a book on the subject. At that point, I ceased my efforts excavating the garden story and turned to these six 'son' stories ... although some published and unpublished material from my Garden of Eden analysis is included in the current study.

I began the formal process of writing the book by examining the commentaries of the people covered in Part I. When I read them I already had a working idea about the J Documentary Hypothesis without the use of that term. That awareness enabled me to read these individual's exegesis through a new perspective. I realized that many of the questions I had raised in my own review of the six stories had been raised before. I realized that some of these people were struggling with the same issues that I faced. I realized that in some cases people were on the brink of being able to posit something resembling the J Documentary Hypothesis without being able to take that final step.

The concerns raised by these exegetes over the son stories are listed at the conclusion of each chapter in Part I. Certain consistencies emerged when all six listings from all six stories were grouped together. Biblical exegetes had identified the questions that need to be answered in the J Documentary Hypothesis.

---

2   My contribution to the published proceedings 'Where's Eden? An analysis of some of the Mesopotamian motifs in Primeval J' reflects the reduced scope of my initial effort; see JoAnn Scurlock and Richard H. Beal, eds, *Creation and Chaos: A Reconsideration of Hermann Gunkel's Chaoskampf Hypothesis* (Winona Lake: Eisenbrauns, 2013), 172–189.

1. They recognized the presence of multiple writers with differing viewpoints within a story such as the Sons of God and the Sons of Noah.
2. They recognized variances between stories such as Kenites versus Sethites and Nimrod versus the Tower of Babel.
3. They recognized unexplained changes in character by an individual such as the cursed Cain in exile versus Cain the city-builder and Noah in the ark versus Noah on land.
4. They recognized connections between stories such as the Sons of Cain and the Tower of Babel being by the same author.
5. They recognized a local flood tradition in the emphasis on the Kenites, Nephilim, and Tower of Babel separate from the universal flood tradition.

Taken as a whole, such considerations demonstrated that the Documentary Hypothesis was insufficient to resolve the discrepancies, inconsistencies and tensions which had been identified within the J narrative.

The situation with J was similar to that which the Pentateuch had posed before the Documentary Hypothesis was developed. Clearly there was a need for a J Documentary Hypothesis. Biblical scholars did struggle to resolve the dilemma and propose one. Over the years they posited J^1 and J^2 and J^e and J^j to account for the appearance of multiple writers. No consensus ever emerged. Even if one had, did such narratives extend beyond the early stories of J into the patriarchal narratives and afterwards as well? Other sigla like K and S briefly emerged as biblical scholars continued to wrestle with the challenge of bringing order to what their own exegesis had revealed. None worked and eventually the effort was abandoned. At present, there is little effort to untangle the various strands within the J narrative. Indeed the trend, especially in Germany, has been to deny the existence of J in the first place.

In academic terms, the current paradigm was inadequate; in more prosaic terms, people were trapped in their ruts. Two formidable obstacles hindered the quest to solve the challenge of J in the post-Gunkel world.

1. The stories were first and foremost political. In general, traditional exegesis approaches the stories from a religious background regardless of the religion of the exegete. Quite bluntly, these stories are not about the fall, the sin of man, the sin of woman, the separation of humanity and the deity, or the degradation of human nature. They were not generic stories about the human species in its entirety but about specific individuals in history or in some cases specific peoples or type of person. The stories of these studies were not the creations of isolated individuals alone in their studies or perhaps only in contact with their fellow academics; they were stories developed in the political arena, they mattered to people in power, and they helped determine who was in power. In this sense, biblical writers were more like Thomas Becket who confronted Henry II or Cardinal Richelieu who supported Henry IV than like the Society of Biblical Literature which is not known by the American President or relevant in the Beltway.
2. While the Wellhausen Documentary Hypothesis is incomplete in deciphering J, the Gunkel Hypothesis is flat-out wrong. These biblical stories are not small remnants from hoary antiquity that were gathered together by unknown persons for ill-defined reasons. They are not a window into Paleolithic or Neolithic times sustained from time immemorial until at last someone put pen to paper or stylus to papyrus and collected the fragments. Instead these stories are about current events and contemporary people expressed through the mechanism of the story in the time before the abstract language of the Greeks and the Enlightenment had been developed.

Hollywood has a better grasp on such storytelling than do biblical scholars. If Thomas Jefferson had lived pre-abstract language, he would not have written the abstract, legalistic Declaration of Independence. He would have told the story of the two Georges (III and Washington), perhaps using different names, where one was the dutiful son who had served the father (in the French and Indian War or Seven Years War) and then displaced him and became the father of his own country in his own right. In telling the story about George Washington becoming the father, Tom well may have created incidents which illustrated what we would consider to be rights or principles but without using such terms. In Hollywood, historical Spartacus and William Wallace were galvanized into action when the women they loved were violated and/or abducted just as Homer's Mycenaeans had been after the abduction of Helen. Women make for superb symbols of a people and provide an audience-accessible way to tell stories of the actual battles for power between men to rule over and protect those people (Book of Esther at Purim). While the writers identified as D and P were not storytellers at all, E and especially J were. Nobody makes a movie based on D or P.

The review in Part I directly contributed to the creation of the J Documentary Hypothesis. In particular, the Gunkel paradigm provides a false starting point for the analysis of the stories. The stories are not myths from hoary antiquity. The stories are not etiological. J was not a collector of tales from the ancient Near East database of mythical motifs. Biblical stories are not derivative. The stories are political in nature and unique to Israel because they arose from the Israelite political experience. To understand the stories, one must understand the political context in which they originated. Specific people at specific points in time created these stories even if they subsequently were removed from that context and became timeless. The chapter on Jerusalem presents that context; now I turn to the weapon used by the political warriors within that arena.

The story of writing

There is a story to be told of the development of the weapon deployed by the writers of the biblical alphabet prose narratives. As mentioned in the Introduction, Friedman attributes a significant amount of writing from garden to Solomon (Gen. 2 to I Kings 2) to a single unnamed individual. The very title of his book, *The Hidden Book in the Bible: The Discovery of the First Prose Masterpiece*, itself tells a story. The J Documentary Hypothesis agrees, questions and builds on the thesis Friedman presented in the opening words of his book.

> 'A great work lies embedded in the Bible, a creation that we can trace to a single author. And I believe that we can establish that it is of great antiquity: it was composed nearly 3000 ago – so it is indeed nothing less than the first work of prose. Call it the first novel if you think it is fiction, or the first history if you think it is factual. Actually, it is a merger of both. But, either way, it is the first. There is no longer work of prose before this anywhere on earth. East or West, so far as I know. We know of poetry that is earlier, but this is the oldest prose literature: a long beautiful exciting story. And the astonishing thing is that, even though it is the earliest lengthy prose composition known to us, it is far from a rudimentary, primitive first attempt at writing. It has the qualities that we find in the greatest literature the world

has produced. Indeed, scholars of the Bible and of comparative literature have compared individual parts of it to Shakespeare and to Homer. Those scholars were right, but they were barely at the threshold of the full work, a composition whose unity and brilliant connection have been hidden by the editorial and canonical process that produced the Bible.'

Friedman boldly charts a course showcasing a seminal creation in human history: the first prose work and one which becomes the basis for the Bible.[3]

Friedman raises several critical points requiring further examination.

1. He envisions the masterpiece as a single act of creation as if it had sprung forth fully-formed from the brow of the author – could there have been precedents, earlier prose pieces perhaps by the same author as he developed his skill?
2. He attributes the masterpiece to a single individual – could there have been multiple writers of different perspectives who contributed to the masterpiece?
3. His Garden to Solomon masterpiece ends with Solomon secure on the throne – could it originally have ended earlier with David seemingly secure on the throne when he planted the ark there?
4. He acknowledges the existence of Israelite poetry prior to the composition of Israelite prose – who wrote such poetry and did they later write in prose?

John Barton refers to the 'enormous ramifications' of Friedman's hypothesis linking J and the Succession Narrative about life during the reign of David. But rather than assign the texts to a lone author as Friedman does, Barton suggests 'a particular tradition of writing narrative prose'. He differentiates this 'deadpan style' from the later novella of Esther, Ruth and Jonah. He does not restrict the texts to a single century, but does refer to 'a golden age for classical Hebrew narrative'. Even as he accepts the historical reality of David, Bathsheba, Barzallai and Athithophel in the story of Absalom's rebellion and Solomon's accession, Barton does not suggest that J and Succession Narrative might both be about the same historical events.[4]

Friedman includes the six son stories of this study in his proposed prose composition with the exception of Gen. 4: 25–26a about the birth of Seth and Enosh. Obviously, he includes far more stories then encompassed here. Before turning to the points raised by Friedman in the opening paragraph of his book, I wish to address some other considerations to the act of writing a prose masterpiece – the development of the alphabet used by the writers.

To analyze the writings or stories in the aftermath of David, there are certain considerations, presumptions, and working hypotheses which must be stated. To begin with, people in the land of Canaan were not unfamiliar with writing. As previously described, the kings and their scribes had written during the Amarna Age and presumably continued to do so until the 12th century BCE when Egypt withdrew from the land. At that point writing to Pharaoh became meaningless. The Canaanites wrote with a Mesopotamian Akkadian

---

3 Friedman, *The Hidden Book*, 3.
4 John Barton, 'Dating the "succession narrative"', in John Day, ed., *In Search of Pre-exilic Israel: Proceedings of the Oxford Old Testament Seminar* (JSOT Sup. Series 406; London: T&T Clark, 2004), 95–106, quotations from 101, 102, and 104.

script but modified the Akkadian language to express their own Canaanite language. This script and language would not become the script and language of the Israelites.

One important feature of the Amarna Letters frequently overlooked in biblical writing is the use of the familial in the salutations between kings. The Great Kings of the world of international diplomacy in the Amarna Era referred to each other as brothers, letters were written to 'my brother'. Relationships operated in familial terms including interdynastic marriages. A marriage between the daughter of a Hittite king and an Egyptian Pharaoh 'provided a biological reality to the metaphor of brotherhood espoused by the rulers of the Late Bronze Age'. The use of kinship terms recasts military and political relations. One can easily imagine a storyteller drawing on this concept. A marriage story could be between biologically real people like David and Bathsheba or it could be about an alliance between Israel and the Aramaeans represented by Jacob and Laban, his father-in-law. While the Great Kings were equals as brothers, a subordinate like the king of Jerusalem, would be a son, meaning obedient to, to either Pharaoh or a deity. In biblical stories, it is always critical to know if the kinship relations in a story are biological, political, or both.[5]

There also had been literate Egyptians stationed in the land of Canaan as part of the imperial rule. Local people had joined the Egyptian administration and become versed in the Egyptian writing as well. Now these Egyptian scribes and/or Canaanites trained as Egyptian scribes faced the dilemma of what to do. Their skills may well have been welcomed by the newly emergent Philistines, the now-freed Canaanite cities, and Israel in some form. Egyptian hieratic numerals and signs are present in 8th–7th centuries BCE Israel and Judah but not their neighbors. It is reasonable to conclude that these numerals entered the Hebrew script prior to the division of the kingdoms and were drawn from the older Egyptian scribal tradition.[6] These numerals would have been essential for economic and administrative documents. The recognition of their presence led Na'aman to conclude 'It is evident that writing had already entered the court of Jerusalem in the tenth century BCE.'[7]

The writing of these Egyptian or Egypt-trained scribes was not the writing of Israel. To begin with, there is the question of the original language used by the Israelite writers. The presumption is that the spoken language was Hebrew. Language itself changes over time as any English-speaking person attempting to read the English of Chaucer readily knows. Even within a single lifetime the meaning of words may change. Accents also change the pronunciation of words. The inhabitants of the land of Canaan who became Israelite only

---

5   Marian H. Feldman, *Diplomacy by Design: Luxury Arts and an 'International Style' in the Ancient Near East 1400–1200 BCE* (Chicago: University of Chicago Press, 2006), 15, 70, 161–163, quotation from 70; see also Mario Liverani, 'The Great Power club', in Raymond Cohen and Raymond Westbrook, eds, *Amarna Diplomacy: The Beginnings of International Relations* (Baltimore: Johns Hopkins University Press, 2000), 15–27.

6   Orly Goldwasser, 'An Egyptian scribe from Lachish and the Hieratic tradition of the Hebrew Kingdoms', *TA* 18 1991: 248–253.

7   Nadav Na'aman, 'The contribution of the Amarna Letters', 22; repeated in 'Sources and composition in the history of Solomon', in Lowell K. Handy, ed., *The Age of Solomon: Scholarship at the Turn of the Millennium* (Brill: Leiden, 1997), 57–79, here 60. By contrast Finkelstein will only acknowledge that an early layer in the David story pre-dates 840 BCE but it was not written at the time and was about David the outlaw, not David the king (Israel Finkelstein, 'Geographical and historical realities behind the earliest layer in the David Story', *SJOT* 27 2013: 131–150).

when David created the kingdom of Israel presumably did not speak Hebrew prior to their inclusion. However according the story of David and Araunah, they did (see Chapter 8). The biblical narrative itself expresses how neighboring languages may be similar yet distinctive with serious consequences:

> **Judges 12: 5** *And the Gileadites took the fords of the Jordan against the Ephraimites. And when any of the fugitives of Ephraim said, 'Let me go over', the men of Gilead said to him, 'Are you an Ephraimite?' When he said, 'No',* [6] *they said to him, 'Then say Shibboleth', and he said, 'Sibboleth', for he could not pronounce it right; then they seized him and slew him at the fords of the Jordan. And there fell at that time forty-two thousand of the Ephraimites.*

For purposes here, it will be presumed that the writers of these stories spoke some form of Hebrew which was similar to but not identical with the language of their non-Israelite neighbors.[8]

Regardless of the language spoken, a second consideration is the language written. Written language such as academic jargon may have only a passing resemblance to spoken language. Furthermore, academic practitioners know they must alter their written and spoken languages when communicating in an academic setting versus one with a general public audience. The presumption here is that the written language was comparable to academic language in that it required special training but that it served as the basis or script for speaking to the general public. A significant difference between then and now is that the ancient genre of communication was in storytelling. The language of abstract expression complete with footnotes and bibliographic references had not been invented ... except in occasional references to the Books of Jashar and the Wars of Yahweh and to various annals and chronicles.[9]

The script itself used in the composition of the stories was the alphabet, the same one that serves as the basis for the English alphabet today. The story of the origin of the alphabet is an ongoing one subject to new archaeological discoveries. At present it appears to have originated in Egypt during the Middle Kingdom by Semites from the land of Canaan (although the region was not called Canaan then by Egypt). According to scholars, these Semites were either educated in the Egyptian language or not educated in the Egyptian language, located either in the eastern deserts or in Sinai, either as a marginalized people or not. These Canaanite people had no writing of their own, observed that Egypt did, and expropriated Egyptian signs to stand for individual sounds. The Egyptians already had done that when sounding out foreign names such as the name for Jerusalem in the Execration Texts. They used roughly 25 uniconsonantal signs but did not jettison their hieroglyphic system of writing for this 'Egyptian alphabet'. Nor did the Semites transfer the symbols the Egyptian's used to express a single sound to the alphabet. They created one for themselves drawing on their exposure to Egyptian writing (see Additional Readings: Alphabet).

---

8   Sanders claims Ugaritic literature is the first known example where a written language seeks to match the spoken language; see Seth L. Sanders, *The Invention of Hebrew* (Urbana: University of Illinois Press, 2009), 4.
9   For the differences between the ancient Near East and Hellenistic Greece on abstract thought in mathematics and philosophy see Peter Machinist, 'The voice of the historian in the ancient Near Eastern and Mediterranean world', *Int* 57 2003: 117–137, here 132–133.

This new written form seems to have remained in virtual hibernation for centuries or roughly until Egyptian domination of the land of Canaan ceased. It was the marginalized script of marginalized people living in the shadow of the syllabic cuneiform correspondence reflected in the Amarna Letters or the intra-Egyptian hieroglyphic/hieratic writing. During the Iron I period, the political vacuum following the Egyptian withdrawal was matched by a written one – comparatively speaking there was no one to whom to send cuneiform-script diplomatic correspondence requesting help. This void allowed native scripts by marginalized peoples (Israel) to develop independent of Egyptian hieroglyphics and Mesopotamian cuneiform. So while there was not necessarily an Israelite 'Noah Webster' casting off British English for American English after the American Revolution, it is reasonable to conclude that an anti-Egyptian people, the Israelites, would have preferred to use its own form of communication, namely the alphabet, rather than hieroglyphics or cuneiform as part of an assertion of their identity.[10]

The practitioners of this new information communication system would have been limited. After all, on a daily basis, the need for writing was minimal. Israel was a community of somewhat isolated hilltop settlements with no king, no temple, and no bureaucracy, the prime sectors necessitating scribal education. In this rural situation, the need for even the most perennial and routine economic documents also would have been limited,. The ordinary Israelite simply did not need to partake of the alphabet system of writing no matter how 'easy' it was to learn (see Additional Readings: Daily Life in Iron I Israel; Literacy).[11]

Writing during this period was for specified circumstances. If an Israelite did need or want writing inscribed on prestige objects, the supplier of such skills in these rural settings were likely to have been the priests. Ryan Byrne suggests, during the Iron I period, elite patronage helped maintain the scribal profession but he does not address the presence of priesthoods (who also might have earned a living in-between festivals by supporting the needs of rich people in a non-state society). Van der Toorn similarly claims the part-time lector priests in Egypt made their living as businessmen when they were off rotation at the temple. One specialized group of people utilizing writing may have been the warrior (guilds) with their inscribed arrowheads. Javelins could also be inscribed. The relationship between the writing-priests and their elite patrons may indicate that the priests were not free agents but dependent on their benefactors. Javelins also could be inscribed. Beyond such circumscribed uses, the outlets for writing to provide a living were limited (see Additional Readings: Arrowheads and Javelins).[12]

---

10 According to Sanders, 'For the first half millennium or so of its history, the main attested use of the alphabet was for marginal people' such as foreign soldiers and laborers (Seth L. Sanders, 'What was the alphabet for? The rise of written vernaculars and the making of Israelite national literature', *Maarav* 11 2004: 25–56, here 33, repeated word for word in his subsequent book, *The Invention of Hebrew*, 40, and related texts in 77–87; see also Orly Goldwasser, 'The advantage of cultural periphery: the invention of the alphabet in Sinai (circa 1840 BCE)', in Rakefet Sela-Sheffy and Gideon Toury, eds, *Culture Contacts and the Making of Cultures: Papers in Homage to Itamar Even-Zohar* (Tel Aviv: Tel Aviv University/Unit of Culture Research, 2011), 255–321, here 286.
11 See David M. Carr, 'The Tel Zayit abecedary in (social) context', in Ron E. Tappy and P. Kyle McCarter, eds, *Literate Culture and Tenth-Century: The Tel Zayit Abcedary in Context* (Winona Lake: Eisenbrauns, 2008), 113–129, here 116. He also avers that the idea of quick acquisition of functional alphabetic competence is a myth.
12 Ryan Byrne, 'The refuge of scribalism in Iron I Palestine', *BASOR* 345 2007: 1–31; Van der Toorn, *Scribal Culture*, 71.

One additional function for writing was in the maintenance of Israel's cultural legacy. People sang the songs, told the stories, celebrated the festivals that kept the anti-Egyptian Israelite identity alive for centuries even though Israel had no king, no temple, and no capital city, an unprecedented configuration for a settled people in its own right. Israel's heritage was maintained through songs or poetry including the previously mentioned Book of Jashar. It was not an alphabet prose narrative although it, or at least portions of it, later became incorporated into one. Catherine Bell observes that:

> 'to maintain the authority and prestige of formalized functions (referring to rituals, feasts, ceremonies...) there must be restricted access to the necessary skills or training, requiring primarily oral transmission with no written materials to facilitate indiscriminate access'.[13]

The most notable biblical example of an individual being inducted into a training program is the story of the Ephraimite child Samuel becoming part of the priests of Shiloh (I Sam. 1). Although the details are not elaborated, it is reasonable to conclude that he learned the traditions of Israel as part of his education. These ritualist specialists provide a logical venue for the transformation from early heroic poetry to prose narratives in the absence of a king and bureaucracy.

Typically one would expect the early poetry to be sung about the human warriors or kings and/or the divine gods and goddesses who ensured the safety and well-being of the people against the forces of chaos. Israel was not immune to this practice even if it did not have a human king. Other cultures praised human kings like Gilgamesh of Uruk, Sargon the Great of Akkad, Tukulti-ninurta of Assyria, Thutmose III, Ramses II, and Merneptah of Egypt, among others. But even the Israelite's heroic songs were scarcely about the achievements of a human king or warrior. They were about the victories of Yahweh: Yahweh over Egypt and Yahweh over Canaanites in the time of Egyptian hegemony. The poetic writing of early Israel is consistent with Friedman's observation that poetry preceded prose in Israel's writing.[14]

The foremost example of Israelite poetic alphabet writing during the interim between Merneptah and monarchy is the Song of Deborah (Judg. 5). The Song of Deborah generally is considered to be one of if not the oldest song in the biblical tradition ... a claim which is disputed. It often has been linked with the Song of the Sea/Song of Miriam (Ex. 15), the Blessing of Jacob (Gen. 49), and the Blessing of Moses (Deut. 33) as representatives of the oldest writing in the Hebrew language. The Song is an example of poetry preceding prose (the narrative story in Judg. 4). It consists of obscure and difficult language and there is the noteworthy absence of Judah in the list of the tribes of Israel. Whether the Song is a unity or was composed over the centuries originating in pre-monarchic times and

---

13 Catherine Bell, *Ritual Theory, Ritual Practice* (New York: Oxford University Press, 1992), 121.

14 It should be noted that Friedman was a student of Frank Moore Cross at Harvard who was a co-student with David Noel Freedman at Johns Hopkins University of William Foxwell Albright. The 'Albright [Scribal] School' strongly supports the idea of poetry during the Iron I period when Israel emerged in history. For heroic poetry in early Israel, see the recent study by Mark S. Smith, a Cross student, which focuses on Iron I Israel where he claims there has been no study that examines it in detail (Mark S. Smith, *Poetic Heroes: Literary Commemorations of Warriors and Warrior Culture in the Early Biblical World* [Grand Rapids: William B. Eerdmans, 2014], 19).

finalized in monarchic times also has been debated. It has been compared to non-biblical royal poems of victory composed after the battle by the Egyptians Thutmose III, Ramses II, and Merneptah and the Assyrians Tukulti-ninurta, Tiglath-pileser I, and Shalmaneser III. It sings to the glory of the triumph of Yahweh and Israel at a time when Israel had no king (see Additional Readings: Song of Deborah).

The Song occurs during a critical void in the written record of Israelite history. The Song of Deborah sings of a battle in north against Canaanites whereas the Book of Jashar song is limited to a battle in the south in the land of Benjamin. Nonetheless, Benjamin participates in this battle at Taanach as part of Israel right along with Ephraim, the tribe of Joshua (Judg. 5: 14). Benjamin, like Ephraim, always was part of Israel while Jerusalem was not. While the Israelite tribes are named in the song, the Canaanite city opponents are not:

> **Judges 5: 19** *The kings came, they fought; then fought the kings of Canaan, at Taanach, by the waters of Megiddo; they got no spoils of silver.*

While Jerusalem was not part of Israel, it is unlikely that it participated in a Canaanite coalition so far to the north.

The Song cuts right to the heart of a key issue in biblical scholarship: the memory of people in the land of Canaan of the Egyptian hegemony during the Late Bronze Age. Na'aman wonders how there could be a 350-year black hole in biblical memory for the era of Egyptian imperialism in Canaan. Coincidentally, on the other side of river, Egyptologist Manfred Bietak bemoans the Egyptological neglect of 'over 300 years' of Hyksos and Asiatic presence in Egypt on New Kingdom culture as if the Egyptian stories of the warriors from across the river and the Hebrew traditions are not connected. Leuchter claims that this time period in Israelite history did not disappear from the Israelite cultural memory. He refers to Canaanite kings in the Late Bronze Age serving as Pharaoh's proxies and he notes the likelihood of long-term collective memories of the tensions between highland Israel and lowland Canaanite cities (see Chapter 9 for the Canaanite coalition in Josh. 10). Robert Miller makes the case that the opening verse in Judges 5: 2 is better translated as 'When Pharaoh ruled' based on the consonants פרע or PR' rather than 'When leaders led'. His interpretation means the song is set in the time when Egypt still ruled the land of Canaan. Since Merneptah mentions Israel in the 13th century BCE and Egypt did not withdraw from the land until the 12th century BCE, there was ample time for Israel to sing songs and rejoice in the failure of Egypt to destroy its seed.[15]

The Song itself has direct Egyptian connections. The commander of the enemy forces in the Song is Sisera. The powers of the cosmos are unleashed against him:

---

15 Manfred Bietak, 'The aftermath of the Hyksos in Avaris', in Rakefet Sela-Sheffy and Gideon Toury, eds, *Culture Contacts and the Making of Cultures: Papers in Homage to Itamar Even-Zohar* (Tel Aviv: Tel Aviv University/Unit of Culture Research, 2011), 19–65, here 21; Mark Leuchter, '"Why tarry the wheels of his chariot?" (Judg 5,28): Canaanite chariots and echoes of Egypt in the Song of Deborah', *Bib* 91 2010: 256–268, here 261; Robert D. Miller II, 'When Pharaohs ruled: on the translation of Judges 5:2', *JTS* 59 2008: 650–654; Na'aman, 'The Exodus story', 64.

Judges 5: 20 *From heaven fought the stars, from their courses they fought against Sisera.*

The ethnic identification of his name has been vexing and unresolved in biblical scholarship. The suggestion that makes the most sense to me is the proposal by Egyptologist Donald Redford that Sisera derives from the shortened version of the name of Ramses III aka Se-se or Sesy or Ssy-r^c. Ramses II also used the *sese* sobriquet. Given the existence of Israel in the land of Canaan during the campaigns of Merneptah and Ramses III, it is more reasonable to conclude that it did retain memories of them than it did not. After all, its existence was on the line. Just because a story has Uncle Sam and a bear does not mean it is about a physically literal event. The same considerations apply with the Kenite wilderness woman smiting Pharaoh in a tent. Israel knew the core Egyptian values and motifs and reversed them (see Additional Readings: 1177 BCE).[16]

One should note that the presence on a relief of an Egyptian king does not necessarily mean that he was physically present at the battle. His vassals may have been largely on their own to manage the Sea People invasions. By implication the same considerations apply to any altercation with Israel. The garrison forces and/or vassals who fought on his behalf signified his symbolic presence even if not a physical one. Indeed, collective action on the part of Canaanite kings without Pharaonic guidance or blessing is unlikely.[17]

Additional connections to the Late Bronze Age may be mentioned. Na'aman begins his analysis of the 350-year Egyptian imperialism with Thutmose III. The 'Napoleon of Egypt''s great victory was at Megiddo, one of the best documented battles from the ancient Near East. Thutmose III seized 924 chariots in that campaign and launched the massive deportation of Canaanites to Egypt. His commencement of the age of hegemony was the alpha to Deborah's omega when it ended with Israel's triumph by the waters of Megiddo in a battle against 900 chariots. Na'aman's suggestion 'that the major event underlying the Exodus tradition is the dramatic Egyptian withdrawal from Canaan after the Egyptian bondage reached its peak during the Twentieth Dynasty' in the 12th century BCE should have been followed by the suggestion of an immediate Israelite reaction to it. The Munchkins did not wait 500 years to sing 'Ding dong, the witch is dead'. The answer to the question posed by Cross, 'Can we really suppose that Israel alone had no singers of tales?' is 'No'. Before there were the laments of trauma and despair there were the songs of victory and celebration against Egypt and its Canaanite 'flying monkeys'.[18]

Whether the Song of Deborah was a war cry in preparation for the battle, a celebration immediately subsequent to it, a celebration after Egyptian withdrawal, or all of the above, is secondary here. It is difficult to imagine that the time of conflict between Egypt and its Canaanite vassals against Israel during the time from Merneptah and Ramses VI, was one of silence. Egypt claimed to have and failed to destroy the seed of Israel, Instead it withdrew from the land of Canaan. The current emphasis in biblical scholarship on writing

---

16 Donald B. Redford, *Egypt, Canaan, and Israel in Ancient Times* (Princeton: Princeton University Press, 1992), 257 n.2; see also Morris, *The Architecture of Imperialism*, 412, 414, for Ramses II as Sese.

17 See Morris, *The Architecture of Imperialism*, 351, 696.

18 Frank Moore Cross, 'Telltale remnants of oral epic in the older sources of the Tetrateuch', in J. David Schloen, ed., *Exploring the Longue Durée: Essays in Honor of Lawrence E. Stager* (Winona Lake: Eisenbrauns, 2009), 83–88, here 87; Na'aman, 'The Exodus story', 65.

in response to trauma should not negate the recognition by previous generations of scholars of Israelite poetic writing to celebrate victory even if Israel did not have a king.[19]

The net result is that during the period between the withdrawal of Egypt and the rise of the Israelite monarchy, writing did not loom large in the life and culture of Israel. The writing which occurred related to economic transactions was limited, routine, and boring. The writing which occurred so rich people could show off their wealth was limited, routine, and boring. The writing which occurred to celebrate and remember the glorious events of Israel's history in the two centuries from its birth in the 13th century BCE to pre-monarchic times in the 11th century BCE was exciting, unique, and sung at cultic settings, special in both space and time. None of these writings were alphabet prose narratives. Something had to happen to push the envelope of the information system in use to elevate it to the next level.

The king

One critical component of the writing equation in ancient times was the king. Even when people gave thanks for life, the alpha male was involved as either the great hunter or the great protector. Even when the people lamented trauma, the alpha male was involved as the source of the failure. Once the position of the alpha male was institutionalized as king, he dominated the discourse even more. Writing dealt directly with him or indirectly as the representative of the deity on earth. Either way the king was the focal point and early Israel did not have a human one.

The importance of the king to writing may be observed in nearby cultures. Normally one thinks of praising the king but we should recognize that there would be times when a king might be taken to task: assassinations, coups, death in battle, defeat, famine all require explanations. Modern scientific answers were not available nor was political science. The explanations needed to be expressed in the language of the times. For the most part that meant in poetry and/or non-alphabetic writing.

The concept of combining literature and politics was neither new nor unique to Israel. Stories set in the past could be about contemporary political situations and conditions at the time of the composition. Authors had the option of delivering political messages in the present through stories set in mythical or historic time. Israel did not invent this techniques. *The Crucible*, *Inherit the Wind*, and *Spartacus*, all from the 1950s, are all stories set in the human past but about the Joe McCarthy political present. All are easily removed from their own historical context now that the McCarthy era is over. None of them was written to be timeless and all presuppose familiarity with a shared cultural and political legacy. Would Macbeth and Vlad the Impaler even recognize who they have become? The technique of indirect attack or commentary through oblique or slightly camouflaged figures is a time-tested one that continues to be effective to this very day.[20]

---

19 Peter Feinman, 'Egypt and Israel: From Ramses II to Ramses VI', paper presented at the annual conference of the Society of Biblical Literature, Atlanta, November 24, 2015.
20 For the combination of politics and literature see, Dean Hammer, *The Iliad as Politics: The Performance of Political Thought* (Norman: University of Oklahoma Press, 2002), 3–46; Mario Liverani, *Myth and Politics*

Long before Israel wrestled with the idea of kingship, Mesopotamia dealt with political and dynastic change. There are Mesopotamian stories set in the historical past but composed to comment on contemporary events. A lament over the destruction of Sumer and Ur also could be about the current transfer of power from the destroyed city to the city where the lament was composed. *The Cuthean Legend* about Naram-sin (2254–2218 BCE) was composed five centuries after the historical events it purports to tell. The original oral tradition eventually had become a fixed written record. Even that lament drew on the century-earlier precedent of a curse levied against Agade with its assault on Naram-sin. These writings suggest that the Akkadian Naram-sin developed into the proverbial whipping boy as the failed king even to non-Akkadian cultures (much as King Jeroboam of the northern kingdom of Israel would become in the Bible).[21]

Another facet of royal Mesopotamian writing dealt with internal divisions. Peter Machinist examines *The Tukulti-Ninurta Epic*. The 13th century BCE Assyrian ruler pushed the envelope of what Assyrian rulers could do. He expanded the borders of the empire even to the inclusion of revered Babylon, a major endeavor for the 'minor' northern upstart. Machinist posits dissension within the Assyrian ranks due both to this violation of the natural order and the threat of 'southern culture' on the native traditions of the northern country. The Epic then was composed not simply to exalt the king but to allay the fears of those Assyrians opposed to his actions. Machinist acknowledges that evidence for this resisters is 'not abundant'. However since Tikulti-ninurta was assassinated, resistance to him is not a far-fetched notion either.

For Machinist, 'literature is essentially a political act, created to explain and justify major political and cultural shifts'. He sees a similar situation with Assyria in Israel where David and Solomon had to address not the Babylonians but the Canaanites who were in the land. Literature was critical in both situations of expressing and resolving conflicts of identity in fluid circumstances that were a change from the past. He specifically cites Ps. 29 as an example of a Canaanite hymn to Baal reworked as a paean to Yahweh (similar to the way Assyrians later replaced Babylonian deity Marduk with Assyrian deity Ashur in *Enuma Elish*). Machinist opines that the continued legacy of the older Canaanite monarchy contributed to this development and that the Melchizedek passage (Gen. 14: 18–24) may be a product of this time. In the biblical case, it is far easier to point to critics of the actions of David and Solomon especially since the kingdom divided. Unfortunately, even though

---

in *Ancient Near Eastern Historiography* (Ithaca: Cornell University Press, 2004), 160–192; Vanderhooft and Winitzer, eds, *Literature as Politics, Politics as Literature*.

21 Machinist, 'The voice of the historian', 124–125, 129; Piotr Michalowski, *Lamentation over the Destruction of Sumer and Ur* (Winona Lake: Eisenbrauns, 1989), 6–9; Barbara Neveling Porter, *Ritual and Politics in Ancient Mesopotamia* (AOS 88; New Haven: American Oriental Society, 2005), 1–6; Jack Sasson, *Judges 1–12* (The Anchor Yale Bible 6D; New Haven: Yale University Press, 2014), 404; Joan Goodnick Westenholz, 'Oral tradition and written texts in the Cycle of Akkade', in Marianna E. Vogelzang and Herman L. J. Vanstiphout, eds, *Mesopotamian Epic Literature: Oral or Aural?* (Lewiston: Edward Mellen Press, 1992), 123–154. For the example of a myth to interpret the historical irruption of the Aramaeans *c.* 1000 BCE and the Babylonian Erra Epic, see W. G. Lambert, 'Old Testament mythology in its ancient Near Eastern context', in J. A. Emerton, ed., *Congress Volume 1986* (SVT 40; Leiden: E. J. Brill, 1988), 124–143, here 129.

he is exactly right, he never elaborated on these insights to identify the pro- and anti-king portions of the biblical text by Canaanite and Israelite authors.[22]

Closer to Israel, the 13th century BCE Ugaritic Baal cycle itself may in fact be an expression of royal politics using diplomatic conventions to address political issues through the familial relationships in mythic form. Mark Smith declares point blank that 'It is well-known that political language dominates the Baal cycle'. The king was its patron. Wayne Pitard views the Baal cycle as a story of royal succession more comparable to Solomon's succession in I Kings 1 than to the cosmic confrontations of the Mesopotamian creation story *Enuma Elish*. The difference is that the story is set on a mythological plane rather than a human one. Seth Sanders touts the Baal epic as inaugurating a new distinctively local literature delivering the message that the king was the crucial figure in the triumph over chaos and the ritualized redemption of Ugarit from disaster. He avers that the history of the marginalized alphabet linked its usage to political expressions. He specifically cites the example of Ugarit where a cuneiform alphabet developed.[23]

Initially, the Ugarit writings were not germane to the Israelite experience – Israel had no king. Still, the precedent had been created. Royal politics were expressed through the cuneiform-based alphabet by the scribal elite in the 13th century BCE. A newly emerging Israelite kingdom in the late 11th century BCE had the option to draw on these techniques. There is no inherent reason why it might not employ an Egyptian-based alphabet that had been around for centuries but not used by existing power structure, for its own royal deliberations. It could even use the alphabet prose narrative to attack the notion of kingship and to create an Israelite counter to the Baal epic once Israel ruled Baal-worshiping people. Canaanite myth could become a Hebrew epic under the right circumstances.[24]

Egypt also deployed such writing to deal with the present. While the Mesopotamian examples are more remote, the Egyptian examples provided Israel the opportunity to learn this technique from the Egyptians especially if Egypt deployed it against them. The 'Quarrel Story of Seqenenre and Apophis' was composed three centuries after those historical figures lived. The story about a confrontation between Egypt and a West Semitic people who had

---

22   Peter Machinist, 'The Tukulti-Ninurta epic and the Bible', *CBQ* 38 1876: 455–482, quotations from 475 and 479.

23   Wayne Pitard, 'Baal's palace and Ugarit's temple in the Baal Cycle', paper presented at the annual conference of the Middle West Branch of the American Oriental Society, February 12, 2011; Wayne T. Pitard, 'The combat myth as a succession story at Ugarit', in JoAnn Scurlock and Richard H. Beal, eds, *Creation and Chaos: A Reconsideration of Hermann Gunkel's Chaos Kampf Hypothesis* (Winona Lake: Eisenbrauns, 2013), 199–205; Sanders, *The Invention of Hebrew*, 50–57; Sanders, 'What was the alphabet for?', 33; Mark S. Smith, *The Ugaritic Baal Cycle Volume I* (SVT 55; Leiden: E. J. Brill, 1994), xxiv; Smith, *Poetic Heroes*, 100; Aaron Tugendhaft, 'How to become a brother in the Bronze Age: an inquiry into the representation of politics in Ugaritic myth', *Fragments* 2 2012: 89–104; Aaron Tugendhaft, 'Unsettling sovereignty: politics and poetics in the Baal Cycle', *JAOS* 132 2012: 367–384; Nicolas Wyatt, 'Ilimilku's ideological programme: Ugarit royal propaganda and a Biblical postscript', *UF* 29 1997: 775–796; Nicolas Wyatt, 'The religious role of the king in Ugarit', *UF* 37 2005: 695–727.

24   The idea of the Canaanite myth becoming a Hebrew epic is part of the legacy of the Frank Moore Cross scribal school at an elite institution (see Sanders, *The Invention of Hebrew*, 222 n100). See also Umberto Cassuto, *Biblical and Oriental Studies: Volume II – Bible and Ancient Oriental Texts* (Jerusalem: Magness Press, Hebrew University, 1975), 69–109.

sojourned to Egypt few in number, had a leader named Jacob, and a tradition of 400 years in the Delta written by the Pharaoh who claimed to have destroyed their seed was not written for a graduate seminar but to address an issue in the present. Mythical Egyptian stories including the 'Contendings of Horus and Seth', the 'Tale of the Two Brothers', and the 'Blinding of Truth by Falsehood', all have been linked to historical circumstances at the onset or demise of the 19th Dynasty. A shift in the focus in a story from Osiris and Horus to Horus and Seth also could be about the new Pharaoh, Ramses IV, succeeding an assassinated one, Ramses III. The stories set in the past and the monuments and reliefs in the present were both political propaganda about the royal present.[25]

Thomas Schneider's observations that the *Tale of Two Brothers* is not a fairy tale intended for amusement and entertainment is valid. He postulates that the Egyptians borrowed from the Ugaritic traditions to fill a gap to deal with the immediate Egyptian political issue of royal succession at the end of the 19th Dynasty. Since the Potiphar incident in the Joseph story clearly borrows from this Egyptian tale, it is reasonable to conclude that the Israelite author also was aware of the dynastic political implications of the story from the time when a Pharaoh claimed to have destroyed Israel. Societies with kings knew about dynastic problems and wrote about. So far, Israel did not have a king.[26]

The intertwining of literature and politics already was an ancient and widespread phenomena by the time Israel first entertained the idea of monarchy. These writings in the other cultures never became a continuous prose narrative encompassing centuries of time until the post-Alexander world. Israel was different from its neighbors. Three primary facts differentiated the Israelite cultural experience from them and became defining factors for the Hebrew Bible. First, Israel debated the very issue of having a human king or not. Second, Israel had a continued existence within the political entity of different points of view even after the monarchy had been established. Third, Israel continued to extend the story over time as new topics of concern arose. The genesis of these traits occurred with the birth of the kingship and they continued even after the kingship ended in Israel and Judah. Again, these differences substantiate why Israel produced the Hebrew Bible and no other culture had an equivalent.

In one sense, the change to prose narratives occurred because there now was a need for a different genre or form of communication. Sanders refers to the 'politics of biblical writing' and asks 'Why did people begin to write about themselves, in their own language,

---

25 Edward Bleiberg, 'Historical texts as political propaganda during the New Kingdom', *BES* 7 1985/86: 5–13; Peter Feinman, 'The Quarrel Story: Egypt, the Hyksos, and Canaan', *Conversations with the Biblical World* 35 2015: 94–127; Susan Tower Hollis, 'The woman in ancient examples of the Potiphar's Wife Motif, K2111', in Peggy L. Day, ed., *Gender and Difference in Ancient Israel* (Minneapolis: Fortress Press, 1989), 28–42, here 35; Leonard H. Lesko, 'Three late Egyptian stories reconsidered', in Leonard H. Lesko, ed., *Egyptological Studies in Honor of Richard A. Parker – Presented on the Occasion of His 78th Birthday, December 10, 1983* (Hanover: Brown University Press by University Press of New England, 1986), 98–103; Georges Posener, *Littérature et Politique dans l'Égypte de la XIIe Dynastie* (Sciences Historiques et Philologiques 307; Paris: Bibliothèque de l'École des Hautes Etudes, 1956); Jean Revez, 'Looking at history through the prism of mythology: can the Osirian Myth shed any light on Ancient Egyptian royal succession patters?', *JEGH* 3.1 2010: 47–71, here 50–60.
26 Thomas Schneider, 'Innovation in literature on behalf of politics: the tale of the two brothers, Ugarit, and 19th Dynasty history', *Agypten et Levante* 18 2008: 1–12.

in alphabetic writing?'[27] He also recognizes 'that there is more than one possible fit between writing an political development'.[28] In this regard, one needs to recognize that reading and writing back then do not equate with the terms as understood today. The Hebrew language originally did not have a separate word meaning 'to read'. Instead, *qara*, meant 'to call out, proclaim'. This definition is consistent with the understanding of these initial writings as part of an oral performance of some kind including both cultic and non-cultic, meaning political, situations. Van der Toorn definitively declares that writing was used mostly to support oral performance including the classic texts from Mesopotamia. Something new had occurred in Israel that caused them to want to call out and proclaim their feelings.[29]

At this point, I wish to express my disagreement with Friedman about Solomon becoming secure on the throne after the death of David as the impetus for the composition of the prose masterpiece that became the basis for the Bible. Instead of security by the king, I see insecurity over the very issue of having a king as the launch point. Instead of celebration of the secure king, I see accusation and castigation of one who would become king after centuries of Israel not having a human king. Instead of Solomon being the key figure, I see Saul as the catalyst for the development of the alphabet prose narrative in Israel. Saul's decision to seek the crown in the time of Philistine domination and the opposition to Saul's decision are the direct causes for the origin of the alphabet prose narrative in Israel. Those two intertwined actions changed the Israelite paradigm. Now the Israel people had matters to discuss, debate, and decide about. There was no existing genre for political exchange when there were differences in opinion. The alphabet prose narrative filled a new niche in human history. It contributed to the uniqueness of ancient Israel.[30]

Once Israel's actions are put in context, one can see that the use of the alphabet prose narrative in the time of Saul simultaneously drew on existing traditions and took them to a new level. However, there is a second element to be considered. These individual alphabet prose narratives coalesced into a single narrative as Friedman indicates. Whether it is his one proposed masterpiece in the time of Solomon or not, my contention is that the six son stories of this study are supplements to an existing narrative. Therefore I am obligated to demonstrate two developments: the origin of the alphabet prose narrative in Israel and the creation of the first continuous alphabet prose narrative in Israel.

---

27 Sanders, 'What was the alphabet for?', 25–26.

28 Seth L. Sanders, 'Writing and Early Iron Age Israel: before national scripts, beyond nations and states', in Ron E. Tappy and P. Kyle McCarter, eds, *Literate Culture and Tenth-Century Canaan: The Tel Zayit Abecedary in Context* (Winona Lake: Eisenbrauns, 2008), 105.

29 See David M. Carr, *Writing on the Tablet of the Heart: Origins of Scripture and Literature* (New York: Oxford University Press, 2005), 120; William M. Schniedewind, *How the Bible Became a Book*, 48; Van der Toorn, *Scribal Culture*, 11–13. The foremost American example of a similar 'calling out' or 'proclaiming' occurred during the American Revolution when an individual would read aloud the latest broadside to an assembled crowd. The equivalent today are the TV talk shows where talking heads exclaim about books and articles on current events the audience has not read.

30 The concept of the Philistines as a catalyst for the formation of Israel identity is not a new one (see Faust, *Israel's Ethnogenesis*, 111–156). Its impact extended beyond considerations of material culture and traditions into the political realm as well with the rise of the monarchy. In and of itself, that development did not make Israel distinctive. The opposition to the monarchy and the retention of both sides of view in the written record did.

My focus is on late 11th/10th century BCE writing. David Carr's advice on the precariousness of drawing conclusions based on the absence of archaeological data bears notice. He considers scholars to have been 'ill-advised' to have done so based on the absence of such data for the 10th century BCE even going so far as to deploy the word 'dangerous'. No matter how many desks, inkwells, or inscriptions one might find in the archaeological record, the leap from such material artifacts to the *Iliad*, Shakespeare, or the Bible would clearly be a giant step. Without the preservation of texts, problematic if on perishable materials, the full flowering of such genius irrevocably would be lost. One may add that his admonitions also attest by implication the role of the individual artist especially in a non-scribal setting.[31]

Mark Smith regards the 10th century BCE as the time of transformation of a pre-monarchic oral poetry society to a monarchic prose narrative society. Specifically, he designates David as the watershed figure emblematic of the shift from the heroic poetry of early Israel to prose narratives during the monarchy. In this regard, he is slightly before Friedman chronologically who affixes the earliest date for the transformation to prose after Solomon became secure on the throne.[32]

In making this claim, Smith posits that the Song of Deborah was composed in two primary units. He dates the initial composition to the Iron I period of early Israel, to a time of various tribal militias who join or decline to participate in a coalition against a Canaanite foe (vassals of Egypt who opposed Israel). The names Yahweh and Israel are conspicuously absent or minimized in this version. By contrast, the added component abounds in references to the two 'signatories' to the covenant. Smith interprets this addition to reflect the development of the monarchical society. The emphasis had become national and not local.[33]

I interpret that very addition to a date just prior to the kingship. What the author has done is to revise the Song of Deborah to deliver an anti-monarchical polemic. He is delivering a message in his present by drawing on a venerated tradition, like adding a verse to an existing song rather than composing a new one. Just as there was no need for a human king to defeat the Canaanite foe in ancient times, so there is no need for a human king to defeat the Philistines in our time. Yahweh had worked water wonders in Egypt, so too he had worked water wonders in the land of Canaan. Peoples in Edom, Moab, Canaan, and Philistia had trembled in terror and dread before Yahweh in the past, so too would they tremble in the present. Yahweh will reign as king for ever and ever (Song of the Sea, Ex. 15: 14–18).

Israel had survived for centuries without a human king. Its seed had not been destroyed by Merneptah. Why change now? Smith's proposed revision of the Song of Deborah occurred during the time when Israel began debating the issue of human kingship. Presumably a keeper of the traditions of the songs of Yahweh triumphant modified a well-known song.

---

31 Carr, 'The Tel Zayit abcedary', 118, 125. Pioske observes that the epigraphic record cannot preclude the possibility of the composition of a larger body of Hebrew texts before the 8th century BCE – particularly in a region noted for its use of perishable writing materials (*David's Jerusalem*, 69).
32 See Smith, *Poetic Heroes*, 284–307, 326–328.
33 Smith, *Poetic Heroes*, 211–266, 287–289.

The song included mention of Benjamin and Ephraim but not Judah. Now it rejected the notion of human king such as Saul from Benjamin since victory was attributed to Yahweh with no king present except for the losers. In contrast to Saul, the early Israelite hero Gideon had it right:

> **Judges 8: 22** *Then the men of Israel said to Gideon, 'Rule over us, you and your son and your grandson also...'*[23] *Gideon said to them, 'I will not rule over you, and my son will not rule over you; Yahweh will rule over you.'*

These revisions occurred before there was a Judah and while the debate over the monarchy raged. A step had been taken towards the development of the continuous alphabet prose masterpiece.

There is a second consideration. In Smith's proposal, Yahweh not only is mentioned, he is pictured as emerging from the wilderness of Seir. The author is vigorously asserting not only the presence of Isra-el and Yahweh, but the equation of Yahweh of the wilderness and El of Canaan. Merneptah names the people Isra-el but provides no information about the deity of the people. King Mesha of Moab in the 9th century BCE similarly identifies Yahweh as the deity of Israel. The open questions are when did a people named after Canaanite El begin to worship Kenite/Shasu Yahweh and why? These questions are outside the scope of this study. However, the calling of the name of Yahweh figures prominently in the Seth story and people speak the name on multiple occasions elsewhere in the son stories. Miriam and Deborah both sing to Yahweh. Even Arunuah and Rahab know his name. The name of the deity of the people very much is an item of contention in the battle for power after the death of David. Smith's proposed revision to the Song of Deborah and Gideon's admonition against human kingship are part of the transition from oral poetry to written prose initiated when Saul sought the kingship.

Saul

Poor Saul. He cannot get a break. The debates among Mesopotamians when kingship first descended from heaven and among Egyptians when the king first ascended the throne have been lost to history assuming they ever even existed in written form in the first place. By contrast, one can find them in the biblical narrative where even the idea of kingship was criticized as a rejection of Yahweh:

> **I Samuel 10: 17** *Now Samuel called the people together to Yahweh at Mizpah;*[18] *and he said to the people of Israel, 'Thus says Yahweh, the God of Israel, "I brought up Israel out of Egypt, and I delivered you from the hand of the Egyptians and from the hand of all the kingdoms that were oppressing you."*[19] *But you have this day rejected your God, who saves you from all your calamities and your distresses; and you have said, "No! but set a king over us." Now therefore present yourselves before the Yahweh by your tribes and by your thousands.*[34]

Volkmar Fritz offers Jotham's Fable (Judg. 9: 8–15) as another example of an anti-monarchic diatribe with no ancient Near East parallel. He delicately deems it a mocking, scathing,

---

34 Volkmar Fritz, *The Emergence of Israel in the Twelfth and Eleventh Centuries BCE* (Biblical Encyclopedia 2; Atlanta: Society of Biblical Literature, 2011), 221–223, quotation from 222.

sarcastic denunciation of the office of king. Fritz posits that it 'originated at the earliest in the early monarchic period when the new form of government must have been asserted against contrary opinions'. The battle over kingship was engaged and responsibility for the Exodus was a battlefield. Saul's quest for the kingship initiated a war of words that continued long after he was dead. It includes the very stories that are the subject of this study.[35]

There is a story to be told about Saul becoming the first king of Israel and Israel told it, both pro and con. The complexities of his life, kingdom, and death will not be unraveled as part of the current study. Suffice it to say, the study presumes the historical existence of Saul as king of Israel consistent with the geographic boundaries delineated in II Sam. 2:9 when his son Ishbaal succeeded him:

> and he made him king over Gilead and the Ashurites and Jezreel and Ephraim and Benjamin and all Israel.

Finkelstein supports the notion that this biblical verse expresses a genuine description of the kingdom of Saul. He compares it to Labayu's Shechem-based kingdom in the Amarna Age, a king who was a thorn in the side to his city-state neighbors and threat to Egyptian control of the trade routes. Ultimately both these highland kings failed in their efforts to expand into the lowlands. Jerusalem was not part of his kingdom nor of the debate on kingship. It is reasonable to conclude that Saul would have his supporters (Benjaminite priests) who could tell his side of the story stressing his successes and legitimacies.[36]

Scholarly opinions on Saul vary. A non-inclusive sample of scholarly deliberations reveal a range of opinions about him as an individual and the writings about him found in I Sam. (Additional Readings: Saul's Rise to Power).

J. Maxwell Miller's analysis of the Saul narrative reveals a deliberate linking of the stories of Saul and David's rises to power.

Diana Edelman focuses on how the Deuteronomist in the 7th century BCE would tell the story of Saul's rise to power while recognizing that Saul did not emerge in history as a character at that time.

Joseph Blenkinsopp despairs that 'access to usable historical information about Saul and his reign has been rendered extraordinarily difficult by politically and theologically

---

35 The situation at the birth of the United States was quite different from the birth of kingship in Egypt or Mesopotamia. The pro- and anti-Constitution opinions of the American people during its creation and the extended ratification process were written down and are studied to this very day. The possession of multiple and contradicting opinions in the ancient Near East where the king tended to monopolize the information system is less frequent. Perhaps the most famous non-biblical example of differing opinions occurred after the battle of Kadesh when the participating Egyptian and Hittite kings remembered the confrontation differently. In biblical traditions, there are the competing biblical and archaeological versions of the actions of Shoshenq, Mesha, Hazael, and Sennacherib to name a few. All these examples are cross-cultural not intracultural as exist in the biblical narrative starting with Saul.

36 Israel Finkelstein, 'The last Labayu: King Saul and the expansion of the first North Israelite Territorial Entity', in Yairah Amit and Nadav Na'aman, eds, *Essays on Ancient Israel in its Near Eastern Context: A Tribute to Nadav Na'aman* (Winona Lake: Eisenbrauns, 2006), 171–187. By contrast, Na'aman considers it a retrojected attempt at historical reality ('The Kingdom of Isbaal' *BN* 84 1990: 33–37; Nadav Na'aman, 'Saul, Benjamin and the emergence of "Biblical Israel" (continued, Part 2)', 335–349, here 347.

inspired polemic' which he traces back to a pro-Samuel Ephraimite prophetic source without identifying when it originated.[37]

In his Anchor Bible Commentaries on I and II Samuel, McCarter identifies a 'Saul Cycle' containing precisely such stories praising him in the savior style of a hero from the Book of Judges. Yet for some reason he dates the cycle to the 9th century and the northern kingdom of Israel provenance even though Benjamin at the that time was part of the southern kingdom of Judah. By contrast, he dates the biblical story of David's rise to power to the time of David himself.

Marsha White more vigorously advocates for the composition of a 'History of Saul's Rise' contemporaneous with that rise and serving as a base text for the story of David's rise to power.

Drawing on White, Leuchter posits pro-Samuel and Saul factions at Shiloh (and Benjamin) dating to the 11th century BCE which continued on afterwards. He proposes a four-level composition process beginning with anti-Saul polemics in Judges to pro-Saul stories based on Samson elements extending to Josianic-era shapings in the 7th century BCE as Shiloh regrouped under the support of David but lost power during the Davidic dynasty. His proposition adds a dimension to polemical writings whereby stories are not necessarily about the person named in the story but someone in the present.

My supposition is that the origin of the monarchy in Israel after the people had existed for over two centuries without one was the true trigger for the development of the alphabet prose narrative in a secular not sacred setting. Differences of opinions among competing political factions is the basis of this study.

Na'aman's casual reference to 'the author of the Saul story-cycle' in contrast to 'the author of the Jacob story-cycle' recognizes that actual individual authors are involved. However, he is constrained because he rejects the possibility of the existence of such writers in 10th century BCE Jerusalem regardless of the political turmoil at that time. Only centuries later could they write about it due to a 'genuine antiquarian literary interest'. On the other hand, he also states

> that scribal activity was introduced in the court of Jerusalem no later than the time of Solomon, and possibly already in David's time ... (which) must have been confined to a small group of scribes in the court of Jerusalem and was mainly used for administrative and diplomatic exchange [why not political as well?].

Na'aman's positions echoes those of Carr who suggests the possibility 'that the shared script tradition in Judah and Israel is an indicator of a shared scribal system that emerged already in the 10th century, when biblical traditions depict both kingdoms as being ruled from Jerusalem by David and Solomon'. His view runs counter to recent trends in biblical scholarship against there being a distinctly Hebrew scribal system in the 10th century BCE or there being a united monarchy.[38]

---

37 Joseph Blenkinsopp, 'The quest for the historical Saul', in James W. Flanagan and Anita Weisboro Robinson, eds, *No Famine in the Land: Studies in Honor of John L. McKenzie* (Claremont: Scholars Press for Institute for Antiquity and Christianity, 1975), 75–99, here 82.

38 Carr, 'The Tel Zayit abecedary', 121 and 122; Nadav Na'aman, 'Saul, Benjamin, and the emergence of

Scholars also have proposed ways in which the Saulide debate unfolded that circumvent Friedman's proposed one prose masterpiece emerging fully-formed in the time of Solomon. Consider for example, one prominent anti-Saul text of terror story using the alphabet pose narrative: the rape in Gibeah, Saul's home and capital of his kingdom, of a Bethlemite woman, from the home of David, who was with a Levite from Ephraim where the priests of Shiloh were based (Judg. 19). Mario Liverani addresses the close connection between the writing of history and the validation of political order and political action in the ancient Near East targeting Judges 19–21 as a possibly pro-Davidic, anti-Benjaminite story from the time of Saul.[39] Yairah Amit declares:

> 'Literature has always been susceptible to involvement in political struggle, so the political mobilization of biblical literature should occasion no surprise... I have chosen to discuss ... the anti-Saul polemic hidden in chs. 19–21 in the book of Judges.'[40]

> '...the confrontation between the house of Saul, whose origin is in Gibeah, and the house of David, whose origin is in Bethlehem Judah, is in fact the core of the story.'[41]

Marc Brettler echoes Amit's statement in seeing the alphabet prose narrative story as an anti-Saul polemic in the use of literature as politics. He wonders why what is seemingly so obvious is rejected by scholars. How can a story which mentions the homes of Samuel, Saul and David not be a political polemic? Of critical importance as well is to recognize that the unnamed female figure also exists by the creation of the author as part of the polemic. Like Lady Liberty, she symbolizes the people. The story is 'a world of unrelenting terror' because that is the message the author wished to deliver in his polemic.[42]

An existing story might even be revised to strengthen its polemical message over time as the battle of words continued. Amit notes that the natural flow of a story may be interrupted by a glaring intrusion using the same stories in the Book of Judges as examples of this motif.

> **Judges 20: 28** *and Phinehas the son of Eleazar, son of Aaron, ministered before it in those days, saying, 'Shall we yet again go out to battle against our brethren the Benjaminites, or shall we cease?'*

"Biblical Israel" [continued, Part 2]', *ZAW* 121 2009: 335–349, here 342–345, quotation 345; Nadav Na'aman, 'The settlement of the Ephraites in Bethlehem and the location of Rachel's tomb', *RB* 121 2014: 516–539, 527; Nadav Na'aman, 'Sources and composition in the history of David', in Volkmar Fritz and Philip R. Davies, eds, *The Origin of the Ancient Israelite States* (JSOT Sup. Ser. 228; Sheffield: Sheffield Academic Press, 1996), 173–186, here 172–173; see also Nadav Na'aman, 'The conquest of Canaan in the Book of Joshua and in history', in Israel Finkelstein and Nadav Na'aman, eds, *From Nomadism to Monarchy: Archaeological and Historical Aspects of Early Israel* (Jerusalem: Israel Exploration Society, 1994), 218–281, here 218).

39 Liverani, *Myth and Politics in Ancient Near Eastern Historiography*, 160–192.

40 Yairah Amit, 'Literature in the service of politics: studies in Judges 19–21', in Henning Graf Reventlow, Yair Hoffman, and Benjamin Uffenheimer, eds, *Politics and Theopolitics in the Bible and Postbiblical Literature* (JSOT Sup. Ser. 171; Sheffield: Sheffield Academic Press, 1994), 28–40, here 28.

41 Yairah Amit, 'The use of analogy in the study of the Book of Judges', in Matthias Augustin and Klaus-Dietrich Schunck, eds, *Wünschet Jerusalem Frieden: Collected Communications to the XIIth Congress of the International Organization for the Study of the Old Testament, Jerusalem 1986* (Frankfurt am Main: P. Lang, 1988), 387–394, here 391.

42 Brettler, 'The Book of Judges', 412–413; Trible, *Texts of Terror*, 65. For an American example, see the ending of the movie version of the French book *The Planet of the Apes* where only the torch of Lady Liberty is visible from the ground.

This individual appears out of nowhere and has nothing to do with the surrounding story. She compares this intrusion with another three-generation sequence of priests who originated in the Exodus now appearing in a story in the Book of Judges:

> **Judges 18: 30** *And the Danites set up the graven image for themselves; and Jonathan the son of Gershom, son of Moses, and his sons were priests to the tribe of the Danites until the day of the captivity of the land.*

Here again a figure appears almost as an afterthought. These two Exodus-based three-generation priesthoods deriving from Moses and Aaron do not just exist here by chance.[43] For purposes in this study, Amit's and Brettler's observations suggest the ongoing long-standing rivalry between these two groups. There was not only a clash between Saul and David but between two political parties/priesthoods who were their advocates, one priesthood based on Moses in Ephraim and another on Aaron in Benjamin who supported Saul. That rivalry was expressed in the war of words in the stories of this study.

As previously mentioned, the rape story even includes a seemingly gratuitous but pointed dig about the Jebusites who were foreigners to Israel.

> **Judges 19: 11** *When they were near Jebus, the day was far spent, and the servant said to his master, 'Come now, let us turn aside to this city of the Jebusites, and spend the night in it'.* [12] *And his master said to him, 'We will not turn aside into the city of foreigners, who do not belong to the people of Israel; but we will pass on to Gibeah'.*

The Levite priest spurns Jebus as foreign for Gibeah, Saul's capital. How could this rape story not be a political polemic expressed through the alphabet prose narrative?

A writer also had the option of attacking someone indirectly. As Amit states:

> The authors of the Old Testament literature did not limit themselves to open polemic. Alongside that overt polemic, they employed the technique of hidden polemic.[44]

One could attack Saul, Solomon or Bathsheba directly by name in a story or one could tell a story which obviously, at least to the audience in its present, targets a living person. Stories could be set in the present or the past or both and still be about the same person or issue. These insights are critical to understanding the meaning of the six son stories of this study. We also may observe that Moses, Aaron and the Jebusites represent three constituencies within the kingdom of Solomon when the stories were written.[45]

---

43 Amit, 'The use of analogy', 389–390.

44 Yairah Amit, 'Hidden polemic in the conquest of Dan: Judges XVII–XVIII', *VT* 40 1990: 4–20, here 4; Amit, 'Literature in the service of politics: studies in Judges 19–21', 28–40. See also J. Gwyn Griffiths, 'Allegory in Greece and Egypt', *JEA* 53 1967: 79–102.

45 Amit posits authors composed for two different audiences: the first was the broad audience of hearers-listeners, which was satisfied with the plot and see obvious implications of the text without any sophisticated commentary; the other was an audience of educated people, familiar with poetics... (Yairah Amit, 'Looking at history through literary glasses too', in Yairah Amit and Nadav Na'aman, *Essays on Ancient Israel in its Near Eastern Context: A Tribute to Nadav Na'aman* (Winona Lake: Eisenbrauns, 2006), 1–15, here 10.

The birth of prose Bible writers

At this point, it is possible to the witness the emergence of three different voices within the Israelite polity. In the previous chapter tracing the history of Jerusalem through to David, we observed the existence of the Canaanite Jebusite community. It continued to exist as part of Israel once the city became the capital of the kingdom but had no need, opportunity, or skill in writing Hebrew prose narratives. That moment would not occur until after the death of David.

Within Israel, two different voices could be heard. The two genealogical intrusions identified by Amit in the polemical writings about kingship represent two political parties/factions/priesthoods. At minimum they were at political war with other but the story in Judges 19–21 and the actions of Saul against the priests of Shiloh (I Sam. 22: 18–19) suggest it was a violent confrontation as well. The two groups may be identified as Moses and Aaron, Joseph or Ephraim and Benjamin, Eleazar/Phinehas and Shiloh. So far the polemical stories were stand-alone stories. They had not cohered into a continuous narrative strand. Something else was needed to spark the creative leap forward.

An unusual if not unique situation had developed. Israel was a people who had existed for centuries without a king and yet who had maintained its identity and cohesion despite a geographically irregular configuration without a capital city. Now in a time of some turmoil due to another people living in the land of Canaan, it developed a monarchy. The monarchy then became basis of the early writings as people who battled for power within those various kingdoms which emerged: Saul's Israel, David's Judah, David's Israel including Judah, the divided kingdoms of Israel and Judah of Benjamin, Jerusalem, and the tribe of Judah. All of these occurrences required explaining and that is exactly what happened through the story format.

Sanders will reject my proposed sequence if he reads it. He delays the Israelite use of the alphabet prose narrative to support the king to the 9th century BCE. Despite his awareness of the example and precedence of the Ugaritic political tradition known to Israel, despite his awareness of the presence of kings earlier than the 9th century BCE, Sanders credits the Assyrian presence beginning with its imperial propaganda, monuments, public performances and rituals as providing the catalyst for West Semitic kingdoms like Israel, Moab and Aram to develop their own alphabetic narratives. His suggestion deferring the Israelite alphabet prose narratives until the Assyrian intrusion is incorrect.[46]

First, he ignores the Egyptian precedent. There is no inherent reason why Egyptian imperial propaganda, monuments, public performances and rituals both in Egypt and Canaan during the Late Bronze Age might not have influenced Israel. It's not as if Egypt did not have political stories like 'The Quarrel Story', 'Contendings of Horus and Seth, the 'Tale of the Two Brothers', and the 'Blinding of Truth by Falsehood'. It is not as if Egypt did not erect monuments in the land of Canaan itself prior to the emergence of the Israelite monarchy. Egyptian monuments at Beth Shan erected by grandfather Pharaoh Seti and son Rameses II were designed to impress the local population and assert Egyptian hegemony.

---

46 Sanders, *The Invention of Hebrew*, 9, 120–122, 149, 160, 216 n39; see also Schmidt, 'A history of Israel's earliest literature', 103–132.

For the locals it was of the utmost importance that they could rely on Pharaoh to protect them whether in person or not. Israelites in the time when grandson Merneptah claimed to have destroyed them would have been able to write based on Sanders' methodology based on the Egyptian experience.[47]

Second, why presume Assyria operated in a vacuum? The Assyrians themselves drew on Egyptian motifs. During the Amarna Period exchanges when the Assyrians first became a great power and member of the club, they had direct contact with Egypt. The ancient Near East was united in an 'international style' that carried over from traditional art artifacts into historical narratives. When the Assyrians finally reached the Upper Sea (the Mediterranean), they placed their own monuments adjacent to the Egyptian ones at Nahr el-Kalb along the Mediterranean coast from centuries earlier by Ramses II. The Ramesside influence on historical narrative in Neo-Assyrians is commonly acknowledged.

The Egyptian historical representations attained a mythical status of cosmic proportions to the Assyrians. Kings waged 'literary warfare' against the forces of chaos as an old order was dying and a new one emerged. The figures of Ramses II at Kadesh and Ramses III against the Sea Peoples loomed large in the impact on other cultures (including Israel). The *Iliad* became part of this scenario with the demise of Troy as the paradigmatic Late Bronze Age walled city echoed the walled city reliefs of Pharaohs Seti I, Ramses II, and Merneptah in 13th century BCE campaigns in Canaan. These depictions were not simply historical reconstructions merely to praise the king, they were cosmic triumphs to celebrate the equivalent of mythical victories in historic times just as the story of Joshua fought the battle of Jericho was. Israel did not need to wait until Assyria reached Israel in the 8th century BCE to know the motif of the destroyed walled city.[48]

Apparently everyone in the ancient Near East and the Aegean except Israel 'got the memo' about casting historical narratives as cosmic triumphs involving the destruction of walled cities. Echoing Gunkel's assertion that Israel produced no Homer (see Part I), Sanders concludes that 'we do not see the specific moment when a brilliant scribe or visionary king decided to inaugurate a new way of writing'. I do. As it turns out Israel did, in fact, have a brilliant scribe and a transformative, visionary, genius king. David had entered the stage of human history.[49]

---

47 For the local importance of the Beth Shan steles see Morris, *The Architecture of Imperialism*, 352–353.
48 For Egypt's influence see Mehmet-Ali Atac, 'The historical memory of the Late Bronze Age in the Neo-Assyrian palace reliefs', in David Nadali, ed., *Envisioning the Past through Memories: How Memory Shaped Ancient Near Eastern Societies* (London: Bloomsbury Academic, 2016), 69–83); Feldman, *Diplomacy by Design*; Marian H. Feldman, 'Assur Tomb 45 and the Birth of the Assyrian Empire', *BASOR* 343 2006: 21–43; Jen Thum, 'When Pharaoh turned landscape into a stela: royal living rock monuments at the edges of the Egyptian world', *NEA* 79 2016: 68–77). For the phrase 'literary warfare', Atac cites Eric Cline, *The Trojan War: A Very Short Introduction* (Oxford: Oxford University Press, 2013), 36.
49 Sanders, *The Invention of Hebrew*, 160.

Chapter 10

WRITERS OF THE BIBLE:
DAVID AND THE SONS OF DAVID

There is no place for the individual genius in biblical scholarship. In this regard the discipline is distinctly different from American history. The latter abounds in biographies, in biographies of people from every walk of life. Without biographies airport book racks would be devoid of historical books. The heart and soul of American history is the quest to document, understand, and tell the story of a remarkable person in history. Except with David, such a quest is fraught with danger in biblical scholarship. There simply is insufficient evidence to tell a person's story except perhaps for the novellas on Joseph, Ruth, and Esther (Additional Readings: David).

David himself is shortchanged in his biographies. There is a gaping hole in his story. The hole is writing. Even people who think he contributed to the lament over the deaths of Saul and Jonathan (II Sam. 1: 18–27), limit his writing to this one instance at the dawn of his royal career. Smith opines that David in the lament, is the most important person to emerge from the early era of Israel. He is more of a 'person' than any other figure in the early Israelite poetry. He is part of the heroic warrior tradition and the exemplar of the next stage in Israel's history. Just as the revised Song of Deborah prepared its audiences for the shift from the tribal identity to the monarchic, the lament promulgated a new communal identity for post-Saulide Israel, one based on David.[1]

There is no attempt to incorporate any other alleged David-writings into the academic biographies of his life. Was he not aware of the Book of Jashar? Of the Book of the Wars of Yahweh? Of the pro- and anti-Saul polemics set in both the present and the past? Was he not aware of the stories of his own rise to power and of his son Absalom's failed attempt? The easy answer is to say 'No, he was not, because he never existed and those stories would not be concocted until centuries later'. A better answer is to present a reasonable, coherent, straightforward account that would be readily acceptable if the Bible were not THE BIBLE. David was not the catalyst for the alphabet prose narrative but he was the artist who pushed the state of the art of information system to new levels.

---

1   Smith, *Poetic Heroes*, 283.

The King David Bible

Part of kingship involves public appearances. Hermann Spieckermann states:

> 'It is precisely the king's performance of cultic duties that conveys the idea of the very essence of kingship… All these cultic services of the king can only be properly understood as being meaningful in order to rule the land and to ward off danger of any kind.'[2]

To put David's manner of public appearances in context, let's first examine what other kings in the area were doing. Egypt, Mesopotamia, and Israel provide three different cultural expressions of the performance by a king and of a god in sacred rituals that demonstrated the preservation and maintenance of the cosmic order. Israel was late to having a king, but when it finally did he had a charismatic warrior who understood theater.

In Egypt, oral performance of the divine and royal inscriptions at the temple may be inferred. The word for 'read' in Egyptian, *šdj*, refers to oral performance. Even when statues of deities were involved it is presumed that divine speech was pronounced by a human priest of the deity. As part of the performance, priests wore masks, human kings and queens dressed in divine regalia, and people danced. In the Mesopotamian tradition, the deity was represented by a statue, the king played himself, and the queen or high priestess accompanied the king during the annual *akitu* victory festival. It is likely that the audience realized that a priest speaking the words of the deity was in fact a human being (Additional Readings: *akitu*, Egyptian Theater).

Daniel Fleming notes that transporting a divine image in a procession was standard operating procedure in the ancient Near East as an annual rite. He suggests that even though the biblical narrative presents the ark story as a singular event involving the king at the sacred center, it describes such a vivid ritual that one would expect it to have been repeated. These processions involved bringing the sacred object outside the city walls before returning it and that significant rites were performed outside the city walls. He proposes the threshing floor outside the city gates as a natural venue for a public assembly in connection with the ritual tradition. The festival celebrated the arrival of Yahweh in Jerusalem linked to figure of David. Fleming is exactly right but the festival was more extended than he realizes.[3] Fleming cites Ps. 132 as envisioning an overlooked ritual procession of the ark.

> **Psalm 132:1** *A Song of Ascents. Remember, O Yahweh, in David's favor, all the hardships he endured;* [2] *how he swore to Yahweh and vowed to the Mighty One of Jacob,* [3] *'I will not enter my house or get into my bed;* [4] *I will not give sleep to my eyes or slumber to my eyelids,* [5] *until I find a place for Yahweh, a dwelling place for the Mighty One of Jacob.'* [6] *Lo, we heard of it in Ephrathah, we found it in the fields of Jaar.* [7] *'Let us go to his dwelling place; let us worship at his footstool!'* [8] *Arise, O Yahweh, and go to thy resting place, thou and the ark of thy might.* [9] *Let thy priests be clothed with righteousness, and let thy saints shout for joy.* [10] *For thy servant David's sake do not*

---

2   Hermann Spieckermann, 'God and his people: The concept of kingship and cult in the Ancient Near East', in Reinhard G. Kratz and Hermann Spieckermann, eds, *One God – One Cult – One Nation: Archaeological and Biblical Perspectives* (BZAW 405; Berlin: Walter de Gruyter, 2010), 341–356, here 347–348.

3   Daniel E. Fleming, 'David and the Ark: A Jerusalem festival reflected in royal narrative', in David S. Vanderhooft and Abraham Winitzer, eds, *Literature as Politics, Politics as Literature: Essays on the Ancient Near East in Honor of Peter Machinist* (Winona Lake: Eisenbrauns, 2013), 75–95, here 75, 76, 85, 92, 93.

turn away the face of thy anointed one. [11] *Yahweh swore to David a sure oath from which he will not turn back: "One of the sons of your body I will set on your throne.* [12] *If your sons keep my covenant and my testimonies which I shall teach them, their sons also for ever shall sit upon your throne."* [13] *For Yahweh has chosen Zion; he has desired it for his habitation:* [14] *"This is my resting place for ever; here I will dwell, for I have desired it.* [15] *I will abundantly bless her provisions; I will satisfy her poor with bread.* [16] *Her priests I will clothe with salvation, and her saints will shout for joy.* [17] *There I will make a horn to sprout for David; I have prepared a lamp for my anointed.* [18] *His enemies I will clothe with shame, but upon himself his crown will shed its luster.*

The psalm indicates that it was possible to combine David, the Davidic dynasty, the ark, the covenant, Zion, the house of the Lord, and a procession in a single poem. It certainly seems an appropriate song to sing as part of the annual New Year festival at the Solomonic temple. But the annual temple ritual is subsequent to the death of David. Naturally, the dating of the psalm is debated as well as it use (Additional Readings: Psalm 132).

Before turning to David, let me cite the example of one larger-than-life luminary from slightly before David. Nebuchadnezzar I (1126–1105 BCE) of Babylon was a warrior king who triumphantly returned to the city and the temple the statue of Marduk which the Elamites previously had captured. The abscondment of deity statues was a tactic of longstanding in Mesopotamia, but the return of a captured one was something special. Examine how Assyriologists portray this great moment in Mesopotamian history and think of the return of the ark of the Lord from the Philistines and its installation at Zion (Additional Readings: Nebuchadnezzar I).

'In devastating the land of Akkad and especially by removing the statue of the patron deity of Babylon, the Elamites had lowered the morale of the country to a state seldom equaled throughout its long history.'[4]

'The outcome of the [victorious] battle [over Elam] was of greater significance for Babylonian morale than for any political or territorial gain... Above all, the cult statue of Marduk was restored to E-sagila amid much popular rejoicing and elaborate ceremonies.'[5]

'On the Marduk Prophecy: The most significant statement concerning the future king is that he will deliver Babylon from the hands of the Elam... The new king will subdue Elam, the dominator of Babylon. As he accomplishes this, he will serve the function of placing Babylonian society in order.'[6]

'The crisis brought on by the Elamite sack of Babylon, the plunder of its gods – particularly the removal of the statue of Marduk – and the ultimate resolution of this crisis by Nebuchadnezzar I's conquest of Elam and subsequent return of Marduk was widely celebrated in Babylonian literature.'[7]

---

4   J. A. Brinkman, *A Political History of Post-Kassite Babylonia 1158–722 BC*, (Rome: Pontificium Institutum, 1968), 105.

5   D. J. Wiseman, 'Assyrian and Babylonia *c.* 1200–1000 BC', in I. E. S. Edwards, ed., *History of the Middle East and the Aegean Region c. 1380–1000 BC* (The Cambridge Ancient History, Vol. 2. Part 2; Cambridge: Cambridge University Press, 1975), 443–481, here 455–456.

6   Tremper Longman III, *Fictional Akkadian Autobiography: A Generic and Comparative Study* (Winona Lake: Eisenbrauns, 1991), 136.

7   J. J. M. Roberts, 'Nebuchadnezzar I's Elamite Crisis in Theological Perspectives', in Maria deJong Ellis, ed., *Essays on the Ancient Near East in Memory of Jacob Joel Finkelstein* (Hamden, CT: Archon Books, 1977),

The literature included the writing of *Enuma Elish*, the great Mesopotamian story of the triumph of cosmos over chaos and of Marduk of Babylon becoming king of the universe, the story recited during the *akitu* festival and procession.[8]

In light of Nebuchadnezzar I, the Israelite version seems quite reasonable.

> **I Samuel 4: 10** *So the Philistines fought, and Israel was defeated, and they fled, every man to his home; and there was a very great slaughter, for there fell of Israel thirty thousand foot soldiers. [11] And the ark of God was captured;*

> **I Samuel 4: 19** *Now his [Eli's] daughter-in-law, the wife of Phinehas, …[22] said, 'The glory has departed from Israel, for the ark of God has been captured.'*

> **II Samuel 6: 14** *And David danced before Yahweh with all his might; and David was girded with a linen ephod. [15] So David and all the house of Israel brought up the ark of Yahweh with shouting, and with the sound of the horn.*

The tradition of the iconic image of the American soldiers raising the flag at Iwo Jima during World War II is an ancient one. For Israel, the Elamites were the Philistines and David was Nebuchadnezzar I. The story of Abram's victory over the Elamites (Gen. 14) was a cosmic one just as it was in Nebuchadnezzar I's Babylon. All Israel rejoiced when David planted the ark at Zion. But the Jebusites were not part of Israel when the Philistines captured the ark and the object had no meaning to them except as a symbol that their city was the capital of the kingdom.

David's contribution to the royal procession was the King David Bible (KDB). It was the social drama embodied in ritual whereby the one individual, King David, sought to express the fundamental values of Israel as he envisioned it. The KDB served as the functional equivalent for Israel of the *akitu* of Marduk or the *zukuru* of Dagan at Emar. It provided an Israelite expression of the cosmic order and role of the Israelite king and people in it. I propose that the KDB was a seven-day fall new year festival celebrating the harvest performed at Zion where the ark of Yahweh substituted for the statue of a deity. The story began in the garden and ended at Zion. The king and the queen performed in the lead human roles each day of the story. A priest spoke the words of Yahweh and narrated the story. During the festival the ark was removed from Zion to the wilderness (the threshing floor) with the king performing as Moses. The next day the ark was carried around the walls with the king performing as Joshua. Finally on the seventh and final day in the last episode, the king performed as himself and the ark was returned to Zion. At the end, the king leaped and danced before the Lord (II Sam. 6:16). The KDB was a story of joyous celebration. It probably was performed only once although it may have been read aloud during the reign of Solomon with the son stories that are part of this study (Additional Readings: Dance).[9]

183–187, here 183; reprinted in J. J. M. Roberts, *The Bible and the Ancient Near East: Collected Essays* (Winona Lake: Eisenbrauns, 2002), 83–92.

8   Related events in American history occurred when the star-spangled banner still waved against the British in the War of 1812, when the flag was raised at Iwo Jima in World War II, and when the flag was flown by the first-responders after 9/11. The emotional power to Israel of David's raising the 'flag' at Zion should not be underestimated.

9   For Israel see, Carr, *Writing on the Tablet of the Heart*, 28, 72–74; Robert D. Miller, 'The performance of oral tradition in Ancient Israel', in Brian B. Schmidt, ed., *Contextualizing Israel's Scared Writings: Ancient Literacy,*

The KDB presents a distinctly different vantage for understanding the biblical stories than traditional scholarship. The gleanings from the field of performance are in marked variance to the ivory tower exegesis presented in Part I which continues to dominate biblical scholarship to this very day. The stories not only are political but physical. They possess a vibrant power best experienced on the stage and not from a piece of paper, a computer screen, or even an oratorically-gifted minister. The KDB was great theater with a stage, props, music, and audience participation ending with a shared meal. The spectacle of the king, the charisma of an individual, the dynamic of inter-personal chemistry, the sacredness of the setting, all are lost once the KDB is removed from its historical context. Bell observes:

> '…human activity is situational, which is to say that much of what is important to it cannot be grasped outside of the specific context in which it occurs. When abstracted from its immediate context, an activity is not quite the same activity.'[10]

Sanders comments that 'no other Near Eastern texts talk like the Bible does' and it is the first one to address the people as a public. Virtually all other literatures were written by and for scribes whereas the Bible speaks to the people. Yet he remains unaware of the theatricality of the original narrative. Reading the text is not the same as seeing it performed be it Shakespeare or the KDB.[11]

One illustrative theatrical example will have to suffice here before turning to the six stories added to this innovative work of genius. Consider the story of Joshua fought the battle of Jericho and the walls came tumbling down. Typically in biblical scholarship, the approach is to interpret the story literally. The story is the word of God and the walls really did fall down miraculously. Or since archaeology confirms that no such walls at Jericho existed at the alleged time of Joshua, the story is bunk and can be safely ignored as history. As previously noted, the destruction of walled cities by the king was one of the great expressions of the triumph of the forces of cosmos over chaos. In the KDB, that motif was expressed in alphabetic prose narrative form and performed.

Now ignore the literally true/literally false approaches in biblical scholarship and treat the story as royal political theater of cosmic triumph and see the difference. As a theatrical experience:

The king (David) performs as Joshua.

The queen (Bathsheba) performs as Rahab, representing the marginalized 99% Canaanite people in the walled cities, subservient to the elites there. She is costumed as Asherah though human.

The queen says to the audience: '*I know that Yahweh has given you the land, and that the fear of you has fallen upon us, and that all the inhabitants of the land melt away before you*' (Josh. 2:9).

The queen appears at a window or ledge on the Large Stone Structure/Stepped Stone Structure high above the crowd outside the walls of the city when she says these words.

Orality, and Literary Production (AIL 22; Atlanta: SBL Press, 2015), 175–196; Pioske, *David's Jerusalem*, 76; C. L. Seow, *Myth, Drama, and the Politics of David's Dance* (HSM 44; Atlanta: Scholars Press, 1989).

10 Bell, *Ritual Theory*, 81.

11 Sanders, *The Invention of Hebrew*, xi, 1.

The spies climb down the walls to the audience below: *Then she let them down by a rope through the window, for her house was built into the city wall, so that she dwelt in the wall'* (Josh. 2:15). The audience sees the rope and the actors (Joab?) climb down.

The men in the name of the king and the deity promise no harm to the inhabitants if they choose not to fight Israel: *'Behold, when we come into the land, you shall bind this scarlet cord in the window through which you let us down; and you shall gather into your house your father and mother, your brothers, and all your father's household. If any one goes out of the doors of your house into the street, his blood shall be upon his head, and we shall be guiltless; but if a hand is laid upon any one who is with you in the house, his blood shall be on our head'* (Josh 2:18–19).

The audience sees the scarlet cord.

The king leads a procession of people and the ark of the Lord around city and they proclaim to the sound of trumpets: *'Shout; for Yahweh has given you the city'* (Josh. 6:16).

What message does the story deliver now? What is the fate of the 99% here? Did the Canaanite people have anything to fear now that they were part of David's Israel? The keys to understanding the story of Joshua fought the battle of Jericho are the mind of David and the means through which he expressed his vision in the performance of the KDB.

David needed to legitimate his position and present his vision of the cosmic order. Not Egypt's vision, not Mesopotamia's vision, not Canaan's vision, but his vision. Long before Alexander unsuccessfully sought to merge the peoples of the east and west into one under his rule, David needed to find some way to combine disparate peoples, heritages, and cultural memories into a single people. To blend all this diversity together into a single whole presented a challenge, a challenge of the highest order. Bell cautions us to recognize that ritualization cannot transform individuals into a community on its own. A one-time event in Jerusalem or a recurring opening procession in the Summer Olympics will not create a unity from a mixed multitude.[12]

Consider the contrasting examples of the United States and Europe. As long as the citizens of the United States accept July 4 as the shared date of the birth of the country they wish to be part of, the American experiment continues. From the moment of its birth, the United States consisted of a demographically diverse multitude who chose to constitute itself as a single people, *e pluribus unum*. Over time, the initial community has expanded to include new generations and peoples who pledge their allegiance to that republic. If the residents cease to do so, the country cannot long endure. By contrast, the European Union has no such moment of shared birth. The European Union has no George Washington, no founding father, no emotional bond to the people. It is not possible to imagine a European Union Olympic team or a European Union World Cup team whereas it is possible to imagine a single American team.

According to David's story of Joshua fought the battle of Jericho, Israel had a defining moment at its birth. Israel also had the capability to expand over time to include additional peoples who had not participated in its conception. The change from the central hills settlements (the Rachel tribes) to the tribes in the Song of Deborah to the kingdom of Saul defined in II. Sam. 2: 9 to the 12-tribe schema encompassing the land of Canaan reflects the ongoing development of the Israelite experiment over the centuries just as the 13–50

---

12 Bell, *Ritual Theory*, 222.

states do for the United States. The story on Day 6 of Rahab who heard what Israel had seen (Josh. 2: 9–12) was part of that development. Everyone then could celebrate on Day 7 when the ark was returned to Zion:

> **II Samuel 6: 18** *And when David had finished offering the burnt offerings and the peace offerings, he blessed the people in the name of Yahweh of hosts,* [19] *and distributed among all the people, the whole multitude of Israel, both men and women, to each a cake of bread, a portion of meat, and a cake of raisins. Then all the people departed, each to his house.*

Here the whole people of Israel return home as one. To blend into one people those who do not share a common experience is a daunting challenge indeed. Oftentimes it requires a war to create a band of brothers and sisters out of biologically unrelated people. David's visionary kingdom was an anomaly that could not be sustained..

Ironically, it is Mesha of Moab in the 9th century BCE who destroyed the sanctuary to Yahweh at Mount Nebo where the founding father was thought to be buried who illustrates what David sought to accomplish. The Mesha Stele (now at the Louvre) often is described as having a similar goal in the land of Moab. In that instance, Mesha of Dibon sought to transform peoples in the land of Moab who had not previously been united. He wanted them to think of themselves as being part of the new and larger kingdom he was creating after he liberated the land from the rule of the Omride dynasty in Israel.

Mesha used the Hebrew script to deliver this message in the Moabite language. Ironically, the Mesha Stele may represent the first attestation of the Hebrew national script presumably learned when Israel ruled the land of Moab. Sanders cautions scholars to 'go beyond the state/nonstate paradigm'. He perceives the Israel state to have recruited writing to argue publicly that it existed, acknowledges founding king Mesha in the 9th century for having done so using a Hebrew script, and denies that Saul and David could have done the same. David is the genius who made the Hebrew Bible possible although it may have required the trauma of Absalom's revolt and death to propel him out of necessity to reach a higher level (Additional Readings: Mesha Stele and Mount Nebo).[13]

The KDB expressed in word, song, performance, processions and location the new world order David asked the people in the land of Canaan to accept. For David, garden to Zion was a single story. For David, Zion was the cosmic center. For David the ark of the Lord was the symbol behind which all people should walk as they did around the walls of the city. For David the KDB was his opportunity to stand revealed before the people he ruled with all his emotions exposed, his hopes expressed, his vision displayed. No king had ever created what David had created. No king ever had dared what David had dared. No king ever had envisioned what David had envisioned. Unbeknownst to him, he had imprinted his celebration on humanity and in ways he never anticipated.

There are larger-than-life figures who impact the world of their times and the world to come. Even similar circumstances can produce different results given different people. Erhard Blum observes,

> 'As Nadav Na'aman pointed out already, the situation under David resembles structurally the picture one gets from the Amarna-letters concerning the LB-city-states. But apparently Davd

---

13 Sanders, 'Writing and Early Iron Age Israel', 98, 107.

surpassed Abdi-chepa and fellows in his power as a charismatic leader and in the efficiency of his loyal troops. At the end the established "United Kingdom" proved to be ephemeral and could not survive the charismatic founder more than one generation.'[14]

Amihai Mazar echoes these ideas on the role of the individual in history. In 2007, he wrote:

> 'The role of the individual personality in history should be taken into account [when evaluating the historicity of the United Monarchy]… Leaders with exceptional charisma could have created short-lived states with significant military and political power, and territorial expansion. I would compare the potential achievements of David to those of an earlier hill-country leader, namely Lab'ayu [of Shechem in the 14th century BCE] … except that he [David] operated in a time free of intervention by the Egyptians or any other foreign power and when the Canaanite cities were in decline. In such an environment, a talented and charismatic leader, politically astute, and in control of a small yet effective military power, may have taken hold of large parts of a small country like the Land of Israel and controlled diverse population groups under his regime from his stronghold in Jerusalem…'[15]

He liked what he said so much that in 2008, he wrote:

> 'David's huge impact on Judean collective memory cannot be explained merely as an invention of later authors. In evaluating the historicity of the United Monarchy, one should bear in mind the role of the individual in history. David may have been one of those leaders with exceptional charisma who might have created a short-lived political entity even without having a very large capital, organized army, and administration.'[16]

Then in 2010, he copied what he had written in 2007 into a new article.[17]

David failed in that effort but his attempt became a lasting legacy. That attempt to control 'diverse population groups under his regime from his stronghold in Jerusalem' was the King David Bible. The same four-dimensional vision that aided his political and military success carried over to his artistic and theological genius. He envisioned the garden to Zion, the Negev to Haran, the Israelites and the Canaanites as part of a single story which he wrote, produced, and directed. All the bibles produced afterwards are based on David's narrative and performance at Zion in Jerusalem. And then he died. Now what?

Priesthoods of the Pentateuch

Who would tell David's story? Or what story would they tell? Who were the political storytellers in the time of Saul, David, and Solomon? In his description of the Documentary Hypothesis delineated in the Introduction, Friedman identified one social function and two groups within that sector. The occupation was priesthood and the JEDP narrative

---

14 Erhard Blum, 'Solomon and the United Monarchy: some textual evidence', in Reinhard G. Kratz and Hermann Spieckermann, eds, *One God – One Cult – One Nation: Archaeological and Biblical Perspectives* (BZAW 405; Berlin: Walter de Gruyter, 2010), 59–78, here 73.

15 A. Mazar, 'The spade and the text', 165.

16 Amihai Mazar, 'From 1200 to 850 BCE: Remarks on some selected archaeological issues', in Lester L. Grabbe, ed., *Israel in Transition: From Late Bronze II to Iron IIa (c. 1250–850 BCE)* (LHBOTS 491; European Seminar in Historical Methodology 7; London: T&T Clark, 2008), 86–120, here 109.

17 A. Mazar, 'Archaeology and the Biblical narrative', 51–52.

was divided between two different priesthoods. The priests of Shiloh/Moses/Ephraim were assigned to the E and D sources. The priests of Jerusalem/Aaron were assigned P and the Redactor. J and J alone was attributed to no priesthood although he often was associated with the Judean monarchy, meaning the Davidic dynasty. J also is the one most routinely referred to as a genius. These ruminations mark the starting point for the attempt to better identify the individuals responsible for the writing of J.

As to the identity of the different priest factions competing in the political arena, there is a general agreement for the names but differences on the relationships and boundaries. Wellhausen, who formulated the Documentary Hypothesis, also developed a priest schema. In a chapter entitled 'The Priests and the Levites', Wellhausen sought to describe these identities. He differentiated the sons of Aaron, the sons of Zadok, and the Levites, one more group than Friedman would do. The sons of Zadok originally were the illegitimate parvenus who superseded the priests of Eli at Shiloh. They could not trace their ancestry in Israel back before David and they then displaced the older priesthood which could [referring to the Zadokite banishment of the Levite priest Abiathar]. The Zadokites then became the legitimate ones particularly with the Solomonic temple. One might expect that they had some explaining to do about this change in status. Wellhausen was exactly right but he never applied his three-priesthood division to the J narrative itself (Additional Readings Priesthoods).[18]Wellhausen's observations, which I did not recall when I started this book, seems better than Friedman's. As William H. Propp notes, only three groups in Israel claimed the mantle of exclusive priests of Yahweh: the Levites, the Aaronids, and the Zadokites. As it turns out English Assyriologist and biblical scholar Archibald Sayce's 19th-century conjecture that multiple voices, including Canaanite and Babylonian, exist within a single narrative was correct but not exactly as he proposed. Combining the observations of Wellhausen, Propp, and Sayce leads to the following working hypothesis used in this study:

> the Zadokites express the Canaanite/Jebusite traditions through the prism of Israelite rule
> the Aaronites/Benjaminites express an Israelite view with a Mesopotamian orientation
> the Levites/Ephraimites express an Israelite view with an (anti-)Egyptian orientation.

The classic text thought to combine these disparate elements is from Ezra:

> **Ezra 7:1** *Now after this, in the reign of Artaxerxes king of Persia, Ezra the son of Seraiah, son of Azariah, son of Hilkiah,* [2] *son of Shallum, son of* **Zadok***, son of Ahitub,* [3] *son of Amariah, son of Azariah, son of Meraioth,* [4] *son of Zerahiah, son of Uzzi, son of Bukki,* [5] *son of Abishua, son of* **Phinehas, son of Eleazar, son of Aaron the chief priest** *–* [6] *this Ezra went up from Babylonia. He was a scribe skilled in the* **law of Moses** *which Yahweh the God of Israel had given; and the king granted him all that he asked, for the hand of Yahweh his God was upon him.*

In this passage, Ezra is introduced as a descendant of Zakok and of Aaron/Eleazar/Phinehas and who is skilled in the law of Moses (Levites). One should note that the trio of Aaron, Eleazar, and Phinehas are the same three Amit observed were inserted into the polemic in Judg. 20: 28 above. They clearly were regarded as the founding fathers of one political party.[19]

---

18 Wellhausen, *Prolegomena to the History of Israel*, 121–151.

19 William H. Propp, 'Ithamar', in *ABD* III: 579–581, here 580; A. H. Sayce, *The 'Higher Criticism' and the Verdict of the Monuments* (London: Society for Promoting Christian Knowledge, 1894), 171–172.

Imagine if at the birth of America, one faction looked to England (Hamilton, the Federalist Party), one faction looked to France (Jefferson, the Republican Party), one faction looked to their own local traditions (Iroquois/Haudenosaunee) and the capital city was located by Lake Onondaga, the center of the Haudenosaunee confederation. The parallel does not work because the Haudenosaunee were insufficiently strong to have a seat at the table of the new political entity. However the ongoing treaty arrangements and identity questions of the Haudenosaunee as Americans who happen to be Haudenosaunee or as the independent nation of Haudenosaunee, the Iroquois Nations, which happens to be located in the United States are directly relevant. The kingdom of David was not homogeneous ethnically, historically, religiously, or in life-style. Truly it was a kingdom of mixed multitudes and the fashioning of one from many was a Herculean challenge in which he ultimately failed.

The recognition of differences is essential for understanding Israelite history, the Hebrew Bible, and the writing of these stories. Recently, Esther Hamori, Union Theological Seminary, reflected on these differences in a posting on the web:

> 'What I would like to emphasize is the presence of diverse perspectives in the Bible, actually diverging viewpoints, on the same issues.
>
> The spectrum of voices in the Bible is astonishing. Writers of biblical texts reflect northern and southern perspectives (Israelite and Judahite); urban and rural; rich and poor; they are priests and poets, shepherds and elite literate professionals in royal scribal circles; people living in Jerusalem and Babylon and Persia and more. It should therefore not surprise us that some of these people differ in how they see the world.'[20]

Although she was not referring to the specific stories that are the subject of this study, the points raised apply here.

Deborah Rooke, Oxford University, who combines her biblical scholarship with a love of Handel's use of the Old Testament, observes:

> 'The absolute limitation of legitimate priestly rights to particular groups is a later development, very probably politically motivated. Doubtless, rivalries over precisely who was entitled to serve in the Jerusalem Temple with its exalted status as national and royal shrine, and later sole legitimate site of worship, required a distinct theological justification and claim to be put forward by the appropriate parties.'[21]

The proposal in this study is the rivalries occurred early, definitely were politically motivated, and began even before Israel had a temple.

Typically, the effort to unravel the question of priest involvement in the writing of the Bible has started with the Levites ... but without identifying how the Levites came to write in the first place or the connection to J who preceded E and D in the Documentary Hypothesis. I propose to draw on existing scholarship to postulate how Levites arrived at

---

20 Esther Hamori, 'Voices of God: religious diversity in the Bible', *Huffington Post*, July 29, 2012, http://www.huffingtonpost.com/esther-j-hamori/religious-diversity-in-the-bible_b_1684798.html

21 Deborah W. Rooke, 'Kingship as priesthood: the relationship between the high priesthood and the monarchy', in John Day, ed., *King and Messiah in Israel and the Ancient Near East: Proceedings of the Oxford Old Testament Seminar* (Sheffield: Sheffield Academic Press, 1998, JSOT Sup. Series 270), 187–208, here 191.

this position of prominence. I do so by combining the scholarship of people who worked independently of each other but in fact each produced pieces of a larger story without realizing it. They illustrate the adage about the whole being greater than the sum of the parts. I confess at times to being pleasurably astounded as I read and then reread some of their writings and realized they were connected.

I start with a major study by Karel van der Toorn entitled *Scribal Culture and the Making of the Hebrew Bible*. Van der Toorn echoes Friedman by also asking up-front 'Who wrote the Bible?' He then asks a critical second question: 'How did the Levites become the professionals of writing among the priests?'[22] Van der Toorn prefaces this question by counseling prudence. In his investigation to answer his own question, he starts at the end of the sequence and works backwards. He states that biblical (Book of Chronicles) and extrabiblical texts from the 4th century BCE into the Hellenistic period afterwards clearly confirm that the Levites were the scribal experts of Jewish society.

He then turns to a Levite assertion in D that uses the past to state a claim in the present citing Deut. 33: 10:

> *They shall teach Jacob thy ordinances, and Israel thy law.*

He interprets the verse to reveal that the northern kingdom references to Israel and Jacob indicate that the Levites performed cultic and teaching functions prior to the destruction of Israel in 722 BCE. Following the fall of the capital city of Samaria to the Assyrians, these Levites migrated south to Jerusalem and sought to re-establish themselves.[23]

That migration brought them into direct confrontation with the Zadokite temple priests. The conflict between these two priesthoods in the same city was expressed through biblical writings. According to van der Toorn, the Levites made their case for equal income from the temple revenues through the words of Moses:

> **Deuteronomy 18: 5** *For Yahweh your God has chosen him out of all your tribes, to stand and minister in the name of Yahweh, him and his sons for ever.* [6] *'And if a **Levite** comes from any of your towns out of all Israel, where he lives – and he may come when he desires – to the place which Yahweh will choose,* [7] *then he may minister in the name of Yaweh his God, like all his fellow-**Levites** who stand to minister there before Yahweh.* [8] *They shall have **equal portions** to eat, besides what he receives from the sale of his patrimony.*

This strong assertion of the ancestral rights of the Levites expressed in the Book of Deuteronomy represented a claim in the time of its writing for equal portions of the temple income to the portions received by the Zadokite temple priests in Jerusalem.[24]

As one might expect that claim was countered with an equally vigorous denunciation of it. Van der Toorn cites the rejection made by Ezekiel on behalf of the Zadokites and in his own words. First Ezekiel castigates the Levites for going astray after idols as had the now-destroyed kingdom of Israel (Ezek. 44: 10). Second it is the sons of Zadok who did not go astray then and who ministered unto the Lord at his sanctuary, meaning the Jerusalem

---

22 Van der Toorn, *Scribal Culture*, 92.
23 Van der Toorn, *Scribal Culture*, 89–92.
24 Van der Toorn, *Scribal Culture*, 93.

(Ezek. 44: 15; see also Ezek. 40: 46, 43: 19, 48: 11). In detailing the responsibilities of these sons of Zadok, Ezekiel clearly distinguishes between these two groups of priests. The Levites were to be punished and demoted for going astray while the sons of Zadok were to remain dominant in the House of Yahweh.[25]

In this analysis, van der Toorn has presented part of the presumptions of this study.

1. The competition between priesthoods for power.
2. The use of writing to express that competition.
3. The use of stories set both in the present and the past in that competition for power.
4. The use of named people delivering the message of the combatants: in one case a person speaking his own words in the present about the present (Ezekiel) and in the other case a person in the past (Moses) speaking 'his own' words about the author's present (an unnamed Levite).

This type of writing and confrontation among priesthoods did not begin after the northern kingdom of Israel was destroyed and the competing priesthoods shared a single city; it originated even before the kingdoms split.

Van der Toorn avers that the Levites in Persian times (6th–4th centuries BCE) had predecessors in late pre-exilic times (mainly the 7th century BCE). He adds that the predecessors of those predecessors 'are shrouded in darkness.'[26] Ironically, it is van der Toorn's very analysis of what these Levites did which sheds light on the writings of those predecessors and ultimately to a fuller answer to the original question of 'Who Wrote the Bible?' He posits a four-tiered Book of Deuteronomy written over a lengthy period repeatedly attuned to shifting historical circumstances. The specific chapters and verses he assigns to each layer each with its own beginning and ending in the Book of Deuteronomy are secondary here to the conceptual model of a multi-layered narrative van der Toorn identifies reflecting changed historical circumstances.

1. *Covenant Edition*: the original edition was created in response to King Josiah's reform *c.* 622 BCE. It constitutes a revision itself of the earlier Covenant Code (Ex. 21–23) and was written by someone fully conversant with the Neo-Assyrian treaty texts of the 7th century BCE, perhaps with the intention of negating them. One may add that the Covenant Code generally is assigned to the E narrative although the Elohist may have incorporated the code into his narrative and not be its originator. None-the-less, van der Toorn's comments are consistent with the E-D link.
2. *Torah Edition*: a utopian document was created to compensate for lost realities between 590–570 BCE, the time of the Babylonian destruction and exile. The king had lost his place of supremacy to be replaced by the priests (Levite not Zadokite). The Torah words were put directly into the mouth of Moses by the author.
3. *History Edition*: an historical edition fused the perspective of the two previous editions. Its creator intended to use the resulting book as the beginning of a larger work of national history from Deuteronomy to II Kings. His consolidated history was a theodicy to explain the Exile and intensely emphasized Moses the prophet.
4. *Wisdom Edition*: the final edition contains an optimistic vision of a national conversion following the return of all Israel from a worldwide diaspora. It was written by a Babylonian

---

25 Van der Toorn, *Scribal Culture*, 93.
26 Van der Toorn, *Scribal Culture*, 96.

Jew early in the Persian period when Cyrus the Great permitted the exiles to return home after 539 BCE.

The Levites responsible for these writings maintained their distinctive identity throughout these centuries including their loyalty to Moses as their patron and ancestor. They were neither Zadokite nor Aaronite priests.[27]

There is no inherent reason why the exact same schema cannot be applied to the period prior to the destruction of the northern kingdom of Israel. It is relevant to the historical circumstances of the Iron II period as well. It's hardly likely that either the kingship or the Levites originated in the 7th century BCE. Can those shadowy predecessors be identified? In fact, over 20 years earlier, Antony Campbell had in effect done exactly that by positing a late 9th-century BCE prophet text. He asserted this Prophet record anticipated the later Deuteronomistic History van der Toorn wrote about. In effect, Campbell had filled in the gap between E and D by introducing a non-Pentateuchal narrative.[28]

The Prophet narrative was intended to demonstrate the course of God's guidance of his people during an exciting and eventful period in their history. The specific chapters and verses assigned to this narrative are not germane to this study either. What is important is Campbell's proposition that 9th-century BCE prophetic views were themselves superimposed on previously existing stories. These now-revised stories themselves later became part of even a larger narrative. One goal was to show that Yahweh's will denied the temple to David. The result diminished the stature of Solomon and excused the northern kingdom for not having it. Based on Campbell's analysis, one might reasonably ask if expressing opposition to the Solomonic temple occurred in the 9th century BCE, could it also have occurred in the 10th century BCE when it was built? If a prophet was responsible for the writing in the 9th century BCE, could an earlier counterpart have done the same in the 10th? The J Documentary Hypothesis answers these questions in the affirmative.

Campbell attributes the prophet narrative to disciples of Elisha, the prophet who succeeded Elijah. The political context then would be when the Jehu dynasty supplanted the Omride dynasty of Ahab and Jezebel in the 840s BCE. The usurpation resembles Jeroboam rejecting Rehoboam, son of Solomon, in creating the northern kingdom of Israel in the 920s BCE with the support of the prophet Ahijah, an important figure in Campbell's prophet narrative. Although Campbell and van der Toorn were not working together (van der Toorn does not list Campbell in his bibliography), the two clearly present a consistent approach beginning in 9th century BCE of Levite priests/prophets writing in the Moses tradition. They wrote on an ongoing basis as historical circumstances changed and required explanation. Sometimes they wrote new stories, sometimes they supplemented existing ones.

Over time, the finished product grew longer and longer as the story of Yahweh's presence in history continued to manifest itself.

---

27 Van der Toorn, *Scribal Culture*, 141–172, 221–224.

28 Antony F. Campbell, *Of Prophets and Kings: A Late Ninth-Century Document (I Samuel 1–2 Kings 10)* (CBQMS 17; Washington, DC: The Catholic Biblical Association of America, 1986), 14–15, 20, 79. McCarter identifies a 'prophetic history' of northern origin which he dates to the 8th century BCE following the destruction of the kingdom (*I Samuel*, 18–23).

At this juncture, I consider it essential to bring together the archaeological record and literary exegesis. To ignore the surrounding events in the historical record undermines the effort to understand the written record in the Bible. Van der Toorn locates some of his proposed layers in specific historical contexts relating to the actions of Babylonia and Persia. These contexts generated biblical writings as the people (and the Levites) sought to understand what was happening and to have hope for the future. By no coincidence whatsoever, a similar situation occurred in the 9th century BCE at time of Campbell's proposed prophet narrative.

Mesha of Moab once again proves instrumental for understanding writing in Israel. The catalytic event for the Prophet Narrative was in the 840s BCE when Mesha destroyed the sanctuary to Yahweh at Mount Nebo. Nebo receives some but not the attention it deserves in understanding the writing of the Bible. The very name Nebo, otherwise called Pisgah (Deut. 3: 27, 34: 1), calls to mind Nabû, the Mesopotamian god of writing. The linkage suggests a mountain dedicated to scribes where there was an sanctuary to Moses and tradition of the burial of the founder of the religion.[29]

Na'aman comments that the 'loss of Nebo to Mesha was a heavy blow to Israel'. There was a temple in the city that must have been associated with the figure of Moses, and served as a major administrative and cultic centre in the region. His observations suggest by the 9th century BCE, traditions about Moses already were established. Perhaps they dated back to the early days of Israel when the Yahweh sanctuary located in the territory of Reuben first was built. Cross suggests there was a Gilgal ritual that symbolically recreated the entrance of Israel from the wilderness across the Jordan into the land eventually settled. A hypothetical procession beginning at the burial site of Moses to Shittim and Baal-Peor before ending at Gilgal in Benjamin where Saul would be coronated links many key names, places, and events from later times. It also highlights the difficulty in ascertaining what associations the audience would make when hearing certain words in a story.[30]

The Moabite deity Chemosh clearly recognized the importance of Nebo to Israel when he designated Mesha to attack it. Logically, the Moabite-identified Israelite sanctuary to Yahweh at Nebo must have been important to Israel too. It is absolutely irrelevant whether or not Moss was buried at Nebo to gauge the trauma to Israel of the destruction of the site where they believed he was buried. No one would claim that since God does not exist therefore the temple destructions by Babylonia and Rome generated no trauma. The same considerations apply to Mesha's destruction at Nebo.

Mesha's destruction of the site therefore would have generated writing to explain who should be held accountable for the loss and to identify who would be called to act against the one responsible for the loss. His violation of the sanctuary of Yahweh demanded a restoration of order and punishment. The story of Jehu with the support of Elijah and Elisha replacing the Omride dynasty (recounted in I Kings 19; II Kings 9–10) needs to be understood within the context of the destruction of the sanctuary to Yahweh at Nebo, the

---

29　For Nebo/Nabû connection; see Schniedewind, *How the Bible Became a Book*, 26.

30　For the wilderness cult see Frank Moore Cross, *Canaanite Myth*, 103–105; Frank Moore Cross, 'Reuben, first born of Jacob', ZAW 100 Supplement 1988: 46–65, here 51–52, reprinted in *From Epic to Canon: History and Literature in Ancient Israel* (Baltimore: Johns Hopkins University Press, 1998), 57–58.

presumed burial site of Israel's founder. Undoubtedly it is not coincidence that there is a story of Elijah at Horeb at the very time the Israelite dynasty failed to protect the sanctuary at the burial site of Moses. Trauma is a catalyst for writing in a storytelling species with the capability to write.

The proposals of Campbell and van der Toon depict a Levite and prophetic writing tradition across the centuries. They wrote in the time of Ahab. They wrote in the time of Josiah. They wrote in the time of the Babylonian exile. They wrote in the time of the Persian restoration. There is no inherent reason why this schema could not be extended back in time to before the kingdom divided or before there even was a king – back to the origin of Israel itself.

I have suggested that Saul's desire to become king of Israel was the catalyst for the development of the alphabet prose narrative. I have suggested that polemical anti-Saul stories which scholars have identified should be dated to this period. The transition from heroic poetry to prose narrative commenced during the time of Saul. Now it is possible to identify the likely candidates for the writers of these texts. The Levites of Shiloh and Ephraim wrote anti-Saul stories; the Benjaminites of Aaron-Eleazor-Phineas wrote pro-Saul stories; the Zadokites were not part of this debate as Jerusalem was not part of Israel yet. They wrote before the KDB existed and supplemented it during the reign of Solomon after David died.

One would be remiss in this investigation of the Levites to Israelite history and biblical writing if one ignored that sometimes the Levites themselves were the subject of stories that portray a distinctly non-priestly picture of them. Typically one thinks of priests in ritualistic settings. They offer sacrifices, maintain the holiness of the sanctuary, and perform rituals at the sacred times. But with the Levites, there is a legacy of violence associated with them as well. The verses typically cited to illustrate that aspect of their identity are:

Genesis 34: 25 *On the third day, when they were sore, two of the sons of Jacob, Simeon and Levi, Dinah's brothers, took their swords and came upon the city unawares, and killed all the males.*

Genesis 49: 5 *Simeon and Levi are brothers; weapons of violence are their swords. [6] O my soul, come not into their council; O my spirit, be not joined to their company; for in their anger they slay men, and in their wantonness they hamstring oxen. [7] Cursed be their anger, for it is fierce; and their wrath, for it is cruel! I will divide them in Jacob and scatter them in Israel.*

Exodus 32: 27 *And he [Moses] said to them, 'Thus says Yahweh God of Israel, "Put every man his sword on his side, and go to and fro from gate to gate throughout the camp, and slay every man his brother, and every man his companion, and every man his neighbor."' [28] And the sons of Levi did according to the word of Moses; and there fell of the people that day about three thousand men.*

Deuteronomy 33: 8 *And of Levi he said, 'Give to Levi thy Thummim, and thy Urim to thy godly one, whom thou didst test at Massah, with whom thou didst strive at the waters of Meribah; [9] who said of his father and mother, "I regard them not"; he disowned his brothers, and ignored his children. For they observed thy word, and kept thy covenant. [10] They shall teach Jacob thy ordinances, and Israel thy law; they shall put incense before thee, and whole burnt offering upon thy altar. [11] Bless, O Yahweh, his substance, and accept the work of his hands; crush the loins of his adversaries, of those that hate him, that they rise not again.'*

Exactly how it came to be that the Levites and violence are so closely linked is not clear.[31]

---

31 Joel Baden, 'The violent origins of the Levites: text and tradition', in Mark A. Leuchter and Jeremy M.

In Mark Leuchter's oral presentation on 'The Fightin' Mushites' two years prior to his published paper, he stated in his abstract:

> 'The priestly line founded by Moses (the 'Mushites' following Cross and others) stands out most prominently in this regard in premonarchic tradition and, subsequently in the northern kingdom... But how did the Mushites establish themselves as a dominant priestly house, and at what point did Moses himself become a typological symbol of the Levites more broadly.'[32]

Leuchter finds his answers in the violent Mushite legacy of Moses slaying the Egyptian taskmaster who beat a Hebrew (Ex.2: 11–22). In that episode, Moses flees to Midian where he marries Zipporah and they have a son Gershom. Leuchter dismisses the biblical 'stranger in a strange land' explanation for the name of Gershom as its true meaning. Citing various scholars, Leuchter links the shared root GRSH (גרש) to the action of the shepherds who 'drove away' the women watering at the well before Moses turned the table on them. Thus the son was named after the action whereby his parents met. Leuchter then suggests that term Gershom was less a name than a title signifying a Mushite who acts to defend the weak be it the Hebrew man in Egypt or the Midianite women in the wilderness. In the remainder of the article, Leuchter elaborates on the continuity of this marital prowess tradition.[33]

It remains for Friedman to firmly push the Levite identity back to the origin of Israel into Egypt itself. In his book on *Who Wrote the Bible?*, Friedman suggests that perhaps of the people who became Israel only the Levites had been slaves in Egypt. He cites the Egyptian names of key Israelites such as Moses and Aaron's grandson Phinehas. Since the Levites in Egypt were mere slaves, Friedman does not address the writing or literacy skills of these marginalized people. Nor does he speculate on how these Levites acquired their violent image if they were slaves in Egypt. Years after that 1987 publication he returned to that subject online and promised a forthcoming book about it. Perhaps since Friedman has identified the Levites as critical to the writing of the Hebrew Bible, the promised book will address the writing legacy these Levites brought with them when they crossed over the river Nile to the promised land.[34]

In the meantime, it is possible to put these pieces together to suggest the critical role of the Levites in the origin of Israel and the writing of the Hebrew Bible. For violent Semites in the land of Egypt there are two realistic choices: the Hyksos and the n'rn.

Hutton, eds, *Levites and Priests in Biblical History and Tradition* (Leiden: Brill, 2012), 103–116; Richard Elliott Friedman, 'Levites and priests in history and tradition', paper presented at the annual conference of the Society of Biblical Literature, San Diego, November 24, 2014; Mark A. Leuchter, 'The Fightin' Mushites' *VT* 62 2012: 479–500.

32 Mark A. Leuchter, 'The Fightin' Mushites', paper presented at the Columbia Hebrew Bible Seminar, March 17, 2010. The published article dates the presentation to February 2010.

33 Leucheter, 'The Fightin' Mushites', 492–494.

34 Friedman, *Who Wrote the Bible?*, 82; Richard Elliott Friedman, 'The historical Exodus: the evidence for the Levites leaving Egypt and the introduction of YHWH into Israel', *The Torah: A Historical and Contextual Approach*, undated, http://thetorah.com/the-historical-exodus/ and 'The Exodus is not fiction: An interview with Richard Elliot Friedman', *Reform Judaism*, undated, http://www.reformjudaism.org/exodus-not-fiction. See also Richard Elliott Friedman, 'Love your neighbor: only Israelites or everyone?', BAR 40/5 2014: 48–52.

N'rn is a Semitic word. They were the soldiers who rescued Ramses II when he marched headstrong into a Hittite trap on the Orontes in Syria in Year 5 (1274 BCE). They appear out of nowhere without explanation and are depicted as Egyptians in a battle relief. Even more amazingly, Ramses credits them for the 'victory' at Kadesh, a battle he also claimed to have won all by himself! The n'rn also appear in the Karnak Inscription of Merneptah. Generally, they are considered to be Canaanites from multiple locations now fighting on behalf of Egypt, but their ethnicity is under debate among Egyptologists. However, the Karnak Inscription clearly differentiates the n'rn from the victorious Egyptian troops as they are likened to each other. One might even inquire why Merneptah chose to compare his Egyptian troops to the n'rn in the first place. Evidently their fighting reputation was well-known (Additional Readings: N'rn).

The Hyksos are an intriguing piece in the puzzle. They were warriors from across the river Nile, who had a 400-year tradition of being in Egypt, a leader named Jacob, knowledge of hieroglyphics, were part of the Egyptian textual record in the time of Ramses II, the traditional Pharaoh of the Exodus, and his son and successor Merneptah, who claimed to have destroyed the seed of Israel. The Hyksos were remembered in ancient times and modern as being connected in some way to the origin of Israel. There is no inherent reason why Hyksos could not have been included in the n'rn who rescued Ramses or their commanding officers (Additional Readings: Hyksos).

According to Manfred Bietak, the excavator Avaris/Pi-Ramesse, the capital city of both the Hyksos and Ramses:

> 'The end of Hyksos rule in Egypt from the historical point of view is a subject rarely addressed in Egyptology... In Egyptology, the impact of Hyksos rule on Egypt has been largely neglected in research if not ignored... [I]t is only logical to postulate that the presence of several ten thousands people of Western Asiatic people in north-eastern Egypt over a period of over 300 years (*c.* 1830–1530 BCE) must have had an impact on successive New Kingdom culture.'[35]

Levite nr'n would have a military heritage but not the writing and cultural experience of the Hyksos who had once ruled Egypt and remained a more elite and educated group. Either way, Friedman's violent slave Levites make more sense if they had a military background.

The Levites are the key to answering the question 'Who Wrote the Bible?' The Friedman-Leuchter/Baden-Campbell-van der Toorn combination provides a straightforward historical reconstruction that is speculative, comprehensive, continuous, and reasonable ... and makes it easier to name the names and explain the contexts of the battle for the throne using the son stories after David died. Consider again Friedman's opening words to *The Hidden Book in the Bible: The Discovery of the First Prose Masterpiece*:

> 'A great work lies embedded in the Bible, a creation that we can trace to a single author. And I believe that we can establish that it is of great antiquity: it was composed nearly three thousand years ago so it is indeed nothing less than the first work of prose. Call it the first novel if you think it is fiction, or the first history if you think it is factual. Actually, it is a merger of both. But, either way, it is the first. There is no longer work of prose before this anywhere on earth. East or West, so far as I know. We know of poetry that is earlier, but

---

35 Bietak, 'The aftermath of the Hyksos in Avaris', 20–21.

this is the oldest prose literature: a long beautiful exciting story. And the astonishing thing is that, even though it is the earliest lengthy prose composition known to us, it is far from a rudimentary, primitive first attempt at writing. It has the qualities that we find in the greatest literature the world has produced. Indeed, scholars of the Bible and of comparative literature have compared individual parts of it to Shakespeare and to Homer. Those scholars were right, but they were barely at the threshold of the full work, a composition whose unity and brilliant connection have been hidden by the editorial and canonical process that produced the Bible.'[36]

I have refined his thesis as follows:

1.   There were earlier prose pieces perhaps by the one author as he developed his skill and that then his writings were encompassed in this larger prose masterpiece.
2.   There were multiple writers of different perspectives whose writings were encompassed in this larger prose masterpiece.
3.   The original continuous prose masterpiece extended from the garden to David seemingly secure on the throne when he planted the ark there. I call this masterpiece the King David Bible (KDB), a continuous, coherent narrative from garden to Zion. It comprises the original J narrative without the supplements such as the six stories of this study. It extended into Joshua as proponents of the Hexateuch have suggested. It concluded with portions of the Ark Narrative (I Sam. 4: 1b–7:1 and II Sam. 6), an independent narrative text identified by biblical scholars.[37]
4.   The Levites maintained the Israelite cultural legacy in poetry before doing so in prose.

As n'rn and especially as Hyksos, the Levites were familiar with royal monuments. They were the subject of royal texts. They were literate. They were warriors. Given this perception and understanding of the Levites as educated warriors in the political arena, when Israel began to consider monarchy as an option, the Levites were ready, their loins were girded for battle and the alphabet prose narrative was their weapon … along with their ally David. Based on these ruminations, one can develop a coherent straightforward sequence bridging the gap from the poetry of early Israel to the alphabet prose masterpiece. It did not happen all at once but in steps over time. There was a progression from Deborah's song to Solomon's narrative in the application of the new state of the art information tool. Over time, people developed their skill in its usage and had the examples of previous writings before them. Initially, Israel had been a people of poetry. When the debate over the monarchy ensued, the writing changed as the venue for the war of words. This sequence starts in the time of Saul and ends exactly where Friedman's proposed masterpiece ends.

> Existing poems were revised (Song of Deborah).
> Oral traditions were revised (Gideon, Jephthah).

---

36 Friedman, *The Hidden Book*, 3.

37 The hexateuch is probably best known in English from Gerhard von Rad, 'The form-critical problem of the Hexateuch', in Gerhard von Rad, *The Problem of the Hexateuch and Other Essays* (New York: McGraw-Hill, 1966), 1–78. For the Ark Narrative see McCarter, *I Samuel*, 23–26; Patrick D. Miller Jr. and J. J. M. Roberts, eds, *The Hand of the Lord: A Reassessment of the "Ark narrative" of 1 Samuel* (Johns Hopkins Near Eastern Studies; Baltimore: Johns Hopkins University Press, 1977); Leonhard Rost, *The Succession to the Throne of David* (Historic Texts and Interpreters in Biblical Scholarship 1; Sheffield: Almond Press, 1982), 6–34; translation of *Die Überlieferung von der Thronnachfolge Davids* (BWANT III 6; Stuggart: W Kohlhammer, 1926).

New polemical metaphorical stories were created (Rape of the Benjaminite concubine)
Cycles or extended narratives were created:

> Saul's Rise to Power
> David's Rise to Power in Judah
> David's Rise to Power in Judah
> David's Rise to Power in Israel
> Absalom's Rise to and Fall from Power
> Solomon's Illegitimate Rise to Power
> Solomon's Legitimate Rise to Power.[38]

Erhard Blum notes that the narratives about David's rise and the various successions are not the collection of folk traditions 'but represent a sophisticated, professional art of storytelling'. He adds that the virulent animosity expressed between Benjamin and the house of David best fits the beginnings of the dynasty before the dynastic principle had been established. It is reasonable to anticipate that Benjamin will figure in the writing of the stories.[39]

The writing was not mythical or folk. The writing was not theological. The writing was not business contractual. The writing was not historical either contrary to Friedman. I mean this in the sense that no one sought to write 'The History of Israel'. The writing was political. It addressed the questions of the present day for which the people needed answers, the actions which required legitimacy, and the fears which need visions of a better tomorrow to calm. The concerns naturally changed over time necessitating new writing to address the new concerns.[40]

Where are the stories of Genesis in this sequence? I contend that stories about these political developments could be set in the present when they occurred, in the past, or both. Friedman postulates that one person wrote a single 'J' narrative concluding with Solomon secure on the throne. White referring to *The Hidden Book of the Bible* concurs with Friedman about the creation of a comprehensive history in the time of Solomon but suggests it drew on existing sources without using the terminology here or the exact breakdown here.[41] The idea of the connection between David and J stories in the Book of Genesis is not new.[42]

---

38 Ancient Egypt was renowned for a genre of royal composition known as *Königsnovelle* or 'king's novel'. These writings focused on the king as the divinely-inspired representative of the country who acted decisively to defend and maintain *ma'at* (see Antonio Loprieno, 'The "King's Novel"', in Antonio Loprieno, ed., *Ancient Egyptian Literature: History and Forms* [Leiden: E. J. Brill, 1996], 277–295). The stories of Saul, David, Absalom, and Solomon display a distinctly different approach which decisively defines the Israelite culture.

39 Blum, 'Solomon and the United Monarchy', 65–67, quotation from 66.

40 According to Sanders, the 'confluence of the alphabet and politics resulted in the first written history of a people' ('What was the alphabet for?' 27). But the initial writing was about events in the present of the authors sometimes told through stories set in the past.

41 White, 'The history of Saul's rise', 272 n.3.

42 See Walter Brueggemann, 'David and his theologian', *CBQ* 30 1968: 156–181; Walter Brueggemann, *David and His Theologian: Literary, Social, and Theological Investigations of the Early Monarchy* (Eugene, OR: Cascade Books, 2011); Walter Brueggemann, 'Kingship and chaos: a study in tenth century theology', *CBQ* 33 1971: 317–332; R. E. Clements, *Abraham and David: Genesis XV and Its Meaning for Israelite Tradition* (London: SCM Press, 1967); Rendsburg, 'The Genesis of the Bible', 16; Gary A. Rendsburg, 'Biblical literature as politics: the case of Genesis', in Adele Berlin, ed., *Religion and Politics in the Ancient Near East* (Bethesda,

The intertwining between the Davidic narrative and the Genesis verses is quite thorough. The next step in this process is to recognize that people writing for and against Solomon by name also could author or supplement existing texts that did not refer to him by name to still tell a story about him including in the Book of Genesis.

Sons of the KDB

'[B]iblical texts did not function primarily as literature or entertainment, and therefore need to be understood within the historical, political matrix in which they arose.'

Marc Z. Brettler, 'Biblical literature as politics: the case of Samuel'[43]

'No study of biblical literature can possibly claim to do justice to the subject if it fails to take account of the world-view of the biblical writers.'

Nahum Sarna, *Understanding Genesis*[44]

Following David's death, the great narrative and festal celebration of Yahweh, Israel, and David, was likely to have been revised as people scrambled for power around the throne in Jerusalem. In the following chapters, four individual participants in the political battle for power after the death of David are detailed. The background of each individual is provided along with their writings and an explanation for the writings. The biblical narrative provides the only source material for these individuals as well as the texts assigned to each of them. A final chapter brings the pieces together as the writings became part of a single biblical narrative. And then the process started all over again as time moved on and new stories needed to told to explain and understand what happened until at last the book was closed and rabbis, ministers, priests, and academics began commenting on it.

Campbell postulates that there was a middle ground between the prose text and the spoken word. A written text could serve as an aide-memoire for the deliverer of the written word to a public audience. In gauging the reception of a story, one should not limit oneself to the written word but take into account the skill of the storyteller. The modern equivalent is an archaeology lecture where one picture (slide) is worth a thousand words but the speaker does not necessarily speak the exact same words each time when presenting the talk. Each individual image serves as an aide-memoire. With some Egyptian stories because of the surviving papyrus copies, it is possible to trace the physical process of writing, to know when the ink ran dry or when the writer refilled the stylus even before it had become dry. Even the performance by the storyteller has been speculatively reconstructed from the extant manuscript.[45]

MD: University Press of Maryland, 1996), 4–70; David S. Sperling, *The Original Torah: The Political Intent of the Bible's Writers* (New York: New York University Press, 1998); Walter Wifall, 'Son of man – a pre-Davidic social class?' *CBQ* 37 1975: 331–340; H. W. Wolff, 'The Kerygma of the Yahwist', *Int* 20 1966: 131–158.

43 Marc Z. Brettler, 'Biblical literature as politics: the case of Samuel', in Adele Berlin, ed., *Religion and Politics in the Ancient Near East* (Bethesda, MD: University Press of Maryland, 1996), 71–92, here 91.

44 Nahum M. Sarna, *Understanding Genesis: The World of the Bible in the Light of History* (New York: Schocken Books, 1966), xxiv.

45 See Antony F. Campbell, 'The reported story: midway between oral performance and literary art', *Semeia*

While examining the writings assigned to a specific person as presented here, one also needs to consider the possibility that even they may not have been written at a single moment. As the political situation unfolded over time, new op-ed pieces may have been needed. There is no inherent reason why all the writings attributed to one person had to be written at one time rather than over the course of the political life of that person. Nor is there any inherent reason to presume these individuals were graduates of elitist scribal schools. In some situations, a father to son model may have been sufficient particularly with the alphabet and for non-bureaucratic settings outside the royal apparatus. Biblical writers were not necessarily an early facsimile of biblical scholars.

The scholars recently have been focusing on the ancient scribal culture to ascertain the writing of the Hebrew Bible. Van der Toorn asserts from the end of the Kassite period in Mesopotamia (mid-12th century BCE), scribal education took place in temple schools as it did in New Kingdom Egypt (1550–1100 BCE). Sanders takes issue with the emphasis by Carr and van der Toorn on the Egyptian and Mesopotamian scribal schools for understanding Israelite scribal culture. Schniedewind also criticizes van der Toorn for being 'trapped in a paradigm that envisions the formation of the Bible among temple scribes during the Persian and Hellenistic periods'.[46]

The model of large-scale bureaucracies with schools in big kingdoms may not be appropriate for a single city or priesthood where father-son might be more realistic ... somewhat like the size in a Sumerian language class today in a graduate school seminar. Rollston reports that a class with four was probably large even in Babylonia, classes could be in open air, and there were scribal families with fathers teaching sons. None of these conditions require a temple or king. For centuries, Israel was a people of no king, no state, no temple, no standing army, and no city but it did have families, open air, songs to sing, stories to tell, and festivals to celebrate. The nexus of writing in pre-monarchic Israel was the priesthood. Therefore Rollston's article on scribal curriculum omits what these priests were writing in the time between Ramses/Merneptah and Saul/David/Solomon to preserve and perpetuate the legacy of Israel.[47]

With all these considerations, suppositions, hypotheses, and conjecture in mind, the four individuals responsible for the six stories of this study added to the KDB can be identified.

1. Zadok, Jebusite J

This individual brought a Canaanite and pro-Egypt perspective to his writings. His involvement with Israel began with David and he had no admiration for Israel's origins in

46 1989: 77–85; R. B. Parkinson, *Reading Ancient Egyptian Poetry among Other Histories* (Malden, Oxford: Wiley-Blackwell, 2009).

46 Sanders, *The Invention of Hebrew*, 182 n.1; William M. Schniedewind, 'Scripturalization in ancient Judah', in Brian B. Schmidt, ed., *Contextualizing Israel's Sacred Writings: Ancient Literacy, Orality, and Literary Production* (AIL 22; Atlanta: SBL Press, 2015), 305–321, here 310; Van der Toorn, *Scribal Culture*, 56, 68. See also Lipiński, 'Royal and state scribes in ancient Jerusalem', 157–164.

47 Christopher A. Rollston, *Writing and Literacy in the World of Ancient Israel: Epigraphic Evidence from the Iron Age* (SBLABS 11; Atlanta: Society of Biblical Literature, 2010); Christopher A. Rollston, 'Scribal curriculum during the First Temple Period', in Brian B. Schmidt, ed., *Contextualizing Israel's Scared Writings: Ancient Literacy, Orality, and Literary Production* (AIL 22; Atlanta: SBL Press, 2015), 71–101.

history centuries earlier. Thanks to David, his city became the chosen one as the capital of the kingdom. He and his Zadokite descendants had home field advantage as long as the Jerusalem temple survived.

2. Abiathar, Shiloh J

Abiathar brought a traditional Israelite perspective to his writings. His involvement with Israel was part of the longstanding heritage of the Levite priests of Moses and the physical manifestation of it was the ark of the Lord, the ark of the covenant. Thanks to David, the ark of Yahweh had been installed at Zion. Zadok had Abiathar exiled but not killed. The father of the alphabet prose narrative had been active in polemical writing since the time of Saul, had the standing in the community, and the writing skills to denounce throughout Israel what had occurred in the Canaanite city of Jerusalem under Pharaoh Solomon. In a sense, he became the first and a most vigorous example of telling truth to power through writing. Only when Israel had a king could someone advocate outside the institutional power structure against what the king was doing.

3. Phinehas, Mesopotamia J

Phinehas also brought a traditional Israelite perspective to his writings but one tempered by the experience of the tribe of Benjamin. Although the Aaronid priesthood was second to the priesthood of Moses, both Israelite priesthoods shared an antipathy to what the Canaanites in Jerusalem were doing. Bathsheba, David's widow, had the wisdom and political skill to recognize the Zadokite failure in winning the support of Israel. She decided that the enemy of her enemy was her friend and that the priesthood of Saul, the first king of Israel, would be a valuable weapon in maintaining her position in the kingdom. Phinehas brought the Mesopotamian tradition into the political arena as expressed in his writing.

4. Ahijah, Prophet J

Ahijah brought a traditional Israelite perspective to his writings and with an increased intensity and emotion. Whereas Abiathar of Ephraim son of Joseph was more Egyptian in his orientation, Ahijah, prophet of Moses, was more closely associated with the wilderness tradition of the Kenites, later called the Midianites, of Zipporah, wife of Moses, and Jethro, her father. He knew what his predecessors had written and rejected both the Canaanite and Mesopotamian approaches.

These writers deployed specific literary techniques in the execution of their political objectives. A writer could add a new beginning and ending to an existing story (Zadok). Writers could create new stories in response to the stories of others (Abiathar, Phinehas, Ahijah). Writers could create a new ending to the first cycle of the KDB (Abiathar, Phinehas, Ahijah). Writers could write more than once (Phinehas, Ahijah). A writer could revise (rewrite) an existing story (Phinehas). A writer could combine the writings (manuscripts) of competing writers (Phinehas). Each of these aforementioned conditions will be presented in the forthcoming chapters.

My hypothesis shifts the approach by Baden to a contemporary setting. He stresses the historical claim intrinsic to each of the JEDP narrative strands. He claims that elevating the historical claim to primary evaluative status actually makes it relatively easy to identify the sources or writers. I propose the same applies to the political claims by each of the writers within the J narrative. To know one's political objectives in the present, enables one to assign verses more easily to each writer. In American terms, the political objectives of Thomas Jefferson and Alexander Hamilton are a better guide to distinguishing their writings than stylistic differences.[48]

These suggestions represent an alternative view to the traditional 'Sumerian King List' linear approach in biblical scholarship. That paradigm posits sequential biblical writers (JEDP) where at any given time there can only be one writer. An alternative view suggests instead that multiple views by contemporary writers in dialog with each other on the fundamental religious and political issues of the day can be expressed in the biblical narrative. One also notes that these individuals are the likely candidates for writing the overtly political narratives involving Saul, David, and Solomon. Collectively their writings and the KDB comprise the continuous coherent narrative ending with Solomon secure on the throne that Friedman hypothesized.

There was no ancient Near East precedent for this type of writing. A story might be revised over time with the Gilgamesh epic being the leading example. But to find this many writers in dialog with each other over so short a period of time in the political arena was unique to Israel and rare in the human experience. Even within Israel, this process was scarcely repeated as circumstances changed. Perhaps the closest parallel is in the Gospels. The three synoptic gospels, Mark, Matthew, and Luke have much material in common and much that is different and at variance with the other gospels as we are reminded each Christmas when holiday displays combine the Jesus birth stories of Matthew and Luke.

A more political comparison is the Constitution of the United States. Article 5 permits the document to be amended. Should changes be appended to the original document or should the original series of articles be rewritten? Does the Constitution permit freedom of religion? How will scholars 3000 years from now know that the answer was 'no' in 1787 and 'yes' in 1791 with James Madison, the father of the Constitution, taking a leading role in both instances? How will they know that one of his proposals in 1789 delaying self-approved Congressional pay raises was not ratified until 1992, two centuries later? Is alcohol to be prohibited or permitted? Even though the document is referred to as THE Constitution, it has changed over time as the political environment changed. So did THE Pentateuch. So did THE J narrative.

Biblical writing did not stop in the 10th century BCE with Ahijah and the division of the kingdom. Political crises occurred again and again over the course of time. The situation was tense when Pharaoh Ahab was king. The situation was tense when Mesha of Moab destroyed the sanctuary to Moses at Mount Nebo. The situation was tense when

---

48 Baden, *The Composition of the Pentateuch*, 106, 117, 26.

Aramaean Hazael of Damascus conquered the land. The situation was tense when Assyria destroyed the northern kingdom of Israel. The situation was tense when Assyria ravaged the land of Judah. The situation was tense when Babylonia destroyed the temple in Jerusalem. One should expect political writing by priests and prophets to have occurred in all these circumstances until the monarchy was no more and it was time to put the pieces together and hope for a savior.

In the history of the ancient Near East, the great kings are remembered not only as warriors but as builders. David is the major exception. His monument was the King David Bible. Exclude them and Israel is no different from any other people; embrace the role of individual human agency and he changed the course of human history. While no one after David could fill his shoes, four people sought to supplement his message as part of Jerusalem Throne Games. Here are their stories.

Chapter 11

ZADOK: JEBUSITE J

The first supplement to the KDB was by Zadok. The identity of Zadok has been a debated one within biblical scholarship. The main area of contention is whether or not Zadok was a Jebusite priest of Elyon. The stakes in the debate are significant. If he was part of pre-Davidic Jerusalem, then his presence during the reigns of David and Solomon represents the ongoing existence of a Canaanite culture in the new capital of Israel. I side with the view that Zadok was a Jebusite priest of Elyon who only became part of Israel when David made it his capital. Only later were the Zadokites incorporated into the Aaronid line. The death of David provided Zadok with the opportunity to co-opt the kingdom of Yahweh and Israel. Zadok became the Canaanite in the story of the sons of Noah who was cursed by those Israelites who favored Israel and Yahweh (see Additional Readings: Zadok).[1]

Zakok wrote his supplement to the KDB after David had died and during the reign of Solomon. According to the biblical narrative this comparatively unknown person played a pivotal role in these historical events. Tracing his history through the canonical record, Zadok first appears in Hebron as part of troops gathered in support of David becoming king of Israel. He is described as:

> **I Chronicles 12: 28** *Zadok, a young man mighty in valor, and twenty-two commanders from his own father's house.*

In this list, he is not part of the Levites, the Aaronids, or the Benjaminites. The forces under his control are small. There is no information about where he does belong. There is no counterpart to this list in the stories of David at Hebron in II Samuel. It implies that perhaps this non-Israelite Jebusite priest had defected to David's side even before he became king of Israel. This mighty man of valor would have been a useful ally in the quest to conquer the seemingly impregnable Zion citadel ... or to pave the way for its peaceful acquisition. While it seems historically unlikely that Zadok did defect, the idea that he became a willing ally on the new king does seem quite reasonable given his future.[2]

According to the biblical narrative, Zadok became part of David's administration:

> **II Samuel 8: 15** *So David reigned over all Israel; and David administered justice and equity to all his people.* [16] *And Joab the son of Zeruiah was over the army; and Jehoshaphat the son of Ahilud was recorder;* [17] *and* **Zadok** *the son of Ahitub and Ahimelech the son of* **Abiathar** *were priests; and Seraiah was secretary;* [18] *and Benaiah the son of Jehoiada was over the Cherethites and the Pelethites; and David's sons were priests.*

---

1   Rendsburg suggests Zadok was Araunah, the Jebusite king from whom David purchase the threshing floor. Araunah is the title of the king and Zadok is the personal name ('Biblical literature as politics', 55–56, 68).
2   See C. E. Hauer, 'Who was Zadok?' *JBL* 82 1963: 89–94.

The original sequence probably designated Abiathar the son of Ahimelech the son on Ahitub leaving Zadok with no genealogy. The revised sequence makes more sense given the relationship among the three in I Sam. 22: 20: *But one of the sons of Ahimelech the son of Ahitub, named Abiathar, escaped and fled after David.* That verse is part of an extended narrative involving Abiathar (see Chapter 12). Whether the change was accidental or deliberate is a separate issue.[3]

One notices here that Zadok and Abiathar were priests. These two people were rivals and their rivalry would be expressed in writing through supplements to the KDB. As royal appointees, these priests may assume the air of being chief priests. One should remain vigilant about not imposing images of other times and apparently similar positions on these designees of David. They were not Popes, Archbishops of Canterbury, or the chief priest of the temple in the Gospels. Rooke's analysis of the writings of P and the Deuteronomist (outside the scope of this study) suggest that Zadok priests focused on the cultic activities in the temple while the Abiathar priests tended to ignore that very role in favor of acting as a prophet. In neither case did political powers accrue to the priest nor did that individual possess a national leadership position. However that does not mean Zadok did not have lofty ambitions of dominating the kingdom through the person of the king.[4]

Zadok next appears again in the canonical record with Abiathar when David flees Jerusalem in the course of Absalom's rebellion.

> **II Samuel 15:24** *And **Abiathar** came up, and lo, **Zadok** came also, with all the Levites, bearing the ark of the covenant of God; and they set down the ark of God, until the people had all passed out of the city.* [25] *Then the king said to **Zadok**, 'Carry the ark of God back into the city. If I find favor in the eyes of Yahweh, he will bring me back and let me see both it and his habitation;* [26] *but if he says, "I have no pleasure in you," behold, here I am, let him do to me what seems good to him.'* [27] *The king also said to **Zadok** the priest, 'Look, go back to the city in peace, you and **Abiathar**, with your two sons, **Ahimaaz** your son, and **Jonathan** the son of **Abiathar**.* [28] *See, I will wait at the fords of the wilderness, until word comes from you to inform me.'* [29] *So **Zadok** and **Abiathar** carried the ark of God back to Jerusalem; and they remained there…* [35] *[David said to Hushai the Archite,] 'Are not **Zadok** and **Abiathar** the priests with you there? So whatever you hear from the king's house, tell it to **Zadok** and **Abiathar** the priests.* [36] *Behold, their two sons are with them there, **Ahimaaz**, **Zadok**'s son, and **Jonathan**, **Abiathar**'s son; and by them you shall send to me everything you hear.'*

The passage gives equal time to the two priests who are entrusted with the sacred responsibility for the transportation of the ark of Yahweh. The sons of both priests are introduced so the relationship extended for another generation.[5]

---

3   For the biblical scholarship on the verse, see Caquot and de Robert, *Les Livres de Samuel*, 448–449; Cross, *Canaanite Myth*, 212–213; John Day, 'The Canaanite inheritance of the Israelite monarchy', in John Day, ed., *King and Messiah in Israel and the Ancient Near East: Proceedings of the Oxford Old Testament Seminar* (JSOT Sup Series 270; Sheffield: Sheffield Academic Press, 1998), 73–78, here 76; McCarter, *II Samuel*, 253–254; Merlin Rehm, 'Zadok', *The Interpreter's Dictionary of the Bible Supplementary Volume* (Nashville: Abingdon, 1976), 976–977, here, 976; Deborah W. Rooke, *Zadok's Heirs: The Role and Development of the High Priesthood in Ancient Israel* (New York: Oxford University Press, 2015), 63–64; Rowley, 'Zadok and Nehushtan', 114; Wellhausen, *Prolegomena*, 126.

4   See Rooke, *Zadok's Heirs*, 11–79.

5   The compositional history of these verses raises the possibility the phrase 'with all the Levites' is an insertion into the original text and the presence of Abiathar is confusing. Jockeying for power through insertions into

In the story of Absalom's rise to and fall from power, these two generations of priests are deeply involved in David's efforts to squash the rebellion against him.

II Samuel 17: 15 *Then Hushai said to* **Zadok** *and* **Abiathar** *the priests, 'Thus and so did Ahithophel counsel Absalom and the elders of Israel; and thus and so have I counseled'.*

After Absalom is killed, Joab, David's general, prepares to send a message to David about the death. At that point Ahimaaz, the son of Zadok speaks up.

II Samuel 18: 19 *Then said* **Ahimaaz the son of Zadok**, *'Let me run, and carry tidings to the king that Yahweh has delivered him from the power of his enemies…* [22] *Then* **Ahimaaz the son of Zadok** *said again to Joab, 'Come what may, let me also run after the Cushite'. And Joab said, 'Why will you run, my son, seeing that you will have no reward for the tidings?* [23] *'Come what may', he said, 'I will run'. So he said to him, 'Run'. Then* **Ahimaaz** *ran by the way of the plain, and outran the Cushite…* [26] *And the watchman saw another man running; and the watchman called to the gate and said, 'See, another man running alone!' The king said, 'He also brings tidings'.* [27] *And the watchman said, 'I think the running of the foremost is like the running of* **Ahimaaz the son of Zadok**.' *And the king said, 'He is a good man, and comes with good tidings'.*

According to the Amarna Letters, Egyptians had stationed Nubians in Jerusalem (see Chapter 8). It is conceivable that Nubians continued to exist in Jerusalem three centuries later and after Egypt had withdrawn. In these verses, Ahimaaz scarcely has an identity of his own as he is routinely identified as the son of Zadok. Presumably he thinks that as the messenger of good tidings, it will reflect well on his father even though Zadok was not the cause of Absalom's death. According to the text, David perceives him as a good man.

There are additional references to Zadok and Abiathar but the action really heats up when David is about to die and the issue of his successor becomes crucial.

I Kings 1: 7 *He [Adonijah, the eldest living son of David] conferred with Joab the son of Zeruiah and with* **Abiathar** *the priest; and they followed Adonijah and helped him.* [8] *But* **Zadok** *the priest, and Benaiah the son of Jehoiada, and Nathan the prophet, and Shimei, and Rei, and David's mighty men were not with Adonijah.*

The text introduces two competing factions in the battle for succession each with priest and warriors. Joab's and Abiathar's connections with David long pre-dated the establishment of the City of David as the capital city of kingdom. They support David's eldest son, Adonijah, a son born in Hebron. The opposing faction includes Zadok, the mighty men (see Chapter 4), and various figures who do not appear in the narrative until David makes Jerusalem his capital. They are not part of David's story with Saul or in Hebron. This faction supports Solomon, the son born to Bathsheba in Jerusalem and with a name sharing the same '*slm*' consonants as the city. The battle lines have been drawn.

The battle then is engaged. The account in I Kings 1 describes the machinations of the competing factions to install their candidate as the new king. As is well known, the pro-Solomon faction triumphs and he becomes king. Indeed, Zadok is front and center when power passes to the new king:

---

the narrative was standard operating procedure for centuries; see Caquot and de Robert, *Les Livres de Samuel*, 531; McCarter, *II Samuel*, 365, 370: Rooke, *Zadok's Heirs*, 70 n.68.

> **1 Kings 1: 38** *So **Zadok** the priest, Nathan the prophet, and Benaiah the son of Jehoiada, and the Cherethites and the Pelethites, went down and caused Solomon to ride on King David's mule, and brought him to Gihon.[39] There **Zadok** the priest took the horn of oil from the tent, and anointed Solomon. Then they blew the trumpet; and all the people said, 'Long live King Solomon!'.*

To the victor belongs the spoils. In the time-honored tradition, the winner in the battle to become king of the mountain dispatches those who hindered his quest. King Solomon replaces David's longtime allies who had backed the wrong son with the people who backed him for the throne:

> **I Kings 2: 35** *The king [Solomon] put Benaiah the son of Jehoiada over the army in place of Joab, and the king put **Zadok** the priest in the place of Abiathar.*

All these references to him give the impression that the name on Zadok's birth certificate was 'Zadok the priest'. The net result of this battle for power is that according to the narrative tradition, Zadok is now the priest of priests in the capital city during the reign of the king who will build the temple.

After this, Zadok the individual disappears from record. De Vaux raises the possibility that Zadok had died early in the reign of Solomon since he is not heard from throughout the life of Solomon (the way Abiathar is with David). His death would have made succession an issue just as it had been when the king died. Rooke posits that Zadok died without ever actually serving in the temple (which does not mean he did not help plan it or see part of its construction). She offers as a candidate Azariah, one of Zadok's sons and an official of Solomon who served as priest in the house which Solomon built in Jerusalem (I Kings 4: 2: I Chr. 6: 10).[6] Zadok's 'house' or family line appears in the time of King Hezekiah (715–686 BCE) as told by the Chronicler but not in II Kings.

> **2 Chronicles 31: 10** *Azariah the chief priest, who was of the **house of Zadok**, answered him [Hezekiah]…*

This reference suggests that centuries later when Assyria invaded the kingdom of Judah in 701 BCE, the priests at the temple in Jerusalem belonged to the Zadokite dynasty.[7]

The continuation of the Zadokite line in the temple another century later is suggested in the comments of Ezekiel describing who can do what there:

> **Ezekiel 40: 46** *and the chamber which faces north is for the priests who have charge of the altar; these are the **sons of Zadok**, who alone among the sons of Levi may come near to Yahweh to minister to him.*

> **Ezekiel 43: 19** *you shall give to the Levitical priests of the **family of Zadok**, who draw near to me to minister to me, says Yahweh GOD, a bull for a sin offering.*

---

6   Roland de Vaux, *Ancient Israel: Its Life and Institutions* (New York: McGraw-Hill Book Company, 1961), 373; Rooke, *Zadok's Heirs*, 69.

7   Bartlett's analysis of Zadok's successors suggests that the position of chief priest was not necessarily an inherited one but that the king selected the best person for the job. He focuses on the rivalry between the Zadokite and Aaronid family lines and considers the reference to the 'house' of Zadok to be a misleading and artificial phrase (see J. R. Bartlett, 'Zadok and his successors at Jerusalem', *JTS* 19 1968: 1–18).

> **Ezekiel 44: 15** *'But the Levitical priests, the sons of **Zadok**, who kept the charge of my sanctuary when the people of Israel went astray from me, shall come near to me to minister to me; and they shall attend on me to offer me the fat and the blood', says Yahweh GOD;*

> **Ezekiel 48: 11** *This shall be for the consecrated priests, the sons of **Zadok**, who kept my charge, who did not go astray when the people of Israel went astray, as the Levites did.*

Two critical observations may be drawn from these verses centuries after the individual Zadok lived.

1. The priesthood running the temple continued to identify with the priest who was present when the temple was built.
2. These Zadokites had rivals known as Levites.[8]

This rivalry including the Aaronids did not commence in the time of Hezekiah or Ezekiel (late 8th to early 6th centuries BCE) or in post-exilic times but was present in the time of David (10th century BCE). The rivalry and battle for power then directly contributed to supplements to the KDB.

Before turning to Zadok's writings (or writing done on his behalf, perhaps by one of his sons), it is necessary to determine who this individual is. As previously mentioned, unlike his rival Abiathar, Zadok appears out of nowhere in the narrative in Jerusalem. Then suddenly he is front and center in the battle for power as the charismatic king is about to die and he anoints the successor Solomon. To understand his writings, more information is needed.

David's choice inevitably would lead to complications, especially after he died. The question here is what was the relationship between Elyon and Yahweh after David died? Or less theologically and more politically, what was the relationship between the priests and people of Yahweh and those of Elyon, between Abiathar and Zadok? The answer to that question may be revealed in two Elyon passages: Gen. 14: 18–20 and Deut. 32: 8–9 written differently in the MT and the LXX versions.

As previously noted, pre-Israel Jerusalem worshiped the deity Elyon. According to this passage, the priest of Elyon and the king of the city were one.

> **Genesis 14: 18** *And Melchizedek king of Salem brought out bread and wine; he was priest of God Most High. [19] And he blessed him and said, 'Blessed be Abram by God Elyon, maker of heaven and earth; [20] and blessed be God Elyon, who has delivered your enemies into your hand!' And Abram gave him a tenth of everything.*[9]

The message of the verse suggests that the Canaanite Jebusites in Jerusalem worshiped Elyon prior to David. The issue of the relationship between the king and the priest for both Melchizedek and the Davidic dynasty has drawn scholarly attention, particularly as it relates to Ps 110: 4:

---

8   White recognizes that the non-Levitical Zadokites had usurped the priesthood in the nation's capital but considers the Zadokites to be authentic Aaronids rather than Jebusite in origin (see Marsha White, 'The Elohistic depiction of Aaron: a study in the Levite-Zadokite controversy', in J. A. Emerton, ed., *Studies in the Pentateuch* (Leiden: E. J. Brill, 1990), 149–159, here 150–151.

9   For the use of this passage as a reflection of priesthood rivalries see Mathews, *Melchizedek's Alternative Priestly Order*, 52–135; Rooke, 'Kingship as priesthood', 197–198; De Vaux, *Ancient Israel*, 374.

Yahweh has sworn and will not change his mind, 'You are a priest for ever after the order of Melchizedek'.

One interpretation is that the psalm legitimates a Jerusalem priesthood through the precedent of Melchizedek. Despite the appeal of this interpretation of passage as means of the Jerusalem priesthood justifying its ancient origin one should proceed with caution. There is no positive evidence so another view is better safe than sorry and to admit ignorance as the origin of Zadok. I choose to interpret the passage as the attempt by a Jebusite who cannot claim authority or legitimacy through Moses (Jethro) or Aaron (Phinehas) to predate those claims with a patriarchal assertion.

The parallels between Abraham and Melchizedek, the warrior shepherd-king of Hebron and Zadok are obvious. The depiction of Abraham, meaning David, acknowledging the god, sanctuary, and priesthood of pre-Israelite Jerusalem presents a powerful message by the author. Zadok seeks to assert the primacy of Elyon over Yahweh in this story set in the past. He follows the example of Bathsheba who asserted the primacy of Solomon over Adonijah but did so in the name of Yahweh. Now that David is dead, Zadok has no restraints on restoring Elyon to his rightful position as king of the pantheon.[10]

The two versions of Deut. 32: 8–9 reflect the divergent path about to unfold in Israelite history (see Additional Readings: Deut. 32: 8–9).

MT: Deuteronomy 32: 8 *When Elyon gave to the nations their inheritance, when he separated the sons of men, he fixed the bounds of the peoples according to the number of the sons of God.* [9] *For Yahweh's portion is his people, Jacob his allotted heritage.*

LXX: Deuteronomy 32: 8 *When Elyon divided the nations, when he separated the sons of Adam, he set the bounds of the nations according to the number of the angels of God.* [9] *And his people Jacob became the portion of Yahweh, Israel was the line of his inheritance.*

The differences between these two different manuscripts has produced its own abundance of scholarly debate. For purposes here to understand Zadok's political intent, three observations are significant:

1. The universal nature of the passage should be understood in terms of the world that mattered to the original author. The focus was not the entire earth as it is known to today or even the ancient Near East. The world then meant the Levant, the land of Canaan, the realm of El in the Canaanite pantheon, the world Israel now dominated.
2. Despite the attempts to equate Elyon and Yahweh, the simpler and more obvious interpretation is that the author is asserting the primacy of Elyon over Yahweh. Elyon is the creator of the world that matters, not Yahweh. The latter is subordinate to the former just as Abiathar was to Zadok after Solomon's accession.
3. Yahweh's people is restricted to being one of multiple peoples in the land. The other peoples in the land of Canaan such as the Jebusites and Amorites among others are not part of the people of Yahweh. This assertion is in direct contradiction to the story of Rahab:

---

10 Lemaire, 'Le "Dieu de Jérusalem" à la lumière de l'épigraphie', 49–58. Num. 24: 16 with mention of Elohim, Elyon, and Shaddai is a classic example of a politician linking diverse constituencies as one.

Joshua 2: 9 *and [Rahab] said to the men, 'I know that Yahweh has given you the land, and that the fear of you has fallen upon us, and that all the inhabitants of the land melt away before you...'*[11] *'...for Yahweh your God is he who is God in heaven above and on earth beneath'.*

In this instance, a Canaanite woman, speaking as a representative of the non-Canaanite elite, the marginal people, speaks glowingly about what Yahweh did in the Exodus and against the Amorites. She uses the same heaven and earth of Gen. 14: 18 but here attributed to Yahweh and not to Elyon. The Zadokite approach directly refutes the role of Yahweh and the Exodus as the basis for the identity of the kingdom and for the subservient position of the Canaanites. Instead Zadok supports the primacy of David who created the kingdom and whom Zadok claims acknowledged the position of Elyon, his Jebusite priesthood, and Zadok.

4. Depending on how one interprets the composition of the MT and LXX versions of Deut. 32: 8–9, even Israel by name does not fare well. Based on the MT version the people are the people of Jacob with no mention of Israel. In the LXX version, the name Israel slips in at the end. In the post-David kingdom, Zadok did not assign any special role to Israel. He acknowledged the presence of the Jacob people, but he did not use the name Israel. When the kingdom divided, even though Jerusalem had been the capital under David and Solomon, the name of the kingdom was Judah from David in Hebron and not Israel the name dating back to the 13th century BCE. Nobody thought of Jerusalem as Israelite. Not the Jebusites who lived there. Not the Israelites who later separated. The story of Jacob becoming Israel (Gen. 32: 28) needs to be understood in response to this context.

Zadok's political agenda displaced Israel, Yahweh, and the Exodus. He put them in their place subordinate to Jerusalem, Elyon, and David.

The battle to install Solomon as the successor to David was only the beginning of Zadok's effort to assert control over the entire kingdom. One would be remiss if one ignored the economic aspects of this political confrontation expressed in theological terms. The diatribes were not simply academic ivory-tower debating points. H. H. Rowley's straightforward clear-cut pronouncement:

> 'I find that Abraham who recognizes the priesthood of Melchizedek corresponds to David who recognizes the priestly office of Zadok, and Melchizedek who blesses Abraham corresponds to Zadok who blesses David'

is incomplete. Gary Rendsburg recognizes that the message of the passage is for Israel not to object to tithing Zadok. While that certainly was Zadok's goal, it was a claim he asserted after David and during the reign of Solomon when the temple to Yahweh had been built. Zadok's assertion of power on behalf of his Canaanite priesthood of Elyon would not go unchallenged. Rooke concludes that Melchizedek was used to foster reconciliation between the Jebusites and the Israelites. She minimizes the economic powerplay initiated by Zadok by mentioning it only in passing in a footnote. Jon Levenson concludes that the passage evidently is an etiology for the tithe thereby suggesting a continuity between the pre-Israelite and Israelite priesthoods in Jerusalem. One is reminded here of the old adage, 'follow the money'.[11]

---

11 Jon Levenson, 'Zion traditions', in *ABD* VI: 1098–1102, here 1101; Rendsburg, 'The genesis of the Bible', 18; Rooke's *Zadok's Heirs*, 89–90; Rowley, 'Melchizedek and David', 485. For an example of the elaborate textual effort ancient priests would undertake to ensure royal support, see Irving Finkel and Alexandra Fletcher,

Zadok was engaged in a blunt grab for power. His assertion that David had blessed his share of the royal revenues is what Zadok wanted the people to believe David had done. In the political parlance of the present, Zadok's action is pure 'spin'. Since David was dead, who was there to contradict him? The only reason Zadok was not taking Yahweh's name in vain was because he did not use it; he made the claim in the name of Elyon who trumped Yahweh. Zadok's assertion that his priesthood was entitled to 10% of the royal revenues was not simply a talking point. It struck right at the heart of the funding for the priesthoods especially if the royal revenues in Solomon's time were substantial, that is, worth fighting over.

The Canaanite-based Jebusites presented a different heritage and values to the Israelite way of life. Up until that time Israel had survived for centuries without a king, whereas Canaanite cities including Jerusalem had one. Up until that time Israel had survived for centuries without a temple, whereas Canaanite cities including Jerusalem had one. Up until that time Israel's relation with Egypt was one of enmity, whereas Jerusalem's was one of vassalage and thanks. Up until that time there was no Canaanite tradition of cities deferring to the ongoing leadership of one Canaanite city whereas now they would have to. Times had changed. Kathleen Kenyon's assertion that the 'successful [military] opposition of the Jebusites [to Israel] was to have an effect on the history of the Israelite tribes that lasted to the end of historic Judaism in Palestine' understates the Jebusite impact. The competition switched to the political arena and the written words remain with us to this very day.[12]

These circumstances demarcated the world Jebusite Zadok inhabited during the reign of David when Jerusalem became the capital of his kingdom. The death of the great leader who had fashioned the kingdom based on his personal ambition, charisma, innovativeness, skill, vision, and genius, meant nothing could be taken for granted now. Even the installation of Solomon as king in Jerusalem did not automatically mean other Canaanite cities or Israelite tribes would accept his rule.[13] The death of the old king traditionally is a time to rebel against the untested novice new king. Solomon's death and the attempt to install Rehoboam as king would prove that point as the kingdom divided. Even with the army behind him, there were considerable, hopefully for him not insurmountable, challenges confronting Zadok.

Part of the way Zadok coped was through an addition to the KDB. His goals were to:

1. Legitimize Queen-mother Bathsheba as regent.
2. Legitimize the Davidic Dynasty.
3. Legitimize the construction of a temple.
4. Ensure his priesthood received its cut of the royal revenues.
5. Replace enmity with Egypt with alliance.

'Thinking outside the box: the case of the sun-god tablet and the cruciform monument', *BASOR* 375 2016: 215–248.

12 Kenyon, *Royal Cities of the Old Testament*, 15.

13 Pioske claims that Jerusalem's previous history as a local non-Israel ruling center was conducive to Israel's acceptance of it as the capital of the kingdom (*David's Jerusalem*, 237). The position taken here is that the opposite occurred and neither the Canaanite cities nor the Israelite tribes supported the primacy of Jerusalem even during David's reign yet alone after the charismatic warrior-king had died.

6. Diminish the status of the Israelites.
7. Diminish the status of Yahweh.

Typically, one expects the founding king to do certain things. In ancient times these actions included founding a city, building a temple, building walls so the people would be safe, and protecting water so the people would survive. David did not do these things. His son Solomon is remembered as the great builder even though he has no legacy as a warrior. A. Mazar plaintively asks, 'if Solomon did not built [*sic*] a temple in Jerusalem, who was responsible...?' The memory of Solomon as the builder of the temple should be considered authentic especially since there is no realistic alternative choice. It seems reasonable that before there could be the trauma over the destruction of the temple there was the celebration of the king building it.[14]

Despite the successful coup, Zadok's position remained precarious. Outside of Jerusalem, Solomon had the allegiance of virtually no one. Merneptah's Israel, the Song of Deborah tribes, David's Judah, and the other Canaanite cities and non-Israelite peoples only had fleeting allegiance to the kingdom David created and now that creator was gone. Zadok did have home-field advantage as long as Jerusalem was the capital and the continued existence of the Zadokites centuries later demonstrate the success of his efforts while many of the surrounding peoples vanished. The Zadokite priesthood was permanently changed by David and it never reverted to being solely Canaanite; but it never became truly Israelite either.[15]

Reconstructed Narrative of Jebusite J

Zadok's supplement to the KDB's first cycle involving the six son stories of this study is provided below. His additions are in italics.

> *Garden story*
> **Gen. 3: 20** *The man called his wife's name Eve, because she was the mother of all living.*
> **Gen. 4: 1** *Now the man knew Eve his wife, and she conceived and bore Cain.*
> **Gen. 4: 2** *And again, she bore his brother Abel.*
>
> *Cain and Abel story*
> **Gen. 4: 25** *And Adam knew his wife again, and she bore a son and called his name Seth*
> **Gen. 4: 26** *To Seth also a son was born, and he called his name Enosh. At that time men began to call upon the name of Yahweh.*
> **Gen. 6: 4** *The Nephilim were on the earth in those days. These were the mighty men that were of old, the men of renown.*
>
> *Local flood story*

---

14 A. Mazar, 'Archaeology and the Biblical narrative', 48; see also David Carr, *The Formation of the Hebrew Bible: A New Reconstruction* (New York: Oxford University Press, 2011), 370; Lester L. Grabbe, 'Reflections on the discussion', in Lester L. Grabbe, ed., *Israel in Transition: From Late Bronze II to Iron IIa c. 1250–850 BCE) Volume 1: The Archaeology* (*LHBOTS* 491; European Seminar in Historical Methodology 7; London: T&T Clark, 2008), 219–232, here 229; Na'aman, 'The contribution of the Amarna Letters', 22; Pioske, *David's Jerusalem*, 112.

15 See Bartlett, 'Zadok and his successors', 10–11.

Exegesis

Zadok's additions to the KDB in the son stories were slight. These additions are now part of two of the son stories presented in Chapters 3 and 4 above. In fact, they are barely stories. Instead they consist more of series of facts that the author states the audience should accept as true. His supplement envelops the existing story of Cain and Abel by providing a new beginning and new ending. It connects the revised story to the garden story. Now Cain and Abel have parents and a younger brother. In so doing, Zadok sought to change the meaning of the narrative to fit the times in which he lived, the reign of Solomon, and not the time of David. In Zadok's conception of the post-David kingdom, there was little place for Yahweh, Israel, or the Exodus.

Rainer Albertz succinctly states: 'The reason why the official Yahweh religion of the Jerusalem temple shows hardly any awareness of the liberation traditions of the early period is that at the latest from the time of Solomon onwards, former non-Israelites gave its tone as priests and theologians'. A deliberate attempt was made by them to obscure the temple connection to the Jebusite sanctuary at the 'threshing floor' by implying the Solomonic temple was a new construction on culturally virgin soil. Albertz attributes these actions to the Jebusites beginning with Zadok who promoted their deity Elyon and the Solomonic temple over Exodus and the ark. The story of the Exodus had become a battleground.[16]

One may observe that Zadok is not a writer in the literary sense. His writings are not the work of an artist. Literary flourishes either were beyond his capability or not relevant. There is no purple prose to sweep people off their feet or to lift their spirits to the heavenly realm. The writing is pointed not inspired. Zadok has a case to present and he presented it. Here is the way it is in the kingdom now that the great king has died; it is our turn now. He proclaims his message to his audience.

Zadok's genealogy introduces two new figures, the second generation Seth, who is himself much younger than his adult brothers, and the third generation Enosh. For his audience, the relationships would call to mind events which had just occurred. Solomon was younger than his two deceased brothers Absalom and Adonijah. Zadok clears the deck so he can introduce the new character to the story and reveal his purposes. This approach reflects a one-to-one correspondence between figures in the writing and actual specific people in history. However while Abel died in the original story, Cain did not so perhaps there is more to it than this.

Another way one could re-interpret Zadok's story and the existing story of Cain and Abel is as one of competing priesthoods. Just as Absalom and Adonijah were older than Solomon, so the priests of Shiloh and Benjamin were part of Israel before Zadok. Indeed Shiloh in Ephraim and Benjamin at Bethel had a long history of competition culminating most recently in the battle over kingship initiated by Saul. Now the Saulide priests of Benjamin seemingly were politically dead thanks to the installation of David by the Shiloh priests of Abiathar. Abiathar himself was in exile. There was a new priesthood within

---

16 Rainer Albertz, *A History of Israelite Religion in the Old Testament Period, Vol. I: From the Beginning to the End of the Monarchy* (Louisville: Westminster/John Knox Press, 1994), 129–138, quotation from 129.

the Israelite arena now, the priests from the Jebusite city that now was the capital of the kingdom. Zadok's supplement was their story.

In no way does this mean that the original story of Cain and Abel was about any of these events. In no way does this mean the figures of Cain and Abel could be understood only one way in the present. In no one does this mean the figures of Cain and Abel should be understood too literally. Zadok was working with an existing story which he framed with a new beginning and new ending. He did not change the story he had inherited. His actions do mean that stories can acquire new meanings and interpretations as circumstances change. One could if one so chose understand these brothers as sons of the king and/or as priesthoods that had backed different people for kingship and lost. Seth was the winner as was Zadok and Seth also was the winner as was Solomon.

Typically in biblical exegesis, this 3-generation sequence of Adam-Seth-Enosh is considered a fragment as Westermann and von Rad did (see Chapter 3).[17] This perception leads to the inevitable follow-up questions about whether one author created this fragment from a longer list or inherited this fragment and then combined it with the alternative Cainite genealogy (see Chapter 2).

1. According to Gunkel, 'The Seth genealogy, originally a variant of the genealogy of Cain, has been combined with it by a collector'. He titled this section of his commentary '4. The genealogy of Seth 4: 25, 26 … 5:29 J^e', in lieu of the now terminated Abel and Cain lines by one of the multiple J writers he had identified. Gunkel proposes a genealogical connection of Adam-Seth-Enosh-Noah.[18]
2. Westermann concurs that the Sethite genealogy was a separate genealogy and that the Cainite and Sethite genealogies each have an independent origin. He notes the common scholarly contrast between the 'pious and god-fearing' Sethites and the 'godless and wicked' Cainites.[19]

Reflecting the consensus, J. M. Miller starkly states: 'Verses 4 25–26 clearly represent only a fragmentary list.'[20]

An alternative view is that a single author proposed a 3-generation Seth sequence that was complete in and of itself. The proposed reconstruction by Jacques Vermeylen is very similar to the one proposed here except that he identifies Noah as a son of Enosh without realizing that Gen. 5: 29 turns out to have originated with another author (see Chapter 13).[21]

The net result is instead of this genealogy being a truncated version of the genealogy in Gen. 5, the latter is an expanded version of the original three-level one in Gen. 4. It makes a difference in understanding the meaning of the text if one is examining the original creation

17 D. T. Bryan, 'A reevaluation of Gen. 4 and 5 in light of recent studies in genealogical fluidity', *ZAW* 99 1987: 180–188, here 185; Von Rad, *Genesis*, 112; Westermann, *Genesis 1–11*, 338; Skinner, *A Critical and Exegetical Commentary on Genesis*, 124–125. For genealogies in general, see Robert R. Wilson, 'The Old Testament genealogies in recent research', *JBL* 94 1975: 169–189, reprinted in in Richard S. Hess and David Toshio Tsumura, eds, *I Studied Inscriptions from Before the Flood: Ancient Near Eastern, Literary, and Linguistic Approaches to Genesis 1–11* (SBTS 4; Winona Lake: Eisenbrauns, 1994), 200–223; Robert R. Wilson, *Genealogy and History in the Biblical World* (New Haven: Yale University Press, 1977).
18 Gunkel, *Genesis*, 54.
19 Westermann, *Genesis 1–11*, 338, 343.
20 J. M. Miller, 'The descendants of Cain: notes on Genesis 4', *ZAW* 86 1974: 162–174, here 166.
21 Jacques Vermeylen, 'La descendance de Caïn et la descendance d'Abel', *ZAW* 103 1991: 175–193, here 178.

of the author versus a truncated version that has been reformulated through a redaction. In terms of Jerusalem, this author was writing at a time when there only was a 3-level dynastic line: king David who was dead, Solomon who was king, and his son Rehoboam who would be king or David who was king and chief priest, Zadok who was chief priest, and Ahimaaz or Azariah, his sons, one of whom would become chief priest after him. The political approach provides a distinctively different context for understanding the meaning of these verses than the mythical folktale from hoary antiquity does.

Genesis 3: 20 *The man called his wife's name Eve, because she was the mother of all living*

As presented here, this verse was not part of the existing garden story. Delitzsch observes that since the time of pioneer modern biblical scholar Georg Heinrich August Ewald (1803–1875), this verse has been regarded as a later interpolation to the garden story.[22] Dillmann and von Rad concur.[23] Speiser's Genesis commentary does not address this issue. Gunkel suggests '(T)he poem stems from another context and another source'.[24] Reuven Kimelman pithily comments that the verse does not flow from the preceding one or into the succeeding one and its absence would not be missed.[25] Westermann comments that 3: 20 is one of a series of verses at the conclusion of the garden story that were loosely attached to it. He recognizes the scholarly unanimity regarding the verse as an insertion and asks, 'If the sentence is an insertion, where can it have come from?'[26]

The answer to the query is provided in the proposed reconstruction. The verse really was not added to the garden story as much as it was the new introduction to revised story of Cain and Abel.[27] Based on Westermann's suggestion that the subsequent verses to 3: 20 in the garden story also were added (by other authors) this raises the possibility that the man and the woman (the king and the queen) were still in the garden as the current story unfolds. In this scenario, all three sons in the story were born in the garden. One son will be murdered in the royal capital, a second will be exiled from the royal capital, and the third son will witness the calling of the name of Yahweh in the royal capital. These developments have important implications for understanding the battle for power in the royal capital after the death of David.

---

22 Delitzsch, *New Commentary on Genesis*, 169.

23 Dillmann, *Genesis*, 81; Von Rad, *Genesis*, 96.

24 Gunkel, *Genesis*, 23.

25 Reuven Kimelman, 'The seduction of Eve and the exegetical politics of gender', *Biblical Interpretation* 4 1996: 1–39, here 37. See also Bauks who thinks the verse is misplaced and better concluded the anthropogony (Michaeloa Bauks, 'Text and reception-historical reflections on transmissional and hermeneutical techniques', in Thomas Dozeman, Konrad Schmid and Baruch Schwartz, eds, *Genesis 2–3, The Pentateuch: International Perspectives on Current Research* [Tübingen: Mohr Siebeck, 2011], 139–168, here 147).

26 Westermann, *Genesis 1–11*, 267–268.

27 Any additional changes to the garden story by this author or the other proposed authors is outside the scope of this study.

Eve

This author names the woman Eve. The use of a proper noun in a narrative which routinely employs the common nouns 'man' and 'woman' strikes Gunkel as odd. He proposes that the verse was an inserted poem of non-Hebrew origins which included the name Eve.[28]

Westermann posits that 'it is quite conceivable that the woman receives her proper name in this new context of the genealogy; the appropriate occasion for this is the birth of a child'.[29] The proper name therefore derives from the change in her status when the female becomes a mother.

Some interpretations are more mythical in orientation. Skinner suggests that since the name of the woman is included in the story whereas the name of the man is not, that this preservation of a distinctive name derives from a more primitive theory of human origins in which the first mother represents the unity of the human race.[30] Howard Wallace wonders if the name is meant to foreshadow her role as the progenitress of mankind or if it is a remnant of an earlier garden story or both.[31] He expresses strong interest in the possible linkage between Eve and the serpent both in ancient times and in modern scholarship. Wallace approvingly quotes Philo's argument that once the words are stripped of their mythical sense what's left are Eve/Life and the serpent/pleasure (*De Agricultura XXII*. 96–97).[32] Scott Layton echoes the perception that the name is a symbolic author-construct as 'Life giver' befitting her role in the story and drawing on shared Hebrew roots with Amorite, Ugaritic, and Phoenician-Punic.[33]

As proposed here, the name is a symbolic construct by the author with political implications. Her name needs to be understood in conjunction with the other names Zadok introduces into the narrative, Seth and Enosh, as well as the descriptive phrase for her which he created. She represents Bathsheba because Zadok dates the origin of the kingdom to David and Bathsheba.

Mother of all living

The phrase 'mother of all living' to describe Eve has drawn extensive scholarly attention. Gunkel also finds the supreme honorific title for the woman odd as she does not have any children as yet.[34] Von Rad suggests that it is a name of honor which presupposes that she already had borne children.[35] Zevit cheekily observes that the woman could not have been the mother of *all* living things since only humans are involved. He may be too literal in his approach.[36]

---

28 Gunkel, *Genesis*, 22-23.
29 Westermann, *Genesis 1–11*, 268.
30 Skinner, *A Critical and Exegetical Commentary on Genesis*, 86.
31 Howard Wallace, *The Eden Narrative* (Atlanta: Scholars Press, 1985), 143.
32 Wallace, *The Eden Narrative*, 148.
33 Scott C. Layton, 'Remarks on the Canaanite origin of Eve', *CBQ* 59 1997: 22–32.
34 Gunkel, *Genesis*, 22–23.
35 Von Rad, *Genesis*, 96.
36 Ziony Zevit, *What Really Happened in the Garden of Eden?* (New Haven: Yale University Press, 2013), 229.

In keeping with Westermann's declaration that the story expresses Israel's separation from traditional mythic concerns, some scholars pursue those myths to highlight the similarities and the differences.

1. Primeval origin of Eve

Westermann uses the naming at birth in this genealogy to deliver a theological point on the Israelite religion. The title 'mother of all living' once joined to a Mother Earth figure that now has been separated from all mythical considerations and simply serves as an expression of the joy of motherhood. This perception is consistent with the understanding that the name 'Eve' drives from the origins of humanity, a topic of concern to him.[37]

2. Mesopotamian parallel to Eve

Scholars also have sought parallels in other mythical traditions, especially from Mesopotamia. Isaac Kikawada compares the Mesopotamian Atra-hasis epic and primeval Genesis 1–11 to posit parallel literary structures in opposition to each other. This dichotomy applies to the honorific name of the Mesopotamian goddess Mami as 'mistress of all the gods' who creates the mankind to do the work formerly done by the gods. Mami's legacy carries over to contrast Eve, 'mother of all the living' and Deborah 'mother in Israel' (Judg. 5: 7). Kikawada compares the male god Enki whose assistance is required for Mami to give birth with Yahweh's assistance to Eve. He concludes that the figure of Mami lay behind the figure of Eve who has been thoroughly demythologized as Westermann stated. Therefore the two beings may be paralleled, the one in the Mesopotamian mythic context and the other in the Israelite demythologized context.[38]

One significant difference emerges from the comparison. The offspring in both the Genesis and Mesopotamian accounts have to work but the nature of work reflects two different visions. The toil of tilling the land by the humans in the biblical account is for their own survival while in the Mesopotamian account it is to serve the gods, meaning to build a temple.

3. Canaanite parallel to Eve

Canaanite mythology brings the cultural parallels closer to home. Wallace acknowledges the various scholarly efforts to connect Eve to a goddess. He praises Kikawada for drawing attention to the similarity between Eve as the 'mother of all living' and Akkadian Mami, 'mistress of the gods' but does not think the connection has been substantiated. In an attempt to identify a connection, he scours the Punic evidence for Tannit and *rbt*, 'lady', following in the wake of a suggestion by Cross. The search proves successful as Wallace is able to trace it back to 'the lady, mistress of Byblos', to Ugarit, a Syrian coastal city, where Asherah, 'the lady who treads on the sea', is frequently referred to in connection with her children, and to Egypt and the goddess Qudshu.[39]

---

37   Westermann, *Genesis 1–11*, 268. See also, Driver, *The Book of Genesis*, 63.
38   Isaac M. Kikawada, 'Two notes on Eve', *JBL* 91 1972: 33–37, here 33.
39   Wallace, *The Eden Narrative*, 149.

Wallace then shifts the focus from Mami to Asherah. In Gen. 4: 1, Eve appears more as the wife of Yahweh than she does of Adam. However, instead of the Eve parallel generating the productivity and fertility associated with Asherah in Canaanite myth, the result is 'death, sterility, and hardship' in the Israelite world. For Wallace, this opposition provides insight into the function of the story: 'This reversal of expectations supports the identification of Eve and Asherah but it also suggests that the identification has been made with a polemical purpose in mind'. The association of Eve with Asherah would be particularly telling politically at a time when the king was dead and his wife ruled as Queen Mother and regent. He does not consider the possibility of two authors with opposite ideologies – the one who praises the woman/queen as Asherah as in this supplement and the one who curses the woman/queen for her hubris and arrogance in another supplement of curses.[40]

4. Good Eve/Bad Eve

The two faces of Eve may help elucidate the meaning of being the 'mother of all living'. This discrepancy between the cursed woman in Gen. 3: 16 and the praised Eve in Gen. 3: 20 has not gone unnoticed. A. J. Williams ponders the issue of why a seemingly positive expression about the woman is present given the context of the curses of the previous verses.[41] At first glance, the naming verse in Gen. 3: 20 lacks the pain one might expect from Gen. 3: 16:

> To the woman he said, 'I will greatly multiply your pain in childbearing; in pain you shall bring forth children, yet your desire shall be for your husband, and he shall rule over you.'

There is no indication in the birth stories in Gen. 4 of any pain in childbearing. For that matter, such pain in childbearing is not part of biblical narrative tradition. One wonders if Gen. 3: 16 even had been written yet and to whom it applied.

The naming of Eve in Gen. 3: 20 more closely resembles the naming which occurs in Gen. 2: 20 even though the actual names are not included there:

> The man gave names to all cattle, and to the birds of the air, and to every beast of the field; but for the man there was not found a helper fit for him.

If the naming of 3: 20 simply had followed the naming in 2: 20, the story would have flowed smoothly and its absence from chapter 3 would not have been noticed. Now the man has simply continued his naming responsibilities extending to the helper with whom he will be one. It's as if for Zadok the garden story from Gen. 2: 25 to 3: 19 did not exist, there is no Fall. When understood in this manner, then being the 'mother of all the living' is the way in which she helped the man, precisely the message which Zadok sought to deliver about Bathsheba's relationship to David that led to the divinely-sanctioned birth of Solomon.

The question of the nature of Eve is one that continues to challenge biblical interpreters. The presentation of this sample of the scholarly exegesis suggests the range of possibilities which have been proposed. For the purposes of this analysis two critical lessons emerge:

---

40 Wallace, *The Eden Narrative*, 152–159, quotations 159.
41 A. J. Williams, 'The relationship of Genesis 3: 20 to the Serpent', *ZAW* 89 1977: 357–374, here, 357.

1.   The interpretations tend to the mythical and generic as though they apply to all women and not political as if the text was about a specific individual at a specific place and point in time.

2.   Even though the interpreters are open to the idea of multiple writers, they have not grasped the possibility of there being divergent opinions about a single figure, in this case, a woman, the queen.

In the political context, the more appropriate issue is what does 'Eve the mother of all living' mean when a woman, Bathsheba, ruled as regent and her son Solomon was king.

Queen mother

To answer this question one needs to consider the role of the queen mother. The term *gĕbîrâ/gĕberet* has been translated multiple ways as 'lady', 'great lady', 'mistress', and 'queen', or as a term of respect for a powerful women. The term also was applied to Asherah making the *gĕbîrâ* her human counterpart. She is the mother to the king as Yahweh is the father. It also could be used for 'queen mother', or in signifying the most significant woman in the kingdom who might be the king's wife or even grandmother. This person plays a prominent position in genealogies as well as diplomacy and politics in the biblical narrative. The primary individual identified as 'queen mother' is Maacah (I Kings 15: 13; II Chr. 15: 16). In II Kings 10: 13, Judeans sent by King Ahaziah inquire of Jehu who has seized power in Israel in a coup about the 'sons of the queen mother'. That women is presumed to be Jezebel the mother of the assassinated Jehoram but also could refer to his wife. The phrase is not one which regularly recurs with each the genealogical description of each king of Israel and Judah (see Additional Readings: Queen Mother).

Based on the evidence from the ancient Near East, the queen mother could reign as regent, participate in the cult, and be involved in political, military, and economic affairs. Whether such powers were institutionalized for all queen mothers or were limited to specific individuals based on their personalities, skills, and circumstances is debated. To a great extent, the resolution does not matter here. With Bathsheba, Israel faced this condition for the first time and there was no precedent. Perhaps Bathsheba simply was 'an extraordinary woman who plays a pivotal role in the outcome' at 'an auspicious and critical moment' of first dynastic succession, a worthy wife to the extraordinary David.[42]

Bathsheba acted quite vigorously on behalf of her son.[43] Her actions should not be

---

42 See Nancy R. Bowen., 'The quest for the historical gĕbîrâ'. *CBQ* 64 2001: 597–618, here 606. In American mythical iconography the character Kathleen Turner plays in *Body Heat* comes to mind now set in the Beltway where she is battling for presidential power that she could not obtain on her own but only through a husband or son.

43 Niels-Erik A. Andreasen, "The Role of the Queen Mother in Israelite Society," *CBQ* 45 1983: 179–194, here 188–189. The suggestion has been made that Bathsheba not only acted politically on behalf of her son but did so literarily, meaning she is the author behind the image of David and accession to the throne of her son (see Baruch Halpern, *David's Secret Demons: Messiah, Murderer, Traitor, King* (Grand Rapids: Eerdmans, 2001), 46; Ernest Axel Knauf, 'The queen's story: Bathsheba, Maacah, Athaliah and the "Historia of Early Kings"', *Lectio Difficilor: European Electronic Journal for Feminist Exegesis* 2 2002) http://www.lectio.unibe. ch/02_2/axel.htm.

surprising. In the biblical narrative, she was introduced first as the daughter of Eliam and then as the wife of Uriah (II Sam. 11: 3). Randall C. Bailey notes that Eliam was one of David's mighty men (II Sam. 23: 34), and by implication a son of Ahithopel, one of David's advisors (see below). In other words, David did not suddenly gaze upon a stranger bathing on yonder roof; rather he was well aware that Bathsheba was part of a politically influential family. This awareness is consistent with his marriages to Michal and Abigail which advanced his political power. The logical conclusion is the biblical story of David and Bathsheba really is about a political marriage arising from deal-making and intrigue and not one of sexual lust. Bailey asks if the marriage occurred after the Absalom Revolt but without considering that Solomon might have been conceived and viewed as a replacement for the deceased beloved son. Bailey's approach agrees with the one taken in this study and indicates that the story of David and Bathsheba is another example of politics as literature, literature as politics. Bathsheba's connections more likely were to pre-Israelite Jerusalem than to Deborah's Israel.[44]

Eliam himself was the son of Ahithophel of Giloh (II Sam. 23: 34), one of a long list of cities assigned to the tribe of Judah (Josh. 15: 51). The site raises fascinating questions on the political factions in Jerusalem. Given its location about 4 miles (6.4 km) from Jerusalem, one might reasonably conclude that it was a daughter village within the Jebusite sphere of influence. Amihai Mazar proposed that the site is an early example of an Israelite fortification from its brief inhabitation during the 12th–11th century BCE when Israel emerged in history. Gösta Ahlström counters that it reflects an indigenous population. He claims that Mazar allowed the Bible to identify the site instead of basing his conclusions on the pottery and architecture which were Canaanite. For Ahlström, the Jebusite city required protection and therefore constructed this fortification.

Continued excavations uncovered an Iron I tower located outside the walls. Mazar notes similarities to other sites like Shiloh but cautions that the inhabitants of Giloh during this transition period might not have identified themselves as Israelites. He also sees resemblances to the Stepped Stone Structure in Jerusalem. Ziony Zevit proposes that the tower should be compared to the one at Mount Ebal and really is an altar. He rejects Volkmar Fritz' proposal of a farmstead due to its hilltop location. Ahlström previously had suggested the lack of accessible water had led to the site's abandonment. Hawkins concurs that the site was unsuitable for a permanent agricultural settlement and supports an at least partially military interpretation with tower as a form of migdol or fortress. All in all quite a lot of attention for a comparatively small short-lived site.

The implications are not so small. I have suggested that in the wake of the Egyptian withdrawal the Jebusites were responsible for their own security. Their efforts included building the Stepped Stone Structure and the Large Stone Structure. Ahlström's perception that the Jebusites built the site for defense and Mazar's view of similarities with the simultaneously-built Stepped Stone Structure support my interpretation. A Jebusite origin to the site for defense purposes makes it possible that the Eliam of Giloh belonged to a

---

44 Randall C. Bailey, *David in Love and War: The Pursuit of Power in 2 Samuel 10–12* (JSOT Sup. Series 75; Sheffield: Sheffield Academic Press, 1990), 87–88, 90, 122–123; Randall C. Bailey, 'Eliam', in *ABD* II: 459–460.

Jebusite military family that aligned with David. Beverly Cushman also raises the possibility that Giloh was a Canaanite city outside Jerusalem and controlled by the Jebusites. She posits that David incorporated Jebusite people and customs into his government while the people of his first kingdom remained in its capital Hebron. In this light, David's marriage to Bathsheba further supports the idea of her being not only from a politically influential family but a Jebusite one (see Additional Readings: Giloh).

Ahithophel joined Absalom's conspiracy against David. When his advice to Absalom was not followed he returned home and hanged himself (II Sam. 15: 12–17: 23). Perhaps Ahithophel had a premonition that if Absalom followed the deliberately bad advice proffered by David's agent Hushai that he would lose and he simply chose not to wait for the end. This storyline suggests that Bathsheba came from a politically active family and was a generation younger than David. As an ambitious woman, she now realized David was a better catch than the princes Amnon, Absalom, or Adonijah were. Bathsheba no more appeared as a bathing beauty babe in the sight of David out of nowhere than Tamar appeared on the roadside before Jacob by chance (Gen. 38: 14).

The narrative storyline continues to portray Bathsheba as a player in the political arena. She helped displace the eldest born son, Adonijah, for the youngest, her son Solomon. Taking a slightly different tact, Solomon was the eldest son born to the king in Jerusalem, a critical datum which may have helped generate local support in the capital city on his behalf. One of the goals here was to establish the primacy of Jerusalem over the other Canaanite cities so having the new king as someone born in the city with no allegiance to any other city helped.

As depicted, Bathsheba's actions may be favorably compared with those of Athirat in the Baal Cycle. In that story, the wife of El successfully intercedes on behalf of the younger son Baal against Yamm, the older heir apparent. Yamm acts too uppity in a direct attack on El's position and authority similar to Adonijah asserting his own kingship while David still lived (I Kings 1: 5–10). By contrast, Bathsheba goes through proper channels through the living king to secure the blessing of the younger son to be king or so the story goes. Whether she really did that is a separate matter. In the royal legitimacy spin, she claims to have followed procedure with one undermining twist. She took the Lord's name in vain, at least according to the author of Solomon's Illegitimate Rise to Power (I Kings 1).[45]

The transfer of mythical motifs, formats, to the human plane is characteristic of Israelite writing. Along the same lines, Adonijah later also beseeches the king through the agency of the mother, Bathsheba. He seeks Abishag the Shunammite, who had warmed David, to be his own wife. In this instance, Solomon has the wisdom to recognize that Adonijah really is asking for the kingdom and Adonijah pays with his life (I Kings. 2: 13–25). Following the murder of Adonijah, Solomon exiles the priest Abiathar and kills Joab, thus severing all ties to the people who had risen to power with David from the time of Saul. Friedman postulates that I Kings 2: 46 then concludes the extended J narrative when 'the kingdom was established in the hand of Solomon'. A similar conclusion is stated in I Kings 2: 12 when 'his kingdom was firmly established' when Solomon first ascends to the throne

---

45 For the Baal Cycle, see Pitard, 'The combat myth', 202–205.

after the death of David. The subsequent series of events seems to be from the author of Solomon's Legitimate Rise to Power.

Bathsheba's involvement with the rule of the kingdom did not cease the moment her son was recognized as king. She was far too vibrant to suddenly disappear from history. She did not go as far as Queen Athaliah as to assume direct power herself (II Kings 11), but she certainly would have served as a precedent for Jezebel following the death of Ahab. Maacah, daughter of Absalom, wife of King Rehoboam, mother of King Abijah, temporarily established the cult of Asherah presumably in the Jerusalem temple to Yahweh. Her efforts illustrate what a queen mother could accomplish. According to the narrative Maacah had been successful in establishing her religion in Jerusalem otherwise her son Asa would not have been able to cut and burn the image of the goddess (I Kings 15: 13). Asa's pro-Yahweh actions may be viewed as part of his effort to win back the northern kingdom by eliminating foreign-cult practices. One may postulate that the political faction supporting Asherah and the actions of Rehoboam had been displaced in favor of the pro-Yahweh priesthood, meaning the Jebusite Zadokites were out and the Israelite Benjaminite Aaronids were back in.[46]

The Asherah connection is significant. Maacah's action reveals extensive power attributed to this queen mother. It also raises the questions of what power the queen herself may have levied even while the king was alive. Bathsheba, wife of David, Pharaoh's daughter, wife of Solomon, Jezebel, wife of Ahab, and Athaliah, wife of Jehoram, may have been forces to reckon with during the reigns of their husbands. Susan Ackerman emphasizes the cultic responsibilities of the queen mother and recognizes the political implications. If the king is the adopted son of Yahweh, the divine father (Ps. 2: 7; II Sam. 7: 14), then who is the divine mother? Her answer is Asherah. The queen mother then as the earthly counterpart to the divine mother legitimates the rule of her son. The king may be dead but the queen mother lives and her physical presence substantiates the claim of her son to the crown. One should recognize that what to Ackerman is Judean royal ideology may have originated as Jebusite royal ideology now asserted following the coup which installed Solomon, an ideology not adhered to by Israelites.[47]

In Bathsheba's case there potentially is more to the Asherah connection than Ackerman realizes. Based on the suggestion that the pre-Israelite city of Jerusalem worshiped Elyon and Asherah, the goddess was no stranger to the residents in the time of Solomon. Zadok, the Jebusite priest of Elyon, was drawing on the traditional values of the Canaanite religion and introducing them into the KDB and Israel. Bathsheba was not simply an ambitious person maneuvering to have her son named king, she became the human representative of Asherah as well just as she had been costumed as the figure of Rahab in the story of Joshua fought the battle of Jericho in the KDB. Bathsheba as Asherah changed the religion of Israel to fit the Canaanite model precisely as Zadok intended to do. The danger of an Israelite king marrying a foreigner was her becoming the representative of a goddess as the king was the representative of a god.

---

46 Andreasen, 'The role of the queen mother', 181; Spanier, 'The queen mother', 194.
47 Susan Ackerman, "The Queen Mother and the Cult in Ancient Israel," *JBL* 112 1993: 385–401, here 400–401.

City

Zadok had more in mind than simply the queen mother, the new king and the temple (see below). There also was the issue of the capital city itself. The possible allusions of Eve to Asherah need to be understood within the geopolitical context even when expressed in mythic terms. Major cities commonly were perceived in feminine terms as the mother of the people. A personified city then might be worshiped as a goddess who was understood to be the consort of the male patron (warrior) god (see Isa 1: 21 Ezek 16 and 23 Hos 1: 2). The city was personified 26 times as *bat siyyôn* 'daughter of Zion' or 'virgin daughter of Zion' in the biblical narrative signifying its feminine identity.[48]

The likelihood is that pre-Israelite Jerusalem already had a feminine identity which automatically carried forward into the Israelite monarchy. The recognition of the Canaanite continuity may be considered the basis for the view that Jerusalem was feminine and would be protected by the male warrior deity. The deity now was Yahweh, represented by the ark, regardless of who the patron deity had been prior to Israelite rule. This development signified what would become an essential component of the Zion ideology with fatal consequences (see below).

Typically Jerusalem's special position is analyzed strictly within an Israelite context. Moshe Weinfeld acutely observes that the designation of Jerusalem as the capital of the kingdom and the building of a temple represented a profound innovation in the history of Israel. The former hill country people now had a royal dynasty and fixed building just like their neighbors. These revolutionary innovations for Israel required religious legitimation. Virgil Rabe foreshadows Weinfeld by asserting that just as there had been opposition to the innovation of the king so there was to the temple. He posits an ancient tent and Shiloh tradition which was preserved by a conservative prophetic circle. The ways of the Canaanite cities had become the ways of Israel after centuries of difference.[49]

These changes were equally a revolutionary innovation for Canaanite cities, too. Now they had to bow down before one Canaanite city. Jerusalem had been part of the Canaanite cacophony of the Amarna Age as cities in the 14th century BCE vied with each other for the favor of Pharaoh. These cities could cooperate when necessary if asked to do so. But to perpetually defer to one city above all others, one which previously held no exalted position in the land of Canaan, was to ask too much. Jerusalem was a comparatively small and isolated outpost removed from the main economic trade and military routes. Zadok needed to establish the primacy of his city in the land and to do so now that the warrior king who had created the kingdom was dead. A story alone was not sufficient but asserting that claim was a prerequisite for maintaining power.[50]

---

48 P. K. McCarter, 'Zion', in *DDD*, 940–942.

49 Virgil W. Rabe, 'Israelite opposition to the temple', *CBQ* 29 1967: 228–233; Moshe Weinfeld, 'Zion and Jerusalem as religious and political capital: ideology and Utopia', in Richard Elliott Friedman, ed., *The Poet and the Historian: Essays in Literature and Historical Biblical Criticism* (Harvard Semitic Studies 26; Chico, CA: Scholars Press, 1983) 75–115, here 75, 87–88, 114.

50 Other stories relate to this situation. In one a woman throws a millstone from the walls of Shechem that crushed Abimelech's skull (Judg. 9:53). In another, the wise woman of Abel of Bethmaacah, 'a city which is a mother in Israel' convinces the people to cut off the head of Sheba son of Birchi and throw it over the wall to Joab (II Sam. 20: 15–22). It is essential to know the authors to ascertain the message being delivered through

In one verse, the author of this supplement has changed the tenor of the narrative. He makes the woman the first named person in the narrative; the man is not named until afterwards. He links stories which had been separate although consecutive into one genealogical sequence. He situates the story in the garden, the cosmic center. Whereas the KDB had focused on the connection between the man and the woman as husband and wife in the garden, here the emphasis shifts to the mother role of the female. The story of Cain and Abel now will be about sons. In other words, the verse reflects the historical context in which it was written in the time of Bathsheba and Solomon. It proclaims the author's drive to legitimate the new political order in the land of Canaan based on Jerusalem, Elyon and Asherah.

Genesis 4: 1 Now the man knew Eve his wife, and she conceived and bore Cain

Westermann sees this verse as a new beginning.[51] It has no immediate connection with what precedes it is intended.[52] The action of the man with Eve, the mother of all living, is sexual as the verb 'to know' frequently is used in biblical texts.[53] This physical act occurs within a social context as the woman is identified as his wife.[54] One presumes that the designation as 'wife' draws on the garden text designating the woman as wife:

> **Genesis 2: 23** *Then the man said, 'This at last is bone of my bones and flesh of my flesh; she shall be called woman, because she was taken out of man'.* [24] *Therefore a man leaves his father and his mother and cleaves to his wife, and they become one flesh.*

Interestingly the proverb has not been fulfilled here unless one considers Yahweh the father of the man and that the man has left him. In a more physical context, the first biblical man to leave his father and his mother is Jacob when he leaves Isaac and Rebekah to eventually meet and marry Rachel (and Leah) in the third cycle.

The result of this knowing is a child named Cain. That figure already existed in the KDB story of Cain and Abel. Zadok provides no additional information about him about except to identify his parents. Cain now is in a subordinate position unlike in the KDB where he exists as an independent adult figure.

Genesis 4: 2 And again, she bore his brother Abel

The second son also already existed in the KDB story of Cain and Abel. Zadok provides no additional information about him either except to identify his parents. The father is not even mentioned here. This is about the least one could write about the birth of the son who will die. The use of the term 'again' has been cited by scholars as an unusual formulation.[55]

---

these symbolic figures.

51 Westermann, *Genesis 1–11*, 288.

52 Dillmann, *Genesis*, 183.

53 Dillmann, *Genesis*, 183; Speiser, *Genesis*, 32; Westermann, *Genesis 1–11*, 288–289.

54 Westermann, *Genesis 1–11*, 288–289.

55 Westermann, *Genesis 1–11*, 292. In the story of Jacob's second visit to Bethel (Gen. 35: 9), Baden notes the use of the word 'again' as a possible addition by the compiler (*The Composition of the Pentateuch*, 216).

Genesis 4: 25 And Adam knew his wife again, and she bore a son and called his name Seth

Scholars have speculated on why the father is referred to by his name instead of with the article as 'the man' as he normally has been. Westermann speculates that the redactor was responsible for the proper noun 'Adam' being used in 4: 25 while the common noun 'the man' was used elsewhere. Wifall contends that 'man' derives from the term used in the Amarna correspondence by Pharaoh to signify the king of the Canaanite city. This usage in Egyptian and Mesopotamian cultures as well as the application to David refers to an elevated class of people, an aristocracy or nobility. The implication is the man or Adam is king in his garden. Interestingly the most famous use of 'man' to designate the leader is with the man (*ish*) Moses (Num. 12: 3) although he is not a king but is meek, more so than any man (*adam*) on the face of the earth (*adamah*) suggesting a different author.[56]

One may speculate on the change in parental naming. Zadok differentiated among the sons. In the first two instances with the existing figures, the relationship is metaphorical and political, not biological and the critical relationship is to Bathsheba, the Queen Mother who rules over them. With the new figure added to narrative, Zadok sought to emphasize David's fatherhood of Solomon. Therefore he named the father so there was no misunderstanding or doubt.

The use of the term 'again' again has been cited as an unusual formulation.[57]

Seth, too, has been the subject of investigation over the derivation of his name. Delitzsch interprets the name to mean 'the appointed' since Seth is a gift of god to continue the line of promise. Dillmann interprets 'Seth' to mean 'setting or slip' for 'god has set for me another'. J. M. Miller postulates that Seth actually was the first born son and the sequence was revised in a redactional effort. As previously mentioned (see Chapter 3), von Rad connects the Sethites here to those in the Balaam tradition (Num. 24: 17) although the English versions sometimes use 'Sheth'.[58] The citation is part of a larger oracle with many relevant names:

> **Numbers 24: 15** *And he took up his discourse, and said, 'The oracle of Balaam the son of Beor, the oracle of the man whose eye is opened,* [16] *the oracle of him who hears the words of God [**El**], and knows the knowledge of the Most High [**Elyon**], who sees the vision of the Almighty [**Shaddai**], falling down, but having his eyes uncovered:* [17] *I see him, but not now; I behold him, but not nigh: a star shall come forth out of **Jacob**, and a scepter shall rise out of **Israel**; it shall crush the forehead of Moab, and break down all the sons of **Sheth** [**Seth**].* [18] *Edom shall be dispossessed, Seir also, his enemies, shall be dispossessed, while Israel does valiantly.* [19] *By Jacob shall dominion be exercised, and the survivors of cities be destroyed!'* [20] *Then he looked on Amalek, and took up his discourse, and said, 'Amalek was the first of the nations, but in the end he shall come to destruction'.* [21] *And he looked on the Kenite, and took up his discourse, and said, 'Enduring is your dwelling place, and your nest is set in the rock;* [22] *nevertheless **Kain** shall be wasted'.*

---

56 See Gunkel, *Genesis*, 54; Westermann, *Genesis 1–11*, 338; Wifall, 'Son of man', 335–336.

57 Westermann, *Genesis 1–11*, 338.

58 Delitzsch, *New Commentary on Genesis*, 201–202; Dillmann, *Genesis*, 208; J. M. Miller, 'The descendants of Cain', 165; von Rad, *Genesis*, 112.

In this oracle, one notes the presence of multiple variations on the name of the deity, the geographical setting in the Negev and Transjordan, the status of Balaam, the combination of Jacob and Israel, and the combination Seth and Cain but not Abel. Clearly this was a well-thought through composition by a skilled politician designed to touch all bases and resonate on many levels with a diverse audience of multiple constituencies.

One should recognize that Zadok's choice of the name Seth did not occur in a vacuum. The name may derive from the Transjordanian Shutu. They were part of a wilderness rivalry between the S(h)utu and the Kenites. The Suteans were part of the Amorite people along with the Haneans and the Yaminites. They were located primarily in the area of Babylonia and the Syrian steppe-pasture west of the Euphrates bend to Palmyra where they spent the winter months with their flocks. The Egyptians mentioned them in the Execration Texts. According to the Amarna Letters, king Labayu of Shechem hired some Suteans to serve as mercenaries. They appear in the Ugaritic texts as well. By the end of the 2nd millennium BCE, their name became intertwined with the Aramaeans who lived in the same areas (see Additional Readings: Suteans).

Based on the presumption that Jebusite Zadok authored the Seth story, his selection of the name 'Seth' needs to be understood within this context. The Sethites or S(h)utu or Suteans were neither Yaminites (Benjaminites) nor Kenites (Cainites). The Seth designation may have served as a means to establish an identity and legacy independent of other peoples within the kingdom of David and Solomon. One may reasonably speculate that the Jebusites were a clan within the Sutean tribe who settled in Jerusalem and served Pharaoh. Certainly it would be nice to have additional information. In its absence one is forced to speculate to create an historical reconstruction. One certainty is that the name would have meant something to the original audience. Zadok used the designation to assert an ancient legacy separate from the competing priesthoods battling for power in Jerusalem.

Genesis 4: 26 To Seth also[59] a son was born, and he called his name Enosh

The name of the son Enosh (אנוש) a collective noun for man as is *adam* (אדם)) raises the possibility that Enosh like Adam once began his own genealogy. The name has been understood to derive from the verb meaning to become weak or fail implying a feeble human.[60]

The dynastic line continues into the third generation through a son born a generation after the first two sons. The change element is that the father names the son who will succeed him. The mother has disappeared. Rehoboam's mother according to the biblical narrative was an Ammonite named Naamah (I Kings 14: 21 and 31). The name only appears elsewhere in the Kenite genealogy (Gen. 4: 22) (see Chapter 14). She is not a factor for this author. As a result, one should consider the possibility that this sentence was inserted into

---

59 This word may be an addition by a scribe since it is not present in the LXX but is in the SP and MT; see Ronald S. Hendel, *The Text of Genesis 1–11: Textual Studies and Critical Editions* (New York: Oxford University Press, 1998), 49.

60 Delitzsch, *New Commentary on Genesis*, 202; Dillmann, *Genesis*, 208; Westermann, *Genesis 1–11*, 339.

the supplement by Zadok (or his son Ahimaaz or Azariah) after the death of Bathsheba, the birth of Rehoboam, and the construction of the temple.

Zadok's disappearance from the story of Solomon has led to the previously mentioned interpretation that he died during Solomon's reign prior to the completion of the Temple. His death would have provided an opportunity for his son to carry on his polemical political writing. Indeed, Robert Pfeiffer proposes that Ahimaaz rather than Abiathar was the author of the story of Absalom's rebellion. He calls him the true 'father of history' half a millennium before Herodotus for creating history as an art in a genre that had not previously existed. Pfeiffer deems his work 'a masterpiece, unsurpassed in historicity psychological insight, literary style, and dramatic power', a depiction resembling that by Friedman for the author of the prose masterpiece. Undoubtedly the death of a political heavyweight who helped make the coup successful would have caused Bathsheba to consider who would now best serve her cause of remaining in power.[61]

Genesis 4: 26 At that time men began to call upon the name of Yahweh

This verse may be rendered literally as 'Then it was begun to call upon the name Yahweh' or 'then there began the calling on the name of Yahweh'.[62] The implication of this verse is that when Cain and Abel brought offerings to the Lord, they did not call his name. Perhaps the omission is because the offerings were an isolated interlude and not a recurring public proclamation.[63] Another possibility is Zadok could not change the story of Cain and Abel which was based on those offerings.

Robert Gordon comments that 'it was not the intention of the MT to associate the beginnings of Yahweh worship specifically with Enosh'.[64] If not Enosh the individual, then who? It would appear to be a more generic allusion to men as translated in the English versions. Now 'men', not an individual, call upon the name of Yahweh. A similar action by the 'sons of men' occurs in the story of the Tower of Babel. By contrast, those men definitely are not seeking to call upon the name of the Lord (see Chapter 14).

The act itself differs from the offerings of Cain and Abel. This calling should not be construed as an act of individuals alone in the woods or the wilderness praying to their deity. Rather it is a collective action by a group of men. The most obvious example of such an action is in a group religious ritual and not an individual burning-bush or prophetic revelation. Implied but not stated is that a collective religious ritual requires someone or a group to organize it, to ensure that everything is kosher in the worship of the Lord.

---

61 Robert Pfeiffer, *The Introduction to the Old Testament* (New York: Harpers & Brothers Publishers, 1948), 357; Rooke, *Zadok's Heirs*, 69.

62 See Robert P. Gordon, 'Who "began to call on the name of the Lord" in Genesis 4: 26B?: The MT and the versions', in Iain Provan and Mark J. Boda, eds, *Let Us Go Up to Zion: Essays in Honour of H. G. M. Williamson on the Occasion of his Sixty-Fifth Birthday* (SVT 153; Leiden: Brill, 2012), 57–68, here 66; Samuel Sandmel, 'Genesis 4: 26b', *HUCA* 32 1961: 19–29, here 19.

63 Dillmann, *Genesis*, 209.

64 Gordon, 'Who "began to call on the name of the Lord" in Genesis 4: 26B?', 66.

Augustus Pfeiffer in 1679 in *Dubia Vexata* may have been the first to recognize that the true meaning signaled the formal commencement of a full-pledged divine cult of Yahweh including public display.[65]

This worship of Yahweh in supposedly primeval times has proved troubling in a way that the offerings of Cain and Abel to Yahweh have not. For Gunkel, the verse demonstrates the true antiquity of the worship of Yahweh:

> 'This note is extremely interesting from a religiohistorical standpoint. It contradicts, at least in wording, the usual assertion (Exod 3: 4; 6: 12) that Moses was the first to employ the name Yahweh. We cannot state the reason for associating the name Yahweh with Enosh. We have here the oldest deliberation about the age of Yahweh worship, and the impression reflected in this note that the same Yahweh traces back to the primeval period and is older than Moses and the people Israel is assuredly correct.'[66]

Westermann similarly locates the setting in primeval times differentiated from the Exodus. He uses this distinction to separate the worship of Yahweh by Israel and the origin of religion among all people which is a part of the human experience dating back to primeval times. They are not calling on the God of Israel but the God who is significant for all humanity.[67]

Speiser suggests a 'plausible solution'. He posits an original worship of Yahweh confined to 'a small body of searchers under the aegis of the patriarchs' which was recorded by J. When Moses fashioned Israel 'out of an amorphous conglomerate of sundry ethnic and tribal elements', he used the religion of the forefathers tied to Promised Land, the religion of the patriarchs who worshiped Moses. As a result, Speiser differentiates the personal revelation to Moses as part of the Exodus nation-building from the older religion of the 'patriarchal pioneers'.[68]

By contrast, J. M. Miller asserts that the worship of Yahweh by name from the very earliest time is one of the distinguishing characteristics of J.[69]

Perhaps Samuel Sandmel has the most constructive advice for the discrepancy on Enosh and Moses on the beginning of the worship of Yahweh by name: 'Of course, the verse clashes. But why emend the text?'[70] Exactly right. Instead of doing everything imaginable to avoid the plain truth of the text, one should recognize that two different views are being expressed. The story set in the past is about the present. The verse represents part of Zadok's attempt to usurp Israel and its religion by undermining it. Zadok wants David and the temple to mark the origin of the kingdom in the land of Canaan and not Moses and the covenant to mark the promise of the land of Canaan to the people Israel.

Gordon observes that calling on the name of the Lord also is something individuals in the biblical narrative do elsewhere.[71] Abraham is the first:

---

65 Cited in Sandmel, 'Genesis 4: 26b', 24.
66 Gunkel, *Genesis*, 54. For the name 'Yahweh' see Chapter 3.
67 Westermann, *Genesis 1–11*, 339, 594, citing the work of Delitzsch, Dillmann, and Gunkel; see also von Rad, *Genesis*, 113.
68 Speiser, *Genesis*, 37–38.
69 J. M. Miller, 'The descendants of Cain', 165.
70 Sandmel, 'Genesis 4: 26b', 29.
71 Gordon, 'Who "began to call on the name of the Lord" in Genesis 4: 26B?', 63–64.

> **Genesis 12: 8** *Thence he removed to the mountain on the east of Bethel, and pitched his tent, with Bethel on the west and Ai on the east; and there he built an altar to Yahweh and called on the name Yahweh.*

Shortly afterwards he does it again:

> **Genesis 13: 3** *And he journeyed on from the Negeb as far as Bethel, to the place where his tent had been at the beginning, between Bethel and Ai, ⁴ to the place where he had made an altar at the first; and there Abram called on the name Yahweh.*

His final time adds some new geographic and political information:

> **Genesis 21: 32** *So they made a covenant at Beersheba. Then Abimelech and Phicol the commander of his army rose up and returned to the land of the Philistines. ³³ Abraham planted a tamarisk tree in Beersheba, and called there on the name Yahweh, the Everlasting [Olam] God.³⁴ And Abraham sojourned many days in the land of the Philistines.*

Isaac also calls on the name of the Lord similar to the previous example of Abraham:

> **Genesis 26:22** *And he moved from there and dug another well, and over that they did not quarrel; so he called its name Rehoboth, saying, 'For now Yahweh has made room for us, and we shall be fruitful in the land'. ²³ From there he went up to Beersheba. ²⁴ And Yahweh appeared to him the same night and said, 'I am the God of Abraham your father; fear not, for I am with you and will bless you and multiply your descendants for my servant Abraham's sake'. ²⁵ So he built an altar there and called upon the name Yahweh, and pitched his tent there. And there Isaac's servants dug a well.*

The alpha-male marking of turf with altars to Yahweh screams of royal political assertions. These political machinations involving the sites of Bethel and Beersheba and the relationship with the Philistines were not part of Zadok's message in his Seth supplement. None the less, these examples of individuals calling on the name of the Lord indicate that the theological significance of calling the name of Yahweh was not the primary focus as the exegetes presume. The patriarchal examples announce the royal marking turf of the kingdom of Yahweh and making alliances outside that kingdom. For Zadok, the turf he wished to mark was the temple at Jerusalem as the cosmic center of the kingdom David had created.

The political approach yields a different interpretation than the mythical one when examining the name that the people are calling. According to traditional exegesis, since the story is set in primeval times it must refer to worship of Yahweh by people in primeval times long before Moses. However, the story is not set in or about primeval times but is about the time in which it was written as the audience knew. That realization changes the approach to understanding this verse.

Zadok's use of 'Yahweh' in the narrative should not be viewed in isolation from the other son stories. The presence of 'Yahweh' in KDB's first cycle of stories or J is fairly well controlled. As a general rule, the narrator employs the name but the characters in the story do not. In other words, in KDB's first cycle, the name Yahweh typically is written but not spoken. As a corollary, the usage tends to be as subject-verb where Yahweh speaks to a human being or acts in some capacity. Deviations from this pattern are few and noticeable.[72]

---

72 Another theory is that humans in J always knew the name of God but did not use it until they were expelled

Genesis 4: 1 *Now Adam knew Eve his wife, and she conceived and bore Cain, saying, 'I have gotten a man with the help of Yahweh'.*

Genesis 4: 26 *To Seth also a son was born, and he called his name Enosh. At that time men began to call upon the name of Yahweh.*

Genesis 5: 29 *and called his name Noah, saying, 'Out of the ground which Yahweh has cursed this one shall bring us relief from our work and from the toil of our hands'.*

Genesis 9: 26 *He [Noah] also said, 'Blessed by Yahweh my God be Shem; and let Canaan be his slave'.*

Genesis 10: 9 *He was a mighty hunter before Yahweh; therefore it is said, 'Like Nimrod a mighty hunter before the Yahweh'.*

There are only these five examples in Gen. 1–11 where the word 'Yahweh' is used by humans.

These examples shed light on the writers who supplemented the original narrative. All five examples of the use of Yahweh here derive from additions to the original KDB narrative. Each addition is not part of some folk or mythical heritage from hoary antiquity but part of the battle for power in the time of the monarchy and the temple where people began to call the name of Yahweh at a set location with a temple priesthood. Only three people use the name Yahweh in speech: Eve giving birth to Cain, the one who names his son Noah, and Noah blessing Shem and cursing Canaan. In the Nimrod example, people collectively speak the name. Quotation marks are used in these four examples in accordance with the writing conventions today. It is reasonable to conclude that these four examples all are the work of a single author as part of his overall vision in supplementing the narrative (see Chapter 13). The Seth usage belongs to Zadok, the author who sought to legitimize the rule of Solomon and the building of the temple on the threshing floor which David had purchased from Araunah the Jebusite.

Once one accepts that these uses of the name 'Yahweh' are part of a political debate, a second conundrum is resolved as well. The verse has to do with the origin of the men who call the name of the Lord and the city/temple where the organized religion is practiced. The author is not a telling a story about the origins of human civilization. He is writing about the direction of the new kingdom of David in the city of Jerusalem. That city had been around 'forever'. It already was populated and built. It already worshiped Elyon and his consort Asherah. The change is not that a city, a population, and a temple existed where none had before. Rather the change is the temple to Yahweh, an organized religion based on Yahweh, now existed where it had not before. Previously, we have seen a story where the men of Shechem 'converted' to Yahweh by being circumcised (see Chapter 8). Here the men of Jebus acknowledge Yahweh as their deity.

The conundrum for rabbis, church fathers, priests, ministers, and biblical scholars about the origin of these men who began to call upon the name of Yahweh was no mystery to the original Jebusite audience. They knew the story was about their present and not primeval times. They were hearing the story at the new temple in Jerusalem built by Solomon, the Jerusalem-born king. The audience was 'the [Jebusite] men'. The Seth addition was a

from the garden (Robert S. Kawashima, '*Homo faber* in J's Primeval History', *ZAW* 116 2004: 483–501, here 496).

story of dynastic and temple legitimation perhaps first told when the Solomon temple was inaugurated or shortly thereafter. How convincing a story of legitimation it was beyond that immediate audience is a separate matter as will be seen with 'the men' who build the Tower of Babel.

The Canaanite population consisted of more than just adult men. Within the male population, there was a special group of warriors. Their allegiance was part of the story Zadok told. Scholars tend to see the story of the sons of God as a unity. This view is incorrect. It began here as a single verse authored by Zadok in his supplement to the KDB. The remaining verses were by other authors (see Chapters 13 and 14).[73]

> **Genesis 6: 4** *The Nephilim were on the earth in those days. These were the mighty men that were of old, the men of renown.*

The idea that Gen. 6: 4 is somehow out of place in its present position is not a new one. Gunkel perceives Gen. 6: 4a to have been added to the story of the sons of God with no inner coherence, like a parenthetical note or an antiquarian gloss. Westermann interprets Gen. 6: 4 as not being a continuation of the sons of God verses as handed down. For him, the verse is not a unity. He sees 4b as the principal sentence in the original narrative context. Another possibility is that originally verse 3 followed verse 4.[74]

The two subjects of the lone verse then are the Nephilim and the mighty men or *gibborim*. These two terms are connected. Are they one and the same? Is one a subset of the other, meaning all Nephilim are *gibborim* but others could be as well? The English translations suggest that relationship as one is capitalized like a proper noun and the other is lower case as a common noun. The challenge is to determine what these terms meant at the time when Zadok introduced into the narrative. What message was he seeking to deliver?

Nephilim

As proposed here, these Nephilim are not connected to the sons of God as those verses had not yet been written. The Nephilim existed prior to the sons of God and are more naturally associated with the mighty men.[75] They definitively are linked to pre-Israelite Canaan. During the Exodus, when the spies return from the land of Canaan and report to Moses, they say:

> **Num. 13: 31** *'We are not able to go up against the people; for they are stronger than we ...*[32] *The land, through which we have gone, to spy it out, is a land that devours its inhabitants; and all*

---

73 Marc Vervenne, 'All they need is love: once more Genesis 6: 1–4', in Jon Davies, Graham Harvey and Wilfred G. E. Watson, eds, *Words Remembered, Texts Renewed: Essays in Honour of John F. A. Sawyer* (JSOT Sup. Series 195; Sheffield: Sheffield Academic Press, 1995), 19–40, here 30–40.

74 Gunkel, *Genesis*, 58; Kraeling, 'The significance and origins of Gen. 6: 1-4', 197, 199 Westermann, *Genesis 1–11*, 366, 377–378. See also J. T. A. G. M. Van Ruiten, 'The interpretation of the flood story in the Book of Jubilees', in Florentino Garcia Martinez and Gerard P. Luttikhurzen, *Interpretations of the Flood* (TBN 1; Leiden: Brill, 1998), 66–85, here 83.

75 Day, *From Creation to Babel*, 82–83.

*the people that we saw in it are men of great stature. [33] And there we saw the **Nephilim** … and we seemed to ourselves like grasshoppers, and so we seemed to them.'*

These Nephilim not only are located in the land of Canaan, they are identified as enemies of Israel. Baruch Levine notes that 'what is most significant about these traditions [of the Nephilim, Rephaim, and Anakites] is consistent identification of these almost mythic creatures as non-Israelite, as having descended from other groups, some identifiable and others not, but decidedly not from Israelite ancestors.'[76] In other words, they are non-Yahweh worshiping peoples of the land of Canaan who opposed Israel (see Additional Readings: Nephilim).

The Rephaim are known from Ugaritic literature where they are identified as ancestors of the Ugaritic kings. They are some of the kings and heroes summoned to appear at a coronation to legitimate the new king. They arrive at the threshing floor and participate in a harvest feast. The Rephaim also have been linked to the Rabbeans tribe within the Suteans, The presence of King Og, the last of the Rephaim kings with his iron bed (Deut. 3: 11), the Valley of Rephaim in major battles involving Abraham (Gen. 14: 5) and David (II Sam. 5: 18, 22 and 23: 13) support the notion that a sub-group of Suteans had settled in the land on both sides of the Jordan and left their mark (see Additional Readings: Rephaim).[77]

Although the Nephilim and the Rephaim are not directly connected in the biblical text or in the archaeological record, there does seem to link between them. Ezekiel says:

> **Ezek. 32: 27** *And they do not lie with the **fallen mighty men** of old who went down to Sheol with their weapons of war, whose swords were laid under their heads, and whose shields are upon their bones; for the terror of the mighty men was in the land of the living.*

The application of the term *nöplîm* or 'fallen' with the *npl* root suggests the Nephilim are dead warrior heroes of old though not necessarily kings like the Rephaim.[78]

The existence of these fallen heroes before and after the Flood raises questions. William Nelson ponders if there might be two traditions about the Nephilim. Hendel posits an author aware of multiple and inconsistent traditions who was constrained by the expectations of the audience to render such oral traditions consistent when written. He baldly declares, 'The function of the Nephilim in Israelite tradition, I submit, is to die [in the Flood]'. Helge Kvanvig understands the story as being 'in the time of the Nephilim' as the setting in Gen. 12: 6b is 'in the time of the Canaanites' and Gen. 13: 7b is 'in the time of the Canaanites and Perizzites'. Still one must wonder why this emphasis on people who supposedly would have been wiped away by the Flood. Driver logically concludes that Dillmann and other commentators are correct in suggesting the story was written without reference to the Flood

---

76 Baruch A. Levine, *Numbers 1–20* (New York: Doubleday, 1993), 378. Anak adds another level to the editorial process and necessitates analyzing the wilderness and conquest traditions in detail which are outside the scope of this study; see David Carr, 'The Moses story: literary-historical reflections', *Hebrew Bible and Ancient Israel* 1 2012: 7–36, here 16; Levine, *Numbers 1–20*, 355, 359.

77 Levine, *Numbers 1–20*, 378.

78 It should be noted that when Pharaoh Seti referred to 'the fallen-ones' he was referring to the 'Shasu [who] are plotting rebellion'. His triumphant expression of victory over these people hardly suggests a heroic image; see Morris, *The Architecture of Imperialism*, 347.

just as the story of the sons of Cain was (Gen. 4: 17–24). Building on these conclusions, one may also aver that the Flood story had not yet acquired its universal or global dimension. When Zadok introduced the Nephilim into the KDB the deluge was still local.[79]

All these Nephilim permutations fall by the wayside in the proposed reconstruction here. This one verse addition in Gen. 6: 4 follows on the sons of Seth supplement which the author already had written. Both texts occurred as part of a single writing which clearly flow together in one seamless story. There are men in the capital who called the name of Yahweh. Then there are these beings called the Nephilim, mighty men who have acquired a name for themselves. They were not an archaic reference which required explanation. Zadok introduced and defined the Nephilim to support his anti-Israelite political agenda where the temple supplants the Exodus as the basis of Israelite identity. He is reaching out to the Canaanite warrior class throughout the land and especially in Jerusalem to resist Israel in the present as they had done in the past on behalf of Pharaoh when Israel first emerged in the land. His supplement legitimates the Solomon, the temple, and the mighty men who helped install Solomon as the new king.[80]

Mighty men

The Nephilim are *gibborim* or 'mighty men'. Westermann considers the origin of the *gibborim* to be the goal of the narrative. He thinks that the 'narrator wants to introduce a class that is utterly superior; persons who are so powerful that, when they a desire a woman because of her beauty, they are not confined by the limits that restrain ordinary mortals'. He claims kings belong to this class of people who see and take citing Pharaoh with Sarah and David with Bathsheba. James Kugel calls them 'ancient superheroes' and agrees that the original purpose of the insertion was to celebrate their birth. Hendel suggests the reference to the men of renown 'presumably triggered well-known associations that are now obscure'. Who were the warriors of renown who were remembered? For Israel, Abram who battled the kings from the east (Gen. 14)? Jacob who took unidentified land from the Amorites by sword and bow (Gen. 48: 22)? Others?[81]

In the biblical tradition, the *gibbor* and *gibborim* are warriors, military leaders and elite fighting men. The named individuals who comprise this vaunted group consist of Nimrod (Gen. 10: 8; see Chapter 6), the first one, Gideon (Judg. 6: 12), Jephthah (Judg. 11: 1),

---

79 Driver, *The Book of Genesis*, 82; Hendel, 'The Nephilim were on earth', 23; Helge S. Kvanvig, 'Gen. 6, 1–4 as an antediluvian event', *SJOT* 16 2002: 79–112, here 83; William B. Nelson, Jr. 'Nephilim', in David Noel Freedman, ed., *Dictionary of the Bible* (Grand Rapids: Eerdmans, 2000), 958–959, here 959.

80 Driver adheres to this more traditional approach. For people of a religious background, the mythic provides an acceptable option. These semi-divine beings did intermarry and produce a race of supposed prehistoric giants that so many peoples had in their traditions. Normally the Hebrew narrators were able to strip the mythological tinge from the folklore but for unknown reasons it remains discernible here (Driver, *The Book of Genesis*, 83).

81 Hendel, 'The Nephilim were on earth', 16; James Kugel, 'The descent of the wicked angels and the persistence of evils', in Gary A. Anderson and Joel Kaminsky, eds, *The Call of Abraham: Essays on the Election of Israel in Honor of Jon D. Levenson* (Notre Dame, IN: University of Notre Dame Press, 2013), 210–235, here 229; Westermann, *Genesis 1–11*, 365, 367, quotation from 367.

Kish but not his son Saul (I Sam. 9: 1), David (II Sam. 17: 10) and the Aramaean Naaman who also is a man of valor (II Kings 5: 1). Valor frequently is associated with a mighty man or men (Josh. 6: 2, 8: 3, 10: 7; Judges 6: 2: II Kings 5: 1 and 24: 14; I Chr.12: 21, 25, 28, 30; II Chr.14: 8; 17:13, 14, 15, 16, 25: 6, 26: 12; Neh.11: 14 and other times simply with a man or men Deut. 3: 18; Josh.1: 4; Judg. 20: 44, 46; I Sam. 10: 26 and 16: 18; II Kings 24: 16; II Chr. 26: 17 and 28: 6.

A group of three warriors of David warrant this designation five times in a single story (II Sam. 23: 8, 9, 16, 17, and 22). Coxon identified the *gibborim* as being 'clearly a race apart from David's champions' under the impression because the story is set in the past therefore it is about the past, as mythical and not historical. Na'aman offers a more institutional explanation. He claims the mighty men of David listed in II Sam. 23 were an officer's rooster which should be dated to David's rule in Jerusalem. This corps first crystalized in the wilderness and became the nucleus for the professional army of the king. He probably is correct in that the term was a generic one employed to designate certain warriors in any army.[82]

Mighty men can fight for and against Israel. They are with Joshua as mighty men of valor (Josh. 8: 3; 10: 7) and against him from the Canaanite cities of Jericho (Josh. 6: 2) and Gibeon (Josh. 10: 2). In addition to the above examples, they frequently appear in stories related to David (II Sam. 10: 7; II Sam. 16: 6, II Sam. 17: 8; II Sam. 20: 7; and I 1: 8, 10) where they help install Solomon at the expense of Adonijah. Later on mighty men of valor are captured by Nebuchadnezzar in the fall of Jerusalem (II Kings 24: 14), valiant to the end.

Unlike proper-noun the term 'Nephilim', the common-noun 'mighty men' was a neutral term applicable to any individual who had acquired a certain level of martial proficiency. The biblical examples of mighty men demonstrate that the term was applied collectively to the warriors who fought for Israel and against Israel. The term was not 'Israelite' in origin. Its application to the armed forces of Jericho and Gibeon suggest it should be understood within the context of the Canaanite culture. These warriors were the top guns of their times, not mythical beings, and there is no trace of euhemerism. All of these mighty men in the biblical texts are human. The humanity of the mighty men further supports the suggestion that all the participants in the sons of God story in Gen. 6: 1-4 should be regarded as human and not mythical or divine beings in some way.

Men of renown

The additional characteristic of 'men of renown' equaling 'men of name' elevates these mighty men to a legendary level. The human effort to acquire a 'name', to become a person of renown, whom others remembered after having fallen and died, may be considered a human response to the absence of eternal life. Warriors across time and space are familiar with this desire. In 2012, an ex-marine explaining why he lived in Hollywood said:

---

82 P. W. Coxon, 'Gibborim', in *DDD*, 345–346; Nadav Na'aman, 'The list of David's officers (šālîšîm)', *VT* 38 1988: 71–79).

'They're going to be making our movies. This is why I came out [to Hollywood]. I wanted to make sure the story's told right. We have to tell the story. We're the ones who know Our Fallen. We have to tell it 'cause this will dictate what happens with the next generation.'

Crockett, Custer, Montcalm, and Montgomery are fallen warriors from American history who live on in paintings, songs, stories, and movies; Leonidas, Spartacus, and Wallace are examples of fallen warriors from outside American history who live on in American culture. The fallen ones were remembered in ancient times as they are today.[83]

While the desire may be universal the manifestation of it tends to be limited. We have Flanders Field and Arlington Cemetery, but in ancient times one fallen hero stands out above the crowd, the hero warrior who became king. To make a 'name' for one's self seems to have been standard operating procedure among the kings of the ancient Near East from the moment writing was invented. Without kings making their name great, Egyptian, Sumerian, Akkadian, Amorite, Kassite, Assyrian, and Babylonian civilizations just would be a lot of plain tombs, pottery, and contracts. Apparently these Canaanite warriors, presumably including kings as well, partook of the same boasting. Other than the warrior shepherds Abram and Jacob from the 2nd millennium BCE, and later warriors like Joshua, Gideon, Baraq, Jephthah, Saul, and David, the land of Canaan is bereft of names of warrior heroes whose names are remembered although they must have existed (Shamgar?).

Who were the Nephilim and gibborim?

The question then must be raised as to the message Zadok was delivering through the introduction of the Nephilim into the KDB. Walter Wifall's suggestion that the *gibborim* or mighty men and *nephilim* originally were pre-Israelite princes of Canaanite city-states from the 2nd millennium BCE bears notice if expanded to include the entire military aristocracy of these political entities.[84] Kugel declares that the 'fame of these ancient heroes was no doubt celebrated in song and story, even if, for one reason or another, most of their legends never made it into the final version of the Bible's history'.[85] A continuation of the use of these terms and concepts into the Hebrew Bible may be seen in David's lament for the fallen Saul and Jonathan in II Sam. 1:

[19] *'Thy glory, O Israel, is slain upon thy high places! How are the **mighty fallen!**...'*

[25] *'How are the **mighty fallen** in the midst of the battle!' Jonathan lies slain upon thy high places.*

[27] *'How are the **mighty fallen**, and the weapons of war perished!'*

These terms therefore acquire a 'band of brothers' tenor among fellow warriors, a bond that unites them despite all other considerations.

---

83 Kraeling, 'The significance and origins of Gen. 6: 1–4', 203; Michael Ware, 'Charlie Sheen's last stand', *Newsweek* July 2 and 9, 2012, 40–45, here 44.

84 Walter Wifall, 'Gen. 6: 1–4 – a royal Davidic myth', *BTB* 5 1975: 294–301, here 298 and 300. See also Hendel, 'Of demigods and the deluge', 23, for a Late Bronze period of oral diffusion.

85 James Kugel, 'The descent of the wicked angels and the persistence of evils', 219.

In earlier times such warriors might have been considered 'maryannu' (see Additional Readings: Maryannu). In later times one might refer to them as knights, not for their equipment but for their position within the military.[86] Perhaps today the term 'special forces' would be more appropriate. These are superbly trained fighting men in the weapons of their time who sometimes assume political leadership positions in recognition of their skill. David was deemed an 'expert in war' (II Sam. 17: 8). Subsequent to Nimrod, who was the first, the designation most frequently is used first for David and then for Joshua. So when the audience heard about a mighty man it is quite possible it would think of Israelites Joshua and David as the most recent examples depending on with what other stories it had heard or that were familiar.[87]

In this instance, Zadok specifically calls attention to one group of mighty men, the Nephilim. These Nephilim were from days of yore prior to the time Israel had its own kings and warrior class. Then Israel's own deceased warrior king (Saul) could be deemed fallen. Zadok promotes as heroes the fallen warriors who were part of the Canaanite legacy. They had resisted the Israelites who had violated the land. The Exodus story was a battlefield.

Conclusion

Zadok's supplement to the first cycle of the KDB in these texts was designed to fulfill his political objectives.

1. Legitimize queen-mother Bathsheba as regent – accomplished through the designation of the woman in the garden as Eve, mother of the living dynasty.
2. Legitimize the Davidic dynasty – accomplished by creating a new dynastic line where Absalom is replaced by a new beloved of David and Adonijah is murdered.
3. Legitimize the construction of a temple – accomplished by dedicating the temple to Yahweh even though it is in a Jebusite city and on a Jebusite site.
4. Ensure his priesthood received its cut of the royal revenues – to be accomplished via a supplement to the KDB second cycle where the priest-king of Salem is tithed (Gen. 14: 18–21).
5. Replace enmity with Egypt with alliance – accomplished by arranging a marriage between Pharaoh's daughter and Solomon (I Kings 3: 1).
6. Diminish the status of the Israelites – accomplished by praising the Nephilim who intimidated them, by referring to Israel as Jacob, and by reducing Israel to being only one of the peoples of the land and not the dominant one (Deut. 32: 8–9).
7. Diminish the status of Yahweh – accomplished by making him subordinate to Elyon, the creator deity of Jerusalem (Deut 32: 8–9).

---

86 See Kraeling, 'The significance and origins of Gen. 6: 1–4', 196. However, even though he wrote of an 'age when a sort of knighthood was in flower', he later referred to them as 'a Western adaptation of the Babylonian tradition of the antediluvian kings' (200).

87 For the mighty men of David see Moishe Garseil, 'David's elite warriors and their exploits in the Books of Samuel and Chronicles', *JHS* 11/5 2011: 1–28, http://www.jhsonline.org; Benjamin Mazar, 'The military élite of King David', *VT* 13 1963: 310–320; Na'aman, 'The list of David's officers (šālîšîm)', 71–79.

Zadok was not subtle about targeting the Israelites of his own time. Presumably he had the military muscle of the current Nephilim or warrior elite on his side. The Nephilim in the present stood with Solomon, Bathsheba, and Zadok at the temple. For this author, these warriors were heroes both in past and in the present. Through the achievement of David and the murder of his general Joab, there were no military forces in the land to challenge Solomon. The constructions attributed to Solomon at Megiddo, Hazor, and Gezer (I Kings 9: 15) may have been more for controlling the domestic population than defending it against external invasion.[88] This author wrote from a politically secure position if he had the audacity to frontally challenge the larger Israelite community. He sought to hijack the Israelite kingdom with its Moses, Exodus, covenant basis and transform it in a Canaanite one centered at his temple in Jerusalem and backed by the Nephilim. Responses to such provocative claims were inevitable.

---

88 Halpern considers Solomon to have been an Egyptian vassal and the Jerusalem elite to have had an Egyptianizing concept of the monarchy. Therefore it would have made sense for Solomon to have adopted the administrative framework previously employed by the Egyptian empire when it ruled Canaan; see *David's Secret Demons.* 219, 291, 397–398. The control points to dominate the land did not change from Egyptian Pharaohs to the Philistines to Solomon.

Chapter 12

ABIATHAR: SHILOH J

Abiathar was a priest of Shiloh where the ark had been located prior to its capture by the Philistines. Everything in this sentence is subject to questioning. As will be seen, the trauma associated with the loss and destruction of the ark remained part of the Israelite legacy. In the approach taken here, that trauma may have been embellished, manipulated, and spun, but it was not invented. To understand his supplement to the KBD, one must understand the context in which it was written. Even before his confrontation with Zadok in Jerusalem over David's successor, he was in alliance with David in a confrontation against Saul. Abiathar's life experiences and his current situation in life directly contributed to what he was trying to accomplish through his writings both before and after David died.

Shiloh

Shiloh looms large in the history of early Israel. The archaeology of Shiloh provides a fascinating story in its own right. The twisting and turning by Israel Finkelstein to be true to the discipline of archaeology and to his personal values would make any contortionist proud. He begins one article with the affirmative declaration that 'there is nothing in the biblical text that can shed light on the history of Canaan in the early Iron I'. The archaeology of the Shiloh site reveals that it had been destroyed and abandoned in the late Iron I (meaning around 1050 BCE). He deems the biblically-described battle of Eben-ezer dated to that time as geographically realistic as recounted in I Sam. 4 and he is unable to provide an explanation of who did it or why it occurred. Nor can he can archaeologically identify the deity worshiped at the highland shrines in the late Iron I which the Bible does as Yahweh.

Finkelstein then acknowledges that regardless of the deity of the author of this story, 'there is no escape, then from the conclusion that there was a strong memory in Judah ... of an early devastated cult place at Shiloh' which the refugees from the destroyed northern kingdom brought with to Jerusalem after 722 BCE. He concludes, 'one issue seems to be quite certain – that the Shiloh traditions preserve old memories...'. He expresses similar ideas another 8 years later. It is difficult to imagine a scholar of Egypt, Assyria, Babylonia, Greece or Rome engaging in such a comparable tortuous fight with himself as Finkelstein does to avoid categorically stating that there was a Yahweh sanctuary at Shiloh which was destroyed by the Philistines in the late Iron I period as the biblical narrative says.[1]

---

1   Israel Finkelstein, 'Shiloh: twenty years later', in Niels Peter Lemche, Morgen Müller and Thomas L Thompson, eds, *Historie og konstruktion: festskrift til Nils Peter Lemche i anledning af 60 års fødselsdagen den*

When Israel first emerged in history in the land of Canaan, it would have been presumptuous for it to proclaim that its deity was king of the land. Pharaoh still ruled Canaan. The campaigns into Canaan of Merneptah (1212 BCE) and Ramses III (1177 BCE) failed to destroy the seed of Israel or dislodge the people. Similarly they demonstrated the ongoing presence of Egypt in the land. The claim that Yahweh was king in the land rang false and was not claimed. When the age of Egyptian hegemony ended with Ramses VI (1139 BCE), Canaanite cities like Jerusalem now were on their own to defend themselves. It was during the subsequent century when Shiloh was in its prime and the claim that Yahweh was king in the (high)lands became believable.

> **Ex. 15: 17** *Thou wilt bring them in, and plant them on thy own mountain, the place, O Yahweh, which thou hast made for thy abode, the sanctuary, Lord, which thy hands have established.* [18] *Yahweh will reign for ever and ever.*

In the biblical text, the people assemble at Shiloh under Joshua for the apportioning of the land to the different tribes (Josh. 13–19). As an historical event, that apportioning is unlikely. However, the Joshua-based allocation at Shiloh does provides an alternative to any royal allocation plan by Solomon in Jerusalem or priestly allocation by Eleazar. A story attributing an allocation of land occurring at Shiloh would have had no validity unless the name was known already. Shiloh continues to be important in the Book of Joshua. It is the gathering place for the Israelite people in Josh. 21 and 22 as well.

Shiloh is the location of an annual feast to the Lord that becomes the center of a story involving a war between Benjamin and Israel.[2]

> **Judges 21: 19** *So they said, 'Behold, there is the yearly feast of Yahweh at **Shiloh**, which is north of Bethel, on the east of the highway that goes up from Bethel to Shechem, and south of Lebonah'.* [20] *And they commanded the **Benjaminites**, saying, 'Go and lie in wait in the vineyards,* [21] *and watch; if the **daughters of Shiloh** come out to dance in the dances, then come out of the vineyards and seize each man his wife from the **daughters of Shiloh**, and go to the **land of Benjamin**.* [22] *And when their fathers or their brothers come to complain to us, we will say to them, "Grant them graciously to us; because we did not take for each man of them his wife in battle, neither did you give them to them, else you would now be guilty"'.* [23] *And the **Benjaminites** did so, and took their wives, according to their number, from the dancers whom they carried off; then they went and returned to their inheritance, and rebuilt the towns, and dwelt in them.*

This passage provides geographical information about the location of Shiloh, anthropological information about mating in a rural agricultural setting, and historical information about the tensions between the tribe of Benjamin which apparently had not gone to Shiloh before and the northern tribes of Israel which did. One may observe similar elements to this story where the daughters of men become wives of the sons of gods (see Chapter 13). The story calls to mind the actions of the daughters of Israel who annually go to the

---

6. september 2005 (København: Museum Tusculanum, 2005), 142–152, quotations from 142, 147, and 150 respectively; Israel Finkelstein, *The Forgotten Kingdom: The Archaeology and History of Northern Israel* (ANEM 5; Atlanta: Society of Biblical Literature, 2013), 23–26, 49–50.

2   Robert Miller declares that Shiloh was the only site with evidence of large-scale interaction with other Israelite sites (Miller II, 'Chieftains of the highland clans', 119).

mountains to lament the daughter of Jephthah (Judges 11: 40). It also is not difficult to see some of these stories as political polemics in the battle over whether Saul of Benjamin should be king (see Chapter 9).

Going forward, Shiloh continues to play a prominent role in pre-monarchic Israelite history in the biblical narrative. It is the location where Eli the priest presides and Hannah dedicates her first-born to the Lord (I Sam. 1–2). Later that son Samuel becomes the leader of the priests of Shiloh and therefore the religious leader of Israel.

> **I Sam. 3: 20** *And all Israel from Dan to Beersheba knew that Samuel was established as a prophet of Yahweh.* [21] *And Yahweh appeared again at Shiloh, for Yahweh revealed himself to Samuel at Shiloh by the word of Yahweh.*

These verses vigorously affirm the connection between Yahweh and his priesthood at Shiloh in biblical memory.

But Israel was not the only newcomer contesting for a place in the land of Canaan. The Philistines had arrived too, so Israel's claim to kingship was precarious. As previously noted, according to the biblical narrative, the apocalyptic showdown occurred at Ebenezer when the ark went forth into battle on behalf of Israel and was captured (I Sam. 4). The archaeological record is consistent with the realistic description of the Israelite defeat *c.* 1050 BCE. One should expect a great deal of recriminations following this defeat including casting blame on who was responsible for causing Yahweh to allow the Philistines to capture the ark. The story of that event itself would serve as a battlefield in the war of words over who bore responsibility for this trauma (see Chapters 13 and 14).

The Philistine destruction of Shiloh became part of the legacy of ancient Israel just as in centuries to come the destruction of the temple in Jerusalem would be. The site effectively vanished from Israelite history save as memory of a once important place that now no longer existed. The transfer of power from Shiloh to Zion and the temple is positively depicted much later in Psalm 78:

> [56] *Yet they tested and rebelled against the **Most High** [Elyon] God, and did not observe his testimonies,*
> [57] *but turned away and acted treacherously like their fathers; they twisted like a deceitful bow.*
> [58] *For they provoked him to anger with their high places; they moved him to jealousy with their graven images.*
> [59] *When God heard, he was full of wrath, and he utterly rejected Israel.*
> [60] *He forsook his dwelling at **Shiloh**, the tent where he dwelt among men,*
> [61] *and delivered his power to captivity, his glory to the hand of the foe.*
> [62] *He gave his people over to the sword, and vented his wrath on his heritage.*
> [63] *Fire devoured their young men, and their maidens had no marriage song.*
> [64] *Their priests fell by the sword, and their widows made no lamentation.*
> [65] *Then the Lord awoke as from sleep, like a strong man [gibbor] shouting because of wine.*
> [66] *And he put his adversaries to rout; he put them to everlasting shame.*
> [67] *He rejected the tent of Joseph, he did not choose the tribe of Ephraim;*
> [68] *but he chose the tribe of Judah, Mount Zion, which he loves.*
> [69] *He built his sanctuary like the high heavens, like the earth, which he has founded for ever.*

The psalm functions as a diatribe against Shiloh and a paean to the exodus, conquest, covenant, Zion, Elyon, the Jerusalem temple, and the Davidic dynasty. For the composer of this song and his audience the memory of the loss of the ark was still fresh and he knew who to blame for that event: the priests of Shiloh.

Given all these associations, it is not surprising that the psalm has been dated to the 10th century BCE as an anti-Shiloh polemic precisely when these issues loomed large in the battle for power. Of course that date has been disputed. Shiloh is located in the land assigned to Ephraim. Intriguingly the psalm denigrates the military prowess of Ephraim:

> **Psalm 78: 9** *The Ephraimites, armed with the bow, turned back on the day of battle.* [10] *They did not keep God's covenant, but refused to walk according to his law.* [11] *They forgot what he had done, and the miracles that he had shown them.*

These mocking words claiming the Ephraimites forgot the Exodus reverse the praise of Ephraim's father Joseph in the Blessing of Jacob:

> **Genesis 49: 23** *The archers fiercely attacked him, shot at him, and harassed him sorely;* [24] *yet his bow remained unmoved, his arms were made agile by the hands of the Mighty One of Jacob (by the name of the Shepherd, the Rock of Israel),*

and to the grandfather Jacob himself:

> **Genesis 48: 22** *'Moreover I [Jacob] have given to you [Joseph] rather than to your brothers one mountain slope which I took from the hand of the Amorites with my sword and with my bow'.*

It is reasonable to conclude that Ephraim's military expertise lay in bow rather than, for example, the sling. One may easily imagine some alpha-male rivalry within the tribes of Merneptah's Israel in the hill country. Now the sanctuary to Yahweh in the land of Ephraim had been lost by the people of the bow providing a window of opportunity for another tribe to seek leadership just as Saul of Benjamin did.[3]

The cultural memory of Shiloh's destruction could be drawn on to address considerations in the present because the peoples involved still lived. Centuries after its destruction, the prophet Jeremiah, who was from the same village Abiathar had been exiled to (Jer. 1: 1), used Shiloh as a warning for Jerusalem in the face of a pending Babylonian invasion.

> **Jeremiah 7: 12** *Go now to my place that was in **Shiloh**, where I made my name dwell at first, and see what I did to it for the wickedness of my people Israel.* [13] *And now, because you have done all these things, says Yahweh, and when I spoke to you persistently you did not listen, and when I called you, you did not answer,* [14] *therefore I will do to the house which is called by my name, and in which you trust, and to the place which I gave to you and to your fathers, as I did to **Shiloh**.*

> **Jeremiah 26: 6** *then I will make this house like **Shiloh**, and I will make this city a curse for all the nations of the earth.* [7] *The priests and the prophets and all the people heard Jeremiah speaking*

---

3   Antony F. Campbell, 'Psalm 78: a contribution to the theology of tenth century Israel', *CBQ* 41 1979: 51–79; R. P. Carroll, 'Psalm LXXVIII: vestiges of a tribal polemic', *VT* 21 1971: 133–150; Mark Leuchter, 'The reference to Shiloh in Psalm 78', *HUCA* 77 2006: 1–31; Phillip Stern, 'The eighth century dating of Psalm 78 re-argued', *HUCA* 66 1995: 41–65. Ps. 132 which also expresses some of that joy, includes the mention of Ephratah, the home of David's people (see Chapter 10).

*these words in the house of Yahweh. ⁸ And when Jeremiah had finished speaking all that Yahweh had commanded him to speak to all the people, then the priests and the prophets and all the people laid hold of him, saying, 'You shall die!⁹ Why have you prophesied in the name of Yahweh, saying, "This house shall be like **Shiloh**, and this city shall be desolate, without inhabitant?"' And all the people gathered about Jeremiah in the house of Yahweh.*

Oh, how the mighty have fallen. Where once the heavens and Israel had meet at Shiloh, now it had become an abandoned site no one visited. Learn its lesson. It is difficult to imagine Jeremiah or anyone else issuing this warning if no one knew Shiloh's legacy.

Shiloh and David

Abiathar's personal experiences are part of the Shiloh heritage. The story of David's rise to power includes Abiathar as a major character. In contrast to Zadok, the biblical account documents a much longer relationship between David and Abiathar back to the time when David held no political power. The link between David and Abiathar requires explanation. David's connection to Abiathar may be understood within the context of David as an Israelite, Ephraite, and Bethlehemite. Bethlehem and Ephratah are different names for the same location (Gen. 35: 19 and 48: 7).

Leuchter suggests that אפרתי in I Sam. 1: 1 usually translated as 'Ephraim' is better translated as 'Ephrati' meaning a man of Ephratah. The pilgrimage of Elkanah and Hannah of Ephraite to Shiloh leading to the birth of Samuel therefore indicates a strong connection between the religious circles of Ephratah-Bethlehem and Shiloh. Japhet suggests that David, the son of an Ephrathite of Bethlehem of the tribe of Judah (see I Sam. 17: 12), belonged to an Ephraimite clan that had migrated south where it came in contact with Calebites such as Nabal and his wife Abigail whom David later married (I Sam. 25) (see Additional Readings: Ephratah).

The implications to these suggestions help tie together various biblical strands. Na'aman concurs and furthermore suggests members of this Ephraimite clan may have migrated to Gilead across the Jordan River as well. He raises the issue of the connection between the ark and Ephratah (Ps. 132: 6) and David's connection to the priests of Shiloh and their most sacred object. He focuses on Rachel, the eponymous ancestress of the tribe of Ephraim and the clan of Ephrathites. She dies from hard labor when giving birth to Benjamin and is buried by what becomes David's birthplace in what is known as Rachel's tomb. Na'aman claims the memory of her death dates to the early Iron Age. Albright earlier had suggested that a colony of Ephrathites had established a settlement in the Bethlehem district and had subsequently built Rachel's Tomb. Rachel's prominent appearance in the third cycle of KDB stories may be traced back to her importance to David's Ephrathite clan in the Bethlehem district which had migrated from Ephraim where the Shiloh priesthood was based.[4]

One should presume that David did not just appear out of nowhere to challenge Saul

---

4   William F. Albright, 'Appendix II: Ramah of Samuel', *AASOR* 4 1922–1923: 112–123, here 118–119 n.6; Na'aman, 'The settlement of the Ephraites', 516–539.

for the throne. David always was Israelite and from a family with wide connections both north and south. If he had been born first, he would have sought the crown before Saul did. It is reasonable to assume David was a person of 'name' for his military exploits. It is reasonable to assume that David felt shortchanged in some way by Saul for his military achievements. It is reasonable to assume that the Shiloh priests had legitimate reasons for reaching out to David to avenge the Benjaminite violation of the Israelite body politic. Of course from the Benjaminite perspective, it is reasonable to assume that they saw Saul as the 'George Washington' of Israel and David as the brilliant-warrior 'Benedict Arnold' who became a traitor by defecting to the Philistines.

The stories of Saul's and David's rise to power reflect these divergent views. It is as if patriot and loyalist or Union and Confederate narratives later had been combined into a single text. The intricacies of the interconnections in the stories motifs in the stories of Jerusalem throne games are overwhelming. One thread leads to multiple additional ones creating a dazzling tapestry of brilliant colors that would take more than a lifetime to unravel and understand. Truly there was nothing even remotely comparable in the ancient Near East and perhaps there never has been anything to rival what the writers of 10th century BCE Israel achieved.

Biblical scholars have gazed into the brilliance of the writings and struggled to see the face of the person or persons behind the light. Rost was perhaps the first to recognize that a single connected narrative work encompassed David's rise to power. Rost wrestles between two candidates, either Abiathar or Ahimaaz (son of Zadok). His leaning towards Abiathar is tempered by the pro-Solomonic words which scarcely could be attributed to him. Rost was not prepared to recognize the presence of two authors, Abiathar and Zadok. Rost also nominated Abiathar as a candidate for the Ark Narrative, the story of David planting the ark at Zion and conclusion of the KDB. Lipiński does recognize a two-stage process in the succession story. He posits a highly skilled author in the Jerusalem court as responsible for the superior prose composition that he had personally witnessed many of the events. His anti-Solomonic polemic subsequently was transformed into a pro-Solomonic work concluding with the same I Kings 2: 46 ending Friedman proposes. Lipiński suggests the priest Abiathar whom Solomon expelled as the original author but does not name the reviser. Rofé proposes an anti-kingship Ephramite strand within Josh. 24 to I Sam. 12. Regardless of the specific verses attributed to this author, Rofé suggestion highlights the work involved in extracting the individual authors from Friedman's proposed prose masterpiece.

If Abiathar began writing in the time of Saul that would make him the father of the alphabet prose narrative. It is difficult to imagine a Zadokite in any time period fabricating the figure of Abiathar in such detail and whose connection to the hero David preceded that of Zadok himself. So while David is the visionary king Sanders claims Israel never had, his teacher Abiathar is the transformative scribe who wrote in the time of Saul, David, and Solomon.[5]

---

5   Edward Lipiński, 'Royal and state scribes in ancient Jerusalem', in J. A. Emerton, *Congress Volume Jerusalem 1986* (SVT 40; Leiden: E. J. Brill, 1988), 157–164), here 159–160; Alexander Rofé, 'Ephraimite versus Deuteronomistic history', in Gary N. Knoppers and J. Gordon McConville, eds, *Reconsidering Israel and Judah: Recent Studies on the Deuteronomistic History* (SBTS 8; Winona Lake: Eisenbrauns, 2000), 462–474; reprinted

Let us recap what is Abiathar is prime candidate to have written in the time of Saul and why his alliance with David succeeded.

> The song or oral tradition of Gideon now includes an admonition for war heroes not to seek the kingship (Judg. 8: 22–23, see Chapter 9).
> The Song of Deborah was revised to stress the role of Yahweh in achieving victory and therefore implicitly to reject the need for a human king (see Chapter 9).
> The oral tradition of Jephthah was revised to become an alphabet prose story on the dangerous folly for a warrior to usurp the role of the priesthood in going into battle on his own initiative.
> A new metaphorical story on the rape of the Bethelemite concubine was written as an anti-Saul polemic (see Chapter 9).

Who is the person best situated to affect these changes and push the envelope of the state of the art information system? In effect, Abiathar in the time of Saul created a 'Book of Saviors' demonstrating that Israel could be victorious without a king. One could later add Samson to this list. Abiathar delivered the message that in those days when there was no king in Israel, thanks to Yahweh, the true king of Israel, the people were triumphant.

Abiathar was the most skilled wielder in the world of the alphabet prose narrative as a weapon of war before David even began his rise to power. Just as the priests of Shiloh reached out to the leading Israelite warrior to stop Saul, so that warrior reached out to Israel's greatest warrior of the word to legitimate his cause. It was a match made in political heaven. Abiathar became David's voice to the people. This recap traces the transformation from oral tradition and poetic songs to the alphabet prose narrative. The recap suggests that it is possible to trace the writing of one individual from the time of Saul to the time of Solomon, to examine the corpus of writing over time by a single person, a rarity in ancient times. Truly Abiathar is one of the unsung people in the history of writing.

According to the narrative, after Saul instigates the slaughter of the priests who oppose him along with their women, children, and animals, David and Abiathar have their first contact:

> **I Sam. 22: 20** *But one of the sons of Ahimelech the son of Ahitub, named **Abiathar**, escaped and fled after **David**.* [21] *And **Abiathar** told **David** that Saul had killed the priests of Yahweh.* [22] *And **David** said to **Abiathar**, 'I knew on that day, when Doeg the Edomite was there, that he would surely tell Saul. I have occasioned the death of all the persons of your father's house.* [23] *Stay with me, fear not; for he that seeks my life seeks your life; with me you shall be in safekeeping.'*

Doeg the Edomite's slaughter of the priests of Moses anticipates Mesha the Moabite's slaughter of the priests at the sanctuary of Yahweh at Nebo. Mesha's actions exist in the archaeological record; Doeg's do not. Mesha's acted against a foreign people; Doeg did not since he was obedient to Saul.

The incident provides sufficient justification to legitimize the Shiloh-David alliance. White posits that it was Saul's unprecedented assumption of the royal prerogative combined with this slaughter of the Shiloh priesthood which necessitated the creation of the coherent

from Daniele Garonne and Felice Israel, eds, *Storia e Tradizioni di Israele: Scritti in Onore di J. Alberto Soggin* (Brescia: Paideia, 1991), 221–235; Rost, *The Succession*, 105–106, 121–122n.12 and 123 n.50. For Abiathar's authorship, see also Caquot and de Robert, *Les Livres de Samuel*, 17–20.

defense of Saul's rise to power. Whether or not the massacre actually occurred is a separate issue. What is relevant here is Saul's effort to be king undermined the authority of the Shiloh priests who considered themselves the only ones authorized by Yahweh to call Israel to war. In the alphabet prose narrative, David is portrayed as deferring to Abiathar's pronouncements while Saul initiates war on his own. Regardless of the actual details contributing to the alliance, it is reasonable to conclude that Abiathar would not have a high regard for Saul or for the Benjaminite priests who sang Saul's praises.[6]

The biblical narrative then recounts a series of adventures in the wilderness by these fugitives from Saul (I Sam. 23 and 30 and the duplicate I Sam. 24 and 26). The scenes with Abiathar involve an ephod through which David inquires of the Lord as to what action he should take (see Additional Readings: Ephod). The Lord then answers David. On a practical level, one needs to inquire as to how the Lord's answer was communicated. There is the traditional VOICE OF GOD interpretation where the heavens speaks in a deep male voice the actual words written in the biblical text. There is the silent voice of God where the supplicant hears in his or her mind the message of the deity which no one else hears. These theological visions are unlikely to reflect what actually occurred when David or any king sought the guidance of the divine.

Then there is the more practical and physical view to be considered. It is the priest himself who spoke the words of the God. His vocalization is standard operating procedure in the ancient Near East: a recognized representative of the deity speaks directly to the king or would-be king in the name of the deity. In this case that would mean Abiathar spoke in the name of Yahweh to David. Abiathar speaking in the name of Yahweh to David should not be considered an example of anthropomorphism. Kings knew the priest or prophet was not Yahweh; so did the audience hearing the story. A human being could speak, touch, and walk with the king in the guise of the deity imparting instructions, blessings, or denunciations without anyone thinking that he was the deity himself. One presumes in these instances that Abiathar had the skill to know what David in his heart wanted to do and was legitimating that decision through his role as priest of Yahweh.

The highlight of Abiathar's life undoubtedly was the first time David installs the ark of Yahweh at Zion. According to the biblical text at some point Abiathar even had carried the ark of Yahweh itself. Although the precise circumstances are not provided, evidently it was an action of such significant importance as to warrant Solomon later sparing his life:

> **I Kings 2: 26** *And to Abiathar the priest the king [Solomon] said, 'Go to Anathoth, to your estate; for you deserve death. But I will not at this time put you to death, because you bore the ark of Yahweh GOD before David my father, and because you shared in all the affliction of my father'.*

Even those who banished him acknowledged his position with David and the ark.[7]

---

6   Marsha C. White, 'The "History of Saul's Rise" and the compositional history of I Samuel 1–14', paper presented at the annual conference of the Society of Biblical Literature, November 20, 2000, Nashville; Marsha White, '"The History of Saul's Rise": Saulide state propaganda in 1 Samuel 1–14', in Saul M. Olyan and Robert C. Culley, *'A Wise and Discerning Mind': Essays in Honor of Burke O. Long* (BJS 325; Providence, RI: Brown Judaic Studies, 2000), 271–292.

7   The use of the ark of Yahweh here versus the ephod in the wilderness stories of Abiathar inquiring of Yahweh for David further supports the notion that originally the ephod and the ark are connected if not synonymous

David's action had a precedent. In ancient times, the person outside the Bible most closely associated with the successful recovery of a captured sacred object that represented the deity and the people was Nebuchadnezzar I (1126–1105 BCE) (see Chapter 10). The Elamite forces of chaos seized the statue of Marduk from Babylon and removed it. The captured object became an Elamite trophy of the conquest exactly as the Philistines later did with the ark. The absconding with the revered symbol was traumatic for Babylon as it would be for Israel. Its return engendered an equally exuberant response as it would for Israel as well. A procession with sacrifices celebrated the reinstallation of the statute of Marduk, the restoration of order, and a return to normal as it would do for Israel. A mythical, not historical, composition called *Enuma Elish*, has been linked to this historical event.

Nebuchadnezzar I's actions were a model for the actions of David when he restored the ark (II Sam. 6). The shame of the defeat by the Philistines was cleansed. The installation was a time of great rejoicing, when songs were sung, tales were told, and food was eaten. This event irrevocably linked the Shiloh priests to both David and the ark at Zion. If life was a movie, this would have been the moment when the heroes go off into the sunset. But life goes on one day at a time just as it did before the climactic moment and when all was said and done, Jerusalem remained a Jebusite city with Zadok waiting for the moment to seize power once the great hero passed from the scene.

The installation marked the transfer of the ark traditions at Shiloh to the new capital of the new kingdom. It was an action of extraordinary cultic significance with Abiathar playing a pivotal role. Whereas Seow envisions a one-time occurrence, Fleming draws on the annual calendric processions of the ancient Near East to propose a recurring public procession with particular emphasis on the subsequent installation of the ark into the Solomonic temple (I Kings 8) to honor the arrival of Yahweh in Jerusalem. The idea of an annual procession is attractive and may have occurred for a short time (see Additional Readings: Sacral Kingship). Three caveats militate against its application here: (1) Solomon lacked the stature and charisma to match David, (2) the kingdom shortly split rendering the non-Jerusalem/non-Jebusite ark secondary to the temple built in Jerusalem which now housed the ark outside public view, (3) the psalms frequently sing praises to Elyon suggesting a continuing Zadokite priesthood presence for whom the ark was secondary.[8] After the successful coup installed Solomon, Abiathar was alone in the capital bereft of supporters. Joab, David's longtime military ally alongside Abiathar, had been put to death by Zadok-ally Benaiah. He then assumed Joab's position as military leader:

> **I Kings 2: 34** *Then Benaiah the son of Jehoiada went up, and struck him down and killed him; and he was buried in his own house in the wilderness.*[35] *The king put Benaiah the son of Jehoiada over the army in place of Joab, and the king put **Zadok** the priest in the place of **Abiathar**.*

(see Karel van der Toorn and Cees Houtman, 'David and the ark', *JBL* 113 1994: 209–231, here 218, 228).
8   Fleming, 'David and the ark', 75–95; McCarter, *I Samuel*, 23–26, 102–139; McCarter, *II Samuel*, 161–184; Seow, *Myth, Drama, and the Politics of David's Dance*; Ben C. Ollenburger, *Zion, The City of the Great King: A Theological Symbol of the Jerusalem Cult* (Sheffield: Sheffield Academic Press, 1983, JSOT Sup. 41), 134; Van der Toorn and Houtman, 'David and the ark', 220–226. For the place of Ps. 99 in this process see, Mark Leuchter, 'The literary strata and narrative sources of Psalm XCIX', *VT* 55: 20–38.

Zadok took Abiathar's place and had him dispatched from the royal capital as previously noted. An additional notation expresses that the action should be understood in the context of a larger issue requiring investigation (see Chapter 14).

> **I Kings 2: 27** *So **Solomon expelled Abiathar** from being priest to Yahweh, thus fulfilling the word of Yahweh which he had spoken concerning the house of Eli in Shiloh.*

This last verse is a tip-off that the war of words to assign blame for the loss of the ark continued. The action harkens back to a prophecy in I Sam. 2: 27–36. That inserted oracle of judgment generally is considered among exegetes to be prophesying the replacement of the House of Eli with another priesthood in the leadership position. Now we see which one, the Zadokites. Combined the prophecy and the fulfillment delivers a sophisticated anti-Israel message through the aegis of the foundational story of Israel, the ark, and its deity.[9]

The end result witnesses the old guard based on Yahweh, Moses, the wilderness, and the covenant banished from the beltway. Long live the new non-Israelite one of Elyon and Asherah, Solomon, Jerusalem, and the temple. The biblical denunciations of the Canaanite religion and way of life spring from this division of original Israelites represented by Abiathar and newcomers under David who did not abandon the Canaanite ways represented by Zadok.[10]

Abiathar's exile did not end the battle for power. Zadok's efforts to foist a Canaanite culture on Israel was not well-received. As the priest of Moses, the priest of Shiloh, Abiathar's voice still carried weight among the Israelites. To challenge Zadok and the mighty men ensconced in the capital in the time of Solomon would not be easy. Military power throughout the land had been depleted necessitating a search for those would stand up against the new world order now being imposed. Abiathar's supplement to the KDB may be considered a call to arms against the foreign rule in Jerusalem, against a reimposition of Egyptian hegemony throughout the Solomonic kingdom. Indeed, this supplement may have precipitated the harsh crack down on the restless Israelite population and the dispersal of royal forces to Gezer, Megiddo, and Hazor by the new 'Pharaoh'. In hindsight, the effort to hamstring the horses of the Israelite Pharaoh and burn his chariots with fire never came to fruition. But a generation later the kingdom would divide as the battle for power continued.

One observes in this story a three-way battle for power. For Abiathar and the remnant of the Shiloh priests, the initial conflict was between Benjamin and Ephraim. These two tribes had been part of Israel from the beginning. They had fought side by side as sung in the Song of Deborah. When Saul sought to become the permanent savior of Israel as king against the Philistines, the rivalry within Israel assumed deadly proportions. With the triumph of David and Abiathar, the latter may have presumed the battle with Benjamin was over, as if Benjamin had died and been buried in a cave never to revive or live on.[11]

---

9   McCarter, *I Samuel*, 92; Rooke, *Zadok's Heirs*, 57–58.

10 Uehlinger correctly notes the intra-Israel conflict over religious practices without recognizing that they arose between peoples who became Israelite centuries apart and after having been in opposition to each other ('The "Canaanites" and other "pre-Israelite" peoples, [Part I]', 565–566).

11 For a survey of the Ephraim/Benjamin polemics in the Book of Judges see Marvin A. Sweeney, 'Davidic polemics in the Book of Judges', *VT* 47 1997: 517–529.

Now he and his Benjamin priest rivals had to contend with a new power bloc, Zadok and Jebusite city of Jerusalem, a city that had opposed the emergence of Israel in the land of Canaan. The wilderness experience between David and Abiathar vastly differed from the urban one between David and Zadok in the city of Jerusalem. The latter was a political one that functioned solely on an institutional basis. There was no personal connection between the king and this priest. He simply served the needs of the king. By contrast, David and Abiathar had bonded during an extended time as fugitives in the wilderness where their lives were in danger. Saul already had wiped out much of Abiathar's world and David clearly was his rock and savior. This more intense and emotional relationship make it unlikely that at the end of David's life he would have abandoned Abiathar for Zadok. It strengthens the argument that Solomon attained power through a coup against the preference of David ... hence Zadok's need to proclaim the opposite.

Abiathar's background was Shiloh where there was no human king while Zadok's position in Jerusalem was the exact opposite. Israel's tradition was one of primarily rural communities and no taxes while the Canaanite way was urban, stratified, and with taxes and forced labor. For two centuries, no one in Israel had the opportunity to abuse power; now kings had the potential to do so. The theological and religious language in the Bible should not obscure the social and political ramifications of installing a king. It is easy to imagine the need one day to amend the Israelite constitution to establish checks and balance to limit the power of the king.

After Abiathar lost the battle for the successor of David, after Adonijah and Joab had been executed, after Abiathar had been exiled, after he had lost control of the ark, where could he turn for help to overcome Zadok and his non-Israelite allies? Could he reach out even to Benjamin, tribe of Saul but also fellow Israelites from the dawn of Israel's existence? Could Joseph and Benjamin reunite against a common foe? The War of Words continued.

Reconstructed narrative of Shiloh J

Gen. 9: 20 *Noah planted a vineyard;* [21] *and he drank of the wine, and became drunk, and lay uncovered in his tent.* [22] *Canaan saw the nakedness of his father, and told his two brothers outside.* [24] *When Noah awoke from his wine and knew what his youngest son had done to him,* [25] *he said, 'Cursed be Canaan; a slave of slaves shall he be to his brothers'.* **10: 15** *Canaan became the father of* [16] *the Jebusites, the Amorites, the Girgashites.*

New end of the first cycle.

Exegesis

Abiathar's supplement to the first cycle of the KDB concluded it. Whereas Zadok had created a new beginning and ending for the story of Cain and Abel, Abiathar created a new ending for the entire cycle. His ending then set the stage for the commencement of the second cycle, the story of the warrior shepherd-king from Hebron. Two separate (papyrus) manuscripts now existed, first the KDB plus Zadok's supplement and second, the KDB plus Abiathar's supplement. Although the actual number of additional words were few, they offered distinct and contrasting views of a world, one based on the Canaanite way of life and one based on Israel. These words were an act of war.

Abiathar, like Deborah before him, sought to rally the Israelites against these Canaanites. Commentators repeatedly have stressed that Canaan was the true target of Noah's (and the author's) ire in this story (see Chapter 5). Contrary to the explanations presented for this hostility, it was not a theological confrontation or a battle against a 'primitive' people. Quite the contrary, Abiathar's denigration of the Canaanites was part of a battle for power in Jerusalem. His disparaging treatment of the Canaanites derives from opposition to the political ambitions of Zadok, the pro-Canaanite author, by Abiathar, the pro-Israelite priest of Shiloh. To understand Abiathar's story, one must keep in mind how it would help him get back in the game.

Abiathar's words are direct and to the point just as Zadok's were. There are a series of actions from planting a vineyard to cursing Canaan that occur with nary an unwasted word or action. The author accomplishes his goals swiftly and efficiently. Noah goes from being the actor, to being acted upon (by the alcohol), to being passive, to being described. The action shifts to Canaan who sees and tells his brothers something. Seeing tends to lead to actions as when the woman in the garden sees the trees were good for food and a delight to the eyes (Gen. 3: 6) and the sons of Gods see that the daughters of men were fair (Gen. 6: 2). This time the seeing leads to the action of telling what one has seen.

The action then shifts back to Noah who awakes, knows what happened, and curses Canaan who is clearly defined demographically. The pace is quick. The author consciously picked these elements, motifs, actions, and names as part of the message he wished to deliver to his contemporary audience. One notes Abiathar's superiority as a storyteller to Zadok. He engages the audience. Zadok issues pronouncements from on high about the way it is going to be in kingdom. Abiathar's response not only is in opposition to the message Zadok delivered but to the style of delivery. One may anticipate that someone in the palace might have the wisdom to discern and be concerned about the effectiveness of Abiathar over Zadok and for the need to reach out to someone who could better counter Abiathar's appeal to an Israelite audience.

The sons of Noah story also raises the issue of its relation to the preceding flood story. As noted by many exegetes, in the J flood story the unnamed sons of Noah are married with children who enter and leave the ark together (Gen. 7: 7 and 8: 18). '[H]ere they are still so young that they live with their father in his tent', meaning politically within his kingdom.[12] The resolution of the different portrayals cannot be accomplished solely through the excavation of the sons of Noah story. To do so requires an investigation of the J flood story in its own right, a major effort not to be undertaken lightly. Here the challenge is to identify the different political entities represented by the three sons and the new political configuration being proposed by Abiathar through this new ending to the flood story and the first cycle of the KDB.

---

12 Gunkel, *Genesis*, 79.

9: 20 Noah planted a vineyard

This vineyard has been a focus of exegetical attention. Gunkel comments, 'The tradition of "Noah, the farmer" is independent of the other in which the first man was already destined to farm the field and in which Cain was already a farmer'. Westermann does not accept this sequence. He makes Noah not the first farmer but the one who elevated the profession of agriculture to viticulture. David Neiman also sees the account as an etiology of viticulture and not agriculture for which there were precedents in Gen. 2: 15 and 4: 2. Lloyd Bailey thinks this reference to Noah which contradicts Gen. 4: 2 is evidence of a new story which some English translations attempt to mitigate while others do not. Pauline Albenda suggests that the incorporation of grapevines into biblical iconography may be comparable to the introduction of a new method of viticulture into Assyria as an expression of fertility (see Additional Readings: Vineyards).

Westermann's Noah knew what his ancestors knew about farming but somehow he was able to take a step forward on behalf of all humanity. For Westermann, the critical point is the advance in human civilization was achieved by a human being and not through a divine action. The contrast between human-initiated and divine-initiated progress is part of the distinguishing characteristics of the J narrative. A similar advance in human civilization occurs by the sons of Cain in Gen. 4: 17–24 (see Chapter 2). The planting of the grape signifies that humanity has moved beyond the drudgery of toiling for the physical necessities of life and now can escape the daily routine with festal drinking in a celebration of life.[13]

Gunkel locates the vintner Noah in Syria or Canaan because that's where he thought viticulture originated. He understands the story as an etiological one consistent with his oral tradition approach.[14] These standard interpretations take the story literally as memory remnants from the dawn of civilized time or a least life centuries ago. The issue here is not getting high on life or the advancement of civilization. The audience was not interested in an anthropology lesson on the civilization of humanity, it wanted to know who to blame right now in their present for the current situation. Which son? Which priesthood? Which political faction? Who should be blessed and who should be cursed?

Yahweh planted a garden in the opening story of the KDB, now Noah plants a vineyard. The same verb is used in both stories: נטע. The audience is supposed to make a connection between the two actions. In Yahweh's situation, he is planting a garden in a pre-existing world. Therefore it is presumed that the materials necessary for a garden existed. Noah's situation is quite different. The flood presumably inundated existing vineyards too. As previously noted, the rabbis postulate that Noah's vineyard derived from Eden (Pirqe Rabbi Eliezer 23). It is highly unlikely that the original storyteller was concerned with this question or that it was relevant to the message he was delivering through this new story.

What did the vineyard mean in the context of this story? Since one can make a Yahweh/garden and Noah or king/vineyard parallel, the odds are the audience would understand the vineyard of Noah as it did the garden of Yahweh.

---

13 Westermann, *Genesis 1–11*, 487.
14 See Gunkel, *Genesis*, 80.

a)   Positive examples – The planting of a vineyard by the lead character in this story may be viewed as something positive and for which people should give thanks to Yahweh for his blessing. For example, see Isaiah 65: 21, Jeremiah 31: 5, Ecclesiastes 2: 4, and Psalm 107: 31 (Table 1). All these examples attest the positive image of a kingdom of plenty and abundance where people live free from the fear of hunger.

b)   Calling card of the Lord – The reappearance of the vineyard may testify to the power and righteousness of the Lord. For example, see Jeremiah 32: 15, Ezekiel 28: 26, and Amos 9: 14 (Table 1). Again these examples illustrate the vision of a prosperous kingdom free from want.

c)   Warning – The absence of the vineyards or inability to reap its rewards may serve as a warning or punishment to the people whereby the land has returned to nature or its fruits will not be available to the planters. For example, see Deut. 28: 39, Amos 4: 9, 5: 11, Micah 1: 6, Zephaniah (Table 1). The Lord could be challenged for not living up to his end of the bargain:

> **Numbers 16: 14** *Moreover you have not brought us into a land flowing with milk and honey, nor given us inheritance of fields and **vineyards**. Will you put out the eyes of these men? We will not come up.*

But the people could be remanded for thinking they were the ones responsible for the bounty from the vines:

> **Deuteronomy 6: 11** *and houses full of all good things, which you did not fill, and cisterns hewn out, which you did not hew, and **vineyards** and olive trees, which you did not plant, and when you eat and are full…*

> **Joshua 24: 13** *I gave you a land on which you had not labored, and cities which you had not built, and you dwell therein; you eat the fruit of **vineyards** and oliveyards which you did not plant.*

The concerns of the people for their vineyards could be very practical and critical in an agricultural society:

> **Nehemiah 5: 3** *There were also those who said, 'We are mortgaging our fields, our **vineyards**, and our houses to get grain because of the famine'. And there were those who said, 'We have borrowed money for the king's tax upon our fields and our **vineyards**. Now our flesh is as the flesh of our brethren, our children are as their children; yet we are forcing our sons and our daughters to be slaves, and some of our daughters have already been enslaved; but it is not in our power to help it, for other men have our fields and our vineyards.'*

These examples attest some of the ways in which vineyards have been used in biblical texts.

There are some stories where vineyards play a role which help shed more light on the intention of the author here. These are stories of power where the vineyard is part of a confrontation with more direct political overtones. Some call to mind motifs in the story of the sons of Noah raising the possibility that they were part of a dialog in various battles for power. In biblical order, not necessarily the order in which they written, such texts include:

> **Genesis 49: 9** *Judah is a lion's whelp; from the prey, my son, you have gone up. He stooped down, he couched as a lion, and as a lioness; who dares rouse him up? The scepter shall not depart from Judah, nor the ruler's staff from between his feet, until he comes to whom it belongs; and to him shall be the obedience of the peoples. Binding his foal to the **vine** and his ass's colt to the choice **vine**, he **washes his garments in wine** and his **vesture in the blood of grapes**;*

In the Blessing of Jacob, Judah receives the kingship using the lion image. It should be noted that the sole time within Israel's history when the question of Judah's kingship was raised was when the northern tribes created a separate kingdom after Solomon died. According to the text, Judah possesses such an abundance of wine that it can use this precious commodity as if it were water. The results are garments died red just as the Phoenician royal garments were died purple. One may debate whether this passage blesses Judah for the kingship or condemns him for his luxurious wasteful royal lifestyle.[15]

> **Judges 9: 26** *And Gaal the son of Ebed moved into Shechem with his kinsmen; and the men of Shechem put confidence in him.* [27] *And they went out into the field, and gathered the grapes from their **vineyards** and trod them, and held festival, and went into the house of their god, and ate and drank and reviled Abimelech.*

At the navel of the universe or cosmic center, Gaal and his men drink the grapes from the vineyard as part of a (new year) festival, presumably are drunk, and curse the name of the father-king. The biblical texts indicate an antipathy towards this wine festival:

> **Judges 9: 27** *And they [the men of Shechem who supported Gaal] went out into the field, and gathered the grapes from their vineyards and trod them, and held festival, and went into the house of their god, and ate and drank and reviled Abimelech.*

This incident bears resemblance to a Canaanite ritual for the feast of grape involving Baal. However in this version, the Baal-figure does not prevail and the El-figure triumphs. This human counterpart to the mythological Canaanite tale touts the supremacy El over Baal, a particularly potent message in a time when Canaanites and Israelites were battling for control of the kingdom. This political polemic reflects an ongoing hostility against those who practiced the Canaanite new year festival. The multilayered polemic where Moses sends the spies in Num. 13: 17–33 includes not only the mention of the Nephilim but the season of the first ripe grapes and the spies cutting a cluster of them. All the references in the story are chosen for a reason in the delivering of a political message.[16]

> **Judges 14: 5** *Then Samson went down with his father and mother to Timnah, and he came to the **vineyards** of Timnah. And behold, a young lion roared against him;*

Samson triumphs in this confrontation against a beast both feared and admired/imitated. His triumph becomes part of a riddle in a deadly confrontation with the Philistines involving the taking of festal garments (Judges 14: 12–19).

---

15 Based on the archaic vocabulary, Hendel dates this text to early in the monarchy, see Ronald Hendel, 'Historical context', in Craig A. Evans, Joel N. Lohr and David. L. Petersen, *The Book of Genesis: Composition, Reception, and Interpretation* (SVT 152; Leiden: Brill, 2012), 51–80, here 52–54.

16 For the Ugaritic new year festival also called the festival of the new wine involving the king, music, song, dance, and food at a sacred center, see Johannes C. de Moor, *New Year with Canaanites and Israelites* (Kampen: Kok, 1972); Baruch A. Levine and J. M. De Tarragon, 'The king proclaims the day: Ugaritic rites for the vintage (KTU 1.41//1.87)', *RB* 100 1993: 76–115; Nicolas Wyatt, *Religious Texts from Ugarit: The Words of Ilimilku and his Colleagues* (Biblical Seminar 53; Sheffield: Sheffield Academic Press, 1998), 97–107, 348–355.

> **Judges 21: 20** *And they commanded the Benjaminites, saying, 'Go and lie in wait in the **vineyards**,* ²¹ *and watch; if the daughters of Shiloh come out to dance in the dances, then come out of the **vineyards** and seize each man his wife from the daughters of Shiloh, and go to the land of Benjamin'.*

In another story involving vineyards, a cosmic center, and a (new year) festival, there also is a violent encounter, this time involving the Benjaminites and the women of the Shiloh. Since the Abimelech story mentions Shechem and Hamor (Judges 9: 28) which calls to mind the story of Dinah involving King Hamor and his son Prince Shechem (Gen. 34), it is reasonable to suggest that all these stories are in dialogue with each other in some way.

Besides divine power, vineyards also may be associated with human power, specifically that of the king. The prophet Samuel warns the people of what a human king would do if Israel chose to follow that path:

> **1 Samuel 8: 14** *He will take the best of your fields and **vineyards** and olive orchards and give them to his servants.* ¹⁵ *He will take the tenth of your grain and of your **vineyards** and give it to his officers and to his servants.*

Then Saul, who becomes that king, claims that if David should become king the very actions Samuel warned of would not be done by David on behalf of the Benjaminite warriors who now chose to follow him against Saul.

> **I Samuel 22: 7** *And Saul said to his servants who stood about him, 'Hear now, you Benjaminites; will the son of Jesse give every one of you fields and **vineyards**, will he make you all commanders of thousands and commanders of hundreds...'.*

This combination of Samuel, Saul, David, Benjamin, Shiloh, Shechem and vineyards provides a potential backdrop for deciphering the figures in and the writers of the story of the sons of Noah.

So in this story of Noah and the vineyard, what associations would come to mind in the audience? Any answer is speculative. In the various prophet citations the vineyards are part of a symbol of the good life, of a land of plenty where stomachs are full, peace rules, and all is well. On the other hand, in the narrative accounts, vineyards are part of various confrontations and struggles among peoples at cosmic centers like Shiloh and Shechem or of power politics. One approach is to assume the author of this supplement to the KDB is drawing on the audiences' familiarity with vineyard stories, cosmic centers, heroes and villains. The heroic Noah who captained the ark community is now drunk at the (new year) grape festival at the cosmic center. In his weakened state he is vulnerable to be violated by those he should be able trust. This author's Noah needs to sober up, get his act together, and hold accountable those who had violated his vulnerability. One may anticipate that he will do so in the remainder of the supplement which is exactly what happens.

9: 21 and he drank of the wine, and became drunk, and lay uncovered in his tent

As Westermann says, '[t]he real action begins in v. 21'. Noah drinks, he becomes drunk, he is naked in his domicile. Gunkel regards Noah's condition as extremely indecent and suggests the use of a tent and not a house was the narrator's oversight. For Westermann the condition of drunkenness was not reprehensible in antiquity. Regardless of the value judgment, without the state of drunkenness there would be no story to tell. In this regard, the verse sets the stage for the action to follow.[17]

9: 22 *Canaan saw the nakedness of his father, and told his two brothers outside*

For the figure of authority to curse Canaan in this story makes it essential to understand exactly who or what is meant by Canaan and what he does. The name is known in the archaeological record primarily as a geographic term based on Egyptian and Ugaritic texts (see Chapter 8). The precise meaning and boundaries of the land of Canaan in the Late Bronze Age has been a source of debate within the field. These texts raise the issue of how the people in the land of Canaan referred to themselves. Since there was no political entity of Canaan except perhaps as an administrative unit of the Egyptian empire, the inhabitants were more likely to refer to themselves as being of a local city or ethnic group such as Jebusite, Gibeonite, Hivite, Girgashite, etc., part of a 'hard core of a cliché-list of pre-Israelite peoples of Palestine and Syria' according to Simons.[18] If the only users of the term 'Canaan' or 'Canaanite' were the Egyptians external to the land, then the use by a writer internal to the land might have applied to those inhabitants who were loyal to Egypt, i.e., enemies of Israel.

In the biblical texts, the terms Canaan and Canaanites are used frequently. In general terms, Canaan is employed in the same geographic sense as the archaeological examples. There is a 'land of Canaan' to which the patriarchs go and the children of Israel possess. On this land lived the Canaanite people but the biblical accounts rarely refer to them in this manner. When Canaanites is used to refer to a people, it frequently is joined with other peoples in the land of Canaan, the implied peoples of the allocation in Deut. 32: 8–9 (see Chapter 11).

Zadok seeks support from the Canaanite side of these encounters while Abiathar reached out to the Israelite. His ire is directed not solely towards the Jebusites in Jerusalem but to all the peoples of the land who are allied with Zadok. His personifies his foe with the character Canaan who interacts with Noah in a reprehensible manner. Biblical exegetes routinely interpret the figure of Canaan as a representative of the Canaanite people and not as an individual human being (see Chapter 5). Driver succinctly states 'Canaan is here not an individual, but the *representatives of the Canaanites*, the native races of Canaan'. One might venture that representational figures are a diagnostic marker for Abiathar as a writer. Whereas Zadok's figures represent specific individuals, Abiathar creates characters who are representatives of a people and who interact with specific individuals such as Canaan the people with Noah the person.[19]

---

17 Gunkel, *Genesis*, 80; Westermann, *Genesis 1–11*, 487.
18 J. Simons, 'The "Table of Nations" (Genesis 10): its general meaning', *OtSt* 10 1954: 155–184, reprinted in Richard S. Hess and David Toshio Tsumura, eds, *I Studied Inscriptions from Before the Flood: Ancient Near Eastern, Literary, and Linguistic Approaches to Genesis 1–11* (SBTS 4; Winona Lake: Eisenbrauns, 1994), 234–253 here 242.
19 Driver, *The Book of Genesis*, 110.

In Abiathar's story, the character of Canaan commits two actions. By implication, both those actions warrant condemnation. Canaan sees what he should not have seen and speaks what he should not have spoken. He has transgressed filial piety. Again, there is a great economy of words here with only a few words being necessary to speak volumes. The verses are quick, short, and very fast-paced.[20]

Since Canaan went outside the tent to speak to his brothers, one presumes that he was inside the tent when he did what he did. The audience is not to imagine that Canaan was walking along minding his own business when he suddenly happen to notice through the open tent (or window) something he should not have seen. His actions were pre-meditated.

Left unmentioned is exactly why Canaan was inside his father's tent in the first place. Westermann presumes that everyone was living together.[21] It seems more likely that the author who deliberately chose to change the venue to 'outside' has already implied that the son was inside. The Midrashic tale of Ham objecting to his father's attempt to produce a fourth son and possibly castrating him may be psychologically more relevant (see Chapter 5).

One approach has been to interpret biblical law as suggesting the vocabulary of the story means the son was guilty of homosexual rape:[22]

> **Leviticus 20: 11** *The man who lies with his father's wife **has uncovered his father's nakedness**; both of them shall be put to death, their blood is upon them.*

By implication then, the son who has uncovered his father's nakedness has committed the equivalent of laying with the wife. Simply seeing nakedness is bad enough. Another possibility is that the action by Ham in the canonical text and Canaan in Abiathar's story was not simply the equivalence of maternal incest, it really was paternal incest.[23]

> **Leviticus 20: 17** *If a man takes his sister, a daughter of his father or a daughter of his mother, and **sees her nakedness, and she sees his nakedness**, it is a shameful thing, and they shall be cut off in the sight of the children of their people; he has uncovered his sister's nakedness, he shall bear his iniquity.*

The midrash (San 70a) of castration to prevent a fourth son from being born [a daughter seems not to have been considered a possibility] provides mitigating circumstances for otherwise uncalled for heinous behavior. In any event, the son has transgressed the basic norms of Judaism.

The specifics of his action really are secondary. Canaan has violated the space of his vulnerable father. At the exact moment of unforeseen circumstances when the son is obligated to honor his father (and mother), he instead dishonors Noah. This dishonoring is foretold by placing Canaan in the tent in the first place. A violation of boundaries has occurred. The decision to enter the tent was in itself a transgression. The audience would understand, especially if the story was being performed in some way, that Canaan deliberately had entered the tent precisely when he should not have. He did not ask for

---

20 Day, *From Creation to Babel*, 159; Gunkel, *Genesis*, 80.
21 Westermann, *Genesis 1–11*, 488.
22 Frederick W. Basset, 'Noah's nakedness and the curse of Canaan: a case of incest?' *VT* 21 1971: 232–237.
23 John Sietze Bergsma and Scott Walker Hahn, 'Noah's nakedness and the curse of Canaan (Genesis 9: 20–27)', *JBL* 124 2005: 25–40.

water as Sisera did of Yael when he entered her tent (Judg. 5: 25). There was no valid reason for him to be inside the tent. At Baal Peor, Phinehas the son of Eleazar the son of Aaron the priest rectified a sexual violation at the tent of meeting and received the covenant of eternal priesthood in return (Num. 25). These stories suggest that sometimes a tent is not just a tent and what happens there is of the highest stakes with significant ramifications.

Gunkel notes the possible connection to the story of Lot's daughters (Gen. 19: 30–38). In this supplement to the Abram or second cycle of the KDB, the father figure, in his new abode after the catastrophic destruction of his former abode, becomes drunk. This father-drunk-from-wine story takes the violation to another level by leaving nothing to the imagination ... and removing any sacredness to the actions by placing the characters in a cave fit for the burial of the dead. This time he is not drunk of his own initiative but because his daughters ply him wine. They do so in order to preserve their offspring (Gen. 19: 32), that is, to continue the family line even if in a perverted way. Devora Steinmetz comments that '(t)he parallel between the Lot story and the vineyard story supports the implication of a sexual violation of Noah by his son'. Von Rad wonders if something more repulsive is being repressed. Westermann's criticism of Gunkel on this verse is quite illuminating. He writes on this breach of custom:

> This is narrated so clearly that is it difficult to understand how exegetes have missed the obvious meaning. H Gunkel writes: 'According to v. 22 Canaan saw his father's shame and communicated it to his brothers. Both are sinful: he should not have looked and at least should not have spoken of it. Gunkel's explanation is within the framework of a Christian individual ethic which holds almost all exegetes captive here.'

Considering what is to come, Noah's cursing of Canaan, it is quite reasonable to suppose that a significant violation of the father by the son had occurred.[24]

Canaan, like Ham and the Philistines, has endured a poor image over the years. This persistence portrayal of the degradation of the Canaanites has made them an easy target to this very day. They are a people doomed to slavery by its vices for following the moral abomination of its distant ancestor. Abiathar's vehement denunciation of the Canaanite priesthood or political faction of Zadok has been transformed into a theological condemnation of cosmic proportions. Here is an example of when not knowing the individual author and the political context can lead one askew.[25]

9: 24 *When Noah awoke from his wine and knew what his youngest son had done to him*

The father awakens naked and alone in his tent ... yet he still knows exactly what had happened to him and who had done it which seems unlikely. Devora Steinmetz suggests

---

24 Gunkel, *Genesis*, 80; Devora Steinmetz, 'Vineyard, farm, and garden: the drunkenness of Noah in the context of primeval history', *JBL* 113 1994: 193–207, here 199 n13; von Rad, *Genesis*, 137; Westermann, *Genesis 1–11*, 488.

25 William F. Albright, *From the Stone Age to Christianity* (Baltimore: Johns Hopkins University Press, 1940), 214; Allen P. Ross, 'The curse of Canaan', *BSac* 137 1980: 223–240, here 235–236.

that Noah precipitated his own humiliation by setting the stage for his violation by his son. This interpretation is consistent with her understanding of sin and fall, where this time the man cannot claim ignorance as Adam and Cain could: 'In this postdiluvean world, a lack of knowledge is no excuse and no defense against the consequences of sin'. This lesson is important because 'Noah's world is our world'. Gunkel considers Canaan not to be an adult, but an undisciplined child. Children were not expected to possess the wisdom to discern good from evil and therefore could not be held accountable as adults for their actions. Westermann's opines that how Noah learned what had been done to him 'is not important for the narrative'. Who else could have violated him other than Canaan? The story takes for granted Canaan's odious nature, one that even the father recognized.[26]

Westermann's point is valid. His own interpretation is to reject the sexual implications and to take the verse literally: the son saw his father's nakedness. The situation is 'murky', after all, where was Mrs Noah when this 'seeing' transpired? In a biography that would matter; in this symbolic political story, it did not. Abiathar's concern is the relationship between the Canaanites led by Zadok whom he despises and David, not a literal action within a biological family. It is the political consequences that are the focus of his story that now ends the first cycle of the KDB.[27]

9: 25 he said, 'Cursed be Canaan; a slave of slaves shall he be to his brothers'

The immediate reaction of the father to the realization of the violation which has been perpetrated against him by his youngest son is to curse him with slavery. Abiathar did not select these words at random. Each word or phrase was carefully picked to deliver a very strong message in the name of David towards the abuse committed by Zadok. If Abiathar was not already exiled, this verse would have caused it; if he was already exiled then this verse defined him as a new Deborah calling on Israel to act against the Canaanites today as they had done so in the past.

Curse

This curse deserves special attention within the development of Israelite religion. G. Palmer Robertson calls it 'the first recorded curse uttered by a human being'. A human being pronounces the curse. What is his authority to so? What power does the curse on a human by a human have? For Driver, the cursing or blessing by the father exerts a real power in charting the course in life for his offspring. Gunkel sees the curse as a proverb about Canaan which now has been incorporated into a story about Ham. Speiser asks if this curse is a reflection of the facts of the time of the telling of story or is it a wishful projection. Certainly it is the main point of the story.

---

26 Gunkel, *Genesis*, 79–80; G. Palmer Robertson, 'Current critical questions concerning the "Curse of Ham" (Gen. 9: 20–27)', *JETS* 41 1998: 177–188, here 179; Steinmetz, 'Vineyard, farm, and garden', 207; Westermann, *Genesis 1–11*, 489.

27 Westermann, *Genesis 1–11*, 488.

The second consideration is the target of the curse. Westermann observes that of the five times Canaan is mentioned in the pericope, it is here where he is the sole and unambiguous individual, identified neither as a son nor as a brother. This observation leads to the realization that 'The name Canaan therefore is attested with certainty only as an individual name, not as part of the series of three sons of Noah'. The key point is that whereas the first cycle of the KDB had ended with Yahweh blessing Noah (Gen. 8: 21–22), the revised cycle now ends with Noah cursing Canaan.[28]

Slave of slaves

The human father not only curses another human, he does so with slavery, Canaan will be the slave of slave, the עבד of עבד, the superlative designation for the lowest of the low.[29] How did this author expect his audience to respond to the term 'slave of slaves'? The term 'slave', outside the legal codes in the Hebrew Bible where its usage is within the realm of the routine, appears in a number of stories in the Bible. One might serve as a handmaid or under the control of taskmasters performing forced labor.

> Hagar is a slave (Gen. 21: 10–13)
> Joseph threatens slavery to Benjamin and then Judah protests (Gen. 44)

Slavery also could occur at the level of a people and not just an individual.

> Israel remembers that it was a slave in Egypt (Deut. 15: 15, 16: 12, 24: 18, 22)
> Israel performs forced labor for Pharaoh Solomon (I Kings 5: 13, 9: 15)
> The house of Joseph performs forced labor for Pharaoh Solomon with Jeroboam as the taskmaster (I Kings 11: 28)
> Israel rebels against forced labor by killing Adoram the taskmaster of Pharaoh Rehoboam (I Kings 12: 18)
> Israel defines its deity in its covenant as one who delivered them from a house (=kingship) of bondage (Ex. 20: 2).

The collective usages tend to be restricted to Pharaoh and Solomon.

In American terms, the collective usages are more analogous to the numerous field slaves on a plantation than to the fewer house slaves who might live in the same building as the master or on a small farm. In ancient times, such slavery is strongly associated with forced labor on behalf of building for a king. In Mesopotamian tradition, serving the gods, meaning the human representative or king, is the very purpose for which human beings were created. In the Epic of Atrahasis, humans are created for the express purpose of toiling for the gods. Any similarity between that mythical toil and the actual toil on behalf of the king in building and maintaining canals, walls, palaces, and temples is not coincidental. It was standard operating procedure throughout the ancient Near East with its stratified societies and royal rule to mobilize forced labor. Israel's DNA was different: forced labor on behalf of the king for his building projects was abhorrent. In the centuries from Pharaoh

---

28 Driver, *The Book of Genesis*, 169; Gunkel, *Genesis*, 79, 81; Robertson, 'Current critical questions', 180; Speiser, *Genesis*, 61; Westermann, *Genesis 1–11*, 483–484, quotation from 484.

29 Gunkel, *Genesis*, 81; Speiser, *Genesis*, 61.

Merneptah claiming to have destroyed Israel (1212–1202 BCE) to the monarchy, Israelites had not labored on behalf of a king. Canaanites in city-states could not make that claim. As Carr pithily comments, 'there is little reason to believe this use of forced labor by Solomon was invented by the biblical authors'.[30]

One observes the abhorrence to forced labor on behalf of the king in the spin undoubtedly issued by an apologist for Pharaoh Solomon:

> **I Kings 9: 20** *All the people who were left of the Amorites, the Hittites, the Perizzites, the Hivites, and the Jebusites, who were not of the people of Israel –* [21] *their descendants who were left after them in the land, whom the people of Israel were unable to destroy utterly – these Solomon made a forced levy of slaves, and so they are to this day.* [22] *But of the people of Israel Solomon made no slaves; they were the soldiers, they were his officials, his commanders, his captains, his chariot commanders and his horsemen.*

What 'day' that was may be debated. When else other than the time of Solomon would there have been the opportunity for a Jerusalem king to enslave various Canaanite peoples in building projects? The point of the spin regardless of the date of composition was to convince Israelites that their ancestors had not endured forced labor under Solomon. Instead the forced labor was imposed on the Amorites, the Hittites, the Perizzites, the Hivites, and the Jebusites who were still slaves to this very day. So despite the Israelite abhorrence of forced labor and slavery and the worship of a deity who delivered them from that condition, slavery and forced labor of Canaanites, non-Israelite peoples in the land, seemed kosher. The slavery specifically of Canaanites appears in several stories.

> Canaanites in the land of Ephraim become slaves doing forced labor (Josh. 16: 10)
> Canaanites in the land of Manasseh become slaves doing forced labor (Josh 17: 13)
> Canaanites in the land of Israel perform forced labor (Judg. 1: 28–35).

These Canaanite examples seem consistent with the curse being fulfilled.

One should note that the story of Rahab offers an alternative to the idea of enslaving the Canaanites in the land.

> **Joshua 6: 25** *But Rahab the harlot, and her father's household, and all who belonged to her, Joshua saved alive; and she dwelt in Israel to this day, because she hid the messengers whom Joshua sent to spy out Jericho.*

Rahab's special treatment is attributed to her assistance to Israel. As previously noted, she had made her position abundantly clear:

> **Joshua 2: 9** *and [Rahab] said to the men, 'I know that Yahweh has given you the land, and that the fear of you has fallen upon us, and that all the inhabitants of the land melt away before you.'*

Rahab recognizes Yahweh and not Elyon as God in heaven above and on earth beneath (Josh. 2: 11). Her action as a representative of the Canaanite people is in sharp contrast to the Canaanite kings who oppose the emergence of Israel in the land compatible with the intentions of Pharaoh Merneptah's express desire to destroy Israel. Israelite hostility against those peoples in the land of Canaan who supported Pharaoh in the 13th century

---

30 Carr, *The Formation of the Hebrew Bible*, 371.

BCE lingered for centuries. When Abiathar cursed the Canaanites in the name of David, he thought it likely that all Israel would rally behind that call.

Without knowing who authored these stories of Hagar, Joseph, Rahab, and Solomon, it is difficult to reconstruct the slavery debate occurring within the Israelite society during the reign of Solomon. Part of that debate involved Abiathar cursing Zadok and his minions in the name of the (deceased) figure of authority with a put-down to the lowest of the low position within that society. These were fighting words that resembled a taunt or throwing down the gauntlet reminiscent of David's taunting of the Jebusites before capturing the city (see Chapter 8). Did Abiathar have the power to back up this curse? Was he acting alone or did he have allies?

Brothers

In this story, only Noah and Canaan are named. They are the protagonist and antagonist of the story, the two figures in conflict with each other, the vulnerable hero and the villain who abuses that vulnerability. The silent supporting cast are not named and take no actions. The author expected the audience to know who the unnamed brothers were.

The audience may have been familiar with some of the brother stories which touch upon slavery, such as Joseph (Gen. 44 involving Joseph, Judah, and Benjamin). If so, then the two unnamed brothers may have been Joseph/Ephraim and Benjamin. These two brothers occupied the hill-country together with expanded settlements at the dawn of Israel in the archaeological record. In other stories, these two brothers fought the kings of Canaan in the Song of Deborah, clashed in the rape at Shiloh and over Saul's kingship, and divided into two different kingdoms a generation after Solomon had his temple vision in the land of Benjamin. Considering the vineyard examples previously cited, these two brothers should be given the first priority for selection of the two unnamed brothers in Abiathar's story.

Or were the two brothers Joseph and Judah also connected in the story of Joseph or Judah and Benjamin who formed the southern kingdom? While it seems likely that the two brothers were from among the more prominent ones in the literature, that is not proof. It does seem reasonable to ask who were the two brothers in the best position to share dominion over the Canaanites and exactly how they would do it? Unfortunately what was obvious to the original audience is a struggle to understand today. Undoubtedly Abiathar, the author of this supplement to KDB, was part of one of the two-unnamed brothers suggesting one brother was Joseph/Ephraim. In this story then he is reaching out to Benjamin to form an Israelite anti-Canaan alliance to wrest control of the kingdom back from Jebusite Zadok and his Canaanite allies.

10: 15 Canaan became the father of the Jebusites, the Amorites, the Girgashites

Uehlinger perceptively recognizes that 'Canaan thus represents from the beginning an almost tragical character in a play that calls him on stage only to be submitted to the permanent fate of slavery'. Canaan represents a number of peoples and the pre-Israelite people are never identified solely as Canaanites. Unfortunately he dates the creation of this figure to post-exilic times with little relevance for the earlier historical periods. As presented here, Abiathar invented this usage as a pejorative in his conflict at a time when Canaanites were still in the land. They were the people in the kingdom who preferred Elyon, Asherah, Nephilim, and the temple and opposed Yahweh, Israel, and the ark.[31]

With this verse, Abiathar clearly delineates the peoples he means to be cursed. His had identified the array of people who comprise the pro-Solomon factions in the battle for power in Jerusalem. Canaan means the Jebusites, the Amorites, the Girgashites. It does not mean the Gibeonites who had figured so prominently in stories of Joshua and David (Josh. 9–10; II Sam. 21). His designation suggests that even though the phrase 'the land of Canaan' encompassed the entire land comparable to Egyptian usage, all the peoples of the land were not considered 'Canaanite' people. The kingdom of Israel therefore may be said to have included a mixed multitude of ethnically diverse peoples: peoples who had been loyal vassals of Egypt and opposed Israel, peoples who had not supported Egypt and joined the Israelite anti-Egyptian coalition. Now all these peoples were supposed to be one big happy family in a single kingdom ruled from the Canaanite city of Jerusalem. Not quite.

Eventually the list of pre-Israelite peoples in the land of Canaan grew. It would become an almost standardized one of seven names which appears in one form or another 27 times in the Hebrew Bible. This enemies list has been likened to the Egyptian convention of designating the enemies who surround it as the 'Nine Bows'. There is a story to be told as to how these biblical variations developed over time. The process began here with Abiathar and the peoples he identified as foes of Israel at the time he wrote this story.[32]

These names had specific meanings to Abiathar and his audience in the time of Solomon.

Jebusites: The Jebusites were the people of Zadok who dominated the city of Jerusalem, the capital city of the kingdom. This story therefore contains a polemic directed squarely against the pre-Israelite people perceived to be enemies of Israel (and friends of Egypt). These people would be quite willing to broker a marriage alliance between Egypt and Jerusalem-ruled Israel which would really enrage the descendants of the original anti-Egypt Israelites.

Girgashites: The Girgashites appear infrequently in the Hebrew Bible and not at all in the archaeological record. They never appear alone but always as part of a litany of peoples in the land of Canaan. In three instances they are one of seven peoples in the land Yahweh promises and delivers through Joshua: Deuteronomy 7: 1; Joshua 3: 10, 24: 11 (see Table 2, below). In all three cases, the Jebusites and Amorites are mentioned as well as are the Canaanites as a separate people. In a promise to Abraham, the Girgashites are one of ten people including the Amorites and Jebusites who roughly comprise the West Semitic world:

31 Uehlinger, 'The "Canaanites" and other "pre-Israelite" peoples, [part I]', 567–568, 578 n.71, quotation 567–568; Uehlinger, 'The "Canaanites" and other "pre-Israelite" peoples, [part II]', 179–195.

32 Edwin C. Hostetter, 'Geographic distribution of the pre-Israelite peoples of ancient Palestine', *BZ* 38 1884: 81–86; Tomoo Ishida, 'The structure and historical implications of the lists of pre-Israelite Nations', *Bib* 60 1979: 461–490; Walter Wifall, 'The foreign Nations – Israel's "Nine Bows"', *BES* 3 1981: 113–124.

Gen. 15: 19 *the land of the Kenites, the Kenizzites, the Kadmonites,* [20] *the Hittites, the Perizzites, the Rephaim,* [21] *the **Amorites**, the **Canaanites**, the **Girgashites** and the Jebusites*

In one instance the Table of Nations description is repeated.

I Chr. 1: 14 *and the **Jebusites**, the **Amorites**, the **Girgashites**.*

These verses provide scant information from which to derive a clear sense of who the Girgashites were beyond their already being somewhere in the land and an enemy of Israel. No geographical information is provided unlike with the Jebusites and no stories as with the Amorites. Perhaps the most one may claim is that they appear to be a local enemy, a people in the same land as Israel just like the Jebusites in Jerusalem and the Amorites all over the map. It is possible that the Girgashites were added to Abiathar's list which originally consisted of only two enemies: the Jebusites and the Amorites.

Amorites: The Amorites frequently appear in the Hebrew Bible and also in the archaeological record across the ancient Near East (see Chapter 8). The biblical Amorites seem more local in scope: 'Moreover I have given to you rather than to your brothers one mountain slope which I took from the hand of the Amorites with my sword and with my bow' (Gen. 48. 22) and 'Thus Israel dwelt in the land of the Amorites. And Moses sent to spy out Jazer; and they took its villages, and dispossessed the Amorites that were there' (Num. 21: 31–32). They are quite prominent in connection with Transjordanians Sihon and Og and are significant in the conquest stories of Joshua (see especially Num. 21, Deut. 2–3, and Josh. 13). This story is about Amorites who are enemies of Israel.

The situation between Israel and the Amorites appears to have been fluid. They attack Gibeon an ally of Israel (Josh. 9) and then suffer defeat at the hands of Yahweh and Joshua (Josh. 9–10). At one point they are depicted in a subordinate position as a former foe:

Judges 1: 34 *The **Amorites** pressed the Danites back into the hill country, for they did not allow them to come down to the plain;* [35] *the **Amorites** persisted in dwelling in Harheres, in Aijalon, and in Shaalbim, but the hand of the house of Joseph rested heavily upon them, and they became subject to forced labor.* [36] *And the border of the **Amorites** ran from the ascent of Akrabbim, from Sela and upward.*

This description locates them in a battlezone and eventually succumbing to domination by the tribe of Joseph. They also are shown in a more positive light after a time of apparent confrontation:

I Samuel 7: 14 *The cities which the Philistines had taken from Israel were restored to Israel, from Ekron to Gath; and Israel rescued their territory from the hand of the Philistines. There was peace also between Israel and the **Amorites**.*

This peace has replaced the previous time of tension between the two peoples. The Amorites are located near the frontlines of the Israelite-Philistine wars and now have chosen to side with Israel.[33]

---

33 Yigal Levin suggests the materially-Canaanite settlements in the Shephelah that continued to exist from the Late Bronze Age into the Iron Age were Amorite; see Yigal Levin, "'And there was peace between Israel and

Frequently the Amorites appear in a litany of peoples of the land, sometimes with the Girgashites but more often not. They do appear frequently with the Jebusites and Canaanites among others as part of the land to be conquered, see Ex. 3: 8, 17; 13: 5; 23: 23; 33: 2; 34: 11; Deut. 20: 17; Joshua 9: 1; Judges 3: 5; I Kings 9: 20; II Chronicles 8: 7; Ezra 9: 1 (Table 2). Excluding Sihon and Og, there appears to be an effort to locate them in the hill country which certainly is where Israel lived, see Num. 13: 29; Joshua 11: 3, 12: 8 (Table 2).

In summary, the original audience knew exactly who the Canaanites, Girgashites, and Jebusites were. One reasonable interpretation is that

> they were peoples who lived in the land where Israel had settled
> they continued to live there even though they were not politically dominant
> they now lived in the tent of Israel, the political kingdom of Israel
> they had been or were joined together in an anti-Israelite combination.

In this story as proposed here, the Canaanites including the Jebusites, Girgashites, and Amorites are the enemy of Israel and presumed allies of Zadok. They ascended to power after David's death and now they were to be put in their place according to the curse of Abiathar in the name of Noah. Now ends the first cycle of the KDB thereby setting the stage for the arrival of the hero warrior-shepherd king at Hebron in the second cycle.

Conclusion

The prolific writer added one, and only one, story to the first cycle of the KDB, a new ending. In his story of the sons of Noah, Abiathar calls for a renewed 'Song of Deborah' alliance against the Canaanite kings. Whereas once that had meant an alliance against the Canaanite vassals of Pharaoh who had opposed Israel, now it meant taking back the kingdom of Israel from the Canaanite usurpation centered in Jerusalem. Abiathar countered the Zadokite texts by advocating against the political coup which had installed Solomon as king. He vehemently cursed precisely those Canaanites who had violated the former king with that coup. Abiathar did so by putting words in the mouth of Noah suggesting that he had the credibility to speak on behalf of the deceased king just as he had when he was the voice of Yahweh when David was alive. This story cursing the anti-Israelite Canaanite faction is a call for military action and a sharing of the kingdom between Joseph and Benjamin. In another generation that would happen but not in a way anticipated by this author. Just because he was reaching out to his brother against the Canaanite faction, did not mean his brother would accept it. Benjamin may have had visions of power of its own.

---

the Amorites" (I Sam. 7: 14): Israelites and Canaanites in Late Iron I', paper presented at annual conference of the Society of Biblical Literature, Hebrew Bible, History, and Archaeology session, November 24, 2014.

Table 1: Sons of Noah

The Vineyard

a) Positive examples – The planting of a vineyard by the lead character in this story may be viewed as something positive and for which people should give thanks to Yahweh for his blessing. For example:

Isaiah 65: 21 They shall build houses and inhabit them; they shall plant vineyards and eat their fruit.

Jeremiah 31: 5 Again you shall plant vineyards upon the mountains of Samaria; the planters shall plant, and shall enjoy the fruit.

Ecclesiastes 2: 4 I made great works; I built houses and planted vineyards for myself;

Psalm 107: 31 Let them thank Yahweh for his steadfast love, for his wonderful works to the sons of men! [32] Let them extol him in the congregation of the people, and praise him in the assembly of the elders. [33] He turns rivers into a desert, springs of water into thirsty ground, [34] a fruitful land into a salty waste, because of the wickedness of its inhabitants. [35] He turns a desert into pools of water, a parched land into springs of water. [36] And there he lets the hungry dwell, and they establish a city to live in; [37] they sow fields, and plant vineyards, and get a fruitful yield.

All these examples attest the positive image of a kingdom of plenty and abundance where people live free from the fear of hunger.

b) Calling card of the Lord – The reappearance of the vineyard may testify to the power and righteousness of the Lord. For example:

Jeremiah 32: 15 For thus says Yahweh of hosts, the God of Israel: 'Houses and fields and vineyards shall again be bought in this land.'

Ezekiel 28: 26 And they shall dwell securely in it, and they shall build houses and plant vineyards. They shall dwell securely, when I execute judgments upon all their neighbors who have treated them with contempt. Then they will know that I am Yahweh their God.

Amos 9: 14 I will restore the fortunes of my people Israel, and they shall rebuild the ruined cities and inhabit them; they shall plant vineyards and drink their wine, and they shall make gardens and eat their fruit.

Again these examples illustrate the vision of a prosperous kingdom free from want.

c) Warning – The absence of the vineyards or inability to reap its rewards may serve as a warning or punishment to the people whereby the land has returned to nature or its fruits will not be available to the planters. For example:

Deuteronomy 28: 39 You shall plant vineyards and dress them, but you shall neither drink of the wine nor gather the grapes; for the worm shall eat them.

Amos 4: 9 'I smote you with blight and mildew; I laid waste your gardens and your vineyards; your fig trees and your olive trees the locust devoured; yet you did not return to me', says Yahweh.

Amos 5: 11 Therefore because you trample upon the poor and take from him exactions of wheat, you have built houses of hewn stone, but you shall not dwell in them; you have planted pleasant vineyards, but you shall not drink their wine.

Micah 1: 6 Therefore I will make Samaria a heap in the open country, a place for planting vineyards; and I will pour down her stones into the valley, and uncover her foundations.

Zephaniah 1: 13 Their goods shall be plundered, and their houses laid waste. Though they build houses, they shall not inhabit them; though they plant vineyards, they shall not drink wine from them.

Table 2: Abiathar's Canaanites

Girgashites

Deuteronomy 7: 1 When Yahweh your God brings you into the land which you are entering to take possession of it, and clears away many nations before you, the Hittites, the **Girgashites**, the **Amorites**, the **Canaanites**, the Perizzites, the Hivites, and the **Jebusites**, seven nations greater and mightier than yourselves

Joshua 3: 10 And Joshua said, 'Hereby you shall know that the living God is among you, and that he will without fail drive out from before you the **Canaanites**, the Hittites, the Hivites, the Perizzites, the **Girgashites**, the **Amorites**, and the **Jebusites**'.

Joshua 24: 11 And you went over the Jordan and came to Jericho, and the men of Jericho fought against you, and also the **Amorites**, the Perizzites, the **Canaanites**, the Hittites, the **Girgashites**, the Hivites, and the **Jebusites**; and I gave them into your hand.

Amorites

Exodus 3: 8 and I have come down to deliver them out of the hand of the Egyptians, and to bring them up out of that land to a good and broad land, a land flowing with milk and honey, to the place of the **Canaanites**, the Hittites, the **Amorites**, the Perizzites, the Hivites, and the **Jebusites**.

Exodus 3: 17 and I promise that I will bring you up out of the affliction of Egypt, to the land of the **Canaanites**, the Hittites, the **Amorites**, the Perizzites, the Hivites, and the **Jebusites**, a land flowing with milk and honey.

Exodus 13: 5 And when Yahweh brings you into the land of the **Canaanites**, the Hittites, the **Amorites**, the Hivites, and the **Jebusites**, which he swore to your fathers to give you, a land flowing with milk and honey, you shall keep this service in this month.

Exodus 23: 23 When my angel goes before you, and brings you in to the **Amorites**, and the Hittites, and the Perizzites, and the **Canaanites**, the Hivites, and the **Jebusites**, and I blot them out.

Exodus 33: 2 And I will send an angel before you, and I will drive out the **Canaanites**, the **Amorites**, the Hittites, the Perizzites, the Hivites, and the **Jebusites**.

Exodus 34: 11 Observe what I command you this day. Behold, I will drive out before you the **Amorites**, the **Canaanites**, the Hittites, the Perizzites, the Hivites, and the **Jebusites**.

Deuteronomy 20: 17 but you shall utterly destroy them, the Hittites and the **Amorites**, the **Canaanites** and the Perizzites, the Hivites and the **Jebusites**, as Yahweh your God has commanded;

Joshua 9: 1 When all the kings who were beyond the Jordan in the hill country and in the lowland all along the coast of the Great Sea toward Lebanon, the Hittites, the **Amorites**, the **Canaanites**, the Perizzites, the Hivites, and the **Jebusites**, heard of this,

Judges 3: 5 So the people of Israel dwelt among the **Canaanites**, the Hittites, the **Amorites**, the Perizzites, the Hivites, and the **Jebusites**;

1 Kings 9: 20 All the people who were left of the **Amorites**, the Hittites, the Perizzites, the Hivites, and the **Jebusites**, who were not of the people of Israel

2 Chronicles 8: 7 All the people who were left of the Hittites, the **Amorites**, the Perizzites, the Hivites, and the **Jebusites**, who were not of Israel.

One prophet links them with a host of abominable people including the Egyptians.

Ezra 9: 1 After these things had been done, the officials approached me and said, 'The people of Israel and the priests and the Levites have not separated themselves from the peoples of the lands with their abominations, from the **Canaanites**, the Hittites, the Perizzites, the **Jebusites**, the Ammonites, the Moabites, the Egyptians, and the **Amorites**.'

Location

Numbers 13: 29 The Amalekites dwell in the land of the Negeb; the Hittites, the **Jebusites**, and the **Amorites** dwell in the hill country; and the **Canaanites** dwell by the sea, and along the Jordan.

Joshua 11: 3 to the **Canaanites** in the east and the west, the **Amorites**, the Hittites, the Perizzites, and the **Jebusites** in the hill country, and the Hivites under Hermon in the land of Mizpah.

Joshua 12: 8 in the hill country, in the lowland, in the Arabah, in the slopes, in the wilderness, and in the Negeb, the land of the Hittites, the **Amorites**, the **Canaanites**, the Perizzites, the Hivites, and the **Jebusites**.

Chapter 13

PHINEHAS: MESOPOTAMIA J

The writer designated 'Phinehas' differs from the previous two writers. Zadok was a Jebusite Canaanite priest of Elyon who became part of Israel when David made his city the capital of the kingdom. He came from a pro-Egyptian, anti-Israel tradition. Abiathar was a Shiloh priest of Moses whose ancestors had been part of Israel since the beginning and who had reached out to David against Benjaminite Saul's efforts to become king. Abiathar's deity was Yahweh and he came from an anti-Egyptian tradition. These two rivals are both mentioned in the biblical narratives of David and Solomon. Their supplements to the KDB express their opposite points of view in the battle of succession after David died.

By contrast, although the name Phinehas does appear in the biblical narrative, it does not appear in the Solomonic era when this proposed supplement was written. Therefore documenting his presence in the biblical narrative is more problematical. His appearances in other time periods should be viewed through the lens of the time in which they were written. Determining when they were written is a challenge in and of itself. Nonetheless, there appears to be information contained within these texts that sheds light on the situation during the reign of Solomon. Typically priesthoods in Israel have been divided into three groups: Mushite/Levite/Shiloh with Abiathar as its representative, Jebusite/Zadokites with Zadok as its representative, and Aaronids. The presumption to be elaborated on is that Phinehas was a Benjaminite priest of Aaron and Eleazar whose ancestors had been part of Israel since the beginning.

Benjamin is unusual among the tribes of Israel. There is archaeological evidence of its existence beyond the land of Canaan or the Cisjordan region. The Mari Letters from the Upper Euphrates in modern northern Syria from the 18th century BCE refer to a Yaminite tribe. Various scholars have linked these Yaminites to Benjamin. Haran served as a cultic center for these people where donkeys were sacrificed. Drawing on the work of Fleming, Hendel stresses the strong connection between the patriarchal names (Serug, Nahor, Terah, and Haran primarily in Gen. 11: 20–32) and the marriage stories to women from Haran and not from Ur (Gen. 24 and 28–29). These links derive from Amorite times and the Yaminite people. The existence of Haran as a cultic center looms large in his analysis. He posits that the Amorite background was updated to refer to Aramaeans living in the same area when the biblical narratives originated (see Additional Readings: Benjaminites/Yaminites).[1]

---

1   Ronald Hendel, *Reading Genesis: Ten Methods* (Cambridge: Cambridge University Press, 2010), 40–42; *Remembering Abraham: Culture, Memory, and History in the Hebrew Bible* (New York: Oxford University Press, 2012), 52–54; 'Historical context', 65–69; see also Astour, 'Benê-iamina et Jéricho', 9–12, for the importance of Haran as a Benjaminite cultic and its link to the name Jericho as a moon-god site. For the connection between the earlier Amorites and the Aramaeans see Daniel Bodi, 'Is there a connection between the Amorites and the Arameans?' *Aram* 26/1 and 2 2014: 383–409.

Some of the most successful political leaders at Mari demonstrated a remarkable interest in storytelling. Sanders cites the Mari diplomatic narratives as artfully crafted in setting scenes, foregrounding characters, and deploying verbal rhythms in ways not found in Mesopotamia. He regards them as examples of the earliest known West Semitic narrative prose as verbal performance addressed to political leaders and collective assemblies of people. Exactly how, when, or why the format migrated to the land of Canaan remains unknown in the archaeological record. It is reasonable to conclude that such people would bring their traditions into the Israelite culture with them.[2]

Regardless of its origin, the tribe of Benjamin became part of Israel right from the beginning. The lands assigned to Benjamin and Joseph were settled simultaneously by new people in new settlements at the dawn of the Iron I period. Benjamin and its land are part of the story of Israel from Joshua right through Judges until I Samuel when Saul of Benjamin becomes king of Israel. The relationship between Joseph/Ephraim and Benjamin has its high points and low points and at times Benjamin seems separate from Israel rather than part of it. That impression may derive from Benjamin's foreign origin and/or choosing not to be part of Israel when the later split in the time of Rehoboam and became its own kingdom (see Additional Readings: Benjamin).

Unlike with Jebusite Zadok but like Shiloh's Abiathar, Benjamin's story and priesthood date back to the origins of Israel in the Exodus. The introduction of Phinehas occurs with a brief biological note with significant implications.

> **Exodus 6: 25** *Eleazar, Aaron's son, took to wife one of the daughters of Putiel; and she bore him Phinehas. These are the heads of the fathers' houses of the Levites by their families.*

Phinehas first appears as part of a three-generation sequence of Aaron, Eleazar, and himself as part of the Exodus. This establishes his bonifides as an Israelite linked to the very origin of Israel. This genealogical sequence raises the possibility at least that the father Eleazar was a figure of some prominence in his own right perhaps as Benjamin's pro-Saul writer in the time of Abiathar and David. This unsubstantiated comment is meant to raise the possibility of the scribal tradition passing on the political writing skills from the father to the son.

According to the biblical text, the father takes, לקח, a wife, just as the sons of God take wives in Gen. 6: 2. In this instance only one of the daughters is taken and her father is identified. Putiel's name with the 'el' ending like 'Isra-el' demonstrates that the son was of good stock on both the mother's and father's side, a point of contention with the priests of Moses whose putative ancestress Zipporah was Kenite/Midianite. The final observation raises the topic of the configuration of the priestly factions within the overall rubric of priests in Israel. Priest houses just like royal houses are dynastic terms.

The next example of Phinehas's presence in the biblical narrative is the critical one for establishment of his legitimacy. An incident at Baal-Peor involving a Midianite woman turns ugly. Fortunately Phinehas rises to the occasion and saves Israel from the punishment it otherwise deserved. For being the savior, Phinehas is awarded an eternal priesthood.

---

2   Sanders, *The Invention of Hebrew*, 73–74.

> **Numbers 25: 7** *When* **Phinehas** *the son of Eleazar, son of Aaron the priest, saw it, he rose and left the congregation, and took a spear in his hand* [8] *and went after the man of Israel into the inner room, and pierced both of them, the man of Israel and the woman, through her body. Thus the plague was stayed from the people of Israel.* [9] *Nevertheless those that died by the plague were twenty-four thousand.* [10] *And Yahweh said to Moses,* [11] '**Phinehas** *the son of Eleazar, son of Aaron the priest, has turned back my wrath from the people of Israel, in that he was jealous with my jealousy among them, so that I did not consume the people of Israel in my jealousy.* [12] *Therefore say, "Behold, I give to him my covenant of peace;* [13] *and it shall be to him, and to his descendants after him,* **the covenant of a perpetual priesthood**, *because he was jealous for his God, and made atonement for the people of Israel."'*

This passage has generated its fair share of scholarship. For political purposes here, one may view the story as one legitimating of the priesthood of Phinehas. The 'priesthood passed to the Aaronids precisely for their service in cleansing Israel from the taint of Midianite rites! The polemical tone could not be stronger or more obvious.'[3] One may interpret this story solely as one which occurred in the wilderness. One may also interpret the story as using the Exodus setting to define a situation in the present. There came a time when the priesthood of Aaron, the brother of Moses, required legitimation. It occurred through the personhood of Phinehas, the actual person who saved Israel at the expense of the outsider Midianites ... or so he and/or his followers claimed (see Additional Readings: Baal-Peor).

The next appearance of Phinehas demonstrates his leadership ability to resolve differences among the tribes of Israel (Josh. 22). He appears in a story where people from Gad, Reuben, and Manasseh living across the Jordan River, meaning not in the land of Canaan, build an altar of great size to Yahweh. The story also includes references to the sin at Peor and to Acahn for his actions involving the spoils from Jericho (Josh. 7). In this supplement, the people reach out to Phinehas as the leader.[4]

> **Joshua 22: 13** *Then the people of Israel sent to the Reubenites and the Gadites and the half-tribe of Manasseh, in the land of Gilead,* **Phinehas** *the son of Eleazar the priest.*

The wrath of Yahweh and the people Israel is stilled when Phinehas and representatives of the three tribes negotiate a settlement:

> **Joshua 22: 30** *When* **Phinehas** *the priest and the chiefs of the congregation, the heads of the families of Israel who were with him, heard the words that the Reubenites and the Gadites and the Manassites spoke, it pleased them well.* [31] *And* **Phinehas** *the son of Eleazar the priest said to the Reubenites and the Gadites and the Manassites, 'Today we know that Yahweh is in the midst of us, because you have not committed this treachery against Yahweh; now you have saved the people of Israel from the hand of Yahweh.'* [32] *Then* **Phinehas** *the son of Eleazar the priest, and the chiefs, returned from the Reubenites and the Gadites in the land of Gilead to the land of Canaan, to the people of Israel, and brought back word to them.*

---

3   Cross, *Canaanite Myth*, 202.

4   The chapter seems to have multiple levels, connections to Num. 25 and Josh. 7, and a strong cultic emphasis, see John S. Kloppenborg, 'Joshua 22: The priestly editing of an ancient tradition', *Bib* 62 1981: 347–371.

The story attests the stature and skill of Phinehas in resolving an inter-tribal dispute. It demonstrates that he recognizes lands outside the promised land of Canaan as being part of the domain of Yahweh. It demonstrates that he accepts the presence of non-centralized altars to Yahweh as not representing acts of treachery, treason, or sin. Phinehas's involvement is consistent with Saul's actions and Ishbaal's kingdom extending across the river. The Aaronid priesthood of Benjamin is reaching out to its Transjordian allies who accept Yahweh.

A similar example of a tribal inclusion into the people Israel with an altar and priest occurs in Judg. 17–18. In this instance the participants are Micah of Ephraim, Jonathan the son of Gershom the son of Moses, and Dan. The issues involved are the same as those in the Phinehas story. In effect, the sons and daughters of the American Revolution vouch for the legitimacy of peoples who were not part of the people in the beginning. Since Israel was founded on an idea and not geography, membership could be extended. People outside the river valleys of Egypt and Mesopotamia could never be Egyptians or Assyrians/Babylonians; people outside the land of Canaan could be Israelites, that is, inducted into the covenant community.

The issue of people who do not have ancestors who participated in the foundational event of the covenant community was a critical one. In American terms, a comparable example occurred at Gettysburg when Lincoln linked the people of the present both native and foreign-born to the fathers of four score and seven years earlier. Similar connections have been expressed in music and movies with Irish-American George M. Cohan when he updated *Yankee Doodle Dandy*, Jewish-American Irving Berlin with *God Bless America*, Sicilian-American Frank Capra with *Mr. Smith Goes to Washington*, *Meet John Doe*, and *It's a Wonderful Life* with Gary Cooper and Jimmy Stewart, and Puerto-Rican-American Lin-Manuel Miranda with the musical *Hamilton*. These examples demonstrate the critical need to update foundational stories to include new peoples in the community even if the ancestors of the newcomers were not part of the original story. The biblical texts witness ancient Israel's struggles with the same issue of reaching out beyond the Rachel tribes of original Israel. Zadokites did not extend a hand of welcome.

There is some but not much information provided on the father Eleazar, one of four sons to Aaron, two of whom died in the unholy performance of their duties (Lev. 10: 1–2).

Numbers 3: 32 *And Eleazar the son of Aaron the priest was to be chief over the leaders of the Levites, and to have oversight of those who had charge of the sanctuary.*

Following the failed rebellion against Moses in the wilderness, Yahweh instructs Moses to select Eleazar, son of Aaron, to perform the necessary cleansing ritual (Num. 16: 36–40). When Aaron dies, his garments are transferred to Eleazar in a ritual of succession (Num. 20: 22–29). Most prominently, Eleazar helps lead, with the blessing of Moses, a military campaign against the Midianites, a story which includes references to Peor and Balaam (Num. 31). Later Eleazar assists Joshua in the apportioning of the land of Canaan among the tribes of Israel in a leadership position at Shiloh (Josh. 14:1, 17:4, 19:51, 21:1). And then he dies.

> **Joshua 24: 33** *And Eleazar the son of Aaron died; and they buried him at Gibeah, the town of* **Phinehas** *his son, which had been given him in the hill country of Ephraim.*

Eleazar, father of Phinehas and Joshua are both reported to have been buried in the hill country of Ephraim (Josh. 24: 30 and 33). The verses in-between recount the story of the bones of Joseph being transported from Egypt to be buried at Shechem on land which Jacob had purchased from the sons of Hamor (Gen. 33: 19). Sorting these verses by author and context is a challenge in its own right. For purposes here, they attest the ongoing battle among priesthoods to validate their legitimacy through stories of heroic founders. One may observe in these endings to the Joshua cycle the same type of supplements which occurred in the first cycle of the KDB starting with Abiathar, the priest of Moses. The end of a papyrus scroll seems to have been an irresistible lure for additions.

One problem here is with the location at Gibeah where Eleazar is buried by Phinehas, his son. According to Josh. 15: 57, Gibeah is assigned to the tribe of Judah. However, it belongs to the inheritance of Benjamin in Josh. 18: 28. In the story of the rape of Bethlehem concubine, Gibeah is located in Benjamin (Judg. 19-20). Gibeah later is identified as the home of Saul (I Sam. 10: 26), the Benjaminite who becomes king. The stories involving Saul overwhelmingly demonstrate that Gibeah was part of Benjamin. There is no story of wilderness Phinehas dying most likely because Solomonic Phinehas still was alive (see Additional Readings: Gibeah).

These wilderness stories of Aaron, Eleazar, and Phinehas reveal the ongoing conflict between the two leading Israelite priesthoods. It did not begin with Saul's becoming king and it did not end when Solomon died and the kingdom separated. Whereas Zadok used a story of Abram and Melchizedek to justify his priesthood, his god Elyon, and his right to a cut of the royal revenues (Gen. 14: 18–20), the Benjaminite priests of Aaron used the Exodus as the battleground to assert the legitimacy of its priesthood and the god Yahweh. By so doing, they also generated a response from the priests of Moses who had a different view of the Exodus, Yahweh, and their priesthood (see Chapter 14). These writings are some of the most intense and profound in the biblical narrative. While the writings do not possess the artistic genius behind the creator of the KDB, they demonstrate skill in their use of the alphabet prose narrative to wage political war across a vast spectrum in time and space.

> **Reconstructed Narrative of Mesopotamia J:** includes the supplements of Zadok and *Abiathar*
> **Gen. 2: 10 A river flowed out of Eden to water the garden, and there it divided and became four rivers.**
> [11] **The name of the first is Pishon**
> [13] **The name of the second river is Gihon**
> [14] **And the name of the third river is Tigris**
>
> **And the fourth river is the Euphrates.**
>
> 3: 20 The man called his wife's name Eve, because she was the mother of all living.
> 4: 1 Now Adam knew Eve his wife, and she conceived and bore Cain, **saying, 'I have gotten a man with the help of Yahweh.'**
> 4: 2 And again, she bore his brother Abel.

Cain and Abel story

4: 25 And Adam knew his wife again, and she bore a son and called his name Seth, **for she said, 'God has appointed for me another child instead of Abel, for Cain slew him.'**

4: 26 To Seth also a son was born, and he called his name Enosh. At that time men began to call upon the name of Yahweh.

5: 29 [The men] called his [Enosh's] name Noah, saying, **'Out of the ground which Yahweh has cursed this one shall bring us relief from our work and from the toil of our hands.'**

6: 1 When men began to multiply on the face of the ground, and daughters were born to them,[2] the sons of God saw that the daughters of men were fair; and they took to wife such of them as they chose.

6: 4 The Nephilim were on the earth in those days, **and when the sons of God came in to the daughters of men, and they bore children to them.** These were the mighty men that were of old, the men of renown.

Universal Flood story

9: 18 The sons of Noah who went forth from the ark were Shem, Ham, and Japheth.

9: 19 These three were the sons of Noah and from these the whole earth was peopled [scattered].

9: 20 *Noah* was the first tiller of the soil. He *planted a vineyard;* [21] *and he drank of the wine, and became drunk, and lay uncovered in his tent.* [22] *Canaan, saw the nakedness of his father, and told his two brothers outside.*[23] Then Shem and Japheth took a garment, laid it upon both their shoulders, and walked backward and covered the nakedness of their father; their faces were turned away, and they did not see their father's nakedness. [24] *When Noah awoke from his wine and knew what his youngest son had done to him,* [25] he said, 'Cursed be Canaan; a slave of slaves shall he be to his brothers.' [26] He also said, 'Blessed by Yahweh my God be Shem; and let Canaan be his slave.' 9[27] God enlarge Japheth, and let him dwell in the tents of Shem; and let Canaan be his slave.

[Shem became the father of Cush and Canaan.] 10: [8]Cush became the father of Nimrod; he was the first on earth to be a mighty man. [9] He was a mighty hunter before Yahweh; therefore it is said, 'Like Nimrod a mighty hunter before Yahweh'. [10]The beginning of his kingdom was Babel, Erech, and Accad and Calneh, all of them in the land of Shinar. *10:[15] Canaan became the father of* [16] *the Jebusites, the Amorites, the Girgashites.*

10: 18 Afterward the families of the Canaanites spread abroad [scattered]. [19] And the territory of the Canaanites extended from Sidon, in the direction of Gerar, as far as Gaza, and in the direction of Sodom, Gomorrah, Admah, and Zeboiim, as far as Lasha

New end of the first cycle.

The analysis here is based on the presumption that the third supplement to the KDB was done by Phinehas, an Amorite Benjaminite priest of Aaron. He came from a pro-Saul priesthood which was in opposition to the Shiloh priesthood of Abiathar. He came from an anti-Canaanite tradition dating back to the time when Israel emerged in history. Bathsheba was skilled in the game of power and her primary concern was that she remain in power. Her loyalty was no longer to those who helped her become the queen mother but to those who would help her remain the queen mother. She well knew that the enemy of your enemy could become your friend. Bathsheba selected Phinehas to be the temple priest because she had the wisdom to recognize the failure and shortcomings of Zadok and the Jebusite priesthood. She remained focused like a laser on her own political viability and decided a skilled Israelite writer who wanted to be in the center of the action was the best choice for the job. His supplement to the KDB needs to be understood in this context.

Phinehas faced a different situation than had Zadok. The facts on the ground were different when this Amorite Benjaminite priest succeeded the Jebusite one. Phinehas's initial concern was not so much who should be king but which priesthood should have the leadership position in the new temple and the kingdom: the Zadokites of Jebus, the exiled priests or prophets of Moses from Ephraim, or his own Saulide priests of Aaron from Benjamin? As a result, Phinehas changed the tenor of the narrative to legitimate his position in the kingdom as a priest of Aaron.

When he initiated his writing, two different manuscripts existed:

1. The KDB + the Zadok supplement including the new beginning and ending to the story of Cain and Abel
2. The KDB + the Abiathar supplement including a new ending to the flood story and therefore to the entire first cycle.

Phinehas combined these two manuscripts into one, refuted both his predecessors, and offered a new vision. To accomplish this reorientation, he modified the supplements of both Zadok and Abiathar adding to both the Cain and Abel and sons of Noah stories, a task made easier by the fact that he was creating a new manuscript. The very process of copying the two manuscripts into one combined manuscript afforded the opportunity to fully integrate his own additions without having to squeeze anything above or below the lines or in the margins.

He then created an entirely new ending for the first cycle by elevating the story to a global level. He shifted his focus from Abiathar and Zadok in the land of Canaan to the place of the Davidic dynasty and Solomonic temple at the height of the kingdom on the larger world stage. To do so, he created a world stage on which his story would unfold, identified the major civilizations in Mesopotamia which had occupied that stage, and prepared the establishment of the kingdom of David in the land of Canaan. This action undermined the Exodus as the sole basis for Israelite deity and elevated Yahweh to a deity who had created the entire world and ruled all of it from the dawn of time. As it turns out, there was only a narrow window of time when he could convincingly deliver this message, but once it had been written, it remained part of the fabric of Israelite/Judean identity even when the historical circumstances mocked its validity.

Phinehas initiated this supplement in three stages. His texts were not all written at once but dealt with different stages in the reigns of Solomon and Rehoboam. The first stage was when Bathsheba dominated as Queen Mother. At this point, Phinehas focused on justifying to her the validity of bringing him to the royal court and temple at the expense of Zadok and Abiathar. The Exodus played an important role in the legitimation of his priesthood. The second stage was after Bathsheba had died and Pharaoh's daughter became the dominant woman in Solomon's life as his queen:

I Kings 3: 1 *Solomon made a marriage alliance with Pharaoh king of Egypt; he took Pharaoh's daughter, and brought her into the city of David...*

For Zadok it was the high point of his international diplomacy; for Israel including Benjamin, such a marriage was fraught with danger. This political alliance and marriage helped inspire Phinehas to raise his sights to a global level worthy of a daughter of Pharoah despite the traditional anti-Egyptian inclinations (see Additional Readings: Pharaoh's Daughter). Of course, his own ambitions as a Benjaminite contributed to his Mesopotamian perspective as well. The final stage occurred during the reign of Rehoboam when everything Phinehas had worked for came undone. He had become an old-timer and his advice was ignored by the princeling.

Phase I: Phinehas in the time of Bathsheba
Genesis 4: 1 *saying, 'I have gotten a man [שיא] with the help of Yahweh.* [5]

When reading this phrase as an addition to the Cain birth story, certain observations come to mind. First is the apparent joy (one would expect) at the birth of the child.[6] While the biblical account is notably sparse in its language, the presumption is that a joyous event is being proclaimed. Second is the contradiction between the birth described here and the birth process exclaimed in the garden as previously mentioned:

Genesis 3: 16 *To the woman he said, 'I will greatly multiply your pain in childbearing; in pain you shall bring forth children, yet your desire shall be for your husband, and he shall rule over you.'*

Far from being a painful process, the birthing seems to be as easy as it was for the Hebrew women in Egypt:

Exodus 1: 19 *The midwives said to Pharaoh, 'Because the Hebrew women are not like the Egyptian women; for they are vigorous and are delivered before the midwife comes to them.'*

One possible explanation to be considered is that both these writings, Zadok's dry statement on the birth of Cain and Phinehas's more exuberant addition, were written before Gen. 3: 16 and Ex. 1: 19 were written.

A third observation is that women do not give birth to adults. Even the rapidly-growing child in science fiction stories who quickly becomes an adult starts out as a child. Yet, the woman gives birth to a man, *ish* (שיא), and not a child according to the Hebrew. The author certainly could have presented a child had he wanted to. The presence of the man is a sign that this is not a biological birth story.[7]

Westermann concludes that the more appropriate translation than 'gotten' or 'acquire' from the verb form קנה is 'to create' which is what Yahweh had been doing all along in the

---

5   It should be noted that the LXX has 'Elohim' and not 'Yahweh'.
6   Dillmann, *Genesis*, 183; Westermann, *Genesis 1–11*, 289.
7   Van Wolde recognizes that שיא normally is not applied when describing the birth of a baby. She connects the choice of the term to the terms in Gen. 3: 16 and 20 about the pain in child-bearing by the mother of all living beings. But she does not recognize that different authors are involved and that they are in dialog; see Ellen van Wolde, 'The story of Cain and Abel: a narrative study', *JSOT* 52 1991: 25–41, here 27. See also von Rad, *Genesis*, 103.

garden. Eve and Yahweh give life to Cain.[8] In Phinehas's version, the man, Cain, created by the woman, Eve is supposed to be obedient to her just as the man, Adam, created by Yahweh in the garden, and was supposed to be to him.

Westermann comments that 'she sees in the child she has borne the (future) man; she boasts therefore that she has brought forth a man in a way that corresponds to the creation of the man by the creator'.[9] His glowing tribute expresses a fanciful attempt to paint a positive image on what scholars perceive to be a biological birth rather than a political expression through representational figures. Also what is not realized here is that the author of this addition already knows what will happen to this man, Cain.

Two other considerations immediately come to mind based on the political analysis being pursued here. First, why does Phinehas have this woman, the Queen Mother, Bathsheba, utter these words; and second, why does she apply them to this son? In more general terms, how does this declaration advance the political cause of the author in the battle for power?

The story exhibits no opprobrium in the woman mentioning the name of God. The woman is accused of no impropriety nor is any implied. There is nothing in the text in any way shape or form which would suggest that the woman's use of the name of Yahweh was inappropriate or that she really gave birth without the help of Yahweh and is only falsely claiming his help. Quite the contrary, she is the first person in the biblical narrative to use his name and it is used in conjunction with a most serious undertaking: the birth of a son. In this regard, the author is paying homage to the queen mother by giving her this honor.

Eve's use of the name of the Lord without reprobation is consistent with the use by Rahab when she welcomes the spies into her home (Josh. 2: 9–11). Since Rahab was not a member of the covenant community, one could argue that she was not subject to the restrictions on the use of word Yahweh. According to the narrative, for a non-participant in the Exodus itself, she seemed quite conversant with what had occurred … and without reading about it either. In the KDB, David delivers the message through Bathsheba performing as Rahab that the Canaanite people are welcome in the community. Phinehas takes it a step further by validating Jebusite Bathsheba performing as Eve as a member of the Yahweh community.

Phinehas is responding to accusations that Bathsheba had used Yahweh's name in vain. In the story of Solomon's illegitimate rise to power, the name of the Lord is bandied about by a host of characters who all appear to be using it in vain according to the author.

> **I Kings 1: 17** *She [Bathsheba] said to him [David], 'My lord, you swore to your maidservant by the **Yahweh** your God, saying, "Solomon your son shall reign after me, and he shall sit upon my throne."'*

> **I Kings 1: 36** *And Benaiah the son of Jehoiada answered the king, 'Amen! May **Yahweh**, the God of my lord the king, say so.* [37] *As **Yahweh** has been with my lord the king, even so may he be with Solomon, and make his throne greater than the throne of my lord King David.'*

Bathsheba almost appears as an outsider herself in her reference to Yahweh as 'your God' rather than 'our God'. Similarly, Benaiah appears as a non-Israelite who joined forces with David at some point during his career:

---

8   Van Wolde, 'The story of Cain and Abel', 28; Westermann, *Genesis 1–11*, 290.
9   Westermann, *Genesis 1–11*, 290.

II Samuel 8: 18 *and **Benaiah** the son of Jehoiada was over the Cherethites and the Pelethites;*

II Samuel 20: 23 *Now Joab was in command of all the army of Israel; and **Benaiah** the son of Jehoiada was in command of the Cherethites and the Pelethites;*

II Samuel 23: 20 *And **Benaiah** the son of Jehoiada was a valiant man of Kabzeel, a doer of great deeds; he smote two warriors of Moab. He also went down and slew a lion in a pit on a day when snow had fallen. ²¹ And he slew an Egyptian, a handsome man. The Egyptian had a spear in his hand; but Benaiah went down to him with a staff, and snatched the spear out of the Egyptian's hand, and slew him with his own spear. ²² These things did Benaiah the son of Jehoiada, and won a name beside the three mighty men.*

Throughout the story of Solomon's illegitimate rise to power, this mighty man is referred to as 'Benaiah the son of Jehoiada' and 'over the Cherethites and the Pelethites' or both. During the reign of Solomon, Benaiah displaced Joab as leader of the Israelite military forces by murdering him (I Kings 2: 34–35) and then killed Shimei, a Benjaminite 'man of the family of the house of Saul' (II Sam. 16: 5; I Kings 2: 46) as well. Depending on when one thinks these verses were written, one can easily conclude that speaking the name of the Lord, the admission of non-Israelites into the center of power, and the selection of who would provide the military muscle for the throne were contentious issues.

As previously mentioned in Zadok's reference to men calling on the name of Yahweh, there are only four instances of people speaking the name in the equivalent of quotation marks in the first cycle of the KDB. All four should be attributed to this one author, Phinehas. The Cain birth story contains his first use. One should also recognize the likelihood that the story of the first revelation of the name Yahweh to Moses at the burning bush had not been written yet nor had the covenant been amended to prohibit it. It is even conceivable that those developments occurred in reaction precisely to these writings by Phinehas and the claims made by Bathsheba and Benaiah. The effort by biblical scholars to seek an explanations for an apparent violation by Eve in primeval times for speaking Yahweh's name should be redirected towards reconstructing the battle for the throne after David's death.

One might then expect that the son born with the help of Yahweh would be the heir or the successful one just as the son of Bathsheba was the one who would inherit the throne. After all, if the Queen Mother gave birth to a son with the assistance of the deity of the people, clearly that son was marked for greatness. One should also keep in the mind that the author and the audience already know the two existing stories. In the original KDB, this first-born son is a murderer who will not inherit the garden but who will be exiled. In the Zadok supplement, Seth, Enosh, and the temple to Yahweh are presented and Cain is exiled as Abiathar had been. The challenge now is to ascertain how these additional modifications assisted Phinehas in shifting the messages of his predecessors to one more favorable to his faction, the Aaronid priesthood.

This divine claim introduced by the author reveals a subtle and sophisticated mind. This is not a folk tale nor is it about a biological birth. The issue here is one of church and state. As long as Israel did not have a king, priests had no institutional constraints placed upon them. With the establishment of the monarchy, Israel now faced that issue.

Priesthoods should be subservient to the king. Typically, priesthoods were not to challenge the authority of the king.

Monarchy changed the priesthood in Israel. Priesthood power and legitimacy no longer derived directly from the deity without any royal interference. The arena is now the capital city and the Queen is calling the shots. The relationship between church and state is being played out through these genealogies and stories. Zadok had been concerned with royal dynastic; but the time of Phinehas, royal succession was not the issue, priestly power was. The priesthoods were obligated to be loyal to the state and in these circumstances that meant to Bathsheba. Abiathar was not obedient to Bathsheba. He reviled her for leading David astray.

The exile of Abiathar and the death of Zadok provided the Benjaminite priests with an opportunity for power. They offered Bathsheba a way to reach out to the Israelite community in a way Jebusite Zadok could not and Shiloh Abiathar would not. Even the legitimacy of the temple could be shown to have Benjamin roots since Solomon's 'I had a dream' vision occurred in Gibeon, the pro-Israelite Canaanite city in the land of Benjamin (I Kings 3: 4–5). Benjamin was willing to pledge its loyalty to the Davidic dynasty even before the kingdom split. But the principle of royal control over the priesthood is a sword of Damocles. It is fine when one's own priesthood is the one chosen. Both Rehoboam and Jeroboam would make their own political choices to the detriment of both the priests of Moses and Aaron (see Chapter 14).[10]

4: 25 *for she said, 'God has appointed for me another child instead of Abel, for Cain slew him.'*

Westermann's observation that such explanation by the mother for her son is scarcely conceivable is exactly right. He alludes to the possibility that verse 4: 25 without some 'additions' corresponds to 4: 1 and should be equally jubilant. That presumed jubilation derives from his understanding of the story being by one writer about biological relationships and not political ones.[11]

Generally biblical scholars presume a biblical author uses only one designation for the deity. Indeed, the designation is one way scholars identify authors and developed the Documentary Hypothesis. Other considerations alter this presumption. First, there is the writing of the revelation of the name to Moses being subsequent to this verse; second, there is existence of a people Israel named after El worshiping a non-Canaanite deity Yahweh; and third, the pre-Israelite people in the capital city of the kingdom did not worshiped Yahweh, they worshiped a Canaanite deity (Elyon and his consort Asherah). Even though David had planted the ark of Yahweh in Zion, Solomon had been born on Elyon turf, not on land that had been part of Israel for centuries.

---

10 The story of Solomon's dream at Gibeon to build the temple has been likened to an Egyptian royal novella (Siegfried Herrmann, 'The royal novella in Egypt and Israel: a contribution to the historical books of the Old Testament', in Gary N. Knoppers and J. Gordon McConville, eds, *Reconsidering Israel and Judah: Recent Studies on the Deuteronomistic History* (SBTS; Winona Lake: Eisenbrauns, 2000), 493–515. Such similarities would be viewed favorably by those who supported the Egyptian alliance and negatively by those who did not.

11 Westermann, *Genesis 1–11*, 338.

Phinehas faced the political dilemma of needing to reach out to various constituencies including to the Elyon-worshiping Jebusites in the capital. Whether or not he coined the term 'elohim', the actual word used in this verse, to be a plural form noun used in the singular cannot be determined from this verse alone. Suffice it to say, he considered it advantageous to attribute Solomon's birth to Elohim rather than to Yahweh. The latter received his due in the already-written next verse with the historically real temple that had been built to him. Yahweh would speak to Solomon in a dream. The wording here allows if one is so inclined to for the residents of the capital city to see their own pre-Israelite deity as the one responsible for the birth of the king who lives in their city. Realistically, 'elohim' marked the maximum extent Phinehas could reach out to non-Yahwists without compromising his own identity as an Israelite.

> *6: 1 When men began to multiply on the face of the ground, and daughters were born to them,* [2] *the sons of God saw that the daughters of men were fair; and they took to wife such of them as they chose.*

> *6: 4 The Nephilim were on the earth in those days,* **and when the sons of God came in to the daughters of men, and they bore children to them.** *These were the mighty men that were of old, the men of renown.*

The additions by Phinehas are about sex. Sex between whom and for what purpose? To answer these questions requires initially working through the supplement following standard exegetical procedures. Only then can one step back and see the whole picture without getting lost in the details. I will preface this foray with the notice that there were strong emotions and long-standing memories involved. This story is but one of many sex stories that may derive from one incident or related ones. When Phinehas wrote this supplement he had scores to settle. The initial portion of the supplement with Cain addresses the political rivalry, now he turned to the tribal one.

Traditionally, the story of the sons of god and the daughters of men is regarded as 'a piece of raw mythology', perhaps the 'most blatant instance' of it in the sacred canon.[12] Brian Doak's claim that this 'short episode has probably engendered as much commentary and speculation as any other in the Hebrew Bible' rings true even though not verifiable.[13] The common opinion is that Gen. 6: 1–4 is one the most mythic portions of the Hebrew Bible. Supposedly egregious behavior involving the crossing of boundaries demonstrated irredeemable sin necessitating the ultimate punishment: the mass murder of the species save for one righteous man and his family in the world's greatest do-over.

This attitude haunts the interpretations of the text. Commentators see sin, evil, degradation, violation of boundaries culminating in the justifiable Flood since there is no hope for humanity but to start anew. Scholars have been tied up in knots seeking to avoid the scandalized truth of gods having sex with woman and producing children … and equally distraught and overwhelmed in anguish if they face that truth. They wonder

---

12 Meredith G. Kline, 'Divine kingship and Genesis 6: 1–4', *WTJ* 24 1962: 187–204, here 187.

13 Brian R. Doak, *The Last of the Rephaim: Conquest and Cataclysm in the Heroic Ages of Ancient Israel* (Ilex Foundation Series 7; Boston: Ilex Foundation and Washington: Center for Hellenic Studies, Trustees for Harvard University; distributed by Cambridge: Harvard University Press, 2012), 55.

why this 'torso' even is in the Bible (see Chapter 4). Doak's perceptive question asking why include the story if it required so much cleansing and still is inappropriate goes to the heart of the methodological flaw in traditional exegesis: the story is not a myth and is not about primeval times. The story is about Israelite human beings in the present.[14]

Furthermore, none of the people in the story did anything wrong. Despite this persistent castigation of the behavior of the participants, the observation that:

> '…on surface nothing in the biblical text of Genesis 6.1–4 demands that the reader understand those verses in a negative light … as depicting some action or event that is considered inappropriate or dubious'

is exactly right. Similarly Archie Wright is right: 'nothing obvious in the narrative would lead the reader to understand that the characters depicted were responsible for bringing the judgment of the Flood'.[15] By contrast, Westermann's comment on this story that 'it is not J's intention to write history but to tell the story of a primeval event' is exactly wrong.[16] Something else is going on than the traditional damnation of humanity for the violation of the divine/human order.

Phinehas would have been aware of the pre-Israelite Canaanite elements in Zadok's supplement with the Nephilim. His own supplement focusing on the sons of God instead transforms the meaning of the Nephilim without deleting any portion of Zadok's addition. In so doing, Phinehas supersedes the Canaanite Jebusite priests of Zadok as he had the Mushites priests of Shiloh with his addition on the birth of Cain. Phinehas choose to introduce the term 'sons of God. into the narrative. One might suspect that the term relates to or represents the author or his people in some way. The sons of God story is not a battle between the sexes, it is a battle between men using sex.

To begin with, the opening verse in this revised sons of God incident does not indicate anything negative will follow.[17]

6: 1 When

With this beginning, the author signals the start of a new story. Westermann sees Gen. 6: 1–2 as forming a pure narrative introduction.[18] He is correct. The author also was obligated to work within the confines of the inherited material. The garden story already

---

14 Doak, *The Last of the Rephaim*, 60.

15 Archie T. Wright, *The Origin of Evil Spirits: The Reception of Genesis 6.1–4 in Early Jewish Literature* (Tübingen, Mohr Siebeck, 2005), 6, 52, quotations from 6. For a survey of scholarship see Carol Kaminski, *Was Noah Good?: Finding Favour in the Flood Narrative* (New York: Bloomsbury, 2014), 28–35 and for her own views on the unity of 6: 1–8 see 24–63.

16 Westermann, *Genesis 1–11*, 381. Soggin declares 6: 1–4 to be a self-contained episode but then avers that the purpose of the text is to show the increase of sin among human beings as a prerequisite for the Flood: to show that humanity deserved the Flood and therefore the story is connected to 6: 5–7 (J. A. Soggin, 'Sons of God(s), heroes, and *nephlim*: remarks on Genesis 6: 1–4', in Michael V. Fox, Victor Hurowitz, Avi Hurvitz, Michael L. Klein, Baruch J. Schwartz and Nili Shupak, eds, *Texts, Temples, and Traditions : a Tribute to Menahem Haran* [Winona Lake: Eisenbrauns, 1996], 135–136).

17 A. Wright, *The Origin of Evil Spirits*, 55.

18 Westermann, *Genesis 1–11*, 366.

existed. The story of Cain and Abel already existed. The son of Seth already existed. He could not delete the existing text. Instead he works around it. Obviously in a linear sense, the sons of God story which this author creates follows the son of Seth story the previous author created. However, that does not necessarily mean it is occurring subsequent to it. By choosing this beginning, one could also construe the sense of the text as 'At the same as the sons of Seth story occurred, there were these other events going on'. After all, in the real world things do occur simultaneously and events do not occur in a vacuum. That is a lot to extract from a single word but the reasonableness becomes clearer as one proceeds through the supplement. Keep in mind the story follows immediately after men begin calling the name of God in the temple.

6: 1 men

These men are the real men or *adam* (אדם) as one finds in the garden story. They are not the *ish* (איש) men he uses to describe the birth of Cain or the *enosh* (אנוש) men Zadok used who called on the name of Yahweh. The exact nuances of the different terms in the Hebrew translated the same in English may be lost to history. It is reasonable to surmise that these choices were not random or accidental. These men are not the enemy or foreigners. Zadok's story of the sons of Seth ends with men calling the name of Yahweh. These men appear out of nowhere and remain nameless. That does not mean their identity was unknown to the audience since the reference is to the audience itself. For example, when an American politician refers to 'the people' or 'We the People' it is not necessary to include the adjective 'American' for the audience to know which people are meant. However, in this story, the focus will not be the males in Zadok's audience calling the name of Yahweh for the first time. It will be about another group of men in the Israelite community and the action they take.

6: 1 began to multiply

This multiplication implies an unmentioned participant in the process. While Eve may be the mother of the all the living, there is no mention here of anyone in the role of mother in this multiplication. It occurs outside the dynastic line.

6: 1 on the face of the ground

This seemingly routine phrase, on the face of the ground, האדמה, the *adamah*, helps draw a line in the sand between the competing priesthoods. It appears elsewhere in the first cycle of the KDB as well. One notes the connection between the men *adam* and the ground *adamah*. The sons of God is their story. The phrase 'face of the ground', appears throughout the first cycle of the KDB.

> Gen. 2: 6 but a mist went up from the earth and watered the whole *face of the ground*
> Gen. 6: 7 So Yahweh said, 'I will blot out man whom I have created from the *face of the ground*...'

Gen. 7: 4 For in seven days I will send rain upon the earth forty days and forty nights; and every living thing that I have made I will blot out from the *face of the ground.*
Gen. 7: 23 He blotted out every living thing that was upon the *face of the ground...*
Gen. 8: 8 Then he sent forth a dove from him, to see if the waters had subsided from *the face of the ground;*
Gen. 8: 13b the waters were dried from off the earth; and Noah removed the covering of the ark, and looked, and behold, the *face of the ground* was dry.

The meaning of the phrase seems to encompass the same geographic expanse as a similar phrase also used in the biblical narrative, 'the face of all the earth' or 'the face of the whole earth' הארץ, the *eretz*, in English.

Gen. 7: 3 and seven pairs of the birds of the air also, male and female, to keep their kind alive upon the *face of all the earth.*
Gen. 8: 9 but the dove found no place to set her foot, and she returned to him to the ark, for the waters were still on *the face of the whole earth...*
Gen. 11: 4 Then they said, 'Come, let us build ourselves a city, and a tower with its top in the heavens, and let us make a name for ourselves, lest we be scattered abroad upon *the face of the whole earth.*'
Gen. 11: 8 So Yahweh scattered them abroad from there over *the face of all the earth...*

These two expressions refer to the entire earth, as least as the term was geographically understood then.

The terms are a diagnostic marker. The author of the Tower of Babel story uses the term *eretz* 'earth', while the author here and in the garden story uses *adamah* 'ground'. Both phrases appear in the Flood story. One explanation is that two authors were involved: one who wrote the Tower of Babel story (see Chapter 14) and the other who used the phrase here and in his other additions while both writers contributed supplements to the Flood story. Phinehas's use of the term 'the face of the ground' may even help prepare for the Flood story. As with the example for 'men', individual writers had different preferences and reasons for the vocabulary choices that are obscured when all the texts are lumped together as 'J.' The Hebrew terms differentiate the warring factions.

6: 1 and daughters were born to them

One presumes that the daughters were not born by the men. The absence of specific reference to the mothers is striking. One could say that the 'men' here refers to all human beings including the women who become mothers but that may be reading contemporary values into the text. The biblical narrative is well aware of women as mothers as they form an essential part of many stories from the garden to Bathsheba. Women not only give birth but play an active role in the lives of men, fathers, brothers, husbands, and sons. The identity of these daughters is another clue in unraveling the message Phinehas was delivering.[19]

---

19 Van Wolde similarly is struck by the absence of the mothers. As it turns out she uses the word 'strikes' whereas I wrote 'striking' without my having borrowed the term her since I had not yet read her book. See Ellen van Wolde, *Words become worlds: semantic studies of Genesis 1–11* (BiIntS 6; Leiden: E. J. Brill, 1994), 72.

6: 2 and 6: 4 the sons of God

Before examining the meaning of 'the sons of God' in this story, one should also recognize that other similar familial and social designations are possible. For example, in the Genesis/ Kings narrative 'man of God' is used to refer to specifically named person or anonymous individual.

> *Man of God*
> Moses (Deut. 33: 1; Josh. 14: 6, *ish*)
> Samuel (I Sam. 9: 6–7–8–10, *ish*): meeting future king Saul
> Shemaiah (I Kings 12: 22, *ish*): prophet providing military advice to king Rehoboam
> Elijah (I Kings 17: 18, 24, *ish*)
> Elisha (II Kings 4 eleven times and in II Kings 13: 19, *ish*)
>
> *man of God (anonymous)*
> Judg. 13: 6, 8 (*ish*): speaking to the wife of Manoah, future mother of Samson
> I Sam. 2: 27 (*ish*): speaking to Eli, prophet at Shiloh
> I Kings 13 (*ish*): 15 examples of a man from Judah at Bethel speaking first to king Jeroboam and then to a prophet of Bethel
> I Kings 20: 28 (*ish*): providing military advice to unnamed king of Israel
> II 23: 16–17 (*ish*): in time of King Josiah referring the incident in I Kings 13 above

In these instances, the figure is human. He frequently operates in a prophetic or cultic manner very often in conjunction with a king and with a special relationship to the deity. These examples should be kept in mind in the effort to ascertain what Phinehas meant when he introduced a similar term into the narrative.

While Zadok focused on the Nephilim as Canaanite mighty men, Phinehas stresses the sons of God, *bene ha'elohim*. Then these sons of God engage not in military actions but in procreation with women who bear a different designation as daughters of men, *benoth ha'adam*. The action definitively is sexual but the biological basis does not invalidate political and social implications (see Additional Readings: Sons of God).

The phrase 'sons of God' has proved problematic both in religion for what it indicates about God and for secular scholars simply wrestling with defining the term. Before seeking to determine its meaning, one should recognize that the author took for granted the audience's knowledge of who they were.[20] Now it has to be reconstructed. Three different interpretations have been applied over the years. The first meaning is the one which occurs to people at first glance and causes the most consternation – that these beings are typical of what one finds in traditional (Greek) mythology. To have divine beings in pagan mythology have sex with humans to produce a mixed being seems standard operating procedure and would not cause a second glance there. However, the story is in the Bible where there is only one god and he does not have children except once if you are Christian and then under special circumstances devoid of sex where he did not take/marry the woman.

As a result, people, beginning in Hellenistic times sought alternative explanations. One was that these beings were Sethites, sons of Seth, the good son who replaced the murdered

---

20 Victor P. Hamilton, *The Book of Genesis* (Grand Rapids: William B. Eerdmans Publishing Company, 1990), 262.

Abel. The second alternative was that they were angels who had fallen, a more acceptable idea than calling them gods. Part of the challenge today derives from attempting to understand what the phrase would have meant to the original audience rather than to a Hellenistic, Christian, rabbinic or academic audience (see Chapter 4).

Archaeology seemingly provided a way to resolve the issue scientifically. The archaeological discoveries at Ugarit on the Syrian coast opened a window into the pre-Israelite Canaanite culture centuries before the Elijah stories and with a completely different perspective – Baal was the good guy! In these stories the god El and his wife Asherah have dozens of sons, there are assemblies of gods, and the idea of plural gods and offspring is commonplace. The Ugaritic tales however do not involve actual sex between beings divine and human. Still, their discovery made it all too convenient to see in the biblical texts an extension of the values and terminology of these Canaanite traditions.

The analysis of Gen. 6: 1–4 in modern times became susceptible to the Ugaritic mythic lens just as Hellenistic giants once slanted biblical exegesis of Nephilim. These sons of god then were divine beings who were members of the Yahweh's heavenly entourage who functioned in various ways.[21] For example, consider these comments by Simon Parker about this story:

> 'Yahweh is conspicuous by his absence from these mythical events … The mythological character of these references [to *gibborim* and Nephilim] leaves no doubt that the divine beings in question in question are the gods of traditional myth known to use from various Near Eastern cultures…'

> 'Thus in Gen. 6: 1–4 the divine beings are portrayed in a reference to a traditional myth (or myths), which is given a place in events leading up to the deluge.'[22]

All of this is predicated on the supposition that the beings in Gen. 6: 1–4 are to be identified as gods comparable to such beings in 'other' myths from the neighboring peoples.

Alternatively, if these sons of god were human, specifically, kings, then this line of analysis has little to do with the understanding the story. David Clines addresses this possibility as one of the three interpretations for the identity of the 'sons of God'. He states that the use of 'son of God' for a human king while well-attested in the ancient Near East was reserved for 'courtly rhetoric and poetic adulation'. Clines perceives this story to be a 'satanic parody of the idea of the image of God in man'. Look what these divine beings on earth have done! Their actions represent an 'exercise of royal violence and despotic authority over other humans'. Based on this interpretation, the prophet who exclaims 'Thou art the man' (II Sam. 12: 7) in the face of such a despotic exercise of royal violence should be praised as should David for acknowledging his transgression, by responding 'I have sinned' (II Sam. 12: 13).[23]

On the other hand, perhaps the author of these verses was not incensed by the actions which had transpired. Perhaps the 'son of God' should be understood as a king:

---

21 Hendel, 'The Nephilim were on Earth', 17.

22 Simon B. Parker, 'Sons of (the) God(s)', in *DDD*, 794–802, here, 796–797. This insight enables Parker to understand Yahweh's position in Deut. 32: 8 and Ps. 82 vis-a-vis the other deities in the council.

23 David J. A. Clines, 'The significance of the "Sons of God" episode (Genesis 6: 1–4) in the context of the Primeval History (Genesis 1–11)', *JSOT* 13 1979: 33–46, quotations from 34, 37.

Ps. 2: 7. *I will tell of the decree of the Yahweh: He said to me, 'You are my son; today I have begotten you.'*

Zevit challenges this statement offering more prosaic explanations. As Baal was adopted by El so the king is adopted by Yahweh. The father-son language expresses a tutorial relationship as one becomes part of a band of prophets with a leader (II Sam. 2: 14).[24]

Based on royal approach, the taking a woman to be a wife could be construed to be within the king's rights. In that case, David, a mighty man, simply should have asserted to the prophet Nathan his right as the king to take the beautiful daughter of man. Why assume everyone supported the prophet's condemnation of David's behavior in the Bathsheba story?[25] This interpretation holds significant implications for understanding the legitimacy of the marriage of David to Bathsheba and of their descendants starting with Solomon. An audience in Jerusalem would have made connections to the political circumstances as it understood them at the time of the story's telling. David Petersen comments on the arbitrary exercise of power by the king in the ancient Near East as an act inviting the wrath of the gods and it being 'particularly important for the writer of Gen. 6: 1–4'. It does not automatically follow that a king who did take a woman was considered to have abused his power.[26]

Meredith Kline also pursues the king option amplifying the position to a sacral level. In his analysis he refers to scholarship about sacral kingship. In particular, Kline cites Ps. 82 along with Ex. 21: 6; 22: 8, 9, 28 as examples within the biblical canon of similar titles for theocratic rulers in Israel. Even though this approach had been suggested in ancient times, Kline is aware that this 'Jewish view' has been 'lightly dismissed in critical surveys of the long debate over the exegesis of Gen. 6: 1–4' even though 'it alone of all the views was on the right track'. His solution links the sons of God pericope to the dynastic Cainite genealogy with its emergence of cities in Gen. 4: 17–24 (see Chapter 2). The sons of God story then condemns the polygamy and tyranny of the princes who are the Nephilim/*Gibborim* born to the royal houses, similar to what transpired in the Sumerian antediluvian traditions.[27]

This line of reasoning finds acceptance within Assyriology. For example, Irene Winter writes:

> 'From the beginning of the attestation of the royal title in the consolidated city-state, well before the determinative for "god" and the divinity were officially and explicitly ascribed to rulers, we have both text and imagery suggesting that the ruler/king was literally represented as a "big man", larger in scale than others, and in a filial relationship to the gods...'[28]

---

24 Ziony Zevit, 'Israel's royal cult in the ancient near eastern *Kulturkreis*', in Gary Beekman and Theodore Lewis, eds, *Text, Artifact, and Image: Revealing Ancient Israelite Religion* (BJS 346; Providence, RI: *BJS*, 2006), 189–200, here 197–199.

25 For an historical Davidic basis to the story see Wifall, 'Gen. 6: 1–4', 294–301.

26 David L. Petersen, 'Genesis 6: 1–4, Yahweh and the organization of the cosmos', *JSOT* 13 1979: 47–64, here 59.

27 Kline, *Divine Kingship*, 191, 193–199, quotation from 194.

28 Irene J. Winter, 'Touched by the gods: visual evidence for the divine status of rulers in the ancient Near East', in Nicole Brisch, ed., *Religion and Power: Divine Kingship in the Ancient World and Beyond* (OIS 4; Chicago: Oriental Institute, 2008), 75–10, here 81. See also, Simo Parpola, 'Sons of god: the ideology of Assyrian kingship', *Odyssey* 2/5 1999: 16–27, 61.

Fellow Assyriologist Jacob Klein anticipates this insight and offers an ethnic and political twist:

> 'Sumerian literature probably composed in the Ur III period (*c.* 2100–2000 BCE) assumes that the Early Dynastic priestly kings of Uruk had been divine or semi-divine beings, descended from gods… Another literary motif frequently invoked as proof of divinity of the Ur III and Isin kings is their claim of divine lineage… The Isin kings, descended from Amorite families, based the legitimation of their kingship solely upon Nippur religious establishment and, with few exceptions, claim to be the sons of Enlil or the well-known Amorite deity Dagan.'[29]

Biblical scholar Rainer Albertz makes the sweeping statement:

> 'In the Near East the king was regarded in one way or another as more or less directly God's representative on earth: as God's creation, the son of God, the image of God or even God himself, who imposed divine rule outside the state and established divine order within, thus guaranteeing the existence of the state.'[30]

Perhaps in a time when angels were messengers and not Michael, when the Greek giants were unknown, and when there were no Jewish rabbis, Catholic priests, Protestant ministers, or university scholars, the original audience of the story of the sons of God was more amenable to seeing the sons of God as kings since the kings were the most important people in their lives.

In these circumstances, one must remain cognizant of the place of biological references in political situations. As previously mentioned, the language of kingship in the ancient Near East employed kinship terms to express such relationships. Kings could be 'brothers' especially as in the Amarna Age. The use of kinship terms in diplomatic correspondence should be understood without any suggestion of biological validity. No dishonesty or deception was implied either. The abstract language of political science had yet to be invented. Assyria's effort to be join the club and be considered a 'brother' to the great kings is a political not biological endeavor. For the relationship between a king and his deity, the use of 'son' was an appropriate way for an individual to proclaim that he is the counterpart on earth and obedient to the deity in the heavens without there being any biological considerations.[31]

David Melvin wonders if perhaps the 'myth which lies behind the text [Gen. 6: 1–4] in its present form, included the divine instruction motif'.[32] Melvin's approach serves as a reminder that the questions of the origins of civilization, acquiring of knowledge, and building of empires are part of a series of son episodes.[33] Kings, or people who become

---

29 Jacob Klein, 'Sumerian kingship and the gods', in Gary Beekman and Theodore Lewis, eds, *Text, Artifact, and Image: Revealing Ancient Israelite Religion* (BJS 346; Providence, RI: Brown Judaic Studies, 2006), 115–131, here 118, 123, 124; for examples of individual kings see 124 n.42, 125, 125 n.43 and n.44.

30 Rainer Albertz, *A History of Israelite Religion in the Old Testament Period* (Louisville: Westminster/John Knox Press, 1994), I: 116.

31 For Assyria's effort to be join the club and be considered a 'brother' to the great kings see Feldman, 'Assur Tomb 45', 37–39; Tugendhaft, 'How to become a brother in the Bronze Age', 93–97.

32 David P. Melvin, 'Divine mediation and the rise of civilization in Mesopotamian literature and in Genesis 1–11', *JHS* 10 2010: Article 17, 2–14, http://www.jhsonline.org/Articles/article_145.pdf, here 12.

33 Robert S. Kawashima, '*Homo faber* in J's Primeval History', *ZAW* 116 2004: 483–501, here 492. See also Petersen on the connection between Gen. 6: 1–4 and Gen. 3 ('Genesis 6: 1–4', 56–58).

kings, frequently play a leadership role in maintaining and preserving civilization. However, whereas in Mesopotamian myths, human civilization arises due to divine intervention, in J human initiative is responsible from the Cainites to Nimrod. The common perception is that these endeavors depict 'an increasing descent of humanity into sin' that reflects poorly on the various aspects of civilization that accompany this decline.[34] However it should be noted that the Cainites who create civilization in Gen. 4: 17–24 and Moses who dispenses justice in Ex. 18 were not kings. Their actions highlight that not everyone within the Israelite body politic accepted the royal model or saw human initiative as a sin.

James Coleran notes that 'the *idea* that men could be and were sons of God runs throughout the whole Old Testament'. He cites such verses as Ex. 4: 22, Jer. 3: 14, 19; 31: 9, 20 and Hos 1: 10/2: 1 among others. He considers them 'a last remnant of a group of just and faithful worshipers of God on a sinful earth; when they fell away into sin (especially due to their intermarrying with the sinful group)'.[35] Part of the reason for multiple expressions on these concerns may be that different constituencies within the Israelite community had different views as to how this was accomplished and that these multiple views now exist within a single narrative.

Even assuming the sons of God was a royal designation, there are problems. This is not a story about an individual king coming into a daughter of man to produce a child. This is not a story about David seeing Bathsheba, wanting her, acting on his lust, and producing Solomon. That scenario is included within the larger rubric of the text but there is no biblical tradition of group royal sex. There are no stories of multiple kings simultaneously taking multiple women to multiply. The 'sons of Gods' story is one of collective sex, consensual sex, and sex which produces children between two groups of humans, male sons of God and female daughters of men. More is involved than simply justifying David's marriage to Bathsheba.

6: 2 and 6: 4 daughters of men (adam)

Daughters do not appear in the stories in the KDB's first cycle except in this story. 'Daughters of men' by that phrase does not appear anywhere else in the text either. Daughters alone appear often in connection to a specific family group such as the daughters of Lot (Gen. 19), Laban (Gen. 28, 29, 31), Jethro (Ex. 2), and Zelophedad (Num. 26–27). Daughters also may be identified by a political entity such as the daughters of Canaan or Canaanites (Gen. 24: 3, 37), Moab (Num. 25: 1), Israel (Deut. 23: 17), Philistines (Judg. 14: 1–2), Shiloh (Judg. 21), and by implication Shechem (Gen. 34). The men of Sodom and Benjamin in particular do not fare well in some of these daughters' stories.

6: 2 were fair

The daughters of men are 'good' *tov* to look at. Rebecca is described the same way. By contrast Sarah and Rachel are described as 'beautiful'.[36] This raises the possibility that this

---

34 Melvin, 'Divine mediation', 11.

35 James E. Coleran, 'The sons of God in Genesis 6, 2', *TS* 2 1941: 488–509, quotation from 506.

36 Carol M. Kaminski, 'Beautiful women or "false judgment?" interpreting Genesis 6: 2 in the context of the

author and the author of the Rebecca story (Gen. 24) concluding the KDB Abram cycle and this sons of God supplement might be the same person. Vocabulary may serve as a diagnostic marker among the priesthoods competing for power.

Van Wolde objects to the double standard. Men who are *tov* are 'good', 'fair', or 'just' in the English translations. Women who are *tov* generally are 'beautiful' or 'attractive'. She thinks the 'goodness' of the women was recognized by the sons of God.[37]

6: 2 to wife or wives

Whether or not the women were taken as wives remains debatable among biblical scholars. Based on convention one expects the *lamed* (ל) prefix to signify their status as wives as belonging to the males.[38] Kraeling constructively suggests the storyteller purified the story by replacing its promiscuity with wives.[39]

6: 2 took

Gunkel unequivocally states that 'the sons of God in their superior might prevailed upon the daughters of men at will'.[40] Regardless of the nature of the sons of God, Gunkel does not envision a relationship comparable to the man and the woman in the garden, Jacob and Rachel at the well, or even David spotting Bathsheba. Such 'taking' also occurs when Yahweh takes the man and puts him in the garden (Gen. 2: 15), when Yahweh takes a rib from the sleeping man (Gen. 3: 6), when the woman takes fruit from the tree (Gen. 3: 6), and when Lamech takes wives (Gen. 4: 19). In fact, the actions of the sons of God and the vocabulary of seeing something good and then taking it bears direct resemblance to the actions of the woman in Gen. 3 suggesting that the author might be same.[41] Nothing wrong had occurred. Any application of force would seem to be superfluous to the story and should be considered eisegesis. Something else is going on here.

Collective sex is a rare phenomenon in biblical stories. One man and one woman is more common. Prominent stories involving the threat of or the actual act of collective sex are violent and heinous.

1.　The anonymous men of Sodom threaten the anonymous daughters of Lot. They are prevented from raping the women due to the intervention of two messengers of Yahweh (Gen. 19).
2.　The anonymous men of Gibeah 'which belongs to Benjamin' (and was Saul's capital) ravage the anonymous concubine of Bethlehem (home of David) leading to the Levite (priest of Shiloh)

Primaeval History', *JSOT* 32 2008: 457–473, here 458–459. Tov also is used for the sister of the wife of Samson (Judg. 15: 2), Saul (I Sam. 9: 2), and Ben-hadad (I Kings 20: 3). The full implications of the application of this term in Gen. 6: 2 and its relation to other biblical texts employing it are outside the scope of this study.

37　Van Wolde, *Words Become Words*, 73.
38　A. Wright, *The Origin of Evil Spirits*, 134–136.
39　Kraeling, 'The significance and origins of Gen. 6: 1–4', 207.
40　Gunkel, *Genesis*, 56.
41　See Lyle Eslinger, 'A contextual identification of the bene *ha'elohim* and benoth *ha'adam* in Genesis 6: 1–4', *JSOT* 13 1979: 65–73, here 66.

to call for avenging this monstrosity (presumably with the assistance of a man of Bethlehem) (Judges 19–20).

3. The anonymous men of Benjamin took the daughters of Shiloh who were dancing the dances at the yearly feast of Yahweh as their wives and rebuilt their tribe (Judges 21).

> **Judges 21: 19** *So they said, 'Behold, there is the yearly feast of Yahweh at Shiloh, which is north of Bethel, on the east of the highway that goes up from Bethel to Shechem, and south of Lebonah'.* [20] *And they commanded the Benjaminites, saying, 'Go and lie in wait in the vineyards,* [21] *and watch; if the daughters of Shiloh come out to dance in the dances, then come out of the vineyards and seize each man his wife from the daughters of Shiloh, and go to the land of Benjamin.* [22] *And when their fathers or their brothers come to complain to us, we will say to them, "Grant them graciously to us; because we did not take for each man of them his wife in battle, neither did you give them to them, else you would now be guilty."'* [23] *And the Benjaminites did so, and took their wives, according to their number, from the dancers whom they carried off; then they went and returned to their inheritance, and rebuilt the towns, and dwelt in them.*

There was bad blood between Benjamin and Ephraim. There was a stain on the Israelite social fabric. The people who had been a band of brothers in the Song of Deborah were competing males at harvest celebration at Shiloh. The memories lingered.

Sometimes the mating process does not work out. Sometimes the cliques, gangs, factions, gathered at a single dance clash. Apparently in at least one instance, the boys of Benjamin crashed the party at Shiloh and ended up with some of the women as mates. In non-academic American mythical terms the genre to which the sons of God story belongs is *West Side Story*. The antipathy may be visceral, even tribal. With his supplement to the Nephilim of Zadok, Phinehas of Benjamin addressed the legacy of that action on behalf of his tribe. His revision sanctifies the sons of God and absolves them of any wrongdoing with the daughters of men. The revision claims the sex was consensual, the mating legitimate, and the community better off for it. The stain of Benjamin has been removed.

This interpretation makes the sons of God not angels, kings, or Sethites but human Benjaminites. That requires some explaining.

First, 'sons' is being used here to define men who are obedient to the father meaning to the king and/or god. The term is being used to express a political concept and not a biological one just as was done with making the adult Cainites/priests of Moses sons of Eve/Bathsheba.

Second, Phinehas uses the term 'Elohim' in his addition to the sons of Seth story (Gen. 4: 25) and in his addition to the sons of God story. These uses are connected as they were part of one story. In the Seth story, the king's obedience to God is pledged by the mother who calls upon him. Similarly Hannah would pledge her son to Yahweh in I Sam. 1: 22. In effect, the author dedicates these sons and the son Seth to the same deity in one continuous story. Benjamin is an ally of Solomon and both serve the same deity Elohim.

Third, the mighty men or warriors making this pledge are not Canaanites from days of old as in Zadok's version. They are not the Cherethites or Pelethites of Benaiah either. Instead they were Israelites pledging their military muscle to the king. Within Israel, the best known warriors were from the tribe of Benjamin, the people of Ehud, Saul, and Judges 20–21.

Benjamin stands with Solomon not Abiathar and Shiloh and it proclaims this commitment throughout the land to the people of Israel in a story. One may anticipate Phinehas will reject Abiathar's offer to share rule in Canaan.

This interpretation is distinctly different from traditional biblical scholarship. It is at marked variance to the mythic, folkloristic, theological sin understandings which prevail. The approach taken here is that the writing was relentlessly political. The cosmic order the story meant to legitimate was not a generic one but the one of a specific king at a specific point in time. The story was not mythic, literary, historical, theological, or about the human condition. The writings were about contemporary political events expressed through the language of the family relationships. Phinehas is pledging loyalty by Benjaminite priesthood and warriors to Bathsheba, Solomon, and temple. He is cleansing his tribe of the mark placed upon it. Think of the text in its political context as one story expressing the view of the ascending political faction at the expense of the Jebusite and Shiloh priesthoods.[42]

To recap Phinehas's supplement [**in bold**] to Zadok so far:

> 3: 20 David called his wife's name Bathsheba, because she was the mother of all living.
> 4: 1 Now David knew Bathsheba his wife, and she conceived and held power over the priests of Moses, the oldest priesthood, **saying, 'I have gotten a man with the help of Yahweh'.**
> 4: 2 And again, she bore his brother Abel.

Cain and Abel story new meaning by implication: Abiathar abuses his power and is exiled; Zadok and the Jebusites are politically dead.

> 4: 25 And Adam knew his wife again, and she bore a son and called his name Seth, **for she said, 'Elohim has appointed for me another child instead of Abel, for Cain slew him'.**
> 4: 26 To Seth also a son was born, and he called his name Enosh. At that time men began to call upon the name of Yahweh at his temple in Jerusalem on the site of the threshing floor.
> **6: 1 When men of Israel began to multiply on the face of the ground, and daughters were born to them,** [2] **the Benjaminites obedient to Elohim saw that the daughters of Shiloh were fair; and they took to wife such of them as they chose.**
> 6: 4 The Nephilim were on the earth in those days, **and when the Benjaminites came in to the daughters of Shiloh and they bore children to them.** These were the mighty men that were of old, the men of renown.

Moving on, one finds that Phinehas has created a new ending to Abiathar's sons of Noah story by revising the ending.

> 9[26] He also said, 'Blessed by Yahweh my God be Shem; and let Canaan be his slave'.

---

42 As it turns out, this approach for the sons of God also was taken in 19th century England. In his analysis of the artistic portrayals of the story then, Steven Holloway suggests these 19th century creations were about 'the political and social fallout of the Napoleonic wars, the industrial revolution, and Evangelical anxieties concerning liberal thought and shifting social mores;' see Steven W. Holloway, 'Imagining the Unspeakable: Genesis 6: 1–4 in the nineteenth century', *PEGLBS* 28 2008: 25–40, here 36. Something similar may have occurred with the analysis from an evangelical perspective by Doedens. He defines the sons of god as 'divine or heavenly beings not otherwise specified' who in later times, especially New Testament times, were identified as angels. He is at pains to show that this was not polytheism since these beings were not worthy to be called gods and the story was in fact about the origin of idolatry which provided a reason for the inevitability of the flood (Doedens, *The Sons of God*, 209–254, 295–299).

This is the second instance of the author having the name 'Yahweh' spoken in quotation marks. Undoubtedly once again, Phinehas did not consider himself to be taking the Lord's name in vain.

The verse does not flow smoothly from Abiathar's curse by Noah in Gen. 9: 25.[43] Translations also may obscure the intent. According to Gunkel, Shem is not blessed but his God is.[44] 'Blessed be Yahweh, the God of Shem'.[45] Speiser notes that one expects the blessing to be aimed at Shem rather than Yahweh leading to various suggestions to no avail as to how to repoint the text to arrive at the desired interpretation.[46] Westermann observes that the majority of interpreters such as Gunkel and von Rad see here a deliberate subtlety in Noah's blessing of the deity and he wonders about in what the blessing over Shem consists. This leads him to conclude 'that the old narrative ended with the curse over Canaan (= Ham)…' and that the verse is secondary since slavery over Canaan was never part of the promise to Israel. In a way, Westermann is correct, the verse is secondary since it was written by Phinehas and Gen. 9: 25 which Westermann regards as the only curse of the original narrative was written by Abiathar, the first author.[47]

While the cursing of Canaan makes sense based on the story, there is nothing which would warrant special treatment for Shem, a figure who is introduced without explanation. One important consideration is the traditional equation of Shem with Israel (see Chapter 5).[48] Westermann concurs with the interpretation that Shem can only mean Israel but regards it as an *ad hoc* construction of no importance.[49] Another consideration is that at this point the meaning of the name might be more circumscribed. Abiathar's story had Canaan and two nameless brothers representing Ephraim and Benjamin, the priests of Moses and Aaron. Phinehas names one of those brothers and has him blessed by Noah. Most likely he meant the now-named brother to represent the Benjaminites, the people of the author. Abiathar's proposal for a shared dominion over the common Canaanite enemy has been rejected for the primacy of the position of Benjamin sanctioned by the king, an audacious assertion in the name of David just as Bathsheba had done on behalf of her son.

Biblical scholars seem reluctant to extend the principle of a named figure in the story actually representing a real people or person in history at the time of the writing. In other words, if Shem could be Israel and Canaan could be the Canaanite people, then who was Noah or Eve? Exactly why it is so easy for scholars to accept an equation of Shem with Israel in the story but to relegate everyone else to hoary antiquity is not clear.

---

43 Westermann, *Genesis 1–11*, 492.
44 Gunkel, *Genesis*, 81.
45 Westermann, *Genesis 1–11*, 482. For similar translations see also Fox, *The Five Books of Moses*, 45; Plaut, *The Torah*, 69; Speiser, *Genesis*, 60. The *HarperCollins Study Bible* and von Rad maintain translations similar to the RSV (Rosenberg, 'Genesis', 16; von Rad, *Genesis*, 135).
46 Speiser, *Genesis*, 61.
47 Westermann, *Genesis 1–11*, 492–493, quotation from 493.
48 Day, *From Creation to Babel*, 141.
49 Westermann, *Genesis 1–11*, 493.

Phase II: Phinehas in the time of Pharaoh's Daughter

Times changed as the kingdom prospered. Instead of looking backward, Phinehas now was able to look ahead. With his second supplement, Phinehas became a writer transformed. He went beyond the local focus of a battle for power with the Zadokites or Abiathar and the Mushites within the land of Canaan to staking out a global position for the kingdom as he saw it. No longer is he on the outside knocking on the door to be admitted into the beltway in a position of power. Now he has arrived and his vision is cosmic.

The Geographical Universe

> *2: 10 A river flowed out of Eden to water the garden, and there it divided and became four rivers.*
> *¹¹ The name of the first is Pishon*
> *¹³ The name of the second river is Gihon*
> *¹⁴ And the name of the third river is Tigris*
> *And the fourth river is the Euphrates*

These verses are not part of the sons of J stories that are the focus on this study. However, they do set the stage for the son stories by this author. This universal stage will become particularly important for the world of the sons of Noah, the Table of Nations and Nimrod. What is so striking about the global vision that begins Phinehas's supplement is the contrast with the ending of first cycle where he outlines the land of Canaan (see below). In so doing he returns the focus to the world of Zadok and Abiathar where the next cycle, the stories of Abram, occurs. But now those stories occur as part of a larger universal story.

The rivers of the garden have been a source of investigation in their own right (see Additional Readings: Genesis 2: 10–14). Westermann succinctly began his analysis of the text with: 'The problem about the passage 2: 10–14 has not yet been clarified. Is it originally part of the narrative 2: 4b–3: 24, or is it a secondary insertion?'[50] John McKenzie acknowledges that Gen. 2: 10–14 is secondary.[51] Carr concurs that Gen. 2: 10–14 disrupts the narrative style of the overall story and is only loosely integrated with its context.[52] Ed Noort suggests that it is a mythic-geographical fragment which probably arose as a learned addition to the original text in an attempt to partially localize the garden.[53]

According to Gunkel, the narrator of these verses believed these four rivers to comprise all the earth's major streams. He likened the four rivers motif to that of the four corners of the world, the four directions of heaven, and the four parts of the earth common in 'the ancient Orient'. Westermann cites this insight. Gunkel did not specifically identify the 'four' motif as Mesopotamian since he includes an Egyptian reference as well. He does,

---

50 Westermann, *Genesis 1–11*, 215.

51 John L. McKenzie, 'The literary characteristics of Genesis 2–3', *TS* 15 (1954) 541–572, here 553–554, reprinted as 'The literary characteristics of Genesis 2–3', in *idem., Myths and Realities: Studies in Biblical Theology* (London: Geoffrey Chapman 1963), 146–181.

52 David Carr, 'The politics of textual subversion: a diachronic perspective on the Garden of Eden Story', *JBL* 112 (1993) 577–595, here 577–578.

53 Ed Noort, 'Gan-Eden in the context of the mythology of the Hebrew Bible', in Gerard P. Luttikhuizen, ed., *Paradise Interpreted: Representations of Biblical Paradise in Judaism and Christianity* (TBN 2; Leiden: Brill, 1999), 21–36, here 28.

however, state that the Nile was not included in these rivers consistent with his perception that there were no Egyptian elements in the primeval tradition.[54]

Gunkel refers to the immaturity of the narrator for his geographical knowledge or lack of knowledge (three times on one page!) and declares it 'entirely improper to attempt to reconcile this system of rivers with actual geography'. Gunkel asserts that the '(a)uthor's world view rests only partially in reality and partially in traditions whose origins cannot be sought, at any rate, in actual geographical circumstances'. Westermann is referring instead to the 'hazy and primitive notions of geography' by the author. He claims to understand why the names and descriptions of the four rivers were so incomprehensible, so vague.[55] Before tackling the nitty-gritty details of each verse, Westermann plaintively inquires:

> 'One must ask if the extraordinary labor that exegetes have expended to establish the geographical details does not begin from a false presupposition. It does more justice to the text to distinguish clearly what is significant and what is not and to set aside hypotheses that are not soundly based.'[56]

Westermann is exactly right. The false presupposition that should be discarded was stated precisely by von Rad:

> 'This passage has no significance for the unfolding action, nor are its elements mentioned elsewhere… It must therefore be considered as originally an independent element which was attracted [do texts have magnetic charges?] to the story of Paradise but without being able to undergo complete inner assimilation [are texts independent life forms seeking to be assimilated into the collective myth?].'[57]

These musings are precisely wrong. Far from having no significance, this insert was vital to the new world-view being promulgated by the author. He transformed the one-river garden of abundance into a four-river format that encompassed the known world and made his story universal. Phinehas's creation of this global stage on which events unfolded forms the basis for the new supplement he was writing during the glory days of the kingdom of Solomon.

Turning to each river in reverse order of appearance:

1. *Euphrates*: This river scarcely required any introduction as it was the great river of the ancient Near East. It was the river to which great warrior Pharaohs like Thutmose I and Thutmose III would brag about reaching; it was the river which the great Assyrian warrior kings would proudly cross on their imperial quests to reach the Upper Sea, the Mediterranean. It was the river which divided the great civilizations of Mesopotamia in the east from the lesser powers of the Levant and Syria, a defining consideration for allocation of peoples as sons of Shem.
2. *Tigris*: This river to the east of the Euphrates became part of the Fertile Crescent, the phrase coined by the American Orientalist James Henry Breasted for a textbook he was writing. He needed a term to label the area and a century later it is still in use. In ancient times, the faster more powerful river was more closely associated with Assyria than Babylonia.[58]

---

54 Gunkel, *Genesis*, 8–9, quotation from 8; Westermann, *Genesis 1–11*, 217.
55 Gunkel, *Genesis*, 9; Westermann, *Genesis 1–11*, 216.
56 Westermann, *Genesis 1–11*, 216.
57 Von Rad, *Genesis*, 79.
58 James Henry Breasted, *Ancient Times: A History of the Early World* (New York: Ginn & Co., 1935, 2nd ed.), 135.

3.   *Gihon*: The Nile River which reaches the land of Cush is the best candidate for the Gihon. It is inconceivable that a biblical author either in the land of Canaan or in Mesopotamia excluded the Nile River from his four-river world view. An author who excluded the Nile would have forfeited his credibility as much as he would have if he had left the sun or the moon out of his heavens. Noort succinctly notes 'when big rivers of antiquity are mentioned, the Nile cannot be missed'. Radday wonders, 'If Scripture intended to name here great rivers, why is the Nile omitted when Torah elsewhere mentions it no fewer than twenty-eight times?' The Nile must have been part of the four-river world-encompassing addition to the narrative along with the Tigris and Euphrates. Indeed, it may be said, that only a Meso-centric person, not in Canaan, and prior to the Amarna age, could have created a four-river world view that excluded the Nile. This biblical author was not such a person.[59]

Similarly efforts to locate the Gihon at Jerusalem are misguided. Jerusalem became the cosmic center with the construction of the temple. The selection of the same name for a river from the garden and the place where Solomon became king:

I Kings 1: 33 *And the king [David] said to them, 'Take with you the servants of your lord, and cause Solomon my son to ride on my own mule, and bring him down to Gihon'*

was deliberate. In this manner the unnamed river of the KDB has been absorbed into the expanded narrative and in support of the Davidic monarchy and Jerusalem temple.

4.   *Pishon*: As it turns out there was there was a fourth significant river located in the ancient Near East. This river recently discovered through satellite imagery has been dubbed the Kuwait River.[60] In his translation of Gunkel's *Schöpfung und Chaos*, K. William Whitney added a helpful footnote on the four rivers being the Euphrates, Tigris, Nile, and Persian Gulf with no mention of the Kuwait River.[61] While mainstream scholarship has yet to digest this river, its discovery has been of interest to evangelicals.[62] This dried-up river apparently flowed northeast across the Arabian peninsula with its mouth near that of the Tigris and Euphrates at the head of the Persian/Arabian Gulf. The Kuwait River appears to have originated adjacent to Mahd edh-Dhahab, 'the Craddle of Gold', an area in the Arabian Peninsula known for its gold. Thus it fits the biblical description of the Pishon. The biblical references to the products of the Havilah were not as Gunkel suggested 'a rather immature method of geographical description' expressed concerning the products of the land, but a savvy means of identifying a land through the products his audience knew first hand even if they did not know the land of

---

59 Noort, 'Gan-Eden', 30; Yehuda T. Radday, 'The four rivers of Paradise', *Hebrew Studies* 23 (1982) 23–31, here 31.

60 I first became aware of the Kuwait River through a brief notice in the *New York Times* under 'Science Watch' by Walter Sullivan, 'Signs of ancient river' March 30, 1993; see also, James A. Sauer, 'The river runs dry: creation story preserves historical memory', BAR 22: 4, 1996: 52–54, 57, 64; James A. Sauer, 'A new climate and archaeological view of the early Biblical traditions', in Michael D. Coogan, J. Cherry Exum and Lawrence Stager, eds, *Scripture and Other Artifacts: Essays on the Bible and Archaeology in Honor of Philip J. King* (Louisville: Westminster, 1994), 366–398, here 381–388; Philip J. King and Lawrence E. Stager, *Life in Biblical Israel* (Louisville: Westminster John Knox, 2001), 171.

61 K. William Whitney, Jr in Gunkel, *Creation and Chaos*, 324 n.90.

62 See Carol A. Hill, 'The Garden of Eden: a modern landscape', *Perspectives on Science and Christian Faith* 52 (2000) 31–46, here 32–38; Edwin M. Yamauchi, *Africa and the Bible* (Grand Rapids: Baker Academic, 2005) 38–39.

origin first hand.[63] The river disappeared beginning post-3500 and by 2000 BCE during a time of increased aridity.[64] The land it had watered did not disappear and Saba/Sheba was part of the world view of the author's audience. The Kuwait River with its fabled riches left its legacy in oral tradition. Such cultural memories may be considered part of Gunkel's 'precompositional stage'.

This revised view reveals the biblical author to have been a sophisticated erudite writer of consummate skill and knowledge. It contradicts Gunkel's perception of him as geographically 'immature'. His vision was not just limited to the immediate world with which Israel was in proximity and related, but the entire and frequently distant world. This conscious addition to the written text set the stage for the additions to follow as this biblical writer crafted a new narrative through the judicious use of proper nouns that transformed a local narrative into a global one. The stories of this stage all are based on this global arena.

> *9: 18 The sons of Noah who went forth from the ark were Shem, Ham, and Japheth.*
> *9: 19 These three were the sons of Noah and from these the whole earth was peopled [scattered].*

In academic exegesis, the story of the sons of Noah itself has been divided into two parts: 9: 18–19 and 9: 20–27. Dillmann and Driver consider 9: 18a and 19 to be the introduction to 9: 20–27 possibly by the redactor with 18b about Ham as the father of Canaan an insert.[65] Gunkel unambiguously assigns 9: 18–19 to the conclusion of J's flood story and attributes the introduction of the sons of Noah to the writer designated as J[j] with the second author designated as J[e]. He observes as others have that Noah 'the farmer and vintner who lies drunk in his tent, seems to be an entirely different figure than the righteous and pious Noah of the Flood legend …'[66] Gunkel follows Budde on their being two sources:

> J[1] – the older non-flood Palestinian story with Noah as the ancestor of Shem, Japheth, and Canaan
> J[2] – the newer Babylonian flood story with Noah as the ancestor of Shem, Ham, and Japheth.[67]

Westermann concurs that the story consists of two self-contained units with 9: 18–19 closing the flood story and introducing the sons.[68] Ross expresses awareness that many commentators think two traditions have been combined but wonders what caused two irreconcilable versions to be united.[69] He calls it a literary bridge between the Flood narrative and the Table of Nations; Neiman suggests the verses could serve as an introduction to Gen. 10.[70] In a sense, the verses are an introduction to a story or rather a continuation of

---

63 Gunkel, *Genesis*, 9. The details would be added later; see Chapter 14.
64 Sauer, 'A new climate', 64.
65 Dillmann, '*Genesis*', 300; Driver, *The Book of Genesis*, 108.
66 Gunkel, *Genesis*, 79.
67 Hermann Gunkel, *Creation and Chaos in the Primeval Era and the Eschaton: A Religion-Historical Study of Genesis 1 and Revelation 12* (Grand Rapids: William B. Eerdmanns Publishing Company, 2006), 95, originally published as *Schöpfung und Chaos in Urzeit und Endzeit: Eine Religionsgeschichtliche Untersuchung über Gen. 1 und Ap. Jon 12*, (Göttingen Vandenhoeck & Ruprecht, 1895).
68 Westermann, *Genesis 1–11*, 482. See also Bailey, *Noah*, 158.
69 Ross, 'The curse of Canaan', 228.
70 David Neiman, 'The date and circumstances of the cursing of Canaan', in Alexander Altman, ed., *Biblical Motifs: Origins and Transformations* (Cambridge: Harvard University Press, 1966), 113–134, here 113; Ross,

theme. Phinehas has established a world stage with four rivers and a global flood; now he must populate it and explain the relationship among its parts.

9: 18 *The sons of Noah who went forth from the ark were Shem, Ham, and Japheth*

This verse creates a new story of going forth. It is an exodus not into the wilderness but into the civilized world. The sons, not the father, are the center of this story. It is what they will or will not do that drives the action and determines the results. The focus is on their battle for power. This is their story. New characters are named thereby raising the question of who the author meant these characters to be. The story does not specifically identify the relationship of Canaan to these three named sons.

9: 19 *These three were the sons of Noah; and from these the whole earth was peopled [scattered]*

Phinehas thinks globally. For him the Flood was universal. His three sons will populate the world. There are no other sons either. No Sethites. No Nephilim. No Cainites. Just these three sons. Undoubtedly, he would have preferred four sons in keeping with the Mesopotamian tradition of the four quarters of the world and the use of four for the rivers of the garden, civilizations of Nimrod, and forces of chaos arrayed against Abram. Apparently he had no choice. He inherited the three-son motif from Abiathar and to create a fourth son from thin air simply would have resulted in a loss of credibility. So he worked within the existing parameters to deliver his message and implicitly relegated the originally named son, Canaan, to a subservient status even without naming his father.

> 9: 20 *Noah* **was the first tiller of the soil. He** *planted a vineyard;* [21] *and he drank of the wine, and became drunk, and lay uncovered in his tent.* [22] *Canaan, saw the nakedness of his father, and told his two brothers outside.* 9 [23] **Then Shem and Japheth took a garment, laid it upon both their shoulders, and walked backward and covered the nakedness of their father; their faces were turned away, and they did not see their father's nakedness.** [24] *When Noah awoke from his wine and knew what his youngest son had done to him,* [25] *he said, 'Cursed be Canaan; a slave of slaves shall he be to his brothers.'* [26] **He also said, 'Blessed by Yahweh my God be Shem; and let Canaan be his slave.** 9 [27] **God enlarge Japheth, and let him dwell in the tents of Shem; and let Canaan be his slave.'**

Noah is the designated the hero. He will be the one to save the people and start again. There is no genealogical link to anyone in the earlier stories because he is a new figure in his own right. Instead, the author redefines the hero of the Flood story by providing a new introduction thereby drawing attention to the person in the present whom Noah represents.

9: 20 *Noah was the first tiller of the soil*

In the Hebrew, Noah is a man of the ground, (*ish hadamah*). Speiser translates the verse as 'Noah, a man of the soil' which is consistent with Cain being the first tiller of the soil

---

'The curse of Canaan', 224–225.

(Gen. 4: 2; *adamah*).[71] In the garden, *hadam* is a man from the ground, *hadamah*. The observation 'that this phrase was chosen to draw an explicit comparison between Noah and Adam' is correct.[72] Even more so, it reveals the intricate dialog among not only the supplementers to the KDB with each other but to the original KDB narrative.

9: 23 *Then Shem and Japheth took a garment, laid it upon both their shoulders, and walked backward and covered the nakedness of their father; their faces were turned away, and they did not see their father's nakedness*

This long verse of four direct actions and two comments presupposes knowledge of the names of the brothers and who they represent. The extensive level of detail is in marked contrast to Abiathar's brief account in 9: 21–22.

The issue is the behavior of the sons. Who should be cursed and who should be blessed? The answer has ramifications for these people in Phinehas's present. It is time to identify the wrongdoing which will occur and assign blame for undoing the success of the father. These sons are the epitome of filial piety. 'The narrator takes obvious pains to present the two brothers as chaste and pious in contrast to Canaan…'[73] No one hearing/reading this verse could fail to realize that the actions of these two brothers are perfectly calibrated to be exactly what they should be in such circumstances. There simply is no way to improve upon the actions of these two brothers. They are exemplary.

9: 27 *God enlarge Japheth, and let him dwell in the tents of Shem; and let Canaan be his slave.*

This verse directly addresses the political configuration at the time of its writing. Scholars have speculated as to exactly what that political configuration was. The author did not introduce vague names of unknown meaning into the story any more than Merneptah did when he mentioned Israel for the first time in the archaeological record. The audience was not expected to be befuddled in confusion and lose track of the storyline amidst the swirl of strange sounds and mystifying names. Phinehas expected the audience to understand the meanings. He would provide the details in what became part of Gen. 10, the Table of Nations, following the story.

His geographic delineations encompassed but extended far beyond Abiathar's restricted vision to the land of Canaan. Now Phinehas sought to redefine the world. Scholars have been seeking to unravel that worldview to identify the peoples cursed.

---

71 Speiser, *Genesis*, 60–61.

72 Anthony J. Tomasino, 'History repeats itself: the "Fall" and Noah's drunkenness', *VT* 42 1992: 128–130, here 129. In this article, Tomasino elaborates on the numerous parallels between Adam in the garden and Noah in the vineyard. While such common motifs exist, to understand them would require excavating the garden story to identify the writers responsible for each one.

73 Gunkel, *Genesis*, 80. See also Dillmann, *Genesis*, 305; Westermann, *Genesis 1–11*, 488.

1. David Neiman

Neiman suggests this depiction related to the conflict of Egypt and Canaan against the Sea Peoples and Israel. He links the three curses of Canaan in 9: 25–97 as a 'passionate expression of hatred and anger' in their excoriation of him. These verses reflect a condition of war and 'constitute a battle cry, the cry of a belligerent engaged in combat against a detested enemy'. However this outcry reflects not an historical situation but a hope or desire for one to come. He likens it to the taunt, a traditional form of the literature of battle whereupon the wish that the enemy be destroyed is expressed out loud. Neiman cites various exchanges between the Achaeans and the Trojans in *The Iliad* (Book XIII: 232–234, 414–416, 620–625) and the Song of Deborah (Judg. 5: 23 and 25–31) as examples. The presence of the taunt has been noted in David's conquest of Jebusite Jerusalem and Abiathar's curse of Canaan in this story (see Chapters 8 and 12). It would appear in the Song of Lamech (see Chapter 14). Neiman's proposed scheme poses a dilemma since he knows there was no war by Israel against the Canaanites following the battle at Tanaach which he dates to *c.* 1180 BCE in the Song of Deborah.[74]

Neiman resolves this dilemma through the Sea Peoples of Japheth. Their movements threatened the land of Canaan from the west in Ramesside times. At the same time, Israel was entering the land of Canaan from the east. The result of this two-pronged effort whether coordinated or coincidental was the common-enemy Canaan being squeezed on both sides. Neiman considers it unlikely that the two attack forces were unaware of each other and therefore they 'willy-nilly' became allies against Canaan in the time of Ramses III. The alleged monarchal origin of the story in J therefore contains the memory of events nearly two centuries earlier, an ancient war cry of what the taunters hoped would happen turns out to have happened as sung in the Song of Deborah. Even though the Philistines, Canaanites, and Israelites existed at the time Neiman proposes the text was written, he does not apply these terms to the author's present.[75]

2. A. Van Selms

Van Selms also thinks the curse to be political and not genealogical from roughly the same period. He dates the linkage of Canaan to Ham to before 1200 BCE from the time of Egyptian hegemony. It more likely drew on the memory of that time than originated in that time. At the time of writing, it served as a reminder to the audience that many Canaanite cities had been loyal vassals of Egypt. His comments about it signifying a Japheth = Philistine 'cooperation' with Israel against the settled Canaanites seems more likely. Van Selms suggests that David drew on an old tradition of Israelite-Philistine cooperation against Canaan when he allied with Achish, the Philistine king at Gath. But if the date of the story is shifted to the 10th century BCE of David, then these Canaanites who had been loyal to Egypt are the ones who resisted David. A logical conclusion is the author is proposing a revival of the anti-Canaanite cooperation in the present. All the ire is directed towards Canaan. Its tone seems confident of the outcome.[76]

---

74 Neiman, 'The date and circumstances of the cursing of Canaan', 121–123, quotations from 113, 121.

75 Neiman, 'The date and circumstances of the cursing of Canaan', 117, 125–132.

76 A. Van Selms, 'The Canaanites in the Book of Genesis', *OtSt* 12 1958: 182–213, here 186–187.

3. Hermann Gunkel

Gunkel looks back even farther in time appropriate for the aetiological story about vintners. He notes the switch from 'Yahweh' to 'Elohim' in the curses and suggests that 'Yahweh's name is only known to Shem, not to Japheth'. For Gunkel, 'Unquestionably, the narrator considers himself a Shemite'; Shem being the tent-dwelling, firstborn, Yahweh-worshiping son. He observes that modern scholars, meaning those who lived over a century ago, concur with Wellhausen in equating Shem with Israel, Japheth with the Phoenicians or Philistines, and the event in question fulfilled by this curse as the subjugation of Canaan attested in the biblical period. Not only did the modern scholars realize this, so would have the original audience: 'Certainly, the ancient Israelite who heard this legend would also have understood the son whose God is Yahweh and who rules Canaan to be the progenitor of his people…'.[77]

However despite this consensus, his judgment is that 'the effort to relate these sayings to Israel's historical situation may be considered a failure'. For Gunkel, Canaan can be both a people and a region. He concludes, 'Hence Noah's blessing points us to a historical situation in which Canaan, i.e. the land from about Taurus to Egypt, was subjugated from the East by a nomadic "Semitic", "Hebrew" people'. He dates the situation of the curse to the 2nd millennium BCE and characterizes it as 'the oldest report in the OT concerning relationships between nations…'. This conclusion leads him to postulate that originally Noah was a Syro-Canaanite, the first farmer and vintner who became the progenitor of the Syro-Canaanite people. He became the father of all humanity when his name was adopted into the Babylonian flood legend that became the basis for the biblical story.[78]

4. Gerhard von Rad

Von Rad takes a more theological approach in a specific historical context. He, too, narrows the focus of the narrative from the Table of Nations: 'But one sees very soon that the actual narrative is talking, not about this *ecumenical* scheme of nations, but about a much more limited *Palestinian* one: Shem, Japheth, and Canaan'. To clarify the matter, he specifically asserts that the Shem who are the people of Yahweh here is not the Shem of Gen. 10: 22. Such an idea is theologically unacceptable although it would be consistent with non-Israelite Nimrod being a mighty hunter before Yahweh in Mesopotamia (see below).[79]

Von Rad also passes value judgments on the sons. He views them as individuals, 'great persons, who were obviously sharply distinguished from one another in the ancient Palestinian region'. With this local focus, von Rad is able to castigate the religious, political, and ethnic foes of Israel: 'The Old Testament indicates in many places the amazement and abhorrence with which the newly arrived Israel encountered the sexual depravity of the Canaanites (cultic prostitution)'. Just as he had with the sons of God, von Rad hones in on the sexual perversity that defines the degenerate people who deserve to be destroyed in the Flood or be conquered in the Conquest. This depiction of the Canaanites and the curse reveal God's will from the beginning that Israel should have the land at some point but

---

77 Gunkel, *Genesis*, 82.
78 Gunkel, *Genesis*, 82–85, quotations from 82 and 84.
79 Von Rad, *Genesis*, 135–136, quotation from 135.

not necessarily now. In-other-words, the story is an aetiological basis for a plan in history that would lead to Israel being in the land of Canaan.[80]

Von Rad seeks to unravel the mystery of the use of Shem for Israel. He concedes 'the use of the name Shem as a designation for Israel is unusual, indeed singular in the Old Testament'. Von Rad is forced to wonder if the word 'Shem' like the word '*Habiru*', the nomadic people of the steppe who became 'the Hebrews', simply fell out of use. With Japheth, von Rad is more sure, equating them with the Philistines.[81] Still he puzzles over the 'spiritual interpretation' of Japheth's dwelling in the tents of Shem in the promised gift of land calling it 'a great riddle in God's guidance in history'. Alas, he must acknowledge, 'the mystery is not revealed, and God's intention remains hidden', a most disquieting thought.[82]

5. Ephraim Speiser

Speiser agrees that 'the background is distinctly local'. He seeks to pinpoint the historical context at the turn of the 12th century BCE with the arrival of the Philistines along the coast as Israel struggled against the entrenched Canaanites. Speiser shares in the condemnation of the older inhabitants of the land for their distasteful practices. He suggests the curse 'must allude to some form of cooperation between the two groups, with Canaan condemned to enslavement by both'.[83]

6. Claude Westermann

Westermann notes the changeover from a story about individuals to one about peoples in the curses: 'Exegetes must confront the fact that the pronouncements deal only with individual peoples and their relationship to each other…'. He then dismisses von Rad's scheme of nations from the Shem-Japheth-Canaan Palestinian context revised to be the ecumenical Shem-Ham-Japheth families of peoples. Westermann recounts various efforts to locate the historical context of the curse drawing on Gunkel's observation that an aetiological narrative starts with the present of the author which he is trying to explain. That historical context is the Davidic-Solomonic kingdom when scholars presume J to have been written. But since Westermann agrees with the equation of the Philistines with Japheth, he is at a loss to explain how Japheth could share in the subjugation of the Canaanites.[84]

His dismissal 'at the ingenious and fanciful attempts' to fit Japheth into an historical scheme is a cautionary warning to all who would seek to do so. Yet, Westermann remains as confused and uncertain about the meaning of curse of Gen. 9: 27 as those he criticizes.

---

80 Von Rad, *Genesis*, 137–138, quotations from 137.

81 Von Rad, *Genesis*, 137–139, quotations from 137. L. Bailey tentatively supports the Philistine etiology based on the presumption that the individuals in the story personify sociopolitical groups addressing the question of why the once-flourishing Canaanite civilization was eclipsed (*Noah*, 159–160).

82 Von Rad. *Genesis*, 139.

83 Speiser, *Genesis*, 62–63, quotations from 62.

84 Westermann, *Genesis 1–11*, 490. The entire approach to identify a politico-ethnic context has been rejected by Robertson who understands the curse in a redemptive-historical context. Canaanites still may be redeemed as Rahab demonstrates and 'from the cursed line of Canaan comes the promised Savior', 'Concurrent critical questions', 182–187, quotation from 186.

For him, this is the one political curse of the three and is about a concrete event yet to occur. It is an independent blessing now attached to the story where only Gen. 9: 25 was original. He agrees with others that Japheth can only mean the Philistines so therefore the political event is the Philistines with Israel putting Canaan under the yoke. 'It is no longer possible to know the origin and original meaning of the blessing over Japheth.'[85]

One faces quite a range of possibilities in this exegesis. Westermann pithily sums up the situation after dismissing the efforts of Gunkel, von Rad, Neiman, and van Selms among others by name stating:

> 'The sweep of the possibilities suggested here is amazing. The historical situations alleged to explain the pronouncements stretch from about the middle of the 2nd millennium to the period after Alexander the Great. There is no methodological basis for further conjectures, as Gunkel's embarrassment should have already made clear. Only a new methodological approach to the text can help.'[86]

Even though he accepts that the curses in 9: 25, 9: 26, and 9: 27 comprise three different writings, he cannot develop a new methodological approach that will account for it.

The proposed writing here provides a new methodological approach that Westermann thinks is needed. Gen. 9: 25 by Abiathar is the original verse of the story. Gen. 9: 26 by Phinehas is his direct response to Abiathar. Gen. 9: 27 also by Phinehas later is part of his vision of the world stage. Phinehas is writing about the 10th century BCE world in which he lives. He is addressing the political circumstances of his present. He is proposing a division of power that expresses the terms he seeks as the reward for becoming the temple priest. His concerns are both local and global. The local refers to the peoples in the immediate vicinity and of direct contact. The global is an assertion of the place of Israel in the world. When a United States president claims it is morning in America and the country is a city on a hill, the correct response is not to calculate the time of day or measure the elevation of his capital city; instead one should verify that he made such claims, seek to understand why the president thought such claims were valid, and determine if they resonated with the audience … and then determine if the president was Dear Leader or if there was a legitimate basis to the claim.

Locally, Phinehas is proposing some sort of division of Canaan between the Japheth-Philistines and the Shemite-Israelites. The situation has changed from the time of Saul. No longer were the Philistines a threat to dominate Israel. And for Benjaminites, Israel was defined by the kingdom of Ishbaal:

> **II Samuel 2: 9** *and he [Abner] made him [Ishbaal] king over Gilead and the Ashurites and Jezreel and Ephraim and Benjamin and all Israel*

which did not included Jerusalem, Judah, or the pro-Egypt/anti-Israel Canaanite cities.

Benjamin felt no compelling need to directly administer traditionally anti-Israelite Canaanite cities. That task could be relegated to the Philistines as long as they deferred to

---

85 Westermann, *Genesis 1–11*, 491, 493, quotation from 493.
86 Westermann, *Genesis 1–11*, 491.

Israel. Phinehas had no objection to Philistine mastery over non-Israelite peoples as long as the Philistines operated within the Israelite tent.

An alliance between the Philistines and Israel is biblically sanctioned. Op-ed pieces on alliances or working arrangements with the Philistines occur with Abraham involving Gerar (Gen. 20), Isaac also involving Gerar (Gen. 26), David (with Gath in I Sam. 21 and 27, the Cherethites and the Pelethites in II Sam. 8: 18), and Shimei (I Kings 2). The first two patriarchs and the first two kings both entered into alliances with the Philistines. The same Benjamin that would become part of the southern kingdom under a Davidic king also could work with the Philistines if that's what it took to gain power in the capital city.

The curses present alternate visions. Abiathar wanted to revert to a premonarchic situation where Ephraim and Benjamin split the land of Canaan but are united as Israel against foreign foes as they had been in the Song of Deborah. Phinehas preferred a division of the entire land of Canaan between Israel and the Philistines. In this division, Benjamin would rule Israel as defined by the kingdom under Ishbaal and the Philistines would administer coastal Canaanite cities which previously had been vassals of Egypt before becoming dominated by the Philistines anyway. This offer was contingent on the Philistines remaining independent but within the Israelite sphere of influence or tent as it had become under David.

> **II Samuel 5: 17** *When the Philistines heard that David had been anointed king over Israel, all the Philistines went up in search of David; but David heard of it and went down to the stronghold.* *[18]* *Now the Philistines had come and spread out in the valley of Rephaim.* *[19]* *And David inquired of Yahweh [without Abiathar], 'Shall I go up against the Philistines? Wilt thou give them into my hand?' And Yahweh said to David, 'Go up; for I will certainly give the Philistines into your hand.'* *[20]* *And David came to Baalperazim, and David defeated them there; and he said, 'Yahweh has broken through my enemies before me, like a bursting flood.' Therefore the name of that place is called Baalperazim.* *[21]* *And the Philistines left their idols there, and David and his men carried them away.*

Regardless of the historicity of this passage, the Philistines well may have accepted this offer from Phinehas. There is no indication in the biblical narrative that the Philistines were a disruptive force in the remaining years of the United Kingdom. Decades after the kingdom split, hostilities resumed between the northern kingdom of Israel against the Philistine city of Gibbethon (I Kings 15: 27 and 16: 15). These ruminations highlight the importance of understanding the Israelite-Philistine relationship from their arrival in the land of Canaan, to the Philistine capture of the ark, to the times of Saul and David. That relationship forms the backdrop for the curses in the story of the sons of Noah (see Additional Readings: Khirbet Qeifaya and Benjamin for Khirbet Ed-Dawwara).

[Shem became the father of Cush and Canaan]

Phinehas's second concern was to define Israel's place in the world at large as he knew it. This proposed addition establishing a global framework vanished when the Table of Nations was expanded (see Chapter 15). He presented no genealogical information on Ham (Egypt) or Japheth (the Philistines). It was the world of Shem which needed some explanation.

Phinehas divides the world of Shem into two parts, Canaan and Mesopotamia or Cush.

The two sons of Shem effectively split the Semitic world into East Semitic and West Semitic, which all things considered, was a quite reasonable division. The Mesopotamian portion east of the Euphrates is to be ruled by Nimrod (see below). The implication is there will be a counterpart to rule the land of Canaan or west of the Euphrates, aka, the Solomonic empire. In effect, he establishes a Yahweh-based world of the ancient Near East with the Canaanite people left out of the grand plan since they were but slaves who opposed Yahweh and Israel. The Benjaminite hatred of the Canaanites dates back at least to when Israel first emerged in the land in the 13th century BCE and the two fought at the Valley of Aijalon as sung about in the Book of Jashar. The animosity had not abated in the centuries since. In the new world order, Israel was the cosmic center and the Canaanites were nothing.

This vision of the world is consistent with the biblical depiction of the world in the time of Solomon:

> **I Kings 4: 34** *And men came from all peoples to hear the wisdom of Solomon, and from all the kings of the earth, who had heard of his wisdom.*

This declaration should not be interpreted to mean that Israel ruled the world. One may refer to New York City as the world's capital without meaning that it is the political capital of the world or that events elsewhere do not happen independently of it. Still just as there is some merit to the exaggerated status New York has in the world, it is equally reasonable to presume that at a particular point in time, Israel with its temple at its capital city could portray itself to its own satisfaction as being the cosmic center. Allies can be thought of as servants if one so desires and trade as tribute. Obviously, in hindsight, this self-proclaimed designation did not stand the test of time ... but it did establish an ideal that was to become part of the Israelite heritage called the Zion tradition.

The effort to exalt the global position of Jerusalem led to the development of the Zion tradition. That tradition glorifies Yahweh, Zion, and the rule of Yahweh's king as expressed in Psalm 2:

> **Psalm 2: 1** *Why do the nations conspire, and the peoples plot in vain?*[2] *The kings of the earth set themselves, and the rulers take counsel together, against Yahweh and his anointed, saying,*[3] *'Let us burst their bonds asunder, and cast their cords from us.'*[4] *He who sits in the heavens laughs; the Lord has them in derision.*[5] *Then he will speak to them in his wrath, and terrify them in his fury, saying,*[6] *'I have set my king on Zion, my holy hill'.*[7] *I will tell of the decree of Yahweh: He said to me, 'You are my son, today I have begotten you.*[8] *Ask of me, and I will make the nations your heritage, and the ends of the earth your possession.*[9] *You shall break them with a rod of iron, and dash them in pieces like a potter's vessel'.*[10] *Now therefore, O kings, be wise; be warned, O rulers of the earth.*

The psalm is practically a taunt (an apparently common motif at that time) or song of warning of what will befall any king who dares to defy the one chosen by Yahweh. It mocks the pretensions of the puny kings and their silly plots.

The issue then is to determine when this tradition originated. John Hayes focuses on the pre-Israelite Jebusite traditions which were carried forward into the Israelite religion. He is especially interested in the psalms (18, 46, 48, 76, 89, 110, and 132 among others) and Gen. 14 that attest the election of Jerusalem even before David installed the ark of Yahweh at Zion. From this he surmises that the tradition of Zion's inviolability preceded Sennacherib's invasion in 701 BCE where he ravaged the land and despoiled the temple but did not destroy the city or displace the Davidic dynasty. While it is reasonable to conclude that Jerusalem boasted of its own city even before David, one should also recognize the likelihood that every Canaanite city tooted and touted itself much like the people in every city with a professional sports team do in their stadium of their team. The change agent was for the first time an indigenous person was king of the entire land of Canaan and the surrounding areas were in decline.[87]

J. J. M. Roberts argues that the Zion tradition was created by Israelite court theologians in the time of David and Solomon. He rejects the notion that it was an inherited tradition from the Jebusites. Typically, the rise to prominence of an imperial deity is accompanied by the rise to prominence of the king who worships that deity. He cites the examples of Hammurabi in Babylon and Sargon the Great in Akkad. In the Israelite version, for Yahweh to become the king at Zion presupposes a human at Zion who attained earthly success. That human was David who installed the ark of Yahweh at Zion.[88] The theologian who established the new vision was Phinehas.

Rémi Lack suggests that the Jebusites never thought of their 760 meter hill as the mountain of God in the Canaanite but it was the actions of the Davidic dynasty which made the idea of *the* cosmic mountain being in Jerusalem plausible, To draw an exact line to separate the Zion tradition into the Canaanite elements from Zadok, the Shiloh tradition which included Canaanite elements (see Chapter 12), and David's genius (the KDB which included an ark procession and enthronement at the new year) may be impossible. The numerous psalms to Yahweh Elyon/Most High express this ongoing theology in Jerusalem.[89]

In the new world order with the temple to Yahweh with his ark as the cosmic center, each people has its place. Phinehas defines the old word order from east of the Euphrates and not the river Nile as in the exodus. He sets the stage for the new world order to be created west of the Euphrates.[90] He is not writing a history but proclaiming a passing of the torch from Mesopotamia to Israel. His message is that time has passed and a new world order has emerged with the Solomonic temple as the cosmic center. One can recognize the

---

87 John H. Hayes, 'The tradition of Zion's inviolability', *JBL* 82 1963: 419–426.

88 J. J. M. Roberts, 'Solomon's Jerusalem and the Zion tradition', in Andrew G. Vaughn and Ann E. Killebrew, eds, *Jerusalem in the Bible and Archaeology: The First Temple Period* (SBLSymS 18 Atlanta: Society of Biblical Literature, 2003), 163–170; see also J. M. Roberts, 'The Davidic origin of the Zion tradition', *JBL* 92 1973: 329–344; J. J. M. Roberts, 'Zion in the theology of the Davidic-Solomonic empire', in T. Ishida, ed., *Studies in the Period of David and Solomon and Other Essays* (Tokyo: Yamakawa-Shuppansha, `1982), 93–108; J. J. M. Roberts, 'Yahweh's foundation in Zion', *JBL* 106 1987: 27–45; see also Ollenburger, *Zion*.

89 Rémi Lack, 'Les origines de Elyon, le tres-haut, dans la tradition cultuelle d'Israel', *CBQ* 24 1962: 44–64, here 59.

90 The Euphrates was a traditional boundary line between east and west from Thutmose I and III and the Mitannians in the 15th century BCE, the Hittites and the Assyrians in the 14th century BCE, the western border of Assyria in the 10th and 9th centuries BCE, and Assyria and the Land of Omri in the 9th and 8th centuries BCE; see J. N. Postgate, 'Royal ideology and state administration in Sumer and Akkad', in *CANE*, 395–411, here 409.

appeal of such a grandiose vision to the (easily-influenced) Israelite king with Pharaoh's daughter as queen with the Gihon (Nile) in Jerusalem.

10: 8 Cush became the father of Nimrod…

10: 8 Cush

The location of Cush has been a source of debate among scholars (see Chapter 6). Generally, the favored choice for this person has been a derivation from the Kassites, the people who ruled Babylon and portions of Mesopotamia from the 16th–12th centuries BCE. They were deposed by the Elamites, the great force of chaos to the civilized world of Mesopotamia. In later times, Cush or Nubia would become more prominent in Israelite and Judahite life necessitating an update the geographical configuration (see Chapter 15).[91]

10: 8 Nimrod

The quest for Nimrod has not been undertaken in isolation from other stories and interests (see Chapter 6). For example, Kline's Nimrod anticipates the climatic episode of defiance in the building of the Tower of Babel. Nimrod is a mighty man thereby linking him to Gen. 6: 4 and he clearly is a king. His 'hunting exploits were not mere sport but a function properly pertaining to his royal office'. Just as the fall of the Cainite dynasty 'led to Noah and the kingdom of the ark' so the fall of Nimrod's rule 'led to Abraham and the kingdom in the [covenantal] promises'. Kline's view of kingship concludes with Jesus Christ (Phil. 2: 9–11 ends the article). His Christian lens does not mitigate the possibility that the Tower of Babel story originated in an environment of sacral kingship, was connected to both the Cainite genealogy and Nimrod in some way, and may have been communicated in a royal-religious setting of some kind. Even though biblical scholars tend to divide texts into manageable size pericopes that can be recited in religious settings, they were not written that way. Instead they were part of longer sequences that can best understood in their entirety and in relation to the narrative writings that preceded them and which followed.[92]

Nonetheless, the attempts to identify a specific individual in history as the basis for the figure of Nimrod (see Chapter 6) have not proved successful. This is not to deny any possible linkage of Nimrod to the word 'Ninurta'[93] (see Additional Readings: Ninurta). It seems reasonable to relate him to the Marduk/Ninurta coalescence in the Babylonian myth of creation but it is problematic to seek to link him to Assyrian Tukulti-ninurta or any other individual king. Albright uses the word 'composite' without identifying the components and this path seems more fruitful.[94] Driver thinks whether Nimrod was

---

91 For the Kassites see Walter Sommerfeld, 'The Kassites of Ancient Mesopotamia: origins, politics, and culture', in *CANE*, 917–930; Diana L. Stein, 'Kassites', in *OEANE*, 271–275.

92 Kline, 'Divine kingship', 201–202, 204, quotations from 201 and 202.

93 Hendel suggests that Ninurta as the city god of Calah probably was the basis for the name Nimrod ('Historical context', 61).

94 William F. Albright, 'The Babylonian matter in the predeuteronomic primeval history (JE) in Gen. 1–11', *JBL* 58 1939: 91–103, here 100.

mythical or historical he became for reasons unknown 'the representative of Babylonian power'.[95] Kraeling searches for a real person in history from the time of Naram-sin but recognized that for Gen.10: 11, 'The figure of Nimrod has here assumed an idealistic nature; it symbolizes the imperialism of the eastern Semites'.[96] Westermann states, 'The net result of all these endeavors is that Gen. 10: 8f intends the type of leader of the early period of Mesopotamia, like Gilgamesh of the epic…'[97] Lipinski thinks he had been created by the Yahwist in Neo-Assyrian times in preparation for the story of the Tower of Babel.[98] Van der Toorn considers the list of Nimrod's cities to be 'a condensed résumé of Mesopotamian history' and Nimrod to be 'a symbol of Mesopotamian political leadership'. He attributes the passage to the redactor.[99] Van der Kooij considers the attempt 'to identify Nimrod with a single monarch of Mesopotamian history' as not 'to be a relevant question'. Rather it was 'a symbolic name', or as Hendel describes it: 'appropriation and epitome of Mesopotamian lore, concentrated around a single archetypal Mesopotamian king'.[100]

These last perceptions better match the vision of Phinehas who created the figure. In the beginning when archaeologists sought to prove the Bible literally true, the quest was to match the individual biblical figure to an individual in history. Various candidates like Sumerian Gilgamesh, Akkadians Sargon the Great and Naram-Sin, and Assyrian Tukulti-ninurta were suggested. But just as Canaan, Japheth, Shem, and Ham were not specific individuals in history but peoples so too was Nimrod. For Phinehas, Nimrod represents the Mesopotamian way of life and it is a way he wanted the Davidic king to emulate.

Nimrod is a composite of multiple traits which define the great king. He is a mighty man, a mighty hunter, a mighty hunter before Yahweh, and king over major cities where each in their own day was a cosmic center. These attributes do not just exist by chance. Quite the contrary. One should understand this description of the traits of the Mesopotamian as representing the essence of the Mesopotamian royal culture. Phinehas is not writing a biography about an individual human being; he is portraying a civilization through the defining characteristics of its great kings. By examining each of the characteristics chosen by the author, one can ascertain the purpose of the insert and the political context in which it occurred. Phinehas is creating a model of how the great king achieves 'name' or eternal renown as a great king. The relentless quest to find Nimrod in the archaeological record precisely because he is only great king of the dawn of human civilizations who is named along with these real cities in the biblical account attests Phinehas's unanticipated success!

---

95 Driver, *The Book of Genesis*, 122.

96 Emil G. Kraeling, 'The origin and real name of Nimrod', *AJSL* 38 1922: 214–220, here 219.

97 Westermann, *Genesis 1–11*, 516.

98 E. Lipinski, 'Nimrod and Aššur', *RB* 73 1966: 77–93.

99   Karel van der Toorn, 'Nimrod before the Bible', in Karel van der Toorn and Pieter W. van der Horst, 'Nimrod before and after the Bible', *HTR* 83 1990: 1–29, here 7–8.

100   Arie van der Kooij, 'The city of Babel and Assyrian imperialism: Genesis 11: 1–9 interpreted in the light of Mesopotamian sources', in Andre Lemaire, ed., *Congress Volume: Leiden 2004* (Leiden: Brill, 2006), 1–17, here 12; Ronald Hendel, 'Genesis 1–11 and its Mesopotamian problem', in Erich S. Gruen, ed., *Cultural Borrowings and Ethnic Appropriations in Antiquity* (Geschichte Oriens et Occidens 8; Stuggart: Franz Steiner Verlag, 2005), 23–36, here 30.

10: 8 *he was the first on earth to be a mighty man*

This verse appears to be a variance with the claim by Zadok about the mighty men of Canaan or Nephilim (Gen. 6:4). Three speculative considerations address this issue. First, the stories did not yet have the genealogical connective link that anchors them chronologically as they exist today. Therefore one could make the case that the Nimrod story occurred prior to the Nephilim story regardless of its position in the linear narrative today. Second, the universal flood wiped out those Nephilim who survived Zadok's local flood and Nimrod, son of Cush, son of Shem, son of Noah, is the first mighty man post-deluge. Neither explanation is completely satisfactory.

A third possibility is, Phinehas had to work with the text as he inherited it. The simple expedient of deleting the Zadok verse was not an option. Phinehas could not erase or delete what already had been written. There may have been an unwritten rule among the writers who supplemented the KDB that one could add but not subtract. In this light, Phinehas is usurping the mighty men of Canaanite tradition with the even mightier men of Mesopotamian tradition. His is as dismissive of the Canaanite claim to have mighty men as the Egyptians were to Canaanites having kings.

10: 9 *He was a mighty hunter before Yahweh; therefore it is said, 'Like Nimrod a mighty hunter before Yahweh'*

This verse contains the third use in the first cycle of the KDB of the name Yahweh being spoken in quotation marks.

For Dillmann, it is evident that verse 9 on Nimrod the hunter breaks the connection with the preceding and succeeding verses. He suggests it derives from oral tradition. It bespeaks the close connection between the hunter of animals and the warrior and is conspicuous in the Assyrian-Babylonian tradition for kings and gods. He rejects the proposals that verse 9 therefore is older than verses 8 and 10f.[101]

Gunkel similarly thinks that Gen. 10: 9 was an independent tradition inserted into the narrative.[102] Westermann concurs in his commentary. He claims that J himself inserted the verse between verses 8 and 10 which he had written.[103] Presumably if there had been quotation marks and bibliographic references, J's actions would have been more discernible. Instead, one may consider that this author added some descriptive material to his proper nouns to help guide the audience into understanding his message and perhaps that is what he did with this hunter 'proverb'. The text suggests that the audience had some sense of who Nimrod was. Similarly, the average person today will recognize the name Attila the Hun and have an image of him without really knowing much about him beyond his being a wreaker of havoc long ago.

The hunting reference is instructive and has drawn the attention of various Assyriologists. Van der Kooij links the hunting motif to Assyria. He cites an inscription from Tiglath-pileser

---

101 Dillmann, *Genesis*, 352–353.
102 Gunkel, *Genesis*, 90.
103 Westermann, *Genesis 1–11*, 516.

I in the 12th century BCE to document this assertion.[104] Tiglath-pileser I introduced the
hunting motif which later became a stereotyped staple of Assyrian royal annals.[105] Dick,
who accepts the Ninurta-Nimrod link, characterizes the hunt as the embodiment of the
Neo-Assyrian kingship in the 1st millennium BCE.[106] This motif therefore stretches over
five centuries from the Middle-Assyrian into the Neo-Assyrian period and cannot be used
to specify a time of origin for the story. Furthermore, Gispen reads the exact same hunting
reference and identifies a dating two millennia earlier than van der Kooij: Gilgamesh
'definitely [was] portrayed as a great hunter' which ties the reference to the account in Gen.
6: 1-4.[107] Gispen uses this insight to understand the 'proverb' in Gen. 10: 9 as a mighty
hunter before Yahweh. '[T]he currency of this expression in Israel proves that the figure
of Nimrod and the stories about him were well known. This points again to Gilgamesh'.[108]
Gispen concludes that Nimrod was based on Gilgamesh and, similar to Jastrow's view that
this king may have served as a model or characterization of subsequent kings.[109]

Westermann augments this idea by emphasizing the importance of kingship to
understanding this proverb. This 'text is concerned with the beginning of great kingdoms'
from an early time.[110] Westermann looks to the time when hunting was serious business
for the survival of the community from the threat of wild animals. As he puts it, 'What
became a sport and pastime in the high cultures was once a necessity that secured the life
of the community.'[111] While the fate of the countries were not literally on the line with the
hunts of Thutmose III in Syria or the Neo-Assyrian kings in their game parks, the successful
hunt by the king symbolically delivered a message of the triumph of order over chaos and
that the king was fulfilling his obligation to provide for the sustenance of the people. Such
assertions were particularly important for a founding king as Nimrod is represented for the
Sumerians, Akkadians, Babylonians, and Assyrians.[112]

Nimrod is not simply a mighty hunter, he is a mighty hunter before Yahweh long

---

104   Van der Kooij, 'The City of Babel and Assyrian imperialism', 1–18, here, 12.

105   Victor Hurowitz and Joan Goodnick Westenholz, 'LKA: a heroic poem of Tiglath-pileser I's Musru-
Qumanu Campaign', *JCS* 42 1990: 1–49, here 1. 49.

106   Michael B. Dick, 'Nimrod as a symbol of Neo-Assyrian kingship', paper presented at the annual
conference of the Society of Biblical Literature, 'Assyriology and the Bible' section, Philadelphia, 2005.

107   W. H. Gispen, 'Who was Nimrod?' in John H. Skilton and Milton C. Fisher, eds, *The Law and the
Prophets: Old Testament Studies Prepared in honor of Oswald Thompson Allis* (Nutley, NJ: Presbyterian and
Reformed Publishing Co., 1974), 207–214, here 210, quotation from 213.

108   Gispen, 'Who was Nimrod?', 213.

109   Morris Jastrow, Jr., *The Religion of Babylonia and Assyria* (New York: Ginn & Co., 1898), II: 515; Gispen,
'Who was Nimrod?', 214.

110   Westermann, *Genesis 1–11*, 518.

111   Westermann, *Genesis 1–11*, 516.

112   This motif continues today in the mythologies of peoples. For example, in the American tradition, Teddy
Roosevelt gained popular renown as a hunter even bequeathing to popular culture the beloved 'Teddy' bear
for an animal he would not shoot. That image resonated with the commander in-chief who talked softly and
carried a big stick, had the right stuff to go into the arena, and claimed the country stood at Armageddon
and battled for the Lord. American presidents who led the fight against science fiction forces of chaos in the
movie *Independence Day* or terrorists in the movie *Air Force One*, both encounters in the skies, continue this
tradition of cosmic triumph and heroic leaders.

before Moses encounters the deity by that name in the wilderness at the Burning Bush.[113] Hom is struck by the fact that Nimrod's prowess is directly subject to Yahweh.[114] That is precisely the point Phinehas wished to make. He is delivering the message that Yahweh is not simply a wilderness deity but a universal one from the dawn of time including over the great cities and empires of Mesopotamia. This claim undermines the primacy of the priests of Moses by enlarging the scope and presence of the Lord. Thanks to this one-upmanship, the Aaronid priests of Benjamin would be second no more. Yahweh's story now begins even earlier than the Exodus and with kings before Saul and David.

10: 10 Babel, Erech, and Accad and Calneh

These suggestions freeing Nimrod from being an individual in history enable one to understand what the biblical writer sought to achieve by adding him to the narrative. Nimrod is king over:

a. Uruk, most ancient of cities and home to Sumerian Gilgamesh
b. Akkad, capital city of Akkadian Sargon the Great (a long-abandoned city still known by name to this author, evidence of his erudition and learning)
c. Babylon, cultural capital of Mesopotamia and capital city of Amorite Hammurabi and Nebuchadnezzar I of Isin
d. Calneh, an unknown site.

It would be nice if Calneh were Calah, the Assyrian capital, with a 'stray' nun or 'n' somehow making its way into the word just as it did in Judges 18: 30. But transforming *kalnēᵇ* into *kālaḥ* is not quite that simple no matter how attractive that transformation might be. On the other hand, what other Mesopotamian city ranked with Uruk, Accad, and Babylon as cosmic centers of great civilizations and empires prior to Nineveh? Excluding Assyria from this worldview seems as unlikely as excluding the Nile from the four rivers of the garden. The biblical author certainly was aware of Assyrians Tukulti-ninurta I as the giant king of the 13th century BCE and Tiglath-pileser I who had reached nearby Lebanon in the 12th.[115] Calah was the primary city for Shalmaneser I, father of Tukulti-ninurta I and for Ashurbanipal II in the 9th century BCE.[116] Perhaps the change to Calneh was made when the Neo-Assyrian cities were added to the narrative and Amos referred to Calneh (Amos 6: 2) (see Chapter 15).

No scholar has been a greater advocate of Tiglath-pileser I's connection to the biblical narrative than Halpern but for David and Solomon, not Nimrod. He devotes a section

---

113 It should be noted that instead of 'before Yahweh', various commentators have considered 'against Yahweh' to be more appropriate particularly given Nimrod's presumed link to the following story of the Tower of Babel.
114 Mary Katherine Y. H. Hom, 2 "'...A mighty hunter before Yahweh": Genesis 10: 9 and the moral-theological evaluation of Nimrod', *VT* 60 2010: 63–68, here 66.
115 The Tukulti-ninurta epic 'reveals the subtle ways in which literature can be made to serve political ends' (Machinist, 'Literature as politics', 455). The age of Tiglath-pileser I also was one of significant scribal activity including both original compositions and the copying of traditional material (Hurowitz and Westenholz, 'LKA', 1).
116 Peter Machinist, 'Assyrian and its image in First Isaiah', *JAOS* 103 1983: 719–737, here 720 n.2.

entitled 'The Image of the King in Royal Propaganda' in his book on David to Tiglath-pileser I's innovative establishment of the model for all subsequent Assyrian kings to follow in how to portray oneself as king. Besides with the Assyrian kings, one finds these attributes most clearly in the Solomonic narrative in I Kings 3–10 and with no subsequent biblical king. Halpern's next section 'The Tiglath-Pileser Principle' extols the Assyrian king for perfecting the 'spin in Near Eastern royal historiography' where the propaganda 'whole' is greater than the sum of the actual parts achieved by the king. He discerns the same spin in the Solomon narrative and even David. Phinehas deserves credit for transferring that Assyrian model to the Israelite kings.[117]

This overview of the cities provides a way to understand the author's intent. These are 'celebrated cities … each having served as a major capital at one time…'[118] They are very reminiscent of the sequential Sumerian King List (see Additional Readings: Sumerian King List] but now with the cities joined under one composite representative individual. The author was doing chronologically in these imperial capitals what had been done geographically in the garden story with the naming of the four rivers (Gen. 2: 10–14). The expansion there to encompass the known world is mirrored here by Phinehas encompassing all time. Nimrod represented the great epochs and heroes of Mesopotamia known to the biblical writer's audience. The author has created a four-period chronology just as there was a four-quartered universe with his rivers and there would be with the four kings of chaos from the east who are cosmically defeated by the king from Hebron (Gen. 14).

Phinehas had enough perspective to recognize different eras in Mesopotamian history symbolized by the capital cities of the major civilizations. Undoubtedly the audience knew what the author meant. Given the cities involved it is difficult to imagine that they would not associate Nimrod with Mesopotamia especially if his name had been pronounced Ki-MaR-Du or even Ni-Mar-Du. The Mesopotamian war deity of empires had been humanized to represent the great royal eras in Mesopotamian history. Gen. 10: 8–10 provides the exemplar or avatar of what a king of the universe should be. As Knohl states, 'He was described as a hero to whom God granted extraordinary might and as the first king of Mesopotamia, who founded the ancient cities of Babel, Erech, Akkad, and Calah'.[119] The author elevated the KDB to a cosmic or universal level that it had not had before. Nimrod achieved in the great Mesopotamian past what Davidic kings were suppose to achieve in the Israelite present. For this author, Nimrod is a hero, a role model, a figure to be emulated.

10: 10 Shinar

All these cities are located in the land of Shinar. The people in Mesopotamia did not use that Greek name in ancient times for the land between the rivers. Locally-derived geographic terms included Sumer in the south at the beginning of the 3rd millennium BCE and Sumer-Akkad by the end of millennium due to the exploits of Sargon the Great

---

117   Halpern, *David's Secret Demons*, 113–132, quotation from 128.
118   B. Oded, 'The Table of Nations (Genesis 10 – a socio-cultural approach)', *ZAW* 98 1986: 14–31, here 27.
119   Knohl, 'Nimrod, son of Cush', 50.

at Akkad, his capital city. Sumer itself consisted of many independent city-states that only sometimes were joined into a single Sumerian entity. Babylon was more centrally located upriver but the city in itself did not include Sumer to the south or Assyria to the north. One suggestion is that Shinar derives from 'Shanhara', the name the Kassites who ruled Babylon *c.* 16th century to 1155 BCE gave to the city.[120] It was a name outsiders created and not a term employed within Mesopotamia itself.[121] This is consistent with the idea that Cush originally derives from the Kassites and that Nebuchadnezzar I who ruled after the Kassites was the recent model for what a great king could accomplish.

As Gunkel noted, Egypt is not mentioned in this listing either.[122]

The past is an important component in understanding Nimrod. Mesopotamian kings themselves were very familiar with the concept of drawing of past greatness. One way for kings to buttress their rule was to claim as their forefathers legendary heroes who were not their ancestor. Assyriologist Piotr Michalowski observes:

> 'By claiming the archetypical king Gilgamesh as his ancestor, Šulgi invented a literary tradition focusing on the legendary hero and establishing his links to a glorious past.'[123]

Objects from the past could be displayed publicly to show a link to the once-great and now deceased kings.[124] A possible illegitimate ruler might even take the name of a legendary king like Sargon II and possess a statue of Gilgamesh. But Nimrod is not the ancestral shepherd of Israel, Abram was and his story would be told the second cycle of the KDB.

Even though Nimrod should not be equated with either Tukulti-ninurta or Nebuchadnezzar I, the examples of those kings provided precedents for the Israelite king. Both the Middle Assyrian and Middle Babylonian king are associated with writings in support of their legitimacy. As noted, the Tukulti-ninurta Epic shows how literature can be made to serve political ends. Certain general observations may be made at the time in which this epic was created which lend themselves to understanding the significance of Nimrod.

1. The epic culminated a sequence for Assyria being accepted in the brotherhood of Great Kings of the Late Bronze Age. The days of being dismissed as a vassal of Babylon were now over.
2. The presumed audience of the epic was likely to have been the royal court and priestly hierarchy in the capital city.

In part, based on these considerations, Peter Machinist concluded that 'literature is essentially a political act, created to explain and justify major political and cultural shifts' and which serves 'as an important means of expressing and resolving' the internal conflicts. The change of relevance for the understanding of Nimrod's role in the biblical epic was

---

120 Ron Zadok, 'The origin of the name Shinar', *ZA* 74 1984: 240–244.

121 Day, *From Creation to Babel*, 171.

122 Gunkel, *Genesis*, 88.

123 Piotr Michalowski,'The mortal kings of Ur: a short century of divine rule in ancient Mesopotamia', in Nicole Brisch, ed., *Religion and Power: Divine Kingship in the Ancient World and Beyond* (University of Chicago OIS 4; Chicago: Oriental Institute, 2008), 33–45, here: 36–37. See also J. J. Finkelstein, 'The genealogy of the Hammurapi dynasty', *JCS* 20 1966: 95–118.

124 Talley Ornan, 'The long life of a dead king: a bronze statute from Hazor in its ancient Near East context', *BASOR* 366 2012: 1–23 here 17.

the shift in the cosmic center from Babylon to Assur as a direct result of Tukulti-ninurta's actions.[125]

Nebuchadnezzar I served as a closer and perhaps more direct precedent for Israelite kings (see Chapter 10). He:

> recovered the captured statue of Marduk from the Elamites,
> built a ziggurat,
> initiated the composition of *Enuma Elish*, the dominant story of Marduk's triumph over chaos and becoming king of the universe
> celebrated the *akitu*, the new year festival which included the recitation of *Enuma Elish* and processions with the statue of Marduk leaving the city and being returned to it.

In the time of David recovering the ark from the Philistines, his son building a temple, the writing of the KDB, and processions involving the ark, it is easy to see how his legacy might have been absorbed into the Israelite cultural legacy and become the figure behind the Nimrod story of Phinehas as the exemplar of Mesopotamian culture and civilization.

Another salient consideration is at the time of the writing all these Mesopotamian cities and kings of the 3rd and 2nd millennia were the cities and kings of the *past*. They were the great kings of renown, the kings of name, not the great king of the present. Gilgamesh, Sargon the Great, Naram-Sin, Hammurabi, Tukulti-ninurta, Tiglath-pileser I, and Nebuchadnezzar I were all dead as were their empires (and Egypt's, too). The inevitable question raised by this presentation for its audience is that given these four great cities of the four kingdoms of the humanized Mesopotamian deity who knew Yahweh, what is to be the great city of the kingdom of Yahweh in the present? Who is the great king of Yahweh in the present of the telling of the story? Who is the mighty hunter before Yahweh in our heritage? The answer was the shepherd who sojourns from Mesopotamia to Hebron and who defeats the forces of chaos in the second cycle of the KDB.

These attributes of Nimrod are essential for determining the authorial intent. They exist in the narrative as a conscious expression of his will and not as mythical fragments floating in oral tradition ether which the writer has snatched from thin air for his composition.

1. The mighty man is the great warrior king.
2. The hunter is a royal symbol of the successful warrior king who establishes the cosmic order from chaos.
3. 'Before Yahweh' indicates that the great warrior king who establishes the cosmic order builds a temple to his deity at the cosmic center.
4. The cities of Uruk, Akkad, Babylon, and probably Calah suggest this composite figure represents all the great eras of the different ethnic groups in Mesopotamia.

The city of the king is the capital of the empire. One city will rule over all others. One city will collect the taxes/tribute from all others. One city will organize the workers from all other cities. The royal infrastructure will be built in the capital city of the new empire. For this author, Nimrod is role model the Israelite king should or is emulating in the city of David.

---

125   Machinist, 'Literature as politics', 471–472, 475, 478–479, quotations from 478–479.

10: 18 Afterward the families of the Canaanites spread abroad [scattered]. ¹⁹ And the territory of the Canaanites extended from Sidon, in the direction of Gerar, as far as Gaza, and in the direction of Sodom, Gomorrah, Admah, and Zeboiim, as far as Lasha

Phinehas now narrows his focus to the land of Canaan. He is obligated to respond to Abiathar's verse which could not be deleted. He takes a more expanded view than Abiathar had. Abiathar simply defined Canaan in terms of three peoples, one of whom can be associated with a city, one perhaps with the hill country, and the third now ill-defined. Phinehas was quite precise in utilizing specific geographic references to define a land and not simply peoples. His Canaan is a 'territory' with a northwest to southwest border and a southeast to northeast border encompassing both sides of the Jordan and including the Philistines. This is the immediate world of concern for the author. Its borders match those of Israel's most ambitious aspirations.[126]

Phinehas's description of the Canaanites in 10: 18–19 draws to a conclusion the first cycle of stories. At first glance this quotidian description of the land of Canaan might seem anticlimactic, a rather pedestrian conclusion to some momentous events. However, one should recognize that he was aware of the second cycle, he knew the story continued. These verses may be likened to the teaser or cliffhanger that concludes a season series leaving the audience to wonder what will happen next.

Phinehas chose to anticipate the next cycle with his ending of the first cycle. He has identified the land of the kingdom, he has established a model for kingship, he has positioned the kingdom within the world arena. Now the stage in the land of Canaan has been set. But the individual hero has not yet entered the stage. The warrior king has not yet made his presence felt. He will do so in the second cycle now with a new introduction preceding the call. The next cycle will commence with Abram, the future warrior-shepherd-king at Hebron leaving the land of Cush to make a name for himself in the land of Canaan. The torch will be passed from the Nimrod civilizations to the Davidic dynasty with a new temple at the cosmic center in Jerusalem and the Aaronid priesthood headed by Phinehas in charge.

Phase III: Phinehas in the time of Rehoboam

> *5:29 [The men] called his name Noah, saying, 'Out of the ground [adamah] which Yahweh has cursed this one shall bring us relief from our work and from the toil of our hands'.*

This speech is the fourth and final instance of the author having the name Yahweh being spoken in quotation marks. Generally this verse is attributed to the J author even though it appears in the midst of an extensive genealogy attributed to the Priest author.[127] Based

---

126 Jack M. Sasson, 'The "Tower of Babel" as a clue to the redactional structuring of the primeval history [Gen. 1–11: 9]', in Gary Rendsburg, Ruth Adler, Milton Arfa and Nathan H. Winter, eds, *The Bible World: Essays in Honor of Cyrus H. Gordon*, (New York: KTAV, 1980), 211–219, here 212.

127 Gunkel, *Genesis*, 133–134; Speiser, *Genesis*, 39; von Rad, *Genesis*, 72; Westermann, *Genesis 1–11*, 359–360.

on the assumption that the verse was placed here during the redaction process (see Chapter 15), the issue then becomes where it had been located previously.[128] It does not smoothly follow from the Lamech story in Gen. 4 (see Chapter 14) although he is the presumed speaker from 5: 28. It does not smoothly follow from the son of Seth story here either although it is part of the Seth line in Gen. 5.[129] Actually it does, once one realizes that the men who called on the name of Yahweh then call up the name of Enosh/Rehoboam and give him this new name as the one who brings relief from toil. Why did Phinehas make this change? What did this new name mean then?

The definition of the name of Noah clearly draws on the images in Gen. 3: 17–19:

> **Gen. 3: 17** *And to Adam he said, 'Because you have listened to the voice of your wife, and have eaten of the tree of which I commanded you, "You shall not eat of it", cursed is the ground [adamah] because of you; in toil you shall eat of it all the days of your life;* [18] *thorns and thistles it shall bring forth to you; and you shall eat the plants of the field.* [19] *In the sweat of your face you shall eat bread till you return to the ground [adamah], for out of it you were taken; you are dust, and to dust you shall return.'*

Hendel suggests that the commonality in the garden story (3: 17–19), Cain and Abel (4: 11–12), 5: 29, Flood (8: 21), and the sons of Noah (9: 20) are all part of a writer's effort to create a literary continuity out of stories that had not been previously linked in Israelite oral tradition.[130] He follows the tradition of Gunkel that J was both a collector and artful writer without recognizing the possibility of multiple writers supplementing a common narrative. The name of Noah seems to draw to a close the punishment inflicted in the garden story upon the man (king), his future is dust not dynasty. Westermann, like others, also makes the connection between Gen. 5: 28–29 and Gen. 3: 17. He again understands it as celebrating the advance of civilization.[131] Turning to a more political approach, the verse suggests under the leadership of this individual the workload of the people in the plural will be lightened. The call for the lightening of the workload appears elsewhere in the biblical tradition.

1. The most famous example occurs in the Exodus story where Pharaoh is a taskmaster who makes the people serve with vigor and hard labor in bitterness (Ex. 1: 11–14). An entire chapter in the Exodus story is devoted to struggle to make bricks with reduced straw (Ex. 5). Clearly here are a people seeking to be delivered from a life of hard labor and bondage.
2. Pharaoh Solomon also used forced labor in his building projects (I Kings 9: 15). The biblical narrative presents two views on the people who were so subjugated. In one version, Israelites

---

128   Kohn suggests the Redactor spliced the J text of the name of Noah into the P genealogy through the addition of Gen. 5: 28b, 'he became the father *of a son*' whereas the remainder of the genealogy uses the actual name of the son instead. The transfer of Lamech from the Cainite to Sethite genealogy cleanses humanity from having been descendants of Cain. See Risa Levitt Kohn, 'Whom did Cain raise? Redaction and J's primeval history', in Richard Elliott Friedman and William H. C. Propp, eds, *Le-David maskil: A Birthday Tribute for David Noel Freedman* (Winona Lake: Eisenbrauns, 2004), 39–46, here 44–45.

129   Westermann, *Genesis 1–11*, 359.

130   Hendel, 'Is the "J Primeval Narrative" an independent composition?', 185; Hendel, '*Leitwort* style and literary structure', 96–97, 104–106.

131   Westermann, *Genesis 1–11*, 360, 487 and that wine will be a comfort for Yahweh's curse.

were exempted while the burden fell to 'All the people who were left of the Amorites, the Hittites, the Perizzites, the Hivites, and the Jebusites, who were not of the people of Israel', (1 Kings 9: 20). By contrast, an alternative view suggests the Israelites experienced forced labor as well since Jeroboam is identified as having been placed in charge by Solomon 'over all the forced labor of the house of Joseph' (1 Kings 11: 28). This version seems more believable in light of what was to come while the former seems like spin designed to cover-up the truth.

3.   Pharaoh Rehoboam sought to use forced labor when it was his turn to rule. The people Israel assembled at Shechem (I Kings 12: 1) which suggests that Jerusalem and Judah were not considered Israel. The narrative clearly states that forced labor over Israel had been part of Pharaoh Solomon's reign:

> **I Kings 12: 4** '*Your father made our yoke heavy. Now therefore lighten the hard service of your father and his heavy yoke upon us, and we will serve you.*'

Pharaoh Rehoboam then consulted his old advisors, aka, the Benjaminite priests of Aaron. They counseled:

> **1 Kings 12: 7** '*If you will be a servant to this people today and serve them, and speak good words to them when you answer them, then they will be your servants for ever.*'

Phinehas had the people call the name Noah for Enosh who was Rehoboam. He defined the name to be relevant to the times. Israel needed a leader who would lighten the load so the people would have a day of rest, so first-born sons could care for their mothers and maintain the farms of their fathers. Zadok's policies had alienated everyone outside the capital city. Abiathar had tapped into that angst. Over time, the anger against Pharaoh Solomon and his Pharaoh's daughter queen mounted. Phinehas now sought to ameliorate the anger of the people against the crown by reducing the crushing blow of forced labor. He recognized the danger to the kingdom if the hardship persisted. He recognized that as one king passed from the scene and an untested one took his place that the people might rise up and revolt. He advised Rehoboam to become a new Noah who would bring relief from their work and save the people. Phinehas was unsuccessful in this quest and the kingdom would not endure. The cursing of one man, the king in the garden, to hard labor (eye for an eye?) and the definition of the name of Noah were part of an ongoing political struggle fought first with words and then with a show of force as the people Israel rallied behind another leader and other words against Pharaoh once again (see Chapter 14).

Postscript

> 9: 18 *Ham was the father of*
> 9: 22 *And Ham, the father of*

Phinehas's glorious image of Solomon's cosmic kingdom proved short-lived. The times were changing both at home and abroad. In Egypt, a new dynasty emerged with dreams of reinvigorating the era of New Kingdom imperialism. In year five of the reign of Rehoboam, son of Solomon, Shishak/Sheshonq invaded the land of Canaan. According to the biblical

narrative he focused on Jerusalem, the capital city where the daughter of the pharaoh he had
replaced ruled as queen. It may be that the Jerusalem/Egypt alliance had been supplanted
by an Israelite/Egypt with Jeroboam who had taken refuge in Egypt:

> **I Kings 11: 40** *Solomon sought therefore to kill Jeroboam; but Jeroboam arose, and fled into Egypt,
> to Shishak king of Egypt, and was in Egypt until the death of Solomon.*

These actions harkened to the bad old days of Israel's origins where Canaanite cities and
its imperialist master fought to destroy the seed of Israel. Now these Canaanite cities in
the guise of the new kingdom Israel once again were the enemy, subservient to Egypt (see
Additional Readings: Shishak).[132]

   This change in circumstances mocked the cosmic pretensions of the Solomonic kingdom.
One of the old powers was back in the imperialism game and in a few decades so would
Assyria. The vision of Phinehas would not be forgotten but it was an ideal that scarcely
matched the current realities. This meant back to the drawing board or revising the biblical
narrative. In recognition of the new political order, the Canaanites through the language
of family to express political relationships, were assigned their place in the world as true
enemies of Israel: Canaan was a son of Ham, obedient to Egypt.

   Biblical scholars tend to agree that this phrase is secondary.[133] Clearly, the sentence calls
the audiences' attention to the link between Ham and Canaan who subsequently will be
cursed.[134] It could not have been written when Rehoboam ascended to the throne. Whether
Phinehas or his successor wrote it cannot be determined. Either way, the division of the
kingdom and Shishak's campaign marked the end of Israel's viability as a world power.
It's almost as if a prophecy of the collapse of Solomon's 'world' kingdom had come true.

---

132   Since Shishak's imperialist venture was not sustained, perhaps it would have been beneficial for Jeroboam
to demonstrate that he was not a lackey of Egypt but a champion of the Exodus. To convince people of such
a claim is another matter and he did not fare well in the biblical narrative.

133   Gunkel, *Genesis*, 79; von Rad, *Genesis*, 135 and Westermann, *Genesis 1–11*, 482.

134   Ross, 'The curse of Canaan', 225; Speiser, *Genesis*, 61.

Chapter 14

AHIJAH: PROPHET J

The final writer in the 10th century BCE sequence of supplements to the KDB was Ahijah, prophet and priest of Shiloh. Blenkinsopp declares 'beyond question' there were 'sources emanating from prophetic groups in the Ephraimite region [which includes Shiloh] who never reconciled themselves to the monarchy'.[1] One may include Abiathar and Ahijah in the list. Ahijah may have been the most intense of these biblical writers. He wore his emotions on his sleeve and held nothing back. For him, the confrontation with the crown was not simply politics as usual. It was visceral.

When Ahijah looked at the surrounding world he was distraught. Israel defined its deity as one who had led them out of Egypt. Israel had survived campaigns by Merneptah and Ramses III. Israel's seed had not been destroyed. Israel had celebrated the withdrawal of Egypt from the land. Israel had established Shiloh as the cosmic center. Israel had created the ark as the symbol of Yahweh's kingship. And Israel had sung songs and told stories every step of the way. Even the loss of the ark had been overcome when the heroic David, student of Abiathar, priest of Moses, created a kingdom in the land of Canaan, installed the ark at Zion, the former stronghold of the enemy, and led the people in joyous procession with the ark. What more could one want? O happy days.

From there it was all downhill. Following the death of David, a Jebusite coup installed Solomon as king. Solomon married an Egyptian princess. Solomon built like an Egyptian Pharaoh, sometimes in the same places as where Egypt had once ruled. Solomon made life harsh and the people served him with rigor. Solomon undid centuries of Israelite existence of no king, no temple, no forced labor, and no taxes. Solomon's temple swallowed up the ark and it disappeared from sight. Albertz postulates that the slave descriptions in the Exodus derive from the experiences of forced labor under (Pharaoh) Solomon. The struggle against forced labor in the present was fought through an appeal to the story of liberation from forced labor in the past. Regardless of the historicity of the Exodus, its story was a viable battleground at the time the northern kingdom of Israel was born. To control the story of the past was to control the future.[2]

Now the priests of Moses were not simply in exile from the Beltway, the arena of power, they were not even playing the game anymore. The Benjaminite priests of Aaron ran the show. They controlled the past, they controlled the story of the Exodus, they controlled the origin of Yahweh. Ahijah's world was crumbling and he needed a savior. He was a writer who seethed. The prophetic movement of no-holds barred challenges to those in power had begun.

---

1   Blenkinsopp, 'The quest for the historical Saul', 80.
2   Albertz, *A History of Israelite Religion*, 45, 142.

In the story of Baal Peor, the battle between the two Israelite priesthoods was formally engaged (see Chapter 13). Phinehas merited a dynastic priesthood while the passive Moses had stood by and watched a Midianite violate the tent of meeting. In Num. 31, the stakes are raised even higher. Now Moses charges Eleazar, the father of Phinehas, with the task of leading the forces of Israel against the kings of Midian. They are specifically enjoined to 'remember the Baal Peor'. The results are brutal, the death total huge, the booty enormous. The foundational event of the Israelite people continually was being used as a battleground to address conditions within the people Israel. The emotions were raw, longstanding, and all-consuming. The writings could be equally focused (see Additional Readings: Midian).

Phinehas's rival Ahijah appears by name in the biblical narrative only in a few specific instances. These passages were not written by him but by those who continued the path he had trod as the struggles against Israelite Pharaohs, as the prophets saw them, continued.[3] The Book of the Saviors became the Book of the Prophet narrative as prophets and kings who listened to them became heroes. The Ahijah writings focus on the figure of Jeroboam, the apparent new Moses who never became one.[4] The text introduces Jeroboam as:

> **I Kings 11: 26** *Jeroboam the son of Nebat, an Ephraimite of Zeredah, a servant of Solomon, whose mother's name was Zeruah, a widow, also lifted up his hand against the king.*

The Hebrew Ephrati (אפרתי) is translated as 'Ephraimite' here following in the tradition of the LXX as if there were an 'm' at the end. While Jeroboam becomes king of the northern kingdom including Ephraim, this translation obscures a potential political connection of grave importance. David already has been linked to Ephratah-Bethlehem and Shiloh has been linked to those locations through the story of Elkanah and Hannah. If Jeroboam is 'Ephrati' too, then he is linked to both the David and the priests of Shiloh as well.[5]

Jeroboam then was a home-grown figure. His selection to oversee the forced labor of the house of Joseph (I Kings 11: 28) may have seemed astute. However, the biblical text has sowed the seeds of dissent. 'House' was a term typically used for a dynasty such as of kings. It is as if Jeroboam had been made king by Solomon over the people he later would become king of when the split into Israel and Judah occurred. Conversely he did not earn the position of power nor was he embraced by the people as Saul had been at Gilgal (I Sam. 11: 15) and David had been at Hebron (II Sam. 5: 1-3). Jeroboam likely was familiar with the story of David's rise to power. The dynastic tradition was not yet well-established and he may harbored ambitions of his own just as David had.

Then Jeroboam met Ahijah.

---

3   To understand Elijah, Elisha, Hosea, and Jeremiah, one must understand Ahijah and what he wrought. This study only covers his writings in the first cycle of the KDB but one should keep in mind his intensity which became part of the legacy of the prophetic tradition.

4   For a compiled list of the Moses/Jeroboam parallels see Carr, *The Formation of the Hebrew Bible*, 477.

5   For the Ephraim/Ephratah issue see, Leuchter, 'Jeroboam the Ephraite', 60–65. He elaborates that the 'breach' which Solomon closes in v.27, פרץ or 'perez' really refers to Perez, a descendant of Judah and ancestor of David (Ruth 4: 18–21; I Chr. 2: 5–15). Leuchter's interpretation means Solomon's action to close the city of David his father in the verse refers not to Jerusalem but to the seizure of Ephratah-Bethlehem.

I Kings 11:29 *And at that time, when Jeroboam went out of Jerusalem, the prophet Ahijah the Shilonite found him on the road. Now Ahijah had clad himself with a new garment; and the two of them were alone in the open country.[30] Then Ahijah laid hold of the new garment that was on him, and tore it into twelve pieces.*

Garment is a literary motif. In Phinehas's supplement to the story of the sons of Noah, Shem and Japheth cover the naked Noah with a garment (Gen. 9: 23), the same term used here. A garment also figures prominently in the incident between Joseph and Potiphar's wife (Gen. 38: 14) and when Tamar wears a widow's garments (Gen. 39). In these instances a different Hebrew term is used although often translated into English the same way. The garments Yahweh makes in the garden for the man and woman (Gen. 3: 21) and Joseph's famous coat of many colors or tunic (Gen. 37: 3) are based on a third term. The common English translation obscures the difference in the Hebrew as with *ish* and *adam* for man. Clearly the garment or clothing motif which appears in additional stories as well is an important one in storytelling and was used by different storytellers.

In the subsequent verses to the passage, the prophet Ahijah effectively commissions Jeroboam as the future king of a ten-tribe nation. When Solomon learns of the event, Jeroboam flees to Egypt where he is welcomed by Pharaoh Shishak (I Kings 11: 40), Sheshonq in the Egyptian archaeological record. The 22nd Dynasty Pharaoh was a Libyan who had supplanted the 21st Dynasty which had provided the Pharaoh's daughter who became Solomon's wife (see Additional Readings: Shishak).

After Solomon died and his son Rehoboam became king, Jeroboam did return. When Rehoboam rebuffed the entreaties of the people over their harsh treatment in the kingdom of bondage, a new ten-tribe kingdom of Israel was created with Jeroboam as king as Ahijah had predicted. The men may have called Enosh 'Noah' in the hope of his ameliorating their oppressive condition, but Rehoboam did not hear.

I Kings 12: 15 *So the king [Rehoboam] did not hearken to the people; for it was a turn of affairs brought about by Yahweh that he might fulfil his word, which Yahweh spoke by Ahijah the Shilonite to Jeroboam the son of Nebat.*

One glimpses in the passage the perspective of hindsight. Someone is bringing order to the past through the creation of a narrative that answers questions in history that are relevant to the present of its composition. In this instance, the message being delivered seems intended to justify revolt against Pharaoh kings of Israel. The author belonged to the prophet party.

One would think that the historical trends now favored the priests of Shiloh. Whereas Abiathar had been exiled into oblivion by Zadok and Solomon, a single generation later the tide seemingly had turned. Now Abiathar's successor had become a king-maker. The second part of the passage, perhaps written at a different time, suggests that Rehoboam's action is part of a divinely-controlled sequence now coming to fruition ... or so the storyteller wants the audience to believe. Unfortunately for Ahijah, the Shiloh priests did not fare well in the new northern kingdom. Among other things, the new king preferred to put his own people in power rather than depend on the old priesthood as previously noted.

I Kings 12: 32 *And he [Jeroboam] placed in Bethel the priests of the high places that he had made.*

Undoubtedly such actions did not please the priest who had placed him in power. Friedman succinctly states:

> 'The priests from Shiloh soon felt betrayed and excluded again… The priests from Shiloh had no place in Jeroboam's religious structure… If the priests of Shiloh were indeed descendants of Moses, their present status, or lack of status, in both kingdoms must have been bitter for them. They had fallen from leadership of the nation to poor, landless dependency.'[6]

In a sense, they had suffered a personal trauma which could be understood as a national trauma since they were the keepers of the nation's cultural legacy. The international situation also conspired against Ahijah. According to the biblical narrative:

> **I Kings 14: 25** *In the fifth year of King Rehoboam, Shishak king of Egypt came up against Jerusalem;* [26] *he took away the treasures of the house of Yahweh and the treasures of the king's house; he took away everything. He also took away all the shields of gold which Solomon had made.*

This invasion occurs subsequent to the time of the six son stories of this study and will not be addressed here.

Ahijah, of course, did not write these stories about himself. Someone(s) did after he had died. There are other more elaborate stories about Jeroboam and Ahijah that seem more reflective of a future war of words in the battle for power (see I Kings 14: 1–18). Nonetheless, these passages provide valuable information about what actually happened during the reigns of Jeroboam and Rehoboam even if told in symbolic and metaphorical terms to relate them to the time of the author when confronted with similar issues. The historical data to be gleaned from these texts are:

1. The Shiloh priests supported David but not Solomon, the ark at Zion but not the temple in Jerusalem.
2. Ahijah the Shiloh priest was a political player in the time of Solomon, Rehoboam, and Jeroboam – like Jeroboam, he had a life prior to the separation of the kingdoms during which he became a person of name in his own right.
3. Ahijah is portrayed as a prophet, as one who speaks the words of Yahweh and whose words become true. His batting average is perfect and the text consistently makes a point of proclaiming the actions which have occurred are according to the words of Yahweh spoken to Ahijah.
4. Regardless of his actual batting average in history, it is reasonable to conclude that during his lifetime he was considered to be a prophet and spokesperson for the Lord.

Ahijah thereby became a forerunner and precedent for future prophets who challenged the authority of the king. In one sense he continued the tradition established by Moses who challenged the authority of Pharaoh. Pharaoh Ahab later faced similar prophetic challenges from Elijah. Such challenges to royal authority were part of what differentiated Israel from other peoples in the ancient Near East.

---

6 Friedman, *Who Wrote the Bible?*, 66. Halpern wrestles with the machinations of the priests of Moses and the priests of Aaron, identifying the priests at Bethel, and the place of Benjamin but without separating the Zadokites from the Aaronids; see Baruch Halpern, 'Levitic participation in the reform cult of Jeroboam I', *JBL* 95 1976: 31–42. Part of the problem here is that the configuration in the time of Jeroboam depends on the decisions made about it in the time of Saul then David and then Solomon.

One may observe here the development of the 9th century prophet narrative suggested by Campbell (see Chapter 10).

The prophetic role differentiated the prophet from traditional cultic priest functions. The political events generated a religious change. Once the priests of Shiloh had had a place to which Israelites would come. The stories of Hannah at Shiloh praying for a son (I Sam. 1) and the daughters of Shiloh at the yearly feast (Judges 21) reflect that former physical basis. Now, the Shiloh priests had no cultic sanctuary to administer. Shiloh had been destroyed by the Philistines, Abiathar had lost the battle for power in Jerusalem, and Ahijah had lost the battle for power in Jeroboam's new kingdom. Their authority as prophets was not placed-based at a sacred structure of some kind as it traditionally is for priests. Their power derived from their message, the words they spoke in the name of the Lord, words that would be written down.

The loss of the ark of Lord at Shiloh to the Philistines proved to be a political battleground for generations to come. Shiloh's legacy was part of the background for Abiathar (see Chapter 12). The focus of attention on the loss of the ark usually is on David's restoration of it from the Philistines. The political repercussions of its loss would have led to finger-pointing: who is to blame for the traumatic act which has occurred? While that question cannot be answered here (God? superior Philistine military might? superior Philistine leadership? the failure of the members of the Israelite coalition to join the battle?), one should consider the names in the narratives written to explain who was at fault.

The following analysis focuses on the names of the leading characters in the story in the loss of the ark. It does not address the proposed existence of an Ark Narrative in I Sam. 4: 1b–7: 1 and II Sam. 6. The exegesis of those verses warrants its own study as has been done in various commentaries, monographs, and articles as noted in Chapter 10.

> **1 Sam. 1: 3** *Now this man used to go up year by year from his city to worship and to sacrifice to Yahweh of hosts at Shiloh, where the two sons of Eli, Hophni and Phinehas, were priests of Yahweh.*

Once again a son story portrays a battleground. Once again biological kinship is not the issue. Once again political relationships are expressed through familial terms and a character might be a cipher for a political faction. Special effort has been made to mention the Egyptian-named Hophni and Phinehas. As sons, they were expected to be obedient to Eli. The Cainites as sons should have been obedient to Eve/Bathsheba and were not; the Benjamin sons of God did pledge loyalty to Solomon and Rehoboam. The son motif expresses both loyalty and disloyalty depending on the story.

In this instance, obedient sons meant to conduct themselves as worthy of being priests at Shiloh. But the character of these two priests was not good.

> **1 Samuel 2: 12** *Now the sons of Eli were worthless men; they had no regard for Yahweh.* [13] *The custom of the priests with the people was that when any man offered sacrifice, the priest's servant would come, while the meat was boiling, with a three-pronged fork in his hand,* [14] *and he would thrust it into the pan, or kettle, or caldron, or pot; all that the fork brought up the priest would take for himself. So they did at Shiloh to all the Israelites who came there.* [15] *Moreover, before the fat was burned, the priest's servant would come and say to the man who was sacrificing, 'Give meat for the priest to roast; for he will not accept boiled meat from you, but raw'.* [16] *And if the*

man said to him, 'Let them burn the fat first, and then take as much as you wish', he would say,
'No, you must give it now; and if not, I will take it by force'. [17] *Thus the sin of the young men*
was very great in the sight of Yahweh; for the men treated the offering of Yahweh with contempt.

In effect, these two brothers are in the tent of Eli, the divinely-designated figure of authority.
They violate his trust and therefore the Lord's as well. Yahweh is not blind, he sees the
truth. This passage functions as an indictment of the priesthood. The guilty ones deserve
opprobrium not praise, to be cut-off not promised an eternal dynasty.

In this story line, Phinehas is not the hero descendant of Aaron in the Exodus who saves
the people who have sinned with the Midianites. Rather he is the subordinate to Eli, the
priest of Shiloh, whom he undermines with his sin of despoiling the Israelite people for
his own gain. These actions lead to the loss of the ark of Yahweh to the Philistines with
whom Phinehas in the present wishes to ally as expressed in his supplement to the story
of the sons of Noah (see Chapter 13). He (the Benjaminites) caused the ruin of Israel in
the past through his corruption, he will do so in the present or already is with the imperial
spoils if he has his way. The war of words continues.

As one might expect, the prognosis for these corrupt and wayward priests was abysmal.
The battle then commences between Israel and the Philistines. The going is not good so
Israel turns to divine help.

I Samuel 4: 4 *So the people sent to Shiloh, and brought from there the ark of the covenant of*
Yahweh of hosts, who is enthroned on the cherubim; and the two sons of Eli, Hophni and Phinehas,
were there with the ark of the covenant of God.

Note again the effort to identify the presence of the sinful sons. They are at the battlefield
and with the ark. They definitely are Israelite as are the Benjaminites (below). One notes
the presence of the cherubim, the guardians of the Garden (Gen. 3: 24) and the inner
sanctuary of the Temple (I Kings 6: 23–35). One notes that it is 'the people', עם, who take
the initiative to act under the banner of the Lord. These verses are laden with imagery and
motifs intricately intertwined with so many other stories that it would challenge Alexander
the Great to unravel the knot of associations. In the ark narrative, the moment of truth
has arrived and it is not only the ark which is lost.

I Samuel 4: 11 *And the ark of God was captured; and the two sons of Eli, Hophni and Phinehas,*
were slain. [12] *A man of Benjamin ran from the battle line, and came to Shiloh the same day, with*
his clothes rent and with earth upon his head. [13] *When he arrived, Eli was sitting upon his seat by*
the road watching, for his heart trembled for the ark of God. And when the man came into the
city and told the news, all the city cried out.

The ark narrative version of the traumatic battle story repeatedly links Hophni, Phinehas,
and the ark. Indeed, the name Hophni only appears in conjunction with Phinehas and as
part of the story of the loss of the ark (I Sam. 1: 3; 2: 34; 4: 4, 11, 17). The author has
chosen a distressed Benjaminite to be the bearer of bad news. After Absalom dies, Amihaaz
son of Zadok seizes the initiative to report the victory but neglects to mention to David
that Absalom is dead (II Sam. 18). What anonymous city is meant in the story where the
people cried out? These writers were neither journalists nor historians but players in the
game of power politics where everything on the stage is selected to deliver message.

I Samuel 4: 17 *He who brought the tidings answered and said [to Eli], 'Israel has fled before the Philistines, and there has also been a great slaughter among the people; your two sons also, Hophni and Phinehas, are dead, and the ark of God has been captured'.*

The shock of the news of the death of Hophni and Phinehas leads to the immediate death of Eli but the impact did not stop there.

I Sam. 4: 19 *Now his [Eli's] daughter-in-law, the wife of Phinehas, was with child, about to give birth. And when she heard the tidings that the ark of God was captured, and that her father-in-law and her husband were dead, she bowed and gave birth; for her pains came upon her.*
²⁰And about the time of her death the women attending her said to her, 'Fear not, for you have borne a son'. But she did not answer or give heed. ²¹And she named the child Ichabod, saying, 'The glory has departed from Israel!' because the ark of God had been captured and because of her father-in-law and her husband. ²²And she said, 'The glory has departed from Israel, for the ark of God has been captured'.

There is no song of Miriam, no song of Deborah, no women singing 'Saul has slain his thousands, and David his ten thousands' following their encounters with the Philistines. Instead the woman of Phinehas pronounces the brutally stark words of ultimate loss: the glory of the Lord has departed from Israel, the ark of the covenant of God has been captured. The trauma of who lost the ark haunted Israelites even over a century after it had occurred. Regardless of when these words were written, they attest the bitter rivalry between the competing Israelite priesthoods (as the Jebusite/Zadokites could not have cared less about who lost the ark).[7]

Some of the names of in the story of the loss of ark reappeared in the time of the stories of Saul.

I Sam. 14:2 *Saul was staying in the outskirts of Gibeah under the pomegranate tree which is at Migron; the people who were with him were about six hundred men, ³ and Ahijah the son of Ahitub, Ichabod's brother, son of Phinehas, son of Eli, the priest of Yahweh in Shiloh, wearing an ephod.*

I Sam. 14:18 *And Saul said to Ahijah, 'Bring hither the ark of God'. For the ark of God went at that time with the people of Israel.*

The name Ahitub appears four times in I Samuel 22 when Saul massacres the Shiloh priests who were obligated to relocate to Nob following the Philistine destruction of their sanctuary. The name appears in connection with his son Ahimelech, who seems to have been in charge there and who is summoned to present himself to Saul prior to the massacre. One of Ahimelech's sons named Abiathar survives the slaughter, escapes, and then joins David thereby beginning their story together (see Chapter 12). Another son given the name 'Ahijah', is depicted as subordinate to Saul and carries the ark as Abiathar did for David. Strangely enough, Zadok later is identified as a son of Ahitub (II Sam. 8: 17) although he has no role in the story and that verse may be garbled.[8]

---

7   What would this sequence of events mean if Steven Spielberg is right and Sheshonq really is the raider of the lost ark? What would it mean if Phinehas and perhaps his successor Hophni were the temple priests in the reign of Rehoboam when the ark was taken? What would it mean if the priests of Aaron were party to the loss of the ark? What would the story of the golden calf mean then?
8   Caquot and de Robert, *Les Livres de Samuel*, 446; McCarter, *II Samuel*, 253–254.

The tangled machinations of proper names demonstrates the ongoing trauma over the loss of the ark and the need to assign blame for that occurrence. People battling for power in the 10th century BCE and later were using the historical loss of the ark to the Philistines in the 11th century BCE to legitimate claims to power in their own times. Those responsible for the loss of the ark in the past were not worthy to be in positions of power in the present. The Zadokites were not part of the conversation since the capture occurred prior to Jerusalem becoming part of Israel. For the priests of Benjamin (Aaron) and Ephraim (Moses), the battle still raged. Phinehas had supplemented the KDB to advance the Benjaminite position; now Ahijah would have his own turn.

Turnabout is fair play as a tactic in the game of power. Phinehas and his supporters had championed the Aaronid priest line in confrontations with the Midianites, the people of the wife of Moses (see Chapter 12). Now the Aaronids are portrayed as calling for the destruction of the Benjaminites.

> **Judges 20: 28** *and Phinehas the son of Eleazar, son of Aaron, ministered before it in those days, saying, 'Shall we yet again go out to battle against our brethren the Benjaminites, or shall we cease?' And Yahweh said, 'Go up; for tomorrow I will give them into your hand'.* [29] *So Israel set men in ambush round about Gibeah.* [30] *And the people of Israel went up against the Benjaminites on the third day, and set themselves in array against Gibeah, as at other times.*

In this text, Saul Town, Gibeah, is to be attacked by all Israel. Israel is to do so upon instructions from the Lord delivered through Phinehas of Benjamin. Biblical authors had wicked senses of humor. They loved to express it by having a character do something exactly opposite to what the actual person advocated. An author could set such a story in the present: Nathan confronted David! Or an author could set a story in past by naming a character with the figure from the present. Phinehas could be a hero or villain in a story set in past depending on the writer's attitude towards him in the present. All these ark-related passages were part of the ongoing war of words in the battles for power between the priests of Benjamin and Ephraim. It had originated prior to Saul even seeking the throne and continued long after these two tribes were in separate kingdoms. The writings of Ahijah simply are one moment in a conflict that spanned centuries.

Ahijah wrote subsequent to the three supplements to the KDB by Zadok, Abiathar, and Phinehas. The two manuscripts which existed when he began were:

> KDB + Zadok + Abiathar + Phinehas (but not necessarily all 3 of his additions)
> KDB + Abiathar.

Ahijah was aware of the extended version authored by Phinehas, but his own writings were limited to supplementing the Abiathar manuscript. Ahijah responded to Phinehas but in a separate manuscript. As a result, his manuscript includes stories that are in direct opposition to and contrary to the views expounded by Phinehas. Centuries later when the two manuscripts were combined into one (see Chapter 15), that action led to the anomalies and tensions that so plagued the rabbis, priests, ministers, and biblical scholars (see Part I).

Reconstructed Narrative of Prophet J: additions to *Abiathar* in **bold**
Cain and Abel story

Gen. 4: 17 Cain knew his wife, and she conceived and bore Enoch; and he built a city, and called the name of the city after the name of his son, Enoch. [18] To Enoch was born Irad; and Irad was the father of Mehujael, and Mehujael the father of Methushael, and Methushael the father of Lamech. [19] And Lamech took two wives; the name of the one was Adah, and the name of the other Zillah. [20] Adah bore Jabal; he was the father of those who dwell in tents and have cattle. [21] His brother's name was Jubal; he was the father of all those who play the lyre and pipe. [22] Zillah bore Tubalcain; he was the forger of all instruments of bronze and iron. The sister of Tubalcain was Naamah. [23] Lamech said to his wives: 'Adah and Zillah, hear my voice; you wives of Lamech, hearken to what I say: I have slain a man for wounding me, a young man for striking me. [24] If Cain is avenged sevenfold, truly Lamech seventy-sevenfold'.

6:[3] Then Yahweh said, 'My spirit shall not abide in man for ever, for he is flesh, but his days shall be a hundred and twenty years.'

Local Flood story
9: 20 Noah planted a vineyard; [21] and he drank of the wine, and became drunk, and lay uncovered in his tent. [22] Canaan saw the nakedness of his father, and told his two brothers outside. [24] When Noah awoke from his wine and knew what his youngest son had done to him, [25] he said, 'Cursed be Canaan; a slave of slaves shall he be to his brothers'. 10:[15] Canaan became the father of [16] the Jebusites, the Amorites, the Girgashites.

11: 1 Now the whole earth had one language and few words.[2] And as men migrated from the east [eastward], they found a plain in the land of Shinar and settled there. [3] And they said to one another, 'Come, let us make bricks, and burn them thoroughly'. And they had brick for stone, and bitumen for mortar. [4] Then they said, 'Come, let us build ourselves a city, and a tower with its top in the heavens, and let us make a name for ourselves, lest we be scattered abroad upon the face of the whole earth.' [5] And Yahweh came down to see the city and the tower, which the sons of men had built. [6] And Yahweh said, 'Behold, they are one people, and they have all one language; and this is only the beginning of what they will do; and nothing that they propose to do will now be impossible for them. [7] Come, let us go down, and there confuse their language, that they may not understand one another's speech.' [8] So Yahweh scattered them abroad from there over the face of all the earth, and they left off building the city. [9] Therefore its name was called Babel, because there Yahweh confused the language of all the earth; and from there Yahweh scattered them abroad over the face of all the earth.

New end of the first cycle.

Ahijah's additions to the narrative related to the son stories are fairly straightforward:

1. He adds a genealogy to the end of the story of Cain and Abel.
2. He adds an introduction to the story of Flood with a verse now part of the Sons of God story (see Chapter 14)
3. He adds a new ending for the first cycle with the story of the Tower of Babel.

Ahijah responded to the writings of Zadok and especially Phinehas. He was aware of the global stage which Phinehas had created and the Mesopotamian legacy which he had incorporated into the narrative. In contrast, Ahijah's stage remains a local one. He rejected both the Canaanite and Mesopotamian motifs of the previous writers. He harkened to a world of no king and no temple where the people were ruled by Yahweh and governed by the covenant (which needed some new amendments due to the abuse of power by the kings).

Ahijah's story then should be seen not as a continuation of Phinehas's Nimrod and Table of Nations but as an alternative to it. The exegetes who linked the stories of the sons of Cain and the Tower of Babel to a parallel account without a universal flood were correct. As Driver recounts about the Tower of Babel:

> 'It connects also very imperfectly with the close of J's narrative of the Flood; for though the incident which it describes is placed shortly after the Flood, the men who gather together and build the city seem to be considerably more numerous than the members of the single family of Noah. In all probability (Dillm[ann]) the story originally grew up without reference to the Flood, or the derivation of mankind from the three sons of Noah, and it has been imperfectly accommodated to the narratives in chs. ix and x [sons of Noah, Nimrod and the Table of Nations]; perhaps indeed, Wellh[ausen] and others are right in conjecturing that originally it belonged to the same cycle of tradition as iv. 17–24 [sons of Cain], in which the continuity of human history seems not to have been interrupted by the Flood...'[9]

One observes here that approximately one century ago, biblical scholars were on the brink of identifying the writings assigned to Ahijah in this study. Two critical considerations hindered their eyes being opened: (i) the belief that the stories arose in hoary antiquity as oral traditions and, (ii) the unawareness that the writing was a supplement to the KDB.

Ahijah also exhibited a literary style not previously expressed by his predecessors in the son stories – he wrote an entirely new story. Zadok limited himself to some small additions surrounding the story of Cain and Abel that were more pronouncements of the new order than stories. Abiathar had written a very short story about the sons of Noah which provided him an opportunity to vent against Zadok and the Canaanites. Phinehas added lots of proper nouns while exonerating his tribe of Benjamin. Ahijah seemed to be following in these footsteps but then he finished with a major story – the Tower of Babel.

Of all the son stories, the Tower of Babel is the one which is a full story in its own right. Ahijah wrote it from scratch and none of the other writers ever revised it or had much chance to. As a story, it can be analyzed as a single unit as the product of one mind in a specific point in space and time. The Tower of Babel as story affords the reader today an opportunity to go inside the mind of politically-involved artist just as one can do with the slightly longer Gettysburg Address of Lincoln. But while America's greatest president sought to maintain the unity of the united States, the prophet of Moses sought to salvage a failed kingdom through renewal of the people of covenant at Shechem as Israel.

Sons of Cain

Some of the same issues generated by the 'truncated' Sethite genealogy have been raised for the Kenite genealogy. They supposedly are fragmentary and perhaps once part of the same list as the Sethites.[10] Not everyone agrees.[11] The resolution of the debate is the

---

9   Driver, *The Book of Genesis*, 133.
10 J. M. Miller, 'The dscendants of Cain', 166–167.
11 Vermeylen, 'La descendance de Caïn', 176. On the unity of the genealogical unit see Bryan, 'A reevaluation of Gen.4 and 5', 184, 186.

same. Neither one was fragmentary and neither one originated elsewhere. The Kenite and Sethite genealogies both were complete as written by their respective authors and were about the present in which they were written. But whereas Zadok's genealogy had a direct 1:1 correspondence with actual people in his present, Ahijah's genealogy drew on Kenite traditions while delivering a bold message using representational figures.

Day observes that while older commentaries generally attribute the Kenite genealogy to be an etiology for the Kenites, newer commentaries do not even mention them here. He seeks to redress that omission.[12] The standard view on the genealogy was expressed by Driver:

> 'The growth of civilization and the origin of what were taken to be primitive institutions or modes of life in the line of Cain. No doubt, the narrator reports faithfully what was currently believed by the Hebrews,and perhaps by the Canaanites before them, about the beginnings of civilization: but the picture, it must be evident, cannot be historical.'[13]

The genealogy in these verses presents an alternative to the urban Mesopotamian view promulgated by Phinehas through his post-universal-flood Nimrod story. By contrast, Kenite Ahijah's view stresses the wilderness as the starting point, as the place of origin and, as will be seen, has scant regard for what the sons of men do in the city.

Westermann posits that the 'obvious interest in the cultural achievements points to the era of David and Solomon'.[14] Von Rad observes that the 'historical background for the material of our narrative is very strange'.[15] Day thinks von Rad was on the right track in linking the story to the Balaam Oracles as previously noted (see Chapter 11):

> **Numbers 24: 17** *I see him, but not now; I behold him, but not nigh: a star shall come forth out of Jacob, and a scepter shall rise out of Israel; it shall crush the forehead of Moab, and break down all the sons of Sheth.*

> **Numbers 24: 22** *nevertheless Kain shall be wasted. How long shall Asshur take you away captive?*

The two verses bring together Cain and Seth in the Transjordan where the Shutu from the Egyptian Execration Texts locate them. The Kenites and Shutu/Sethites were real peoples and neighbors whose name and/or traditions along with the Amalekites became part of the Israelite story.[16]

Cain then is the embodiment or ancestor of the Kenites who still existed at the time of von Rad's J:

> **I Samuel 15: 6** *And Saul said to* **the Kenites**, *'Go, depart, go down from among the Amalekites, lest I destroy you with them; for you showed kindness to all the people of Israel when they came up out of Egypt'. So* **the Kenites** *departed from among the Amalekites.*

> **I Samuel 27: 10** *When Achish asked, 'Against whom have you made a raid today?'. David would say, 'Against the Negeb of Judah', or 'Against the Negeb of the Jerahmeelites', or, 'Against the Negeb of* **the Kenites**.'

---

12 Day, *From Creation to Babel*, 51–52, 60.
13 Driver, *The Book of Genesis*, 68.
14 Westermann, *Genesis 1–11*, 589, see also 56.
15 Von Rad, *Genesis*, 107.
16 Day, *From Creation to Babel*, 55–57.

> **I Samuel 30: 26** *When David came to Ziklag, he sent part of the spoil to his friends, the elders of Judah, saying, 'Here is a present for you from the spoil of the enemies of Yahweh';* [27] *it was for those in Bethel, in Ramoth of the Negeb, in Jattir,* [28] *in Aroer, in Siphmoth, in Eshtemoa,* [29] *in Racal, in the cities of the Jerahmeelites, in* **the cities of the Kenites,** [30] *in Hormah, in Borashan, in Athach,* [31] *in Hebron, for all the places where David and his men had roamed.*

The narratives of both Saul and David portray the Kenites positively ... and it was Jael, the Kenite who was a hero in the Song of Deborah:

> **Judges 5: 24** *'Most blessed of women be Jael, the wife of Heber* **the Kenite,** *of tent-dwelling women most blessed.'*

It is reasonable to conclude that these Kenites had traditions about their own history and origin. It is also reasonable to conclude that a priest of Moses and therefore of Zipporah, the Kenite wife of Moses, too, would have access to those traditions as well. For Ahijah defining Israel's precovenant existence beginning with the Kenites was a counterpoint to Phinehas's emphasis on Mesopotamia. The Kenite genealogy was not a self-contained unit but part of a larger supplement created as an act of will to assert the primacy of the Kenites against the Jebusite Zadokites and Benjaminite Aaronids. For a priest and prophet of Moses and by extension of his Kenite wife Zipporah, the writing on the Kenite line was of supreme importance.

4: 17 Cain knew his wife, and she conceived and bore Enoch; and he built a city, and called the name of the city after the name of his son, Enoch

The opening verse of the story of the sons of Cain appears out of place. Two contradictory images of Cain are expressed: Cain the unsettled fugitive and Cain the apparent city builder. It calls into question whether the author of the ending of the story of Cain and Abel as it exists now:

> **Genesis 4: 16** *Then Cain went away from the presence of Yahweh, and dwelt in the land of Nod, east of Eden*

was the same author who wrote the Kenite genealogy which now follows. The negative aspersion seems more appropriate to one seeking to cast out the Kenites the way Sarah called upon Abram to cast out Hagar and Ishmael into the wilderness (Gen. 21). One also notes that the curse of Cain:

> **Genesis 4: 11** *And now you are cursed from the ground, which has opened its mouth to receive your brother's blood from your hand*

plays no role whatsoever in the Ahijah pericope as if it was not part of the KDB version he inherited either.

The emphasis on the progress of human culture represented by the construction of the city in the verse presupposes the continuity of human history. It is at variance with the global disruption of the flood which necessitates a restart. These observations contribute to scholars concluding that the diversity of the component parts in Gen. 4 is made comprehensible only through positing multiple authors.[17] For purposes here, the most familiar of those components, the story of Cain and Abel, omitted from this study as it was part of the KDB along with the garden and the Flood. The people reading/hearing the Kenite component would already have been familiar with the original story of Cain and Abel but not necessarily all the verses in the current version.

4: 17 Cain knew his wife and she conceived and bore

Although the issue of the origin of Cain's wife has so troubled commentators (see Chapter 2), the simple conclusion here is that it was a matter of utter indifference to the author. Hendel observes that within the story there is no problem about the origin of the wife. He attributes the problem arising only when independent stories were linked in a chronological sequence and chides the early interpreters who posited Cain marrying his sister.[18] The stories of the KDB first cycle were not about primeval times so the issues of the people Cain feared or from where his wife came were irrelevant. In the KDB-Abiathar-Ahijah narrative, Cain never was the only person on earth or part of the only family on earth.

Unlike the births to Eve, Enoch's birth and the ones to follow occur without any reference to the divine. These are the births of regular people, not kings who presume to represent God on earth. Ahijah's supplement is people-based and not king-based right from the start.

4: 17 Enoch

Enoch belongs to the wilderness tradition as do the Kenites.

> **Genesis 25:4** *The sons of Midian were Ephah, Epher, Hanoch [Enoch], Abida, and Eldaah. All these were the children of Keturah.*

> **Genesis 46:9** *and the sons of Reuben: Hanoch [Enoch], Pallu, Hezron, and Carmi.*

The English translations obscure the repeated use of the name. Whether the audience of the story would have made connections to these wilderness locations is difficult to determine. At least for the author, these locations are consistent with the message he delivers of the wilderness basis for Israel. Enoch is a non-royal person of the wilderness but will undertake royal-like actions with the building of a city.

4: 17 and he built a city

In the Mesopotamian tradition, the city was the definer of civilized life. It was located at the center of the universe. It divided the ordered world from the surrounding world of chaos, the civilized world from the primitive world of the nomad. The physical manifestation of that differentiation was the wall which surrounded the city. On one side of the wall lived beings who resembled animals in their way of life, figures like Enkidu from the Gilgamesh Epic and Martu the Amorite. On the other side were the human beings who had progressed

---

17 Bryan, 'A revaluation of Gen.4 and 5', 184; Dillmann, *Genesis*, 179–182; Gunkel, *Genesis*, 40–41; Vermeylen, 'La descendance de Caïn', 179; von Rad, *Genesis*, 110; Westermann, *Genesis 1–11*, 325.
18 Hendel, '*Leitwort* style', 96.

from chaotic savagery of wilderness life to the exalted state of civilized beings who built things like a canal, palace, and temple. The great Gilgamesh walked the wall of Uruk at the beginning and end of his story. The great Hammurabi through his law code has become the symbol of the civilized Mesopotamian way of life ... except that he was an Amorite, too! Still the city exemplified what civilize people could do and Bedouin nomads could not.[19]

Given this cultural perception in Mesopotamia, the building of city was an action of great importance in its politics and myths.

> [The great gods, the Igigi] designed a city,
> [The Igigi] laid its foundation.
> [The Anunnaki] designed the city of Kish,
> [The Anunnaki] laid its foundation,
> The Igigi made its brickwork firm.
> (Etana I, 1–5)[20]

The Mesopotamian tradition exalts the building of city. Phinehas draws on that legacy in his Nimrod story. Finding comparable praise for the construction of a city in the kingdom of Israel is more difficult. In the archaeological record, cities are more associated with the Canaanites in the land than the Israelites who emerge there at the end of the Late Bronze Age in hill-top settlements. The landscape was full of cities that worshiped Baal and were loyal to Egypt.

The most prominent example of an Israelite king building a city probably is by the 9th century king Omri and it is reported without fanfare.

> **I Kings 16: 24** *He bought the hill of Samaria from Shemer for two talents of silver; and he fortified the hill, and called the name of the city which he built, Samaria, after the name of Shemer, the owner of the hill.*

André LaCocque attributes great importance to the fact that 'when Enochville is built, the text is uncannily silent about to whom or to what the city is dedicated'. Omri apparently did not dedicate his capital city to a deity either. Nor did David. Perhaps that was part of the Israelite tradition that distinguished Israel from other peoples.[21]

The Israelite destruction of city garners more attention. After the fall of Jericho with its walls, the people are put on notice:

> **Joshua 6: 26** *Joshua laid an oath upon them at that time, saying, 'Cursed before Yahweh be the man that rises up and rebuilds this city, Jericho. At the cost of his first-born shall he lay its foundation, and at the cost of his youngest son shall he set up its gates'.*

Woe to one who would violate this curse. As Abiathar's Noah curses Canaan, the author of Josh. 6: 26 curses the rebuilder of a Canaanite city (and later Joshua curses the Gibeonites who have deceived the Israelites Josh. 9: 23).

---

19 For the distinction between the city and the countryside in Mesopotamian life see, Marc Van De Mieroop, *The Ancient Mesopotamian City* (New York: Oxford University Press, 1997), 42–62.

20 Stephanie Dalley, *Myths from Mesopotamia* (Oxford: Oxford University Press, 1989), 190.

21 André LaCocque, *Onslaught against Innocence: Cain, Abel, and the Yahwist* (Eugene, OR: Cascade Books, 2008), 129.

I Kings 16: 34 *In his days Hiel of Bethel built Jericho; he laid its foundation at the cost of Abiram his first-born, and set up its gates at the cost of his youngest son Segub, according to the word of Yahweh, which he spoke by Joshua the son of Nun.*

Just as with Ahijah the prophet of Moses, the words of Joshua the successor of Moses are fulfilled.

The city itself serves as a marker. It is another one of the motifs combatants in the political battle for power used numerous times. *Ir* (עיר) appears here and in the Tower of Babel story. The same term for city is used 10 times in the story of Sodom and Gomorrah (Gen. 18–19) and seven times in the story of Dinah at Shechem (Gen. 34). Both stories contain disturbing sexual events. The other most frequent occurrences of the term in military incidents involves Joshua at Jericho then Ai (Josh. 6 and 7). Needless to say, in none of these stories is the image of a city favorable. Perhaps the most positive images of a city are when the servant of Abraham goes to Mesopotamia and brokers an alliance with Nahor after meeting Rebekah at the well (Gen. 24) and the city of David itself. Otherwise the city does not fare too well.[22]

The action in building a city does not displease the Lord.[23] There is nothing inherently wrong or evil in the construction of a city. Perhaps the most recent example for Ahijah would have been the construction of the fortress site Khirbet Qeiyafa near the Philistine city of Gath, a city which may have been destroyed and not rebuilt by the time Ahijah wrote (see Additional Readings: Khirbet Qeiyafa). In archaeology, the Midianites are known for the building of a city in the wilderness. The city named Quarrayah is located in northwest Arabia. Its distinctive pottery is called Midianite ware and it appears precisely at the same time Israel emerges in history. While the city lacks the majesty and splendor of the glorious cities of Mesopotamia, it attests the secular reality of a wilderness city-building as a cultural legacy. Time and time again, Ahijah turns to the wilderness in pride, it is the place where Israel began (see Additional Readings: Midian).

The undertaking of the city construction here is a human initiative in contrast to the Mesopotamian tradition. The contrast may be reflective of an ambiguous attitude towards the city by Israel. In biblical scholarship, the presence of the city-builder may be a secondary element in the genealogy.[24] These perceptions are incorrect. The two major son story supplements by Ahijah to the first cycle contain city-building elements. Since one individual is responsible for both accounts, it makes more sense to compare them than to discount them. In the first story, Ahijah praises the legacy of his own people and undermines by implication the derogatory wilderness putdowns by others. There is no mention of building a tower or temple here. In the second story, Ahijah launches a frontal assault directly aimed at the Mesopotamian legacy written after Phinehas had raised the stakes from a local stage to a global one (see below).

---

22 Patrick Miller, 'Eridu, Dunnu, and Babel: a study in comparative mythology', in Richard S. Hess and David Toshio Tsumura, eds, *I Studied Inscriptions from Before the Flood: Ancient Near Eastern, Literary, and Linguistic Approaches to Genesis 1–11* (SBTS 4; Winona Lake: Eisenbrauns, 1994), 143–168, here 157.
23 Hamilton, *The Book of Genesis*, 238.
24 J. M. Miller, 'The descendants of Cain', 168 n.17; Patrick Miller, 'Eridu, Dunnu, and Babel', 159–160.

4: 17 *and called the name of the city after the name of his son, Enoch*

The act of naming the city is the only naming act in Ahijah's supplement until the city of Babel is named without a specified 'namer' (Gen. 11: 9). The Ahijah text eschews such actions for living things.

The routine commencement of a genealogy suffers here from the confusion of who is the builder of the city. Without an ending of 'in his own name', meaning Enoch named the city after himself, one would think that Cain and not Enoch was the builder of the city. Drawing on his distinctively psychological perspective, LaCocque considers Cain to have been the builder of 'Enochville', a city of refuge built by a murderer to harbor a refuge, a nest of brigands, and a haven for the lonely.[25]

For Westermann, the natural human evolution sequence is from agriculture to city. Since Cain was a farmer, then he likely was not simultaneously a builder of a city. In genealogies, the advancement of human civilization is demonstrated through successive generations. Therefore, Westermann concludes Enoch was the original builder of the first city. He suggests that the name 'Enoch' means 'founder' so one cannot trace a specific place or city or person to the founder of the city named 'founder'. Westermann takes issue with Delitzsch asserting that Israel did not consider the cities and urban civilization *a priori* as negative.[26]

Cain's naming the city after the son of the builder is considered remarkable. One might add that the builder Solomon did not change the name from the city of David to the city of Solomon even though according to the biblical narrative, the son was the greater builder than the father. Babylon never became the city of Hammurabi or Nebuchadnezzar I. The Assyrians Tukulti-ninurta (*Kār-Tukulti-Ninurta*) and Sargon II (*Dur-Šarrukin*) did name their new cities after themselves so the link between a city name and its builder needs to be evaluated on a case by case basis.

4: 18 *To Enoch was born Irad; and Irad was the father of Mehujael, and Mehujael the father of Methushael, and Methushael the father of Lamech*

This verse differs from the previous one. It lists in rapid fashion a series of descendants who seemingly lack Hebrew names and more likely are to be Babylonian of unknown meanings according to biblical exegetes.[27] One can only speculate as to why Ahijah included these names beyond that they all may have been part of the Kenite tradition. Two sons have names ending in El. It is a little bit surprising to see a deity name known from the land of Canaan in names from outside the land of Canaan. The juxtaposition raises the possibility the names are author-created and not tradition-inherited. At first glance there might seem to be a connection to the Kenite woman Yael or Jael in the Song of Deborah (Judges 5: 24) but despite the similarity in English, the Hebrew spelling is different and her name has no divine connotations.

---

25 LaCocque, *Onslaught against Innocence*, 125–126. Bryan and Westermann consider Enoch to be the likely builder (Bryan, 'A reevaluation of Gen.4 and 5', 187; Westermann, *Genesis 1–11*, 327).

26 Westermann, *Genesis 1–11*, 327–328.

27 Dillmann, *Genesis*, 200; Westermann, *Genesis 1–11*, 328–329.

Ahijah's Lamech is quite different from the Lamech in the bare-boned P genealogy (Gen. 5). Here, he will become a boastful figure who exudes the threat of violence (see below). By contrast the P Lamech has been attached to Phinehas's definition of the name of Noah who will remove the stain of the curse of man and alleviate the burden of his daily life.[28]

Richard Hess postulates that Lamech is the new Cain who concludes one genealogical line while beginning his own. The two mentions of Cain at the beginning and end of the chapter form an inclusio and the numbers 7 and 77 represent completion of the genealogy from Adam. The process continues when the apparently same author in 5: 29 completes the genealogical line of Seth before the line of Noah commences and in the attribution of 777 years to Lamech's lifespan. Hess's cannot find a root *lmch* (למך) in the West Semitic lexical lists which leads him to suggest that these middle consonants in the Hebrew alphabet were selected to represent the joining of the two halves of the alphabet as Lamech appears in the P and J genealogies.[29]

Philip Davies postulates that Noah is a descendant of J Lamech and therefore of Cain. The logical conclusion is in the J narrative all humanity are descendants of Cain and not Seth. Obviously such an interpretation has implications for the message being delivered about human nature. Davies is not vouching for the validity of J's negative portrayal of humanity as the descendants of a murderer, he is informing his audience of what the text really says. One gets the impression that he enjoys revealing the 'true' message of the Bible proclaiming human descent from such reprobates. The failure to recognize that Lamech in 4: 23–24 and Noah's name in 5:29 are from two different writers inevitably has led to misunderstandings.[30]

4: 19 And Lamech took two wives; the name of the one was Adah, and the name of the other Zillah. 20 Adah bore Jabal; he was the father of those who dwell in tents and have cattle. 21 His brother's name was Jubal; he was the father of all those who play the lyre and pipe. 22 Zillah bore Tubalcain; he was the forger of all instruments of bronze and iron. The sister of Tubalcain was Naamah.

These verses mark a change from previous ones. The four verses are all part of a single entity linked to the previous verse solely by the name Lamech. Westermann confidently claims that the function of this portion of the genealogy was to delineate the early history of the community. It serves to reveal the basic tenets of human history prior to the emergence of political structures. People work, people multiply, people progress and people do so without the presence of a king. For Westermann, the concept is of great significance for the understanding of the Old Testament. Such civilizing activities were an essential and necessary part of human history that occurred prior to the development of political structures and the division of humanity into separate peoples each with its own national

---

28 Frank Anthony Spina, 'The "ground" for Cain's rejection (Gen. 4): ᵃdāmāh in the context of Gen1–11', *ZAW* 104 1992: 329–332, here 328–329.
29 Richard S. Hess, 'Lamech in the genealogies of Genesis', *BBR* 1 1991: 21–25.
30 Philip R. Davies, 'Sons of Cain', in *A Word in Season: Essays in Honour of William McKane* (JSOT Sup. 42; Sheffield: JSOT Press, 1986), 35–56.

history.[31] LaCocque attributing the origin of civilization in these verses to the 'sinister descendants of Cain [the murderer]' is a classic example of eisegesis. The likelihood is that Ahijah decided to incorporate the existing Lamech tradition into the narrative to support the wilderness not Canaanite or Mesopotamian origin of Israel.[32]

4: 19 And Lamech took two wives; the name of the one was Adah, and the name of the other Zillah.

The meaning of the names of the two wives of Lamech cannot be explained with certainty.[33] The presence of two wives has led to discussion on the place of polygamy in early human society. Its presence with the patriarchs, especially Jacob, the first man to leave his mother and his father to marry, reveals that the issue has no place in their stories. It warrants no comment whatsoever. However, commentators note that polygamous households in the biblical stories suffer unpleasant and disruptive consequences.[34]

4: 20 Adah bore Jabal; he was the father of those who dwell in tents and have cattle. 21 His brother's name was Jubal; he was the father of all those who play the lyre and pipe.

The two sons Jabal and Jubal along with Zillah's son Tubal (next verse) all seem to have similar-sounding names.[35] The names have been derived from the verb 'to bring forth, to bear fruit' which has nothing to do with their professions and from 'ram' suggesting 'ram's horn'. Ada's sons Jabal and Jubal belong to the nomadic way of life with no judgment implied about it. Westermann observes that the link between musicians and herdsmen is worldwide. Skinner observes that the text refers to the oldest and simplest musical instruments. Dillmann rejects the notion that since the first-born of Lamech is a nomad that therefore the creators of the list perceived nomadic life as the flower of all culture, were themselves nomads, or even considered themselves descendants from Jabal.[36]

4:22 Zillah bore Tubalcain; he was the forger of all instruments of bronze and iron. The sister of Tubalcain was Naamah

Zillah's son Tubalcain launches the technological revolution. Westermann agrees with Gunkel that the double name derives from their being two people involved. He dismisses any link to the family tree of the Kenites and points out that it is only here that the Cain is associated with the smith, the meaning of his name. 'Cain' is a common noun linked to metal working, to shaping or fashioning something in metal more frequently referred

---

31 Westermann, *Genesis 1–11*, 329–330.
32 LaCocque, *Onslaught against Innocence*, 134.
33 Westermann, *Genesis 1–11*, 331.
34 Hamilton, *Book of Genesis*, 238.
35 For Driver the similar-sounding names attest the artificial character of the genealogy but he has no explanation as to why these names were chosen (*The Book of Genesis*, 69).
36 Dillmann, *Genesis*, 201–202; Hamilton, *Book of Genesis*, 239–240; Skinner cited in Westermann, *Genesis 1–11*, 331.

to as a 'smith'.[37] One may then proceed to analyze the role of the smith in non-industrial societies or at the dawn of human civilization. By contrast, J. M. Miller suggests that 'Cain' probably was added and the name originally was simply 'Tubal'. The conclusion is that there were two Cains known in Palestinian folklore: Cain the city builder and Cain the ancestral smith.[38] Another anomaly is the depiction of Tubalcain as a 'forger' or 'sharpener'. In the previous verse, the two sons were described as 'the father of those' who used what had been created. By contrast, here the father role has been eliminated, the inventor himself is the user.[39]

Westermann comments that Israel emerged in history at a time during the transition from the Bronze Age to the Iron Age. Consequentially, it would have recognized that metallurgy was not simply a primeval development. Nonetheless, one should not ignore the fact that the origin of metallurgy frequently was regarded a seminal event in the history of humanity even in ancient times including with the Sumerians, the Greeks, and the Romans. No negative connotations are contained in the announcement of this technological breakthrough and there is no Prometheus here to be punished for what he had done for the humans (see Additional Readings: Smith).[40]

Naamah has been understood to mean 'pleasant', 'graceful', 'gorgeous', or 'gracious'.[41] She has no story and is not the founder of an occupation or skill. Driver comments that she must have been a well-known figure in Hebrew folk-lore.[42] By perhaps no coincidence whatsoever, she bears the same name as the Ammonite mother of Rehoboam (I Kings 14: 21, 31), the king at the time the Kenite genealogy was written. Previously an Ammonite threat aided in Saul's rise to power when he combated it (I Sam. 11). While Joab was fighting the Ammonites on David's behalf, Bathsheba made her presence known (II Sam. 11). After getting Lot drunk, his second daughter becomes pregnant by him and bears Benammi, the father of the Ammonites (Gen. 19: 38). Undoubtedly Ahijah was drawing on the negative associations of the Ammonites in their historical relations to Israel in the time of Saul, David, Solomon, and Rehoboam expressed through his writing. His exact purpose in his name selection remains a mystery.

This observation leads to one clear distinction for the modern interpreter. Phinehas used real rivers, real cities, and a composite of real kings to deliver his message. Unfortunately with Ahijah, the names are obscure. His reasons for selecting them are locked in his now-deceased mind. Unfortunately, his exact reasons for choosing these particular names and their meaning to his audience may never be known.

---

37 Driver, *The Book of Genesis*, 63; Speiser, *Genesis*, 30; Westermann, *Genesis 1–11*, 289.
38 J. M. Miller, 'The descendants of Cain', 168–169; Westermann, *Genesis 1–11*, 332.
39 Westermann, *Genesis 1–11*, 332. Hendel notes the absence of textual variants leading to the conclusion that 'this or something like it was the original text'; see *The Text of Genesis 1–11*, 48.
40 Westermann, *Genesis 1–11*, 333–334.
41 Driver, *The Book of Genesis*, 70; Hamilton, *The Book of Genesis*, 239.
42 Driver, *The Book of Genesis*, 70.

4: 23 Lamech said to his wives: 'Adah and Zillah, hear my voice; you wives of Lamech, hearken to what I say: I have slain a man for wounding me, a young man [boy] for striking me. [24] *If Cain is avenged sevenfold, truly Lamech seventy-sevenfold'.*

According to Westermann, Gunkel quotes Wellhausen's interpretation as becoming the generally accepted exegesis: 'The boasting of the father of one branch of the family tree over against the others does not need any particular audience. And just as the Arabs are accustomed to preen themselves and boast in the presence of their wives, so does Lamech'.[43] Gunkel refers to the 'fierce vengeance' of the song by a 'boastful proud warrior who does not allow himself to be intimidated and who does not fear the enemy' but who is at home in the desert. Here blood vengeance is not condemned and the wild ferocity engenders not horror to the audience but delight in the majestic strength of the hero.[44]

Other scholars express similar interpretations. Skinner attributes the song to 'the fierce implacable spirit of revenge that forms the chief part of the Bedouin code of honour'. Speiser regards the 'Song of the Sword' as distinct in form and content from the earlier passages. It is the cry of the vengeful tribesmen which has its origins not in Mesopotamia but quite possibly from the area where the Kenites lived. Stanley Gevritz characterizes the song as one expressing overweening pride, an arrogant self-conceit and disdain for customary retribution skillfully rendered by the poet.[45]

According to Westermann, these verses belong to a cycle of secular songs from oral tradition which often were found in story books. Specifically, it is a braggart song intended to frighten enemies and is only loosely connected to the previous passage.[46] He suggests that the song does not reflect an action which has occurred but stands as a threat, a warning of the horrific retribution a violator would receive. In a sense it is a text of terror intended to terrify the hearer just as Goliath's taunt (in Hebrew?) was supposed to do to David:

> **I Samuel 17: 44** *The Philistine said to David, 'Come to me, and I will give your flesh to the birds of the air and to the beasts of the field'.*

It is a bragging in the face of one's enemies intended to strike terror by boldly announcing something he would do without hesitation if under duress.[47]

Westermann finds parallels in other short songs which have survived the early period of Israel's history:

> **Exodus 15: 21** *And Miriam sang to them: 'Sing to Yahweh, for he has triumphed gloriously; the horse and his rider he has thrown into the sea'.*

---

43 Cited in Westermann, *Genesis 1–11*, 336 without specific bibliographic information.

44 Gunkel, *Genesis*, 52.

45 Stanley Gevirtz, 'Lamech's song to his wives', in Richard S. Hess and David Toshio Tsumura, eds, *I Studied Inscriptions from before the Flood: Ancient Near Eastern, Literary and Linguistic Approaches to Genesis 1–11* (Sources for Biblical and Theological Study 4; Winona Lake: Eisenbrauns, 1994), 399–415, here 405, reprinted from *Patterns in the Early Poetry of Israel* (Studies in Ancient Oriental Civilization 32; Chicago: University of Chicago Press, 1963), 25–34; Skinner, *A Critical and Exegetical Commentary on Genesis*, 120; Speiser, *Genesis*, 37.

46 Westermann, *Genesis 1–11*, 326.

47 Hamilton, *Book of Genesis*, 241; Westermann, *Genesis 1–11*, 336–337.

Judges 15:16 *And Samson said, 'With the jawbone of an ass, heaps upon heaps, with the jawbone of an ass have I slain a thousand men'.*

I Samuel 18:7 *And the women sang to one another as they made merry, 'Saul has slain his thousands, and David his ten thousands'.*

These parallels make Westermann wonder if the third verse of the Song of Lamech originally belonged to it.[48] The implications are critical since the verse combines the names Cain and Lamech into one verse sustaining a link to both the story of Cain and Abel and to the genealogy. One wonders who is being taunted and warned in the present.

4: 23 Lamech said to his wives: 'Adah and Zillah, hear my voice; you wives of Lamech, hearken [give ear] to what I say [my speech]: I have slain a man for wounding me, a young man [boy] for striking me'

The song begins with a call to 'hear', a common vocabulary term for a summons to listen.[49] The combination of hear/give ear and voice/my speech frequently appears in Hebrew poetry.[50] LaCocque wonders why the character sings like a strutting peacock to his receptive audience, the two women, without recognizing the true audiences for the song. While the character Lamech addresses the song to his women, the performer Ahijah is addressing it to both his immediate audience whom he is energizing for the fight to come and to the foe who will hear of these defiant words.[51]

Westermann considers the presence of a man and a boy, *ish* (אשׁ) and *yeled* (ילד), as synonymous parallelism and not evidence for two confrontations.[52] For Gervitz, the combinations appears odd since there would appear to be no honor in striking a boy. Normally in poetic parallelism, the two terms, here man and boy, are equated. To resolve the disjuncture, Gervitz identifies multiple examples in biblical and non-biblical texts including Egyptian, Greek, and Akkadian attesting the youth of warriors in ancient times. He concludes that the song's reference in Lamech's proud victory is over a 'very-young warrior, an upstart would-be hero'.[53] He does not use the term 'na'ar', also a reference to a young man but which is applied to soldiers as well.

The Canaanite division of *n'rn* figured prominently in the rescue of Ramses II when he marched headstrong into a trap set by the Hittites at Kadesh (see Additional Readings: *N'rn*). These *n'rn* have been equated with the Hebrew na'ar and Ugaritic *n'r*. The term is normally translated as young man or is accompanied by the adjective 'little' for a child. These young men of military age also may be considered soldiers. For example if the young men who accompany David are his warriors (I Sam. 25: 12) than those who accompany Abigail probably are too (I Sam. 25: 14) as are the Amalekites who flee from David's men (I Sam. 30: 17). The young men are arms bearers in Judg. 9: 54; I Sam. 14: 1; II

48 Westermann, *Genesis 1–11*, 334, citing the work of Gervitz below.
49 Westermann, *Genesis 1–11*, 334.
50 Gervitz, 'Lamech's song to his wives', 406–408.
51 LaCocque, *Onslaught against Innocence*, 138–139.
52 Westermann, *Genesis 1–11*, 335.
53 Gervitz, 'Lamech's song to his wives', 409–415, quotation from 415.

Sam. 18: 15 and 19: 18. After reviewing the uses of the term in various biblical settings, John MacDonald concludes that the most appropriate designation is the medieval use of 'squire'.[54]

Patrick Miller elaborates on Gervitz's observation by pointing out a plural usage of *yeled* for the young men who counsel Rehoboam:

> **I Kings 12: 6** *Then King Rehoboam took counsel with the old men, who had stood before Solomon his father while he was yet alive, saying, 'How do you advise me to answer this people?'* [7] *And they said to him, 'If you will be a servant to this people today and serve them, and speak good words to them when you answer them, then they will be your servants for ever'.* [8] *But he forsook the counsel which the old men gave him, and took counsel with the* **young men** *who had grown up with him and stood before him.*

These young men have been compared to the young arms-bearing men of the kingdom who advise Gilgamesh after he resists the advice of the old-timers in the upper chambers about whether to war or not.[55] There appears to be a related use of the term as *yelide harapa* (II Sam. 21: 18) as Philistine enemies of David. They have been interpreted as a group of warriors by association or membership rather than birth or kin. These men become a band of brothers united in their devotion to Rapha as Rephaim. Such a military designation suggests a Canaanite or non-Israelite heritage. It would further separate Israelites and the new king (see Additional Readings: Yeled).

Given the confrontational context the point of Lamech's song is clear: Rehoboam has rejected the advice of the old men who had served his father (Phinehas and the Benjaminites) in favor of the cohort-chums-princelings young men with whom he grew up in royal splendor. Rehoboam is far removed from the reality of kingship, from the requirements of leadership, from the necessity of proving himself. He has been too busy with his princelings enjoying the good life in the palace. Now for the first time in his life he has come face-to-face with the stark reality of command. The character in the story acts as if just by saying something, even if it is truly absurd, it will happen. Or is he daring the people to rebel against his declaration that a bad situation will get even worse and there is nothing the people can do but accept their fate? In the Song of Lamech, Ahijah has taunted the manhood of the would-be king and his princelings for the soft palace life of leisure they led by mocking them to grow a pair. The colloquial terminology better reflects Ahijah's message than the academic and matches the words of Rehoboam.

> **I Kings 12: 10** *And the young men who had grown up with him said to him, 'Thus shall you speak to this people who said to you, "Your father made our yoke heavy, but do you lighten it for us"; thus shall you say to them, "My little finger is thicker than my father's loins"'.*

So spoke an immature leader about his penis size millennia ago before his kingdom divided.

---

54 John MacDonald, 'The status and role of the na'ar in Israelite society', *JNES* 35 1976: 147–170); see also Cutler B. MacDonald, 'Identification of the na'ar in the Ugaritic Texts', *UF* 8 1976: 27–35.
55 Abraham Malamat, 'Kingship and the council in Israel and Sumer: a parallel', *JNES* 22 1963: 247–253.

4: 24 'If Cain is avenged sevenfold, truly Lamech seventy-sevenfold'

Gervitz deems the exaggeration 'pretentious bravado'. Lamech presumes an even greater measure of revenge than his 'infamous forebear'.[56]

Westermann builds on Gervitz's suggestion that the verse originally may have been prose added with the specific purpose of connecting the song of Lamech and the story of Cain. It is only here that the idea of revenge is introduced. The song as a number of exegetes have realized is not concerned with blood vengeance in the strict institutional sense. Instead it exults in boasting about grossly exaggerated retribution for non-lethal injuries which were a violation of honor. The song intimidates through its threat of horrific retribution and strikes terror in one's enemies. Gunkel's claim that the author lived in a softer, more civilized time who saw the song as a sign of the frightful decay of the human race making the Flood necessary is exactly wrong.[57] Quite the contrary, Ahijah wanted certain people, the young men of Rehoboam, to be afraid, to be very afraid. With Ahijah's stark assertion, the Kenite genealogy concludes bringing the story of Cain to a close.[58] The concluding remark suggests that the next verse by Ahijah will begin a new story where the fears will be fulfilled and his enemies will be washed away.

The stakes in the present were substantial. Building on the analysis of the previous verse, the tensions truly were building to a boiling point at the meeting between Rehoboam and all Israel at Shechem (I Kings 12: 1). Rehoboam has faced his moment of truth. He flees back to Jerusalem from Shechem and the rebellion is underway (I Kings 12: 18b). Shemaiah, the man of God, talks Rehoboam out of war and the kingdom divides (I King 12: 21–24). Thus the word which the Lord spoke to Ahijah of Shiloh is fulfilled in what may be an addition to the story by his pro-prophet admirers (I Kings 12: 15).

Zadok's Seth concludes the Cain and Abel sequence with people calling on the name of the Lord in the temple in the time of Enosh, son of Seth; Ahijah concludes with a warning and taunt by Lamech, descendant of Cain. In his exegesis of the taunt in the Abimelech story (Judg. 9), Sasson employs the more colloquial term 'trash talk'. Such phraseology better conveys the actions of Ahijah against Rehoboam than the more academic 'taunt'. Battle lines were being drawn. The Cainites whom Phinehas had gleefully banished into oblivion for their disobedience to the crown are back and they are not alone. Israel stands with them. The Song of Lamech concludes on the brink of this action. Ahijah's next story was likely to be catastrophic for his enemies.[59]

6: 3 Then Yahweh said, 'My spirit shall not abide in man for ever, for he is flesh, but his days shall be a hundred and twenty years'

This verse has generated its own problems in scholarly discourse. Wright deems 6: 3 'perhaps the most troublesome verse of 6.1–4' as if the entire pericope was not one of

---

56 Gervitz, 'Lamech's song to his wives', 410.
57 Gunkel, *Genesis*, 53.
58 Westermann, Genesis 1–11, 335–337.
59 Sasson, *Judges 1–12*, 396.

challenge![60] Gunkel considers the verse to begin abruptly, to have only a loose relationship to its context. He wonders why the sons of God are not punished although they are the primary sinners.[61] Westermann echoes Gunkel's interpretation in rather strong language declaring that the insertion 'has no relationship to the original course of the story'.[62] He wonders if there was a version of the story which is now obscured that would elucidate the verse. He sees a connection with the limitation on human life in Gen. 3: 22 and the building of the Tower of Babel.[63] In a political context that would suggest that this author limits the power of the king, is a proponent of checks and balances on executive power, and is aghast at the idea of:

> **II Samuel 7: 13** *He shall build a house for my name, and I will establish the throne of his kingdom for ever. [14] I will be his father, and he shall be my son.*[64]

The 120 years has been the source of debate. Dillmann rejects the traditional interpretation that mankind received a respite of 120 years before destruction from the Flood. Instead it is a general decree limiting the duration of human life. Quite simply, the author was unaware of the patriarchal stories containing longer lifespans.[65] The number has been compared to the 1200 years in the Mesopotamian story of Athrahasis and linked to the mention of 120 years in a folktale from Emar for the lifespan of an individual.[66]

The perception that the verse is not integral to the story of the sons of God is correct. The verse neither illuminates a lacuna nor resolves an ambiguity. It does not advance the narrative. The realization of its irrelevance therefore generates the question of what it is doing here. The verse did not simply exist as a standalone text either. Before it became part of the sons of God story it was part of something else. Removing it simply sustains the dilemma of where it belongs. It is not a continuation of the Kenite genealogy either.

One should not overlook the performance of the story. Most likely the locale for delivering the message is Shechem, the navel of the universe, where the people have gathered to decide whether or not to accept Rehoboam as king over Israel. Ahijah advocated 'No!'.

---

60 A. Wright, *The Origin of Evil Spirits*, 75. Cassuto anticipates Wright's observation that no improper action has occurred by declaring of the words of the Lord 'if properly understood, contain not a single word of reproof or rebuke', the offspring are mortal and will die as humans do ('The sons of God', 25–26, quotation from 25).

61 Gunkel, *Genesis*, 57.

62 Westermann, *Genesis 1–11*, 366.

63 Westermann, *Genesis 1–11*, 373–374, 382; see also Hendel, 'Of demigods and the deluge', 24.

64 One may debate whether the withdrawal of the Lord's spirit from the king refers to a specific individual or is meant as a generic comment on the institution of kingship; see Doedens, *The Sons of God*, 46.

65 Dillmann, *Genesis*, 239–240. The shortened lifespan approach is more typical (see Day, *From Creation to Babel*, 91–92).

66 Clines, 'The significance of the "sons of God"', 42; Jacob Klein, 'The "bane" of humanity: a lifespan of one hundred twenty years', *Acta Sumerlogica* 12 1990: 57–69. To add to the mystery of the verse, the suggestion has been made that the Assyrian root *šag~mu*, 'to bellow, howl', provided the basis for שׁגם with the preposition ב added. That interpretation renders the verse consistent with the Atrahasis story where the clamor or noise generated by these sons of gods precipitated a divine response – the Deluge. The noise functions as a signal that the creation is out of order. The suggestion has not met with wide acceptance. See Clines, 'The significance of the "sons of God"', 40; Day, *From Creation to Babel*, 90–91, 94; Kvanvig, 'Gen.6, 1–4 as an antediluvian event', 107–110.

He called to limit the monarchy to three generations. The priest/prophet of Moses and Yahweh was the human being speaking in the name of Yahweh to an assembled Israelite audience. The Song of Lamech taunted the kingship of Rehoboam. The verse is a warning. Time's up Rehoboam.

Then the Flood occurs. Ahijah responds to the post-diluvial vision of Phinehas. His proposal that the Mesopotamian model of king, temple, and building was the true path for Israel is rejected. Ahijah's next story is the local flood story in his KDB-Abiathar manuscript and not the universal flood in the Phinehas manuscript with its sons of God story. The three-generation 120-year verse countermands the promise of an eternal dynasty. The Mesopotamian deluge motif normally is used on behalf of the king to extol his marital prowess. Ahijah turns it topsy turvy. The days of the united kingdom are over.

Tower of Babel

Of all the son stories included in this study, the story of the Tower of Babel is the longest and most continuous narrative by a single author. It is suggestive of the stories which may have been produced as supplements to the KDB in other cycles where writers felt freer to compose their own stories. The unity or lack of unity of the story has been the subject of debate. Gunkel proposes the story consists of two recensions involving a tower and a city. Westermann identifies Gunkel as the first to propose the dual hypothesis and notes that many scholars have followed his suggestion including it would seem Westermann himself. Von Rad hedges his bet claiming that the story was an independent narrative which the Yahwist took over. Other scholars take issue with this approach or the idea of multiple layers (see Additional Readings: Tower of Babel). The analysis here is based on the unity on the story which contributes to its importance as the one true complete story in the first cycle of KDB son stories.[67]

As a single story of some length, it has attracted attention for its artistic composition. It may be said to 'reflect the concrete realities of ancient Mesopotamia, a cradle of civilization' with true to life details while simultaneously being 'an artistic portrayal that transcends the ancient cultural setting and hence becomes a paradigm of human life in all times and places'. The skill evidenced in the Babel composition has drawn praise as 'a masterpiece of narrative art'.[68] The story contains distinct themes of city and tower which are stylistically distinct in the narrative due to the literary skill of the artist.[69] Von Rad's assessment, cited by Joel Baden, refers to the story as being 'boldly hewn and recast' older material.[70] Despite

---

67 Gunkel, *Genesis*, 94–102; von Rad, *Genesis*, 150; Westermann, *Genesis 1–11*, 536–539.

68 Bernhard W. Anderson, 'Chapter 10 The Tower of Babel: unity and diversity in God's creation', in *From Creation to New Creation* (Minneapolis: Fortress Press, 1994), 165–178, here 168. For an admiration of the artistic skill of the author, see J. F. Fokkelman, *Narrative Art in Genesis: Specimens of Stylistic and Structural Analysis* (Amsterdam: Van Gorcum, 1975), 11–45.

69 Joel Baden, 'The Tower of Babel: a case study in the competing methods of historical and modern literary criticism', *JBL* 128 2009: 209–224, here, 217.

70 Von Rad, *Genesis*, 148; Baden, 'The Tower of Babel', 218.

the soaring rhetoric, it is unlikely that Ahijah had such grandiose intentions in mind. His concern was more local and immediate.

Baden's admonition citing John Barton on the necessity of using both historical and literary skill if a text is to be adequately interpreted is exactly right.[71] Gnuse sagely advises: 'One should not expect the storyteller to relate in heavy-handed fashion all the details that would turn a symbolic parable into an historical narrative'.[72] Knowing the author and the historical context in which literature is produced is essential to understanding its origin. The giant works of literature were not written to be timeless. The same considerations apply to Ahijah in his story of the Tower of Babel. He wrote it to mark the end of the first cycle and clearly he wanted to leave the stage with a bang.[73]

11: 1 Now the whole earth had one language (lip) and few words (one speech)

Westermann interprets the beginning of the story to be the equivalent of 'Once up on a time'. It means 'There was a time when' the world did not have a multiple of languages. He observes that even the Sumerian tale of everyone speaking the same language only could occur in a geographically limited area. He suggests that there actually had been such times and experiences but that it is no longer possible to reconstruct them. Such times came to an end when revolutionary upheavals brought together people who spoke different languages. 'It was only the transition from the small, self-sufficient group to the larger social unities that demanded constant commerce with those who spoke other languages that gave rise to this question'. The implication is that there was no original language for humankind and the search for one should cease.[74]

For Theodore Hiebert, the opening verse establishes the theme of the story as language, in particular the existence of a single uniform language spoken by all people. He rejects the traditional sin and punishment for excessive pride interpretations for one based on the origins of cultural differences. In this regard, Hiebert may be said to be a running dialog with purveyors of a harsh approach to the story.[75]

More perceptively, LaCocque observes a resonance of the harmony which once had prevailed in the garden. The implication of that observation is a similar sequence of events – the humans will do something they should not do and pay the consequences. One might add that perhaps the same author contributed to the outcomes of both stories.[76]

---

71 Baden, 'The Tower of Babel', 223, citing John Barton 'Historical criticism and literary interpretation: is there any common ground', in Stanley E. Porter, Paul M. Joyce and Davie E. Orton, eds, *Crossing the Boundaries: Essays in Biblical Studies in Honour of Michael D. Goulder* (Leiden: Brill, 1994, Biblical Interpretation Series 8), 3–15, here 15.

72 Robert Gnuse, 'The Tale of Babel: parable of divine judgment or human cultural diversification?' *BZ* 54 2010: 229–244, here 234.

73 LaCocque suggests that the author deliberately wanted to end the primeval history on a negative note; see André LaCocque, *The Captivity of Innocence: Babel and the Yahwist* (Eugene, OR: Cascade Books 2010), 8.

74 Westermann, *Genesis 1–11*, 542–543.

75 Theodore Hiebert, 'The Tower of Babel and the origin of the world's cultures', *JBL* 126 2007: 29–58, here 33.

76 LaCocque, *The Captivity of Innocence*, 40.

Contrary to the global vision of some exegetes, Ahijah operated in a smaller playing field. His world was the immediate one of Israel in the land of Canaan. It was a world of multiple nations, perhaps as many as seven, and multiple tribes that did not necessarily speak identically as the famous Shibboleth/Sibboleth example (Judg. 12: 5) documents.

The Amarna Letters reveal the shared use of the cuneiform script and the Akkadian language among all the kings in the land of Canaan. That time was centuries ago. A new era was emerging where peoples wrote in Ammonite, Aramaean, Canaanite/Phoenician, Edomite, Hebrew, and Moabite. Abiathar had ended the first cycle with:

Gen. 10: 15 *Canaan became the father of* [16] *the Jebusites, the Amorites, the Girgashites.*

Abiathar defined the stage on which Ahijah operated. He knew of the larger world stage Phinehas had created and now he was responding to it in his own way.

11: 1 whole earth

Whereas Phinehas preferred the term ground, *adamah* (אדמה) which resonated with Zadok's Adam (אדם), Ahijah used earth, *eretz* (ארץ) to convey the same meaning without any allusion to Adam. The possible nuances of the differences in meaning or use of these terms is difficult if not impossible to ascertain. One can discern the existence of varied terms such as garments/tunics and Yahweh/Elohim without always being able to understand the divergent uses.

11: 1 one language

The idea of a world with one language has Sumerian precedents in 'Enmerkar and the Lord of Aratta' although it should not be construed as a source for the story. The interpretation of the Sumerian myth referring to a past stage has been questioned in favor of it presenting an idealized version of a future stage once everyone acknowledges Sumerian superiority by adapting the Sumerian language and civilization.[77] One speculation has been that the original language was Hebrew which is after all the language God uses when speaking in the story.[78] The idea that one language truly means unanimity imposed by an imperial authority may be an example of eisegesis although that might be what the original Sumerian myth meant.[79] Perhaps one should consider the position of the English language today. It is one thing for English to be the universal language of discourse between peoples and quite another for it to be the sole language of every individual or the language used in the home.

Multiple languages could be a source of fear.[80] For example:

---

77 Bendt Alster, 'An aspect of "Enmerkar and the Lord of Aratta"', *RA* 67 1973: 101–110; Samuel N. Kramer, 'Man's Golden Age: a Sumerian parallel to Genesis XI: 1', *JAOS* 63 1943: 191–193; Samuel N. Kramer, 'The Babel of tongues: a Sumerian version', *JAOS* 88 1968: 108–111; LaCocque, *The Captivity of Innocence*, 14–15.

78 Kugel, *How to Read the Bible*, 86. It certainly was the language the teller of the story used.

79 See van der Kooij, 'The city of Babel and Assyrian imperialism', 8.

80 André LaCocque, 'Whatever happened in the Valley of Shinar?: a response to Theodore Hiebert', *JBL* 128 2009: 29–41, here 39–40; Allen P. Ross, 'The dispersion of the nations in Genesis 11: 1–9', *BSac* 138 1981: 119–138, here 120.

> **Deuteronomy 28: 49** *Yahweh will bring a nation against you from afar, from the end of the earth, as swift as the eagle flies, a nation whose language you do not understand.*

> **Isaiah 33: 19** *You will see no more the insolent people, the people of an obscure speech which you cannot comprehend, stammering in a tongue which you cannot understand.*

> **Jeremiah 5: 15** *Behold, I am bringing upon you a nation from afar, O house of Israel, says Yahweh. It is an enduring nation, it is an ancient nation, a nation whose language you do not know, nor can you understand what they say.*

Difficult as it may be to understand, people in ancient times may have looked askance at the presence of foreign-speaking 'others' within their own communities.

11: 2 And as men migrated from/to the east, they found a plain (בקעה), in the land (ארץ) of Shinar and settled there

The word 'men' is presumed although not in the passage because the action of migrating is a verb in the third person masculine plural. No noun is used to designate them. One should consider that the action of these men relates to the men of Gen. 4: 26 who call on the name of Yahweh in Zadok's supplement. That calling occurred at a structure, specifically the just-completed Solomonic temple.

The direction of the migration is subject to the preferences of the English translator. For example, Lot 'journeyed east' (Gen. 13: 11) meaning 'to the east' not 'from the east' even though the same verb נסע is used in both stories. Some translations consistently use 'journeyed' in both verses and not 'migrated' as in the Babel story. Day, Delitzsch and Dillmann interpret the verse to mean the men journeyed east from the perspective of the author in Palestine. The eastward direction is contrary to the common translations 'from the east' which puts them east of Babylon to begin with. The journey to the east seems more likely for Ahijah. It contrasts Phinehas's story of Abram's journey to the west from Mesopotamia as if the story of Israel's origin begins there. Going east is consistent with Abiathar's narrative which is set in the land of Canaan.[81]

The movement east in Gen. 11: 2 connects the Babel story to non-son KDB stories in the first cycle:[82]

> the garden is in the east (Gen. 2: 8)
> the garden is guarded in the east by the cherubim (Gen. 3: 24)
> Cain dwells east of Eden (Gen. 4: 16)

All four examples of the 'east' are related but without analyzing the stories of the garden and Cain and Abel, it is not possible to ascertain the precise connection. All one can say here is that the selection of the migrations/journeys and east are part of the political negotiation involved here just as 'ground' and 'earth' were. In the Tower of Babel story, the eastward migration enables Ahijah to render the Mesopotamian civilizations secondary or derivative and to mock the achievements there given what is to come.

---

81 Day, *From Creation to Babel*, 170; Delitzsch, *New Commentary on Genesis*, 348; Dillmann, *Genesis*, 391.
82 See Hendel, '*Leitwort* style', 100.

'Plain' similarly has multiple meanings. In the geographic context of traveling east from Canaan, one eventually arrives at the plains of Mesopotamia. In the literal sense, this word choice seems appropriate. But it also may be considered superfluous. There was no inherent reason to designate the area found as a plain. Was the land the men had departed from a plain also? The allusions associated with the word transforms it from raw geographical data into a political motif. The plain has negative connotations within the land of Canaan:

> **Joshua 17: 16** *The tribe of Joseph said, 'The hill country is not enough for us; yet all the **Canaanites who dwell in the plain** have chariots of iron',*

> **Judges 1: 19** *And Yahweh was with Judah, and he took possession of the hill country, but he could not drive out the **inhabitants of the plain**, because they had chariots of iron.*

> **Judges 1: 34** *The Amorites pressed the Danites back into the hill country, for they did not allow them to come down to the **plain**.*

Clearly the plains in the land of Canaan are lands belonging to the enemy, to people in the Canaanite cities who possess superior arms. The problem is although the English translation is the same, the Hebrew word is not. Despite the vocabulary variance, the value denoted by the geographic setting still was derogatory. By the time of Ahijah, Israel existed for centuries in the hill country. It had no real experience of living in cities on a plain or building towers, temples, and palaces.

Shinar adds to the foreignness of the setting. Shinar had appeared previously in the story of Nimrod (see Chapter 13).

> **Genesis 10: 10** *The beginning of his kingdom was Babel, Erech, and Accad, all of them in the land of Shinar.*

The analysis of that verse noted the suggestion that the term derives from the name the ruling Kassites gave to the city of Babylon. The one Nimrod verse contains two names that are part of the story of the Tower of Babel. In the biblical narrative, Shinar appears only three other times outside Nimrod and Babel. It appears twice in the Abram's war against the kings of the east, another story with numerous proper names:

> **Genesis 14: 1** *In the days of Amraphel **king of Shinar**, Arioch king of Ellasar, Chedorlaomer king of Elam, and Tidal king of Goiim.*

> **Genesis 14: 9** *with Chedorlaomer king of Elam, Tidal king of Goiim, Amraphel **king of Shinar**, and Arioch king of Ellasar, four kings against five.*

and once in the booty Achan takes at Jericho:

> **Joshua 7: 21** *'when I saw among the spoil a beautiful mantle from **Shinar**, and two hundred shekels of silver, and a bar of gold weighing fifty shekels, then I coveted them, and took them; and behold, they are hidden in the earth inside my tent, with the silver underneath.'*

Shinar appears as a place of importance and significance. It is reasonable to conclude there is a connection among these Shinar stories.

Westermann detects the residue of an itinerary in the Babel story. It describes the transition from nomadic to sedentary life. But it leaves the people unidentified and the location vague just as the east is in garden and Cain and Abel stories (Gen. 2: 8 and 4: 16). The settlement location of Shinar is defined as the whole of Mesopotamia. The Mesopotamian definition is consistent with his view of the stories being about the civilizing of the human species in primeval times.[83]

Hiebert points out that these men are to be considered the ancestors of humanity and not just Babylon. Therefore he rejects the notion that the story simply satirizes the folly of the Babylonians and instead is about the dispersion of the human race.[84]

In Ahijah's telling, it is important to remember that while he is responding to Phinehas, he is supplementing Abiathar's version. In Ahijah's manuscript, there is no temple building by Seth, no global flood, and no sons of Noah dividing the world in a table of nations. In his manuscript, there is simply a story here of an unnamed group journeying eastward to Mesopotamia where they will build something. These men are separate from the sons of Cain in the earlier story who already built a city which did not have a tower. Instead, Ahijah alludes to the men who built the temple in Jerusalem in Zadok's text. He sets his story in the same location as the Nimrod story. The Tower story thus rejects the action of Zadok's Seth and the model of Phinehas's Nimrod. There always was a connection between the Nimrod and Babel stories but not exactly the one Josephus and the rabbis thought.

11: 3 And they said to one another, 'Come, let us make bricks, and burn them thoroughly'. And they had brick for stone, and bitumen for mortar. ⁴ Then they said, 'Come, let us build ourselves a city, and a tower with its top in the heavens, and let us make a name for ourselves, lest we be scattered abroad upon the face of the whole earth'.

At last the action begins with the decision by the people to build a city and a tower. Since Mesopotamia had bitumen but not stone, the building proceeded with the materials easily accessible to the builders (see Additional Readings: Bitumen). The biblical description favorably compares with the Mesopotamian one for the identical action for the ziggurat (see Chapter 6). Dillmann admires the 'remarkably picturesque style' of the biblical author who writes not with hyperbole 'but (with) a characterisation of the builders' bold, aspiring spirit, for which the sky itself is not too high nor beyond reach'. Nonetheless, the author wishes to convey the men's arrogance.[85]

In these verses, there is no indication that the people did something wrong. The Tower did not become an example of the dangers of overweening pride leading to destruction cited by biblical prophets and poets.[86] The men did do something wrong but that can only be perceived in the context of the storyteller's tale. In Zadok's supplement, men began to call on the name of Yahweh meaning a place for cultic ritual had been established with the Solomonic Temple. That verse was not part of the KDB-Abiathar-Ahijah narrative. Now those men are calling for a building to make their own name great, not the name

---

83 Westermann, Genesis 1–11, 543–544.
84 Hiebert, 'The Tower of Babel', 34.
85 Dillmann, *Genesis*, 392. Westermann expects the decision in verse 4 to precede the execution of the decision in verse 3 (*Genesis 1–11*, 545).
86 Anderson, *From Creation*, 170, 172.

of Yahweh. Even though two separate manuscripts existed, the meaning in one cannot be properly determined without reference to the other.

One would be remiss if one ignored the cultural power of the tower. Such a tower was prerequisite for being taken seriously as a major city in the Babylonian world. The focus on the major one in Babylon obscures the fact every major city in Mesopotamia had one.[87] The edifice complex is an enduring feature of the human psyche. It lives on such as in the competition in New York City to build the highest sky-scrapers in the world during the late 19th and early 20th centuries. The battle for bragging rights then spread across the globe. It expanded from every major American city having a professional sports stadium based on the technology of the early 20th century to a city having one based on the technology of the early 21st century. It expanded to a city and a nation seeking to host an Olympics. The idea of asserting bragging rights through the construction of towers with one's name on it or it being the tower at the center of the world is not alien to modern times. The Babel story taps into the same desires that continue to exist to this very day. People knew ziggurats existed and knew the awe of their achievement even if they had never been to the Eiffel Tower or the Empire State Building. For the audience, the tower building was an OMG moment but with no deity to bless the endeavor: those men are going to build what!?

Strikingly there is no royal presence in the building effort either. The story is in sharp contrast to the Nimrod tradition where Babylon is identified as a royal city.[88] Hiebert expands on this realization to reject the interpretation of the story as a critique of empire. Its focus is not the suppression of differences but the origin of differences themselves.[89] One might also add that the famed Siloam Inscription from Hezekiah's tunnel does not mention the king either. However, despite the focus on the pride by the actual workers who built the tunnel, clearly the project was initiated by royal command. That in itself does not permit the assumption that a king was behind the actions here.

11: 3 And they said to one another

Ahijah uses the term *ish* for man. Previously Lamech had killed a man where Ahijah used the same term as well. He also has them speaking to each other. For the first time, an author presents the view from the ground up, of people making collective decisions. They did not inquire of the Lord as to the course of action to take and no priest of Yahweh or Moses guided them. They made their decision on their own.

11: 3 Come, let us

Westermann observes the same interjection 'Come' in Ex. 1:10 spoken by Pharaoh.[90]

---

87 Ross, 'The dispersion', 123–125.
88 Anderson, *From Creation*, 172.
89 Hiebert, 'The Tower of Babel', 35.
90 Westermann, *Genesis 1–11*, 545.

Exodus 1: 10 *'Come, let us deal shrewdly with them, lest they multiply, and, if war befall us, they join our enemies and fight against us and escape from the land.'*

The similarity suggests the possibility of the same author although more than a single word is needed to substantiate the link.

11: 3 make bricks

The verb root used here *lbn* (לבן) specifically is associated with the making of bricks rather than the making of anything else.[91] Brick-making also is part of the biblical narrative. Following the passage from the Book of Exodus just cited, the Hebrews have their own encounter with the world of brick-making:

Exodus 1: 13 *So they made the people of Israel serve with rigor,* [14] *and made their lives bitter with hard service, in mortar and brick, and in all kinds of work in the field; in all their work they made them serve with rigor.*

Potentially therefore, the audience hearing of the brick-making in the Babel story might automatically associate it with the bad memories of the Exodus account or the other way around.[92] When the storyteller reached the story of oppression in the house of bondage, it may have called to mind the earlier story of the Tower of Babel as well as the audience's own situation in the present.

11: 3 and burn them thoroughly

Typically the biblical description of the brick-making process has been claimed as an illustration of the familiarity of the author with the actual actions involved in making bricks. The manufacture of bricks in the land of Canaan was a millennia old tradition going back to Neolithic times (9th–8th millennium BCE) but bricks were sun-dried not kiln-fired. That technique was developed later in Mesopotamia in the 4th millennium BCE with bitumen as the normal mortar.[93]

11: 3 And they had brick for stone, and bitumen for mortar

The phrase has been considered a gloss. It provides an explanation for the ingredients that is consistent with the Akkadian texts.[94] Westermann characterizes the sentence as a parenthetical note directed toward the reader or listener. It is not part of the decision-making process but provides explanatory technical information about the building which accomplishes two ends:

---

91 Giogetti, 'The "mock building account" of Genesis 11: 1–9', 9.
92 See LaCocque, 'Whatever happened in the Valley of Shinar?', 35–46; LaCocque, *The Captivity of Innocence*, 29.
93 Walton, 'The Mesopotamian background of the Tower of Babel account and its implications', 163.
94 Giorgetti, 'The "mock building account"', 9.

1. It contrasts the building techniques in Mesopotamia with the Palestine way of using stone and mortar rather than bricks and bitumen
2. It demonstrates the knowledge of the narrator.[95]

The parenthetical note therefore provides the author with the opportunity to razzle-dazzle the audience with his acumen. The non-academic terminology employed here alludes to the theatricality of the storytelling performance easily lost amidst the learned analysis of the erudite. The inclusion of such technological knowledge is the equivalent of the science fiction movies of the mid-20th century where the Albert-Einstein-looking character stands before a blackboard of equations, or of *2001, A Space Odyssey*, where the visual overload of display monitors that no pilot could comprehend, or the computer screens and projections of the more recent movies. Even in a religious story, speaking scientific can be very authoritative.

Bitumen was an expensive resource. Its use was restricted to buildings of significance like temples, palaces, and government structures. Even when bitumen was used, these expensive bricks were limited to the outer surfaces. The cheaper sun-dried mud bricks were used for the parts not seen.[96] It's easy to overlook the significance of the use of kiln-fired bitumen-mortared brick in the ancient context.

Bitumen appears elsewhere in the biblical narrative.

> **Genesis 14: 10** *Now the Valley of Siddim was full of **bitumen** pits; and as the kings of Sodom and Gomorrah fled, some fell into them, and the rest fled to the mountain.*

> **Exodus 2: 3** *And when she could hide him no longer she took for him a basket made of bulrushes, and daubed it with **bitumen** and pitch; and she put the child in it and placed it among the reeds at the river's brink.*

Once again it is reasonable to conclude that these usages were part of ongoing conversations about kingship, the Solomonic temple, and the Exodus as the basis of Israelite identity, a conversation that continued beyond the supplements to the first cycle of the KDB.

11: 4 *Then they said, 'Come, let us…*

The verse is the third instance of the people deciding and collaborating on their own.

11: 4 *…build ourselves a city…*

The construction of city from scratch was a rare phenomenon in Mesopotamia. Some of the leading kings partook of this activity: Sargon the Great (Akkad), Tukulti-ninurta (*Kär-Tukulti-Ninurta* named after himself), Ashurnasirpal II (Calah, rebuilt from Shalmaneser I), and Sargon II (Dur-Šarrukin also named after himself).[97] Akhnaton built Amarna for

---

95 Westermann, *Genesis 1–11*, 546.
96 Walton, 'Mesopotamian background of the Tower of Babel', 163.
97 See Alessandra Gilbert, 'On Kār Tukultī-Ninurta: chronology and politics of a Middle Assyrian Ville Neuve', in Dominik Bonatz, Rainer M. Czichon and F. Janoscha Kreppner, eds, *Fundstellen: Gesammelte Schriften zur Ärchäologie und Geschichte Altvorderasiens: ad honorem Hartmut Kühne*

his capital. Alexander Joffe adds that disembedded capitals generally collapse with the collapse of the founder using Akhnaton's Amarna as the classic example.[98] Perhaps the most common examples today of the abandonment of one-time one-use glorified cities are the villages constructed for the summer Olympics.

The act of building a city was not necessarily well received by the powers that be. According to the Chronicle of the Esagila and the Chronicle of Ancient Kings, Sargon of Akkad violated the city of Babylon when he built his new city as an alternative to it. His hubris led to the god Enlil withdrawing his blessing followed by a revolt.[99] One may interpret these texts as an attack on Sargon II in the present for his building of a new city drawing on his identification with Sargon the Great building Akkad.[100] Since Sargon II died a disastrous death on the battlefield without his body being recovered, polemics against him after the fact rang true. Marc van de Mieroop posits that Mesopotamian kings were reluctant to boast about building a city (in contrast to other physical constructions) because such an act was reserved to the gods and was an act of *hubris* if human-initiated. Restorations were fine but human-initiative in such matters was disastrous.[101]

Directly relevant to the methodological approach used in this study, Van de Mieroop proposes that within the Assyrian political entity there were competing voices using the past to exclaim contrary messages in the present. Sargon the Great had become the exemplar of the successful ruler in Mesopotamian tradition. Therefore when Sargon II used the name of his famous predecessor, he was consciously seeking to bask in the limelight of that success. The Sargon Geography composed in the time of the Neo-Assyrian king presents an idealized view of a world empire in the name of Sargon the Great but applying to the present empire. In this example, a text praises the current king in the name of the revered hero king. This praise would have been offered while Sargon II was alive and did dominate the known world (or most of it). After his ignominious death, his legacy was re-evaluated in the negative. It seems unlikely that Sennacherib, his son and successor, would so mock the achievements of his father, but someone in Assyria did. A shared past could be used to depict opposite viewpoints.[102]

These 'disembedded capitals' resulted from the actions by new elites with the intention of undercutting competing factions and to 'create new patterns of allegiance and authority'.[103]

(Wiesbaden: Harrassowitz, 2008), 177–186; Van De Mieroop, *The Ancient Mesopotamian City*, 53–54.

98   Alexander H. Joffe, 'Disembedded capitals in western Asian perspective', *CSSH* 40 1998: 549–580, 552–556.

99   The texts are quoted in Giorgetti, 'The "mock building account"', 11–12.

100   Marc van de Mieroop, 'Literature and political discourse in Ancient Mesopotamia: Sargon II of Assyria and Sargon of Agade', in Barbara Böck, Eva Cancik-Kirschbaum and Thomas Richter, eds, *Munuscula Mesopotamica: Festschrift für Johannes Renger* (AOAT 267; Münster: Ugarit-Verlag, 1999), 327–339, here 335–338.

101   Van de Mieroop, *The Ancient Mesopotamian City*, 55–61.

102   Van de Mieroop, 'Literature and political discourse', 333–334. The reverse also is possible in hindsight. Hezekiah's tribute to Sennacherib in 701 BCE to forestall the destruction of the temple and Jerusalem (II Kings 18: 13–16) may have looked wise after Sennacherib and his sons ravaged Babylon and Thebes. At that point only the Davidic dynasty and Solomonic temple remained untouched compared to Babylonia and Egypt; certainly something to celebrate.

103   Joffe, 'Disembedded capitals', 549.

Solomon's Jerusalem like Herod's Jerusalem (or Baron Haussmann's Paris or Robert Moses's New York City) were not new cities built from scratch. Yet the constructions by these people reshaped the existing cities. There also can be money to be made by the people in charge of the development. The building of Solomon's wall, Solomon's temple, Pharaoh's daughter's palace afforded the opportunity for a new non-Israelite building elite to emerge atop a more stratified society. Now the prophet had more than just a single king to rail against.

11: 4 …and a tower…

The tower in question is called a migdol (מגדל). In the biblical narrative this term generally applies to a military or watch tower and not to a ziggurat. Von Rad sagely notes that the tenor of the story would be different if the word was translated as 'fortress' but then admits the actual purpose of the structure is not specified in the story.[104] A counter to that assertion is that there were no ziggurats in Canaan or Israelite life so there was no term for one. Therefore Israel had the option of either borrowing a foreign term or adapting a indigenous term.[105] The exact same situation has occurred in modern Hebrew as there were no ancient terms for supermarket, telephone, automobile, computer, or internet to list a few examples.

But while there were no ziggurats per se, there had been towers at Ugarit. They were part of the temples to Baal and Dagan. Each temple rested on a platform approximately 18 meters high and rituals occurred on them. The Ugarit acropolis itself was 20 meters high. The temple towers on the acropolis were a defining characteristic of the city visible from far out to sea. After the city was destroyed around 1186 BCE, it was abandoned and the people scattered.[106]

Millennia before ziggurats and biblical narratives, there was a Neolithic tower at Jericho (8300–7800 BCE). It had 22 steep steps leading to a platform built from local stones. A massive stone wall enclosed the city and tower. So far based on the archaeological record the Jericho tower was unique in the Neolithic era and for the entire ancient Near East at the time. It is quite possible that for centuries it was the highest structure built by men. One may reasonably conjecture that a mud-bricked superstructure capped the tower and ritual activities were performed there. The Jericho tower did not become the model for subsequent religious edifices in the land of Canaan but it does match what developed in Mesopotamia. Exactly what was visible or its legacy in the time of Solomon is unknown.[107]

---

104   Von Rad, *Genesis*, 151.

105   Day, *From Creation to Babel*, 173; Walton, 'The Mesopotamian background of the Tower of Babel', 155–156.

106   Marguerite Yon, 'Ugarit', in *OEANE*, 255–262, here 260.

107   See Ofer Bar-Yosef, 'The Walls of Jericho: an alternative interpretation', *CA* 27 1986: 157–162; Ofer Bar-Yosef, 'The Neolithic Period', in Amnon Ben-Tor, ed., *The Archaeology of Ancient Israel* (New Haven: Yale University Press, 1992), 10–39, here 15–17; Amihai Mazar, *Archaeology of the Land of the Bible: 10,000–586 BCE* (New York: Doubleday, 1990), 41–42.

11: 4 ...*with its top in the heavens...*

The heavenly destination helps situates the story in Babylon. However, that does not necessarily mean the author or audience was or had been there. Westermann comments that the biblical usage does not negate the possibility that an actual visual experience of the mighty Babylonian ziggurats had not occurred. But it does not require it either.[108]

The presence across multiple cultures and centuries of the parallel phrase on raising the head of the tower to the heavens reveals a widespread usage of a standard motif. Echoes of the verse may be found in the archaeological record from *Enuma Elish*, Nabopolassar, Nebuchadnezzar, and Esarhaddon. The action in the verse traditionally is what is presented as being an act of hubris where man seeks to violate his place at the expense of God. The supposed sin continues a long tradition beginning in the garden that not even the Flood could change. Man just would not learn to stop trying to usurp God's heavenly position and therefore needs to be punished again and again.

By contrast, Hiebert counters without using this term that 'top in the heavens' simply was the ancient way of referring to a building that scrapes the sky. It therefore becomes an ancient cliché for height and is no more a declaration to scale the heavens in an arrogant revolt against divine authority than the modern skyscraper is.[109]

One should not overlook the local connotations to the story. Similar imagery exists in the famous Jacob dream of a ladder (stairway) to heaven at Bethel, the House of El (God):

> **Genesis 28: 12** *And he dreamed that there was a ladder (stairway) set up on the earth [eretz not ground/adamah], and the top of it reached to heaven; and behold, the angels (messengers) of God were ascending and descending on it!*

> **Genesis 28: 17** *And he was afraid, and said, 'How awesome is this place! This is none other than the house of God, and this is the gate of heaven.'*

The popular image of what Jacob saw is a ladder. This interpretation of *sull~m* is a longstanding one dating back to the LXX. This view has been questioned for practical reasons: how can angels (messengers) in the plural ascend and descend simultaneously? The closest equivalent to this imagery is the ziggurat which does include a stairway where such actions easily can occur. The 'impression is made that the narrator wishes to express that communication between heaven and earth is established by an initiative from on high, on the part of God'.[110] That 'impression' is the precise opposite of the situation in the Tower of Babel story where humans initiate the action. Contrary messages are being delivered.

The Bethel story is part of the Jacob cycle. To analyze that cycle to determine the original stories, the supplements, and its development is a massive task. For the purposes here, one

---

108   Westermann, *Genesis 1–11*, 547–548. LaCocque insists the story is a polemic against Babylon and its empire and only could have written based on the experience with Babylon (LaCocque, *The Captivity of Innocence*, 5, 15–20).

109   Hiebert, 'The Tower of Babel', 37–39; Theodore Hiebert, 'Babel: babble or blueprint? Calvin, cultural diversity, and the interpretation of Genesis 11: 1–9', in Wallace M. Alston, Jr. and Michael Welker, eds, *Reformed Theology: Identity and Ecumenicity II: Biblical Interpretation in the Reformed Tradition* (Grand Rapids: William B. Eerdmans, 2007), 127–145, here 138.

110   Coral Houtman, 'What did Jacob see in his dream at Bethel?' *VT* 27 1977: 337–352, here 351.

observation deserves notice. The geographical frame of the story has Jacob leaving Beersheba for Haran and stopping at Bethel (Gen. 28: 10 and 19). Haran has been identified as central tribal meeting place in the heartland of Amorite Yaminite territory (see Chapter 13). This is consistent with the interpretation of Phinehas as a Benjaminite and suggests as a working hypothesis he be considered a candidate for at least the story's frame. The consequences of the story were first, to legitimize the site where the dream occurred analogous to Solomon's temple dream in the land of Benjamin (I Kings 3: 5), second, to legitimate the priesthood at Bethel, and third to support an alliance among the peoples at Beersheva, Bethel, and Haran or the Calebite Shasu, Benjaminites, and Aramaeans.

The Bethel passages support my proposal that David had the option of selecting the city to be his capital of Israel (see Chapter 8). Decades later Jeroboam did choose it for a cultic site. The verses of temple dreams, the changing of Jacob's name to Israel, and the birth of Benjamin, were all part of the battle for power among the priesthoods over the identity of Israel. Bethel joined the Exodus and the loss of the ark as one of the battlegrounds. Control over the places deemed sacred provides another diagnostic marker among the combatants. Ironically, it is the biblical Jacob story more than the Abram story which is connected to the Tower of Babel story.[111]

11: 4 ...and let us...

This phrase expresses the fourth collective action of the people – journeying, making bricks, building a city, and now something apparently less physical, less tangible.

11: 4 ...make a name for ourselves, lest we be scattered abroad upon the face of the whole earth'

The act of making a name for oneself plays out in multiple biblical and non-biblical texts. It has been equated with the standard operating procedure in the ancient Near East for victorious kings erecting a boundary stela in recognition of their exploits with their image on it along with their name.[112] The previous mention of a great name in the son stories was by Zadok on behalf of the great Canaanite warriors who were the mighty men of old (Gen. 6: 4, see Chapter 11). The most frequent citation among exegetes involves Abram and it is spoken by Yahweh.

> **Genesis 12: 2** *And I will make of you a great nation, and I will bless you, and make your **name** great, so that you will be a blessing.*

---

111   Harland's interpretation that the structure really was a *mgdl* or tower as a large strong defensive building for protection which also served to unify the people as in Judges 9: 50–57 does not address the cosmic sense to the story (P. J. Harland, 'Vertical or horizontal: the sin of Babel', *VT* 48 1998: 515–533, here 529). The language of the story is more mythic than martial.

112   John T. Strong, 'Shattering the image of God: a response to Theodore Hiebert's interpretation of the story of the Tower of Babel', *JBL* 127 2008: 625–634, here 628–633.

This verse touches on the same themes as in the Tower of Babel story with the focus on the divine promise over the human assertion. The key to understanding the verse is to determine the priest who is saying the words of Yahweh and king who is the recipient of them. Other examples demonstrate the varied use of the 'name' motif for humans. It could be a warning of what will be lost:

> **Joshua 7: 9** *For the Canaanites and all the inhabitants of the land will hear of it, and will surround us, and cut off our **name** from the earth (eretz); and what wilt thou do for thy great **name**?"*

The implication of this verse is that certain actions risked the destruction of the seed of Israel or loss of its name. The transgressions by Achan leading to this inquiry of Yahweh by Joshua involved the mantle from Shinar having been coveted by Achan and buried under his tent (Josh. 7: 21).

Name could be a reminder of what God has done for the people Israel.

> **II Samuel 7: 23** *What other nation on earth (eretz) is like thy people Israel, whom God went to redeem to be his people, making himself a **name**, and doing for them great and terrible things, by driving out before his people a nation and its gods?*

Name could announce the great warrior hero who did make a name for himself.

> **II Samuel 8: 13** *And David won a **name** for himself. When he returned, he slew eighteen thousand Edomites in the Valley of Salt.*

One notes the accrual of name to two individuals here, Abram and David, and to Israel. Typically the 'name' accrues to an individual and not to a people. One would expect a king like Nimrod to partake of this tradition and indeed in biblical exegesis he frequently was presumed to be the leader behind the building of the tower.

Westermann comments that the narrator gives no indication that there is anything inherently wrong with seeking to make a name for oneself. Indeed, the concern that one be remembered after death is part of the fabric of life for a family or community. He even notes the possible impact on nomads coming into contact with the great empires of the ancient Near East and wanting what those civilizations had. The acquisition of fame through the construction of enormous buildings was standard operating procedure in the world which included ancient Israel. Even today it remains possible to imagine seeking to acquire 'name' for posterity by inscribing their name on a building. Westermann considers the final clause about the scattering of people to be an addition which does not harmonize the preceding motives for the construction of the tower.[113]

For Hiebert, making a name expresses a positive endeavor with no sign of self-centeredness, vanity, or insubordination. In this instance it refers to the heart of the human project to construct a tower: the goal of cultural homogeneity. The explicit statement of the builder's motive warrants primary attention which it has not received.[114] Here is an example of the importance of the interpreter to understanding this verse. Should the starting point be considered hoary antiquity, David and the 10th century BCE, exilic

---

113 Westermann, Genesis 1–11, 548–549.
114 Hiebert, 'The Tower of Babel', 35–36, 40–41.

times, or the 21st century CE? Different responses will occur dependent on where the investigation begins.

The second part of the clause raises the issue of being globally scattered in contradiction to having a great name. The goal of building a strong city will be undermined by being spread over the earth which is to be viewed negatively.[115]

The scattering concept automatically links this story with the scattering in the sons of Noah story (Gen. 9: 18–19) and the Canaanites (Gen. 10: 18).[116] It is reasonable to conclude that the author of this story was in dialog with or responding to the world view expressed by another author. It also should be noted that פוץ 'to scatter' or 'to spread' may be understood more as a descriptive term rather than a pejorative action.

11: 5 And Yahweh came down to see the city and the tower, which the sons of men had built. [6] And Yahweh said, 'Behold, they are one people, and they have all one language; and this is only the beginning of what they will do; and nothing that they propose to do will now be impossible for them. [7] Come, let us go down, and there confuse their language, that they may not understand one another's speech'. [8] So Yahweh scattered them abroad from there over the face of all the earth, and they left off building the city. [9] Therefore its name was called Babel, because there Yahweh confused the language of all the earth; and from there Yahweh scattered them abroad over the face of all the earth

The second part of the narrative introduces the only named figure in the story.[117] Yahweh's intervention becomes central. Yahweh reflects, decides, and intervenes with a specified effect. Although the section is coherent, Westermann, among others, sees it as blending two original, self-contained, and independent motifs: dispersion over the face of the earth and the confusion of languages.[118]

Van Wolde takes issue with the ease by which exegetes savage the humans for daring to breech the heavens and invade the realm of the Lord. She decries the admiration for the divine action whereby the unity of the human community is annihilated. Where is the sin of the humans? What is the hubris? Her points are well-taken ... if the Tower of Babel was a standalone allegory written by someone today. Unfortunately for her eagerness to present a positive spin on the story, she has removed it from its life situation. Ahijah at Shechem is championing the division of the kingdom. The men of Jerusalem (with Canaanite help from Hiram) have built what should not have been built. Yahweh needs no human king. Yahweh needs no temple. Ahijah in the name of Yahweh now is calling upon all Israel to act.[119]

---

115 LaCocque, *The Captivity of Innocence*, 32; Van der Kooij, 'The city of Babel and Assyrian imperialism', 5.

116 Hendel offers these similarities as examples of an author creating a literary continuity and not of multiple authors in dialog with each other on a common issues (see '*Leitwort* style', 101).

117 LaCocque, *The Captivity of Innocence*, 9.

118 Westermann, *Genesis 1–11*, 549.

119 Van Wolde, 'Words become words', 94.

11: 5 *And Yahweh came down to see the city and the tower*

The location of the deity has changed from the walking in the garden to the heights of the heavens. Westermann deems the portrayal of a descending deity as characteristic of primeval times and declares it is not the remnant of an astral religion. He contrasts the intervention of a descending deity to punish humankind with the intervention of a descending deity to deliver Israel in the Exodus story:

> Exodus 3: 8 *and I have come down to deliver them [my people] out of the hand of the Egyptians, and to bring them up out of that land to a good and broad land, a land flowing with milk and honey, to the place of the Canaanites, the Hittites, the Amorites, the Perizzites, the Hivites, and the Jebusites.* [One notes the absence of the Girgashites.]

The odds are these two descents are being contrasted whether by the same writer or by one responding to the other.[120]

11: 5 *which the sons of men had built*

The terminology changes here. The men are not *ish*, they are sons of the *adam;* they are not sons as in sons of God addition. The similarity between the sons of God and daughters of men in Gen. 6 with the sons of men/Adam is an example of another *leitwort*.[121]

One notes in the story of the Rape of the Bethlemite Concubine that the rapists are 'men of the city' with the city specifically being identified as Gibeah of Benjamin (Judg. 19: 22). In the potential rape at Sodom, the would-be perpetrators also are 'men of the city' (Gen. 19: 4). In this story the city is Babylon, but one cannot help but wonder if all these stories are part of the same dialog. The city has changed from Saul's capital to Solomon's. They have built something that the Israelite god, unlike the Mesopotamian or Canaanite gods, has no desire for. Perhaps they should have consulted Yahweh, meaning the priests of Yahweh, meaning Abiathar before undertaking this task. After all David inquired of the Lord through the auspices of Abiathar; these sons of *adam*/men did not. Here one may observe the pending doom for those who build without divine authorization. One is reminded of the fate of Jephthah's daughter after the father, the hero warrior against the Ammonites, failed to inquire of the Lord before undertaking a military campaign (Judges 11). People should consult the priests of Yahweh first about actions to be taken otherwise there will be a price to pay.

11: 6 *And Yahweh said, 'Behold, they are one people, and they have all one language; and this is only the beginning of what they will do; and nothing that they propose to do will now be impossible for them'*

The word 'Behold' serves as a warning of dire things to come. It functions as a rhetorical reflection of regret or sorrow. The Lord reflects on the actions of the humans. That reflection leads to a decision. However the decision is not based on the tower but the unity of the

---

120   Westermann, *Genesis 1–11*, 550.
121   Hendel, '*Leitwort* style', 106–107.

language. It anticipates that there will be no limit to what they may accomplish in the future, specifically the fear that they will become like God as expressed in the garden story (Gen. 3: 22) when Yahweh also said, 'Behold'. Humans were not satisfied and were willing to try to force their way into the heavens thereby demonstrating the same hubris as the couple in the garden. Both groups then were to live where they were.[122] According to Hiebert, this first divine response to the actions of the humans provides the key to understanding the entire story. God responds to the homogeneity of humanity. He directly connects it with the opening statement in verse 1. The statement in-and-of itself is not a judgment on human pride. Hiebert objects to translators creating a negative spin by implying a future threat which is not supported by the sentence's syntax. He understands the sentence to be referring what the humans already have planned and begun to do rather than to some unknown future action.[123]

Typically, exegetes imagine the Lord is speaking to his divine council here and in the next verse. Such a perception overlooks that in this world, it is a flesh and blood human being speaking in the name of Yahweh in the performance of the story. Previously Abiathar had been the voice of Yahweh to David and Israel. The torch has been passed. Now Ahijah, priest of Yahweh shifts in the story to his prophet-like-Moses voice about what is to come. He addresses not members of a divine council but the audience standing in front of him who have assembled to decide whether or not to accept Rehoboam as their king.

What happens to Israel if the Canaanites, the Hittites, the Amorites, the Perizzites, the Hivites, the Girgashites, and the Jebusites, the people of our world, all act as one on behalf of the king? Where is Israel if the non-Israelites in the land of Canaan operate as single entity? Will we cease to exist as a people, our name vanished, our seed destroyed, our heritage forgotten, if the men of the king in the capital city have their way? What will these people who opposed the emergence of Israel in the land in the time of Merneptah and afterwards do if they are united as a single people with one voice in a single kingdom? What are 'we' Israel going to do about it? The stakes were high and not abstract, mythical or theological. In the real world, a decision by the people Israel needed to be made and it needed to made now. Listen to Yahweh. Listen to the voice of his prophet standing before you and calling on you to act.

Yahweh's descent here to see what trouble the people are up to should be compared to the descent of Moses in the intensely polemical story of the golden calf (Ex. 32).

11: 7 *Come, let us go down, and there confuse their language, that they may not understand one another's speech*

This verse has raised questions on the unity of the narrative. In verse 5 Yahweh has come down to see the city whereas now he is in the heavens.[124] Westermann rejects the idea that

---

122 LaCocque, *The Captivity of Innocence*, 34; Westermann, *Genesis 1–11*, 551–552.

123 Hiebert, 'The Tower of Babel', 42–46.

124 Van der Kooij, 'The city of Babel and Assyrian imperialism', 2–3; Pierre Swiggers, 'Babel and the confusion of tongues', in Armin Lange, Hermann Lichtenberger and Diethard Römheld, eds, *Mythos im Alten Testament und seiner Umwelt: Festschrift für Hans-Peter Müller zum 65. Geburtstag*, (BZAW 278; Berlin: Walter de Guyter, 1999), 182–195, here 183.

the verse contains a polytheistic approach. In verse 5, it is Yahweh in the singular who descends and so it should be understood here. This verse and the following verse represent the conflating of the two motifs in the later stage: the confusion of language and the dispersion stories. In the Table of Nations, the division of humanity into a plurality of languages and people is a consequence of the blessing of God on those who survived the flood; here it is portrayed negatively.[125]

By contrast, for Hiebert, God's actions mirror and reverse the actions of the people with no negative spin being justified no matter how often exegetes do that.[126]

One still needs to grapple with why the central theme of the story was the change from one world language to many.[127] The men in Ahijah's story had journeyed eastward from the land of Canaan. During the reign on Solomon, the kingdom of Israel had served as a focal point within its region. It was centered amidst a swirl of activities from trade with Sheba to sailing the seas with Tyre. Solomon was dominant and even the Hebrew script seems to have spread across the Jordan River. But by the end of Solomon's reign or the beginning of Rehoboam's, the world had collapsed. Instead of Jerusalem being the focal point, newly emerging political states began to develop their own capitals, languages, and scripts. The course of the empire was in ruins. The perceptual unity of a world from the River of Egypt to the Great River dissolved until 853 BCE when these peoples banded together at Qarqar in Syria to resist the Assyrian invasion led by Shalmaneser III. That event was still 70 years into the future. What was Israel to be now that it did not dominate the region nor did anyone else?

11: 8 So Yahweh scattered them abroad from there over the face of all the earth, and they left off building the city

For Hiebert the dispersal or scattering is descriptive devoid of pejorative connotations. It is not punitive and there is no mention of the tower in the cessation of construction, only the city.[128]

11: 9 Therefore its name was called Babel, because there Yahweh confused the language of all the earth; and from there Yahweh scattered them abroad over the face of all the earth

A conclusion ends the storytelling. For van der Kooij, the spreading out over the face of the earth is the goal of the story.[129] Mission accomplished. According to Westermann, the verse is quite independent and the narrative is complete without it. The older form of the narrative as best reconstructed was not etiological. The Babylon element is a late accretion which is in contrast to the Babylon reference in the Nimrod story (10: 10). In

---

125   Westermann, *Genesis 1–11*, 552.
126   Hiebert, 'The Tower of Babel', 46–49.
127   Day, *From Creation to Babel*, 178.
128   Hiebert, 'The Tower of Babel', 46, 49–50.
129   Van der Kooij, 'The city of Babel and Assyrian imperialism', 7.

fact. Westermann deems this play on words an 'amateurish "popular etymolog(y)"'. Once the historical writing commences in the Old Testament, they cease.[130]

One may reasonably conjecture that the wordplay on the 'Babel' and 'Babylon' would have resonated with the original audience But the verb expressing the confusing of the language *bll* (בלל) does not derive from the noun *bbl* (בבל).[131] The question then arises as to what Babylon meant to the audience of the story. Babylon as the cradle of civilization in the ancient Near East is one logical impression. In and of itself, that does not make Babylon evil. The destruction of the Solomonic temple in 586 BCE by Babylonia certainly renders Babylon in the negative. A story written in the aftermath of Nebuchadnezzar II or Nabonidus easily could portray Babylon as evil.[132] The image of the whore of Babylon, the mother of harlots from the Book of Revelation chapter 17 similarly casts a shadow on the image of the city.

Is that image appropriate for understanding the story of the Tower of Babel? Hiebert obviously answers in the negative claiming Babylon is receiving a bad rap. There is no censure of Babylon here or in the Nimrod story … and there is no censure of Nimrod either since he is a hero (which was true for Phinehas, see Chapter 13). For Hiebert, then, this story at the end of the primeval age is not the climax of human sin and divine judgement that has dominated rabbinic, patristic, and academic exegesis. Instead it serves foundationally for the theme of cultural differentiation and diversity as part of God's design for a multicultural world. It reveals an understanding of the depth of the human need for identity and cultural solidarity amidst a diverse world.[133]

Hiebert very much is a person of the time of lunar landings, global warming, and multiculturalism. The story of the Tower of Babel provides him with the opportunity to tell a wondrous tale of the divinely-introduced diversity of humanity. It should be celebrated across the globe by the dispersed and scattered descendants of the tower's builders who now harmoniously can build a better tomorrow if given the chance in a kumbaya world. Regardless of what one may think of his global vision for the 21st century CE, it has virtually nothing to do with Ahijah's Israelite view in the 10th century BCE.

Ahijah was not an ivory tower intellectual, patristic exegete, or midrashic rabbi. Instead he was a player in the battle for power in the city of Jerusalem in the kingdom of Israel in the time of Solomon then Rehoboam and Jeroboam. Phinehas already had completed his supplement. It ended with the dispersal and scattering of the descendants of the sons of Noah across the entire real world as it was actually known. In so doing, Phinehas set the stage for the next cycle, the entrance of the hero of Hebron. David would create the kingdom where his son Solomon would build the temple at the cosmic center at the

---

130   Westermann, *Genesis 1–11*, 553–554.

131   Gnuse, 'The Tale of Babel', 235; Hiebert, 'The Tower of Babel', 47.

132   Gnuse, 'The Tale of Babel', 235, 244.

133   Hiebert, 'The Tower of Babel', 50–58 and 'Babel: babble or blueprint?', 138–139. Hiebert's rosy view has led to a counter responses. For LaCocque's views on the meaning of the story of the Tower of Babel see 'Whatever happened in the Valley of Shinar?' and *The Captivity of Innocence*. See also Strong, 'Shattering the image of God', defining the building as an attack on the deity contrary to Hiebert.

Jebusite city. Phinehas wrote during good times for his priesthood until he pleaded with Rehoboam to lighten the load of oppression over Israel.

Ahijah knew this and of the additional stories to come in the KDB with its Zadok-Abiathar-Phinehas supplements. He offered an alternative to the vision of Phinehas. Both told stories which drew on the legacy of Nebuchadnezzar I, the 12th century BCE, warrior hero who restored the captured statue of Marduk from the Elamite forces of chaos, built a ziggurat, and fostered a mythic story of cosmic proportions that legitimated his rule. Both told stories of Shinar, the name the Kassites had used for Babylon, to conclude their supplements to the first cycle of the KDB. The unity Phinehas offered was through the king and temple; Ahijah's alternative was one based on the people, the people in the audience at Shechem debating whether or not to accept Rehoboam as king and if not, then what. Phinehas saw Nebuchadnezzar I has a model to replicate; Ahijah saw him as another empire which had ceased to exist.

The story of the Tower of Babel may be understood as a 'mock building account intended as a polemic against royal ideology. This means the story deliberately follows the structure and format one would find a genuine Mesopotamian building account but subverts the imperial hubris contained within it.[134] The format from Sumerian times in the 3rd millennium BCE to Neo-Babylonian times in the 1st millennium BCE remained fairly constant and has been reconstructed by Assyriologists.[135] Knowing that standard provided an opportunity to deliberately reverse it if one was so inclined.

> 'The Tower of Babel story appropriates and inverts the Mesopotamian ideology of the ziggurat (which) served as a cosmic axis, linking heaven and earth... In the Tower of Babel story, the significance of the cosmic axis is turned upside-down.'[136]

> 'Genesis 11: 1–9 was originally composed as a diatribe against Mesopotamian royal ideology **[as practiced by Solomon and supported by Phinehas]**. These kings misused their power to create a unified world order and boasted about it in their massive building inscriptions **[bold added]**.'[137]

The story of the Tower of Babel is no more about the Babylonian ziggurat than the story of Samson destroying the Philistine temple is about a Philistine temple.

The primeval paradigm obscures the meaning of the story. Consider this interpretation by von Rad:

> 'The story in its present form must be understood primarily from the great primeval context into which the Yahwist has placed it. Basically it no longer concerns Babylon and the impressions this world city made on men... What the narrative portrays is sometime thoroughly primeval; it shows how men in their striving for fame, alliance, and political development set themselves against God'.[138]

---

134 Giogetti, 'The "mock building account"', 1–20.
135 See Victor Avigdor Hurowitz, *I Have Built You an Exalted House: Temple Building in the Bible in Light of Mesopotamian and North West Semitic Writings* (JSOT Sup. 115; Sheffield: Sheffield University Press, 1992).
136 Hendel, 'Genesis 1–11 and its Mesopotamian problem', 31.
137 Giogetti, 'The "mock building account"', 20.
138 Von Rad, *Genesis*, 151.

These observations were made by someone who thinks the Yahwist wrote in the time of Solomon without considering the possibility of someone at that time being opposed to what was being done. Von Rad knows about the Kenite genealogy, he knows about the Kenite cities in the time of David (I Sam. 10: 29), he knows the Kenite story does not fit smoothly and seems superfluous given the Flood , but he cannot recognize that there might be a Kenite (Moses) voice in the narrative.[139]

Hendel notes the perceptive rabbinic commentators who linked Nimrod's name (derived from Ninurta) with the Hebrew root *mrd* 'to rebel' to the Tower of Babel rebellion story. He calls this writing 'mimicry' meaning a subtle inversion in writing delivering a message of rebellion. Hendel dates this call for insurrection related to Nimrod to Assyrian times. The story mimics/inverts the Mesopotamian world order and the Mesopotamian ideology of the ziggurat.[140] Another possibility is that the author of the Tower of Babel story was writing in opposition to the Nimrod author and calling for an insurrection within the Israelite community against those who sought to emulate Mesopotamia at the new cosmic center in Jerusalem. The Solomonic temple was not sanctioned by Yahweh regardless of the Benjamin 'I had a dream', spin.

The Tower of Babel, the longest continuous composition by a single author of these supplements, really is a 'foundational story' and 'one of the most forceful mythical accounts in the Old Testament'. A foundation for what?[141]

Conclusion

De Vaux observes that the differing accounts of Aaron's role during the Exodus reflect a struggle between different groups of priests. J. Matthews strongly separates, distinguishes between, and casts as rivals the priesthoods based on Aaron and Jethro (Moses). In this regard, his view is consistent with the approach of Frank Moore Cross and his students who identify the rival Mushite and Aaronid priesthoods. They focus on the story of the golden calf (Ex. 32). Frolov touts Jonathan, the son of Abiathar, as continuing the Shiloh priesthood at Bethel under the auspices of Jeroboam while Ahijah pursued his more prophetic inclinations. One also needs to factor in the original distinction between the Aaronids and the Zadokites. In this three-way conflict among the proponents of Melchizedek, Phinehas, and Jethro, the battle for control of Bethel, assigning responsibility for the loss of the ark were critical to the writing in the 10th century and not just for the six stories that are the subject of this study. Old grudges did not die and new ones were created.[142]

---

139   Von Rad, *Genesis*, 110.
140   Hendel, 'Genesis 1–11', 30–33.
141   Quotations from Swiggers, 'Babel and the confusion of tongues', 189 and 190.
142   See Cross, *Canaanite Myth*,198–199; De Vaux, *Ancient Israel*, 395; Serge Frolov, '"Days of Shiloh" in the Kingdom of Israel', *Biblica* 76 1995: 210–218; Halpern, 'Levitic participation in the reform cult of Jeroboam I', 31–42; J. Matthews, *Melchizedek's Alternate Priestly Order*; Theophile James Meek, 'Aaronites and Zadokites', *AJSL* 45 1929: 149–166. A subtext to this discussion is the implication for Christianity to having Abraham pay homage to this uncircumcised pre-covenantal priest; see Jakob J. Petuchowski, 'The controversial figure of Melchizedek', *HUCA* 28 1957: 127–136.

Was there another way people could act together and become one without a king and temple? For Ahijah the answer was 'Yes', through the covenant. Jebusite Zadok and the Zadokites legitimated their priesthood through the story of Melchizedek (Gen. 14: 18–20), Elyon and the warrior shepherd king from Hebron who chose Jerusalem. Their story began with David. Benjaminite Aaronids legitimated their priesthood through the story of Phinehas (Num. 25: 6–13), Yahweh, and saving the people in the wilderness. Their story began with the Exodus. Ahijah legitimated the priesthood of Shiloh and the prophets of Moses through the story of Jethro, the father-in-law of Moses (Ex. 18: 13–27). That story began with the Exodus as well.

Ahijah championed an alternative to rule by the king, an alternative to rule by the temple priests, an alternative to a stratified society where wealth accumulated to the 1% in the Beltway. People did not belong to the king 24/7. People had the right to continue the homestead of the father and to care for their mother when the father died. Kings did not have the right to covet. Kings did not have the right to steal. Kings did not have the right to commit adultery. Kings did not have the right to murder. Kings did not have the right to bear false witness. Why should there even be human kings? And if there were, there should be checks and balances on the potential abuse of power. Ahijah did not know the term constitutional monarchy but he knew the concept. He did know the term 'covenant' and that it needed to be amended. The priests of Shiloh transformed into the prophets of Moses by calling truth to power with the challenge to Pharaohs Solomon and Rehoboam. The tradition of 'J'Accuse', 'Have you no sense of decency, sir', and standing before a tank with a flower had been born.[143]

And so ended Ahijah's version of the first cycle of the KDB.

---

143   For Ahijah's continuing Abiathar's fight, see Cohen, 'The role of the Shilonite priest', 92–93.

Chapter 15

CONCLUSION: REDACTING
THE KDB SUPPLEMENTS

This journey began with an examination of the Documentary Hypothesis. Part I reviewed how ancient, rabbinic, and leading modern scholars in their Genesis commentaries understood six different son stories. Although several of them suspected the presence of more than one writer within the J narrative, none of them successfully produced a comprehensive J Documentary Hypothesis that has stood the test of time. In this study, I have proposed a comprehensive J Documentary Hypothesis. It is based on the King David Bible and four supplements to it by four different people after David's death. I have used the six son stories as case studies for a model or template which can be extended to additional stories in subsequent cycles and the other stories in the misnamed 'Primeval' cycle.

Writing did not cease with the death of these four individuals but it was not continuous either. Following the tumult of the 10th century BCE, supplementing the KDB dwindled to a halt. The issues of creating a monarchy, succession, and building a temple became either irrelevant or redefined with the division into the two kingdoms. The battle for power in Jerusalem became a minor issue when Jerusalem had no power or very little power beyond its city walls. Under these circumstances, the writings dealing with issues of 10th-century BCE politics were effectively mothballed.

For the Jebusite Zadokites, life returned to much as it had been prior to David. Jerusalem functioned as a more-or-less independent city-state perhaps dominating the surrounding villages just as it had prior to the existence of Israel. The traditions of singing the praises to Elyon, Most High (and perhaps Asherah) resumed with a thin Yahweh veneer. Jerusalem had the temple, its own priesthood, and the king and that trio continued intact for centuries until the Babylonian destruction in 587/586 BCE. The city remained pro-Egypt as the cultural legacy of its pre-Israelite identity lingered.

For the Benjaminites and the priests of Aaron, its moment in the sun ended all too soon. The first Israelite king had been Benjaminite but now Benjamin was not even part of Israel any more. It had gambled on Solomon and had won only temporarily. For a while in the political vacuum of the ancient Near East, there was the opportunity for the kingdom of Israel to become and hopefully remain, a kingdom of power, prominence, and importance. That dream proved short-lived. The Mesopotamian-based Benjaminite vision held no sway for the small-minded princelings who dominated the city of Jerusalem post-Solomon and who saw no further than their own immediate greed and power. The Benjaminites who had been part of Israel since the beginning, still thought of itself as part of Israel even if others did not. These Benjaminites remained pro-Mesopotamia as the cultural legacy of its pre-Israelite identity lingered.

For the Ephraim priesthood of Shiloh and Moses, it had no powerbase. It had lost its link to the Davidic dynasty. It had no role in the temple. It had no role in the new northern kingdom of Israel which it had helped create, only to be tossed aside by a king who wanted his own people in power. Kings, like presidents, premiers, and prime ministers only want to hear advice from people who will tell them what they want to hear. The outsider-prophets of Moses received another blow when Mesha the Moabite channeled the worst of the Philistines and Saul by destroying the Moses sanctuary at Nebo and massacring the priests of Moses situated there. This trauma triggered a call to arms which contributed to the overthrow of the dynasty of Ahab and Jezebel and renewed writing of truth to power, of challenging the king be he Pharaoh of Egypt, Pharaoh Solomon, or Pharaoh Ahab. The priests of Moses had been part of Israel since the beginning. They had no official power; the influence of Ahijah, Elijah, Hosea, and Jeremiah derived from the perception of them that they spoke for Yahweh, the deity responsible for the creation of Israel.

For the tribe of Judah representing the kingdom David first created, the situation also returned to pre-Israelite conditions. David's Judah capital Hebron had not been subordinate to Jerusalem during the Bronze Age of Egyptian hegemony. It had its own tradition of greatness with the descendants of the Anak (Num. 13: 22); the Hebrew warrior Abram (Gen. 14: 13), and the Calebites who displaced the Anakites with the authorization of Ephraimite Joshua (Josh. 15: 14 and Judg. 1: 10). These Calebites had a connection to David prior to his conquest of Jerusalem and an affinity to their fellow Yahweh-worshipers in the northern kingdom of Israel.

And then Israel was no more. The destruction of the northern kingdom of Israel validated the prophecies of Hosea. It also led not merely to Israelites being deported by Assyria but to refugees fleeing south to Judah. The city of Jerusalem expanded. Now it contained substantial numbers of peoples with different traditions and backgrounds. Zadok may have exiled Abiathar but now the people of Israel for the first time and in significant numbers populated Jerusalem. It was not just a Jebusite city anymore. Somehow, all these people needed to learn to live with one another. That included melding their stories together, becoming one people before Assyria would strike again.

One might wonder then, how all these alternative stories presented in this study which later caused rabbis, priests, ministers, and scholars such anguish could exist side-by-side in a single continuous narrative. The answer as presented here is, they did not originally. One individual did create, as an act of conscious will, a unified narrative with multiple cycles, the KDB; he was a genius. After he died and Solomon became king, these supplements were added to his narrative. This led to two separate narratives. Both began with the original KDB narrative:

> KDB + Zadok + Abiathar + Phinehas
> KDB + Abiathar + Ahijah

These similar but different narratives were maintained separately by the prophets of Moses in the northern kingdom and the priests of the temple in the southern kingdom.[1]

---

1 The supposedly fragmentary Elohist narrative which has withdrawn into virtual nothingness in modern scholarship most likely always was a full-fledged coherent narrative with many stories from the original J

The two manuscripts contained obvious differences.

> One had a Sethite genealogy based on specific people at the time of its composition, the other had a Kenite genealogy based on representative ancestral figures.
>
> One had a universal Flood superimposed on the original local flood story while the other kept the local flood story.
>
> One praised Babylon for its success, the other mocked it for its collapse.
>
> One had people call the name of Yahweh before Moses, the other did not.

The stories always were part of the supplemented KDB narrative and never were standalone stories. They were not oral traditions from hoary antiquity but contemporary creations of will by players in the battle for the throne in Jerusalem after the death of David.

Any redaction or merger which did occur would not follow the ivory-tower paradigm of the lone scholar wrestling with multiple manuscripts or sources to create a single entity. The merger of the narratives into one narrative involved at minimum two people, one from each narrative tradition. The committee would have examined the narratives story by story, verse by verse, line by line, word by word, letter by letter to ensure that each side had its traditions included in the master narrative now being created, an effort where literary concerns and consistency were secondary to political/theological ones.[2]

Although the two manuscripts were merged with all the stories being retained, in practical terms for the six stories of this study, it was the writings of Ahijah which were combined with the KDB + Zadok + Abiathar + Phinehas narrative. This process was relatively straightforward.

> **Sons of Cain** (4: 17–4: 24) – the story remained following the story of Cain and Abel where it had been and now preceded the story of Seth.
>
> **Sons of God** (6: 3) – the verse introducing the Flood story was inserted into the story of the sons of God even though it had nothing directly to do with the story. Exactly why it happened is not clear and requires at least an excavation of the Flood story itself to determine. One possibility is that it did not happen at this time but remained part of 6: 5–7. The placement of the verse in the midst of the sons of God story may have caused an editorial addition in 6: 4, 'also afterward', to smooth the flow.
>
> **Sons of Men** (Tower of Babel) (11: 1–9) – the story remained the concluding story of the first cycle now following Nimrod and the Table of Nations.

All things considered, the merger of the stories covered in this study was fairly easy.

narrative starting in the garden. The extant traditional fragments attributed to E represent the differences with the KDB-Zadok-Phinehas narrative and overlooks the identical stories save for the name of the deity.

2   Sanders opines that 'the Pentateuch stands out from every other pre-Hellenistic text from the ancient Near East in its narrative incoherence' (Seth L. Sanders, 'What if there aren't any empirical models for Pentateuchal criticism?' in Brian B. Schmidt, ed., *Contextualizing Israel's Sacred Writings: Ancient Literacy, Orality, and Literary Production* (AIL 22; Atlanta: SBL Press, 2015), 281–304, here 287, 294). Political compromises operate under different rules than academic productions. Imagine if instead of the 14 articles in the book in which Sanders' article appears, they all had been combined into one. The lack of narrative coherence would be quite noticeable and indeed book reviews of such books often note the lack of unity in such compilations. In this biblical example, there were only two narratives which had to be combined.

In addition to the merger, an updating occurred. The world of concern had changed since the 10th century BCE when the stories were composed. By the time of Hezekiah, the issues of the existence of the Davidic dynasty and the Solomonic temple were no longer debated. Both remained and were functional. The world scene had changed. Mesopotamia was not simply a concept about activities in a far off land, it was an immediate threat having destroyed the kingdom of the north, deported people from Israel, and deported people to Israel. The geographic scope had changed while the geographic knowledge of the terms used by Phinehas required explanation if the new manuscript was going to be presented to the people. The Kassites had disappeared from sight and the Cushites now ruled Egypt and opposed Assyria. The narrative needed to reflect current realities.

As a result, additional information [in **bold**] was included in the narrative to help make the text more accessible and to cover the world of concern in the present.

> **Genesis 2: 11** The name of the first is Pishon; **it is the one which flows around the whole land of Havilah, where there is gold;** [12] **and the gold of that land is good; bdellium and onyx stone are there.** [13] The name of the second river is Gihon; **it is the one which flows around the whole land of Cush.** [14] And the name of the third river is Tigris, **which flows east of Assyria.** And the fourth river is the Euphrates.

Descriptive information elaborated on the barebone names which Phinehas had used to define the world stage. The Pishon in Arabia and the Gihon in Egypt and Nubia/Cush were identified in more detail. The Tigris received a brief note reflecting the current threat from Assyria and the well-known Euphrates required no additional information. The world stage remained the same now more clearly defined and included the mention of Assyria, Havilah, and Cush.

The redactors were good editors who recognized the insertion of Cush into the description of the rivers in the garden story warranted changes elsewhere in the narrative as well.

Sons of Noah

The disappearance of the Kassites and the immediate presence and involvement of the Cushites in Judean history altered the geographical landscape. Shem as the father of the eastern (Cush) and western (Canaan) Semites no longer made sense now that the Cushites from Nubia ruled Egypt. The new scenario incorporated this shift plus added lands now better known than they had been centuries earlier (in **bold** supplementing the existing *Abiathar*/Phinehas narrative).

> **Genesis 10: 1 Ham** became the father of Cush. [8]Cush became the father of Nimrod; he was the first on earth to be a mighty man. [9]He was a mighty hunter before Yahweh; therefore it is said, 'Like Nimrod a mighty hunter before Yahweh'. [10]The beginning of his kingdom was Babel, Erech, and Accad, all of them in the land of Shinar. [13]**Egypt** became the father of **Ludim, Anamim, Lehabim, Naphtuhim,** [14]**Pathrusim, Casluhim (whence came the Philistines), and Caphtorim.** [15]Canaan became the father of Sidon his first-born, and Heth, [16]the Jebusites, the Amorites, the Girgashites. **Sidon his first-born, and Heth,** [17]**the Hivites, the Arkites, the Sinites,**

[18]the Arvadites, the Zemarites, and the Hamathites. <u>Afterward the families of the Canaanites spread abroad.</u> <u>[19]And the territory of the Canaanites extended from Sidon, in the direction of Gerar, as far as Gaza, and in the direction of Sodom, Gomorrah, Admah, and Zeboiim, as far as Lasha</u> [21]To Shem also, the father of all the children of Eber, the elder brother of Japheth, children were born. [24]Arpachshad became the father of Shelah; and Shelah became the father of Eber. [25]To Eber were born two sons: the name of the one was Peleg, for in his days the earth was divided, and his brother's name was Joktan. [26]Joktan became the father of Almodad, Sheleph, Hazarmaveth, Jerah, [27]Hadoram, Uzal, Diklah, [28]Obal, Abimael, Sheba, [29]Ophir, Havilah, and Jobab; all these were the sons of Joktan. [30]The territory in which they lived extended from Mesha in the direction of Sephar to the hill country of the east.

With these additions, the redaction committee brought the world map of the biblical narrative up-to-date with current world knowledge.

Nimrod

> Genesis 10: 11 *From that land he went into Assyria, and built Nineveh, Rehobothir, Calah, and* [12] *Resen between Nineveh and Calah; that is the great city.*

Part of that updating meant revising the empire of Nimrod in accordance with the reality of the Assyrian empire. The capital cities of Calah of Ashurnasirpal II and Shalmaneser III in the 9th century BCE and Nineveh of Sennacherib in the 8th century BCE became part of Nimrod's domain. One would have expected to find Dur-Sharrukin, modern Khorsabad, the new capital city from Sargon II named after himself to have been included as well. After all, Sargon II claimed victory over Israel. Perhaps it was in some as yet undecipherable way. It should also be noted that the construction and his death on the battlefield occurred precisely when this update was being formulated.

Van der Kooij makes a strong case for dating these additional verses to the time of Sargon II and the building of his new capital city Dur-Sharrukin. In his view, the entire Nimrod section was composed at one time in contrast with the two-stage composition suggested here. He also attributed the passage to being a comment on Assyrian actions. By contrast, Knohl proposes a reworking of the existing Nimrod tradition in Sargonic times parallel to the Assyrian reworking of Sargon the Great traditions in Neo-Assyrian time. He points out the parallels as noted by various scholars between the change of perception of Sargon the Great and Sargon II following the latter's failed attempt to build a new city. Both proposals are consistent with the time when the proposed redaction committee functioned.[3]

The replacement of Calah in the original Nimrod story with Calneh now can be explained. Calah, unlike Nineveh and Khorsabad, had been an important city in Middle Assyrian kingdom of Tukulti-ninurta and Tiglath-pileser I. It also figured at the beginning of the Neo-Assyrian empire of Ashurnasirpal II and Shalmaneser III. The city needed to be included in the Nimrod update to reflect the Neo-Assyrian empire in the time of Hezekiah, king of Judah, as part of the redaction. But it could not appear twice in the narrative. Fortuitously,

---

3   Knohl, 'Nimrod, son of Cush', 51–52; Van der Kooij, 'The city of Babel and Assyrian imperialism', 8–11, 14–17.

there was a vaguely similar substitute city which could be used to replace the original Calah. Amos mentions it when referring to the Assyrian empire and its looming threat:

> **Amos 6: 1** *Woe to those who are at ease in Zion, and to those who feel secure on the mountain of Samaria, the notable men of the first of the nations, to whom the house of Israel come!² Pass over to **Calneh**, and see; and thence go to Hamath the great; then go down to Gath of the Philistines. Are they better than these kingdoms?*

At the time of the redaction, Calneh was a known entity. The redaction committee therefore relocated Calah in the original Nimrod story in the new verse and replaced it with Calneh in the old verse.⁴

The story of Nimrod illustrates how a story can be reused and reconfigured. A story may 'fit' multiple time periods.⁵ Van der Kooij's fitting of the dispersal of humanity in the Tower of Babel to Sargon II's deportations represents only one fitting, not the only one. The dispersals equally may be viewed in the prism of the collapse of the empire of Nebuchadnezzar I with its ziggurat at Babylon and creation of the *Enuma Elish* story touting Marduk. Nebuchadnezzar I, with his military successes, returning the captured religious object, construction projects, and narratives of legitimacy and achievement, created a model for the Israelite kings. He was the last great Babylonian king prior to the origin of the Israelite state. Empires leave legacies of their collapse as well as their success. The fall of the Akkadian empire under Naram-sin became a defining lesson for the ancient Near East, so too the fall of Rome for Western Civilization. Phinehas drew on the success of Nebuchadnezzar I to provide a model for the Davidic king; the fall of the empire provided a prophet with the opportunity to warn what would happen to the Solomonic empire if it followed that path. The warning that proved consistent with what did in fact happen no doubt enhancing Ahijah's status and legacy.

Sargon's unexpected and unprecedented death on the battlefield in 705 BCE without recovery of his body similarly suggested a negative cosmic judgement had been rendered against him and the Assyrian empire. It may have been the reminder that the message of the Nimrod story still applied. The suggestion here is that the post-Nebuchadnezzar I world better fits the time for the origin of the story with a Sargon II addendum centuries later to reflect new developments of Assyria ruling the world. In this scenario, at the time of origin, the vacuum in Mesopotamian (and Egyptian) power created a window of opportunity for a new cosmic center to be established in the land of Canaan.⁶

It is easier to *first* make the case for being a cosmic center when there is no competition for

---

4   Isaiah expresses similar thoughts to Amos but refers to Calno (Isaiah 10: 9).
5   For the 'fitting' and reuse of stories in multiple geographical and temporal settings see Benjamin D. Sommer, 'Dating Pentateuchal texts and the perils of pseudo-historicism', in Thomas B. Dozeman, Konrad Schmid and Baruch J. Schwartz, eds, *The Pentateuch: International Perspectives on Current Research* (FAT 78; Tübingen: Mohr Siebeck, 2011), 85–108.
6   Kenneth A. Kitchen, 'The controlling role of external evidence in assessing the historical status of the Israelite united monarchy', in V. Philips Long, David W. Baker and Gordon J. Wenham, eds, *Windows into Old Testament History: Evidence, Argument, and the Crisis of 'Biblical Israel'*, (Grand Rapids: William B. Eerdmans, 2002), 111–130; Kenneth A. Kitchen, *On the Reliability of the Old Testament*, (Grand Rapids: William B. Eerdmans, 2003), 98–107.

the position then when there is. The Chinese conception of China as the 'middle kingdom' arose at a time when it was the center of the universe as it knew it. It did not originate during the ages of European colonialism or American superpower status which China then retrojected to an imagined past. Assyria's world rule forced the Israelite effort to redefine its position within that changed world or disappear from history as its neighbors did. Israel's view of itself in history did not originate in Assyrian, Babylonian, Persian, Hellenistic, or Roman times. It began with David's success and adapted to changing circumstances.

With this revision, the redaction combining and updating the six son stories of the KBD was completed.

This study has shown that the traditional understandings of the origins of these son stories were at variance with the historical context in which they were created. Far from being oral folk tales from hoary antiquity about the origins of human civilization or about sin and the separation from God, they were instead supplements to the KDB as weapons of war in the battle for the Jerusalem throne. They were political writings by the people who were the top players in the beltway battle, the leaders of the different combatants. When Israel first emerged in history, Pharaoh Merneptah claimed to have destroyed the seed of Israel and wrote (or had written) a story set in past of a Hyksos-Egypt confrontation. He was not writing history, he was playing politics. So it was with the Israelite writers as well.

Multiple authors with different points of view dialoged and combated each other in the political arena in an attempt to make the other eat his words. This form of communication should be familiar to scholars. It is exactly what occurs in journal articles where scholars respond to the lunacy of another scholar by quoting the predecessor's words, reversing the interpretation, making the bozo eat his/her words. Such communications occurred in biblical times too, but without the academic footnote paraphernalia that enables one to know where one writer ends and the other begins. The result appears confusing unless one can untangle the different voices visible on a single printed page.

It is exciting to be able to delve into the minds of these authors as they debated and fought over crucial issues to creating a people. Through these writings one gains insight into the minds of specific individuals in history and of their struggle to bring order to chaos and triumph in the game of power politics. The level of debate within Israel truly was extraordinary. We are privileged if not blessed to have the writings of these giants who wrestled with the issues that continue to define us to this very day.

ADDITIONAL READINGS

The topics below are arranged in alphabetical order. The readings in each topic provide the background information for the writing in the book. When authors were quoted or when they supplied direct information about a particular point, then the full bibliographic data is included in a footnote in the text.

1177 BCE (see **Iron Age I**)

This year is the consensus date for Ramses III's Year 8 campaign to Canaan. It serves as a useful transition point for the end of the Late Bronze Age (1550–1200 BCE) and beginning of the Iron Age (1200–586 BCE), not for the technology changes but for the political ones. It marks the decline of the Great Kings of the Amarna Letters (see below) and the rise of new political entities in the region. The campaign occurred subsequent to the presence of Israel in the land of Canaan (see Merneptah) and prior to the monarch. For the conditions behind the momentous events surrounding the year 1177 BCE and for that year itself see:

Bunimovitz, Shlomo, 'The problem of human resources in Late Bronze Age Palestine and its socioeconomic implications'. *UF* 26 1994: 1–20.
Cline, Eric H., *1177 BC: The Year Civilization Collapsed* (Princeton: Princeton University Press, 2014).
Drews, Robert, *The End of the Bronze Age: Changes in Warfare and the Catastrophe ca. 1200 BC* (Princeton: Princeton University Press, 1993).
Langgut, Dafna, Finkelstein, Israel and Litt, Thomas, 'Climate and the Late Bronze Age collapse: new evidence from the southern Levant'. *TA* 40 2013: 149–175.
Yurco, Frank J., 'End of the Late Bronze Age and other crisis periods: a volcanic cause?', in Emily Teeter and J. A. Larson, eds, *Gold of Praise: Studies on Ancient Egypt in Honor of Edward F. Wente* (SAOC 58, Chicago: Oriental Institute, 1999), 455–463.

Akitu

The *akitu* marks the 11-day New Year festival where the ziggurat was the center of attention. One may gain insight into human cultures throughout the world and in all times through how they choose to recognize and celebrate the new year. The awareness of this extended public event at the cosmic center revolving around the king, processions, and a story contributed to the formation of the King David Bible. For the *akitu* see:

Bidmead, Julye, *The Akitu Festival: Religious Continuity and Royal Legitimation in Mesopotamia* (Piscataway, NJ: Gorgias Press, 2014).
Jacobsen, Thorkild, 'Religious drama in Ancient Mesopotamia', in Hans Goedicke and J. J. M. Roberts, eds, *Unity and Diversity: Essays in the History, Literature, and Religion of the Ancient Near East* (Baltimore: Johns Hopkins University Press, 1975), 65–97.
Klein, Jacob, 'Akitu', in *ABD* I: 138–140.

Lambert, W. G., 'The conflict in the Akītu house'. *Iraq* 25 1963: 189–190.

Pallis, Svend Aage, *The Babylonian Akîtu Festival* (København, Hovedkommissionaer: A.F. Høst, 1926).

Sommer, Benjamin D., 'The Babylonian Akitu festival: rectifying the king of renewing the cosmos'. *JANES* 27 2000: 81–95.

Van der Toorn, Karel, 'The Babylonian new year festival: new insights from the cuneiform texts and their bearing on Old Testament study', in J. A. Emerton, ed., *Congress Volume Leuven 1989* (Leiden: Brill, 1991), 331–344.

Alphabet (see Literacy)

The alphabet we use today has its origins in Egypt in the second millennium BCE as part of the interaction between Semitic people from the Levant who had no writing system and the Egyptians who did. For the still developing and debated story on that process see:

Carr, David M., 'The Tel Zayit abecedary in (social) context', in Ron E. Tappy and P. Kyle McCarter, Jr., eds, *Literate Culture and Tenth-Century: The Tel Zayit Abcedary in Context* (Winona Lake: Eisenbrauns, 2008), 113–129.

Diringer, David, *The Story of the Aleph Beth* (New York: Thomas Yoseloff, 1960).

Diringer, David, *The Alphabet: A Key to the History of Mankind*, Vol I (London: Hutchinson of London, 1968, 3rd edition).

Gardiner, Alan, 'The Egyptian origin of the Semitic alphabet'. *JEA* 1916: 1–16.

Goldwasser, Orly, 'An Egyptian scribe from Lachish and the Hieratic tradition of the Hebrew kingdoms'. *TA* 18 1991: 248–253.

Goldwasser, Orly, 'Canaanites reading hieroglyphs: Horus is Hathor? – the invention of the alphabet in Sinai'. *Egypt and the Levant* 16 2006: 121–160.

Goldwasser, Orly, 'How the alphabet was born from hieroglyphs'. BAR 26/2 2010: 40–53.

Goldwasser, Orly, 'The advantage of cultural periphery: the invention of the alphabet in Sinai (circa 1840 BCE)', in Rakefet Sela-Sheffy and Gideon Toury, eds, *Culture Contacts and the Making of Cultures: Papers in Homage to Itamar Even-Zohar* (Tel Aviv: Tel Aviv University/Unit of Culture Research, 2011), 255–321.

Goldwasser, Orly, 'The miners who invented the alphabet – a response to Christopher Rollston'. *JAEI* 4/3 2012: 9–22.

McCarter, P. Kyle, Jr., 'The early diffusion of the alphabet'. *BA* 37 1974: 54–68.

Millard, Alan, 'Alphabetic writing, cuneiform and linear reconsidered', *Maarav* 14 2007: 83–93.

Naveh, Joseph, *Early History of the Alphabet: An Introduction to West Semitic Epigraphy and Paleography* (Jerusalem: Magness Press, 1982).

Rollston, Christopher A., 'The probable inventors of the first alphabet: Semites functioning as rather high status personnel in a component of the Egyptian apparatus'. *ASOR blog*, August 28, 2010, http: //asorblog.org.

Sanders, Seth L., 'What was the alphabet for? The rise of written vernaculars and the making of Israelite national literature'. *Maarav* 11 2004: 25–56.

Sanders, Seth L., *The Invention of Hebrew* (Urbana: University of Illinois Press, 2009).

Sanders, Seth L., 'Iron Age Israel: before national scripts, beyond nations and states', in Ron E. Tappy and P. Kyle McCarter, eds, *Literate Culture and Tenth Century Canaan: The Tel Zayit Abecedary in Context* (Winona Lake: Eisenbrauns, 2008).

Sass, Benjamin, 'The genesis of the alphabet and its development in the second millennium BC –twenty years later', *De Kemi à Birit Nari* 2 2005: 147–166.

Amarna Letters

The discovery of the Amarna Letters in 1887 changed our knowledge of the international diplomacy of ancient times. The fortuitous abandonment of this diplomatic 'file drawer' when Amarna was abandoned as the capital provides entry into the actual diplomatic exchanges which occurred beyond the propaganda set pieces on royal monuments. In some ways, they may be considered the first hacked diplomatic emails. They leave us wondering how much more is being missed because we are limited to little more than a decade (1340s–1330s BCE) of such correspondence. For the Amarna Letters see:

Cohen, Raymond and Westbrook, Raymond, eds, *Amarna Diplomacy: The Beginnings of International Relations* (Baltimore: Johns Hopkins University Press, 2000).

For the language and script see:

Moran, William L., 'The Syrian scribe of the Jerusalem Amarna Letters', in Hans Goedicke and J. J. M. Roberts, eds, *Unity and Diversity: Essays in the History, Literature, and Religion of the Ancient Near East* (Baltimore: Johns Hopkins University Press, 1975), 146–166.
Rainey, Anson F., 'Who is a Canaanite? A review of the textual evidence', *BASOR* 304 1996: 1–15, here 12.
Von Dassow, Eva, 'What the Canaanite cuneiformists wrote'. *IEJ* 53/2 2003: 196–217.
Von Dassow, Eva, 'Canaanite in cuneiform'. *JAOS* 124 2004: 641–674.

Amarna Letters and Jerusalem

This study focuses on Jerusalem so the presence of the city in the letters sheds light on the city which David made his capital. For the Amarna Letters and Jerusalem see:

Bodi, Daniel, 'Outraging the resident-alien: King David, Uriah the Hittite, and an El-Amarna parallel'. *UF* 35 2003: 29–56.
Cahill, Jane, 'Jerusalem at the time of the United Monarchy: the archaeological evidence', in Andrew G. Vaughn and Ann E. Killebrew, eds, *Jerusalem in the Bible and Archaeology: The First Temple Period* (SBLSymS 18; Atlanta: Society of Biblical Literature, 2003), 13–80, here 27–33.
Cline, Eric H., *Jerusalem Besieged: From Ancient Canaan to Modern Israel* (Ann Arbor: University of Michigan Press, 2004), 18, 313n11.
Feigin, Samuel I., 'Abd-Ḥeba and the Kashi: the attempted assassination of Abd-Ḥeba'. *JQR* 34 1944: 441–458.
Finkelstein, Israel, 'The sociopolitical organization of the central hill country', in Avraham Biran and Joseph Aviram, eds, *Biblical Archaeology Today, 1990: Proceedings of the Second International Congress on Biblical Archaeology, Jerusalem, June–July 1990* (Jerusalem: Israel Exploration Society, 1993), 119–131.
Finkelstein, Israel, 'The territorial-political system of Canaan'. *UF* 28 1986: 221–255.
Izre'el, Shlomo, 'The Amarna Letters from Canaan', in *CANE*, 2411–2419.
Na'aman, Nadav, 'The origin and historical background of several Amarna Letters'. *UF* 11 1979: 673–684.
Na'aman, Nadav, ' Economic aspects of the Egyptian occupation of Canaan'. *IEJ* 31 1981: 172–185.
Na'aman, Nadav, 'On gods and scribal traditions in the Amarna Letters'. *UF* 22 1990: 247–255.
Na'man, Nadav, 'Canaanite Jerusalem and its central hill country neighbors in the second millennium BCE'. *UF* 24 1992: 275–291.
Na'aman, Nadav, 'The network of Canaanite Late Bronze kingdoms'. UF 29 1997: 599–626.
Na'aman, Nadav, 'The contribution of the Amarna Letters to the debate on Jerusalem's political position in the tenth century BCE'. *BASOR* 304 1996: 17–27.
Na'aman, Nadav, 'Jerusalem in the Amara Period', in Caroline Amould-Béhar and André Lemaire, eds, *Jerusalem Antique et Medievale: Mélanges en l'honneur d'Ernest-Marie Laperrousaz* (Paris: Peeters, 2011), 31–48.
Na'aman, Nadav, 'Jerusalem's political position in the tenth century BCE'. *BASOR* 304 1996: 17–27, here 21.
Na'aman, Nadav, 'The Shephelah according to the Amarna Letters', in Israel Finkelstein and Nadav Na'aman, eds, *The Fire Signals of Lachish: Studies in the Archaeology and History of Israel in the Late Bronze Age, Iron Age and Persian Period in Honor of David Ussishkin* (Winona Lake: Eisenbrauns, 2011), 281–299.
Pioske, Daniel D., *David's Jerusalem: Between Memory and History* (New York: Routledge, 2015), 218–222.

Amorites

The irony of the Amorites is that when they first appeared in history as a people it was as subhumans while a short time later one of them, Hammurabi, became the exemplar of civilized Mesopotamian life studied by school children to this very day. The Amorites appear across a vast stretch of land in the ancient Near East in the first half of the 2nd millennium BCE, are closely associated with the city Mari on the Euphrates, and nomadism. According to Ezekiel, the Amorites are the father of Jerusalem.

Buccellati, Giorgio, *The Amorites of the Ur III Period* (Naples: Istituto Orientale di Napoli, 1966).
Buccellati, Giorgio, 'Amorites', in *OEANE*, 107–111.
Fleming, Daniel E., 'The Amorites', in Bill T. Arnold and Brent A. Strawn, eds, *The World Around the Old Testament* (Grand Rapids: Baker Academic, 2016), 1–30.
Gelb, I. J., 'The early history of the West Semitic peoples'. *JCS* 15 1961: 27–47.
Geus, C. H. J. de, 'The Amorites in the archaeology of Palestine'. *UF* 3 1971: 41–60.
Haldar, Alfred, *Who Were the Amorites?* (Leiden: Brill, 1971).
Kamp, Kathleen and Yoffee, Norman, 'Ethnicity in ancient Western Asia during the early second millennium BC: archaeological assessments and ethnoarchaeological prospectives'. *BASOR* 237 1980: 85–104.
Liverani, Mario, 'The Amorites', in D. J. Wiseman, ed., *Peoples of Old Testament Times* (Oxford, Clarendon Press, 1973), 100–133.
Luke, J. Tracy, ' "Your father was an Amorite" (Ezek. 16: 3, 45): an essay on the Amorite problem in Old Testament traditions', in H. B. Huffmon, F. A. Spina and A. R. W. Green, eds, *The Quest for the Kingdom of God: Studies in Honor of George E. Mendenhall* (Winona Lake: Eisenbrauns, 1983), 221–237.
Mendenhall, George E., 'Amorites', in *ABD* I: 199–202.
Zarins, Juris, 'Jebel Bishri and the Amorite homeland: the PPNB phase', in O. M. C. Haex, H. H. Curves and P. M. M. G. Akkermans, eds, *To the Euphrates and Beyond: Archaeological Studies in Honour of Maurits N. Van Loon* (Rotterdam: Balkema, 1989), 29–51.

Arrowheads and Javelins (see Literacy)

People write on all sorts of physical objects so you never know in an archaeological excavation where writing may appear. During a certain window in time in Iron Age I (1200–1000 BCE), arrowheads and javelins became part of the story in writing in Israel.

Ryan Byrne, 'The refuge of scribalism in Iron I Palestine'. *BASOR* 345 2007: 1–31.
Cross, Frank Moore, *Leaves from an Epigrapher's Notebook: Collected Papers in Hebrew and West Semitic Paleography and Epigraphy* (HSS 51; Winona Lake: Eisenbrauns, 2003), 200–202.
Hess, Richard S., 'Arrowheads from Iron Age: personal names and authenticity', in K. Lawson Younger, ed., *Ugarit at Seventy-Five: [Proceedings of the Symposium Ugarit at Seventy-Five held at Trinity International University, Deerfield, Illinois, February 18–20, 2005 under the auspices of the Middle Western Branch of the American Oriental Society and the Mid-West Region of the Society of the Biblical Literature]* (Winona Lake: Eisenbrauns, 2007), 113–129.
Milik, J. T. and Cross, Frank Moore, 'Inscribed javelin-heads from the period of the judges: a recent discovery in Palestine'. *BASOR* 1954 134: 5–15.
Smith, Mark S., *Poetic Heroes: Literary Commemorations of Warriors and Warrior Culture in the Early Biblical World* (Grand Rapids: William B. Eerdmans, 2014), 26–27, 296–298.
Van der Toorn, Karel, *Scribal Culture and the Making of the Hebrew Bible* (Cambridge, MA: Harvard University Press, 2007), 71.

Asherah (see **Baal**, **El**, **Elyon**, **Ugarit** and **Yahweh**)

Asherah was a word best known from the Bible until the discoveries at Ugarit (see below) opened up the Canaanite world. Her presence in the Canaanite tradition provides a background to the religion of the city David made his capital and to Isra-el given her identity as the consort of El.

Ackerman, Susan, 'At home with the goddess', in William G. Dever and Seymour Gitin, eds, *Symbiosis, Symbolism, and the Power of the Past: Canaan, Ancient Israel, and their Neighbors from the Late Bronze Age through Roman Palaestina* (Winona Lake: Eisenbrauns, 2003), 455–468.

Binger, Tilde, *Asherah: Goddesses in Ugarit, Israel and the Old Testament* (London: Sheffield Academic Press, 1997).

Day, John, 'Asherah in the Hebrew Bible and northwest Semitic literature'. *JBL* 105 1986: 385–408.

Day, John, 'Asherah', in *ABD* I: 483–487.

Day, John, *Yahweh and the Gods and Goddesses of Canaan* (JSOT Sup. Series 265; Sheffield: Sheffield Academic Press, 2000), 42–67.

Dever, William G., 'Asherah, consort of Yahweh? New evidence from Kuntillet 'Ajrûd'. *BASOR* 255 1984: 21–37.

Dever, William G., *Did God Have a Wife? Archaeology and Folk Religion in Ancient Israel* (Grand Rapids: William B. Eerdmans, 2005).

Hadley, Judith M., *The Cult of Asherah in Ancient Israel and Judah: The Evidence for a Hebrew Goddess* (University of Oriental Publications 57; Cambridge: Cambridge University Press, 2000).

Hestrin, Ruth, 'Understanding Asherah – exploring Semitic iconography'. BAR 16/5 1991: 50–59.

Margalit, Baruch, 'The meaning and significance of Asherah', *VT* 40 1990: 264–297.

Mastin, B. A., 'Yahweh's Asherah, inclusive monotheism and the question of dating', in John Day, ed., *In Search of Pre-exilic Israel: Proceedings of the Oxford Old Testament Seminar* (JSOT Sup. Series 46; London: T&T Clark International, 2004), 326–351.

Olyan, Saul M., *Asherah and the Cult of Yahweh in Israel* (Atlanta: Scholars Press, 1988).

Patai, Raphael, 'The goddess Asherah'. *JNES* 24 1965: 37–52.

Smith, Mark S., 'Chapter 3: Yahweh and Asherah', in *The Early History of God: Yahweh and the Other Deities in Ancient Israel* (Grand Rapids: William B. Eerdmans, 1999), 108–147.

Wiggins, Steve A., *A Reassessment of 'Asherah': A Study According to the Textual Sources of the First Two Millennia BCE* (AOAT 235; Neukirchen-Vluyn: Neukirchener, 1993).

Wyatt, Nicolast, 'Asherah', in *DDD*, 99–105.

Baal (see **Asherah**, **El**, **Ugarit** and **Yahweh**)

As with Asherah, Baal was a word best known from the Bible until the discoveries from Ugarit revealed that he was a hero in Canaanite myths. At times, the characteristics associated with Israelite Yahweh resemble those of Canaanite Baal. A traditional key distinction has been Baal's association with the seasons and fertility compared to Yahweh as a deity who acted in history. The climactic rain showdown between the Elijah and the prophets of Baal (I Kings 18) signifies Yahweh's supremacy over Baal in that area as well. Yahweh's post-Flood promise of perpetual seasons (Gen. 8: 22) represents an assertion which does not even acknowledge the existence of Baal. For Baal see:

Day, John, 'Baal', in *ABD* I: 545–549.

Herrmann, Wolfgang, 'Baal', in *DDD*, 132–137.

Kapelrud, Arvid, *Baal in the Ras Shamra Texts* (Copenhagen, G.E.C. Gad, 1952).

Oldenburg, Ulf, *The Conflict between El and Ba'al in Canaanite Religion* (Leiden: Brill, 1969).

Smith, Mark S., 'Interpreting the Baal Cycle'. *UF* 18 1986: 313–339.

Smith, Mark S., *The Ugaritic Baal Cycle Volume I: Introduction with Text, Translation and Commentary of KTU 1.1–1.2* (SVT 55, Leiden: Brill, 1994).

For the relation between Baal and Yahweh see:

Cross, Frank Moore, *Canaanite Myth and Hebrew Epic: Essays in the Religion of Israel* (Cambridge MA: Harvard
    University Press, 1973), 145–194.
Day, John, *Yahweh and the Gods and Goddesses of Canaan* (JSOT Sup. Series 265; Sheffield: Sheffield Academic
    Press, 2000), 68–127.
Smith, Mark S., 'Chapter 2: Yahweh and Baal', in *The Early History of God: Yahweh and the Other Deities in
    Ancient Israel* (Grand Rapids: William B. Eerdmans, 1999), 65–107.

Baal-Peor (Numbers 25)

Num. 25 is a textual tel with disputed layers and dates that attracts attention because of the violence,
the violence against a woman, and the connection to other texts of terror. Based on the approach
taken in this study, it should be viewed as a political story where no actual human beings were hurt
in its telling. The story is important in this study due to the presence of Phinehas whom I identify
as one of the writers who supplemented the King David Bible. His contribution to the son stories
in the first KDB cycle are analyzed in this book. Biblical commentaries on the Book of Numbers
include this story. In addition see:

Collins, John J., 'The zeal of Phinehas: the Bible and the legitimation of violence'. *JBL* 122 2001: 3–21.
Cross, Frank Moore, *Canaanite Myth and Hebrew Epic: Essays in the Religion of Israel* (Cambridge MA: Harvard
    University Press, 1973), 202.
Levine, Baruch A., *Numbers 21–36: A New Translation with Introduction and Commentary* (AB 4A; New York:
    Doubleday, 2000), 279–303.
Monroe, Lauren A. S., 'Phinehas' zeal and the death of Cozbi: unearthing a human scapegoat tradition in
    Numbers 25: 1–18'. *VT* 62 2012: 211–231.
Monroe, Lauren A. S., 'Disembodied women: the sacrificial language in the accounts of the deaths of Bat
    Jephthah, the Behtlehemite concubine the Midianites'. *CBQ* 75 2013: 32–52.
Reif, S. C., 'What enraged Phinehas? A study of Numbers 25: 8'. *JBL* 90 1971: 200–206.
Sivan, Helena Zlotnick, 'The rape of Cozbi (Numbers XXV)'. *VT* 51 2001: 69–80.

Benjamin (*see also* Benjaminites/Yaminites, Saul's Rise to Power)

The youngest son of Jacob in the genealogy is part of the oldest and original component of Israel.
Its history is witnessed by the hill country settlements, its presence in the Song of Deborah, the
location for the battle in the Book of Jashar, and the dream of Solomon. Benjamin is particularly
important in the development of the Hebrew Bible as the tribe of Saul and for the actions of its
priesthood. For a discussion on Benjamin's place in Israel see:

Finkelstein, Israel, 'Saul, Benjamin and the emergence of 'Biblical Israel': an alternative view'. *ZAW* 123 2011:
    348–367.
Na'aman, Nadav, 'Saul, Benjamin and the emergence of 'Biblical Israel (Part 1)'. *ZAW* 121 2009: 211–224.
Na'aman, Nadav, 'Saul, Benjamin and the emergence of 'Biblical Israel (continued, Part 2)'. *ZAW* 121: 335–349.

Finkelstein suggests the one-period fortified site of Khirbet Ed-Dawwara in the 11th–10th century
BCE on the eastern fringe of the Benjamin hill country may have been connected with the resistance
to Philistine rule and also may be associated with Gilgal (where Joshua crossed the Jordan and Saul
was anointed but he is not sure); see:

Finkelstein, Israel, 'Excavations at Khirbet Ed-Dawwara: an Iron Age site northeast of Jerusalem'. *TA* 17 1990:
    163–208.

By contrast, Na'aman suggests the site was a Philistine stronghold:

Na'aman, Nadav, 'Ḥirbet ed-Dawwāra – a Philistine stronghold on the Benjamin desert fringe'. *ZDPV* 128 2012: 1–9.

The site of Khirbet Qeifaya (see below) may also be associated with the kingdom of Saul. The history of the Benjaminite-Philistine relationship is crucial to understanding the story of the sons of Noah and the history of Saul and David.

The continued presence of Saul in biblical writing attests the continued importance of Benjamin and the continued conflict among the priesthoods even when Israel/Judah no longer had a king. The writings in Persian times continue the conflicts of the 10th century BCE that are the subject of this study. Given the Benjaminite affinity for Mesopotamian traditions expressed in this study, the differing fates for Benjamin and Jerusalem under the Babylonians is part of a tradition of long duration. For the later situation, see:

Davies, Philip R., *The Origins of Biblical Israel* (London: T&T Clark International, 2007), 105–115.
Davies, Philip R., 'The trouble with Benjamin', in Robert Rezetko, Timothy H. Lim, and W. Brian Aucker eds, *Reflection and Refraction: Studies in Biblical Historiography in Honour of A. Graeme Auld* (SVT 113; Leiden: Brill, 2007), 93–111.
Giffone, Benjamin D., 'Sleeping dogs: Benjamin-Judah relations in the Persian Period and the Chronicler's portrait of Saul', unpublished paper presented at the annual conference of the SBL Mid-Atlantic Region, March 15, 2013.
Giffone, Benjamin D., *"Sit at my right hand": The Chronicler's Portrait of the Tribe of Benjamin in the Social Context of Yehud* (LHBOTS 628; London: Bloomsbury T&T Clark, 2016).
Jonker, Louis, 'Of Jebus, Jerusalem and Benjamin: the Chronicler's *Sondergut* in 1 Chronicles 21 against the background of the late Persian era in Yehud', in Paul S. Evans and Tyler F. Williams, eds, *Chronicling the Chronicler* (Winona Lake: Eisenbrauns, 2012), 81–102.
Lipschits, Oded, 'The history of the Benjamin region under Babylonian rule'. *TA* 26 1999: 155–190.
Lipschits, Oded, 'Achaeminid imperial policy, settlement processes in Palestine, and the state of Jeruslaem in the middle of the fifth century BCE', in Oded Lipschits and Manfred Oeming, eds, *Judah and the Judeans in the Persian Period* (Winona Lake: Eisenbrauns, 2006), 19–52.

Benjaminites/Yaminites (see Benjamin)

The connection between the biblical Benjaminites and the Amorite Yaminites only was revealed through the discovery of the Mari Archives when the Yaminites became known. The Benjaminite-Mari connection is an essential component to the Mesopotamian cultural orientation of its priesthood in contrast to the Egyptian and Canaanite influences of the other factions within the Israelite polity. For the Yaminites, Benjaminites, and Israel see:

Astour, Michael, 'Benê-iamina et Jéricho'. *Sem* 9 1959: 5–20.
Bodi, Daniel, 'Is there a connection between the Amorites and the Arameans?' *Aram* 26/1 and 2 2014: 383–409.
Fleming, Daniel E., 'Mari and the possibilities of biblical memory'. *Rev Assyriol Archeol Orient* 92 1998: 41–78.
Fleming, Daniel E., *The Legacy of Israel in Judah's Bible: History, Politics, and the Reinscribing of Tradition* (New York: Cambridge University Press, 2012), 145–149.
Hendel, Ronald S., *Reading Genesis: Ten Methods* (Cambridge: Cambridge University Press, 2010), 40–42.
Hendel, Ronald S., *Remembering Abraham: Culture, Memory, and History in the Hebrew Bible* (New York: Oxford University Press, 2012), 52–54.
Hendel, Ronald S., 'Historical context', in Craig A. Evans, Joel N. Lohr and David. L. Petersen, eds, *The Book of Genesis: Composition, Reception, and Interpretation* (SVT 152; Leiden: Brill, 2012), 51–80, here 65–69.
Lemaire, André, 'La haute Mésopotamie et l'origine des Benê Jacob'. *VT* 34 1984: 95–101.

Malamat, Abraham, *Mari and the Bible: A Collection of Studies* (Jerusalem: Hebrew University, 1975).
Malamat, Abraham, *Mari and the Bible* (Leiden: Brill, 1998).

Bethel

As the second most frequently mentioned city in the Hebrew Bible after Jerusalem, Bethel has a long and complicated story to tell. The actions of Jeroboam making it a sanctuary city for the new northern Kingdom of Israel, Josiah of Judah's actions there, and the story connecting them (I Kings 13) are all subsequent to the story of the Tower of Babel and are not addressed in this study. However, they are indicative of the milieu in which the story was written prior to Jeroboam's action. On the issue of the ziggurat Jacob saw in his dream at Bethel and its meaning, in addition to the Genesis commentaries see:

Carr, David M., 'Genesis 28,10–22 and transmission-historical method: a reply to John Van Seters'. *ZAW* 111 1999: 399–403.
Henderson, A., 'On Jacob's vision at Bethel'. *ET* 4 1893: 151–152.
Houtman, Coral, 'What did Jacob see in his dream at Bethel?'. *VT* 27 1977: 337–352.
Hurowitz, Victor Avigdor, 'Babylon in Bethel – new light on Jacob's dream', in Steven W. Holloway, ed., *Orientalism, Assyriology and the Bible* (HBM 10; Sheffield: Sheffield Phoenix Press, 2006), 436–448.
Millard, Alan R., 'The celestial ladder and the gate of heaven (Gen. Xxviii 12, 17)'. *ET* 78 1966: 86–87.
Van Seters, John, 'Divine encounter at Bethel (Gen.28,10–22) in recent literary critical study of Genesis'. *ZAW* 110 1998: 503–513.
Wyatt, Nicolas, 'Where did Jacob dream his dream?' *SJOT* 1990: 44–57.

For Jacob at Bethel in Gen. 35, in addition to the Genesis commentaries see:

Baden, Joel S., *The Composition of the Pentateuch: Renewing the Documentary Hypothesis* (Anchor Yale Reference Library; New Haven: Yale University Press, 2012), 230–245.

For Bethel as a major cultic site for Israel see:

Davies, Philip R., *The Origins of Biblical Israel* (London: T&T Clark International, 2007), 159–171.
Day, John, *Yahweh and the Gods and Goddesses of Canaan* (JSOT Sup. Series 265; Sheffield: Sheffield Academic Press, 2000), 34–41.
Gomes, Jules, *The Sanctuary of Bethel and the Configuration of Israelite Identity* (Berlin: Walter de Gruyter, 2006).
Hyatt, J. Philip, 'The deity Bethel and the Old Testament'. *JAOS* 59 1939: 81–98.
Knauf, Ernst Axel, 'Bethel: the Israelite impact on Judean language and literature', in Oded Lipschitz and Manfred Lipschitz, eds, *Judah and the Judeans in the Persian Period* (Winona Lake: Eisenbrauns, 2006), 291–349.
Langston, Scott M., *Cultic Sites in the Tribe of Benjamin* (Theology and Religion 200; New York: Peter Lang, 1998).
Matthews, Victor H., 'Back to Bethel: geographical reiteration in biblical narrative'. *JBL* 128 2009: 149–165.
Pioske, Daniel, 'Retracing a remembered past: methodological remarks on memory, history, and the Hebrew Bible'. *BibInt* 23 2015: 291–315, here 308–309.
Yarden, Leon, 'Aaron, Bethel, and the priestly menorah'. *JJS* 26 1975: 39–47.

Bethel was archaeologically prominent during the same Iron I period as Shiloh, its neighbor to the north:

Finkelstein, Israel, and Singer-Avitz, Lilly, 'Reevaluating Bethel'. *ZDPV* 125 2009: 33–48, here 43.

Bitumen

Bitumen is an intriguing topic to me. It appears three times in the Hebrew Bible. It is a material in the construction of the Tower of Babel (Gen. 11: 3). It protects infant Moses in his basket floating on the waters Moses (Ex. 2: 3). It is found by the Dead Sea where some of the Sodom and Gomorrah kings fall into the bitumen pits and presumably drown (Gen. 14: 10), perhaps the first 'I'm melting, I'm melting' scene in literature, a millennial-old precursor to the Wicked Witch in the Wizard of Oz. I suspect the same person wrote all three biblical verses hence the interest to me. For the use of bitumen see:

Abraham, Herbert, *Asphalts and Allied Substances – Their Occurrences Modes of Production, Uses in the Arts and Methods of Testing* (New York: D. Van Nostrand, 1920, 2nd edition).
Barton, George, 'On binding – reeds, bitumen, and other commodities in ancient Babylonia'. *JAOS* 46 1926: 297–302.
Danby, Arthur, *Natural Rock Asphalts and Bitumens: Their Geology, History, Properties and Industrial Applications* (London: Constable, 1913)
Forbes, R. J., *Bitumen and Petroleum in Antiquity* (Leiden: Brill, 1936).

Camp Meetings

Camp meetings are an expressly American phenomenon of the early 1800s. These mostly Methodist events brought together the people in rural America to joyously celebrate the harvest, let off steam, and find mates. They live on in the state fairs. They speak to the reality that we are social beings who periodically need to leave our isolated ruts and encounter other people over food, music, storytelling, and sex just as they did in ancient Israel at various locations like Shiloh and Baal-Peor. For the American version see:

Bruce, Dickson D., Jr., *And They All Sang Hallelujah: Plain-Folk Camp-Meeting Religion, 1800–1845* (Knoxville: University of Tennessee Press, 1974).
Eggleston, Edward, *The Circuit Rider: A Tale of the Heroic Age* (Charles Schribner's Sons, 1878).
Eslinger, Ellen, *Citizens of Zion: The Social Origins of Camp Meeting Revivalism* (Knoxville: University of Tennessee Press, 1999).
Gustafson, Sandra, *Eloquence Is Power: Oratory and Performance in Early America* (Chapel Hill: University of North Carolina Press, 2000).
Johnson, Charles A., 'Frontier camp meeting: contemporary and historical appraisals, 1805–1840'. *MVHR* 37 1950: 91–110.
Johnson, Charles A., *The Frontier Camp Meeting: Religion's Harvest Time* (Dallas: Southern Methodist University Press, 1955).

Canaan (see Canaanite City-States)

Obviously the land of Canaan figures prominently in any attempt to reconstruct Israelite history. Defining exactly what it consisted of, who lived there, and how they lived has become part of the discussion about Israel in a new way. Instead of being reviled in a series of derogatory epithets, they have become a people worthy of study on their own right. Nonetheless, the relation between the Canaanites and the Israelites remains a point of contention within biblical scholarship. In this study, the Canaanite voice appears in the Hebrew Bible through the presence of Canaanites in the city David chose to make his capital. For Canaan see:

Faust, Avraham, *Israel's Ethnogenesis: Settlement, Interaction and Resistance* (London: Equinox, 2006), 93–94.

Fritz, Volkmar, *The Emergence of Israel in the Twelfth and Eleventh Centuries BCE* (Biblical Encyclopedia Vol. 2; Atlanta: Society of Biblical Literature, 2011), 76–78.

Grabbe, Lester L., '"Canaanite": some methodological observations in relation to biblical study', in George J. Brooke, Adrian H. W. Curtis and John F. Healy, eds, *Ugarit and the Bible: Proceedings of the International Symposium on Ugarit and the Bible, Manchester, September 1992* (Münster: Ugarit-Verlag, 1994), 113–122.

Hackett, Jo Ann, 'Canaan', in *OEANE*, 408–409.

Hackett, Jo Ann, 'Canaanites', *OEANE*, 409–412.

Hasel, Michael G., 'Pa-Canaan in the Egyptian New Kingdom: Canaan or Gaza?' *JAEI* 1 2009: 8–17.

Hostetter, Edwin C., 'Geographic distribution of the pre-Israelite peoples of ancient Palestine'. *BZ* 38 1994: 81–86.

Killebrew, Ann E., *Biblical Peoples and Ethnicity: An Archaeological Study of Egyptians, Canaanites, Philistines, and Early Israel, 1300–1100 BCE* (SBLABS 9; Atlanta: Society of Biblical Literature, 2005), 93–148.

Lemche, Niels Peter, *The Canaanites and their Land: The Tradition of the Canaanites* (JSOT Sup. Series 110, Sheffield: JSOT, 1991).

Lemche, Niels Peter, 'City-dwellers or administrators: further light on the Canaanites,' in André Lemaire and Benedikt Otzen, eds, *History and Traditions of Early Israel: Studies Presented to Eduard Nielsen, May 8th 1993* (SVT 50; Leiden: Brill, 1993), 76–89.

Lemche, Niels Peter, 'Where should we look for Canaan? A reply to Nadav Na'aman'. *UF* 28 1996: 767–772.

Mazar, Benjamin, 'Canaan and the Canaanites'. *BASOR* 102 1946: 7–12.

Na'aman, Nadav, 'The Canaanites and their land: a rejoinder'. *UF* 26 1994: 397–418.

Rainey, Anson F., 'Who is a Canaanite? A review of the textual evidence'. *BASOR* 304 1996: 1–15.

Sparks, Kenton L., *Ethnicity and Identity in Ancient Israel: Prolegomena to the Study of Ethnic Settlements and their Expression in the Hebrew Bible* (Winona Lake: Eisenbrauns, 1998), 97–104.

Tammuz, Oded, 'Canaan – a land without limits'. *UF* 33 2001: 501–543.

Tubb, Jonathan, *Canaanites* (Norman: University of Oklahoma, 1998).

Uehlinger, Christoph, 'The "Canaanites" and other "pre-Israelite" peoples in story and history (Parts I and II)'. *FZPhTh* 46 1999: 546–578 and 47 2000: 173–198.

Van Selms, A., 'The Canaanites in the Book of Genesis'. *OtSt* 12 1958: 182–213.

Vaux, Roland de, 'Le pays de Canaan'. *JAOS* 1968: 23–30.

Canaanite City-States (see **Canaan**)

The political organization within the land of Canaan is another topic of discussion within biblical studies. During the Late Bronze Age/New Kingdom prior to the emergence of Israel, Canaan was subject to Egyptian hegemony. It was configured into a series of city states. Instead of Hazor, Megiddo, Shechem, Jerusalem, and Gezer think of Boston, New York, Philadelphia, Baltimore, and Charleston during the colonial era in the United States although over a much greater distance. Each American city dominated its own immediate area but there were vast spaces in-between them. Some cities got along better with England than others. For the Canaanite city-state configuration see:

Finkelstein, Israel, 'The sociopolitical organization of the central hill country in the second millennium BCE', in Avraham Biran and Joseph Aviram, eds, *Biblical Archaeology Today 1990, Pre-Congress Symposium Supplement: Proceedings of the Second International Congress on Biblical Archaeology, Jerusalem, June–July 1990)* (Jerusalem: Israel Exploration Society, Israel Academy of Sciences and Humanities, 1993), 119–131.

Finkelstein, Israel, 'The territorial-political system of Canaan in the Late Bronze Age'. *UF* 28 1996: 221–255.

Na'aman, Nadav, 'The network of Canaanite Late Bronze kingdoms and the city of Asdod'. *UF* 29 1997: 599–626.

Sugarman, Michael, 'Trade and power in Late Bronze Age Canaan', in J. David Schloen and Lawrence E. Stager eds, *Exploring the Longue Durée: Essays in Honor of Lawrence E. Stager* (Winona Lake: Eisenbrauns, 2009), 439–448.

Daily Life: Iron I Israel (1200–1000 BCE)

Besides kings there was life for the 99%. Ancient Canaan was a socially stratified society where upward mobility was scarcely a concept yet alone a reality. Since Israel had no king, it had no forced labor, taxes, or beltway bureaucrats. Undoubtedly the absence of these signs of civilization made it attractive to Canaanites who might vote with their feet. For the daily life of Israelites during the Iron I period see:

Borowski, Oded, *Daily Life in Biblical Times* (Leiden: Brill, 2003).

Hopkins, David C., *The Highlands of Canaan: Agricultural Life in the Early Iron Age* (SWBA Series 3; Sheffield: JSOT Press, 1985).

King, Philip J., and Stager, Lawrence E., *Life in Biblical Israel* (Library of Ancient Israel; Louisville: Westminster John Knox Press, 2001).

London, Gloria, 'A comparison of two contemporaneous lifestyles of the late second millennium BC'. *BASOR* 273 1989: 37–55.

Meyers, Carol, *Discovering Eve: Ancient Israelite Women in Context* (New York: Oxford University Press, 1988).

Meyers, Carol, *Rediscovering Eve: Ancient Israelite Women in Context* (New York: Oxford University Press, 2013).

Stager, Lawrence E., 'The archaeology of the family in Ancient Israel'. *BASOR* 260 1985: 1–35.

Van der Toorn, Karel, 'Nine months among the peasants in the Palestinian highlands: an anthropological perspective on local religion in the Early Iron Age', in William G. Dever and Seymour Gitin, eds, *Symbiosis, Symbolism, and the Power of the Past: Canaan, Ancient Israel, and their Neighbors from the Late Bronze Age through Roman Palaestina, Proceedings of the Centennial Symposium, W. F. Albright Institute of Archaeological Research and American Schools of Oriental Research, Jerusalem, May 29/31, 2000* (Winona Lake: Eisenbrauns, 2003), 393–410.

Dance

Since David danced before the ark of the Lord, dancing is part of the story. While we read the biblical texts today, they arose in a time of oral storytelling and performance that could include music and dancing. For the dance see:

Collon, Dominique Collon, 'Dance in Ancient Mesopotamia'. *NEA* 66 2003: 96–102.

Gabbay, Uri, 'Dance in textual sources from Ancient Mesopotamia'. *NEA* 66 2003: 103–104.

Garfinkel, Yosef, *Dancing at the Dawn of Agriculture* (Austin: Texas University, 2003).

Garfinkel, Yosef, 'The earliest dancing scenes in the Near East'. *NEA* 66 2003: 84–95.

Mazar, Amihai, 'Ritual dancing in the Iron Age'. *NEA* 66 2003: 126–117, 129–132.

Seow, C.L., *Myth, Drama, and the Politics of David's Dance* (HSM 44; Atlanta: Scholars Press, 1989).

Spencer, Patricia, 'Dance in Ancient Egypt,' *NEA* 66 2003: 111–121.

Tubb, Jonathan N., 'Phoenician dance,' *NEA* 66 2003: 122–125.

David

Of all the individuals in the Bible, David is the easiest one to be the subject of a biography. In recent years there have been numerous attempts to chronicle and understand his life plus innumerable articles and monographs about facets of his life. For example see:

Baden, Joel, *The Historical David: The Real Life of an Invented Hero* (San Francisco: HarperOne, 2013).

Bailey, Randall C., *David in Love and War: The Pursuit of Power in 2 Samuel 10–12* (JSOT Sup. Series 75; Sheffield: Sheffield Academic Press, 1990).

Davies, Philip, '"House of David" built on sand'. BAR 20/4 1994, 54–55.

Fleming, Daniel E., *The Legacy of Israel in Judah's Bible: History, Politics, and the Reinscribing of Tradition* (New York: Cambridge University Press, 2012).

Fleming, Daniel E., 'David and the ark: a Jerusalem festival reflected in royal narrative', in David S. Vanderhooft and Abraham Winitzer, eds, *Literature as Politics, Politics as Literature: Essays on the Ancient Near East in Honor of Peter Machinist* (Winona Lake: Eisenbrauns, 2013), 75–95.

Halpern, Baruch, *David's Secret Demons: Messiah, Murderer, Traitor, King* (Grand Rapids: Eerdmans, 2001).

Kirsch, Jonathan, *King David: The Real Life of the Man Who Ruled Israel* (New York: Ballantine Books, 2000).

McKenzie, Steven L., *King David: A Biography* (New York: Oxford University Press, 2000).

Seow, C. L., *Myth, Drama, and the Politics of David's Dance* (HSM 44; Atlanta: Scholars Press, 1989).

Wright, Jacob L., *David, King of Israel, and Caleb in Biblical Memory* (New York: Cambridge University Press, 2014).

Obviously the list could be vastly expanded. Without the proper name in the title or book, it would be difficult to discern from the content that David is in fact the subject given the wide disparity of opinions about him. For purposes of this study, David changed the course of human history when he created the King David Bible.

Deut. 32: 8–9 (see **Elyon**)

All biblical commentaries on the Book of Deuteronomy include these verses. In addition they typically appear in studies on Elyon (see below). The source of interest in the verses derives from implications due to the different versions in the MT and LXX. The relationships among Elyon, Yahweh, Israel, and Jacob within Canaan goes to the heart of the different voices and factions within the Israelite political entity battling of power in Jerusalem. For the debate on these verses see:

Gerald Cooke, 'The sons of (the) God(s)'. *ZAW* 76 1964: 22–47.

Heiser, Michael S., 'Deuteronomy 32: 8 and the sons of God'. *BSac* 158 2001: 52–74.

Roberts, J. J. M., 'The religio-political setting of psalm 47'. *BASOR* 221 1976: 129–132.

Smith, Mark S., *God in Translation: Deities in Cross-Cultural Discourse in the Biblical World* (Grand Rapids: William B. Eerdmans, 2010), 139–143, 195–212.

Skehan, Patrick W., 'The structure of the Song of Moses in Deuteronomy (Deut. 32: 1–43)'. *CBQ* 13 1951: 153–163.

Stevens, David E., 'Does Deuteronomy 32: 8 refer to "sons of God" or "sons of Israel"?' *BSac* 154 1997: 131–141.

Wyatt, Nicolas, 'The seventy sons of Athirat, the nations of the world, Deuteronomy 32.6B, 8–9, and the myth of divine election', in Robert Rezetko, Timothy H. Lim and W. Brian Aucker, eds, *Reflection and Refraction Studies in Biblical Historiography in Honour of A. Graeme Auld* (Leiden: Brill, 2007), 547–556.

Ebal, Mount

Mount Ebal is a scary discovery in biblical archaeology. The existence of an altar from the time of Ramses II to Ramses III consistent with the story of Joshua is too frightening to be taken seriously. Not taking the biblical account seriously historically is one of the bedrock axioms of modern biblical scholarship. On the other hand, there is no reasonable explanation why an obscure short-lived site from early Israel, like Ebal, would even be remembered yet alone included in the biblical narrative unless something of importance had happened there. Typically isolated farmsteads and watchtowers are not the focus of biblical stories and Israelite memories. If it really was an altar, who knows what else in the Bible might be true as well? For the altar at Mount Ebal see:

Hawkins, Ralph K., *The Iron Age I Structure on Mt. Ebal: Excavation and Interpretation* (BBR Supplements 6; Winona Lake: Eisenbrauns, 2012).

Kepmpinski, Aharon, 'Joshua's altar – an Iron Age I watchtower'. BAR 12/1 1986: 42–53.

Pitkänen, Pekka Matti Aukusti, *Central Sanctuary and Centralization of Worship in Ancient Israel from Settlement to the Building of Solomon's Temple: A Historical and Theological Study of the Biblical Evidence in Its Archaeological and Ancient Near Eastern Context* (Ph.D. dissertation, Cheltenham and Gloucester College, 2000), 148–164 (published Piscataway: Gorgias, 2003).

Pitkänen, Pekka Matti Aukusti, *Joshua* (AOTC 6; Nottingham: Apollos, 2010), 192–204.

Zertal, Adam, 'Has Joshua's altar been found on Mt. Ebal?'. BAR 11/1 1985: 26–43.

Zertal, Adam, 'An Early Iron Age cultic site on Mount Ebal: excavation seasons 1982–1987'. *TA* 13–14 1986–1987: 105–165.

Zertal, Adam, 'A cultic center with a burnt-offering altar from Early Iron Age I period at Mt. Ebal', in Matthias Augustin and Klaus-Dietrich Schunck, eds, *Wünschet Jerusalem Frieden: Collected Communications to the XIIth Congress of the International Organization for the Study of the Old Testament, Jerusalem 1986* (Frankfurt am Main: P. Lang, 1988), 137–147.

Zertal, Adam, 'Ebal, Mount', in *ABD* II: 255–258.

Zertal, Adam, '"To the land of the Perizzites and the giants": on the Israelite settlement in the hill country of Manasseh,' in Israel Finkelstein and Nadav Na'aman, eds, *From Nomads to Monarchy: Archaeological and Historical Aspects of Early Israel* (Jerusalem: Israel Exploration Society, 1994), 47–69.

Zevit, Ziony, *The Religion of Ancient Israel: A Synthesis of Parallactic Approaches* (London: Continuum, 2001), 196–201.

Egyptian Theater

As one might expect, Egypt was a society of public performances. In addition to the royal procession and celebrations, in addition to the royal proclamations, edicts, and military victories read aloud on Pharaoh's behalf by authorized people, there also were storytellers who educated and entertained local populations. Of course, if someone were too good a speaker, the individual might be considered a threatening rabble-rouser who needed to be punished! Speaking skills are not germane to the biblical stories in this study but would play a role in the story of Moses. For the theatrical experience in Egypt see:

Baines, John, 'Public ceremonial performance in Ancient Egypt: exclusion and integration', in Takeshi Inornata and Lawrence S. Cohen, eds, *Archaeology of Performance: Theater of Power, Community, and Politics* (London: Rowman and Littlefield, 2006), 261–302.

Bleiberg, Ed, 'Historical text as political propaganda in the New Kingdom'. *BES* 7 1985–1986: 5–13.

Frankfort, Henri, *Kingship and the Gods: A Study of Ancient Near Eastern Religion as the Integration of Society and Nature* (Chicago: University of Chicago Press, 1978), 123–139

Gillam, Robyn, *Performance and Drama in Ancient Egypt* (London: Duckworth, 2005).

Loprieno, Antonio, 'The King's Novel', in Antonio Loprieno, ed., *Ancient Egyptian Literature: History and Forms* (Leiden: Brill, 1996), 277–295.

Redford, Donald B., 'Scribe and speaker', in Ehud Ben Zvi and Michael H. Floyd, eds, *Writing and Speech in Israelite and Ancient Near East Prophecy* (SBLSymS 10; Atlanta: Society of Biblical Literature, 2000), 145–218.

Spalinger, Anthony, 'Königsnovelle and performance', in Vivienne G. Callender, L. Bareš, M. Bárta, and J. Janák, eds, *Times, Signs and Pyramids: Studies in Honour of Miroslav Verner on the Occasion of his Seventieth Birthday* (Prague: Czech Institute of Egyptology, Faculty of Arts Charles University, 2011), 350–374.

Wolinkski, Arlene, 'Egyptian masks: the priest and his role'. *Archaeology* 40 1987: 22–29.

Wyatt, Nicolas, 'The religious role of the king in Ugarit', in K. Lawson Younger Jr., ed., *Ugarit at Seventy-Five: Proceedings of the Symposium Ugarit at Seventy–Five Held at Trinity International University, Deerfield, Illinois, February 18–20, 2005* (Winona Lake: Eisenbrauns, 2007), 41–74, here 58.

The extensive references to performances at Edfu in Ptolemaic times occurred centuries later and are excluded here.

El

While El always has been known from the biblical account, the Ugarit discoveries revealed that he had an extensive life as a Canaanite deity. Part of the biblical discussion has been how much of his Canaanite attributes continued over to his becoming the deity of the new people Israel? In particular, scholars have examined El's relationship to Baal and Asherah as three Canaanite deities versus the relationship as one Israelite and two Canaanite deities. A pivotal series of questions are when did he become equated to the non-Canaanite deity Yahweh and why. For El in the Canaanite pantheon see:

Cross, Frank Moore, *Canaanite Myth and Hebrew Epic: Essays in the History of the Religion of Israel* (Cambridge: Harvard University Press, 1973), 1–43.

Day, John, *Yahweh and the Gods and Goddesses of Canaan* (JSOT Sup Series 265; Sheffield: Sheffield Academic Press, 2000), 13–41.

Hermann, Wolfgang, 'El', in *DDD*, 274–280.

L'Hereux, Conrad E., *Rank Among the Canaanite Gods: El, Ba'al, and the Reph'im* (HSM 21; Missoula: Scholars Press, 1979).

Miller, Paul D., 'El the warrior'. *HTR* 60 1967: 411–433.

Moor, Johannes C. de, 'El, the creator', in Gary Rendsburg, Ruth Adler, Milton Arfa and Nathan Winter, eds, *The Bible World: Essays in Honor of Cyrus H. Gordon* (New York: KTAV Publishing House and Institute of Hebrew Culture and Education of New York University, 1980), 171–187.

Oldenburg, Ulf, *The Conflict between El and Ba'al in Canaanite Religion* (Leiden: Brill, 1969).

Pope, Marvin H., *El in the Ugaritic Texts* (SVT 2; Leiden: Brill, 1955).

Pope, Marvin H., 'The status of El at Ugarit'. *UF* 19 1987: 219–230.

Smith, Mark S., 'Recent study of Israelite religion in light of the Ugaritic texts', in K. Lawson Younger Jr., ed., *Ugarit at Seventy-Five: Proceedings of the Symposium at Seventy-Five held at Trinity International University, Deerfield, Illinois, February 18–20, 2005* (Winona Lake: Eisenbrauns, 2007), 1–25.

Elyon (see Deut. 32: 8–9, El)

The deity Elyon does not appear often in the narrative sections of the Hebrew Bible, more so in the psalms. In this study he is regarded as the pre-Israelite deity of the Jebusites in Jerusalem whose presence continued on into the Hebrew Bible through the actions of the Zadokites. His story then directly relates to the figure of Melchizedek in Gen. 14 where Elyon is his god. For Elyon see:

Cooke, Gerald, 'The sons of (the) God(s)'. *ZAW* 76 1964: 22–47.

Day, John, 'The Canaanite inheritance of the Israelite monarchy', in John Day, ed., *King and Messiah in Israel and the Ancient Near East: Proceedings of the Oxford Old Testament Seminar* (JSOT Sup. Series 270; Sheffield: Sheffield Academic Press, 1998), 72–90, here 78–80.

Elnes, E. E. and Miller, P. D., 'Elyon', in *DDD*, 293–299.

Lack, Rémi, 'Les origines de Elyon, le tres-haut, dans la tradition cultuelle d'Israel'. *CBQ* 24 1962: 44–64.

Lemaire, André, 'Le "Dieu de Jérusalem" à la lumière de'épigraphie', in Caroline Amould-Béhar and André Lemaire, eds, *Jerusalem Antique et Medievale: Mélanges en l'honneur d'Ernest-Marie Laperrousaz* (Paris: Peeters, 2011), 49–58, here 54–55.

Mathews, Joshua G., *Melchizedek's Alternative Priestly Order: A Compositional Analysis of Genesis 14: 18–20 and Its Echoes through the Tanak* (Winona Lake: Eisenbrauns, 2013).

Muilenburg, James, 'The history of the religion of Israel', in *The Interpreter's Bible* (Nashville: Abingdon Press, 1952), 292–348, here 296–297.

Römer, Thomas, *The Invention of God* (Cambridge MA: Harvard University Press, 2015), 78–79, 127–128.

Levi Della Vida, Giorgio, 'Elyon in Genesis 14 18–20'. *JBL* 6 1944: 1–9.

References to Melchizedek are not included in this list.

Ephod

The ephod factors into biblical stories as a conduit between human and the divine. Determining exactly what it is has proved more problematic. The detailed biblical description of the use of the ephod has been deemed accurate and serves as a model for other inquiries to Yahweh. Based on the use of the ephod in I Sam. 2: 28, 14: 3, 22: 18, 23: 6 and 9, and 30: 7, scholars interpret this ephod to be a physical object which could be carried and not the priestly linen vestment it is elsewhere. Deborah Rooke deems Abiathar to be David's 'resident ephod consultant,' which sounds somewhat like the pollsters of American presidential candidates seeking to divine the will of the people. Given this description of Abiathar as the voice of Yahweh to David, Abiathar is the logical candidate to have performed as the voice of Yahweh in the performance of the KDB by David. For the ephod see the Samuel commentaries for these verses. In addition see:

Na'aman, Nadav, 'David's sojourn in Keliah in light of the Amarna Letters'. *VT* 60 2010: 87–97, here 90.

Rooke, Deborah, *Zadok's Heirs: The Role and Development of the High Priesthood in Ancient Israel* (New York: Oxford University Press, 2015), 62.

Van der Toorn, Karel, and Houtman, Cees, 'David and the ark'. *JBL* 113 1994: 209–231, here 210–219.

Ephratah

This village often confused with Ephraim in English translations and linked to Bethlehem turns out to be an important one in understanding David's origins, his connections to the Shiloh priesthood, and to the Calebites in the south. Avi Offer wonders if the Ephrathites did not originate from the south of the Ephraim hill country. Gunnar Lehmann posits that Judah consisted of two main family groups, a Calebite group centered at Hebron and an Ephratah group centered at Bethlehem. David's marriage to Abigail should be seen in the political context in which it occurred. Before there was a narrative of David's rise to power as king of Israel in Jerusalem, there would have been a shorter narrative of his rise to power as king of Judah at Hebron. The same person very well may have written both narratives. For Ephratah the village and the Ephratites see:

Albright, William F., 'Appendix II – Ramah of Samuel'. *AASOR* 4 1922–1923: 112–123, here 118–119n.6.

Demsky, Aaron, 'The clans of Ephrath: their territory and history'. *TA* 13 1986: 46–59.

Japhet, Sara, 'Was David a Judahite or an Ephraimite? Light from the genealogies', in Iain Provan and Mark Boda, eds, *Let us Go Up to Zion: Essays in Honour of H. G. M. Williamson on the Occasion of his Sixty-Fifth Birthday* (Leiden: Brill, 2012), 297–306.

Lehmann, Gunnar, 'The united monarchy in the countryside: Jerusalem, Judah, and the Shephelah during the tenth century BCE', in Andrew G. Vaughn and Ann E. Killebrew, eds, *Jerusalem in the Bible and Archaeology: The First Temple Period* (SBLSymS 18; Atlanta: Society of Biblical Literature, 2003), 117–162, here 144–145.

Leuchter, Mark, 'Jeroboam the Ephraite'. *JBL* 125 2006: 51–72, here 60–61.

Na'aman, Nadav, 'The settlement of the Ephraites in Bethlehem and the location of Rachel's tomb'. *RB* 121 2014: 516–539.

Offer, Avi, '"All the hill country of Judah": from a settlement fringe to a prosperous monarchy', in Israel Finkelstein and Nadav Na'aman, eds, *From Nomadism to Monarchy: Archaeological and Historical Aspects of Early Israel* (Jerusalem: Israel Exploration Society, 1994), 92–121, here 120.

For the Bethlehem-Ephratah connection see Gen. 35: 16, 19; 48: 7; Ruth 4: 11; I Chr. 4: 4; Micah 5: 2. For the Caleb-Ephratah connection see I Chr. 2: 24, 50. For David's rise to power as king of Judah see any commentary on I Samuel and:

Levenson, Jon D., 'I Samuel 25 as literature and history'. *CBQ* 40 1978: 11–28.

Execration Texts

These texts showcase the Egyptian use of voodoo to control the emergence of new peoples in lands the Egyptians considered their own. Despite the magic and occasional campaigns such as to Shechem, the valiant Egyptian effort proved unsuccessful and the Amorites did settle in what became the land of Canaan. For the Execration Texts see:

Ben-Tor, Amnon, 'Do the execration texts reflect an accurate picture of the contemporary settlement map of Palestine?', in Yairah Amit and Nadav Na'aman, eds, *Essays on Ancient Israel in its Near Eastern Context: A Tribute to Nadav Na'aman* (Winona Lake: Eisenbrauns, 2006), 63–87.

Cline, Eric H., *Jerusalem Besieged: From Ancient Canaan to Modern Israel* (Ann Arbor: University of Michigan Press, 2004), 16–17.

Posener, Georges, 'Syria and Palestine *c.* 2160–1780 BC: relations with Egypt', in I. E. S. Edwards, C. J. Gadd and N. G. L. Hammond., eds, *The Cambridge Ancient History Volume 1, Part II* (Cambridge: Cambridge University Press, 1971), 532–558, here 547–558.

Redford, Donald B., 'Execration and execration texts', in *ABD* II: 681–682.

Redford, Donald B., *Egypt, Canaan, and Israel in Ancient Times* (Princeton: Princeton University Press, 1992), 87–93.

Gen. 2: 10–14

Although not directly part of the son stories in this study, I propose that the four-rivers of the world were part of the supplement by Phinehas. He globalized the stage. This action directly impacts the story of Nimrod which is part of this study as well as the sons of Noah and the Tower of Babel. All Genesis commentaries include these verses. In addition see:

Breasted, James Henry, *Ancient Times: A History of the Early World* (New York: Ginn, 1935, 2nd edition), 135.

Carr, David M., 'The politics of textual subversion: a diachronic perspective on the Garden of Eden story'. *JBL* 112 1993: 577–595.

Feinman, Peter, 'Where is Eden?', in JoAnn Scurlock and Richard H. Beal, eds, *Creation and Chaos: A Reconsideration of Hermann Gunkel's Chaos Kampf Hypothesis* (Winona Lake: Eisenbrauns, 2013), 172–189.

Hill, Carol A., 'The Garden of Eden: A Modern Landscape'. PSCF 52 2000: 31–46.

King, Philip J. and Stager, Lawrence E., *Life in Biblical Israel* (Louisville: Westminster John Knox, 2001), 171.

McKenzie, John L., 'The literary characteristics of Genesis 2–3'. *TS* 15 (1954) 541–572, here 553–554, reprinted as 'The literary characteristics of Genesis 2–3,' in John L. McKenzie, *Myths and Realities: Studies in Biblical Theology* (London: Geoffrey Chapman 1963), 146–181.

Noort, Ed, 'A Gan-Eden in the context of the mythology of the Hebrew Bible', in Gerard P. Luttikhuizen, ed., *Paradise Interpreted: Representations of Biblical Paradise in Judaism and Christianity* (TBN 2; Leiden: Brill, 1999), 21–36.

Radday, Yehuda T., 'The four rivers of paradise'. *HS* 23 1982: 23–31.

Sauer, James A., 'The river runs dry: creation story preserves historical memory'. BAR 22: 4, 1996: 52–54, 57, 64.

Sauer, James A., 'A new climate and archaeological view of the early biblical traditions', in Michael D. Coogan, J. Cherry Exum and Lawrence Stager, eds, *Scripture and Other Artifacts: Essays on the Bible and Archaeology in Honor of Philip J. King* (Louisville: Westminster, 1994), 366–398.

Sullivan, Walter, 'Signs of ancient river'. *NYT* March 30, 1993.

Whitney, K. William, Jr., in Hermann Gunkel, *Creation and Chaos in the Primeval Era and the Eschaton* (Grand Rapids: William B. Eerdmans, 2006), 324 n.90.

Yamauchi, Edwin M., *Africa and the Bible* (Grand Rapids: Baker Academic, 2005) 38–39.

Gen. 14 (The Kings from the East)

At the dawn of biblical archaeology in the late 1800s, the story of Gen. 14 presented an irresistible lure to salivating archaeologists eager to demonstrate a scientific link between the archaeological record and the Bible. The figures in this chapter and Nimrod dominated the archaeological discourse. William Foxwell Albright, the dean of biblical archaeology, devoted studies on the identity of these figures from the 1920s to the 1960s and that effort alone became a chapter in a dissertation. Every one of the biblical writers analyzed in this study had a hand in the composition of this pericope in cycle 2 of the KDB on Abram. Excavating the passage would have greatly added to the length of this book. All Genesis commentaries deal with this story and the list of articles on it could be greatly expanded. For some early explorations of Gen. 14 see:

Hardwick, Stanley E., *Change and Constancy in William Foxwell Albright's Treatment of Early Old Testament History and Religion, 1918–1958* (Ph.D. dissertation, New York University, 1958), 130–190.

Pinches, Theophilus G., 'Certain inscriptions and records referring to Babylonia and Elam and their rulers, and other matters'. *JTVI* 29 1897: 43–90.

Pinches, Theophilus G., *The Old Testament: In Light of the Historical Records and Legends of Assyria and Babylonia* (London: Society for Promoting Christian Knowledge, 1902), Chapter VI, Abraham – a *short* account of this period, with the story of Amraphel, Arioch, and Tidal, (emphasis added), 192–241.

Sayce, A. H., 'The fourteenth chapter of Genesis'. *ET* 4 1892: 14–19.

Sayce, A. H., *The 'Higher Criticism' and the Verdict of the Monuments* (London: Society for Promoting Christian Knowledge, 1894), 160–171.

Sayce, A. H., *Patriarchal Palestine* (London: Society for Promoting Christian Knowledge, 1895), 65–80.

Sayce, A. H., 'Archaeological commentary on Genesis [XIV]'. *ET* 8 1897: 461–465.

Sayce, A. H., 'The archaeology of Genesis XIV'. *ET* 17 1906: 498–504.

Sayce, A. H., 'The Chedor-laomer tablets'. *PSBA* 28 1906: 193–200 and 247–251.

Sayce, A. H., 'The Chedor-laomer tablets'. *PSBA* 29 1907: 7–17.

Gibeah

Gibeah is an important city as the capital of Saul's kingdom. For the debate over the location of the site of biblical Gibeah in contrast to biblical Geba or Gibeon see:

Albright, William F., 'Excavations and results at Tell el-Fûl'. *AASOR* 4 1923: 1–89.

Albright, William F., 'A new campaign of excavations at Gibeah of Saul'. *BASOR* 52 1933: 6–12.

Arnold, P. A., *Gibeah: The Search for a Biblical City* (JSOT Sup. Series 79; Sheffield: Sheffield Academic Press, 1990).

Miller, J. M., 'Geba/Gibeah of Benjaminin'. *VT* 25 1975: 145–166.

Schniedewind, William M., 'The search for Gibeah: notes on the historical geography of central Benjamin', in Aren M. Maeir and Pierre de Miroschedi, eds, *I will Speak Riddles of Ancient Times: Archaeological and Historical Studies in Honor of Amihai Mazar on the Occasion of His Sixteeth Birthday* (Winona Lake: Eisenbrauns, 2006), 711–722.

Giloh

Giloh was a small short-lived settlement near Jerusalem in the Iron I period. Its identity as Jebusite or Israelite has significant repercussions for the ethnic heritage of Bathsheba and the political meaning of David's marriage. For the site of Giloh see:

Ahlström, Gösta W., 'Giloh: a Judahite or Canaanite settlement'. *IEJ* 34 1982: 170–172.

Ahlström, Gösta W., *The History of Ancient Palestine* (Minneapolis: Fortress Press, 1993), 356–357.

Cushman, Beverly W., 'The politics of the royal harem and the case of Bat-Sheba'. *JSOT* 30 2006: 327–343, here 336–337.

Fritz, Volkmar, *The City in Ancient Israel* (Sheffield: Sheffield Academic Press, 1995), 57.

Hawkins, Ralph, 'Giloh and the Iron Age I cultic landscape,' unpublished paper presented at the Middle West Branch of the American Oriental Society, February 17, 2007.

Killebrew, Ann E., *Biblical Peoples and Ethnicity: An Archaeological Study of Egyptians, Canaanites, Philistines, and Early Israel, 1300–1100 BCE* (SBLABS 9; Atlanta: Society of Biblical Literature, 2005), 165.

Mazar, Amihai, 'Giloh: an early Israelite settlement near Jerusalem'. *IEJ* 31 1981: 1–36.

Mazar, Amihai, 'Jerusalem and its vicinity in Iron Age I', in Israel Finkelstein and Nadav Na'aman, eds, *From Nomadism to Monarchy: Archaeological and Historical Aspects of Early Israel* (Jerusalem: Israel Exploration Society, 1994), 70–91, here 83.

Zevit, Zionyt, *The Religion of Ancient Israel: A Synthesis of Parallactic Approaches* (London: Continuum, 2001), 97–198 n.122.

For Bathsheba's father from Giloh, see:

Bailey, Randall C. 'Eliam', in *ABD* II: 459–460.

Habiru/Hebrew

The alleged connection between the *habiru* from the Amarna Letters and the Hebrews originated at the moment the Egyptian texts were translated in the late 1800s. At this point, it generally is recognized that term is not an ethnic one but a social one referring to stateless people. The fascination with equating the terms may obscure the issue of the meaning of the term Hebrew itself. For the ongoing debate see:

Cazelles, Henri, 'The Hebrews', in D. J. Wiseman, ed., *Peoples of Old Testament Times* (Oxford: Clarendon Press, 1973), 1–28.

Greenberg, Moshe, 'Hab/piru and Hebrews', in Benjamin Mazar, ed., *The World History of the Jewish People, Vol II: The Patriarchs* (New Brunswick: Rutgers University Press, 1970), 188–200.

Gottwald, Norman, *The Tribes of Yahweh: A Sociology of the Religion of Liberated Israel, 1250–1050 BCE* (Maryknoll: Orbis Books, 1979), 401–425.

Lemche, Niels Peter, 'Habiru, Hapiru', in *ABD* III: 6–10.

Lemche, Niels Peter, 'Hebrew', in *ABD* III: 95.

Na'aman, Nadav, 'Ḫabiru and Hebrews: the transfer of a social term to the literary sphere'. *JNES* 45 1986: 271–288.

Rainey, Anson F., 'Unruly elements in Late Bronze Age society', in David Noel Freedman and Avi Hurvitz, eds, *Pomegranates and Golden Bells: Studies in Biblical, Jewish, and Near Eastern Ritual, Law, and Literature in Honor of Jacob Milgrom* (Winona Lake: Eisenbrauns, 1995), 481–486.

Hazor

The sheer size of the site makes Hazor an important city in Israel. The targeted mutilation of Egyptian statues in the 13th century BCE around the time Israel emerged in history also makes for an irresistible site for historical reconstructions. For the debate on the destroyers and Hazor's position see:

Ben-Tor, Amnon, 'The fall of Canaanite Hazor – the "who" and "when" questions', in Seymour Gitin, Amihai Mazar and Ephraim Stern, eds, *Mediterranean Peoples in Transition: Thirteenth to Early Tenth Centuries BCE* (Jerusalem: Israel Exploration Society, 1998), 456–467.

Ben-Tor, Amnon, 'Hazor and the chronology of northern Israel: a reply to Israel Finkelstein'. *BASOR* 317 2000: 9–15.

Ben-Tor, Amnon, 'The sad fate of statues and the mutilated statues of Hazor', in Seymour Gitin, J. Edward Wright, and J. P. Dessel, eds, *Confronting the Past: Archaeological and Historical Essays on Ancient Israel in Honor of William G. Dever* (Winona Lake: Eisenbrauns, 2006), 3–16.

Ben-Tor, Amnon, and Ben-Ami, Doron, 'Hazor and the archaeology of the tenth century BCE'. *IEJ* 48 1988: 1–37.

Ben-Tor, Amnon, and Zuckerman, Sharon, 'Hazor at the end of the Late Bronze Age: back to basics'. *BASOR* 350 2008: 1–6.

Bienkowski, Piotor, 'The role of Hazor in the Late Bronze Age'. *PEQ* 117 1987: 50–61.

Finkelstein, Israel, 'Hazor and the north in the Iron Age: a low chronology perspective'. *BASOR* 314 1999: 55–70.

Finkelstein, Israel, 'Hazor at the end of the Late Bronze Age'. *UF* 37 2005: 341–349.

Kitchen, Kenneth A., 'Hazor and Egypt: an egyptological and Ancient Near-Eastern perspective'. *SJOT* 16 2002: 309–313.

Malamat, Abraham, 'Hazor "the head of all those kingdoms"'. *JBL* 79 1960: 12–19.

Malamat, Abraham, 'Northern Canaan and the Mari texts', in James A. Sanders, ed., *Near Eastern Archaeology in the Twentieth Century: Essays in Honor of Nelson Glueck* (New York: Doubleday, 1970), 164–177, reprinted in Abraham Malamat, *Mari and the Bible: A Collection of Studies* (Jerusalem: Hebrew University, 1975), 20–32.

Malamat, Abraham, 'Trade relations between Mari and Hazor (state of research, 2002)', in Seymour Gitin, J. Edward Wright and J. P. Dessel, eds, *Confronting the Past: Archaeological and Historical Essays on Ancient Israel in Honor of William G. Dever* (Winona Lake: Eisenbrauns, 2006), 351–355.

Schäfer-Lichtenberger, 'Hazor – a city state between the major powers'. *SJOT* 15 2001: 104–122.

Yadin, Yigael, *Hazor: The Head of All Those Kingdoms* (London: Oxford University Press, 1972).

Zarzecki-Peleg, Anabel, 'Hazor – a Syrian city-state in Mitanni's orbit?' *UF* 43 2011: 337–567.

Holy Land

In the second half of the 19th century, the reality of the Holy Land as a place that existed and could be visited sank in especially in England and the United States. Steamships made visiting possible and truly the journey was perceived to be one not only in space but in time. In particular, people saw themselves walking the land the patriarchs and matriarchs had walked. To see the primitive past was a primary focus of the visits and contributed to the detriment of the people living there in the present. They were not stock figures in some Holy Land Museum Park. The degrading views of the ancient peoples of the land by modern scholars would be particularly pronounced in the exegesis of the sons of Cain (Song of Lamech), sons of God, and sons of Noah. A different form of degradation would be expressed in the story of Nimrod. For western visitation to the Holy Land in the late 19th century see:

Ben Arieh, Yehoshua, *The Rediscovery of the Holy Land in the Nineteenth Century* (Jerusalem: Magness Press, 1979).

Davis, John, *The Landscape of Belief: Encountering the Holy Land in Nineteenth Century American Art and Culture* (Princeton: Princeton University Press, 1996).

Davis, Moshe, ed., *With Eyes Toward Zion: Scholars Colloquium on American – Holy Land Studies* (New York: Arno Press, 1977).

Klatzker, David, *American Christian Travelers to the Holy Land, 1821–1939* (Ph.D. dissertation, Temple University, 1987).

Kuklick, Bruce, *Puritans in Babylon: The Ancient Near East and American Intellectual Life, 1880–1930* (Princeton: Princeton University Press, 1996).

Long, Burke O., *Imagining the Holy Land: Maps Models and Fantasy Travels* (Bloomington: Indiana University Press, 2003).

Silberman, Neil Asher, *Digging for God and Country: Exploration, Archeology, and the Secret Struggle for the Holy Land, 1799–1917* (New York: Knopf, 1982).

Hyksos

The Hyksos ruled Egypt during the Second Intermediate Period, roughly 1650–1550 BCE, as the 15th Dynasty. Little was known about them archaeologically until Manfred Bietak began excavating at the Hyksos capital city best known as Avaris. His excavations revealed a Middle Bronze Age city comparable to those in the land of Canaan. Since at least the 3rd century BCE and probably earlier, there have been people who have thought the Hyksos were connected in some way to the Exodus. For the Hyksos see almost anything by Bietak for the last three decades. See in particular:

Bietak, Manfred, 'The aftermath of the Hyksos in Avaris', in Rakefet Sela-Sheffy and Gideon Toury, eds, *Culture Contacts and the Making of Cultures: Papers in Homage to Itamar Even-Zohar* (Tel Aviv: Unit of Culture Research Tel Aviv University, 2011), 19–65.

Bietak, Manfed, 'On the historicity of the exodus: what Egyptology today can contribute to assessing the sojourn in Egypt', in Thomas E. Levy, Thomas Schneider and William H. C. Propp, eds, *Israel's Exodus in Transdisciplinary Perspective: Text, Archaeology, Culture, and Geoscience* (Heidelberg-New York-Dordrecht-London: Springer, 2015), 17–36.

Marée, Marcel, ed., *The Second Intermediate Period (Thirteenth-Seventeenth Dynasties): Current Research, Future Prospects* (OLA 192; Leuven: Peters, 2010).

Oren, Eliezer D., ed., *The Hyksos: New Historical and Archaeological Perspectives* (University Museum Symposium Series 8; Philadelphia: University Museum, University of Pennsylvania, 1997).

Redford, Donald B., 'The Hyksos invasion in history and tradition'. *Or* 39 1970: 1–51.

Redford, Donald B. and Weinstein, James, 'Hyksos', in *ABD* III: 341–348.

Ryholt, K. S. B., *The Political Situation in Egypt During the Second Intermediate Period* c. *1800–1550 BC* (Copenhagen: K.S.B. Ryholt and Museum Tusculanum Press, 1997).

Van Seters, John, *The Hyksos: A New Investigation* (New Haven: Yale University Press, 1966).

Israelite History – Iron I (1200–1000 BCE)

This time period marks the emergence of Israel in history. Even without the Hebrew Bible there would be a story to tell about these people but it would be a little more difficult. For Israel in this period see:

Bloch-Smith, Elizabeth, 'Israelite ethnicity in Iron I: archaeology preserves what is remembered and what is forgotten in Israel's history'. *JBL* 122 2003: 410–425.

Bloch-Smith, Elizabeth and Nakhai, Beth Alpert, 'A landscape comes to life: the Iron I period'. *NEA* 62 1999: 62–92, 101–127.

Faust, Avraham, *Israel's Ethnogenesis: Settlement, Interaction and Resistance* (London: Equinox, 2006).

Faust, Avraham, 'How did Israel become a people? The genesis of Israelite identity'. BAR 35/6 2009: 62–69, 92–94.

Feinman, Peter, 'Egypt and Israel: from Ramses II to Ramses VI,' unpublished paper presented at the annual conference of the Society of Biblical Literature, Atlanta, November 24, 2015.

Finkelstein, Israel, *The Archaeology of the Israelite Settlement* (Jerusalem: Israel Exploration Society, 1988).

Finkelstein, Israel, 'Ethnicity and origin of the Iron I settlers in the highland of Canaan: can the real Israel stand up?' *BA* 59 1996: 198–212.

Finkelstein, Israel and Na'aman, Nadav, eds, *From Nomadism to Monarchy: Archaeological and Historical Aspects of Early Israel* (Jerusalem: Israel Exploration Society, 1994).

Frendo, Anthony J., 'Five recent books on the emergence of ancient Israel: a review article'. *PEQ* 124 1992: 144–151.

Fritz, Volkmar, *The Emergence of Israel in the Twelfth and Eleventh Centuries BCE* (Biblical Encyclopedia, Vol. 2; Atlanta: Society of Biblical Literature, 2011).

Halpern, Baruch, 'The dawn of an age: Megiddo in the Iron Age I', in J. David Schloen and Lawrence E.

Stager, eds. *Exploring the Long Durée: Essays in Honor of Lawrence E. Stager* (Winona Lake: Eisenbrauns, 2009), 151–163, here 157.

Halpern, Baruch, *The Emergence of Israel in Canaan* (Chico: Scholars Press, 1983).

Halpern, Baruch, 'The settlement of Canaan', in *ABD* V: 1120–1143.

Hawkins, Ralph K., *How Israel Became a People* (Nashville: Abingdon Press, 2013).

Hess, Richard S., 'Early Israel in Canaan: a survey of recent evidence and interpretations'. *PEQ* 125 1993: 125–142.

Killebew, Ann E., *Biblical Peoples and Ethnicity: An Archaeological Study of Egyptians, Canaanites, Philistines, and Early Israel, 1300–1100 BCE* (SBLABS 9; Atlanta: Society of Biblical Literature, 2005), 149–185.

Levin, Yigal, '"And there was peace between Israel and the Amorites" (I Sam 7: 14): Israelites and Canaanites in Late Iron I', unpublished paper presented at annual conference of the Society of Biblical Literature, Hebrew Bible, History, and Archaeology session, November 24, 2014.

Mazar, Amihai, 'Jerusalem and its vicinity in Iron Age I', in Israel Finkelstein and Nadav Na'aman, eds, *From Nomadism to Monarchy: Archaeological and Historical Aspects of Early Israel* (Jerusalem: Israel Exploration Society, 1994), 70–91.

Mazar, Amihai Mazar, 'From 1200 to 850 BCE: remarks on some selected archaeological issues', in Lester L. Grabbe, ed., *Israel in Transition: From Late Bronze II to Iron IIa (c. 1250 850 BCE)* (LHBOTS 491; European Seminar in Historical Methodology 7; London: T&T Clark, 2008), 86–120.

Miller, Robert D., II, 'Identifying earliest Israel'. *BASOR* 333 2004: 55–68.

Miller, Robert D., II, *Chieftains of the Highland Clans: A History of Israel in the 12th and 11th Centuries BC* (Grand Rapids: William B. Eerdmans, 2005).

Na'aman, Nadav, 'The conquest of Canaan in the Book of Joshua and in history', in Israel Finkelstein and Nadav Na'aman, eds, *From Nomadism to Monarchy: Archaeological and Historical Aspects of Early Israel* (Jerusalem: Israel Exploration Society, 1994), 218–281.

Pitkänen, Pekka, 'Ethnicity, assimilation and the Israelite settlement'. *TynBul* 55 2004: 161–182.

Rainey, Anson F., 'Whence came the Israelites and their language?' *IEJ* 57 2007: 41–64.

In addition, every history of Israel will cover this period.

Jerusalem: Middle Bronze Age Archaeology

The first half of the 2nd millennium BCE marks the beginning of significant archaeological remains in the city of Jerusalem related to the background of the city David would later make his capital. For Jerusalem in this time period see:

Cahill, Jane, 'Jerusalem at the time of the United Monarchy: the archaeological evidence', in Andrew G. Vaughn and Ann E. Killebrew, eds, *Jerusalem in the Bible and Archaeology: The First Temple Period* (SBLSymS 18; Atlanta: Society of Biblical Literature, 2003), 13–80, here 21–26, 73–83.

Na'aman, Nadav, 'Canaanite Jerusalem and its central hill country neighbours in the second millennium BCE'. *UF* 24 1992: 175–291.

Reich, Ronny and Shukron, Eli, 'Light at the end of the tunnel'. BAR 25/1 1999: 22–33, 72.

Reich, Ronny and Shukron, Eli, 'The history of the Gihon spring in Jerusalem'. *Levant* 36 2004: 211–223.

Reich, Ronny and Shukron, Eli, 'A new segment of the Middle Bronze fortification in the city of David'. *TA* 37 2010: 141–153.

Reich, Ronny and Shukron, Eli, 'The Middle Bronze Age II water system in Jerusalem', in Caroline Amould-Béhar and André Lemaire, eds, *Jerusalem Antique et Medievale: Mélanges en l'honneur d'Ernest-Marie Laperrousaz* (Paris: Peeters, 2011), 17–29.

Khirbet Qeifaya

The recently excavated site of Khirbet Qeifaya overlooking the Valley of Elah where the story of David and Goliath is set is forcing a renewed look at the origins of the Israelite monarchy. The one-level site dated to 1020–980 BCE places it in the time of Saul and/or David. The discovery of cultic installations/rooms and inscriptions including with the name Ishbaal, son and successor of Saul, at a possibly military site on the border with Philistia has led to contentious exchanges about who built it, when, and why. I suspect it is a window into the achievements of Saul as king that have been downplayed by a pro-Davidic author. For the fight over Khirbet Qeifaya see:

Dagan, Yehudah, 'Khirbet Qeiyafa in the Judean Shephelah: some considerations'. *TA* 36 2009: 68–81.
Finkelstein, Israel and Fantalkin, Alexander, 'Khirbet Qeiyafa: an unsensational archaeological and historical interpretation'. *TA* 39 2012: 38–63.
Finkelstein, Israel and Piasetzky, Eli, 'Khirbet Qeiyafa: absolute chronology'. *TA* 37 2010: 84–88.
Galil, Gershon, 'The Hebrew inscription from Khirbet Qeiyafa/Neta'm: script, language, literature and history'. *UF* 2009 41: 194–242.
Garfinkel, Yosef and Ganor, Saar, 'Khirbet Qeiyafa: Sha'arayim'. *JHS* 8/22 2008: 1–10, jhs.2008.v8.a22.
Garfinkel, Yosef and Ganor, Saar, 'Khirbet Qeiyafa in survey and in excavations: a response to Y. Dagan'. *TA* 37 2010: 67–78.
Garfinkel, Yosef, Ganor, Saar and Hasel, Michael, 'The contribution of Khirbet Qeiyafa to our understanding of the Iron Age Period'. *Strata* 28 2010: 39–54.
Garfinkel, Yosef, Ganor, Saar and Silver, Joseph Baruch, 'Rejected! Qeiyafa's unlikely second gate'. BAR 43/1 2017: 37–43, 59.
Garfinkel, Yosef, Golub, Mitka R., Misgav, Haggai and Ganor, Saar, 'The 'Išba'al inscription from Khirbet Qeiyafa'. *BASOR* 373 2015: 217–233.
Garfinkel, Yosef and Kang, Hoo-Goo, 'The relative and absolute chronology of Khirbet Qeiyafa: very Late Iron Age I or very Early Iron Age'. *IEJ* 61 2011: 171–183.
Levin, Yigal, 'The identification of Khirbet Qeiyafa: a new suggestion'. *BASOR* 367 2012: 73–86.
Millard, Alan, 'The ostracon from the days of David found at Khirbet Qeiyafa'. *TynBul* 62 2011: 1–13.
Na'aman, Nadav, 'In search of the ancient name of Khirbet Qeiyafa'. *JHS* 8/21 2008: 1–8, jhs.2008.v8.a21.
Pioske, Daniel D., 'Memory and its materiality: the case of Early Iron Age Khirbet Qeiyafa and Jeruslaem'. *ZAW* 127 2015: 78–95.
Puech, Émile, 'L'ostracon de Khirbet Qeyafa et les débuts de la royauté en Israël'. *RB* 2010 117: 162–184.
Rollston, Christopher, 'The Khirbet Qeiyafa ostracon: methodological musings and caveats'. *TA* 38: 2011: 67–82.
Singer-Avitz, Lily, 'The relative chronology of Khirbet Qeiyafa'. *TA* 37 2010: 79–83.
Tubb, Jonathan, 'Editorial: Early Iron Age Judah in the light of recent discoveries at Khirbet Qeiyafa'. *PEQ* 142 2010: 1–2.

Large Stone Structure (see **Stepped Stone Structure**)

The Large Stone Structure in the City of David has become another battleground among biblical scholars. Whether it is dated earlier then the time of David or later has implications for Israelite history as it relates to the United Monarchy of David and Solomon. I consider it to be a Jebusite structure built after Egyptians withdrew from the land and before David made Jerusalem his capital. For the Large Stone Structure see:

Faust, Avraham, 'The Large Stone Structure in the City of David: a reexamination'. *ZDPV* 126 2010: 116–130.
Faust, Avraham, 'Did Eilat Mazar find David's palace?' BAR 38/5 2012: 47–52,70.
Finkelstein, Israel, 'Has King David's palace been found?' *TA* 34: 142–164.
Finkelstein, Israel, 'The "Large Stone Structure" in Jerusalem: reality versus yearning'. *ZDPV* 127 2011: 1–10.

Mazar, Amihai, 'The spade and the text: the interaction between archaeology and Israelite history relating to the tenth–ninth centuries BCE', in H. G. M. Williamson, ed., *Understanding the History of Ancient Israel* (Oxford: Oxford University Press, 2007), 143–171, here 152–153.

Mazar, Amihai, 'Jerusalem in the 10th century BCE: the glass half full', in Yairah Amit and Nadav Na'aman, eds, *Essays on Ancient Israel in its Near Eastern Context: A Tribute to Nadav Na'aman* (Winona Lake: Eisenbrauns, 2006), 255–272, here 257–265.

Mazar, Amihai, 'Archaeology and the biblical narrative: the case of the United Monarchy', in Reinhard G. Kratz and Hermann Spieckermann, eds, *One God – One Cult – One Nation: Archaeological and Biblical Perspectives* (BZAW 405; Berlin: Walter de Gruyter, 2010), 29–58, here 40–46.

Mazar, Eilat, 'Did I find King David's palace?' BAR 2006 32/1: 16–27, 70.

Na'aman, Nadav, 'Biblical and historical Jerusalem in the tenth and fifth–fourth centuries BCE'. *Bib* 93 2012: 21–42, here 26–28.

Late Bronze Age (1550–1200 BCE)

The Late Bronze Age is an academic construct that roughly corresponds with the Egyptian New Kingdom (18th and 19th Dynasties). In political terms it commences with the ouster of Hyksos rule ending the Second Intermediate Period and begins centuries of Egyptian conquest and hegemony in the land of Canaan. That hegemony ends around 1139 BCE and the 1200 BCE figure derives from the widespread collapse and disarray experienced from the Aegean to Mesopotamia around that time. The Late Bronze Age contributed to the formation of Israel and the memories of this period became part of the Hebrew Bible. For the 'world' situation during this period including Egypt, Canaan, and their legacy see:

Atac, Mehmet-Ali, 'The historical memory of the Late Bronze Age in the Neo-Assyrian palace reliefs', in David Nadali, ed., *Envisioning the Past through Memories: How Memory Shaped Ancient Near Eastern Societies* (London: Bloomsbury Academic, 2016), 69–83.

Bar, Shay, Kahn, Dan'el and Shirley, J. J., eds, *Egypt, Canaan and Israel: History, Imperialism, Ideology and Literature – Proceedings of a Conference at the University of Haifa, 3–7 May 2009* (CHANE 52; Leiden: Brill, 2011).

Feldman, Marian H., 'Assur Tomb 45 and the birth of the Assyrian empire'. *BASOR* 343 2006: 21–43.

Feldman, Marian H., *Diplomacy by Design: Luxury Arts and an 'International Style' in the Ancient Near East 1400–1200 BCE* (Chicago: University of Chicago Press, 2006).

Gitin, Seymour, Mazar, Amihai and Stern, Ephraim, eds, *Mediterranean Peoples in Transition: Thirteenth to Early Tenth Centuries BCE* (Jerusalem: Israel Exploration Society, 1998).

Liverani, Mario, 'The Great Power club', in Raymond Cohen and Raymond Westbrook, eds, *Amarna Diplomacy: The Beginnings of International Relations* (Baltimore: Johns Hopkins University Press, 2000), 15–27.

Thum, Jen, 'When Pharaoh turned landscape into a stela: royal living rock monuments at the edges of the Egyptian world'. *NEA* 79 2016: 68–77.

Ward, William A. and Joukowsky, Martha Sharp, eds, *The Crisis Years: The 12th Century BC from Beyond the Danube to the Tigris* (Dubuque: Kendall Hunt, 1992).

For Egypt during this period see:

Dodson, Aidan, *Poisoned Legacy: The Fall of the Nineteenth Egyptian Dynasty* (Cairo: American University Press in Cairo, 2010).

For Canaan during this period of Egyptian hegemony see:

Bunimovitz, Shlomo, 'Social-political transformations in the central hill country in the Late Bonze-Iron I transition', in Israel Finkelstein and Nadav Na'aman, eds, *From Nomadism to Monarchy: Archaeological and Historical Aspects of Early Israel* (Jerusalem: Israel Exploration Society, 1994), 179–202, here 195–202.

Hasel, Michael G., *Domination and Resistance: Egyptian Military Activity in the Southern Levant, c. 1300–1185 BC* (Leiden: Brill, 1998).

Higginbotham, Carolyn, *The Egyptianization of Ramesside Palestine* (Ph.D. Dissertation, Johns Hopkins University, 1994).

Killebrew, Ann E., *Biblical Peoples and Ethnicity: An Archaeological Study of Egyptians, Canaanites, Philistines, and Early Israel, 1300–1100 BCE* (SBLABS 9; Atlanta: Society of Biblical Literature, 2005), 21–92.

Morris, Ellen, *The Architecture of Imperialism: Military Bases and the Evolution of Foreign Policy in Egypt's New Kingdom* (Leiden: Brill, 2005).

Na'aman, Nadav, 'The Exodus story: between historical memory and historiographical composition'. *JANER* 11 2011: 39–69, here 44–55.

Oren, Eliezer, '"Governors' residences" in Canaan under the New Kingdom'. *JSSEA* 14 1984: 37–56.

Redford, Donald B., *Egypt, Canaan, and Israel in Ancient Times* (Princeton: Princeton University Press, 1992), 125–237.

Singer, Itamar, 'Egyptians, Canaanites, and Philistines in the period of the emergence of Israel', in Israel Finkelstein and Nadav Na'aman, eds, *From Nomadism to Monarchy: Archaeological and Historical Aspects of Early Israel* (Jerusalem: Israel Exploration Society, 1994), 282–338.

Weinstein, James, 'The Egyptian empire in Palestine: a reassessment'. *BASOR* 241 1981: 1–29.

Literacy (see **Alphabet**)

Part of the debate about the writing of the Hebrew Bible is: who are the people in Israel capable of reading and writing at a given point in time? Literacy generally is defined for these purposes as not who can complete a fill-in-the blank form with simple information (date, name, address, phone number, email address, credit card number, etc.), but who can read and write narrative prose. The actual numbers in ancient societies are considered quite limited as a percentage of the population. For literacy see:

Byrne, Ryan, 'The refuge of scribalism in Iron I Palestine'. *BASOR* 345 2007: 1–31.

Carr, David M., *Writing on the Tablet of the Heart: Origins of Scripture and Literature* (New York: Oxford University Press, 2005).

Haran, Menahem, 'On the diffusion of literacy and schools in ancient Israel', in J. A. Emerton, ed., *Congress Volume Jerusalem 1986* (SVT 40, Leiden: Brill, 1988), 81–95.

Hess, Richard S., 'Writing about writing: abecedaries and evidence for literacy in ancient Israel'. *VT* 56 2006: 342–346.

Lemaire, André, 'Levantine literacy *c.* 1000–750 BCE', in Brian B. Schmidt, ed., *Contextualizing Israel's Scared Writings: Ancient Literacy, Orality, and Literary Production* (AIL 22; Atlanta: SBL Press, 2015), 11–45.

Lipiński, Edward, 'Royal and state scribes in ancient Jerusalem', in J. A. Emerton, ed., *Congress Volume Jerusalem 1986* (SVT 40; Leiden: Brill, 1988), 157–164.

Parkinson, R. B., *Reading Ancient Egyptian Poetry among Other Histories* (Malden-Oxford: Wiley-Blackwell, 2009).

Rollston, Christopher A., *Writing and Literacy in the World of Ancient Israel: Epigraphic Evidence from the Iron Age* (SBLABS 11; Atlanta: Society of Biblical Literature, 2010).

Rollston, Christopher A. 'Scribal curriculum during the first temple period', in Brian B. Schmidt, ed., *Contextualizing Israel's Scared Writings: Ancient Literacy, Orality, and Literary Production* (AIL 22; Atlanta: SBL Press, 2015), 71–101.

Maryannu

Maryannu, possibly a Hurrian-derived term, were known as elite chariot warriors particularly from Egyptian lists of captives from the land of Canaan. For the source documents see:

Pritchard, James B., *Ancient Texts Relating to the Old Testament* (Princeton: Princeton University Press, 1955), 22, 237, 241, 262.

For historical interpretations see:

Ahlström, Gösta W., *The History of Palestine* (Minneapolis: Fortress Press, 1993), 173, 211, 213, 235, 346.

Drews, Robert, *The Coming of the Greeks: Indo-European Conquests in the Aegean and the Near East* (Princeton: Princeton University Press, 1988), 59–60, 155–157.

Morrison, Martha, 'Hurrians', in *ABD* III: 335–338.

Redford, Donald B., *Egypt, Israel, and Canaan in Ancient Times* (Princeton: Princeton University Press, 1992), 136,195,198.

Merneptah's Canaanite Coalition versus Israel
(see Merneptah Stele and Merneptah: Cour de la Cachette)

The Merneptah Stele mentions Israel and three Canaanite cities. It does not necessarily list all the Canaanite cities which rose up in opposition to Egyptian rule; nor does it mention the allied Canaanite cities which provided ground support to him. For the political situation at the time Merneptah claimed to have destroyed the seed of Israel see:

Kahn, Dan'el, 'A geo-political and historical perspective of Merneptah's policy in Canaan', in Gershon Galil, Ayelet Gilboa, Aren M. Maeir and Dan'el Kahn, eds, *The Ancient Near East in the 12th–10th centuries BCE: Culture and History: Proceedings of the International Conference, held at the University of Haifa, 2–5 May, 2010* (AOAT 392; Münster: Ugarit-Verlag, 2012), 255–268.

Manassa, Colleen, *The Great Karnak Inscriptions of Merneptah: Grand Strategy in the 13th Century BC* (YES 5; New Haven: Yale University Press, 2003).

Na'aman, Nadav, 'The Egyptian-Canaanite correspondence', in Raymond Cohen and Raymond Westbrook, eds, *Amarna Diplomacy: The Beginnings of International Relations* (Baltimore: Johns Hopkins University Press, 2000), 125–138, here 137.

Na'aman, Nadav, 'Praises to the Pharaoh in response to his plans for a campaign to Canaan', in Tzvi Abusch, John Huehnergard and Piotor Steinkeller, eds, *Lingering over Words: Studies in Ancient Near Eastern Literature in Honor of William L. Moran* (Atlanta: Scholars Press, 1990), 397–405.

Biblical scholarship has focused on a literary analysis of the Merneptah Stele text itself as it relates to Israel.

Merneptah: Cour de la Cachette
(see Merneptah's Canaanite Coalition versus Israel and Merneptah Stele)

In 1978, Egyptologist Frank J. Yurco began advocating that reliefs on a wall at Karnak that had been attributed to Ramses II really belonged to his son Merneptah. He then suggested that the pictures illustrated the very campaign in the Merneptah Stele mentioning Israel. If true, then Merneptah left not only the first mention of Israel in the archaeological record but the first images. There has been general agreement that Yurco is correct in his recognition of the true Pharaoh responsible for the images but debate over which images are of Israel and what the significance is. For the Cour de la Cachette see:

Brand, Peter J., 'Usurped cartouches of Merenpah at Karnak and Luxor', in Peter J. Brand and Louise Cooper, eds, *Causing His Name To Live: Studies in Egyptian Epigraphy and History in Memory of William J. Murnane* (CHANE 37; Leiden: Brill, 2009), 30–48.

Brand, Peter J., 'The date of the war scenes on the south wall of the great hypostyle hall and the west wall of the Cour de la Cachette at Karnak and the history of the late Nineteenth Dynasty', in Mark Collier and Steven Snape, eds, *Ramesside Studies in Honour of K. A. Kitchen* (Bolton: Rutherford Press, 2011), 51–84.

Rainey, Anson F., 'Rainey's challenge'. BAR 17/6 1991;56–60, 93.

Yurco, Frank J., 'Merneptah's Palestinian campaign'. *JSSEA* 8 1978: 70.

Yurco, Frank J., 'Merneptah's Canaanite campaign'. *JARCE* 23 1986: 189–215.

Yurco, Frank J., '3,200-year-old picture of Israelites found in Egypt'. BAR 16 1990: 20–38.

Yurco, Frank J., 'Yurco's response'. BAR 17/6 1991: 61.

Merneptah Stele
(see **Merneptah's Canaanite Coalition versus Israel** and **Merneptah: Cour de la Cachette**)

The discovery of the Merneptah Stele in 1896 with its mention of Israel was big news. For reports from that time see:

Breasted, James Henry, 'The latest from Petrie'. *Biblical World* 7/2 1896: 139–140.

Breasted, James Henry, 'The Israel tablet'. *Biblical World* 9 1897: 62–68.

ET 7 1896: 387–388, 445–447, 548–549; 8 1896: 76.

Petrie, W. M. Flinders, 'Egypt and Israel'. *Contemporary Review* 69 1896/Jan.–June: 617–627.

Petrie, W. M. Flinders, *Six Temples at Thebes* (London: Bernard Quaritch, 1897), 26–30.

Since then there has been an ongoing debate about what Merneptah meant and what actually happened.

Mesha Stele and Mount Nebo

According to biblical tradition (Deut. 34), Moses was buried at Mount Nebo in Moab. The Mesha Stele specifically mentions a sanctuary to Yahweh at Nebo in the 9th century BCE while the biblical account in II Kings 3 of the same Israelite campaign against Mesha does not. For the burial site of Moses at Nebo (Deut. 34) see:

Cortese Enzo, and Niccacci, Alviero, 'Nebo in biblical tradition', in Michelle Piccirillo and Eugenio Alliata, *Mount Nebo: New Archaeological Excavations 1967–1997* (Jerusalem: Franciscan Printing Press, 1998), 53–64.

For Mesha's actions see:

Bernhardt, Heinz, 'The political situation in the east of Jordan during the time of King Mesha', in Adnan Hadido, ed., *Studies in the History and Archaeology of Jordan*, Vol. I (Amman: Department of Antiquities, 1982), 163–167.

Clermont-Ganneau, M., 'La stèle de Mésa: examen critique du texte'. *JA* 9 1887: 72–112.

Dearman, Andrews, ed., *Studies in the Mesha Inscription and Moab* (SBLABS 2; Atlanta: Scholars Press, 1989).

Emerton, J. A., 'The value of the Moabite stone as an historical source'. *VT* 52 2002: 483–492.

Lemaire, André, 'La stèle de Mésha et l'histoire de l'ancien Israël', in Daniele Garrone and Felice Israel, eds, *Storia e Tradizioni di Israele: Seritti in onore di J. Alberto Soggin* (Brescia: Paideia, 1991), 143–169.

Na'aman, Nadav, 'King Mesha and the foundation of the Moabite monarchy'. *IEJ* 47 1997: 83–92.

Na'aman, Nadav, 'Royal inscription versus prophetic story: Mesha's rebellion according to biblical and Moabite historiography', in Lester L. Grabbe, ed., *Ahab Agonistes: The Rise and Fall of the Omri Dynasty* (LHBOTS 421; London: T&T Clark, 2005), 145–183, here 173.

Routledge, Bruce, 'The politics of Mesha: segmented identities and state formation in Iron Age Moab'. *JESHO* 43 2000: 221–256.

Routledge, Bruce, *Moab in the Iron Age: Hegemony, Polity, Archaeology* (Philadelphia: University of Pennsylvania Press, 2004), 27–40, 114–153, 213–221.

Sanders, Seth L., 'What was the alphabet for? The rise of written vernaculars and the making of Israelite national literature'. *Maarav* 11 2004: 25–56, here 55.

Schmidt, Brian B., 'Memorializing conflict: toward an Iron Age "shadow" history of Israel's earliest literature', in Brian B. Schmidt, ed., *Contextualizing Israel's Sacred Writings: Ancient Literacy, Orality, and Literary Production* (AIL 22; Atlanta: SBL Press, 2015), 103–132, here 121–124.

Midian

Despite the harsh wilderness image in northwest Arabia, there turns out to have been a flourishing city in what is known as the land of Midian, modern Quarrayah. The widespread distribution of its distinctive pottery into the Negev, Sinai, and the Arabah attest a city linked to a larger economic zone and the production of copper. In this study, the existence of Midian relates to the sons of Cain, the geographic setting for the narrative, and city building.

Bawden, Garth, 'Painted pottery of Tayma and problems of cultural chronology in Northwest Arabia', in John Sawyer and David Clines, eds, *Midian, Moab and Edom: The History and Archaeology of Late Bronze and Iron Age Jordan and North-West Arabia* (JSOT Sup. Series 24; Sheffield: Sheffield Academic Press, 1983), 37–52.

Coats, George W. 'Moses in Midian'. *JBL* 92 1973: 3–10.

Dumbrell, William J., 'Midian – a land or a league?' *VT* 25 1975: 323–337.

Knauf, Ernst Axel, 'Midianites and Ishmaelites', in John E. A. Sawyer and David J. A. Clines, eds, *Midian, Moab and Edom: The History and Archaeology of Late Bronze Age and Iron Age Jordan and North-West Arabia* (JSOT Sup. Series 24; Sheffield: JSOT Press, 1983), 147–162.

Mendenhall, George E., 'Midianites', in *ABD* IV: 815–818.

Parr, Peter, 'Qurayya', in ABD V: 594–596.

Parr, Peter, 'Contacts between north-west Arabia and Jordan in the Late Bronze and Iron Ages', in Adnan Hadidi, ed., *Studies in the History and Archaeology of Jordan* (Amman, Jordan: Dept of Antiquities, 1982), I: 127–133.

Rothenberg, Beno, and Glass, Jonathan, 'Midianite pottery', in John Sawyer and David Clines, eds, *Midian, Moab and Edom: The History and Archaeology of Late Bronze and Iron Age Jordan and North-West Arabia* (JSOT Sup. Series 24; Sheffield: Sheffield Academic Press, 1983), 65–124.

Nebuchadnezzar I

Nebuchadnezzar I is an unsung figure in biblical scholarship. At the end of the 19th and beginning of the 20th centuries, archaeologists had yet to reveal who he was in contrast to such figures as Gilgamesh, Sargon the Great, and Hammurabi. These other personages were incorporated into various hypothesises related to the history of Israel and the writing of the Hebrew Bible. Nebuchadnezzar I missed out on this formative period of exegetical formulation. Ironically, of all the aforementioned figures, his example is the one which probably had the most impact on David and the biblical writers after his death. For Nebuchadnezzar I see:

Brinkman, J. A., *A Political History of Post-Kassite Babylonia 1158–722 BC* (Rome: Pontificium Institutum, 1968).

Lambert, W. G., 'The reign of Nebuchadnezzar I: a turning point in the history of Ancient Mesopotamian religion', in W. S. McCullough, ed., *The Seed of Wisdom: Essays in Honor of Th. J. Meek* (Toronto: University of Toronto Press, 1964), 3–13.

Longman, Tremper, III, *Fictional Akkadian Autobiography: A Generic and Comparative Study* (Winona Lake: Eisenbrauns, 1991).

Miller, Patrick D., Jr. and Roberts, J. J. M., *The Hand of the Lord: A Reassessment of the 'Ark Narrative'* (Baltimore: Johns Hopkins University Press, 1977), 10–16, 77–85.

Roberts, J. J. M., 'Nebuchadnezzar I's Elamite crisis in theological perspectives', in Maria deJong Ellis, ed., *Essays on the Ancient Near East in Memory of Jacob Joel Finkelstein* (Hamden: Archon Books, 1977), 183–187, reprinted in J. J. M. Roberts, *The Bible and the Ancient Near East: Collected Essays* (Winona Lake: Eisenbrauns, 2002), 83–92.

Wiseman, D. J., 'Assyrian and Babylonia *c.* 1200–1000 BC', in I. E. S. Edwards, ed., *History of the Middle East and the Aegean Region c. 1380–1000 BC* (Cambridge Ancient History 2/2; Cambridge: Cambridge University Press, 1975), 443–481.

For the legacy of Nebuchadnezzar I into Assyrian and Persian times see:

Nielsen, John P., 'Marduk's return: Assyrian imperial propaganda, Babylonian cultural, and the *akitu* festival of 667 BC', in Martin Bommas, Juliette Harrison and Phoebe Roy, eds, *Memory and Urban Religion in the Ancient World* (London: Bloomsbury, 2012), 3–32.

Nielsen, John P., '"I overwhelmed the king of Elam": remembering Nebuchadnezzar I in Persian Babylonia', in Jason M. Silverman and Caroline Waerzeggers, eds, *Political Memory in and After the Persian Empire* (ANEM 13; Atlanta: SBL Press, 2015), 53–73.

Nephilim (see also Sons of God)

The Nephilim are a key character in the story of the sons of God. In addition to the exegesis on them in the Genesis commentaries, there have been various studies seeking to ascertain their true nature. The Nephilim are part of every commentary on Numbers as well. In addition see:

Coxon, P. W., 'Nephilim', in *DDD*, 618–620.

Doak, Brian R., *The Last of the Rephaim: Conquest and Cataclysm in the Heroic Ages of Ancient Israel* (Ilex Series 7; Boston: Ilex Foundation and Washington: Center for Hellenic Studies, Trustees for Harvard University/Cambridge: Harvard University Press, 2012), 53–70.

Doak, Brian, 'The embarrassing and alluring biblical giant', http: //www.bibleinterp.com/articles/2015/12/doa398002.shtml.

Hendel, Ronald S., 'The Nephilim were on the Earth: Genesis 6: 1–4 and its near eastern context', in Christoph Auffarth and Loren T. Stuckenbruck, eds, *The Fall of Angels* (TBN 6; Leiden: Brill, 2004), 11–34, here 30–32.

Hess, Richard S., 'Nephilim', in *ABD* IV: 1072–1073.

Kilmer, Anne Draffkorn, 'The Mesopotamian counterparts to the biblical Nĕpīlîm', in Edgar W. Conrad and Edward G. Newing, eds, *Perspectives on Language and Text: Essays and Poems in Honor of Francis I. Andersen's Sixtieth Birthday July 28, 1985* (Winona Lake: Eisenbrauns, 1987), 39–43.

Kugel, James Kugel, 'The descent of the wicked angels and the persistence of evils', in Gary A. Anderson and Joel Kaminsky, eds, *The Call of Abraham: Essays on the Election of Israel in Honor of Jon D. Levenson* (Notre Dame: University of Notre Dame Press, 2013), 210–235.

Levine, Baruch A., *Numbers 1–20* (AB 4A; New York: Doubleday, 1993), 378.

Mussies, Gerard, 'Giants', in *DDD*, 343–345.

Nelson, William B, Jr., 'Nephilim', in David Noel Freedman, ed., *Dictionary of the Bible* (Grand Rapids: Eerdmans, 2000), 958–959

Ware, Michael, 'Charlie Sheen's last stand'. *Newsweek* July 2 and 9, 2012, 40–45, here 44.

Wright, G. E., 'The troglodytes of Gezer'. *PEQ* 69 1937: 67–78.

Wright, G. E., 'Troglodytes and giants in Palestine'. *JBL* 57 1938: 305–309.

Nimrod

Nimrod, of course, is the central figure in the story about Nimrod. He differs from the other figures in the stories of this study due to the archaeological search to link the biblical and Mesopotamian records as detailed in Part I. He also is part of every Genesis commentary. In addition see:

Albright. William F., 'The Babylonian matter in the predeuteronomic primeval history (JE) in Gen.1–11'. *JBL* 58 1939: 91–103, here 100.

Day, John, *From Creation to Babel: Studies in Genesis 1–11* (London: Bloomsbury, 2013), 16–189.

Dick, Michael B., 'Nimrod as a symbol of neo-Assyrian kingship,' unpublished paper presented at the annual conference of the Society of Biblical Literature, Assyriology and the Bible section, Philadelphia, November, 21 2005.

Gispen, W. H., 'Who was Nimrod?', in John H. Skilton and Milton C. Fisher, eds, *The Law and the Prophets: Old Testament Studies Prepared in honor of Oswald Thompson Allis* (Nutley: Presbyterian and Reformed Publishing Co., 1974), 207–214.

Hirsch, Emil G., Seligsohn, M. and Bacher, Wilhelm, 'Nimrod', in Joseph Jacobs, ed., *The Jewish Encyclopedia* (New York: Funk & Wagnalls, 1906), 309–311.

Hom, Mary Katherine Y. H., '"...A mighty hunter before Yahweh": Genesis 10: 9 and the moral-theological evaluation of Nimrod'. *VT* 60 2010: 63–68.

Knohl, Israel, 'Nimrod, son of Cush, king of Mesopotamia, and the dates of P and J', in Chaim Cohen, ed., *Birkat Shalom: Studies in the Bible, Ancient Near Eastern Literature, and Post-Biblical Judaism, Presented to Shalom M. Paul on the Occasion of His Seventieth Birthday* (Winona Lake: Eisenbrauns, 2008), 45–52.

Kraeling, Emil G., 'The origin and real name of Nimrod'. *AJSL* 38 1922: 214–220.

Lipiński, Edward, 'Nimrod and Aššur'. *RB* 73 1966: 77–93.

Machinist, Peter, 'Assyria and its image in First Isaiah'. *JAOS* 103 1983: 719–737, here 720 n2.

Machinist, Peter, 'Nimrod', in *ABD* IV: 1116–1118.

Speiser, E. A., 'In search of Nimrod', in J. J. Finkelstein and M. Greenberg, eds, *Oriental and Biblical Studies: Collected Writings of E. A. Speiser* (Philadelphia: University of Pennsylvania Press, 1967), 41–52, reprinted in Richard Hess and David Toshio Tsumura, eds, *I Studied Inscriptions from before the Flood: Ancient Near Eastern, Literary, and Linguistic Approaches to Genesis 1–11* (SBTS 4; Winona Lake: Eisenbrauns, 1994), 270–277.

Sommerfeld, Walter, 'The Kassites of ancient Mesopotamia: origins, politics, and culture', in *CANE*, 917–930.

Stein, Diana L., 'Kassites', in *OEANE*, 271–275.

Van der Horst, P. W., 'Nimrod after the bible', in Karel van der Toorn and P. W. van der Horst, 'Nimrod before and after the bible', *HTR* 83 1990: 1–29 here 16–29.

Van der Toorn, Karel, 'Nimrod before the bible', in Karel van der Toorn and Pieter W. van der Horst, 'Nimrod before and after the bible', *HTR* 83 1990: 1–29, here 1–16.

Ninurta

Ninurta is a lesser known Mesopotamian warrior-deity later eclipsed by Marduk. His name has been associated with the derivation of Nimrod. For Ninurta see:

Annus, Amar, *The God Ninurta: in the Mythology and Royal Ideology of Ancient Mesopotamia* (SAAS 14; Helsinki: Neo-Assyrian Text Corpus Project 2002).

Cooper, Jerrold, *The Return of Ninurta to Nippur* (Rome: Pontificium Institutum Biblicum, 1978).

Lambert, W. G., 'Ninurta mythology in the Babylonian epic of creation', in K. Hecker and W. Sommerfeld, eds, *Keilschriftliche Literaturen: Rencontre Assyriologique Internationale, Münster, 8.–12.7.1985* (Berlin: Dietrich Reimer, 1986), 55–60.

Penglase, Charles, *Greek Myths and Mesopotamia: Parallels and Influence in the Homeric Hymns and Hesiod* (London: Routledge, 1994), 49–72.

Porter, Barbara N., 'The anxiety of multiplicity: concepts of divinity as one and many in ancient Assyria', in Barbara N. Porter, ed., *One God or Many? Concepts of Divinity in the Ancient World* (Chebeague Island, Maine: Transactions of the Casco Bay Archaeological Institute, 2000), 211–271.

N'rn

The n'rn provide an alternate view to the traditional one of Hebrew slavery in Egypt. Along with the Hyksos, these warriors from across the river in the time of Ramses add to the political mix confronting the Pharaoh at that time particularly since he owed his life to them ... and they knew it. For the role of these Semitic soldiers in the showdown with the Hittites at the Battle of Kadesh see:

Goedicke, Hans, 'Considerations of the Battle of Kadesh'. *JEA* 52 1966: 71–80.
Kitchen, Kenneth A., *Pharaoh Triumphant: The Life and Times of Ramesses II* (Warminster: Aris & Phillips, 1982), 60.
Manassa, Colleen, *The Great Karnak Inscriptions of Merneptah: Grand Strategy in the 13th Century BC* (YES 5; New Haven: Yale University Press, 2003), 53.
Morris, Ellen, *The Architecture of Imperialism: Military Bases and the Evolution of Foreign Policy in Egypt's New Kingdom* (Leiden: Brill, 2005), 362–366.
Obsomer, Claude, 'La Bataille de Qadech de Ramsès: les *n'arin, sekou tepy* et questions d'itinéraires,' in Christina Karlshausen and Claude Obsomer, eds, *De la Nubie à Qadech: La Guerre dans l'Égypte/From Nubia to Kadesh: War in Ancient Egypt* (Brussels: Safran, 2016), 81–168.
Schulman, Alan, 'The N'RN at the Battle of Kadesh'. *JARCE* 1 1962: 47–52.
Schulman, Alan, 'The N'RN at Kadesh once again'. *JSSEA* 11 1981: 7–19.
Spalinger, Anthony, 'Notes on the reliefs of the Battle of Kadesh', in Hans Goedicke, ed., *Perspectives on the Battle of Kadesh* (Baltimore: Halgo, 1985), 1–42, here 3.
Zudhi, Omar, 'Benteshina and the n'rn division'. *JSSEA* 8 1977–1978: 141–142.

One may also make the case that the Egyptians merely appropriated a Semitic term but applied it to Egyptians. The n'rn then can be understood as specially chosen Egyptian soldiers (see Morris and Obsomer above).

Pharaoh's Daughter

The marriage between Solomon and Pharaoh's daughter is another contentious issue in biblical scholarship even if one accepts the existence of Solomon. The position here is that Solomon was real and really did marry Pharaoh's daughter. As a fabrication one wonders who would have been fooled by it; on the other hand, consider the millions of people who believe a native-born Christian American President really was a foreign-born Moslem. The position here is that for Zadok, the marriage was a return to the Egyptian–Canaanite relationship with an enhanced position for the new kingdom; for Phinehas, it exhibited the world stage on which he envisioned the new kingdom; for Ahijah, it represented a step backward necessitating a call for a new exodus. Commentaries on I Kings address this issue as generally do histories of Israel. In addition for Pharaoh's daughter as wife of Solomon (not the Pharaoh's daughter who rescued Moses) see:

Carr, David M., *The Formation of the Hebrew Bible: A New Reconstruction* (New York: Oxford University Press, 2011), 368–369.
Cohen, Shaye J. D., 'Solomon and the daughter of Pharaoh: intermarriage, conversion, and the impurity of women'. *JANES* 16–17 1984–85: 23–37.
Fritz, Volkmar, 'Solomon and Gezer', in Seymour Gitlin, J. Edwatd Wright and J. P. Dessel, eds, *Confronting the Past: Archaeological and Historical Essays on Ancient Israel in Honor of William G. Dever* (Winona Lake: Eisenbrauns, 2006), 303–307.

Jeon, Yong Ho, 'The retroactive re-evaluation technique with Pharaoh's daughter and the nature of Solomon's corruption in I Kings 1–12'. *TynBul* 62 2011: 15–40.

Kitchen, Kenneth A., *The Third Intermediate Period in Egypt (1100–650 BC)* (Warminster: Aris & Phillips, 1973), 280–282.

Lemaire, André, 'Salomon et la fille de Pharaon: un problème d'interprétation historique', in Aren M. Maeir and Pierre de Miroschedi, eds, *I Will Speak Riddles of Ancient Times: Archaeological and Historical Studies in Honor of Amihai Mazar on the Occasion of His Sixteeth Birthday* (Winona Lake: Eisenbrauns, 2006), 699–710.

Na'aman, Nadav, 'Sources and composition in the history of Solomon', in Lowell K. Handy, ed., *The Age of Solomon: Scholarship at the Turn of the Millennium* (Studies in the History and Culture of the Ancient Near East 11; Leiden: Brill, 1997), 57–80, here 63–64, 77.

Priesthoods

The priesthoods comprise the political factions battling for power after the death of David and are the creators of the six son stories of this study. Typically they are viewed more from a religious perspective than as political parties and players in the game of power politics in the Israelite Beltway. Part of the debate concerns the king functioning as high-priest, the lack of political power by a cultic priest, and the lack of cultic power beyond the sanctuary in Jerusalem. The conflicts among the priesthoods continued long after the 10th century BCE setting for this study. For the debate on the configuration of priesthoods see:

Allan, Nigel, 'The identity of the Jerusalem priesthood during the exile'. *Heythrop Journal* 23 1982: 259–269.

Baden, Joel, 'The violent origins of the Levites: text and tradition', in Mark A. Leuchter and Jeremy M. Hutton, eds, *Levites and Priests in Biblical History and Tradition* (Leiden: Brill, 2012), 103–116.

Blenkinsopp, Joseph, *Gibeon and Israel: The Role of Gibeon and the Gibeonites in the Political and Religious History of Early Israel* (Cambridge: Cambridge University Press, 1972).

Cody, Aelred, *A History of Old Testament Priesthood* (AnBib 25; Rome: Pontifical Biblical Institute, 1969).

Cohen, Martin A., 'The role of the Shilonite priesthood in the United Monarchy of ancient Israel'. *HUCA* 36 1965: 39–98.

Cross, Frank Moore, *Canaanite Myth and Hebrew Epic: Essays in the Religion of Israel* (Cambridge MA: Harvard University Press, 1973), 195–215.

Friedman, Richard Elliott, 'The historical Exodus: the evidence for the Levites leaving Egypt and the introduction of YHWH into Israel', in *The Torah: A Historical and Contextual Approach*, undated, http: //thetorah.com/the historical exodus/.

Friedman, Richard Elliott. 'The Exodus is not fiction: an interview with Richard Elliot Friedman'. *Reform Judaism*, undated, http: //www.reformjudaism.org/exodus-not-fiction.

Friedman, Richard Elliott, 'Levites and priests in history and tradition,' unpublished paper presented at the annual conference of the Society of Biblical Literature, San Diego, November 24, 2014.

Friedman, Richard Elliott, 'Love your neighbor: only Israelites or everyone?'. BAR 40/5 2014: 48–52.

Frolov, Serge, '"Days of Shiloh" in the kingdom of Israel'. *Bib* 76 1995: 210–218.

Halpern, Baruch, 'Levitic participation in the reform cult of Jeroboam I'. *JBL* 95 1976: 31–42.

Leuchter, Mark A., 'The Fightin' Mushites', unpublished paper presented at the Columbia Hebrew Bible Seminar, March 17, 2010.

Leuchter, Mark A., 'The Fightin' Mushites'. *VT* 62 2012: 479–500.

Meek, Theophile James, 'Aaronites and Zadokites'. *AJSL* 45 1929: 149–166.

Morgenstern, Julian, 'A chapter in the history of the high-priesthood'. *AJSL* 55 1938: 1–24, 360–377.

Nelson, Richard D., 'The role of the priesthood in the Deuteronomistic history', in Gary N. Knoppers and J. Gordon McConville, *Reconsidering Israel and Judah: Recent Studies on the Deuteronomistic History* (Winona Lake: Eisenbrauns: 2000), 179–193; reprinted from J. A. Emerton, ed., *Congress Volume Leuven, 1989* (SVT 43; Leiden: Brill, 1991), 132–147.

Polk, Timothy, 'The Levites in the Davidic-Solomonic empire'. *Studia Biblica et Theologica* 9 1979: 3–22.

Popp, William H., 'Ithamar', in *ABD* III: 579–581.

Rehm, Merlin, 'Levites and priests', in *ABD* IV: 297–310.

Robinson, Robert B., 'The Levites in the pre-monarchic period'. *Studia Biblica et Theologica* 8 1978: 3–24.

Rooke, Deborah W., 'Kingship as priesthood: the relationship between the high priesthood and the monarchy', in John Day, ed., *King and Messiah in Israel and the Ancient Near East: Proceedings of the Oxford Old Testament Seminar* (JSOT Sup. Series 270; Sheffield: Sheffield Academic Press, 1998), 187–208.

Rooke, Deborah W., *Zadok's Heirs: The Role and Development of the High Priesthood in Ancient Israel* (New York: Oxford University Press, 2015).

Vaux, Roland de, *Ancient Israel: Its Life and Institutions* (New York: McGraw-Hill, 1961), 358–403.

Wellhausen, Julius, *Prolegomena to the History of Israel* (Atlanta: Scholars Press, 1994, reprint 1885 edition), 121–151.

White, Marsha C., 'The Elohistic depiction of Aaron: a study in the Levite-Zadokite controversy', in J. A. Emerton, ed., *Studies in the Pentateuch* (Leiden: Brill, 1990), 149–159.

Yarden, Leon, 'Aaron, Bethel, and the priestly menorah'. *JJS* 26 1975: 39–47.

Psalm 78 (see **Psalm 132** and **Sacral Kingship**)

Psalm 78 like Psalm 132 (below) is part of the battle for power among the competing priesthoods. The story of Israel could be expressed in poetry at festivals and celebrations. Not all polemics were in narrative format.

Campbell, Antony F. 'Psalm 78: a contribution to the theology of tenth century Israel'. *CBQ* 41 1979: 51–79.

Carroll, R. P., 'Psalm LXXVIII: vestiges of a tribal polemic'. *VT* 21 1971: 133–150.

Leuchter, Mark, 'The reference to Shiloh in Psalm 78'. *HUCA* 77 2006: 1–31.

Stern, Phillip, 'The eighth century dating of Psalm 78 re-argued'. *HUCA* 66 1995: 41–65.

Psalm 132 (see **Psalm 78** and **Sacral Kingship**)

The debate about this psalm focuses on its depiction of an actual procession and if so, its date of origin. The development of the alphabet prose narrative for political purposes did not eliminate heroic poetry. Its focus shifted from a human warrior to a divine one and the poetry as psalms became part of the royal ritual ... especially when nobody had the stature to perform the KDB after David died.

Bentzen, Aage, 'The cultic use of the story of the ark in Samuel'. *JBL* 67 1948: 37–53.

Fretheim, Terrence E., 'Psalm 132: a form-critical study'. *JBL* 86 1967: 289–300.

Hillers, Delbert R. 'Ritual procession of the ark and Ps 132'. *CBQ* 30 1968: 40–55.

Kruse, Heinz, 'Psalm CXXXII and the royal Zion festival'. *VT* 33 1983: 279–297.

Laato, Antti, 'Psalm 132 and the Development of the Jerusalemite/Israelite Royal Ideology'. *CBQ* 54 1992: 49–66.

Patton, Corrine L., 'Psalm 132: a methodological inquiry'. *CBQ* 57 1995: 643–654.

Queen Mother

The Queen Mother adds a comparatively new area of study with the rise of feminist biblical scholarship. At a time when dynastic succession was through the wife of the male leader, the woman behind the throne deserves close scrutiny. Just as the position of king was new to Israel so too was the position of queen. Several of David's wives have stories of their own especially Michal, daughter of Saul, and Abigail, wife of an important Calebite. The best known wife, of course, is Bathsheba, the one who was there at the end and whose son succeeded David. If David changed the course of human history through the creation of the KDB than Bathsheba becomes one of the most significant women in human history as well. For the position of Queen Mother see:

Ackerman, Susan, 'The Queen Mother and the cult in ancient Israel'. *JBL* 112 1993: 385–401.

Ackerman, Susan, *Warrior, Dancer, Seductress, Queen: Women in Judges and Biblical Israel* (Anchor Bible Reference Library; New York: Doubleday, 1998), 128–180.

Ackerman, Susan, 'At home with the goddess', in William G. Dever and Seymour Gitin, eds, *Symbiosis, Symbolism, and the Power of the Past: Canaan, Ancient Israel, and their Neighbors from the Late Bronze Age through Roman Palaestina* (Winona Lake: Eisenbrauns, 2003), 455–468, here 460–461.

Andreasen, Niels-Erik A., 'The role of the Queen Mother in Israelite society'. *CBQ* 45 1983: 179–194.

Ben-Barak, Zafrida, 'The status and right of the *gĕbîrâ*'. *JBL* 110 1991: 23–34, reprinted in Athalya Brenner, ed., *Feminist Companion to Samuel and Kings* (Sheffield: Sheffield Academic Press, 1994), 170–185.

Cushman, Beverly W., 'The politics of the royal harem and the case of Bat-Sheba'. *JSOT* 30 2006: 327–343.

Knauf, Ernest Axel, 'The queen's story: Bathsheba, Maacah, Athaliah and the "historia of early kings"', *Lectio Difficilor: European Electronic Journal for Feminist Exegesis* 2 2002) http://www.lectio.unibe.ch/02_2/axel.htm.

Na'aman, Nadav, 'Queen Mothers and ancestors cult in Judah in the first temple period', *Berührungspunkte: Studien zur Sozial- und Religionsgeschichte Israels und seiner Umwelt; Festschrift für Rainer Albertz zu seinem 65. Geburtstag* (AOAT 350; Münster: Ugarit-Verlag, 2008), 479–490.

Smith, Carol, '"Queenship" in Israel? The cases of Bathsheba, Jezebel and Athaliah', in John Day, ed., *King and Messiah in Israel and the Ancient Near East: Proceedings of the Oxford Old Testament Seminar* (JSOT Sup. Series 270; Sheffield: Sheffield Academic Press, 1998), 142–162.

Smith, Mark S., *Poetic Heroes: Literary Commemorations of Warriors and Warrior Culture in the Early Biblical World* (Grand Rapids: William B. Eerdmans, 2014), 462–463 n157.

Spanier, Ktziah, 'The Queen Mother in the Judean royal court: Maacah – a case study', in Athalya Brenner, ed., *Feminist Companion to Samuel and Kings* (Sheffield: Sheffield Academic Press, 1994), 186–195.

Wyatt, Nicolas, 'Asherah', in *DDD*, 99–105, here 104.

In Ugarit, only one woman could hold the title 'queen'. When her husband the king died, she retained that title. The wife of the son who became king assumed the title of queen only upon the death of her mother-in-law:

Soldt, William H. van, 'Ugarit: a second millennium kingdom on the Mesopotamian coast', in *CANE*, 1255–1266, here 1260).

For the view that scholars have read too much into this term see:

Bowen, Nancy R., 'The quest for the historical *gĕbîrâ*'. *CBQ* 64 2001: 597–618.

Rephaim

The Rephaim like the Nephilim were one of those mysterious people who occasionally appeared in the Hebrew Bible without explanation. The discoveries at Ugarit which shed light on Asherah, Baal, and El, also helped identify the Rephaim. For the Rephaim see:

Caquot, André, 'Les Rephaim Ougaritiques'. *Syria* 37 1960: 75–93.

Dijkstra, Meindert, 'The legend of Danel and the Rephaim'. *UF* 20 1988: 35–52.

Doak, Brian R., *The Last of the Rephaim: Conquest and Cataclysm in the Heroic Ages of Ancient Israel* (Ilex Series 7; Boston: Ilex Foundation and Washington: Center for Hellenic Studies, Trustees for Harvard University; distributed by Cambridge: Harvard University Press, 2012).

Ford, J. N., 'The "living Rephaim" of Ugarit: quick or defunct'. *UF* 24 1992: 73–101.

Hauer, Christian E., Jr., 'Jerusalem, the stronghold and Rephaim'. *CBQ* 32 1970: 571–578.

Helzter, Michael, *The Suteans* (Seminar Di Studi Asiatics Series Minor XIII; Naples: Instituto Universitario Orientale, 1981), 109–112.

L'Heureux, Conrad E., *Rank Among the Canaanite Gods El, Ba'al, and the Repha'im* (HSM 21; Missoula: Montana: Scholars Press, 1979).

Rouillard-Bonraisin, Hedwige, 'Rephaim', in *DDD*, 692–700.

Smith, Mark S., *Poetic Heroes: Literary Commemorations of Warriors and Warrior Culture in the Early Biblical World* (Grand Rapids: William B. Eerdmans, 2014), 137–161, 314–322.

Sacral Kingship (see **Psalm 78** and **Psalm 132**)

The sacral kingship in ancient times is a topic very much intertwined with the role of ritual. It is through rituals that the sacred nature of the position is revealed. If a person becomes king or queen or President and no one sees it, has anything happened? There is a Myth and Ritual school and the voluminous readings on that topic will not be listed here. At first glance, the KDB is a natural fit for the enthronement festivals consistent with the Myth and Ritual School, even more so than the sole act of installing the ark of Lord at Zion which concludes the KDB. However the KDB did not become a ritual because (i) no subsequent king had the stature, standing, and charisma of David, (ii) the kingdom split in two thereby rendering irrelevant much of the message of the performance, and (iii) it was a visionary expression of a single individual based on his own life experiences that did not lend itself to routine repetition. The priests responsible for the royal festivals recognized the fallacy of attempting to replicate the David experience and wisely reverted to the more traditional royal psalms ceremony. For the sacral kingship directly related to the biblical world, see such works as:

Anderson, G. W., 'Some aspects of the Uppsala achool of Old Testament study'. *HTR* 43 1950: 239–256.

Crim, Keith R., *The Royal Psalms* (Richmond: John Know Press, 1962).

Engell, Ivan, *Studies in Divine Kingship in the Ancient Near East* (Uppsala/Oxford: Blackwell, 1967).

Hooke, S. H., ed., *Myth and Ritual: Essays on the Myth and Ritual of the Hebrews in Relation to the Culture Pattern of the Ancient East* (Oxford: Oxford University Press, 1933).

Hooke, S. H., ed., *Myth, Ritual and Kingship* (Oxford, Clarendon Press, 1958).

Johnson, A. R., *Sacral Kingship in Ancient Israel* (Cardiff: University of Wales Press, 1967, 2nd edition).

Knight, Douglas, *Rediscovering the Traditions of Israel: The Development of the Traditio-Historical Research of the Old Testament, with Special Consideration of Scandinavian Contributions* (SBLDS 9; Missoula: Society of Biblical Literature/Scholars Press, 1975).

Merrill, Arthur L. and Spencer, John R., 'The "Uppsala school" of biblical studies', in W. Boyd Barrick and John R. Spencer, eds, *In the Shelter of Elyon: Essays on Ancient Palestinian Life and Literature in Honor of G. W. Ahlstrom* (JSOT Sup. Series 31; Sheffield: Sheffield Academic Press, 1984), 13–26.

Miller, Patrick D., Jr. and Roberts, J. J. M., *The Hand of the Lord: A Reassessment of the 'Ark Narrative' of 1 Samuel* (Johns Hopkins Near Eastern Studies; Baltimore: Johns Hopkins University Press, 1977).

Miller, Robert D., II, 'The performance of oral tradition in ancient Israel', in Brian B. Schmidt, ed., *Contextualizing Israel's Scared Writings: Ancient Literacy, Orality, and Literary Production* (AIL 22; Atlanta: SBL Press, 2015), 175–196.

Moor, Johannes C. de, *New Year with Canaanites and Israelites* (Kampen: Kok, 1972).

Morgenstern, Julian, 'A chapter in the history of the high-priesthood'. *AJSL* 55 1938: 1–24.

Mowinckel, Sigmund, *The Two Sources of the Predeuteronmic Primeval History (JE) in Gen. 1–11* (Oslo: I kommisjon hos J. Dybwad, 1937).

Mowinckel, Sigmund, *He That Cometh* (New York: Abingdon Press, 1954).

Mowinckel, Sigmund, *The Psalm's in Israel's Worship* (New York: Abingdon Press, 1962).

Oden, Robert A., Jr., 'Myth in the OT', in *ABD* IV: 956–960.

Petersen, Allan Rosengren, *The Royal God: Enthronement Festivals in Ancient Israel and Ugarit?* (JSOT Sup. Series 259; Copenhagen International Seminar 5; Sheffield: Sheffield Academic Press, 1998).

Zevit, Ziony, 'Israel's royal cult in the ancient Near Eastern kulturkreis', in Gary Beekman and Theodore Lewis, eds, *Text, Artifact, and Image: Revealing Ancient Israelite Religion* (BJS 346; Providence, RI: Brown Judaic Studies, 2006), 189–200.

Salem

A deity based on the name 'Salem' is part of the pre-Davidic story of Jerusalem; see:

Barton, George, 'A liturgy for the celebration of the spring festival at Jerusalem in the age of Abraham and Melchizedek'. *JBL* 53 1934: 61–78.
Ginsberg, H. L., 'Notes on "the birth of the gracious and beautiful gods"'. *JRAS* (no. vol. num.), 1935: 45–72.
Handy, Lowell K., 'Shalem', in *ABD* V: 1152–1153.
Huffmon, Herbert B., 'Shalem', in *DDD*, 755–757.
Hutzli, Jürg Hutzli, 'The meaning of the term 'îr dāwīd in Samuel and Kings'. *TA* 38 2011: 167–178.
Kirkland, J. R., 'The incident at Salem: a re-examination of Genesis 14: 18–20'. *Studia Biblica et Theologica* 7 1977: 3–23.
Petuchowski, Jakob J., 'The controversial figure of Melchizedek'. *HUCA* 28 1957: 127–136.
Virolleaud, Ch., 'La naissance des dieux gracieux et beaux. Poème Phénicien de Ras-Shamra'. *Syria* 14 1937: 128–151.

Saul's Rise to Power

In this study, the issue is less the history of Saul than his impact for the development of the alphabet prose narrative. The opposition to him by the Shiloh priests may be considered the onset of the form of writing that would become the basis for the Hebrew Bible. For Saul see:

Blenkinsopp, Joseph, 'The quest for the historical Saul,' in James W. Flanagan and Anita Weisboro Robinson, eds, *No Famine in the Land: Studies in Honor of John L. McKenzie* (Claremont: Scholars Press for Institute for Antiquity and Christianity, 1975), 75–99.
Edelman, Diana, 'The Deuteronomist's story of King Saul: narrative art or editorial policy', in C. Brekelmans and J. Lust, eds, *Pentateuchal and Deuteronomistic Studies: Papers Read at the XIIIth IOSOT Congress, Leuven 1989* (BETL 94; Leuven: Leuven University Press, 1990), 207–220.
Edelman, Diana, *King Saul in the Historiography of Judah* (JSOT Sup. Series 121; Sheffield: Sheffield Academic Press, 1991).
Finkelstein, Israel, 'The last Labayu: King Saul and the expansion of the first north Israelite territorial entity', in Yairah Amit and Nadav Na'aman, eds, *Essays on Ancient Israel in its Near Eastern Context: A Tribute to Nadav Na'aman* (Winona Lake: Eisenbrauns, 2006), 171–187.
Leuchter, Mark, '"Now there was a [certain] man": compositional chronology in Judges–1 Samuel'. *CBQ* 69 2007: 429–439.
McCarter, P. Kyle, Jr., *I Samuel* (AB 8; Garden City: Doubleday, 1980), 26–27, 29.
McCarter, P. Kyle, Jr., 'The apology of David'. *JBL* 99 1980: 489–504.
Miller, J. Maxwell, 'Saul's rise to power: some observations concerning I Sam. 9: 1–10: 16; 10: 26–11: 15 and 13: 2–14: 46'. *CBQ* 36 1974: 157–174.
Na'aman, Nadav, 'The kingdom of Isbaal'. *BN* 84 1990: 33–37.
White, Marsha C., 'The "History of Saul's Rise" and the compositional history of I Samuel 1–14', unpublished paper presented at the annual conference of the Society of Biblical Literature, November 20, 2000, Nashville.
White, Marsha C., '"The History of Saul's Rise": Saulide state propaganda in 1 Samuel 1–14', in Saul M. Olyan and Robert C. Culley, eds, *'A Wise and Discerning Mind': Essays in Honor of Burke O. Long* (BJS 325; Providence: Brown Judaic Studies, 2000), 271–292.

For the continuing legacy of Saul in alphabet prose narratives as political polemics into later times, see:

Amit, Yairah, 'The Saul polemic in the Persian Period', in Oded Lipschits and Manfred Oeming, eds, *Judah and the Judeans in the Persian Period* (Winona Lake: Eisenbrauns, 2006), 647–661.

Berger, Yitzhak, 'Esther and Benjaminite royalty: a study in inner-biblical allusion'. *JBL* 129 2010: 625–644.

Brettler, Marc, 'Megillat Esther: reversing the legacy of King Saul'. *The Torah*,http: //thetorah.com/megillat-esther-reversing-the-legacy-of-king-saul/.

Edelman, Diana, 'Did Saulide-Davidic rivalry resurface in early Persian Yehud?', in M. Patrick Graham and J. Andrew Dearman, eds, *The Land that I will Show You: Essays on the History and Archaeology of the Ancient Near East in Honor of J. Maxwell Miller* (JSOT Sup. Series 343: Sheffield: JSOT Press, 2001), 69–91.

Ehrlich, Carl, and White, Marsha C., eds, *Saul in Story and Tradition* (FAT 47; Tübingen: Mohr Siebeck, 2006).

Jonker, Louis C., 'Revisiting the Saul narrative in Chronicles: interacting with the Persian imperial context?', *OTE* 23/2 2010: 283–305.

Sabo, P. J., 'Seeking Saul in Chronicles', in Paul S. Evans and Tyler F. Williams, eds, *Chronicling the Chronicler* (Winona Lake: Eisenbrauns, 2012), 43–63.

Shasu

The connection of the Shasu, a wilderness people known to Egypt and with a deity named Yahweh, to Israel has been the subject of academic debate. Yahweh marching from Seir (Deut. 33: 2; Judg. 5: 4), the close connection of Seir and Esau (Gen. 33; Deut. 2), the presence of the Kenites Zipporah and Yael all are suggestive of a link between Israel and peoples of the wilderness. The circumcision ceremony with Zipporah (Ex. 4: 24–26) is consistent with the idea of an alliance between the two peoples perhaps based on shared anti-Egyptian values. They may have become Calebites and Judahites who do not appear in the Song of Deborah but who are part of the first kingdom of David. Their connection to Merneptah's Israel in the central highlands was stronger than to the Jebusites. For the Shasu see:

Axelsson, Lars Eric, *The Lord Rose up from Seir: Studies in the History and Tradition of the Negev and Southern Judah* (ConBOT 25; Stockholm: Almquist & Wiksell, 1987).

Giveon, Raphael, 'The Shosu of the late XXth Dynasty'. *JARCE* 8 1969–1970: 51–53.

Giveon, Raphael, *Les Bédouins Shosu des Documents Égyptiens* (Documenta et Monumenta Orientis Antiqui 18; Leiden: Brill, 1971), 70–75.

Hawkins, Ralph, *How Israel Became a People* (Nashville: Abingdon Press, 2013), 70–75.

Hoffmeier, James K., *Ancient Israel in Sinai: The Evidence for the Authenticity of the Wilderness Tradition* (New York: Oxford University Press, 2005), 240–243.

Levy, Thomas E., Adams, Russell B. and Muniz, Adolfo, 'Archaeology and the Shasu nomads: recent excavations in the Jabal Hamrat Fidan, Jordan', in William H. C. Propp and Richard E. Friedman, eds, *Le-David Maskil: A Birthday Tribute for David Noel Freedman* (Winona Lake: Eisenbrauns, 2004), 63–89.

Rainey, Anson F., 'Amarna and later aspects of social history', in William G. Dever and Seymour Gitin, eds, *Symbiosis, Symbolism, and the Power of the Past: Canaan, Ancient Israel, and their Neighbors from the Late Bronze Age through Roman Palestina, Proceedings of the Centennial Symposium, W. F. Albright Institute of Archaeological Research and American Schools of Oriental Research, Jerusalem, May 29/31, 2000* (Winona Lake: Eisenbrauns, 2003), 169–187, here 178–184.

Rainey, Anson F., 'Whence came the Israelites and their language?' *IEJ* 57 2007: 41–64, here 55–58.

Redford, Donald B., *Egypt, Israel, and Canaan in Ancient Times* (Princeton: Princeton University Press, 1992), 269–280.

Ward, William A., 'The Shasu "Bedouin": notes on a recent publication'. *JESHO* 15 1972: 35–60.

Ward, William A., 'Shasu', in *ABD* V: 1165–1167.

Shechem

All things considered, if during the second millennium BCE, one had to predict which Canaanite city, especially in the highlands, was likely to become the dominant one following Egyptian withdrawal from the land, the answer more likely would have been Shechem than Jerusalem. For Shechem see:

Anderson, Bernard W., 'The place of Shechem in the Bible'. *BA* 20 1957: 10–32.

Boling, Robert G., 'Who is Š-K-M? (Judges IX 28)'. *VT* 13 1963: 479–482.

Boling, Robert G., *Judges* (AB 6A; Garden City: Doubleday & Company, 1975), 165–185.

Campbell, Edward F., Jr., 'Two Amarna notes: the Shechem city-state and Amarna administrative terminology,' in Frank Moore Cross, Warner Lemke and Patrick Miller, Jr., eds, *Magnalia Dei: The Mighty Acts of God* (New York: Doubleday, 1976), 39–54.

Campbell, Edward F., Jr., 'Judges 9 and biblical archaeology', in Carol L. Meyers and Michael O'Connor, eds, *The Word of the Lord shall Go Forth: Essays in Honor of David Noel Freedman in Celebration of his Sixtieth Birthday* (Special Volume Series ASOR 1; Winona Lake: Eisenbrauns, 1983), 263–27.

Campbell, Edward F., Jr. and Ross, James, 'The excavation of Shechem and the biblical tradition'. *BA* 25 1963: 2–27.

Clements, R. E., 'Baal-Berith of Shechem'. *JSS* 13 1968: 21–32.

Endris, Vince, 'Yahweh versus Baal: a narrative-critical reading of the Gideon/Abimelech narrative'. *JSOT* 33 2008: 173–195.

Farber, Zev, 'Jerubaal, Jacob and the battle for Shechem: a tradition history'. *JHS* 13/12 2013: 1–25, jhs.2013.v13.a12.

Finkelstein, Israel, 'The last Labayu: King Saul and the expansion of the first north Israelite Territorial entity', in Yairah Amit and Nadav Na'aman, eds, *Essays on Ancient Israel in its Near Eastern Context: A Tribute to Nadav Na'aman* (Winona Lake: Eisenbrauns, 2006), 171–187.

Finklestein, Israel, and Naaman, Nadav, 'Shechem of the Amarna period and the rise of the northern kingdom of Israel'. *IEJ* 55 2005: 172–193.

Heffelfinger; Katie M., '"My father is king": chiefly politics and the rise and fall of Abimelech'. *JSOT* 33 2009: 277–292.

Lewis, Theodore J., 'The identity and function of El/Baal Berith'. *JBL* 115: 401–423.

Mazar, Benjaminr, 'Shechem – a city of the patriarchs', in Shmuel Aḥtuv, ed., *Biblical Israel: States and People* (Jerusalem: Magnes Press, Hebrew University, 1992), 42–54.

Mulder, Martin J., 'Baal-Berith', in *DDD*, 141–144.

Sasson, Jack M., *Judges 1–12* (Anchor Yale Bible 6D; New Haven: Yale University Press, 2014), 373–405.

Stager, Lawrence E., 'The Shechem temple: where Abimelech massacred a thousand'. BAR 29/4 2003: 26–35, 66–69.

Stager, Lawrence E., 'The fortress temple at Shechem and the "house of El, cord of the covenant"', in Prescott H. Williams, Jr. and Theodore Hiebert, eds, *Realia Dei: Essays in Archaeology and Biblical Interpretation in Honor of Edward F. Campbell, Jr. at his Retirement* (Atlanta: Scholars Press, 1999), 228–249.

Toombs, Lawrence E., 'Shechem: problems of the early Israelite era', in Frank Moore Cross, ed., *Symposia Celebrating the Seventy-Fifth Anniversary of the Founding of the American Schools of Oriental Research (1900–1975)* (Cambridge: American Schools of Oriental Research, 1979), 69–83.

Wright, G. R. H., 'Temples at Shechem'. *ZAW* 80 1966: 1–35.

Wright, G. R. H., 'The mythology of pre-Israelite Shechem'. *VT* 20 1970: 75–82.

Wright, G. R. H., 'Shechem, the "navel of the land"'. *BA* 20 1957: 2–10.

Wright, G. R. H., 'Shechem and league'. *VT* 21 1971: 572–603.

Wright, G. R. H., 'Joseph's grave under the tree by the omphalos at Shechem'. *VT* 22 1972: 476–486.

For the royal Canaanite vintage story which may provide the background for the feast in Judg. 9 at Shechem see:

Levine, Baruch, and Tarragon, J. M. De, 'The king proclaims the day: Ugaritic rites for the vintage (KTU 1.41//1.87)'. *RB* 1983: 76–115.

Shiloh

Finkelstein, Israel, 'Shiloh: twenty years later', in Niels Peter Lemche, Morgen Müller, Thomas L Thompson, eds, *Historie og konstruktion: festskrift til Nils Peter Lemche i anledning af 60 års fødselsdagen den 6. september 2005* (København: Museum Tusculanum, 2005), 142–152.

Finkelstein, Israel, *The Forgotten Kingdom: The Archaeology and History of Northern Israel* (ANEM 5; Atlanta: Society of Biblical Literature, 2013).

Miller, Robert D., II, *Chieftains of the Highland Clans: A History of Israel in the 12th and 11th Centuries BC* (Grand Rapids: William B. Eerdmans, 2005), 119.

Shishak/Sheshonq/Shoshenq

The attempt to reconcile the Egyptian accounts of the invasion of Sheshonq, the biblical Shishak, and the archaeological discoveries has generated an ongoing plethora of academic reconstructions. The Egyptian records suggest Pharaoh Sheshonq marched north and not to Jerusalem but the incomplete itinerary list is very problematic and may be more of a copy from the lists of previous warrior Pharaohs rather than an actual campaign document. The archaeological discoveries in the northern kingdom raises the possibility that Israel and Egypt now were allies with Judah perhaps paying the price. The continued presence of the Philistines along the coast Sheshonq needed to traverse raises another set of questions. His invasion marks the end of the supplements to the KDB by the authors identified in this study. For a discussion on Sheshonq's campaign see:

Ahlström, Gösta W., 'Pharaoh Shoshenq's campaign to Palestine', in André Lemaire and Benedikt Otzen, eds, *History and Tradition of Early Israel: Studies Presented to Eduard Nielsen, May 8th, 1993* (SVT 50; Leiden: Brill, 1993), 1–16.

Evian, Shirley Ben-Dor, 'Shishak's Karnak relief – more than just name rings', in Shay Bar, Dan'el Kahn and J. J. Shirley, eds, *Egypt, Canaan and Israel: History, Imperialism, Ideology, and Literature: Proceedings of a Conference at the University of Haifa, 3–7 May 2009* (CHANE 52; Leiden: Brill, 2011), 11–22.

Finkelstein, Israel, 'The campaign of Shoshenq I to Palestine: a guide to the 10th century BCE polity'. *ZPDV* 118 2002: 109–135.

Finkelstein, Israel, and Piasetzky, Eliazer, 'The Iron I–IIA in the highlands and beyond: ¹⁴C anchors, pottery phases and the Shoshenq campaign'. *Levant* 38 2006: 45–61.

Grabbe, Lester L., 'From Merneptah to Shoshenq: if we had only the bible…', in Lester L. Grabbe, ed., *Israel in Transition 2: From Late Bronze II to Iron IIa (c. 1250–850 BCE): The Texts* (LHBOTS 521; European Seminar in Historical Methodology 8; London: T&T Clark, 2008), 62–129, here 84–86.

Grabbe, Lester L., 'Reflections on the discussion', in Lester L. Grabbe, ed., *Israel in Transition 2: From Late Bronze II to Iron IIa (c. 1250–850 BCE): The Texts* (LHBOTS 521; European Seminar in Historical Methodology 8; London: T&T Clark, 2010), 219–232, here 227.

Kitchen, Kenneth A., 'The Shoshenqs of Egypt and Palestine'. *JSOT* 93 2001: 3–12.

Levin, Yigal, 'Did Pharaoh Sheshonq attack Jerusalem?' BAR 39/4 2012: 42–52, 56.

Mazar, Benjamin, 'The campaign of Pharaoh Shishak to Palestine'. *Volume du Congress Strassburg, 1956*, SVT 4 1957: 57–66.

Redford, Donald B., *Egypt, Israel, and Canaan in Ancient Times* (Princeton: Princeton University Press, 1992), 312–315.

Ussishkin, David, 'Notes on Megiddo, Gezer, Ashdod and Tel Batash in the tenth to ninth centuries BC'. *BASOR* 277/278 1990: 71–91, here 72–73.

Wilson, Kevin A., *The Campaign of Pharaoh Shoshenq I into Palestine* (FAT 2/9; Tübingen: Mohr Siebeck, 2005).

Smith

Perhaps the best way to understand the smith in ancient times is to think of the nuclear scientist from Nazi Germany after the war or the Pakistani nuclear scientist and the spread of nuclear weapons today. For the role of the smith in society see:

McCarter, P. Kyle, Jr., 'Cain and the Kenites,' unpublished lecture for the Biblical Archaeological Society, Philadelphia, May 27, 1993.

McNutt, Paula M., *The Forging of Israel: Iron Technology, Symbolism, and Tradition on Ancient Society* (SWBA 8; Sheffield: Almond, 1990).

McNutt, Paula M., 'The Kenites, the Midianites, and the Rechabites as marginal mediators in ancient Israelite tradition'. *Semeia* 67 1994: 109–132.

McNutt, Paula M., 'In the shadow of Cain'. *Semeia* 87 1999: 45–64.

Song of Deborah

The Song of Deborah may be the most frequently cited biblical text to situate the early history of Israel after Merneptah and before the monarchy. As expected, the dating of the composition and whether it is a unity or not have been debated. See:

Ackerman, Susan, *Warrior, Dancer, Seductress, Queen: Women in Judges and Biblical Israel* (Anchor Bible Reference Library; New York: Doubleday, 1998), 27–180.

Albright, William F., 'The earlier form of Hebrew verses'. *JPOS* 2 1922: 69–86, here 72–83.

Albright, William F., 'The Song of Deborah in light of archaeology'. *BASOR* 62 1936: 26–31.

Caquot, André, 'Les tribus d'Israël dans le Cantique de Débora (Juges 5, 13–17)'. *Sem* 36 1986: 47–70.

Craigie, P. C., 'The Song of Deborah and the Epic of Tikulti-Ninurta'. *JBL* 88 1969: 253–265.

Craigie, P. C., 'Deborah and Anat: a study of poetic imagery (Judges 5)'. ZAW 90 1978: 374–381.

Cross, Frank Moore, and Freedman, David Noel, *Studies in Ancient Yahwistic Poetry* (Missoula: Scholars Press, 1975), 3–42.

Fritz, Volkmar, *The Emergence of Israel in the Twelfth and Eleventh Centuries BCE* (Biblical Encyclopedia, Vol. 2; Atlanta: Society of Biblical Literature, 2011), 139–157, 211–215, 242.

Halpern, Baruch, *The Emergence of Israel in Canaan* (Chico: Scholars Press, 1983), 8, 91, 117.

Halpern, Baruch, *The First Historians: The Hebrew Bible and History* (University Park, PA: The Pennsylvania State University Press, 1996), 76–103 (first published New York: Harper & Row, 1988).

Leuchter, Mark, '"Why tarry the wheels of his chariot?" (Judg 5,28): Canaanite chariots and echoes of Egypt in the Song of Deborah'. *Bib* 91 2010: 256–268.

Miller, Robert D., II, 'When Pharaohs ruled: on the translation of Judges 5: 2'. *JTS* 59 2008: 650–654.

Sasson, Jack M., *Judges 1–12* (Anchor Yale Bible 6D; New Haven: Yale University Press, 2014), 276–323, 493–505, 513–522.

Schloen, David, 'Caravans, Kenites and *casus belli*, enmity and alliance in the Song of Deborah'. *CBQ* 55 1993: 18–39.

Smith, Mark S., 'Why was "old poetry" used in Hebrew Narrative? Historical and cultural considerations about Judges 5', in Marilyn J. Lundberg, Steven Fine and Wayne T. Pitard, eds, *Puzzling Out the Past: Studies in Northwest Semitic Languages and Literature in Honor of Bruce Zuckerman* (CHANE 55; Leiden: Brill, 2012), 197–212.

Smith, Mark S., *Poetic Heroes: Literary Commemorations of Warriors and Warrior Culture in the Early Biblical World* (Grand Rapids: William B. Eerdmans, 2014), 211– 266.

Taylor, J. Glenn, 'The Song of Deborah and two Canaanite goddesses'. *JSOT* 23 1982: 99–108.

Younger, K. Lawson, Jr., 'Heads! Tails! Or the whole coin! Contextual method and intertexual analysis: Judges 4 and 5', in K. Lawson Younger, Jr., William W. Hallo and Bernard F. Batto, eds, *The Biblical Canon in Comparative Perspective: Scripture in Context IV* (Lewiston: Edward Mellen Press, 1991), 109–146.

Wright, Jacob L., 'War commemoration and the interpretation of Judges 5: 15b–17'. *VT* 61 2011: 505–521.

Wright, Jacob L., 'Deborah's war memorial: the composition of Judges 4–5 and the politics of war commemoration'. *ZAW* 123 2011: 516–534.

Sons of God (see **Nephilim**)

The sons of God are the lead character in the story of the sons of God analyzed in this study. All Genesis commentaries deal with the identity of these beings. In addition for the sons of God see:

Albertz, Rainer, *A History of Israelite Religion in the Old Testament Period* (Louisville: Westminster/John Knox Press, 1994), I: 116.

Alexander, Philip S., 'The Targumim and early exegesis of "sons of God" in Genesis 6'. *JJS* 23 1972: 60–71.

Bremmer, Jan M., 'Remember the Titans!', in Christoph Auffarth and Loren T. Stuckenbruck, eds, *The Fall of Angels* (TBN 6; Leiden: Brill, 2004), 35–60.

Cassuto, Umberto, 'The episode of the sons of God and the daughters of Man', in *Biblical and Oriental Studies Volume I: The Bible* (Jerusalem: Magnes, 1973), 17–28.

Clines, David J. A., 'The significance of the "sons of God" episode (Genesis 6: 1–4) in the context of the "primeval history" (Genesis 1–11)'. *JSOT* 13 1979: 33–46.

Coleran, James E., 'The sons of God in Genesis 6, 2'. *TS* 2 1941: 488–509.

Collins, John J., 'The sons of God and the daughters of Men', in Marti Nissinen, *Sacred Marriages: The Divine: Human Sexual Metaphor from Sumer to Early Christianity* (Winona Lake: Eisenbrauns, 2008), 259–274.

Day, John, *From Creation to Babel: Studies in Genesis 1–11* (London: Bloomsbury, 2013), 77–97.

Doedens, Jaap, *The Sons of God in Genesis 6: 1–4* (dissertation Theologische Universiteit van de Gereformeerde Kerken, 2013), 89–178.

Eslinger, Lyle, 'A contextual identification of the *bene ha'elohim* and *benoth ha'adam* in Genesis 6: 1–4'. *JSOT* 13 1979: 65–73

Goff, Matthew J. 'Ben Sira and the giants of the land: a note on Ben Sira 16: 7'. *JBL* 129 2010: 645–655.

Hanson, Paul D., 'Rebellion in heaven, Azazel, and euhemeristic heroes in I Enoch 6–11'. *JBL* 96 1977: 185–233.

Hendel, Ronald S., 'Of demigods and the deluge: toward an interpretation of Genesis 6: 1–4'. *JBL* 106 1987: 13–26.

Holloway, Steven W., 'Imagining the unspeakable: Genesis 6: 1–4 in the nineteenth century'. *PEGLMBS* 28 2008: 25–40.

Kaminski, Carol, *Was Noah Good? Finding Favour in the Flood Narrative* (New York: Bloomsbury, 2014), 28–35.

Klein, Jacob, 'The "bane" of humanity: a lifespan of one hundred twenty years'. *Acta Sumerlogica* 12 1990: 57–69.

Klein, Jacob, 'Sumerian kingship and the gods', in Gary Beekman and Theodore Lewis, eds, *Text, Artifact, and Image: Revealing Ancient Israelite Religion* (BJS 346; Providence: Brown Judaic Studies, 2006), 115–131.

Kline, Meredith G., 'Divine kingship and Genesis 6: 1–4'. *WTJ* 24 1962: 187–204.

Kraeling, Emil G., 'The significance and origins of Gen. 6: 1–4'. *JNES* 6 1947: 193–208.

Kugel, James L., *The Bible as It Was* (Cambridge MA: Harvard University Press, 1997), 110–114.

Kugel, James, 'The descent of the wicked angels and the persistence of evils', in Gary A. Anderson and Joel Kaminsky, eds, *The Call of Abraham: Essays on the Election of Israel in Honor of Jon D. Levenson* (Notre Dame: University of Notre Dame Press, 2013), 210–235.

Kvanvig, Helge S., 'Gen.6: 1–4 as an antediluvian event'. *SJOT* 16 2002: 79–112.

Melvin, David P., 'Divine mediation and the rise of civilization in Mesopotamian literature and in Genesis 1–11'. *JHS* 10/17 2010 1–14, jhs.2010.v10.a17.

Melvin, David P., 'The Gilgamesh traditions and the pre-history of Genesis 6: 1–4'. *PRSt* 38/1 2011: 23–32.

Parker, Simon B., 'Sons of (the) god(s)', in *DDD*, 794–802.

Parpola, Simo, 'Sons of God: the ideology of Assyrian kingship'. *Odyssey* 2/5 1999: 16–27.

Petersen, David L., 'Genesis 6: 1–4, Yahweh and the organization of the cosmos'. *JSOT* 13 1979: 47–64.

Scodel, R., 'The Achaean wall and the Mmyth of destruction'. *HSCP* 86 1982: 33–50.

Soggin, J. A., 'Sons of God(s), heroes, and Nephilim: remarks on Genesis 6: 1–4', in Michael V. Fox, Victor Hurowitz, Avi Hurvitz, Michael L. Klein, Baruch J. Schwartz and Nili Shupak, eds, *Texts, Temples, and Traditions: a Tribute to Menahem Haran* (Winona Lake: Eisenbrauns, 1996), 135–136.

Spero, Shubert, 'Sons of God, daughters of Men?' *JBQ* 40 2012: 15–18.

Stuckenbruck, Loren T., 'The origins of evil in Jewish apocalyptic tradition: the interpretation of Genesis 6: 1–4 in the second and third centuries BCE', in Christoph Auffarth and Loren T. Stuckenbruck, eds, *The Fall of Angels* (TBN 6; Leiden: Brill, 2004), 87–118.

Van Gemeren, Willem A., 'The sons of God in Genesis 6: 1–4 (an example of evangelical demythologization)'. *WTJ* 43 1981: 320–348.

Van Ruiten, J. T. A. G. M., 'The interpretation of the flood story in the Book of Jubilees', in Florentino Garcia Martinez and Gerard P. Luttikhurzen, *Interpretations of the Flood* (TBN 1; Leiden: Brill, 1998), 66–85, here 83.

Van Wolde, Ellen, *Words Become Worlds: Semantic Studies of Genesis 1–11* (BiIntS 6; Leiden: Brill, 1994), 63–74.

Vervenne, Marc, 'All they need is love: once more Genesis 6: 1–4', in Jon Davies, Graham Harvey, and Wilfred G. E. Watson, eds, *Words Remembered, Texts Renewed: Essays in Honour of John F. A. Sawyer* (JSOT Sup. Series 195; Sheffield: Sheffield Academic Press, 1995), 19–40.

Wellhausen, Julius, *Prolegomena to the History of Israel* (Atlanta: Scholars Press, 1994; reprint of 1885 edition), 317.

Wickham, L. R., 'The sons of God and the daughters of Men: Genesis VI 2 in early Christian exegesis'. *OtSt* 19 1974: 135–147.

Wifall, Walter, 'Gen. 6: 1–4 – a royal Davidic myth'. *BTB* 5 1975: 294–330.

Winter, Irene J., 'Touched by the gods: visual evidence for the divine status of rulers in the ancient Near East', in Nicole Brisch, ed., *Religion and Power: Divine Kingship in the Ancient World and Beyond* (OIS 4; Chicago: Oriental Institute, 2008), 75–10, here 81.

Wright, Archie T., *The Origin of Evil Spirits: The Reception of Genesis 6.1–4 in Early Jewish Literature* (Tübingen, Mohr Siebeck, 2005).

For an exceptionally vigorous defense of the perception of an invasion by Satan and fallen angels see:

Deffinbaugh, Robert L., 'The sons of God and the daughters of Men (Genesis 6: 1–8), https: //bible.org/seriespage/sons-god-and-daughters-men-genesis-61-8.

Stepped Stone Structure (see Large Stone Structure)

The controversy over the dating of the Stepped Stone Structure and the Large Stone Structure (above) go hand in hand. See:

Cahill, Jane, 'Jerusalem at the time of the United Monarchy: the archaeological evidence', in Andrew G. Vaughn and Ann E. Killebrew, eds, *Jerusalem in the Bible and Archaeology: The First Temple Period* (SBLSymS 18; Atlanta: Society of Biblical Literature, 2003), 34–53.

Finkelstein, Israel, 'The rise of Jerusalem and Judah: the missing link', in Andrew G. Vaughn and Ann E. Killebrew, eds, *Jerusalem in the Bible and Archaeology: The First Temple Period* (SBLSymS 18; Atlanta: Society of Biblical Literature, 2003), 81–101, here 84–87.

Lehmann, Gunnar, 'The United Monarchy in the countryside: Jerusalem, Judah, and the Shephelah during the tenth century BCE', in Andrew G. Vaughn and Ann E. Killebrew, eds, *Jerusalem in the Bible and Archaeology: The First Temple Period* (SBLSymS 18; Atlanta: Society of Biblical Literature, 2003), 117–162, here 134–136.

Mazar, Amihai, 'Jerusalem in the 10th century BCE: the glass half full', in Yairah Amit and Nadav Na'aman, eds, *Essays on Ancient Israel in its Near Eastern Context: A Tribute to Nadav Na'aman* (Winona Lake: Eisenbrauns, 2006), 255–272, here 269–270.

Mazar, Amihai, 'The spade and the text: the interaction between archaeology and Israelite history relating to the tenth–ninth centuries BCE', in H. G. M. Williamson, ed., *Understanding the History of Ancient Israel* (Oxford: Oxford University Press, 2007), 143–171, here 152–153.

Mazar, Amihai, 'Archaeology and the biblical narrative: the case of the United Monarchy', in Reinhard G. Kratz and Hermann Spieckermann, eds, *One God – One Cult – One Nation: Archaeological and Biblical Perspectives* (BZAW 405; Berlin: Walter de Gruyter, 2010), 29–58, here 34–40.

Steiner, Margaret, 'The evidence from Kenyon's excavations in Jerusalem: a response essay', in Andrew G. Vaughn and Ann E. Killebrew, eds, *Jerusalem in the Bible and Archaeology: The First Temple Period* (SBLSymS 18; Atlanta: Society of Biblical Literature, 2003), 347–363.

Sumerian King List

The genealogical list of Sumerian kings pre- and post-flood is an irresistible lure for biblical scholars. The apparent similarities to the format in Gen. 1–11 with a flood in the middle naturally draws attention. By contrast there are no elongated genealogies in the KDB or the stories of this study. It is as if they subsequently were fitted into a genealogical framework. For the Sumerian King List see:

Jacobsen, Thorkild, *Sumerian King List* (Chicago: University of Chicago Press, 1939).

Marchesi, Gianni, 'The Sumerian king list and the early history of Mesopotamia'. *Quaderni di Vicini Oriene* 5 2010: 231–248.

Michalowski, Piotor, 'History as charter: some observations on the Sumerian king list'. *JAOS* 103 1983: 237–248.

Suteans

The Suteans are a lesser-known people who nonetheless can contribute to the understanding of biblical stories, particular involving Cain and Seth. For the Suteans see:

Day, John, *From Creation to Babel: Studies in Genesis 1–11* (London: Bloomsbury, 2013), 56 n10.

Helzter, Michael, *The Suteans* (Seminar Di Studi Asiatics Series Minor XIII; Naples: Instituto Universitario Orientale, 1981).

Luke, John Tracy, *Pastoralism and the Politics of the Mari Period: A Critical Re-examination of the Character and Political Significance of the Major West Semitic Tribal Groups on the Middle Euphrates, ca. 1828–1758 BC* (Ph.D. Dissertation, University of Michigan, 1965), 105–138.

Vidal, Jordi, 'Sutean warfare in the Amarna Letters', in Jordi Vidal, ed., *Studies on War in the Ancient Near East: Collected Essays on Military History* (Münster: Ugarit-Verlag, 2010), 95–103.

Threshing Floor

The threshing floor is an easily overlooked place of importance in social, cultural, religious, and political life in ancient times as if those modern classifications really are appropriate. It is easy in urban life with little direct contact with the land and the vagaries of the agricultural cycle to miss the significance of the threshing floor to ancient Israel. For the threshing floor see:

Aranov, Maurice Moshe, *The Biblical Threshing-Floor in the Light of the Ancient Near Eastern Evidence: Evolution of an Institution* (Ph.D. dissertation, New York University, 1977).

Drinkard, Joel E., Jr., 'Threshing floor', in *New Interpreter's Dictionary of the Bible* (Nashville: Abingdon Press, 2000), 588–589.

Griffen, Susan M., 'Threshing floors: a response to Joanna Brooks'. *ALH* 22 2010: 454–458.

Matthews, Victor H., 'Entrance ways and threshing floors'. *Fides et Historia* 19 1987: 25–40, here 29–32.

Matthews, Victor H., 'Memory lingers: definition and redefinition of space in ancient Israel', unpublished paper presented at the annual meeting of the Society of Biblical Literature, November 19, 2011.

McCarter, P. Kyle, Jr., *II Samuel*, (AB9, Garden City: Doubleday, 1984), 511–512.

Smith, Sidney, 'The threshing floor and the city gate'. *PEQ* 78 1946: 5–14.

Tobolowsky, Andrew, 'Where doom is spoken: threshing floors as places of decision and communication in biblical literature'. *JANER* 16 2016: 95–120.

Waters, Jamie L., *Threshing Floors in Ancient Israel: Their Ritual and Symbolic Significance* (Minneapolis: Fortress Press, 2015).

Yeivin, Shmuel, 'The threshing floor of Araunah'. *Journal of Educational Sociology* 36 1963: 396–400.

For the ritual act of threshing see:

Littauer, M. A., and Crouwel, J. H., 'Ceremonial threshing in the ancient Near East: 1. Archaeological evidence'. *Iraq* 1990 52: 15–19.

Tower of Babel

The Tower of Babel is a leading character in one of the stories in this study. All Genesis commentaries include a section on the story. The archaeological sources are presented in Chapter 7 in Part I. See also:

Alster, Bendt, 'An aspect of "Enmerkar and the Lord of Aratta"'. *RA* 67 1973: 101–110.

Anderson, Bernhard W., 'Chapter 10 the Tower of Babel: unity and diversity in God's creation', in *From Creation to New Creation* (Minneapolis: Fortress Press, 1994), 165–178.

Baden, Joel, 'The Tower of Babel: a case study in the competing methods of historical and modern literary criticism'. *JBL* 128 2009: 209–224.

Bar-Yosef, Ofer, 'The walls of Jericho: an alternative interpretation'. *CA* 27 1986: 157–162.

Bar-Yosef, Ofer, 'The Neolithic Period', in Amnon Ben-Tor, ed., *The Archaeology of Ancient Israel* (New Haven: Yale University Press, 1992), 10–39.

Dalley, Stephanie, *Myths from Mesopotamia* (Oxford: Oxford University Press, 1989), 190.

Day, John, *From Creation to Babel: Studies in Genesis 1–11* (London: Bloomsbury, 2013), 167, 173–175.

Fokkelman, J. F., *Narrative Art in Genesis: Specimens of Stylistic and Structural Analysis* (Amsterdam: Van Gorcum, 1975), 11–45.

Gelb, I. J., 'The name of Babylon', in Richard S. Hess and David Toshio Tsumura, eds, *I Studied Inscriptions from Before the Flood: Ancient Near Eastern, Literary, and Linguistic Approaches to Genesis 1–11* (SBTS 4; Winona Lake: Eisenbrauns, 1994), 266–269, reprinted from *JIAS* 1 1955: 1–4.

George, A. R., 'The Tower of Babel: archaeology, history and cuneiform texts', *AfO* 51 2005–2006: 75–95.

Gilbert, Alessandra, 'On Kār Tukultī-Ninurta: chronology and politics of a middle Assyrian Ville Neuve', in Dominik Bonatz, Rainer M. Czichon and F. Janoscha Kreppner, eds, *Fundstellen: Gesammelte Schriften zur Archäologie und Geschichte Altvorderasiens: ad honorem Hartmut Kühne* (Wiesbaden: Harrassowitz, 2008), 177–186.

Giogetti, Andrew, 'The "mock building account" of Genesis 11: 1–9: polemic against Mesopotamian royal ideology'. *VT* 64 2014: 1–20.

Gnuse, Robert, 'The tale of Babel: parable of divine judgment or human cultural diversification?' *BZ* 54 2010: 229–244.

Harland, P. J., 'Vertical or horizontal: the sin of Babel'. *VT* 48 1998: 515–533.

Hendel, Ronald S., 'Book review of Christoph Uehlinger, *Weltreich und 'eine Rede': Eine neue Deutung der sogerannten Turmbauerzählung (Gen.11,1–9)*'. *CBQ* 55 1993: 785–787.

Hiebert, Theodore, 'The Tower of Babel and the origin of the world's cultures'. *JBL* 126 2007: 29–58.

Hiebert, Theodore, 'Babel: babble or blueprint? Calvin, cultural diversity, and the interpretation of Genesis

11: 1–9', in Wallace M. Alston, Jr. and Michael Welker, eds, *Reformed Theology: Identity and Ecumenicity II: Biblical Interpretation in the Reformed Tradition* (Grand Rapids: William B. Eerdmans, 2007), 127–145.

Hurowitz, Victor Avigdor, *I Have Built You an Exalted House: Temple Building in the Bible in Light of Mesopotamian and North West Semitic Writings* (JSOT Sup. Series 115; Sheffield: Sheffield University Press, 1992).

Hurowitz, Victor Avigdor, 'Babylon in Bethel: new light on Jacob's dream', in Steven W. Holloway, ed., *Orientalism, Assyriology and the Bible* (HBM 10; Sheffield: Sheffield Phoenix Press, 2006), 436–448.

Jastrow, Morris, Jr., Price, Ira Maurice, Jastrow, Marcus, Ginzberg, Louis and McDonald, Duncan B., 'Tower of Babel', in Joseph Jacobs, ed., *The Jewish Encyclopedia* (New York: Funk & Wagnalls, 1906), 395–398.

Joffe, Alexander H., 'Disembedded capitals in Western Asian perspective'. *CSSH* 40 1998: 549–580.

Kramer, Samuel N., 'Man's Golden Age: a Sumerian parallel to GenesisXI: 1'. *JAOS* 63 1943: 191–193.

Kramer, Samuel N., '"The Babel of tongues": a Sumerian version'. *JAOS* 88 1968: 108–111.

LaCocque, André, 'Whatever happened in the Valley of Shinar? A response to Theodore Hiebert'. *JBL* 128 2009: 29–41.

LaCocque, André, *The Captivity of Innocence: Babel and the Yahwist* (Eugene: Cascade Books 2010).

Mazar, Amihai, *Archaeology of the Land of the Bible: 10,000–586 BCE* (New York: Doubleday, 1990), 41–42.

Miller, Patrick, 'Eridu, Dunnu, and Babel: a study in comparative mythology', in Richard S. Hess and David Toshio Tsumura, eds, *I Studied Inscriptions from Before the Flood: Ancient Near Eastern, Literary, and Linguistic Approaches to Genesis 1–11* (SBTS 4; Winona Lake: Eisenbrauns, 1994), 143–168.

Ross, Allen P., 'The dispersion of the nations in Genesis 11: 1–9'. *BSac* 138 1981: 119–138.

Sasson, Jack M., 'The "Tower of Babel" as a clue to the redactional structuring of the primeval history [Gen. 1–11: 9]', in Gary Rendsburg, Ruth Adler, Milton Arfa and Nathan H. Winter, eds, *The Bible World: Essays in Honor of Cyrus H. Gordon* (New York: KTAV, 1980), 211–219.

Strong, John T., 'Shattering the image of God: a response to Theodore Hiebert's interpretation of the story of the Tower of Babel'. *JBL* 127 2008: 625–634.

Swiggers, Pierre, 'Babel and the confusion of tongues', in Armin Lange, Hermann Lichtenberger and Diethard Römheld, eds, *Mythos im Alten Testament und seiner Umwelt: Festschrift für Hans-Peter Müller zum 65. Geburtstag* (BZAW 278; Berlin: Walter de Guyter, 1999), 182–195.

van der Kooij, Arie, 'The story of Genesis 11: 1–9 and the culture of ancient Mesopotamia'. *BO* 53 1996: 27–38.

van der Kooij, Arie, 'The city of Babel and Assyrian imperialism: Genesis 11: 1–9 interpreted in light of Mesopotamian sources', in André Lemaire, ed., *Congress Volume Leiden 2004* (SVT 109; Brill Academic Publishers, 2006), 1–17.

Van De Mieroop, Marc, *The Ancient Mesopotamian City* (New York: Oxford University Press, 1997), 42–62.

Van De Mieroop, Marc, 'Literature and political discourse in ancient Mesopotamia: Sargon II of Assyria and Sargon of Agade', in Barbara Böck, Eva Cancik Kirschbaum and Thomas Richter, eds, *Munuscula Mesopotamica: Festschrift für Johannes Renger* (AOAT 267; Münster: Ugarit Verlag, 1999), 327–339.

Walton, John H., 'The Mesopotamian background of the Tower of Babel account and its implications'. *BBR* 5 1995: 155–175.

Van Wolde, Ellen, *Words Become Worlds: Semantic Studies of Genesis 1–11* (BiIntS 6; Leiden: Brill, 1994), 84–109.

Ugarit and Ugaritic Texts

The discovery of a Canaanite voice transformed biblical stories. Now it was possible to hear the other side of the story for figures like Baal and Asherah or to read stories about the desire for a son from non-Patriarchal kings. In addition to specific proper nouns continuing into the biblical tradition from the Canaanite one, various motifs did so as well. One could even postulate that biblical literature simply continued Ugaritic precedents. However, this perception fails to account for the development process which occurred in Israelite alphabet prose narratives from the time of Saul to Solomon. For the city of Ugarit see:

Soldt, William H. van, 'Ugarit: a second millennium kingdom on the Mesopotamian coast', in *CANE*, 1255–1266.

Yon, Marguerite, 'Ugarit', in *OEANE*, 255–262.

For the Ugaritic Texts see:

Cassuto, Umberto, 'Biblical and Canaanite literature', in *Biblical and Oriental Studies: Volume II The Bible and Ancient Oriental Texts* (Jerusalem: Magnes, 1975), 16–59.

Day, John, 'Ugarit and the Bible: do they presuppose the same Canaanite mythology and religion?', in George J. Brooke, Adrian H. W. Curtis and John F. Healey, eds, *Ugarit and the Bible: Proceedings of the International Symposium on Ugarit and the Bible, Manchester, September 1992* (Münster: Ugarit-Verlag, 1994), 35–52.

Gray, John, *The Legacy of Canaan: The Ras Shamra Texts and Their Relevance to the Old Testament* (Leiden: Brill, 1965, 2nd edition).

Olmo Lete, Johannes Gregorio del, *Canaanite Religion: According to the Liturgical Texts of Ugarit* (Winona Lake: Eisenbrauns, 2004).

Pardee, Dennis, 'Ugaritic inscriptions', in *OEANE*, 264–266.

Parker, Simon, *The Pre-Biblical Narrative Tradition; Essays on the Ugaritic Poems Keret and Aqhat* (SBLRBS 24; Atlanta: Scholars Press, 1989).

Pitard, Wayne T., 'Baal's palace and Ugarit's temple in the Baal Cycle', unpublished paper presented at the annual conference of the Middle West Branch of the American Oriental Society, February 12, 2011.

Pitard, Wayne T., 'The combat myth as a succession story at Ugarit', in JoAnn Scurlock and Richard H. Beal, eds, *Creation and Chaos: A Reconsideration of Hermann Gunkel's Chaos Kampf Hypothesis* (Winona Lake: Eisenbrauns, 2013), 199–205.

Smith, Mark S., 'Mythology and myth-making in Ugaritic and Israelite literatures', in George J. Brooke, Adrian H. W. Curtis and John F. Healy, eds, *Ugarit and the Bible: Proceedings of the International Symposium on Ugarit and the Bible, Manchester, September 1992* (Ugaritisch-biblische Literatur 11; Münster: Ugarit-Verlag, 1994), 293–341.

Smith, Mark S., *The Ugaritic Baal Cycle Volume I* (SVT 55; Leiden: Brill, 1994).

Tugendhaft, Aaron, 'How to become a brother in the Bronze Age: an inquiry into the representation of politics in Ugaritic myth'. *Fragments* 2 2012: 89–104.

Tugendhaft, Aaron, 'Unsettling sovereignty: politics and poetics in the Baal Cycle'. *JAOS* 132 2012: 367–384.

Wyatt, Nicolas, *Religious Texts from Ugarit: The Words of Ilimilku and his Colleagues* (Biblical Seminar 53; Sheffield: Sheffield Academic Press, 1998), 97–107, 348–355.

Wyatt, Nicolas, 'Ilimilku's ideological programme: Ugarit royal propaganda and a biblical postscript'. *UF* 29 1997: 775–796.

Wyatt, Nicolas, 'The religious role of the king in Ugarit'. *UF* 37 2005: 695–727.

In addition *NEA* 63 2000 issue is devoted to Ugarit.

Valley of Aijalon

The standing still of the sun and the moon in the biblical text provides a potential astronomical, not archaeological, verification through science of a biblical story. The attempt to substantiate a link has proven problematical. If the answer is not to be found in astronomy, then what does the Bible mean? One presumes the audience knew even if the meaning was metaphorical in some way. Maybe the astral terms were symbols of something on earth? The search for answers continues. For purposes here, the poetry in the Book of Jashar expresses the pre-prose narrative style of writing that eventually was subsumed by the new style, quite literally in this case as it became part of the new narrative. All Joshua commentaries includes a section on this passage. In addition see:

Astour, Michael, 'Benê-iamina et Jéricho'. *Sem* 9 1959: 5–20.

Christensen, Duane L., 'Jashar', in *ABD* III: 646–647.

Holladay, John S., Jr., 'The day(s) the moon stood still'. *JBL* 87 1968: 160–178.

Margalit, Baruch, 'The day the sun did not stand still: a new look at Joshua X 8–15'. *VT* 42 1992: 466–491.

Oeste, Gordon, '"A day like no other" in the context of Yahweh War: Joshua 10: 14 and the characterization of Joshua'. *JETS* 57 2014: 689–702.

Römer, Thomas, *The Invention of God* (Cambridge, MA: Harvard University Press, 2015), 126–127.

Sawyer, John F. A., 'Joshua 10: 12–14 and the solar eclipse of 30 September 1131 BC'. *PEQ* 104 1972: 139–146.

Schniedewind, William M., *How the Bible Became a Book* (New York: Cambridge University Press, 2004), 52–56.

Walton, John, 'Joshua 10: 12–15 and Mesopotamian celestial omen texts', in A. R. Millard, James Hoffmeier and David W. Baker, eds, *Faith, Tradition, and History: Old Testament Historiography in its Near Eastern Context* (Winona Lake: Eisenbrauns, 1994), 181–190.

Vineyards

Vineyards like threshing floors are not simply random background props for a story. Authors choose their props wisely for the messages they deliver even without verbalization. So it was in ancient times as well. In addition to Genesis commentaries on the sons of Noah, see:

Albenda, Pauline, 'Grapevines in Ashurbanipal's garden'. *BASOR* 215 1974: 5–17, here 14.

Bailey, Lloyd R., *Noah: The Person and the Story in History and Tradition* (Columbia: University of South Carolina Press, 1989), 158–159, 227 n4.

Neiman, David, 'The date and circumstances of the cursing of Canaan', in Alexander Altman, ed., *Biblical Motifs: Origins and Transformations* (Cambridge MA: Harvard University Press, 1966), 113–134, here 114–115.

For a brief overview of the deleterious effects of viticulture described in the Hebrew Bible see:

Sasson, Jack M. 'The blood of grapes: viticulture and intoxication in the Hebrew Bible', in Lucio Milano, ed., *Drinking in Ancient Societies: History and Culture of Drinks in the Ancient Near East* (Padua: Sargon srl, 1994), 399–419.

For a broader look at wine and society see:

Brown, John Pairman, 'The Mediterranean vocabulary of the vine'. *VT* 19 1969: 146–170.

Yahweh

For the subject of Yahweh in the non-biblical record see the Shasu (above). While some of these readings address the meaning of Yahweh within the Israelite religion, the primary purposes for listing them are to demonstrate the existence of Yahweh outside the Bible and of the need to combine archaeology and biblical text to provide a fuller understanding of the meaning of the deity to Israel and in the Bible. For the deity of Yahweh see:

Cross, Frank Moore, *Canaanite Myth and Hebrew Epic: Essays in the Religion of Israel* (Cambridge MA: Harvard University Press, 1973), 60–144.

Day, John, *Yahweh and the Gods and Goddesses of Canaan* (JSOT Sup. Series 265; Sheffield: Sheffield Academic Press, 2000), 13–41.

Mettinger, Trygvve N. D., 'The elusive essence: YHWH, El and Baal and the distinctiveness of Israelite faith', in Erhard Blum, Christina Macholz and Ekkehard W. Stegeman, eds, *Die Hebräische Bibel und ihre Zweifache Nachgeshicichte: Festschrift für Rolf Rendtorff zum 65. Geburstag* (Neukirchen-Vluyn: Neukirchener, 1990), 393–417.

Mettinger, Trygvve N. D., 'Yahweh Zebaoth', in *DDD*, 920–924.

Smith, Mark S., *The Early History of God: Yahweh and the Other Deities in Ancient Israel* (Grand Rapids: William B. Eerdmans, 1999).

Van der Toorn, Karel, 'Yahweh', in *DDD*, 910–919.

Yeled

Think of the various meanings 'boy' might have depending on who is saying it and to or about whom. To determine the precise nuance of a term in another language is difficult enough in the present. To do so for a people thousands of years ago who themselves may have employed it in different ways over the years is even more problematic. Since the term is used in the Song of Lamech and for the advisors of Rehoboam, ascertaining the meaning is part of the effort to understand the son stories of this study. All the Genesis commentaries include it for the former story and all the I Kings commentaries do for the latter. In addition for the meaning of *yeled* see:

Evans, D. Geoffrey, 'Rehoboam's advisers at Shechem, and political institutions in Israel and Sumer'. *JNES* 25 1966: 273–279.

L'Heureux, Conrad E., 'The Ugaritic and biblical Rephaim'. *HTR* 67 1974: 265–274.

L'Heureux, Conrad E., "The *yĕlidê hārāpâ*' – a cultic association of warriors'. *BASOR* 221 1976: 83–85.

MacDonald, Cutler B., 'Identification of the na'ar in the Ugaritic texts'. *UF* 8 1976: 27–35.

MacDonald, John, 'The status and role of the na'ar in Israelite society'. *JNES* 35 1976: 147–170).

McCarter, P. Kyle, Jr., *II Samuel* (AB 9; Garden City: Doubleday, 1984), 449–450.

Miller, Patrick, '*Yeled* in the Song of Lamech'. *JBL* 85 1966: 477–478, here 477.

Rofé, Alexander, 'Elders or youngsters? Critical remarks on I Kings 12', in Reinhard G. Kratz and Hermann Spieckermann, eds, *One God – One Cult – One Nation: Archaeological and Biblical Perspectives* (Berlin: Walter de Gruyter, 2010), 79–89.

Willesen, Folker, 'The yālîd in Hebrew society'. *ST* 12 1958: 192–210.

Zadok

For the discussion on the identity of Zadok including the debate on his being a Jebusite priest of Elyon, his descendants, and the impact of the Israelite takeover of the city by David see:

Bartlett, J. R., 'Zadok and his successors at Jerusalem'. *JTS* 19 1968: 1–18.

Browker, J. W., 'Psalm CX'. *VT* 17 1967: 31–41.

Cody, Aelred, *A History of Old Testament Priesthood* (AnBib 25; Rome: Pontifical Biblical Institute, 1969), 88–93.

Cross, Frank Moore, *Canaanite Myth and Hebrew Epic: Essays in the Religion of Israel* (Cambridge MA: Harvard University Press, 1973), 209–214.

Day, John, 'The Canaanite inheritance of the Israelite monarchy', in John Day, ed., *King and Messiah in Israel and the Ancient Near East: Proceedings of the Oxford Old Testament Seminar* (JSOT Sup. Series 270; Sheffield: Sheffield Academic Press, 1998), 73–78.

Gammie, John, 'Loci of the Melchizedek tradition of Genesis 14: 18–20'. *JBL* 90 1970: 385–396.

Hauer, C. E., 'Who was Zadok?' *JBL* 82 1963: 89–94.

Judge, H. G., 'Aaron, Zadok, and Abiathar'. *JTS* 7 1956: 70–74.

Mathews, Joshua J., *Melchizedek's Alternative Priestly Order: A Compositional Analysis of Genesis 14: 18–20 and Its Echoes throughout the Tanak* (BBR Supplements 8; Winona Lake: Eisenbrauns, 2013).

Meek, Theophile James, 'Aaronites and Zadokites'. *AJSL* 45 1929: 149–166.

Olyan, Saul, 'Zadok's origins and the tribal politics of David'. *JBL* 101 1982: 177–193.

Rehm, Merlin, 'Zadok', in *The Interpreter's Dictionary of the Bible Supplementary Volume* (Nashville: Abingdon, 1976), 976–977.

Rendsburg, Gary A., 'The internal consistency and historical reliability of the biblical genealogies'. *VT* 40 1990: 185–206, here 197.

Rooke, Deborah, *Zadok's Heirs: The Role and Development of the High Priesthood in Ancient Israel* (New York: Oxford University Press, 2015), 64–69.

Rosenberg, Roy, 'The god Ṣedeq'. *HUCA* 36 1965: 161–177.

Rowley, H. H., 'Zadok and Nehustan'. *JBL* 58 1939: 113–141.

Rowley, H. H., 'Melchizedek and Zadok Gen. 14 and Ps. 110', in Walter Baumgartner, Otto Eissfeldt and Karl Elliger, eds, *Festschrift Alfred Bertholet* (Tübinngen: J.C.B. Mohr, 1950), 461–472.

Rowley, H. H., 'Melchizedek and David'. *VT* 17 1967: 485.

Smith, Robert Houson, 'Abram and Melchizedek (Gen.14 18–20)'. *ZAW* 77 1965: 129–153.

Tournay, Raymond, 'Le Psaume CX'. *RB* 67 1960: 5–41, here 18–29.